Aeschylean Tragedy

AESCHYLEAN TRAGEDY

Alan H. Sommerstein

Duckworth

First published in 2010 by
Gerald Duckworth & Co. Ltd.
90-93 Cowcross Street, London EC1M 6BF
Tel: 020 7490 7300
Fax: 020 7490 0080
info@duckworth-publishers.co.uk
www.ducknet.co.uk

© 2010 by Alan H. Sommerstein

All rights reserved. No part of this publication may be reproduced, stored in a retrieval system, or transmitted, in any form or by any means, electronic, mechanical, photocopying, recording or otherwise, without the prior permission of the publisher.

A catalogue record for this book is available from the British Library

ISBN 978 0 7156 3824 8

Typeset by Ray Davies
Printed and bound in Great Britain by
CPI Antony Rowe, Chippenham and Eastbourne

Contents

Preface to the Second Edition

This new edition has been thoroughly revised to take account of developments in scholarship, and in my own thinking on Aeschylus, since the first edition was published in 1996. In contrast to the policy adopted in the first edition, important references to modern scholarship are now given in the text or endnotes in the conventional way (though the Bibliographical Guide at the end of the book should be treated as an essential complement to these). A sentence of my original preface (below) has thus been rendered obsolete and misleading, and has been deleted.

I am most grateful to Duckworth for agreeing to publish the volume, to Deborah Blake for the most helpful role she has played throughout as editorial director, and to the original publishers, Levante Editori of Bari, for giving permission for the republication.

Alan Sommerstein
Nottingham, September 2009

Preface to the First Edition

As I complete this book I think of all the teachers, colleagues and students who have helped me to love and, so far as I have been able, to understand Aeschylus, from Martin Lowry who gave me my first acquaintance with him thirty years ago to Elizabeth Randle who, by reaching the same conclusions independently, made me feel that there might be something in the reconstruction of the Danaid trilogy which will be found in Chapter 6. I think also of all the great scholars whose ideas likewise underlie what is here presented and whom I have never had the privilege of meeting.

The book is intended for all who are interested, from whatever angle, in the tragedies of Aeschylus, a majority of whom will not be in a position to read his plays in Greek. Accordingly, all quotations, both from Aeschylus and from other authors, are given in translation. For the same reason no attempt has been made here to offer a systematic discussion of Aeschylus' language and style.

I am grateful to Cambridge University Press for granting me permission to include in Chapters 7 and 12 adapted versions of parts of the introduction to my edition of *Eumenides*, published by the Press in 1989.

I thank especially Alex Garvie and Bernhard Zimmermann, who read the whole book in its penultimate draft and many of whose suggestions I have incorporated. Neither of them is to be held responsible for any shortcomings in the book, which are due entirely to my own oversight, obstinacy, or obtuseness.

I dedicate this book to my students, past, present and future, and to all those like them throughout the world, who, often in face of the ignorant obloquy of their peers (and sometimes of the ignorant obstruction of schools, education authorities and governments) have chosen to study the world of antiquity. I wrote it for their sake, and I hope it does for them a little of what the scholars of whom I spoke before have done for me.

Alan Sommerstein
Nottingham, September 1994

Note to the Reader

Greek names and words

No rigid convention for the representation of Greek names in English is capable of being maintained. By one possible convention we would be forced to call Athens 'Athenai', and the greatest Greek philosophers 'Platon' and 'Aristoteles'; by another, to speak of the goddesses of destiny as the 'Moerae', and those of death, at much risk of confusion, as the 'Ceres'. In this book, *names* of people and places have in general been latinized in the manner which has long been customary in works not designed exclusively for specialists, but a closer transliteration has been used where thought desirable in the interest of communicative efficiency. On the other hand Greek *words*, other than proper names, are precisely transliterated (and printed in italics). The main conversion-equivalences between the two conventions are as follows:

Latinized	*Transliterated*
c	k
ch	kh (*or* ch)
ae	ai
oe	oi
u	ou
y	u (*or* y)
-us	-os
-um	-on

Translations

All translations in this book are my own, unless otherwise stated.

Fragments

Fragments of Aeschylus and other tragedians are cited from *Tragicorum Graecorum Fragmenta* (Göttingen, 1971-2005); if a fragment is numbered differently in my Loeb edition (Sommerstein 2008), both numbers are given. Fragments of comedy are cited from *Poetae Comici Graeci* (Berlin, 1983-). Fragments of lyric poets included in D.A. Campbell, *Greek Lyric* vols II-V (Cambridge MA, 1988-93) are cited by the continuous numbering of that collection (abbreviated as *GL*); those of Sappho and Alcaeus are cited from Campbell's vol. I (Cambridge MA, 1982). Where fragments of other authors are referred to, the editor's name is given ('Fowler' refers to R.L. Fowler, *Early Greek Mythography I: Texts* [Oxford, 2000]; 'Jacoby' refers to F. Jacoby *et al.*, *Die Fragmente der griechischen Historiker* [Berlin/Leiden, 1923-]).

Abbreviations

In general, the names of ancient authors and texts are written out in full, with the exception of the surviving plays of the Aeschylean corpus, which may be abbreviated as *(The)* ***Pers.****(ians)*, ***Seven*** *(against Thebes), (The)* ***Supp.****(liant Maidens)*, ***Ag.****(amemnon)*, ***Cho.****(ephoroi)*, ***Eum.****(enides)*, and ***Prom.****(etheus Bound)*. In Chapter 8, however, which is concerned with several plays all of whose titles include the name Prometheus, the title of the surviving play is abbreviated as *Bound*.

Other abbreviations used (mainly of journal titles in the Bibliography) are as follows:

AJP	*American Journal of Philology*
BCH	*Bulletin de Correspondance Hellénique*
BICS	*Bulletin of the Institute of Classical Studies, University of London*
BMCR	*Bryn Mawr Classical Review*
CA	*Classical Antiquity*
CAG	*Commentaria in Aristotelem Graeca* (Berlin, 1882-1909)
CGITA	*Cahiers du Group Interdisciplinaire du Théâtre Antique*
CJ	*Classical Journal*
C&M	*Classica et Mediaevalia*
CP	*Classical Philology*
CQ	*Classical Quarterly*
CR	*Classical Review*
CSCA	*California Studies in Classical Antiquity*
CW	*Classical World*
G&R	*Greece and Rome*
GL	D.A. Campbell, *Greek Lyric* vols. II-V (Cambridge MA, 1988-93)
GRBS	*Greek, Roman and Byzantine Studies*
HSCP	*Harvard Studies in Classical Philology*
ICS	*Illinois Classical Studies*
IG	*Inscriptiones Graecae*
JHS	*Journal of Hellenic Studies*
LCM	*Liverpool Classical Monthly*
LIMC	*Lexicon Iconographicum Mythologiae Classicae* (Zürich, 1981-99)

MH	*Museum Helveticum*
M-W	R. Merkelbach and M.L. West, *Fragmenta Hesiodea* (Oxford, 1967)
PCA	*Proceedings of the Classical Association*
PCPS	*Proceedings of the Cambridge Philological Society*
QUCC	*Quaderni Urbinati di Cultura Classica*
REG	*Revue des Études Grecques*
RhM	*Rheinisches Museum für Philologie*
SBAW	*Sitzungsberichte der Bayerischen Akademie der Wissenschaften*
TAPA	*Transactions of the American Philological Association*
WJA	*Würzburger Jahrbücher für die Altertumswissenschaft*
YCS	*Yale Classical Studies*
ZPE	*Zeitschrift für Papyrologie und Epigraphik*

Notes

The notes to the text are placed at the end of each chapter.

1

The Life and Times of Aeschylus

Aeschylus, the dramatist who made Athenian tragedy one of the world's great art-forms, was born in or about 525/4 BC[1] at Eleusis in western Attica, a town famous as the home of an immensely popular mystery-cult of Demeter and Persephone. His ancient biographer reports that his father Euphorion was of aristocratic birth, and it is at any rate certain that in later years the family followed the lifestyle of the leisured class: surviving vase inscriptions proclaim, in the traditional manner of Greek upper-class homoeroticism, the beauty of Aeschylus' younger son Euaeon (Beazley 1963:1579).

The state of Athens (whose territory had long comprised the whole of Attica, including Eleusis) had been for over twenty years under the personal rule first of Peisistratus and then, following his death in 528/7, of his son Hippias. They were what Greeks called *tyrannoi* – that is, individuals who seized power by force or stratagem and ruled as *de facto* monarchs. Greek *tyrannoi* as a class earned the hatred both of the aristocrats whom they ousted from power and (at least at Athens) of the democrats who were soon to succeed them, and Aeschylus himself can be found using *tyrannos* and its derivatives in the pejorative sense which they still bear (e.g. *Ag.* 1355, 1365; *Cho.* 973). Most Athenians, however, appear to have accepted the rule of Peisistratus and Hippias at the time: once Peisistratus was firmly established in power Athens enjoyed perhaps the longest peace in its independent history and a growing prosperity. Like several *tyrannoi* elsewhere, the family was particularly noted for its patronage of the arts. Peisistratus (or according to other accounts his son Hipparchus) created, as a regular feature of the quadrennial summer festival of the Great Panathenaea, a competition for rhapsodes, professional reciters of the *Iliad* and *Odyssey*, and he was believed in later antiquity to have been responsible for standardizing the text of the two epics.[2] Another new artistic competition which he instituted, probably in the 530s, ten years or so before Aeschylus' birth, was a contest at the spring festival of the City Dionysia in performing the comparatively new poetic-musical genre called *tragôidia*, tragedy.[3]

The origins of *tragôidia* are not our present concern. At this stage of its existence it was an enactment of a story from heroic legend by an individual performer (called the *hypokritês* or 'respondent') and a chorus perhaps already (as in Aeschylus' time) of twelve members. The chorus sang and danced; the *hypokritês* may sometimes have done so too, but more usually he spoke, either direct to the audience or in dialogue with the chorus or its leader. The chorus represented a group of persons affected by the events of the story, such as elders of a city or slaves in a household; the *hypokritês* might impersonate not only the hero of the story but also (at different times during the performance) other characters, anonymous messengers bringing news of 'offstage' events, even perhaps gods. All the performers were male, and at this date all the *dramatis personae* they represented were male also: female parts, we are told, were an innovation by Phrynichus, whose career began about 510 (*Suda* φ762). In the early days the leading tragic dramatist was Thespis, of Icaria in north-eastern Attica. Thespian one-actor tragedy may seem primitive to us; it would undoubtedly have seemed primitive to Athenians of (say) the late fifth century; but it is striking that *Agamemnon*, produced as late as 458, which many have considered Aeschylus' masterpiece, is in at least one sense Thespian for most of its length. Only during 327 of *Agamemnon*'s 1673 lines is more than one *hypokritês* present on stage, and only during about 64 lines, or four per cent of the play, do *hypokritai* actually engage in dialogue with one another (914-57, 1654-73).

Such, at any rate, was the dramatic art which Aeschylus could have witnessed at the City Dionysia competitions of his boyhood. But by the time he had come of age, the civic framework within which that art was practised had been utterly transformed.

At the Panathenaea of 514 Hipparchus, the brother of Hippias, was assassinated by Harmodius and Aristogeiton. His death seems to have been the result of a private quarrel (Thucydides 6.54-9; Aristotle, *Constitution of Athens* 18); but the exiled opponents of the ruling family were emboldened by it to an attempt to return to Attica and overthrow Hippias, their failure was followed by increased repression, and eventually in 510 the opposition appealed to Sparta, the strongest power in Greece and the traditional enemy of *tyrannoi*. After a first abortive attempt, the Spartans under king Cleomenes forced Hippias to surrender and go into exile with his whole family. But the Athens to which the émigrés returned was almost as different from the Athens of the days before Peisistratus as the France to which the Bourbons returned in 1815 was from the France of 1788. Being generally at odds with much of the aristocracy, the *tyrannoi* had not unnaturally cultivated other strata of society, and had also admitted many non-citizens to membership of the *polis*[4] – new factors in the game of political power, about which the traditional rules of that game had nothing to say. The crisis came two years after the fall of Hippias. Cleisthenes, of the Alcmeonid family, had been defeated in the election to the chief magistracy (the archonship) by his rival Isagoras. He sought the support of the common people (the *dêmos*) with the promise, apparently, of greatly increasing their political power. Isagoras appealed to Sparta, which at once ordered the expulsion of Cleisthenes and his family and sent Cleomenes with a small armed force to Athens. But now Isagoras overplayed his hand. Secure in Cleomenes' support, he tried to banish every possible opponent, and to concentrate all power in the hands of his own faction. But he found he did not have enough of a following even among the upper class. The Council refused to disband itself. Isagoras and the Spartans occupied the Acropolis, where they were besieged by the people for two days and then surrendered. Cleisthenes and the *dêmos* were masters of Athens.

In the next few years the whole political system of Attica was reorganized. The basis of the new system was the *dêmos* (English 'deme') in another sense of the word, the local community – hamlet, village, town, or district of the city – in which every citizen was henceforth to be registered, and the name of which increasingly became regarded as part of his own official name. Aeschylus, registered on coming of age in the deme of Eleusis, was now often called not just *Aiskhulos Euphoriônos* but *Aiskhulos Euphoriônos Eleusînios*. The Council, the army, the magistracies, all were organized around the 139 demes and the ten new, artificial 'tribes' (*phylai*) into which they were grouped. So too was the City Dionysia. In 501 the competitions for dithyrambic choruses[5] at this festival were made tribal, the winning tribe in each of the two contests (for boys and men) being listed each year in the festival records, for which 501 was regarded as a new beginning.[6] This innovation did not apply to the tragic competition, in which there may perhaps simply not have been enough individuals with the required combination of expertise as poets, composers, choreographers, directors and actors to make a tribal contest a practical possibility.

It was in this new 'democratic' City Dionysia that Aeschylus made his début as a tragic dramatist, probably in 499.[7] Three outstanding practitioners, Pratinas, Choerilus and Phrynichus, were already active, and the newcomer was not to win first prize for another fifteen years. It is uncertain whether any plays from this early period of Aeschylus' activity were preserved for posterity to read:[8] of the work of Phrynichus, far more popular at the time, only some late plays seem to have survived into later generations[9] – his *Capture of Miletus* (493 or 492) is famous, or notorious, only because the historian Herodotus (6.21.2) had occasion to mention it, for not a word of its text survives. Perhaps it was not until a few years later, possibly in the early or middle 480s, that the scripts of tragic dramas began to be copied and preserved.

Before then, and before Aeschylus at last reached the top rank of his profession, other and momentous events had occurred. The capture of Miletus by the Persians in 494, which had been the occasion of Phrynichus' celebrated play, had marked the end of a major revolt by some of the Greek *poleis* of Asia Minor against Persian rule. At one stage Athens had given active (though limited) support to the revolt, and the Persians, who already controlled the northern shore of the Aegean, were thus provided with a justification for establishing themselves in Greece proper. In 490 a

Persian expedition crossed the Aegean to attack Eretria and Athens – accompanied by the now elderly Hippias. Eretria (on the island of Euboea) was quickly taken and its population enslaved; but when the Persians landed at Marathon in eastern Attica they were decisively defeated by the Athenians under Callimachus and Miltiades, in a battle which Athenians ever after regarded as the most glorious event in their whole history. Aeschylus fought in the battle, and one of the 192 Athenian dead was his brother:

> In this struggle ... Cynegeirus son of Euphorion seized hold of an enemy ship by the sternpost, and fell when his hand was severed by an axe (Herodotus 6.114).

A year or two after Marathon there was a major political upheaval at Athens and a move towards a more self-confident, assertive, anti-élitist democracy. Miltiades, who had failed to capture the island of Paros, was put on trial, heavily fined, and, unable to pay, died in prison soon afterwards. Then in 488/7 the Assembly of all adult male citizens, the sovereign body of democratic Athens, took three significant decisions. One was that the holders of the nine chief magistracies should no longer be elected by vote but chosen by lot from a list of 100 candidates – thus making it unlikely that any prominent politician would in future hold one of these prestigious positions. The second was to put into operation, for the first time, the machinery of 'ostracism' created twenty years before by Cleisthenes, whereby the people annually had the optional right to vote to expel one citizen from Athenian territory for ten years without charge or trial: in the next six years five men were thus expelled, including two of the three leading politicians of the period. The third was to introduce, as part of the official programme of the City Dionysia, a contest for choruses performing the rumbustious, undignified entertainment that came to be known as *kômôidia*, comedy, which specialized in debunking satire of the prominent and the pretentious. All these decisions are clearly of a populist nature and seem to be part of a considered programme, and it is likely that they should be associated with the name of Themistocles. He was certainly the gainer by the successive ostracisms (despite repeated efforts by his enemies, including the mass-production of pre-inscribed ballots, to turn them against him), and it was he who a few years later (483-480) was mainly responsible for the creation of a great Athenian navy, which did much to shift the balance of political power in Athens towards those who served as oarsmen because they could not afford the hoplite equipment necessary for military service on land.

It was in the middle of this period, in the spring of 484, that Aeschylus at last won first prize in the tragic competition at the City Dionysia. From now to the end of his career he won first prize thirteen times in all;[10] especially after the death of Phrynichus in 473/2 he may have been victorious almost every time he competed. By now tragedy was becoming prestigious enough for an embryo reading public to have come into existence, perhaps at this stage mainly confined to other literary artists in Athens and elsewhere, so that some scripts of plays from this period survived for later generations to read. We cannot, however, identify the plays concerned, with the possible exception of the tetralogy based on the *Iliad* (see n. 8).

In 481/0 another Persian expedition, under the command of king Xerxes himself, advanced by land and sea against Greece with the object of conquering the whole country. The Athenians, who over the previous few years had built up the largest navy in Greece, abandoned their city, evacuated their population and put every available man on board their ships, and we can be certain that Aeschylus was present at the naval battles of Artemisium and Salamis in the late summer of 480 – which gives his account of the latter battle in *The Persians* a unique status: there is perhaps no other battle in ancient history of which we possess a substantial eyewitness account written down so soon after the event for the ears of an audience most of whom had been eyewitnesses themselves. As an Athenian hoplite Aeschylus will also have taken part in the final defeat of the Persian invaders on land at Plataea in the summer of 479.

The Greeks were victorious; but Athens was destroyed – houses, public buildings, walls, temples demolished, looted and burnt. Yet her prestige was higher than it had ever been, and when the Greek allies (mainly from Asia Minor and the Aegean islands), who were continuing the war at sea against the Persians, sensed that Sparta was reluctant to make a long-term commitment to support them, they offered the leadership of their alliance to Athens, and the Athenians accepted. From this time, in 478, begins the period of Athenian maritime domination of the Aegean region, which was to last for most of the rest of the fifth century and was to make Athens, before the end of Aeschylus' life, the most powerful *polis* Greece had ever seen.

In Athens the Persian invasion had led to a closing of ranks, with those previously ostracized being recalled and some of them given high commands. But with the Persian threat removed, personal and policy rivalries soon came to the surface again. Two main groups can be discerned. Of one group Cimon, the son of Miltiades, was the unchallenged leader. His policy was to take the offensive against the Persians with the object of driving them out of reach of all areas of Greek population, to maintain the alliance with Sparta established in 480, and to uphold the political and constitutional *status quo* and especially his own ascendancy. In all these aims he was fairly consistently successful until 462. His main rivals at first were Xanthippus (who had prosecuted Miltiades over the Paros affair) and Themistocles. Themistocles was deeply suspicious of Sparta, and was instrumental, soon after the Persian retreat, in effecting the rebuilding of the walls of Athens and of her port Peiraeus despite Spartan diplomatic opposition. Soon, however, his popularity waned, especially when Cimon began to gain spectacular military successes from 476 onwards; some time late in the 470s Themistocles was ostracized, and in the 460s we begin to find other figures in antagonism with Cimon – Pericles, the son of Xanthippus (born about 495), and a somewhat older man of unknown family named Ephialtes. All this time Athens was steadily consolidating both the power of her alliance in and beyond the Aegean and her own power within the alliance itself, which became more and more an instrument for advancing specifically Athenian interests.

It was during this period that Aeschylus firmly established himself as the outstanding tragic dramatist in Athens. According to his ancient *Life* he was well enough known as early as 476/5 to be invited to Sicily by Hieron, *tyrannos* of Syracuse, who was then founding the new city of Aetna and commissioned Aeschylus to produce *The Women of Aetna* for the occasion. At that time, however, Phrynichus was probably still the leading figure in the field – indeed he had just won first prize with a production financed by no less a person than Themistocles (Plutarch, *Themistocles* 5.5) – and it is on the whole more likely that the Sicilian première of *The Women of Aetna* took place some years later (see below) and that an ancient scholar wrongly associated it with the known date of Aetna's foundation.

It was almost certainly in 473 that Phrynichus died, after a career of some forty years; at any rate Aeschylus, feeling himself Phrynichus' successor, began his *Persians* (see Chapter 4), produced in the spring of 472, with a salute to Phrynichus' memory in the form of a near-quotation of the opening line of *his* play of four years earlier on the same theme. This production by Aeschylus was financed by the young Pericles, and won first prize.

There is ancient evidence, going back to Eratosthenes (third century BC),[11] that *The Persians* was produced again at Syracuse under the auspices of Hieron; there is reason to believe that this visit took place in 470 and that it also featured the production of *The Women of Aetna*. This was the year when Hieron, on winning the chariot-race at the Pythian Games, caused his name to be proclaimed not as 'Hieron of Syracuse' but as 'Hieron of Aetna'. Pindar, celebrating the victory in the ode now known as the *First Pythian*, recalled the victories achieved over the Persians by Athens at Salamis and by Sparta at Plataea and linked them with the almost simultaneous victory of Hieron and his brother Gelon over the Carthaginians at Himera as having 'pulled Greece back from grievous servitude'. It would chime very well with this publicity campaign on Hieron's part if he also sponsored productions, by the greatest dramatist of the day, of a play or plays[12] celebrating recent victories over the 'barbarians'[13] and another which, to quote the *Life of Aeschylus*, 'gave an augury of a good life to those who joined the newly-founded city' of Aetna. Perhaps one production was staged at Syracuse and the other at Aetna itself.

About the same time a new tragic dramatist, Sophocles, nearly thirty years younger than Aeschylus, was making his début. Plutarch, in his life of Cimon (8.8-9), tells a story set at the City Dionysia of 468. Sophocles, he says, was putting on his first production; there were quarrels and taking of sides among the spectators; the presiding magistrate, instead of selecting judges for the contest by lot as was usual, invited the ten generals (one of whom was Cimon) to act as judges, and they awarded the first prize to Sophocles. Plutarch implies, and the ancient *Life of Aeschylus* explicitly states, that Aeschylus was one of the defeated competitors. There is independent evidence that Sophocles won his first victory in 468 (*Parian Marble* A 56), but the participation of Aeschylus in that contest may be a later 'improvement' of the story: certainly Plutarch does not inspire our confidence here when he ascribes Aeschylus' final departure from Athens (which did not occur till a decade later) to pique at this defeat!

Two surviving plays of Aeschylus formed part of productions with which he won first prize in the 460s. In 467 he won with *Laius*, *Oedipus*, *Seven against Thebes* and *The Sphinx* (see Chapter 5), defeating two sons of famous fathers, Aristias son of Pratinas (who competed with his father's plays, Pratinas having presumably died not long before) and Polyphrasmon son of Phrynichus; and in an uncertain year, possibly 463, he won with *The Egyptians*, *The Suppliant Maidens*, *The Danaids* and *Amymone* (see Chapter 6 and §12.2), defeating Sophocles and Mesatus.

In the late 460s substantial alterations seem to have been made both in the rules of the dramatic competition and in the physical environment in which they took place (see Chapter 2), including the introduction of a scene-building (*skênê*) at the back of the acting area, of two special-effects devices (the *ekkyklêma* and *mêchanê*), and of a third speaking actor. Ancient scholars, from Aristotle onwards, disputed endlessly whether Aeschylus or Sophocles was responsible for these innovations. In one sense at least, neither was. The innovations, which may have been associated with some remodelling of the theatre as a whole, called for public expenditure, and must therefore have been authorized by a decree of the Assembly, made on the recommendation of the Council and on the motion, probably, of some active politician – though no doubt advice was taken from the leading dramatists on how the money available for the purpose could best be spent. In the absence of any surviving plays by Sophocles from this period, we cannot tell whether he or Aeschylus was more enthusiastic about these new theatrical resources. All we can say is that by 458 Aeschylus was employing them with as much expertise as if he had been handling them for the whole of his working life. He may have used them, or some of them, in up to three earlier productions: fragments of three lost plays – *The Edonians*, *The Priestesses* and the satyr-play *The Sacred Delegation* (see Chapter 9)[14] – suggest the existence of a scene-building, and in *The Weighing of Souls* (whose authenticity, however, is doubtful) there is evidence both for a three-actor scene (involving Zeus, Eos and Thetis) and for the use of the *mêchanê* (by Eos when she came to take away the body of her son Memnon). Aeschylus thus appears to have embraced the theatrical innovations of the late 460s with enthusiasm and exploited them with some audacity.

The year 462/1 brought fundamental changes in the external and internal politics of Athens, which will be considered more fully later (see §12.1): the abandonment of the alliance with Sparta in favour of one with Sparta's traditional enemy Argos, the ostracism of Cimon, and the removal of the last remaining constraints on popular sovereignty. In the next few years – despite the assassination of Ephialtes, the main promoter of the new policies – the people's state was further consolidated and a daring foreign policy pursued which by 459 had led Athens into war with Aegina, with Sparta and her allies, and with Persia all at the same time, as a single year saw Athenians fighting and dying in Europe, in Asia and in Africa.[15] Many echoes of these developments, some of them extraordinarily explicit by the standards of tragedy, were incorporated by Aeschylus in his *Oresteia* (comprising *Agamemnon*, *Choephoroi*, *Eumenides* and the satyr-play *Proteus*; see Chapter 7) which won first prize at the City Dionysia in the spring of 458.

Not long afterwards Aeschylus again travelled to Sicily. As he was never to return, legends later grew up about his having become estranged from his Athenian public, but no credence need be given to these. We do not know who invited him to Sicily (Hieron was now dead), nor how many cities he visited, nor what plays he produced, nor what plays he had prepared for production at Athens after his anticipated return; only that he died and was buried at Gela in 456/5. An epitaph is preserved which the ancient biographer of Aeschylus ascribes to the Geloans, though another tradition[16] held it to be by Aeschylus himself. It may be translated thus:

> At Gela, rich in wheat, he died, and lies beneath this stone:
> Aeschylus the Athenian, son of Euphorion.
> His valour, tried and proved, the mead of Marathon can tell,
> The long-haired Persian also, who knows it all too well.

One is entitled to be sceptical about the authenticity of ancient poets' epitaphs (all the more so when they are said to have written them personally), but in this case there is cause to be sceptical about scepticism. It is hard to believe that anyone at a *later* date would have concocted an epitaph for Aeschylus that made no reference whatever to his art.[17] Aeschylus, to be sure, can hardly have himself composed an epitaph that specified the place of his death; but it will probably have been commissioned by the Geloans from a member of his family, and its wording will have been in accordance with what his family knew had meant most to him, commemorating him not as a poet, but as a loyal and courageous Athenian who had fought that Athens might still be free.[18]

Scepticism is rather more in order about a number of other anecdotes, mostly undated, that figure in Aeschylus' ancient biography. Only one of these is worth recording, mainly because of its early attestation; it is referred to casually by Aristotle in his *Nicomachean Ethics* as if already well known:

> [The doer of an act] may not realize what he is doing; as people say they were 'carried away while speaking', or 'did not know it was a secret' (as in the case of Aeschylus and the Mysteries) (*Eth. Nic.* 1111a8-10 tr. Thomson).

This implies that Aeschylus was at some time accused, formally or informally, of having divulged secrets, connected with the Mysteries of Demeter and Kore at Eleusis, that were supposed to be concealed from all except initiates of the cult. An ancient commentator on the Aristotelian passage[19] specifies five plays (none of which has survived) in which Aeschylus 'seems' to have done this, and quotes from Aristotle's contemporary Heracleides Ponticus a sensational story of how Aeschylus narrowly escaped being put to death on stage for revealing such secrets, took refuge at the altar of Dionysus, and was eventually put on trial and acquitted, 'mainly because of what he had done in the battle of Marathon'.

Eleusis was both Aeschylus' home town and the home of the Mysteries, and Aristophanes in *The Frogs* exploits this connection to good effect: the chorus of the play is composed of initiates enjoying a blissful afterlife in a privileged region of Hades, and Aeschylus' prayer before his contest with Euripides is 'Demeter who nurtured my mind, may I be worthy of thy Mysteries' (*Frogs* 886-7). Some of the imagery in the *Oresteia* has been thought, probably rightly, to derive from this cult,[20] though none of it is signalled as such (neither the Mysteries nor Eleusis nor even Demeter is mentioned anywhere in the trilogy) and none of it could reasonably be regarded as illicit divulgation, since no non-initiate could even be aware of its connotations. To judge by what Aristotle's commentator says about the five other plays, their sole connection with the Mysteries, so far as later scholars could discover, consisted in some more than passing reference to Demeter.

There is thus no reason to believe that Aeschylus was guilty of what he is said to have been accused of. It does not follow, however, that the story of the accusation is pure legend. As the late Sir Kenneth Dover has put it in another connection, 'the adage that there is no smoke without fire is not applicable to the Athenian law-courts'.[21] Aeschylus, as we shall see more fully in Chapter 12, was a politically committed dramatist and a supporter successively of Themistocles, Ephialtes and Pericles. In the tense atmosphere of, say, the middle and late 460s, when Ephialtes and Pericles were seeking to undermine the ascendancy of Cimon through prosecutions,[22] it is not inconceivable that Cimon or one of his associates tried to attack his rivals indirectly through a prosecution of a man in the public eye who was well known to be an associate of theirs, as twenty-five or thirty years later

Pericles was attacked through prosecutions of friends of his who were well known to the public but were not active in politics (Pheidias, Anaxagoras, Aspasia).[23] If so, Aeschylus was acquitted; had he been convicted, the penalty would certainly have been death, as it was in later cases where similar charges were brought. It will not have taken long for the story to acquire the legendary embroidery found in later accounts.

Various ancient sources preserve sayings ascribed to Aeschylus, of varying degrees of credibility. The best attested is one that has no connection with his art:

> When Aeschylus was watching a boxing contest at the Isthmian Games, and the spectators shouted out when one of the boxers was hit, he nudged Ion of Chios and said 'Do you see what training does? The man who was struck is silent, and the spectators cry out!' (Plutarch, *Moralia* 79e).

Ion was a versatile writer of the fifth century who published a collection of reminiscences of famous people he had met; he was probably born in the late 480s and first visited Athens in the 460s. Our story implies that he and Aeschylus were visiting the Isthmian Games together, perhaps in 464 or 462,[24] which suggests that they had become close friends.

The other sayings attributed to Aeschylus all relate to his art. Some of them are commonplaces that might fit any poet, but two have a degree of individuality. One tells of a polite refusal by Aeschylus to compose a paean for the people of Delphi:

> He said that there already existed an excellent one composed by Tynnichus, and that to put one of his own beside it would be like comparing a modern cult-statue with an ancient one. The old images, crudely made as they were, were reckoned divine; the new ones, made with great artistry, were admired but did not give the same impression of divinity (Porphyry, *On Abstinence* 2.18).

The other is the only substantive comment he is recorded as having made on his tragedies: that they were 'slices of fish taken from the great banquets of Homer' (Athenaeus 8.347d; see Chapter 10). Both these may perhaps likewise come from Ion of Chios.[25] A small point in favour of their authenticity is that they share a tone of good-humoured self-depreciation. We do not know whether Aeschylus ever actually wrote paeans or other free-standing lyric poems, but in the Hellenistic period there circulated under his name at least two elegiac epitaphs[26] and also a longer elegy in honour of those who died at Marathon.[27]

The number of plays he composed is uncertain: our sources give figures ranging from 70 to 90. We know of 80 titles of plays attributed to Aeschylus, and one or two more have been plausibly inferred from other evidence: some of these titles may in fact be alternative names for the same play, some of the plays may be wrongly attributed (one was actually labelled in antiquity as 'spurious') and some genuine plays, especially early ones, may never have gone into circulation as reading texts. The following sifted catalogue attempts to list, once only, all the plays which we know to have been ascribed by ancient scholars to Aeschylus. The plays are listed under the titles by which they are referred to in this book; alternative titles are added in brackets.[28] Production dates are given where known, and titles of plays which survive complete are printed in capitals. I have attempted to describe briefly what is known or plausibly conjectured about each of the non-extant plays in volume iii of Sommerstein 2008.

AGAMEMNON (458; see Chapter 7).
Amymone (463?; satyric; see end of §6.2).
The Archeresses (*Toxotides*).
The Argo, or The Oarsmen (probably satyric).
Atalanta.
Athamas.
The Award of the Arms (*Hoplôn Krisis*).
The Bassarids (= *The Bacchae*?)
The Bone-gatherers (*Ostologoi*) (see Chapter 10).
The Cabeiri.
Callisto.
The Carians, or Europa.
Cercyon (satyric).
The Chamber-makers (*Thalamopoioi*) (probably satyric; see Chapter 10).
The Children of Heracles (*Heracleidae*).
CHOEPHOROI (*The Libation Bearers*) (458; see Chapter 7).
Circe (satyric; see Chapter 10).
The Cretan Women.
The Danaids (463?; see Chapter 6).
The Daughters of the Sun (*Heliades*).
The Edonians.
The Egyptians (463?; see Chapter 6).
The Eleusinians.
The Epigoni.
The Escort (*Propompoi*).
EUMENIDES (458; see Chapter 7).
The Ghost-raisers (*Psykhagôgoi*) (see Chapter 10).
Glaucus of Potniae (*Glaukos Potnieus*) (472).
Glaucus the Sea-god (*Glaukos Pontios*) (probably satyric).
The Heralds (*Kêrykes*) (satyric).
Hypsipyle.
Iphigeneia.
Ixion (probably satyric).
Laius (467; see Chapter 5).
The Lemnian Women (*Lêmniai*).[29]
The Lion (*Leôn*) (satyric).

Lycurgus (satyric).
Memnon.
The Myrmidons (see Chapter 10).
The Mysians.
Nemea (perhaps satyric).
The Nereids (see Chapter 10).
The Net-Haulers (*Dictyulci, Diktyoulkoi*) (satyric; see Chapter 9).
Niobe (see §11.4).
The Nurses of Dionysus (*Trophoi, Dionysou Trophoi*) (probably satyric).
Oedipus (467; see Chapter 5).
Oreithyia (perhaps satyric).
Palamedes.
Penelope (see Chapter 10).
Pentheus.
The Perrhaebian Women (*Perrhaibides*).
THE PERSIANS (*Persae*) (472; see Chapter 4).
Philoctetes.
Phineus (472).
The Phorcides.
The Phrygians (*Phryges*), *or The Ransoming of Hector* (see Chapter 10).
The Phrygian Women (*Phrygiai*).[30]
Polydectes.
The Priestesses (*Hiereiai*).
PROMETHEUS BOUND (*Promêtheus Desmotês*) (see Chapter 8).
Prometheus the Fire-bearer (*Promêtheus Pyrphoros*; probably identical with *Prometheus the Fire-kindler [Promêtheus Pyrkaeus]* and, if so, satyric and produced in 472; see §8.4).
Prometheus Unbound (*Promêtheus Lyomenos*) (see Chapter 8).
Proteus (458; satyric; see end of §7.3).
The Sacred Delegation, or At the Isthmian Games (*Theôroi or Isthmiastai*) (satyric; see Chapter 9)
Semele, or The Water-carriers.
THE SEVEN AGAINST THEBES (467; see Chapter 5).
Sisyphus the Runaway (probably satyric).
Sisyphus the Stone-roller (probably satyric).
The Sphinx (467; satyric; see Chapter 5).
THE SUPPLIANT MAIDENS (*Supplices, Hiketides*) (463?; see Chapter 6).
Telephus.
The Thracian Women.
The Weighing of Souls (*Psykhostasia*).
The Women of Aetna (*Aitnaiai*).[31]
The Women of Argos (*Argeiai*).[29]
The Women of Salamis (*Salaminiai*).[29]
The Wool-carders (*Xantriai*).
The Youths (*Neaniskoi*).

Many of these plays were, or may have been, produced in connected sequences (tetralogies); these will be discussed in Chapter 3.

The Aeschylean corpus as known to us thus comprises some 78 plays, about a quarter of them (exactly the proportion we should expect, given the structure of the City Dionysia programme) certainly or probably satyr-plays.[32] The figure of 90 for Aeschylus' total output, offered by the tenth-century *Suda* lexicon, if not a scribal error may derive from the festival records and include plays that did not survive into the Hellenistic period. During the early centuries of the Christian era most of the plays gradually ceased to be read and copied, and long before the tenth century (the date of our oldest medieval manuscript of Aeschylus, known as the Mediceus, now in the Laurentian library at Florence) only seven were still in existence. More recently, papyrus discoveries have restored to us substantial portions of *The Net-Haulers* and *The Sacred Delegation*, and other papyri, together with many ancient quotations and references, give us greater or lesser degrees of information about the vast majority of the other 'lost' plays.

Aeschylus' ancient *Life* says that he won thirteen victories in the dramatic competition 'and not a few after his death'; the *Suda* lexicon credits him with 28 victories, which, if correct, must include the posthumous ones.[33]

Aeschylus left two sons, Euphorion and Euaeon, both of whom themselves became tragic poets. Euphorion is reported to have won four first prizes with previously unperformed plays by his father (*Suda* ε3800), and since it is hardly a plausible supposition that Aeschylus had composed sixteen new plays in the last three years of his life, it was not unreasonable for West to suspect[34] that on some at least of these occasions Euphorion was actually producing his own work under his father's name; it may have been with one such production that he won first prize in 431, defeating both Sophocles and Euripides (Euripides' plays included *Medea*).[35] Of Euaeon's professional life nothing is known; but his good looks are the theme of about a dozen vase-inscriptions of the 440s. This evidence suggests a substantial age-gap between the brothers, with Euphorion born no later than about 480, Euaeon no earlier than about 467.

In addition to his previously mentioned brother, Cynegeirus, Aeschylus had a sister who married one Philopeithes and became the ancestress of a long line of tragic dramatists.[36] The first of the dynasty was Philocles, whose known period of activity extends from about the 430s until after 410. He is said to have written 100 plays, and on one occasion he defeated Sophocles when the latter's production included *Oedipus the King*.[37] He was thought, however, to have an unpleasant style, and was nicknamed 'Gall' and 'Briny'. Philocles had a son Morsimus and probably another son Melanthius: both were tragic poets (Melanthius may have been an actor also), both were active in the last three decades of the fifth century, both were lampooned in comedy, from which we learn that Morsimus was a small man and practised as an eye-doctor, while Melanthius had a skin disease and was fond of good food. Philocles may have lived *c.* 480-405, Morsimus *c.* 450-400.

Morsimus' son, Astydamas, first entered the dramatic competition in 398 but won little distinction; he lived to be sixty, so his dates may be taken as *c.* 423-363. He in turn left two sons, a second Astydamas and a second Philocles; the latter is an obscure figure, but the former was one of the leading tragic dramatists of the fourth century. He won his first victory in 372, when he cannot have been much over twenty-five, and was still at the height of his fame in 340 when he was awarded the signal honour of a bronze statue of himself in the theatre. In all he won fifteen victories, and he is credited with no less than 240 plays (many of which must have been produced outside Athens).[38] It is tempting to conjecture that when Lycurgus (who dominated Athenian finance and administration from 338 to 326) sought to establish an official text of the three great fifth-century tragedians for future revivals, it was to Astydamas, as the heir of Aeschylus, that he turned for copies of Aeschylus' scripts – for Aeschylus' plays, being much less often revived than those of Sophocles or Euripides, will have been considerably harder to come by in the 330s. If so, it is to Astydamas that we owe the preservation of no small part of what remains of Aeschylean drama.[39]

Notes

1. Dates given in this form refer to the Athenian calendar year, which normally began and ended soon after midsummer. Our sources give, or rather imply, various dates for Aeschylus' birth, but 525/4 is the only one which is attested more than once (*Suda* αι357, with π2230; *Parian Marble* A 48 and 59), and it is consistent with our other evidence about the chronology of Aeschylus' career. It may well, however, have been reached by the common ancient chronological practice of taking a notable event in a person's career (in this case Aeschylus' first victory in 485/4) as his *floruit* and assuming he was then forty years old, and it should not be regarded as more than approximately correct.

2. [Plato], *Hipparchus* 228b (crediting Hipparchus); Cicero, *De Oratore* 3.137; *Palatine Anthology* 11.442; Pausanias 7.26.13 (all crediting Peisistratus). See Janko 1992: 29-32.

3. This traditional date for the institution of the tragic competition has been queried by Connor 1990 and by Scullion 2002: 81, but Osborne 1993 and Sourvinou-Inwood 1994 have argued on independent grounds that the competition is likely to date from the time of Peisistratus. Certainly 'it was the general belief … from as far back as we can see … that Thespis lived under Pisistratus' (M.L. West 1989: 253).

4. *Polis* (plural *poleis*) will often be left untranslated. It denotes an independent political unit, able to make its own laws, and focused on a (normally fortified) urban centre; it is commonly translated as 'city', 'state' or 'city-state'. See Hansen 2006.

5. Dithyrambs were performances of song and dance, originally (but by the fifth century not always) in honour of Dionysus, by a chorus of fifty in circular formation.

6. These records were later published on stone, and have in part survived as *IG* ii² 2318.

7. It was during the 70th Olympiad (Suda π2230) – which ran from 500 to 496 – and Aeschylus was twenty-five years old (*Suda* αι357).

8. It is now widely held that some very early plays of Aeschylus *did* survive, and that the famous Achilles trilogy (see §10.1) was among them (Döhle 1967, Kossatz-Deissmann 1981: 106-14, Garzya 1995: 46-7, Michelakis 2002: 22n.1, 31n.21). This is because a series of vase paintings, the earliest of which are dated by art historians to the 490s, show Odysseus addressing an Achilles who is muffled up in his cloak as the Aeschylean Achilles is known to have been (Aristophanes, *Frogs* 911-12). It would then follow, however, that one of Aeschylus' most celebrated productions – and a popular one at the time, if it really did stimulate all this artistic activity – did not win first prize; and I would ask, with M.L.West 2000: 341n.11: 'does anyone trust vase datings to within five years?' There is another series of vase paintings, beginning about the same time, clearly linkable to the companion play *The Nereids*.

9. There are only five plays of Phrynichus from which ancient authors quote fragments.

10. Each production comprised four plays (see Chapter 3), so that fifty-two of Aeschylus' plays (perhaps about 60% of his total output, see pp. 10-13) formed part of victorious productions.

11. Scholia to Aristophanes, *Frogs* 1028.

12. See pp. 45, 62-5, on the tetralogy of 472.

13. In an ancient Greek context 'barbarian' (*barbaros*) means 'non-Greek' or 'non-Greek-speaking'.

14. The two last-mentioned plays may have been produced together; and either this production, or one of the others here discussed, may have been posthumous.

15. The 177 dead from one of the ten tribes, killed in six different theatres of war 'in the same year', are commemorated in *IG* i^3 1147.

16. Athenaeus 14.627c; Pausanias 1.14.5.

17. Michael Hendry has called to my attention the parallel case of the epitaph of Thomas Jefferson, which describes him as 'author of the Declaration of American Independence, of the Statute of Virginia for Religious Freedom, and father of the University of Virginia' – and no more: even if we did not know positively that Jefferson had prescribed this wording himself, we could have inferred it with near-certainty from the epitaph's failure to mention that he had also been President of the United States.

18. In addition, one feature of the epitaph's language (the use of *alsos* to mean, not 'grove' or 'sacred precinct', but 'level expanse'), is otherwise found only in poetry of the period 480-410 BC and is particularly characteristic of Aeschylus; see Sommerstein 1996.

19. *CAG* xx 145.23-32.

20. See Bowie 1993: 24-6, with references to earlier literature.

21. Dover 1968: xx.

22. See Aristotle, *Constitution of Athens* 23.2 and Plutarch, *Cimon* 14.3-5.

23. Plutarch, *Pericles* 31-2.

24. So Jacoby 1947: 3-4.

25. M.L. West 1985: 78n.25 suggested Ion as source for the 'slices from Homer' remark.

26. One is preserved in the *Palatine Anthology* (7.255), and a line from another is quoted by Theophrastus, *Enquiry into Plants* 9.15.

27. It is mentioned by his ancient biographer, and cited (at second hand) by Plutarch, *Moralia* 628d-e.

28. Where two titles are shown in the form 'A or B' this implies that the play is actually referred to as 'A or B' in at least one ancient source. Other alternative designations listed here mostly reflect the varying habits of modern scholars who may transliterate, latinize or anglicize the Greek titles.

29. For this play, and also for *The Women of Argos* and *The Women of Salamis* (see below), a minority of our sources give the title the ending *-oi* instead of *-ai*, indicating a male rather than a female chorus. The medieval catalogue of Aeschylus' plays (see next note) is in the minority each time, and twice it is in a minority of one.

30. We know of this play only from the catalogue of Aeschylus' plays found in some medieval manuscripts, where it is listed as *Phrygioi*. Either this title is no more than a variant form of *Phryges*, or, as here assumed, we are again dealing with a confusion of the endings *-oi* and *-ai*, to which this catalogue is particularly prone (see previous note).

31. The title means only 'female Aetnaeans', and these may well in fact have been, not women of the city, but nymphs of the mountain (Grassi 1956: 208-9; Lucas de Dios 2008: 186). The medieval catalogue mentions both a 'genuine' and a 'spurious' play of this name. There is no other reference to a second play; possibly Aeschylus, having originally produced the play in Sicily, revised the script for a later Athenian production, and later scholars supposed that the revision was not his work.

32. Many scholars have also posited a play about Cycnus on the evidence of Aristophanes, *Frogs* 963, and one about Tennes (the eponymous hero of the island of Tenedos) on the evidence of a papyrus fragment (*Oxyrhynchus Papyrus* 2256 frr. 51-3 = Aesch. fr. dub. 451o Radt).

33. But see Biles (forthcoming) for a persuasive attack on the ancient tradition (scholia to Aristophanes, *Acharnians* 10 and *Frogs* 868; *Life of Aeschylus* 13; Philostratus, *Life of Apollonius* 6.11; Quintilian 10.1.66) that a decree was passed permitting the posthumous restaging of Aeschylean plays in the City Dionysia tragic competition.

34. M.L. West 1990b: 67-72; 2000.

35. For the possibility that Euphorion may have been the author of *Prometheus Bound* and *Prometheus Unbound* – and may have produced them in 431 – see §8.5.

36. Their genealogy is given in a scholium to Aristophanes, *Birds* 281.

37. Hypothesis II to *Oedipus the King*, citing Dicaearchus (fr. 80 Wehrli).

38. *IG* ii^2 2325.44, 2318.314, 2320.3-6; Diogenes Laertius 2.43; *Suda* α4264-5, σ161 . The compiler of the *Suda*, though he knew there were two tragedians named Astydamas, seems to have misattributed to the elder some information that actually related to the younger.

39. Even two generations later the family still held a leading place in the Athenian theatrical world; in 278/7 we find another Astydamas, probably a grandson of the mid-fourth-century dramatist, going to Delphi on a delegation from the Athenian Artists of Dionysus, and securing from the Amphictiony a decree confirming certain privileges enjoyed by the guild (*IG* ii^2 1132).

2

Aeschylus' Theatre

2.1. The performing space

We have basically four sources of information about the physical layout and equipment of the theatre in which Aeschylus' plays were originally produced. The first, and least reliable, consists of explicit statements by (mostly late) writers about the conditions of theatrical production. The second source is the actual physical remains of the Theatre of Dionysus, under the southern face of the Athenian Acropolis, where the performances took place; unfortunately, owing to subsequent reconstructions, the evidence these provide about the fifth century, especially its first half, is slight and ambiguous. The third source, to which increasing attention has been paid in recent years, is the remains of *other* early theatres, especially those in other parts of Attica; their layout is often much less obscured by later alterations, but it must not be forgotten that they were designed for much smaller audiences and probably for a more restricted range of types of performance. And the fourth is the evidence of the plays themselves, principally those which survive complete but also, under due caution, those for which we have only indirect information together with fragments of text.

Considering first the surviving plays, and leaving aside for the time being the doubtfully authentic *Prometheus Bound* (on which see §8.3), we find, as Wilamowitz (1886) was the first to see, a clear division between the *Oresteia* and the rest. In the *Oresteia* – as in every surviving play of Sophocles, Euripides,[1] Aristophanes and Menander – the text, during at least part of the action, makes a clear distinction between an 'outside' area, the normal acting space, and an 'inside' area – usually but not always a building or buildings – of which the façade and entrance are visible to the audience but the interior normally is not (though interior scenes may be presented in certain circumstances: see below). In *Agamemnon* and the second half of *Choephoroi* the 'inside' area represents the palace of the Atreidae at Argos; in the opening scenes of *Eumenides* it represents the temple of Apollo at Delphi; and in each of the three plays characters are seen to go 'in' and come 'out'. With one doubtful exception, nothing of this sort occurs in *The Persians* or *Seven against Thebes* or *The Suppliant Maidens*. Susa, Thebes, Argos presumably have each a royal palace, but in each play this is assumed to be somewhere at a distance; in each of the three plays there is a holy place within the acting area, but in none of them is it a built temple; in *Supp.*, where the scene is set on the seashore, there is no sign of the cave which in later tragedies and satyr-plays[2] seems an invariable accompaniment to a seashore scene; characters arrive and depart, but their departure is never spoken of as 'going in' nor their arrival as 'coming out'. In short, everything proceeds as though, from the time of the *Oresteia* onwards, the theatrical environment included a building, with a door or doors, which could be taken, according to the requirements of particular plays, as representing a house, palace, temple, hut, etc., or a cave, or (as for example in Sophocles' *Oedipus at Colonus*) a wood or grove or thicket; and as though in the three Aeschylean plays known to be earlier than the *Oresteia* this building was not yet in existence.

The 'one doubtful exception' to this generalization occurs in *Pers.* 140-1. At the beginning of this play the chorus enter, chanting in 'marching anapaests'; then they sing eleven lyric stanzas; then, in anapaests once more, they decide, as they put it, to 'sit down in this ancient building' and deliberate. Is this 'ancient building' a part of the theatrical environment, identical with the building we find in the *Oresteia* and later? Various considerations make this unlikely. The later scene-building is almost always associated with the individual characters and not with the chorus. The chorus here could not go into an actual building and sit down, because to go into a building would be to leave the acting area, so we would have to assume that they were about to enter the building but are prevented by the appearance of the Queen (seen approaching at 150); yet by that point the subject for deliberation has already been propounded in some detail (144-9), as if the councillors were already seated and ready to begin their business. Moreover, the building is never mentioned again throughout the play. Its treatment is in no way parallel to that of the scene-building in later drama, and it is most unlikely to be the same entity. We know that at the beginning of Phrynichus' play on the same theme a eunuch had been preparing chairs for the councillors to sit on (Hypothesis I to *Persians*), and it is reasonable to suppose that Aeschylus gave his councillors chairs as well: a Greek dramatist would hardly allow distinguished Persians (presented in this play as a people given to luxurious living) to sit on the ground if it could be avoided (unless they were in mourning – and the play has not reached that stage yet). Either then there was some purely conventional symbolization of a building (such as a screen placed behind the chairs, and removed with them when they were no longer needed), or else the building was left entirely to the spectators' imagination.[3] At any rate the passage cannot safely be used as evidence for the existence of a scene-building in 473/2.

What *can* we say about the theatrical environment for these earlier Aeschylean plays? There must, in the first place, have been an area for the evolutions of the chorus – to use the word that later became regular, an *orkhêstra* or dance-floor. The shape of the early *orkhêstra* is disputed. In later theatres, such as the famous one at Epidaurus, the *orkhêstra* tends to be circular, and until recently it was nearly always assumed that this was also true of the fifth-century Athenian theatre. Since 1974, however, attention has been drawn to the tendency of other known fifth-century theatres, such as that at Thoricus in south-east Attica, to have an *orkhêstra* of roughly rectangular or trapezoidal form, wider than it was deep, and it has been argued that the physical evidence from the Theatre of Dionysus points the same way. Such an *orkhêstra* would have to be able to accommodate the choruses of dithyramb, consisting of fifty performers and dancing in circular formation; for a long time scholars favouring the quadrilateral *orkhêstra* ignored this constraint, but Goette 2007 posits an *orkhêstra* of about 24x19 metres,[4] which would satisfy the requirement. Such a shape for the *orkhêstra* would also be consistent with the evidence of Aristophanes, *Frogs* 441, which seems to speak of it as 'the sacred circle of the goddess' (441): in such a context *kyklos* 'circle' will not have been used with geometrical precision, and Goette's rectangular *orkhêstra* would be at least as circle-like as the *agora* of most Greek cities[5] and considerably more so than that of Athens. On present evidence, I cautiously favour an *orkhêstra* of approximately this shape for the fifth-century Athenian theatre.

The *orkhêstra* will have been approached by side passages from east and west (referred to as *eisodoi* in fifth-century comedy) for the entrance and exit of actors and chorus. Later writers tell us that the two passages were associated by convention with particular points of origin or destination (the market-place, the harbour, the countryside, etc.). This convention in its developed form may well be of Hellenistic date, but in at least some Aeschylean plays it is not difficult to associate the two *eisodoi* with contrasting directions of approach: in *Pers.* the direction of the palace (east?) and the direction whence the Messenger and Xerxes return from the war (west, cf. 232?); in *Supp.* the city and the harbour.

In all the three early plays there is evidence for the existence, somewhere in the acting area, of an elevated place, usually spoken of as a rock (*pagos*) or a mound (*okhthos*). In *Pers.* this *okhthos* (660) represents the burial-mound of Darius. In *Seven* it is called 'this acropolis' (240); on it are statues of the city's gods, and to it the chorus flock to beseech their aid until Eteocles orders them to 'get away from the statues' (265). In *Supp.* Danaus advises his daughters to sit at 'this *pagos* which belongs to the assembled gods' (189) and where stand their images and a common altar for them all (222). They stay there until the Argive king persuades them to move to 'this level meadow' (508), which must be the *orkhêstra*; later however we find that Danaus is again on the rock, 'this lookout post that welcomes suppliants' (713), from which he sees the Egyptian ships approaching, and when eventually the Egyptians arrive the girls 'flee to protection' (831), evidently to the sanctuary afforded by the images and altars. Where might this elevation have been?

An attractive theory advanced in 1972 by N.G.L. Hammond was based on the supposed archaeological datum that there had existed at one time, near the eastern *eisodos*, a natural outcrop of rock. Its height was unknown, but its base area was put at about 25 square metres. Hammond argued that this rock still existed in the Aeschylean theatre, and that it constituted the *pagos/okhthos* of the earlier plays. This theory made the staging of some passages rather difficult: if the chorus were on the rock when an actor entered via the eastern *eisodos*, he would either come face to face with them while still in the entrance-passage and out of view of most of the audience, or else would have to approach them from behind, go *past* them to reach the centre of the *orkhêstra*, and then make a U-turn in order to address them. It was eventually shown by Scullion (1994: 46-7) to be based on a misunderstanding of the archaeological evidence.

One would on the whole expect that if there were any choice in the matter, the *pagos/okhthos* would be placed symmetrically with respect to the two *eisodoi*, i.e. either in the centre of the *orkhêstra* or else behind it in the area later occupied by the scene-building and its frontage. And some considerations might seem to tell strongly in favour of the former alternative. Firstly, the *pagos/okhthos* does not seem to have immediately disappeared when the scene-building was added, and other changes perhaps made, in Aeschylus' later years: in the *Oresteia*, produced after that time, the whole of the first half of *Cho.* is centred on the burial-mound of Agamemnon (called an *okhthos* in line 4) in much the same way as *Pers.* 598-851 is centred on that of Darius.

Secondly, it is likely that throughout the history of the theatre there was a structure of some sort (sometimes called the *thymelê*, a term already found in this connection in one fifth-century text[6]) in the centre of the *orkhêstra*, around which the circular dithyrambic choruses danced; and this could well have served as a focus of action in tragedy as well. It has usually been supposed that the *thymelê* had a 'real-life' ritual function as an altar of Dionysus which would make it inappropriate for it to be also employed in a range of fictive dramatic functions as the focus of a sanctuary of another god or gods, let alone as a tomb; however, Rehm 1988 has argued very persuasively that this notion of a 'ritual altar' is nothing but a modern dogma without evidential support, and Wiles 1997: 70-2, 191, has argued on archaeological and linguistic grounds that the *thymelê* was not an altar at all but merely some kind of physical marker of the centre of the *orkhêstra*, which could however have property objects, including altars, placed on it. Since the *pagos/okhthos* is consistently spoken of as being elevated, we would have to assume that the earth surrounding the *thymelê* was banked up somewhat – not necessarily to a great height, but enough to mark the area out clearly as being above the body of the *orkhêstra*. It would be easy to place near the *thymelê* one or more images of deities in accordance with the requirements of any particular play.

Thirdly, placing the *pagos/okhthos* in the centre of the *orkhêstra* seems to fit well with some of the evidence from play-texts. It makes it possible to stage scenes in which the *pagos/okhthos*, with its altar or tomb, is entirely surrounded by a chorus; such a staging is explicitly attested for an unknown play of Aeschylus (fr. 379) and is highly probable for the 'binding song' of *Eum.* 307-96. And it enables one, as Rehm shows, to posit a continuity between the staging of suppliant scenes in Aeschylus' time and in the later fifth century, when choruses are still found supplicating at altars (as in Euripides' *Children of Heracles* and *Suppliant Women*).

However, a problem for any such assumption, at least in the 'early' Aeschylean theatre, is posed by another feature of theatrical topography which is called for by the script of Aeschylus' oldest surviving play. In *The Persians* the ghost of Darius, called up from the underworld, emerges, so the text invites us to suppose, from the top (659) of his burial-mound, and his own words make it clear that he has come from under the earth (683, 685, 697) and returns thither at the end of the scene (839). It is of course possible in principle that the actor simply enters from the side and ascends the mound, but this is unlikely: the heroic dead were felt to be present *in* their tombs – that indeed is why Darius is summoned, and offerings poured to him, at this particular place – and he ought not therefore to enter as if arriving from somewhere else. One might then be tempted to suppose that the ghost rose through a hole in the soil of the mound, the performer having got there by an underground passage whose other entrance lay somewhere at or beyond the edge of the *orkhêstra*. Such passages, built in stone, existed in some later theatres under the name of 'Charon's steps'; but there is no evidence at all that one existed in the Athenian theatre at any time in its history, let alone in the fifth century. Hence the *pagos/okhthos* from which Darius seemed to emerge cannot have been in the centre of the *orkhêstra*.

The only solution that I can see is one proposed by Bieber 1961 and revived by Scullion 1994: 70n.9: that the tomb-mound was built up against the *back wall* of the *orkhêstra* terrace (which must, for safety reasons, have stood a metre or so above the level of the *orkhêstra* itself) and that the ghost climbed a ladder placed behind it. This then was doubtless the *pagos/okhthos* in *Seven* and *Supp.* as well (cf. Sandin 2003: 15-19). Once the back of the *orkhêstra* was occupied by the scene-building, the *pagos/okhthos* must have been moved somewhere else – presumably then to the centre of the *orkhêstra*.[7] It is then necessary to assume that Aesch. fr. 379, where a chorus of women is instructed to 'stand all round this altar [in] an endless [i.e. circular] band, and pray', must come from a play produced after the creation of the scene-building.

To the environment thus far described the *Oresteia* adds a scene-building. I say 'adds' because nothing seems to have been subtracted: all the features of the earlier theatre remain available. The *pagos/okhthos* is shifted to the centre of the *orkhêstra*, around the *thymelê*, but in its new position it serves much the same functions. The elevation represents a burial-mound in *Cho.* as it did in *Pers.*, and Orestes and Electra beg

Agamemnon's ghost to appear to them there (*Cho.* 489-96); their prayers are not answered, and indeed it may no longer have been possible for a ghost actually to appear from 'underground' in the way Darius' ghost did. In *Eum.*, to be sure, a ghost does appear, that of Clytaemestra, but she does not emerge from her tomb (for the action is set at Delphi, not at Argos where she was buried) and she may simply have come on stage along one of the *eisodoi*.[8] Later in *Eum.* (235-489) the mound may function as a sanctuary and place of supplication, as in *Supp.*, when Orestes appeals to Athena and the Erinyes sing their 'binding song' around him; and in *Ag.* it may be towards the *thymelê* that the Herald turns when he addresses the 'assembled gods' of Argos (513) whom Danaus and Pelasgus had designated by the same expression in *Supp.* (189, 242).

The features of the scene-building (*skênê*), of which we learn from the *Oresteia*, are as follows. The building was capable of representing either a palace or a temple. It had one main door, presumably in the centre of its façade; and analysis of *Cho.* 875ff. strongly suggests that there was also at least one other door (see §7.6.6). If so, there is likely, for symmetry, to have been a third door on the opposite side.[9] In addition, the roof was accessible to the actors (*Ag.* 1-39). All this is consistent with, though it does not of course prove, the hypothesis that the scene-building of 458 was similar in all essentials to that of the 420s and later, which is known to us principally from Euripides and Aristophanes.

There has been a long and sterile argument over whether in Aeschylus' time (or indeed thereafter) there was an elevated platform ('raised stage') between the scene-building and the *orkhêstra*. There is, in my opinion, evidence in the play-texts (and also in art) for the existence of such a platform from about 422 onwards[10] – though even then, and *a fortiori* earlier, there was easy access in both directions between the *orkhêstra* and the house. Earlier than that there is no clear evidence, and all we can say is that if there was a platform it can hardly have been raised by more than a couple of steps. It is perhaps likeliest that there always was a platform. As we have seen, there was an elevated place in the acting area before there was a scene-building, so that dramatists and audience were used to the idea of a significant contrast of levels; moreover the scene-building was behind the *orkhêstra* and further from the audience, and a little added height would increase the visibility and prominence of those performers who were near the building. This effect could be put to good use in *Agamemnon*, where time and again Clytaemestra, coming out of the palace, would visually dominate the Elders or the Herald or Aegisthus below her in the *orkhêstra*.

In the later fifth century two 'special-effects' devices were used in the theatre, the flying-machine (*mêkhanê* or *kradê*) and the so-called *ekkyklêma*.[11] The flying-machine, essentially a crane, was used for airborne entries, such as those of Bellerophon in Euripides' play of that name and Perseus in his *Andromeda* (parodied by Aristophanes in *Peace* and *Thes-*

mophoriazusae respectively), and for such scenes as the escape of Medea by flying chariot; later also for the interventions of what, long afterwards, came to be called *dei ex machina*. The *ekkyklêma*, a platform on wheels which could be rolled out of the central door of the scene-building, was used in tragedy mainly for the revelation of tableau-like interior scenes, in comedy also for a variety of other purposes.

It is disputed whether these devices were already in use at the end of Aeschylus' career; Taplin 1977: 442-7 in particular, though hesitantly, denied him both of them. Yet the scenes for which the use of the *ekkyklêma* has generally been posited in the *Oresteia* – Clytaemestra over the bodies of Agamemnon and Cassandra (*Ag.* 1372ff.), Orestes over the bodies of Clytaemestra and Aegisthus (*Cho.* 973ff.), Orestes beset by the Erinyes at Delphi (*Eum.* 64ff.) – seem precisely parallel to scenes in later tragedy where its use is not now seriously disputed. Taplin argued that in these later scenes the impending use of the device is carefully signalled by what seems to be a well-established convention,[12] and there are no such signals in the *Oresteia* scenes; but this may indicate merely that in 458 the convention in question was not yet established. The object of the conventional cues was to make it clear to the audience that the tableau they were about to see was meant to be *inside* the background building. In the *Oresteia* this purpose is served by other, less stereotyped methods: in *Ag.* by the bathtub and by Clytaemestra's statement that 'I stand where I struck' (1379); in *Cho.*, more subtly, by the almost perfect repetition of the stage-picture from *Ag.*; in *Eum.* by the fact that the scene portrayed is precisely that which the Pythia, a moment previously, reported having seen inside the temple (see further §7.6.2).

Regarding the *mêkhanê* there is considerably more room for uncertainty. It is suspicious that the two plays in the Aeschylean corpus where its use seems virtually certain – *Prometheus Bound* (see §8.3) and *The Weighing of Souls* (see pp. 7-8 above) – are both, for quite other reasons, of doubtful authenticity. There is some case for giving Athena a flying entrance in *Eumenides* (397), but it is far from conclusive. While, therefore, it seems highly likely that the *ekkyklêma* was introduced at the same time as the scene-building, in the late 460s, the *mêkhanê* may be of somewhat later origin.[13]

2.2. Performers and properties

The performers of Aeschylean tragedy comprised a chorus, two or three speaking actors (*hypokritai*), an unlimited number of mutes, and (by no means least) a piper to accompany the songs. The chorus consisted of twelve members (*khoreutai*): Sophocles, according to his ancient *Life*, increased the number to fifteen, but the debate among twelve speakers in *Ag.* 1348-71 shows that this happened after 458. The *khoreutai* were ordinary citizens, selected and trained by the *khorêgos* or sponsor of the production in conjunction with the author-director and possibly with a specialist trainer; they were probably always young men, aged between eighteen and thirty.[14] Since music and singing were an important part of traditional Greek education, and since every year 500 boys under eighteen performed in dithyrambic contests at the City Dionysia alone and many more at other festivals, there will always have been a substantial pool of candidates with a basic competence in the required skills. We are told that unlike the 'circular' choruses of dithyramb, tragic choruses danced in a rectangular formation, though this should not be regarded as a rigid rule: certain ritualistic scenes focused on the *thymelê* (above, p. 22) cry out for a circular formation, and in others (above all the entry of the chorus in *Seven*) the dancing may have been designedly chaotic. By a convention which probably went back to the earliest days of drama, the leader of the chorus (the *hêgemôn* or *koryphaios*[15]) could represent the whole group in dialogue with the actors; he often has quite an important speaking part (in *Ag.* he speaks 148 lines, more than anyone else in the play except Clytaemestra), though he only very rarely delivers a long set speech. Since in addition the chorus-leader was a full participant in all the songs and dances of the chorus as a whole, and must in practice have found himself largely responsible for their moment-to-moment direction on stage, he bore arguably a heavier burden than any of his fellow-performers – and seems not to have gained as much honour by it as he deserved: authors, *khorêgoi*, pipers, leading actors, might all win fame, but in the whole classical period we do not know the name of a single tragic *koryphaios*.[16] We may well, though, suspect that a remark on the chorus-leader's importance, made by the fourth-century orator (and *khorêgos*) Demosthenes, deserves a fair degree of credence:

> You know, I am sure, that if the leader (*hêgemôn*) is taken away, the rest of the chorus is done for (Demosthenes, *Against Meidias* 60).

In some plays, both by Aeschylus and by later dramatists, there is more than one chorus. In such cases one chorus is always clearly the principal one: it enters early in the play, it remains present continuously or almost continuously until the end, it sings repeatedly, and its leader has a speaking part. A subsidiary chorus will normally be present, and sing, in one scene only, and (at least in tragedy) its leader will not be given words to speak. Two surviving plays of Aeschylus have subsidiary choruses. In *Eum.* a chorus of the female temple-staff of Athena take part in the final procession and sing the concluding lyrics. In *Supp.* the concluding lyrics take the form of a dialogue between the main chorus of the daughters of Danaus and a subsidiary chorus whose identity is disputed (see §6.1); it is also possible that earlier in the play (836ff.) the Egyptian herald is accompanied by a chorus of Egyptian soldiers. We have no firm evidence for any conventions regarding the size of such subsidiary choruses.

The tragedies of the sixth and early fifth centuries had only one speaking actor other than the chorus-leader, and Aeschylus himself is said to have added a second; a third actor was introduced, either by Aeschylus or by Sophocles, in the late 460s, and is employed in the *Oresteia*. There are moments in that trilogy when one feels Aeschylus would have liked to go even further: many have suggested that he actually uses a fourth actor at one moment of *Choephoroi* (but see §7.6.6), and in *Eumenides* the chorus-leader virtually functions as a fourth actor in the trial scene. Yet at the same time he remains capable of writing brilliant drama for a single actor and chorus, as in the greater part of *Agamemnon*. It had always been possible for the same actor to take different parts in successive scenes, but in the two-actor plays the number of speaking parts remains small (four in *Pers.*, two or three in the genuine portion of *Seven*, three in *Supp.*); *Ag.* has six (seven if 1651 is spoken by the captain of Aegisthus' bodyguard), *Cho.* seven or eight, *Eum.* five. For comparison, the number of speaking parts in Sophocles' surviving plays ranges from five to nine; Euripides' *Phoenician Maidens* has eleven, as does the pseudo-Euripidean *Rhesus* (and Aristophanes' *Acharnians* and *Birds* each have twenty-two!)

In addition to the speaking and singing performers there could be an unlimited number of silent performers.[17] A ruler, for example, would normally be accompanied by servants, of whom no notice would be taken by the characters unless they become relevant to the action. Thus we know that Clytaemestra has maids with her in *Ag.* 855ff., because they are needed to spread the crimson cloth before Agamemnon (908ff.): nowhere else in the play is any reference made to her being attended, but nevertheless it is likely that she *was* attended in the earlier scenes as a noble woman appearing in public normally would be (cf. *Cho.* 712ff.). In the murder-tableau (*Ag.* 1372ff.), on the other hand, Clytaemestra must certainly be alone with the two corpses. The *Oresteia* in particular also contains other groups of non-speaking performers who make a vital contribution to the structure and effect of the drama (see §7.6.5). Sometimes, contrariwise, the *absence* of expected attendants can be put to dramatic use, as when in *Pers.* 598ff. the Queen enters without her suite to bring offerings to Darius' grave, and when later the shattered Xerxes returns alone from the expedition on which all Asia had gone forth.

All the performers were male. There may have been some tendency for certain actors to specialize in female roles: in the four plays certainly by Aeschylus that have female actor-parts it is each time possible to distribute the parts in such a way that no actor plays both male and female characters.[18] No such principle can be applied, in general, to Sophocles or Euripides (or to *Prometheus Bound*).

Only one of Aeschylus' performers can be individually identified with certainty, namely Aeschylus himself, who we can safely assume was a principal actor in his own plays. This had always been one of the responsibilities of the author-composer-choreographer-director, as stories about

Thespis indicate; Sophocles, we are told, was the first dramatist *not* to perform in person, allegedly because he had a weak voice (*Life of Sophocles* 4). It is significant that a separate prize began to be awarded to the best actor in the tragedies at the City Dionysia about 450, a few years after Aeschylus' death.[19] Curiously enough nothing is recorded in ancient sources about Aeschylus' own acting; we have various statements about other actors he is said to have employed, but most if not all of these probably in fact refer to later performers who took leading roles in revivals or adaptations of Aeschylean plays.

All the performers wore what are conventionally called masks, but are better spoken of as headpieces, since they combined the functions of mask and wig. The masks in general will not have had the grotesque features found in some later artistic representations of tragic costume: their function was no more than to conceal the actor and identify the character. In most cases they will probably have been straightforward type-representations in accordance with the usual conventions of portraiture in art – men's skin dark, women's pale; young men smooth-faced, men in their prime bearded, old men white-haired and/or partly bald. But many plays will have had some masks of striking individuality: the swarthy complexions of the Danaids, at once African and unfeminine – and surprisingly appropriate, as it transpires, to these maidens who first reject marriage and then, when compelled to submit, murder their husbands – and the still darker features (cf. *Supp.* 719, 745, 888) of their Egyptian pursuers; possibly a somewhat feminine appearance for the unmanly Aegisthus, who is more than once called a 'woman' by his enemies (*Ag.* 1625, *Cho.* 304-5); the gashed cheeks of the chorus of *Choephoroi* (*Cho.* 24-5, 425-6); and the 'fearsome faces' of the Erinyes (*Eum.* 990).[20]

Since tragedy was invariably set in a milieu remote in time or (as in *Pers.*) remote in place from ordinary life, its costume also was more elevated than that of ordinary life (or of comedy). In relation to kings we hear in particular of a garment called the *xystis*, heavy, coloured and richly ornamented, which off the stage was scarcely worn except by charioteers in festival processions. But our Aeschylean texts are sufficient evidence that there was a great deal of variation. The Persian queen, having made her first entry in all the finery that Greek imagination could associate with an Asian empress, returns at *Pers.* 598 plainly dressed (cf. 607-8). Xerxes comes home in torn garments (834-6, 1018, 1030) and presently his counsellors rend their clothes likewise (1060). In *Seven* Eteocles probably wears shorter and lighter garments than tragic kings usually did; this helps, like his early speeches to the army and to the chorus, to mark him as a vigorous young man of action, and obviates the need for him to remove an outer garment when he arms himself in 676-719 (see §5.2). In *Supp.* the Danaids and their father, and likewise the Herald and those who accompany him, will have worn a Greek dramatist's idea of Egyptian costume: we hear of a 'Sidonian veil' of linen (120-1), of 'barbarian robes and headdresses' (235, cf. 431-3), and later, in connection with the men, of dark limbs standing out against white clothes (719-20) – which suggests that, for contrast, the Danaids' own clothes were brightly coloured. King Pelasgus, on the other hand, is dressed so plainly that the Danaids cannot tell whether he is ruler, priest or private citizen (247-8). In the *Oresteia* costume is eloquent in many ways (see §7.6.3) and especially through a three-way colour contrast: white, the colour of rejoicing and of Apollo, worn probably by most characters but especially by Cassandra, the Pythia and Apollo himself; black, the colour of death and mourning, worn by Electra and the chorus in *Choephoroi* and later by the Erinyes; and red or crimson (*phoinix*), a colour with multiple associations (royalty, luxury, blood), prominent among the colours of the cloth on which Agamemnon walks into his palace and probably also of the robes he is wearing, later seen in the blood-stains on the entangling robe through which he was stabbed – and later still, at the end of the trilogy, the colour of the new garments that symbolize the Erinyes' new status as accepted residents (*metoikoi*) at Athens taking part in a procession like that at the Panathenaic festival. All in all, there cannot have been much risk of monotony as far as costume was concerned in the Aeschylean theatre; Euripides' notorious 'ragged' heroes can be seen in this respect as following rather than flouting an older tradition.

It is not always easy to draw a line between 'costumes' and 'properties': on which side of such a line should we place Orestes' and Pylades' travel-bundles (*Cho.* 560, 675), or Xerxes' empty quiver (*Pers.* 1020-2), or the Danaids' suppliant-branches? There is no need to attempt to list here the wide variety of properties utilized in Aeschylus' plays, often to enormous dramatic effect; attention will be drawn to some of them in the discussions of particular plays (see especially §7.6.4). A few words may, however, be said here about one kind of 'property' of which Aeschylus seems to have been particularly fond, namely wheeled vehicles.

At least twice, and probably three or even four times, an Aeschylean ruler makes his or her entry to the scene in such a vehicle. The first such instance is that of the Persian Queen, and the manner in which it is handled suggests that the convention was already well established: the vehicle is not even mentioned in the scene in which it appears (*Pers.* 150ff.), and we only know about it because in a later scene, when the Queen re-enters in humbler style, she makes a point of mentioning (*Pers.* 607) that this time she has no vehicle. The second certain case is that of Agamemnon. Translators and commentators sometimes speak of him as arriving in a chariot, but in the text (*Ag.* 906, 1039) the vehicle is called an *apênê*, which properly means a four-wheeled carriage or wagon, and this is confirmed by 1054 which indicates that there were seats in it. The third case is that of Pelasgus in *The Suppliant Maidens*. Nothing is said about his means of transport when he enters at 234, but before his arrival Danaus has mentioned wheels, chariots and horses (181-3), and there seems little point in his talking thus if no vehicles are going to appear when the Argive army does arrive. It is not clear whether Pelasgus again arrives in a chariot at 911, though in that crowded scene it is perhaps more likely that he does not (see §6.4).

The use of vehicles serves different purposes in different plays. In *Pers.* it has primarily to do with the stereotype of oriental luxury; it also picks up the picture drawn by the chorus of Xerxes pursuing his enemies in a 'Syrian chariot' (84), and contrasts with his entry at the end of the play, alone, on foot, denuded of men, of wealth, and of the 'pavilion on wheels' (1000-1) in which he set forth. In *Supp.* the implications are military: the vehicle is not a travelling carriage but a chariot of war, and when the king drives it he has a retinue of soldiers. In *Agamemnon* too we might have expected a chariot, since Agamemnon is a military conqueror. But we do not get one. Instead we are presented with another Priam (cf. 918-20, 935-6) – or even perhaps with another, though a successful, Xerxes; and by giving Agamemnon an *apênê* Aeschylus makes it possible for Cassandra to ride with him, thus evoking the idea of a wedding procession. Agamemnon is bringing home a bride – to a house that has a wife in it already.

There is, by the way, no reason to doubt that these vehicles were drawn by actual animals. Aristophanes refers (*Frogs* 963) to an Aeschylean Memnon 'with bells on his horses' harness'; in *Supp.* 183 Danaus specifically mentions that he sees horses approaching, while the chorus of *Pers.* mention horses seven times before the entry of the Queen (14, 18, 26, 29, 32, 106, 126). For Greeks the horse – which was extremely expensive to keep and was of no practical use except in sport and war – was a symbol both of luxury and, because of the importance of chariots in the *Iliad*, of military prowess, significances one or both of which are appropriate to all the passages discussed above. These are not the only animals to appear on stage in surviving Aeschylean drama, for in *Eum.* one or more sacrificial beasts form part of the final procession (1006).

2.3. The spectators

The audience of Aeschylean drama was by most modern theatrical standards (though not by those of, say, Verona) a very large one. Recent excavations suggest that the capacity of the fifth-century theatre may have been considerably less than had usually been thought, but it may still have amounted to seven thousand or possibly more[21] – enough to make quite a respectable football crowd, and perhaps a little like one in other respects as well (average age, overwhelming predominance of one sex, liking for alcoholic refreshment, tendency to make unruly noises and possibly throw missiles at performers who displeased them, need for active policing – by stewards equipped with rods and empowered to use them). They were all, or almost all, male; the fifth- and fourth-century evidence indicates that while women were not formally debarred from attending the theatre, few women *of citizen status* ever actually went (Sommerstein 1980b: 16, 2001: 223). They were of all ages: characters in comedy addressing the audience, when they refer to the various groups composing it, nearly always make special mention of the young boys, and given ancient mortality rates it is likely that those under eighteen formed quite a high proportion of the total. Many will not have been Athenian citizens at all: there were many free non-citizens (*metoikoi*) resident at Athens,[22] and in addition there will have been some visitors from abroad, though probably not so many as in later decades when the City Dionysia became a show occasion of Athenian imperialism attended by delegations from all the 'allied' states. The audience will not of course have been perfectly representative of the Athenian community, even disregarding women and slaves. No self-selected sample could ever be so – and that includes the sovereign Assembly which in theory comprised all adult male citizens. There is, however, some reason to believe (see Sommerstein 1997) that in Aeschylus' time the citizen part of the theatre audience was much closer to being a fair cross-section of the citizen body as a whole than it became later in the century when comic dramatists like Cratinus and Aristophanes repeatedly scored successes with vicious political satire on Pericles, Cleon, and other leaders in the radical democratic tradition. Aeschylus could at all times, with only a mild degree of idealization, think of himself as presenting the actions and ideas of his plays to the whole Athenian people; and in *Eumenides* he makes Athena and the Erinyes, all but explicitly, treat the theatre audience as if it *were* the Athenian people.

Among this audience a special status inevitably attached to the judges of the dramatic competition. These were ten in number; like so many other ten-man bodies in the Athenian democracy, they were chosen by lot (from a larger panel which had been appointed by the Council, at least partly on the nomination of the *khorêgoi*) and comprised one member of each of the ten 'tribes' making up the citizen body. They constituted a 'jury' in the literal sense, for they were sworn to judge impartially. At the end of the tragic competition (which may well have extended over three days) the ten judges voted individually for the best chorus – for in theory the competition was, and always remained, a contest between choruses, though in practice the judges will have taken all aspects of the productions into account. It became a proverb that victory 'lay in the lap of *five* judges', and this expression, or something like it, probably goes back to fifth-century comedy (Cratinus fr. 177, Lysippus fr. 7); it most likely indicates that only five of the judges' votes (presumably drawn at random) were actually counted. This practice may have been seen as a precaution against corruption, or as a means of giving the gods (through the lottery process) a share in determining the winner, or as serving both purposes at once. It is not likely that the vote was often close:[23] references to the judges and the judging in comedy and by Plato[24] indicate that the jury were often heavily influenced by the expressed views of the ordinary spectators (no doubt they were as likely to be booed for an unpopular verdict as boxing judges are today). Above everything else, Greek tragedy was an art-form for the people. This does not preclude great sophistication and subtlety in its construction, on a large and a small scale. But if we find ourselves having to assume that an idea essential to the understanding of a play is one that would in all probability have gone far over the head of the man in the Athenian street, we are probably on a wrong track.

Notes

1. Except for *Rhesus*, which is abnormal in other respects also and is probably a fourth-century composition (see Liapis forthcoming).

2. Such as Sophocles' *Philoctetes*, and Euripides' *Andromeda* (parodied by Aristophanes in *Thesmophoriazusae*; cf. Eur. fr. 118 = *Thesm.* 1018).

3. Similarly in Aeschylus' *Myrmidons* Achilles, for most of the early part of the play, was sitting silent and muffled on stage (Aristophanes, *Frogs* 911-24), and the audience were in effect informed at the start that he was sitting *inside* his hut (Aesch. fr. 131.3-4); this scene was echoed in the third play of the same trilogy, *The Phrygians* (*Life of Aeschylus* 6).

4. Goette does not actually state these dimensions, but they can be read off his scale plan of the theatre (p. 117).

5. 'The circle of the *agora*' appears to have been a poetic cliché (Sophocles, *Oedipus the King* 161; Euripides, *Orestes* 919).

6. Pratinas *GL* 708.2 (from a dithyramb or satyr-play): 'what outrage has come against the noisy *thymelê* of Dionysus?'

7. Scullion 1994: 72 acutely notes that according to *Cho.* 322 Agamemnon's tomb is 'in front of the palace'; cf. already Garvie 1986: xli-xliii.

8. The only ghost-character in surviving later tragedy, Polydorus in Euripides' *Hecuba*, does not emerge from 'underground' but appears aloft (*Hecuba* 30-2), probably by means of the *mêkhanê* (he speaks of himself as *aiôroumenos* 'suspended as if on a swing').

9. Later tragedy used the side doors very little if at all; later comedy used them extensively. The earliest comedy known to have used all three doors is Eupolis' *Autolycus* (fr. 48), produced in 420.

10. The earliest textual evidence is probably in Aristophanes' *Wasps* (1341-4), produced in 422, and in Euripides' *Electra* (489-92), datable on metrical grounds *c.* 420. The earliest artistic evidence is a chous from Anavyssos (Attica), dated *c.* 420, showing a comic performer on a stage approached by steps (illustrated e.g. in Taplin 1993 pl. 8.25A).

11. The ancient name for this device is unknown; the word *ekkyklêma* 'wheeling-out' is late in attestation, and strictly it denotes not the device but an occasion on which it is used. However, the verb *ekkyklein* 'to wheel out' was a familiar theatrical term by 425 (Aristophanes, *Acharnians* 408-9).

12. Along the lines of 'open the doors, so that you/I may see ...' (cf. Euripides, *Hippolytus* 808; Sophocles, *Electra* 1458ff.).

13. Apart from *Prometheus Bound* and *The Weighing of Souls*, the earliest clear evidence for the use of the *mêkhanê* is in Euripides' *Medea* (1317ff.), produced in 431.

14. In Plato's *Laws* (665b), the character Cleinias (a Cretan) finds the idea absurd that a chorus in honour of Dionysus might be composed of men over thirty,

and the 'Athenian Stranger', the authoritative figure in the dialogue, agrees that *prima facie* it is, though he undertakes to justify the proposal.

15. *Koryphaios* means 'headman', and has no connection with *khoros* 'chorus'; spellings like 'choryphaeus', which have occasionally found their way into learned journals, are barbarisms.

16. *IG* i^3 969 gives us the names of the *khoreutai* (or, as the inscription itself says, *tragôidoi*) in a (presumably successful) production of plays by Euripides, perhaps that with which he won his first victory in 441, and the name heading the list is Python; but there are only fourteen names in all, at a time when a full tragic chorus numbered fifteen. Either (i) Python was the *koryphaios* and the inscriber accidentally omitted one of his colleagues from the list, or (ii) Socrates of Anagyrus, the *khorêgos*, led his chorus in person, or (iii) he drafted in an experienced *koryphaios* from outside his deme and omitted his name from this local dedication, as he also omitted the names of the solo actors. Ghiron-Bistagne 1976: 121 and P.J. Wilson 2000: 133 both favour solution (ii) while recognizing that (iii) is possible.

17. Later, it would seem, referred to as 'spear-carriers' (*doryphoroi* or *doryphorêmata*) – as their modern equivalents sometimes are too!

18. Except in *Agamemnon*, where, if there is a one-line part for the captain of the bodyguard (see above), either he or Aegisthus must have been played by the actor who had earlier taken the role of Cassandra. It is tempting to suggest that the Cassandra actor played Aegisthus (see below, and §7.6.4, on other ways in which this character is or may be presented as unmasculine).

19. Inferable from the line count in *IG* ii^2 2318.

20. They were probably not 'fearsome' in their actual features, but only because they were festooned with snakes (which most likely formed part of the mask/headpiece itself); in post-458 vase paintings, doubtless inspired by the *Oresteia*, the faces of the Erinyes resemble (aside from the snakes) those of ordinary young women. See Revermann 2006: 286n.64.

21. The best presentation in English of the case for a smaller theatre is by Csapo 2007: 97-100 with Goette 2007; Mitchell-Boyask 2008, however, has pointed out that 'one could [still] argue compellingly for [a total capacity of] around 10,000, [including] many ... on the slope above the theater'.

22. It is noteworthy that two of Aeschylus' surviving plays feature the honourable reception into a *polis* of a group of *metoikoi* (cf. *Supp.* 609, 994; *Eum.* 1011, 1018).

23. As to what may have happened if two competitors gained equal votes, either for first or for second place, see Marshall and van Willigenburg 2004.

24. Aristophanes, *Knights* 546-50, *Birds* 445-6; Plato, *Gorgias* 502b-d, *Laws* 659a.

3

The Tetralogy

In the account of the tragic competition at the City Dionysia given in the preceding chapter, one feature was left unmentioned. It was a rule of the competition that each competitor should present four plays, namely three tragedies and one satyr-play.[1] Modern scholars sometimes apply the term 'tetralogy' to all such four-play sequences, but ancient practice seems to have been to restrict *tetralogia* (and likewise its pendant *trilogia*) to the *connected* sequences discussed below.

In the second half of the fifth century the usual practice was for each of the four plays to be self-contained, and audiences seem not to have looked for any obvious connection between them. Euripides competed in 438 with *The Cretan Women*, *Alcmaeon in Psophis*, *Telephus* and *Alcestis*, and in 431 with *Medea*, *Philoctetes*, *Dictys* and the satyr-play *The Reapers*. But in Aeschylus' time the usual, though not the invariable, practice was different. The tendency was to make the three plays of the tragic sequence present successive episodes of a single chain of legend, after which the satyr-play would present another story from the same saga complex (though this was not necessarily, and indeed not usually, an actual sequel to what had gone before). Such a connected sequence of plays was called, at least from Aristotle's time, a 'four-plotter', a *tetralogia*, and the tighter sequence comprising the three tragedies came to be known as a *trilogia*. Henceforward in this chapter the terms 'tetralogy' and 'trilogy' will be used in these senses.

We know, from the surviving list of the plays he produced in 472 (*Phineus*, *The Persians*, *Glaucus of Potniae*, and *Prometheus [the Fire-bearer]*) that Aeschylus did not always present tetralogies as above defined,[2] and we know that some dramatists after his time occasionally did. Aeschylus' own nephew, Philocles, composed a tetralogy then or later known as the *Pandionis*, and an inscription records a victory by Sophocles with a production called the *Telepheia*. Euripides in 415 competed unsuccessfully with a sequence of plays on episodes in the Trojan saga – *Alexandros*, *Palamedes* and *The Trojan Women* – with connections which, while not so close as in most Aeschylean trilogies, are clearly detectable, followed by a satyr-play *Sisyphus* which may also have been linked, Sisyphus being by some accounts the father of Odysseus who had a prominent and discreditable role both in *Palamedes* and, offstage, in *The Trojan Women*.[3] Nevertheless, in post-Aeschylean dramaturgy the tetralogy seems to have been very much the exception; in Aeschylus it is going only slightly beyond the evidence to say that the tetralogy is the rule, and it has for long, and rightly, been regarded as a characteristic feature of his work.

Not that he necessarily invented it. There is definite evidence that his great older contemporary, Phrynichus, sometimes presented connected sequences of plays. We hear of a play of his called *The Egyptians* (but set at Argos) and another called *The Danaids*: there can be little doubt that these two plays were connected and that they dramatized the same legend (though no doubt in a different way) as Aeschylus' Danaid trilogy. A less clear case is provided by Phrynichus' play or plays about the Persian War. That his *Phoenician Women* dealt with this subject is well known. But we know also of another play with three alternative titles – *The Just Men*, *The Persians*, or *The Assessors* (*Sunthôkoi*); and, as was pointed out by Taplin 1977: 63n.2, what we are told about the opening of *The Phoenician Women*, in which a eunuch was preparing chairs for 'those who sit with the ruling power', would actually be far better suited to this other play. It is thus likely that we have again two plays in sequence. The first was set at some Phoenician city, with a chorus of Phoenician women,[4] the wives (by the play's end, the widows) of men serving in Xerxes' fleet; its centrepiece can hardly have been other than the arrival of news of Salamis. The second play was set at Susa. The chorus consisted, as in Aeschylus' *Persians*, of royal councillors, 'those who sit with' Xerxes. We are told that the defeat of Salamis was already known in Susa at the start of the play; perhaps hopes of ultimate success were then revived by the return of the King with news that Mardonius' army was still in control of most of Greece and poised for a decisive battle – only to be dashed by news of the disaster of Plataea. In each of these two cases we only have evidence for *two* plays in sequence; but we know so little of Phrynichus' *oeuvre* anyway (only about ten titles are known) that the lack of an identifiable third play is not a suspicious feature. It may be added that in 467 Phrynichus' son, Polyphrasmon, competed unsuccessfully with a tetralogy which the festival records listed as the *Lycurgeia*.

Four connected tetralogies by Aeschylus are attested in ancient sources, and a further seven can be reconstructed with a high degree of probability. The following discussion owes much to the work of Timothy Gantz (1979, 1980), even where its conclusions are different from, or less cautious than, his.

The four securely *attested* tetralogies are:

(1) The *Oresteia* (see Chapter 7), produced in 458, comprising *Agamemnon*, *Choephoroi*, *Eumenides* and the satyr-play *Proteus*; the first three plays survive virtually complete.

(2) The Danaid tetralogy (see Chapter 6), comprising *The Egyptians*, *The Suppliant Maidens* (which survives), *The Danaids* and the satyr-play *Amymone*.

(3) A tetralogy on the House of Laius (see Chapter 5), produced in 467, comprising *Laius*, *Oedipus*, *Seven against Thebes* (which survives) and the satyr-play *The Sphinx*.

(4) The *Lycurgeia*, comprising *The Edonians*, *The Bassarids*, *The Youths* and the satyr-play *Lycurgus*; the tetralogy is mentioned in Aristophanes' *Thesmophoriazusae* (135), and an ancient commentator on the passage lists the four plays.

Of the seven *reconstructible* tetralogies, no less than four are based, as is the *Oresteia*, on the saga of the Trojan War and its aftermath, and each of the four is based on a different poem of the 'epic cycle': respectively, the *Iliad*, the *Aethiopis*, the *Little Iliad*, and the *Odyssey* (the *Oresteia* is based on part of a fifth epic, the *Nostoi*).[5]

(5) The Iliadic tetralogy, comprising *The Myrmidons*, *The Nereids*, *The Phrygians* and a satyr-play which may have been *The Chamber-makers*, and

(6) The Odyssean tetralogy, comprising *The Ghost-raisers*, *Penelope*, *The Bone-gatherers* and the satyr-play *Circe*, will be fully discussed in Chapter 10.

(7) Two plays, *Memnon* and *The Weighing of Souls*, can be assigned with confidence to a sequence based on the *Aethiopis*, the epic sequel to the *Iliad*. *The Weighing of Souls* included the famous scene of Eos (mother of Memnon) and Thetis (mother of Achilles) pleading for their respective sons' lives before Zeus, followed by the death of Memnon and the coming of Eos to take away his body. *Memnon* must therefore clearly have preceded it, and probably presented the arrival of Memnon at Troy[6] and his killing of Antilochus, which doomed him to be the victim of Achilles' revenge. What of another play to complete the trilogy? In the first edition of this book I suggested that Aeschylus continued the story to include the death of Achilles, and that the play in question may have been *The Phrygian Women*; since then M.L. West 2000: 347-50 has argued that *Memnon* was the *second* play of the trilogy and that the first was *The Carians or Europa* (Europa being the mother of Sarpedon, another hero of divine parentage who was killed fighting as an ally of the Trojans). West also argues, more controversially, that of the three plays only *Memnon* was actually by Aeschylus, the other two having been composed by his son Euphorion to serve as its prequel and sequel. He admits, however, that 'the subject of the *Europa* [is] not closely connected with that of the Memnon plays' (p. 350). At any rate it is likely that the Aeschylean corpus, as known in the late fifth century and thereafter, included a trilogy centred on the fight between Memnon and Achilles. No relevant satyr-play can be identified.

(8) In the Trojan saga the death of Achilles was followed by the contest for his armour between Odysseus and Ajax, which led to the latter's suicide. Three plays by Aeschylus were concerned with this story, and they almost certainly formed a trilogy. *The Award of the Arms* presented the contest itself: Thetis appeared in person to put up the prize for competition, and Ajax (for the first time in Greek literature so far as we know) insultingly called Odysseus the son not of Laertes but of Sisyphus (fr. 175). *The Thracian Women* included the death of Ajax, which was reported by a messenger (according to the usual tragic convention, which Sophocles in his *Ajax* ingeniously violated). The other related play, if as is likely it was called *The Women of Salamis* (*Salaminiai*) rather than *The Salaminians* (*Salaminioi*), will have been set in Salamis, not at Troy, and may have dealt with the return home of Ajax's brother Teucer and his expulsion by his father who blamed him for Ajax's death – a subject later handled by Sophocles in his *Teucer*. No relevant satyr-play can be identified.

(9) There is fairly substantial evidence concerning four plays based on the story of Dionysus' birth at Thebes, his return to Greece from Asia, and the death of the Theban king Pentheus, the story whose climax is the subject of Euripides' *Bacchae*. Our information about the four plays is in essentials as follows.

Semele or The Water-carriers. Semele, daughter of Cadmus, is pregnant, and in a state of daemonic possession. The women of the chorus lay their hands on her belly (a traditional procedure for easing delivery) and become possessed themselves. They are 'water-carriers' probably because, the birth of Semele's child being apparently imminent, they have come bringing water for the ritual washing of the baby. But the birth never takes place: Hera, as we learn from Plato's *Republic* (381d), enters in the guise of a mendicant priestess[7] and, as later versions of the myth indicate, tempts Semele to ask Zeus to visit her in his full divine splendour; the result is her death and, as mortals suppose, the death of her child also (cf. fr. 221). In fact, however, as the audience will be aware, the infant Dionysus was snatched from the flames by Zeus.

The Wool-carders. This play had something to do with Pentheus' death on Mount Cithaeron (fr. 172b), and the chorus consisted of women who at some stage were driven insane by the goddess of madness, Lyssa, who appeared in person (fr. 169); but the title suggests that at the outset they were normal women doing normal women's work. The play may thus, as Dodds (1960a: xxxi) argued, 'have ended where Euripides' *Bacchae* begins, with the retreat of the Theban women to Cithaeron ... and Pentheus' threat to pursue them'. Since the ancient lexicographers who quote fr. 169 refer to the women as bacchants, it was presumably Dionysus himself who sent Lyssa against them, angered no doubt by the refusal of the Thebans, under Pentheus' influence, to recognize him as a god.

Pentheus. The ancient synopsis of Euripides' *Bacchae* says that its story, that of Pentheus' death at the hands of the Theban bacchants, had been treated in Aeschylus' *Pentheus*. In Euripides' treatment the bacchants were led by Pentheus' own mother Agaue and her sisters, after he had gone to Cithaeron to spy on them, himself disguised as a bacchant: it has been shown by Jennifer March (1989) that the evidence of fifth-century art points decisively to this having been an innovation by

Euripides, and that in the earlier form of the myth Pentheus *led the Theban army* against the bacchants, who defeated him under the 'generalship' of Dionysus. Aeschylus seems to refer to such a battle in *Eumenides* (25-6), and it is probably to his own *Pentheus* that he is alluding. It is unlikely that Aeschylus made Pentheus die by his mother's hand: fifth-century vase paintings, as March points out, when they name the leader of the Theban bacchants, call her not Agaue but Galene.[8]

The Nurses of Dionysus suggests itself as a possible satyr-play for this tetralogy, and certainly the reward of Dionysus' nurses, who were rejuvenated (along with their husbands) by Medea at Dionysus' request (fr. 246a), would make a pointed contrast with the punishment of Pentheus. The husbands, who are not mentioned in other accounts of this story, were probably no other than the satyrs, who are often associated in poetry and art with the nurture of the young Dionysus.

(10) Three plays are known to have dealt with the aftermath of the expedition of the Seven against Thebes. *The Eleusinians* corresponded closely to Euripides' *Suppliant Women* and featured Theseus as a main character, securing from the Thebans the restoration of the bodies of the Seven by persuasion and not (as in Euripides) by force. Since they were apparently buried at Eleusis (Plutarch, *Theseus* 29.5), *The Women of Argos* may have preceded *The Eleusinians* and presented the arrival at Argos of news of the failure of Adrastus' original expedition, with Capaneus (fr. 17) and the rest of the Seven being mourned in their absence. For a third play the obvious candidate is *The Epigoni*, on the renewal of war against Thebes by the sons of the Seven. Another play that has been associated with this group is *Nemea*: no fragment has been preserved, but Aeschylus is known (fr. 149a) to have mentioned somewhere the founding of the Nemean Games 'in honour of Archemorus the son of Nemea', and more than one version of the story of Archemorus[9] links him with Adrastus and/or the Seven against Thebes. Athletics are a favourite theme of satyr-plays (see Chapter 9 for an Aeschylean example), so this *might* be the satyr-play that followed this 'Adrastus trilogy'.

(11) Four plays have a connection with Jason and the Argonauts, and they appear to have centred on the Argonauts' visit to Lemnos, the subject in particular of *Hypsipyle* which included a reference to the oath exacted from the Argonauts by the Lemnian women to have intercourse with them as soon as they disembarked. The oath itself (taken, we are told, before the ship was allowed to come to land) could hardly have been included in the play and must have been referred to retrospectively. Nothing is directly known of the plot of *The Lemnian Women*, but it is very likely to have dealt with the episode which made 'Lemnian deeds' a byword for horrendous crime throughout the Greek world, the murder by the Lemnian women of their husbands (cf. *Cho.* 631-8); the Argonauts arrived some time after this event, so this play will have preceded *Hypsipyle*. *The Cabeiri* – named after a group of minor divinities, worshipped especially on Lemnos and nearby islands, who apparently formed the chorus – included a catalogue of the Argonauts (fr. 97a), at least one of whom at some point in the play appeared drunk, and the Cabeiri, according to Plutarch, 'playfully threatened that the house would run short of vinegar'; this might suggest that it was a satyr-play, but Athenaeus (*Intellectuals at Dinner* 10.428f) clearly believed it to be a tragedy. A catalogue of the Argonauts would be surprising if they had appeared previously in the trilogy; so perhaps the order of the plays was *The Lemnian Women, The Cabeiri, Hypsipyle*, with *Hypsipyle* maybe centring on Jason's discovery of the Lemnian women's crime and his abandonment of Hypsipyle and departure from the island (Gantz 1993: 345-6). Of *The Argo, or The Rower(s)*, we know is that there was mention of Iphys or Tiphys, the Argonauts' helmsman, and of the speaking beam which Athena placed in the *Argo*'s hull: the context in which fr. 20 is quoted by Philo (*That Every Virtuous Man is Free* 143) shows that this beam is said to have 'groaned aloud' when a slave stepped on board the ship. Since none of the Argonauts was a slave, we may well suspect that this play was a satyr-drama in which the satyrs tried to usurp the role of Jason's crew, as (for example) they usurped the role of Theban councillors in *The Sphinx* (see §5.5); the play will then probably have been set at the port of departure, Iolcus.

In at least three more cases we can see a clear connection between two plays but it is hard to find a third to partner them, and the question arises whether we should admit the possibility of a 'dilogy' – that is, of a production comprising two linked plays, a third unconnected tragedy, and a satyr-play which might or might not have a connection with the dilogic pair. Gantz refused to countenance the possibility; and it is certainly true that we have no positive evidence for it. We know of productions whose component tragedies were all related, and productions whose component tragedies were all unrelated; we do not know of productions containing two related tragedies and an odd one out. This lack of evidence may, however, be accidental. After all, out of a total of sixty or seventy four-play productions by Aeschylus, Sophocles and Euripides, there are only twelve of which we can identify with fair confidence all the component tragedies.[10] Since our evidence makes it clear that at least down to 415 tragic dramatists were free to choose between offering one three-play unit and three one-play units, it is arbitrary to deny them the possibility of an intermediate option. We must of course bear in mind that some plays have quite possibly been lost without trace; but if we find a two-play sequence that does seem to be complete with a beginning and end, we should not feel obliged to posit a third play merely to make up a statutory number. Where a dilogy appears to have a satyr-play associated with it, we may assume that for the sake of continuity these three plays were put on second, third and fourth in the production sequence, the unrelated play being performed first.

(12) In one case a surviving play appears to have been part of a dilogy: for *Prometheus Bound* and its sequel *Prometheus Unbound* see §8.4.

(13) Three plays of the Aeschylean corpus are known to have presented phases of the Perseus legend. One, *The Net-Haulers*, was a satyr-play, and we now have fairly substantial papyrus fragments of it (see Chapter 9); it dealt with the arrival at the island of Seriphos of the chest in which Danaë, with her infant son Perseus, had been cast adrift by her father Acrisius. *The Phorcides* obviously had to do with Perseus' encounter with the Phorcides or Graeae in his quest for the Gorgon's head. It is hard to envisage the Graeae appearing on stage in a tragedy in their traditional form – three old women with only one eye and one tooth between them (cf. *Prom.* 794-7), and it seems likely that Perseus' encounter with them (together with his subsequent confrontation with Medusa herself) was narrated rather than enacted (cf. frr. 261, 262).

Where does this leave the third play, *Polydectes*? Polydectes was the wicked king of Seriphos, who, desiring to force Danaë into marriage, sent Perseus on a quest intended to be fatal in order to deprive her of her protector, and whom Perseus on his return turned to stone by means of the Gorgon's head. In principle, therefore, *Polydectes* might either precede or follow *The Phorcides*. Not one word survives of *Polydectes* to help us decide. One possibly relevant consideration is the setting of *The Phorcides* in a remote part of the world: there are unlikely to have been many characters in the play other than Perseus and the chorus,[11] and there may thus have been both scope and need (as in *Prometheus Bound*) for long speeches by the hero providing information ostensibly for the chorus but really for the audience. This would suggest that *The Phorcides* was the *first* play in a connected sequence, and that the opportunity was taken to fill in the antecedents of its action by means of retrospective narrative. The sequence of the production will thus have been: an unconnected opening play, *The Phorcides*, *Polydectes*, *The Net-Haulers*.

(14) Finally, two plays are linked by the figure of Telephus: the play which bore his name, and *The Mysians* which had a chorus of his compatriots. That *The Mysians* was about Telephus is confirmed by the mention in it of Oeus, a village near Tegea in Arcadia (fr. 145), since it was from Tegea, having killed his maternal uncles there, that Telephus came to Mysia in Asia Minor; being a polluted manslayer, he was forbidden to speak to anyone (cf. *Eum.* 448-50), and while he probably opened the play with a soliloquy (cf. fr. 143) he may then have remained silent for a considerable time until purified and accepted by the Mysians. The other play, *Telephus*, seems to have followed *The Mysians*, and to have been set, like Euripides' *Telephus*, at Argos, where Telephus came to seek a cure for the wound inflicted on him by Achilles during a Greek attack on his territory; Agamemnon was a character in the play (fr. 238). It has more than once been suggested that *Iphigeneia*, whose action is presumed to have been set at Aulis and whose mythical 'date' is shortly after that of *Telephus*, was the third play of a Telephus trilogy; but such a trilogy would be very loosely knit: what has Iphigeneia to do with Telephus' uncles? Rather, we may have here another dilogy: *The Mysians* may well have contained a substantial narrative of Telephus' early tribulations in Arcadia, while his visit to Argos, the healing of his wound by Achilles' own spear, and his agreement (in return for this service) to guide the Greek fleet to Troy, are normally the effective end of his story.

Because of the *Oresteia* and the Theban trilogy, we tend to think of the trilogy form as typically associated with the tracing of a long series of tragic doings from generation to generation; but our evidence suggests that this may well be an accident of preservation, since of the remaining nine Aeschylean trilogies discussed above, only one (#10) follows this pattern. Rather, the typical function of the trilogy is to dramatize an extended action centred on a single person or group. All Greek tragedians faced the problem of fitting the complexities of heroic saga into the limiting framework of the theatre, with its restrictions on length of performance and number of actors and its reluctance to countenance a change of scene or a long time interval within a single 'play'. The most obvious methods are two. One is to dramatize only the concluding, climactic portion of the story, bringing the rest in by way of retrospect: this technique is favoured by Sophocles, as in *The Women of Trachis*, *Ajax* and *Oedipus the King*. Another is to concentrate on the events of a short period (normally a single day) and make these events highly complex, with many characters involved and many changes of direction; this is Euripides' practice in several of his latest plays (*The Phoenician Maidens*, *Orestes*, *Iphigeneia at Aulis*) and may have become standard in the fourth century (when comedy too was developing in the same direction). This second method, however, is difficult enough even with three actors,[12] and with two it is virtually impossible. In Aeschylus the normal method of making the action complex is more akin to that of epic. The trilogy, like epic, can stretch out its action. It enables the dramatist to have, if he wishes, three different localities, three different days' action, and three different choruses.[13] It makes possible drama on an entirely different scale to that on which Sophoclean or Euripidean tragedy was conceived. The *Oresteia* is more than twice as long as the longest other work of Greek drama that survives; in number of lines it is comparable to an average play of Shakespeare, and in actual performance, because of the two intervals and the high proportion of sung and danced scenes, it will probably have taken longer. The Aristotelian model of tragedy envisages a single 'action' involving a transition from good to bad fortune or the reverse. The trilogy form makes possible a kind of tragedy involving a sequence of partly independent actions with multiple changes of fortune; and it necessitates giving the action a different kind of rhythm, for it will normally be desirable to provide a climactic event for each part of the trilogy, which must nevertheless (except in the third part) not have the effect of a full close.

There does not appear to have been any master plan to which all or even most Aeschylean trilogies were constructed – nor should we expect there to have been. In the past the aesthetically very satisfying zigzag pattern of the *Oresteia* exercised great influence on conjectural reconstructions of other trilogies, partly because it *was* aesthetically satisfying but mainly because the *Oresteia* happened to be available in its entirety. Nevertheless, it is possible to see across quite a few trilogies a movement from more barbaric to more civilized behaviour – to put it in very general terms.

The Achilles-trilogy (#5) begins with the hero as the slave of his passions – his resentment against Agamemnon, his love for Patroclus, and presently, when Patroclus is killed, his grief and his vengeful hatred of Hector. He continues thus well into the last play, when the repeated motif of his long silence (see §10.1) emphasizes that the position is essentially the same as it was at the outset of the trilogy; but in the end – having lost a loved one through his refusal to listen to the persuasion of friends like Phoenix – he listens to the persuasion of an enemy, Priam, who has himself lost a loved one, and gives up for honourable burial the corpse he has been outraging. That development, admittedly, was implicit in the *Iliad* itself; but then we find Aeschylus (#6) significantly altering the ending of the *Odyssey* to produce a similar development, and the Odysseus who has massacred the suitors overcomes the anger of their kinsfolk by persuasion (see §10.2).

In the first play of the Danaid trilogy (#2) a dispute between two brothers leads to civil war in Egypt. In the second play, the surviving *Suppliant Maidens*, the sons of Aegyptus, or their agents, try to seize the Danaids by force, and Argive support for their victims leads to war being declared between Egypt and Argos. At the beginning of the third play it is discovered that the Danaids, compelled to submit to marriage against their will, have themselves appealed to force and treacherously murdered their bridegrooms – all but one. That one, Lynceus, seems to have won the affection of his bride Hypermestra, and we know that he, the one who used persuasion (cf. *Supp.* 1040) and not force, became king of Argos and founder of a new royal house.

The *Oresteia* (#1) begins with character after character taking vengeance. In every case the victim of vengeance has deserved punishment, but in every case too the avenger's own motives are impure and the vengeance itself is executed brutally. In the second play Orestes takes a vengeance equally brutal and even more horrific, but at least he can and does truly say, as none of his predecessors could, that he had no reasonable alternative. In the third play the justice of Orestes' action (in the given circumstances) is recognized, and it is accepted that it would be wrong that he should suffer for it, but recognized too (in the votes of half the jury) is the horror of the act; and the institution of lawcourts, deciding on the basis of argument whether punishment is appropriate, ensures that direct personal vengeance will no longer be needed, while the Erinyes themselves, the very embodiments of wrathful *talio*, are harnessed to the cause of the good order and prosperity of the *polis*. As we shall see later (§§7.9, 11.6), there is some reason to believe that this shift from violence to persuasion takes place not only in the human world but also in the mind of Zeus.

All these trilogies include catastrophic events, but all end, as it were, on something of an upbeat, on the establishment or re-establishment of some aspect of a stable social order; so perhaps did the Lycurgus group (#4), if M.L. West 1990b: 46-7 and Seaford 2005 are right to suggest that it ended with a recognition that the cults of Apollo/Helios and of Dionysus, whose rivalry had brought Lycurgus and probably also Orpheus to a catastrophic fate, should not be regarded as mutually exclusive. There is, however, another group which seem to end in the lamentation of unmitigated disaster. The Theban trilogy (#3) is the best attested example, but the Pentheus group (#9) and the Memnon group (#7) seem to have been similar; while in the Ajax group (#8) and the Adrastus group (#10) the action moves not away from, but towards, violence and destruction. The disaster precipitated by Ajax's reaction to the award of Achilles' arms to Odysseus does not end with his death: it also engulfs the innocent Teucer whom Ajax can never have wished to harm. In *The Women of Argos*, Theseus succeeds in persuading the Thebans peaceably to surrender the bodies of the Seven; in *The Epigoni* a new war breaks out which will end, we know, in the total destruction of Thebes.

John Herington (1965, 1970) argued, on the basis of the *Oresteia* and the Danaid trilogy (and of the Prometheus plays which he regarded as genuine works of Aeschylus), that the more 'progressive', optimistic pattern was typical of Aeschylus' last years, and recent interpretations of the *Lycurgeia*, which also appears to be a late work (see p. 7), might seem to confirm his suggestion. The Iliadic trilogy, however, is almost certainly much earlier, and it is not safe to posit any sharp chronological division between the two patterns.

It may well be idle to seek deep reasons for the creation of the trilogy form – particularly since we do not know who created it or when. Somebody – whether Aeschylus himself, Phrynichus, or another – tried a bold experiment; it was highly successful; the experiment was then repeated and imitated. Essentially it may have been a matter of scale. Aristotle says (*Poetics* 1449a19-20) that tragedy began with 'small plots and ludicrous diction'. The second phrase is highly problematic, but the first, as the context shows, at least includes the idea of shortness. Surviving Aeschylean plays, with the exception of *Agamemnon*, are indeed shorter than even the briefest Sophoclean and Euripidean tragedies.[14] To a Greek there was a strong connection between size and importance, and Aeschylus or another may well have felt that to become a major art-form tragedy needed, as it were, an ampler canvas.

The reign of the tetralogy lasted, it would seem, for some twenty or twenty-five years. Then, as we have seen, apart from occasional reversions, it was abandoned. Why? The best approach to an answer is to ask, once again, what a dramatist would gain by the change from a tetralogy to four separate plays, and once the question is asked the answer is obvious: he would gain variety. The tetralogist puts all his eggs in one basket. If he is Aeschylus he probably as a rule gets away with it, but a dramatist without Aeschylus' assured supremacy might well prefer to hedge his bets. One spectator (or judge) may like a play of one type, another may prefer something different; why not try to please both? By the 450s there was no longer any need to assert the status of tragedy as a major art-form, for it was generally accepted as such; meanwhile, too, the introduction of a third actor had greatly extended the plot possibilities of the single play. And so it was that the tetralogy, more or less, died with Aeschylus.

Appendix: Scenes, time intervals and choruses in Aeschylean trilogies

The table on the next page gives the following information, so far as it is known or can be inferred with reasonable probability, for each play in each of the eleven trilogies discussed above: **(1)** the location of the action; **(2)** the identity of the chorus (italics denote a female chorus); **(3)** in the case of the second and third plays of a trilogy, the time interval supposed to have elapsed since the action of the preceding play. It will be noted **(1)** that nearly always at least two of the plays are set in the same place, **(2)** that the three choruses are hardly ever all of the same gender, **(3)** that there is some evidence that it is regular for the chorus of the first play to be male and that of the second female, and **(4)** that the duration of the action may range from a few days to twenty years or more, but in no case does it span more than one generation-interval (although, as in the Theban trilogy, the principal *characters* of the three plays may belong to three different generations).

Note that the sequence of plays in trilogies #7 and #11 is particularly uncertain.

1	Agamemnon Argos Argive elders	Choephoroi Argos *Palace slaves* 7 years	Eumenides Delphi/Athens *Erinyes* Few days/few months
2	Egyptians Egypt Egyptian elders?	Suppliant Maidens Argos *Danaids* About a month?	Danaids Argos *Danaids* About a month?
3	Laius Thebes Theban elders?	Oedipus Thebes ? 20-25 years	Seven against Thebes Thebes *Theban maidens* A few months
4	Edonians Edonia Edonian elders?	Bassarids Edonia *Edonian bacchants* Few days?	Youths Edonia Edonian youths ?
5	Myrmidons Before Troy Myrmidons	Nereids Before Troy *Nereids* 1 day	Phrygians Before Troy Priam's attendants 12 days
6	Ghost-raisers Lake Avernus Local priests	Penelope Ithaca *Maidservants?* 7 years	Bone-gatherers Ithaca Suitors' kinsmen 1 day
7	Carians Caria Carian elders?	Memnon Before Troy Trojans? 1 or 2 months?	Weighing of Souls Before Troy Memnon's soldiers? 1 day?
8	Award of the Arms Before Troy Greek soldiers?	Thracian Women Before Troy *Thracian captives* 1 day?	Women of Salamis Salamis *Salaminian women* Few months
9	Semele Thebes *Semele's maids or friends*	Wool-carders Thebes *Theban women* About 20 years	Pentheus Thebes ? Few days
10	Women of Argos Argos *Argive women*	Eleusinians Eleusis Eleusinian men Few days	Epigoni Argos? ? 10 years
11	Lemnian Women Lemnos *Lemnian women*	Hypsipyle Lemnos *Lemnian women?* Few months?	Cabeiri Lemnos Cabeiri Few days?

Notes

1. By 438, as Euripides' *Alcestis* shows, the satyr chorus for the fourth play was no longer obligatory; it continued, however, to be usual at least till the end of the century.

2. Although there is reason to believe that at least the first three plays of the 472 production were in fact thematically connected; see §4.2.

3. He may have presented another connected suite of plays in or about 410 – *Hypsipyle* (dramatizing an episode in the march of Adrastus and the Seven from Argos to Thebes), *The Phoenician Maidens* and *Antigone*. These three plays are mentioned together in a scholium to Aristophanes, *Frogs* 53 (where the title *Antigone* has been corrupted to *Antiope*, a play which on metrical grounds is to be dated considerably earlier – see Cropp and Fick 1985: 75-6); and significantly, a parody of *The Phoenician Maidens* by the comic poet Strattis included an adaptation of the opening lines of *Hypsipyle* (Strattis fr. 46). We cannot identify the accompanying satyr-play; probably it was one of the eleven or so Euripidean satyr-plays of which even the titles have been lost without trace.

4. Unusually for a female chorus, they are away from their home towns, Sidon and Aradus (Phrynichus fr. 9); perhaps they have come to, say, Tyre in the expectation that the Phoenician component of the Persian fleet will soon be returning there, victorious.

5. The remaining major cyclic epic on the Trojan War, the *Cypria*, had too little unity (covering as it did the whole story from its beginnings at the wedding of Peleus and Thetis to the eve of the *Iliad*) to be capable of forming a tragic trilogy; but Aeschylus used its material in *Telephus*, *Iphigeneia* and *Palamedes*.

6. Cf. fr. 300 Radt, which Sommerstein 2008 (following M.L. West 2000: 344) prints among the fragments of *Memnon* (and renumbers 126a).

7. A papyrus fragment (fr. 168 Radt = 220a Sommerstein) gives us part of this scene; Hera's opening words in it are quoted by one ancient scholar, Asclepiades, as coming from *The Wool-carders*, but Asclepiades' citations are notoriously unreliable, and there is no other evidence for Hera having a role in that part of the myth.

8. Another play that has sometimes been linked to this group is *The Archeresses*, whose subject was the death of Actaeon (son of Semele's sister Autonoe), turned into a stag and torn apart by his own hounds after he had offended Artemis (or, in some versions, Zeus); for Stesichorus (*GL* 236) and the mythographer Acusilaus (fr. 33 Fowler) his offence was to have courted Semele, and it is thus in principle possible that *The Archeresses* was the first play of a trilogy and *Semele* the second; but what can then be done with *The Wool-carders* and *Pentheus*? They are unlikely to be two names for one and the same play, since Galen cites both of them separately in the same passage (*Commentary on Hippocrates' Epidemiae Book VI*, xvii a 880.8-14 Kühn).

9. Including that of Euripides (in his *Hypsipyle*).

10. These are tetralogies **(1-6)** above, together with Aeschylus' production of 472, Sophocles' *Telepheia*, Euripides' productions of 438, 431 and 415, and the posthumous production of his last plays by the younger Euripides.

11. One of these was probably Perseus' divine patron Athena, near whose birthplace, Lake Tritonis, the play was apparently set; the chorus may have consisted of nymphs of the lake, who figure in some mythographic accounts (e.g. Pherecydes fr. 11 Fowler) and some artistic representations (e.g. *LIMC* Perseus 88 [sixth century]).

12. In the final scene of *Orestes* there are *seven* characters present, four of whom, with speaking roles elsewhere in the play, perforce remain silent.

13. For details (so far as known or inferable) of the choruses and dramatic locations of the component plays of Aeschylean trilogies, and the time intervals between their actions, see Appendix to this chapter.

14. An exception is Euripides' *Children of Heracles*, which, partly for this reason, has often been thought to be incomplete as it now stands (but see Allan 2001: 35-7, 220-7).

4
The Persians

The Persians was produced in 472, the accompanying plays being ostensibly unrelated in subject (but see §4.2); the production, comprising *Phineus*, *The Persians*, *Glaucus of Potniae* and the satyr-play *Prometheus the Fire-Bearer*, won first prize. The *khorêgos* was Pericles, then aged about twenty-two.

4.1. The play

The Persians is the only surviving Greek tragedy that is not based on a story from the inherited corpus of myth. It was produced seven and a half years after the battle of Salamis which is narrated in it, and probably four years after Phrynichus' sequence of Persian War plays. In the meantime Phrynichus had probably died, and right at the start of the play Aeschylus marks his debt to his predecessor, now no longer his rival, by virtually quoting Phrynichus' opening line. One of Phrynichus' plays had opened with a eunuch preparing chairs for a council meeting, and his prologue-speech had begun:

> These are the <   > of the Persians, who have gone long since to Greece ... (Phrynichus fr. 8).

Aeschylus, not wishing to repeat the effect too closely, has no eunuch, and if there are chairs (see §2.1) they are already prepared and awaiting their occupants. As in *The Suppliant Maidens*, and as in some lost plays (*The Myrmidons* certainly, *Niobe* probably; see §§10.1 and 11.4), there is no prologue: the play begins with the entrance of the councillors themselves as chorus, chanting in 'marching anapaests'. And they commence:

> These [i.e. we] are called the Trustees of the Persians
> who are departed to the land of Greece ... (1-2).

Only one significant change from Phrynichus' words, but it is an ominous one: instead of *bebêkotôn* 'gone' they say *oikhomenôn* 'departed', a verb which has a strong tendency to imply 'never to return'. This is a note that will be struck many times again, both in these opening utterances of the chorus (where the same verb reappears at 12 and 60) and later in the play.

The chorus, like so many later tragic choruses, consists of old men; their costumes will have reflected the Greek idea of how Persians of high rank would dress, and are likely to have been of a luxurious and, in Greek eyes, perhaps somewhat effeminate kind. The idea of luxury is given verbal prominence too at an early stage, when the Persian capital is described as 'wealthy and full of gold' (3).

After identifying themselves, the first thing the chorus tell us is that they are anxious about the return of king Xerxes and his army (8-11), 'for all the strength of the Asian race is departed' (12-13) and no news of any kind has come from them. They proceed to give a long list (21-58) of the peoples and the great warriors who have gone on the expedition – Persians, Egyptians, Lydians, Mysians, Babylonians. In another context this might have emphasized the seemingly irresistible power of the army, but here it is explicitly introduced in order to show how completely

> the flower of the men of Persia's land are departed,
> and all the land of Asia that nursed them
> grieves for them with a longing that burns (59-62)

– particularly the wives and mothers of the soldiers (63-4), who remain unseen, though much spoken of, throughout the play (with the exception of Xerxes' own mother), but who, like the chorus of Phrynichus' *Phoenician Women*, will have passed from tense anxiety to crushing bereavement before it ends.

The chorus have now reached their permanent station in the *orkhêstra*, and from the conventional anapaests of a marching entrance they shift to full-blown song. With a fine and significant incongruity the martial power of the Persian army is described (65-113) in the 'ionic' metre (based on the unit ∪ ∪ – –), whose usual associations in tragedy are not only Asiatic but also *feminine*, and which we know was extensively used by Phrynichus' female Phoenician chorus. For four stanzas – perhaps for six[1] – the tone is one of power and confidence. Xerxes' 'city-sacking army' must by now have crossed into Europe, bridging the Hellespont and 'placing a yoke on the neck of the sea' (72: thus casually and unconcernedly do the Elders refer to what will later be seen as the very emblem of Xerxes' *hybris*[2]). The 'bold ruler of Asia ... a man equal to a god' (73-80) is leading his forces by land and water 'against every country', bringing 'war of the deadly bow' to combat with 'renowned men of the spear' (85-6): here even a spectator (had there been any) who did not know the outcome in advance might well wonder whether it was not riding for a fall to speak of one's ruler as equal to a god, and whether one could be so sure that bowmen would have the beating of spearmen. But not, it seems, the Elders. Though anxious about the lack of news, they have not envisaged the possibility that the news, when it does come, could be anything but good. The Persian army is, after all, unchallengeable (91-2). But here the Elders involve themselves in a contradiction. They portray the invincibility of the army by comparing it to a mighty river or to the waves of the sea (87-90): yet they have already said, and a moment later they repeat (109-13), that the army itself has conquered the sea. Either the sea is conquerable, or it is not. If it is, then the Persian army which resembles it may be conquerable too. If it is not, the 'bold' Xerxes has acted with dangerous rashness in challenging it. Nor does the chorus's language in 102-13 inspire great confidence in their insightfulness. Divine Destiny, they sing, has given to the Persians the power to win battles and destroy cities on land (102-7), and in addition they have 'learned' to cross the sea, 'trusting to thin-drawn cables and to contrivances for the transport of armies'. Do the efforts of engineers really deserve to be considered as trustworthy as the decrees of Destiny?

It is at this moment that confidence suddenly gives place to apprehension:

> But what mortal man can escape
> the guileful deception of a god?
> Who is so light of foot
> that he has power to leap easily away?
> Beguiling men at first with fawning kindliness,
> Ruin leads them into her nets,
> from which no mortal can escape or flee (93-100).

This stanza is still in ionics, but the thought that a god may be guilefully leading the Persians to their doom now changes the Elders' mood completely, and abruptly (93-100 is a strophe with no antistrophe to answer it[3]) the ionics change to pensive trochees. 'My heart is torn with fear,' they sing (114-15), and cries of woe, and talk of the rending of garments, foreshadow the final scenes of the play. The conclusion of the choral entrance-song (*parodos*) reverts to its beginning, finishing (133-9, cf. 13, 63-4) with the picture of the wife in bed alone, waiting, hoping, yearning – the same picture that will be so effectively exploited, more than once, fourteen years later in *Agamemnon*. It is very characteristic of Aeschylus to mark the end of a structural unit (which may be anything from a single speech, or a section of one, to an entire play or trilogy) with an echo of its beginning in word, thought or action, a feature often referred to as *ring-composition*.

The chorus now decide to sit down and deliberate. There is, in fact, nothing for them to deliberate about – but perhaps it is noteworthy that in stating the topic for discussion, their leader for the first time explicitly recognizes the possibility that 'the strength of the spear's head has prevailed' (148-9). The expression shows that they are thinking in terms of a land battle. These, indeed, are the terms in which they have been thinking throughout: there has been mention of naval forces from time to time (19, 39, 54, 77, 83), but the sea has been thought of primarily as an obstacle which has been overcome by the bridging of the Hellespont, and there has been no awareness that the *enemy* have any ships at all.

At this point the Queen is seen approaching. This is not Xerxes' wife but

Xerxes' mother. As a matter of historical fact Xerxes' mother was Atossa, daughter of Cyrus, but it is doubtful whether Aeschylus knew this: his chorus hail the Queen as 'wife of a god and mother of a god' (157) but not as daughter of a god, and later Darius will speak at some length in praise of Cyrus (767-72) without giving any indication that Cyrus was his father-in-law. In the play she is simply Darius' widow and Xerxes' mother, representative of all those millions[4] of mothers and wives of whom we have already heard. She arrives in a vehicle, probably a covered carriage, robed and attended as befits 'oriental' royalty; and the councillors fall on their faces before her (152), in that species of homage which Greeks called *proskynêsis* and which they abhorred the idea of paying to any mortal human. In doing so they involve themselves in another contradiction:

> You were the bedfellow of the Persians' god, and you are the mother of their god,
> unless the old guardian deity of our host has now changed his stance (157-8).

If Xerxes is indeed a god, he should not be dependent on the favour of any other 'guardian deity'; he should be immune from mortal vicissitudes. If on the other hand the chorus are merely using extravagantly honorific language, any Greek could have told them how dangerous such presumption was.

The Queen's heart too is being torn by fear (161-2) lest the royal house be destroyed by the surfeit of its own prosperity (163-4), and in particular lest something may have happened to 'the eye of the house', her son (168-9). She has had a dream, which she relates to the chorus; a dream which, as we will find, foreshadows everything that will happen in the play.

She saw two beautiful women, sisters, one dressed as a Persian, the other as a Dorian, who 'in accordance with the fall of the lot' (186-7) were inhabitants of the barbarians'[5] and the Greeks' country respectively. Although these details form only the setting for the dream, they are dwelt on at some length (seven lines) and are of great interest in two respects. In the first place, as already stated, the Greek woman is spoken of as wearing *Dorian* dress. In other words, she is not specifically an Athenian; if anything, she is Spartan.[6] Right at the outset Aeschylus seems to go out of his way to make it clear that his audience are not to think of the Persian defeat as primarily an Athenian victory; later, the climax of the play's most solemn scene will be the prophecy by Darius' ghost of the disaster that will befall the Persians at Plataea 'beneath the Dorian spear' (817). Secondly, the two women are *sisters* (185-6). What Achilles and Priam discovered at the end of the *Iliad*, Aeschylus in effect tells his audience at the beginning of a play that they might all too easily read (as many modern critics have done) as demonstrating and proclaiming the innate superiority of Greeks to the lesser breeds of Asia: your enemies were your kin, because, like you, they were human, and the vast destruction that you wreaked upon them, deserved though it was, was also a tragedy. It was only by 'the fall of the lot' that you were Greek and they were barbarian; had the lot fallen the other way, you would have been the barbarians and they the Greeks. Would you then have resisted the temptation to act as Xerxes acted? Rarely can ethnic chauvinism have been so effectively punctured by a couple of words.

To return to the Queen's dream. The two sisters quarrelled (188-9). Xerxes' reaction was to try to restrain and mollify them; but then he yoked them to his chariot. The Persian woman submitted, but the Greek resisted, tore the harness apart and broke the yoke in half (194-6). Xerxes fell out of the chariot; his father Darius appeared by his side, pitying him; and when Xerxes saw Darius, far from being comforted he rent his garments. On waking, the Queen very naturally tried to avert the threat of disaster by sacrifices (201-4); but almost at once she saw an evil omen – an eagle, the royal bird, fleeing from a hawk, but being caught and timidly submitting to being clawed and plucked (205-10). All this has put her in terror. For if her son succeeds he will be an admired man, but if he fails – and thereupon we expect to hear 'he will be held in contempt' or the like. Instead we get an ingenious anticlimax which says all there is to say about the difference between a free and an unfree society:

> If he fails, the community cannot hold him to account,
> and in any case, if he returns safe, he will rule this land (213-14).

This conclusion, like various other touches in the play, is designed to mislead the audience about what will happen when Xerxes does at length return.

The chorus give the Queen the best advice they can. She should pray again to the gods, pour drink-offerings to Earth and the departed, and invoke the help of the shade of Darius (though there is no suggestion at this stage of actually summoning him up to earth). The Queen agrees to do all this; but before going home to do so, she asks the Elders a few questions about the enemy her son has gone to meet, and they unwittingly present her, and us, with the reasons – wholly *secular* reasons – why the expedition is bound to fail and the Queen's rituals and prayers to be in vain (230-45). There are certain facts about Greece, and in particular Athens (here mentioned separately for the first time in the play), which Xerxes seems to have ignored. Athens is strong enough to have defeated a Persian army in the past (at Marathon). Her soldiers use the spear and not the bow (and most of Aeschylus' adult spectators had had enough first-hand experience against both weapons to know which they would less like to face). She has ample financial resources, too, in the shape of the Laureium silver mines (the output of which, as the audience knew, paid for her navy, of whose existence the Elders remain unaware); and her people 'are not called the slaves or the subjects of any man' – which the Queen assumes to be a weakness, but which the Elders suspect, and the audience know, to be a strength. 'What you say,' comments the Queen, 'is food for fearful thought for the parents of those who have gone there' (cf. 63) – parents of whom she is one. The Elders had recommended rituals by which the dangerous dream and omen might perhaps be neutralized; but what is the prescribed ritual for neutralizing a political and military blunder? It is, in any case, too late. The long-awaited messenger is approaching.

In a tone full of grief (it is unlikely to be coincidental that the first six lines all begin with a vowel of *o* timbre[7]) the Messenger announces the news of the total defeat of Persian power. A verb, and a sentence, that we had heard before reappears with added meaning, reinforced by a play on words: 'The flower of the Persians (*Persôn*) is fallen (*peson*) and departed' (252, cf. 59-60). The chorus at once fall to lamentation; but when presently we hear the word Salamis (273), we realize that sooner or later there will be more to come which no one yet dreams of. If this is the Persian reaction to Salamis, what will they do or say when they hear about Plataea? And now we learn of another and a far greater military blunder. It was not after all a contest of bow and spear:

> The bow was an utter failure, and the whole host
> perished, brought low by *the rams of ships* (278-9).[8]

From now to the end of the play these ships, of whose existence the Persians had been unaware, will continually haunt their thoughts.

The story must already have been current at Athens how, after the burning of Sardis in 499 in which Athenians had taken part, Darius ordered a slave to remind him daily to 'remember the Athenians' (Herodotus 5.105). It is probably with an ironic allusion to this tale that the Messenger is now made to say:

> O Salamis, most hateful name to hear!
> Ah, how I groan when I *remember Athens*! (284-5).

And the chorus take up his words:

> Yes, Athens hateful to her foes.
> We can well *remember*
> how many of the women of Persia
> they bereaved of sons and husbands, dead in a futile cause (286-9).

The Queen has so far said nothing. This is normal early tragic convention: it is regular for new arrivals to address the chorus first even when another actor is present. But we are long past what may be called the naïve stage of this convention. Aeschylus is conscious that it *is* a convention, and he actively exploits it, making the Queen explain that she was utterly dumbfounded by the disaster. Her first anxiety is obviously for her son, but she does not (are we to understand she dares not?) ask directly about his fate; instead she asks 'Who is not dead, and which of the leaders must we mourn?' (296-7). The Messenger, of course, immediately tells her what he knows she wants to know first, that Xerxes is alive; but without a pause he launches into a catalogue – the second great muster-roll of the play – of nineteen commanders who have perished. As in the similar catalogue of the *parodos*, emphasis is laid on their diverse nationalities: in very truth Asia seems to have been emptied of men.

With this catalogue begins a long scene which consists entirely of narrative. The messenger-speech always remained a regular feature of tragedy, and probably had been so from the earliest days of the genre, but nowhere do we find a messenger-speech like this one. It is really a series of four speeches (302-30, 353-432, 435-71, 480-514), punctuated by interventions from the Queen, each speech presenting a new angle on the disaster and increasing its gravity yet further, a point which the Messenger himself makes repeatedly: 'Of the many evils that were there to report, I have mentioned only a few' (330); 'If I were to speak for ten days without a break, I could not complete the tale of suffering' (429-30); 'Know well that the tale of woe is not yet half told' (435); and even at the very end, 'All this is true, and much of the evil that god brought down upon the Persians I have omitted to tell' (513-14). It is a crushing cumulation of catastrophe.

The Queen cannot understand how it can have happened. Was it the numbers of the Greek navy that gave them the confidence to join battle? No, says the Messenger, in numbers the 'barbarians' were far superior, but 'some god destroyed our host, weighting the balance not by chance nor impartially: the gods preserve the city of the goddess Pallas' (345-7). Then Athens has not, after all, been sacked? The reply we expect is: 'It has indeed been wasted with fire.' The reply we get is the one that Themistocles had given, shortly after the sack had happened (Herodotus 8.61.2): 'While she has men, she has an impregnable wall' (349).

Asked whether Xerxes or the Greeks began the battle, the Messenger says that events were set in motion by 'the appearance from somewhere of an avenging spirit or an evil deity' (353-4). But having given this theological explanation, he then proceeds to give a perfectly secular explanation both of the battle and of the defeat which is full and sufficient in itself. As we shall see more fully later (Chapter 11), Aeschylean gods are not 'supernatural'. They *are* nature. They act not against, but by means of or in parallel with, the forces of the material world and the motives of human beings.

And so the mysterious 'avenging spirit or evil deity' turns out to be none other than Themistocles or his slave (the Messenger says merely 'a Greek man from the Athenian forces'), coming to Xerxes with his false story that the Greeks intended to take to flight (cf. Herodotus 8.75). Xerxes, we are told, 'did not understand the deception of the Greek or the resentment of the gods' (361-2). It would have been surprising if he had. What the supposed traitor told him was what he had expected would happen in any case. Of course the Greeks were going to flee. What else could they possibly do, outnumbered more than three to one?

In what follows, as much space is devoted to the night before the battle (361-85) as to the naval engagement itself (408-32). The Persian admirals were told to block all the Greeks' escape routes, at the price of losing their heads if the Greeks did get away. The orders were carried out in a disciplined manner (374-5); discipline and order (Greek *kosmos*), or the lack of it, are a major theme of the whole of the Messenger's narrative. Every oarsman and every marine boarded his ship; every ship took up its designated station; they waited and watched and patrolled all night, and absolutely nothing happened (384-5). The point would be well taken without needing to be spelt out: with the Persians and their naval allies tired and frustrated as they were, they had lost the battle before it began.

As day broke, at long last, sounds were heard from where the Greek fleet lay (388ff.). But they were not sounds of panic but sounds of music: the note of the trumpet, and the paean, the universal Greek battle-hymn. It was the Persians who were struck by fear (391). Presently there were other sounds: words of command, the splash of oars (396-7) – and then they saw them, the right wing leading 'in good order and well arrayed' (399-400), the rest following on, and all together crying out stirring words on which was based the greatest of modern Greek patriotic songs:

> Forward, sons of the Greeks!
> Set free your country, set free your wives and children,
> the abodes of your fathers' gods and the tombs of your ancestors:
> now it is all or nothing! (402-5).

In the vivid description that follows of the battle itself, the reasons for the Persian defeat – still utterly secular reasons – continue to be pinpointed. The very numbers of the Persian forces, in which such confidence had been placed hitherto (9, 25, 40, 46, 73, 83, 88, 334-44, 352), told against them, as they were too closely packed in a narrow space and could not come to each other's help (413-14); indeed they rammed each other and sheared off each other's oars, while the Greeks attacked in well-planned order (417) from all sides, until the Persians, or what was left of them, 'turned tail in disorderly flight' (422).

There is a grim coda to the account. There were thousands of shipwrecked survivors in the waters around Salamis. The Greeks neither rescued them nor left them to drown: instead they clubbed them to death 'like tunny or some other catch of fish' (424) with any handy piece of floating timber, until night, coming on for the second time in this speech, blotted out the scene of slaughter. It is not usual (or was not, until our own time) for an author, who believes himself and his countrymen to have been victorious in a just cause, to go out of his way to remind them of their own atrocities; but whatever Aeschylus the man may have thought of this massacre, Aeschylus the tragedian is presenting it not as something done by the Greeks but as something suffered by the Persians, the result of Xerxes' folly, as will be made explicit when he finally arrives home to be execrated as the killer of all who died on that day, a day of more death than the world had ever seen (431-2).

And yet, says the Messenger, that is not half the tale: there has been another and even greater disaster. Are we going to hear about Plataea now? The Messenger's summary (441-4) is tantalizing: he simply says that the most outstanding of the Persians, those who were noblest, bravest and most trusted by the King, have perished shamefully and ignominiously. It is only when he gives the tale in full that he turns out to be speaking not of Plataea (there will be many more false climaxes before we reach that) but of the battle of Psyttaleia, a minor part of the Salamis action. It is treated here at such length not because of its military importance, which was slight,[9] but because it was exclusively a *Persian* disaster – and in particular a disaster for the Persian *nobility*, to which the chorus, be it remembered, also belong. What we call the Persian navy consisted mainly, as Aeschylus' audience knew, of Phoenicians, Egyptians and other subject peoples; the force landed on Psyttaleia, by contrast, was one hundred per cent Persian, and it was destroyed to the last man (464, cf. Herodotus 8.95) – destroyed in part, too, by the Persians' own favourite weapon, the bow and arrow (460-1). The one weapon which the Greeks, as this play tells the tale, did *not* use at Salamis was the one the Persians feared, the spear; that will come into its own only at Plataea (817).

When Xerxes saw the fate of the force on the island, he cried out in lamentation (465), tore his garments (cf. 199), and sent his land army orders to withdraw – or rather 'let them go in disorderly flight' (470). No mention is here made of the fact that a large army was left in Greece under Mardonius:[10] Aeschylus is reserving that for later (it is first mentioned by Darius' ghost, to the amazement of the chorus, at 796), and at present what matters is to emphasize the *totality* of the defeat at Salamis.

The Queen blames a 'hateful divinity' (472) for frustrating her son's attempt to avenge the defeat of Marathon. She asks what has happened to the surviving ships; the Messenger briefly tells her that they too 'have taken to flight, in no good order' (480-1), and then, without being asked, goes on to speak of the land army. His first words about it are exquisitely misleading: 'What was left of the army found death in the land of the Boeotians.' Now at last is he going to speak of Plataea? No, as he continues, we find he is talking about the retreat of the main force, marching north, dogged by hunger and thirst, through region after region, river and plain and mountain and marsh, until they come to Thrace. There, for the first time, it seemed that the gods had smiled on them. An unseasonable cold snap froze the river Strymon, and even 'those who had formerly held the gods of no account' bowed down and prayed to them (497-9). But once again the god was tempting them to their doom: the sun's rays melted the ice, and many of them perished. This is the only one of all the disasters of the expedition which is presented as being due to a direct divine intervention. It is a mirror-image of the bridging of the Hellespont with which the expedition began. At the Hellespont, Xerxes (impiously, as we shall learn) tried to turn water into land. At the Strymon, the gods themselves do the same, the impious become pious too late, and the seal is put on the army's ruin. The Messenger ends with a comment on the grievous succession of blows that a god has inflicted on the Persians, and the chorus echo his words (513-16); but on the evidence presented it would be equally true to say that the Persians have been destroyed partly by the Greeks and partly by themselves.

The Messenger probably departs immediately he has finished speaking, and the Queen is left to contemplate the fulfilment of her dream. Once again (cf. 249-54), Aeschylus emphasizes a speaker's grief by a phonetic contrivance: the first *eleven* lines of the Queen's speech (517-27) all begin with a vowel, and the first six of them with a vowel of *o* or *u* timbre. She decides, in spite of everything, to carry out the suggested programme of prayer and sacrifice, in the hope at least of averting further disasters. She leaves for the palace to fetch the requisites for the ritual, with the following instructions to the chorus:

> After these events, which we must take to be true, it is your duty
> to contribute true and faithful counsel;
> and if my son comes here before I return,
> speak soothingly to him and escort him to the palace,
> lest to these evils he add yet further evil (527-31).

This is the first mention of the impending return of Xerxes, towards which the whole of the rest of the play is directed. It is a case of 'false preparation': spectators are likely to assume that Xerxes will be the next character to appear, and their sense of expectation, and of the characters' anxiety, will increase when he fails to appear. The Queen is not specific as to the 'yet further evil' which she fears, but since it is apparently an action by Xerxes of which she is apprehensive, the impression is likely to be created that she supposes he may commit suicide to avoid the shaming prospect of facing again the Persian people to whom he has done such immense harm.

The chorus now, first in recitative anapaests and then in lyrics punctuated by exclamations of grief, lament the disaster, again emphasizing the sorrows of Persian mothers and wives (537-45), again speaking of the emptying of Asia (549). They begin by ascribing the catastrophe to 'King Zeus', but Zeus's action was not arbitrary: he has destroyed the army of the Persians 'who numbered so many *and boasted so greatly*' (533). And thereafter they lay all the stress on two factors: Xerxes and ships:

Xerxes took them[11] – popoi!
Xerxes their slayer – totoi!
Xerxes recklessly staked all
on boats of the sea ... (550-3).

Dark-prowed, linen-winged,
ships took them – popoi!
ships their slayers – totoi!
ships rammed to utter wreck (559-62).

The cause of the disaster, on the human level, was the attempt by Xerxes to conquer on the sea when the destiny of Persia was to conquer on land (cf. p. 47). As a result he has not only left thousands of corpses to be devoured by the fish, not only left houses to mourn for their menfolk, parents for their children, the old for the young, but ruined the Persian empire itself (584-94): the peoples of Asia (let alone Europe) no longer obey Persian laws, no longer pay tribute, no longer prostrate themselves before the representatives of Persian authority, and even presume – crowning proof of imperial impotence – to exercise freedom of speech (591-3). Such despair is premature (even the Ionian Greeks revolted only after Mycale a year later), but it points the moral of the song so far as Xerxes is concerned: by trying, against destiny, to conquer the sea, he has risked the loss of his land empire.

Before the song, it had been left uncertain whether the next event would be the arrival of Xerxes, or the return of his mother with her offerings. It is the latter. This time there is no carriage and no royal splendour (607-8): she comes on foot, simply dressed, and alone, without even a single maid, herself carrying in one hand a vessel containing the drink-offerings for the gods below and the shade of Darius (609-15) and in the other an olive branch wreathed with flowers (616-18). Her explanation for the change is that the sudden turn of fortune has terrified her (598-606): presumably we are to understand her as fearing that any further display of luxury may arouse divine resentment and lead to yet further misfortune. The offerings, as we have heard, are to avert this (526). But that is not all. The Queen asks the chorus, not only to sing a hymn to the gods below to accompany the offerings, but also to 'summon up the divine Darius' (620-1). She does not say for what purpose; but we have to some extent been prepared by a mention of Darius in the preceding choral song:

Why was Darius so successful in those days
when he was the lord of our citizen bowmen,
the beloved leader of Susiana? (554-7).

And as the invocation commences, the mound at the rear of the *orkhêstra* becomes the burial-mound of Darius; and in the introductory anapaests of the chorus, we are told (if we had not guessed it already) why the dead king is being called up from below:

> If he knows any further cure for our troubles,
> alone of mortals he can tell us their end (631-2).

In a wild mixture of metres, in which the ionic rhythm (see p. 46) is most prominent, the chorus call on the nether powers to let Darius rise to earth, frequently speaking of him as if he were a god or nearly a god, uttering semi-articulate cries, falling on the ground and beating it with their hands.[12] On the last words of the song, lamenting the loss of the 'ships, no ships, no ships' (680), the ghost of Darius rises from his tomb (see §2.1), in the full splendour of Persian royal apparel. For the second time in the play the Elders fall on their faces, in such awe of their old ruler that they are unable even to look at him (694), let alone to break to him their terrible news. Darius turns instead to his Queen, who in a stichomythic[13] dialogue tells him of the disaster. At first he simply asks questions, and in reply he is told what we already know; the first significant exchange comes when the Queen mentions the bridging of the Hellespont:

> QUEEN
> He devised means to yoke the strait of Helle, so as to have a passage across.
> DARIUS
> And he accomplished this, so as to close the great Bosporus?[14]
> QUEEN
> So it was. Some deity, I suppose, had touched his wits.
> DARIUS
> Alas, a mighty deity attacked him indeed, to put him out of his right mind!
> QUEEN
> It is there to see in the outcome, what evil he has brought to pass (722-6).

We had heard before of the bridging of the Hellespont, but not in such terms as these. The chorus, indeed, had seemed quite proud of it (113-14). The Queen had not mentioned it before, but she had seen, in her dream, Xerxes attempting to 'yoke' Persia and Greece together (190-1) – and we now see that this symbolized not only the attempt to subjugate the Greeks to his rule, but also the physical joining of Asia and Europe, the turning of sea into land, of the water-passage, the Bos*poros*, into a dry passage (*poros*) for his troops. Both Xerxes' mother and his father see this attempt as a sign of mad folly – though perhaps it is not yet entirely clear why.

Aeschylus gave himself a slight problem as regards the ghost of Darius. He wanted Darius to be initially ignorant of recent events; but he also wanted him to be able to prophesy other disasters that would come in the near future. The circle is squared by the ingenious device of having Darius recognize in what has happened the partial fulfilment of certain oracles once given to him (739-41, 800-2), whose complete fulfilment is now, he declares, unavoidable. The prophecy had not specified when or in what generation the disaster would come, and Darius had hoped it would be long delayed; but Xerxes, a young man in a hurry, has hurried on the ruin of his country (742-4). He thought himself a match for the gods (but then did not the chorus once think him so too?) ...:

> hoping to restrain by fetters, like a slave,
> the flow of the sacred Hellespont, the divine stream of Bosporus,
> altering the nature of the passage (*poros*), girding it
> with hammered shackles, making a great pathway for a great army,
> imagining in his lack of judgement, mortal that he was,
> that he could lord it over all the gods, including Poseidon. What is this
> but a sickness of mind that possessed my son? I fear that all my wealth,
> gained with such toil, may be overturned and plundered by the first
> comer (745-52).

That little strip of salt water between Abydos and Sestos is more than water now: it is a symbol, the symbol of Persia's destiny to dominate Asia and Asia alone. In crossing it and entering Europe, Xerxes was defying that destiny; and since he could never have brought so vast an army across by conventional means, he was compelled to make the defiance manifest by putting fetters on the sea. Poetry is here, in the well-known words of Aristotle (*Poetics* 1451b5-6), 'more philosophical than history', since as a matter of historical fact Darius had himself conquered extensive regions of Europe and had even penetrated beyond the Danube – and what is more, he too had turned sea into land to do it, with the help of Greek engineers (see Herodotus 4.87-9). Faced with this inconvenient set of facts, Aeschylus has done with history what he and other dramatists always do with myth: he has rewritten it to suit his purpose. Darius, according to him, never crossed the Straits or even the river Halys in central Asia Minor (864-6); yes, he did conquer Thrace, the Aegean islands, and Cyprus (868-97), but he did so by deputy and without serious fighting, the armies returning home 'successful without toil or suffering' (861-3). There is no mention of Scythia, and (in the second half of the play) none of Marathon. The *hybris* of Xerxes has to be presented as something entirely new.

And as so often, it has both divine and human causes (cf. §11.3). On the one hand, 'a mighty deity' took away Xerxes' wits. On the other hand, as the Queen tells her husband, certain 'base men' (753, 757) had been taunting Xerxes with his inactivity and with failing to increase the patrimony he had inherited, and these reproaches goaded him into marching against Greece. In that case, says the ghost, these unnamed persons are responsible for the greatest disaster to have emptied Susa of men since the beginning of Persia's history – which he proceeds to recount (762-86), presenting a long and unbroken record of success and (on the whole) virtue, under six kings who in a century or more have not done as much harm to their country as Xerxes has done in a few months by acting (as we now learn, 783) in defiance of his father's specific advice.

The relevance of the long historical excursus has been thought open to some question, particularly since of Darius' five predecessors only one (Cyrus) is credited with any specific achievement. But the speech has a distinct function in the organization of the scene. The idea of the total collapse of Persian power – which, only a moment ago, not only the chorus and the Queen but even Darius himself were in very real fear of – has served its purpose and will not appear again. The historical review – in the calmer iambic metre replacing the tenser, more agitated trochaic tetrameters of the preceding dialogue – helps us to forget it, so that in 790-5 Darius can advise that no further expedition should be sent to Greece, and the chorus-leader can suggest that 'a picked force, easy to transport' might yet achieve something – advice that would be needless, a suggestion that would be absurd, if the whole Persian empire were really disintegrating.

This exchange is itself a transition, designed to lead up to the revelation – an utter shock for the chorus – that there is still a Persian army in Greece and that this too will be destroyed. The shadow of Plataea, long seen in the distance by the audience, has at last spread across the path of the characters. Darius' prophecy is the climax of the play thus far. He was summoned up in the hope that he would be able to give some 'further cure for our troubles, [since] alone of mortals he can tell us their end' (631-2). Now he tells it – in a speech where many familiar ideas from earlier in the play reappear, and in which, for the first and only time, we hear of Xerxes' crimes against the Greek people and their gods. Is it not the case, the chorus-leader asks Darius, that the whole 'barbarian' army has crossed back over the Hellespont from Europe?

> But few of many, if one may trust
> the divine prophecies regarding these present events;
> for oracles are not fulfilled by halves.
> And if they are true, then Xerxes, persuaded by vain hopes,
> is leaving behind a selected portion of his army.
> They remain where Asopus waters the plain with his streams
> and gives welcome enrichment to the Boeotian soil;
> where the fate awaits them to suffer a crowning disaster
> to punish their *hybris* and godless arrogance.
> For when they came to the land of Greece they did not scruple
> to plunder the images of the gods and to burn their temples;
> altars have vanished, and the shrines of the gods
> are ruined, uprooted, wrenched from their foundations.
> Therefore, having done evil, no less evil
> are they suffering and shall yet suffer, nor has the fountain of woe
> yet dried up, no, suffering is still gushing forth.
> So great will be the sacrifice of clotted lifeblood
> on the soil of Plataea beneath the Dorian spear.
> To the third generation the heaps of corpses
> will signify without words to the eyes of men
> that one who is mortal should not have arrogant thoughts;
> for when *hybris* blooms out it bears fruit

> in ruin, whence one reaps a harvest full of tears.
> Such is the punishment of these acts; look on it,
> *remember Athens* [cf. 285] and remember Greece, and let none
> despise the fortune that is his,
> and in his passion for more lose the abundance he possesses.
> Zeus is truly the chastiser of pride
> that is boastful to excess; he calls all to stern account (800-28).

As Salamis was the punishment of Xerxes for invading Europe, so Plataea (where Xerxes was not present) is to be the army's punishment for sacrilege. At Salamis the dead were devoured by the fish (577-8) or washed up on surrounding shores (272-3, 421, 595-7); at Plataea they will be exposed in their thousands to the sight of all. Darius' words 'Zeus ... calls all to stern account' recall and undermine the Queen's optimistic prognosis in 213 ('if he fails, the community cannot hold him to account'). Perhaps the community cannot – though the Elders will at least reproach and admonish him, with Darius' encouragement (829-31). But even a despot remains accountable – to heaven.

Darius, as just stated, asks the councillors to admonish Xerxes to mend his ways, and he asks the Queen to meet her son on his return with new clothes, since his old ones are in rags (832-6). She too is to try to 'soften him with words in kindly fashion' (837), since she is the only person to whom he is likely to listen. Darius then returns to the underworld, taking leave of his old advisers with these words:

> And to you, elders, farewell: even amid troubles
> give pleasure to your souls day by day,
> since wealth brings no benefit to the dead (840-2).

This may seem a rather cynical and anticlimactic conclusion to this solemn and sombre scene; but we must remember what Darius had said earlier about the wealth and honour amassed by his predecessors and himself, an inheritance which they are now powerless to prevent Xerxes from squandering. What then was the point of their labours? Are not toil and frugality meaningless? If their fruits are going to be dissipated anyway, you might just as well dissipate them yourself and enjoy the short-term benefits. Darius, it must be remembered, whatever the chorus may call him, is not superhuman. He knows the future, not by special insight, but from oracles as any mortal might. The rapid fulfilment of those oracles (at the time of Salamis, Darius had been dead less than six years) has undermined his whole philosophy of existence – and he replaces it by a philosophy of meaninglessness. We need not, and should not, automatically assume that he is *right* to do so.

Some have been equally offended by the Queen's reaction to what she has heard: that what pains her most is the sorry state of her son's clothing. On this we must remember, first, that she *is* after all his mother – and, as previously suggested, the representative of all the other Persian mothers and wives whom we do not see;[15] and secondly, that an Athenian audience would not have too much difficulty in supposing that it would be a terrible disgrace for a king, and especially a Persian king, to be seen in public in torn and ragged clothing. Moreover, the whole conclusion of the Darius scene has a vital function in building up expectations about the scene that is to follow. What we are led to expect is roughly this. The Queen will return with new clothes for her son. Xerxes will arrive, in rags and lamenting. He will be admonished (though deferentially as befits his status) by the Elders and comforted by his mother, and will put on new royal robes for his entry into the city. Alternatively, perhaps Xerxes will arrive first (cf. 529) and his mother come back shortly afterwards to soothe and reclothe him. Neither of these things happens, and the actual final procession will make the strongest of contrasts both with what we were expecting and with the majestic figure of Darius that we have just seen.

First, however, the chorus sing an ode that elaborates the theme of the contrast between the successful career of Darius and the calamitous reign of his son. With a seemingly godlike ability to act at a distance – without crossing the Halys, almost without leaving Susa (865-7) – he conquered Thrace, the shores of the Hellespont and Bosporus, and ruled all the Greeks of Ionia, Cyprus and the Aegean: some of his island subjects[16] are listed in another of the play's notable catalogues (882-97) which ends, significantly, with the Cypriot Salamis. Something has already been said about the artistic distortion of history in regard to Darius' conquests, and this catalogue may give more food for thought on the subject. In the first place, we now find that Darius did actually acquire a maritime empire, and we may wonder why the Persians were permitted by the gods to sail in ships to Cypriot Salamis – and indeed to Andros (887) which lies seven miles from the coast of Euboea and thirty miles from that of Attica – but not to Saronic Salamis. And if we are invited to follow Darius' troops so far, we can hardly help recalling also that they did land in Euboea and in Attica – and what happened to them: it may be possible to blot from memory the invasion of distant Scythia, but an Athenian audience cannot be expected to forget about Marathon, particularly when they have been reminded of it earlier in the play and when it gives the lie to the claim made at the beginning and end of this song (858ff., 901ff.) that Darius' armies never knew defeat. There are two possible explanations for this anomaly, which need not be regarded as mutually exclusive. In the first place, there is a parallel in the treatment of Agamemnon in the *Oresteia*. The Argive elders are often very critical of Agamemnon while he is alive, but once he is dead he is remembered (except by Clytaemestra) as a great, successful and revered king whose faults are forgotten, basically because they are as nothing to those of his usurping successors. If Agamemnon's capture of Troy can be remembered and his loss on the expedition of almost his whole army ignored, we can surely forgive it if the Persian elders overlook a mere 6,000-odd dead at Marathon, when Xerxes' losses must be taken to have run into the hundreds of thousands. Secondly, it may well be significant that the scope, and even the classification, of the Persian dependencies recalled in this song corresponds closely to that of the maritime alliance which had been formed in 478/7 under Athenian leadership (see further §12.3). On the one hand this appeals to Athenian patriotic pride: *we*, the Athenian spectator is invited to feel, are the inheritors of the dominion that Darius held and Xerxes lost. On the other hand it embodies an implicit warning: *we* are now in the position of Darius; we have acquired the hegemony of this vast region, almost without thinking about it; we could lose it, if we are not careful, as easily as Xerxes did – and then it might be our turn to lament, as the Persians do now:

> now we are enduring the decisive reversal of all this by the gods in war,
> quelled by grievous blows inflicted at sea (904-7).[17]

Upon these words, Xerxes enters: alone, on foot, and in rags. He *may* be carrying a bow, the emblem in this play of the Persian warrior; but no bow is actually referred to in the text, only a quiver – which is empty (1020-2). This time, we may be sure, the councillors do *not* prostrate themselves before the royal presence. On the contrary, it is Xerxes who nearly collapses to the ground (913) with the shame he feels before them, and he wishes he had perished with his army. In a different sense from the usual one, he has brought the land of Asia to its knees (929-30). The chorus spare him not one word of respect, and in their very first utterance address him as the slayer of his country's youth 'who heaped Hades with Persians' (923-4).

Xerxes accepts the reproach at once (931-3) and asks the chorus to lament with him; this lament begins at 950 and continues till the end of the play, Xerxes being its leader. It is doubtless significant that for Greeks collective lamentation was traditionally the province of *women* – as indeed it had been in Phrynichus' *Phoenician Women*. We may still half expect that at some point Xerxes' mother will appear with new clothes; but as the scene goes on, it becomes clearer and clearer that this would be inappropriate and irrelevant. One does not wear new clothes on a day of mourning; and it may be added that, as Greeks well knew (cf. *Cho.* 28-31, also *Supp.* 120-1), in much of the Near East an important sign of mourning was precisely the rent garment.

The lament falls into three sections. The first section (950-1001) is dominated by the chorus, who sing three-quarters of it. From their lips we hear yet again a long list of commanders who set out with Xerxes and have not returned: 'Where are they? … Did you leave them behind? … We miss them!' (956-61, 978-85, 992-1001). Xerxes can say nothing except to admit they are all gone, to reproach himself, and to recall with sorrow the names of the Greeks, of Salamis and of Athens.

In the second section of the lament (1002-37) the tone becomes more broken and sobby, few utterances exceeding a dozen syllables. It is now that Xerxes displays his empty quiver and the rents in his clothes. At 1038 he and the Elders begin, very slowly, to move away towards the palace, still singing their antiphonal lament. The Elders utter wild cries of grief, beat their breasts (1046, 1054), tear their beards (1056), rend their clothes (1060), pluck out their hair (1062), and Xerxes enters his city as if in a funeral procession, as in almost the last words of the play we are again reminded of the vital factor for which the Persians' advance calculations had not allowed, the 'three-banked boats' by which they were destroyed (1074-5). In general the content of the lament is extremely repetitious, both within itself and of ideas from earlier in the play: it is the mood that is significant. Xerxes is the first representative of a type that will become common in later tragedy, the survivor of a catastrophe who has lost all that makes survival worth while: Creon in Sophocles' *Antigone*, and Jason in Euripides' *Medea*, are notable examples.

Such is the nemesis[18] of Persian power, the work of an avenging deity but also (or one could equally well say 'and therefore') an exemplification of the law well known to every thinking Greek from Solon to Thucydides and beyond, that success feeds ambition, and that the hardest thing in the world is to know when to stop. And that law does not apply only to Persians. This Xerxes is not a bad man. The traditional barbarities of the tyrant – either in real life or on the stage – are conspicuously absent from his portrayal. Even the destruction of Greek sanctuaries is blamed on the army collectively, not on him personally (809-15), and it is they rather than he who pay for it. The worst thing that anyone ascribes to Xerxes is the threat to behead the admirals if the Greek fleet escaped from Salamis (369-71) – a threat which in the end was not carried out, and which in any case was no worse in principle than the death penalty which so great an Athenian as Miltiades had narrowly escaped for failing to capture Paros (Herodotus 6.136). It is the Greeks, if anyone, who are portrayed as murderers. Xerxes is merely weak and vain; in some ways not unlike the Agamemnon whom Aeschylus was to portray fourteen years later. It is even conceivable that Aeschylus may have been attempting the seemingly impossible feat of inducing his audience to feel compassion for the man who had burnt their city, and for the great nation whom his folly and ambition had brought to ruin.

4.2 The tetralogy[19]

The four plays which Aeschylus produced in 472 BC – *Phineus, The Persians, Glaucus of Potniae*[20] and *Prometheus the Fire-Bearer* – seem at first sight like a completely miscellaneous collection of unrelated dramas, such as became common later in the fifth century; comparable, for example, to Euripides' productions of 438 (*The Cretan Women*,[21] *Alcmeon in*

Psophis, Telephus, Alcestis) or of 431 (*Medea, Philoctetes, Dictys, The Reapers*). Phineus was a blind Thracian prophet who was persecuted by the Harpies who persistently snatched away his food (cf. *Eum.* 50-1) until he was visited by the Argonauts; two of their number, Zetes and Calaïs (sons of Boreas, the North Wind, and of the Athenian princess Oreithyia), chased away and killed the Harpies. Glaucus[22] kept a team of horses which he fed on human flesh; when he was competing in the chariot-race at the funeral games of Pelias, he crashed and was eaten by his horses. There is a feeble connection between these two stories, since it was Pelias who sent Jason on what he hoped was the impossible mission of bringing back the Golden Fleece, and he died through the wiles of Medea after Jason's return from the expedition; but what connection has the Persian War with either of them, and why should a play about it be placed *between* them? Attempts have been made from time to time to trace linkages between the plays of this production (e.g. Deichgräber 1974, Flintoff 1992, Moreau 1993, Perysinakis 2000), but none has been at all convincing. I believe, however, that two surviving fragments can provide us with clues that will lead to a surprising solution.

The two fragments are frr. 25a and 40a. The latter is cited by Hesychius from *Glaucus of Potniae* (though most editors before Radt emended Hesychius' text, for no good reason, in order to ascribe the fragment to *Glaucus the Sea-god*).[23] It refers to a 'harbour of Xiphirus' (the name may well be corrupt), which Hesychius seems to say was at or near Rhegium, on the Italian side of the Strait of Messina. We know there was another mention of Rhegium in Aeschylus (fr. 402), saying that it was so named because this was where Sicily was *broken off* (*aporrhagênai*, from the verb *rhêgnynai* 'break') from Italy by an earthquake or earthquakes, and this may well come from the same context.

The other fragment (25a) is quoted by a scholiast on Pindar (*Pythian* 1.78 [153]) simply from Aeschylus' *Glaucus*, without specifying which of the two plays of that name is meant. In it a character says that he[24] washed himself in 'fair streams' and came to Himera (or possibly to the river Himeras) with its high cliffs. The city of Himera, and the river Himeras on which it stood, were in northern Sicily.

It would be too much of a coincidence for there to have been two plays about two different characters of the heroic age named Glaucus, both firmly located in mainland Greece, in each of which mention was made of places in Sicily and southern Italy which played no part in Greek heroic saga at all.[25] We may assume, therefore, at least provisionally, that all the Sicilian/Italian references come from *Glaucus of Potniae*. What might this play have to do with Sicily – and in particular with Himera? Its action was set at Glaucus' home, for news of the fatal chariot-race was brought by a messenger to Glaucus' wife.[26] Neither Glaucus nor any other mortal character in the play would have had reason to travel to Sicily and back. The speaker of fr. 25a must therefore be a god; perhaps he has returned from a visit to Sicily in response to a prayer by Glaucus' wife or by the chorus, just as Athena in *Eumenides* (397-404) returns from a visit to the Troad in response to a prayer by Orestes. In a play that had so much to do with horses, Poseidon Hippios, the god of horses, would be an appropriate god for this purpose.

Now to any Greek in 472 BC, the name Himera would have been associated above all with the victory gained there eight years earlier – on the same day as the battle of Salamis, or so it was later said (Herodotus 7.166) – by Gelon of Syracuse over the Carthaginians, a victory which Pindar (*Pythian* 1.75-80) mentions alongside those of Salamis and Plataea. And Poseidon was doubly involved in this victory. The action that decided the day – the killing of the Carthaginian commander, Hamilcar, and the firing of his fleet – was performed by a detachment of Syracusan *cavalry*, which took Hamilcar by surprise while he was engaged in offering sacrifice *to Poseidon*[27] (Diodorus Siculus 11.21.4-11.22.1). We may note, too, that references to Rhegium, such as those in frr. 40a and 402, would also fit Poseidon: he was the god of earthquakes, such as those which had allegedly sundered Sicily from the mainland.

One can see no reason why Poseidon, or any other god, should have been sent by the dramatist to Himera, except to provide him with an excuse for making prophetic mention of Gelon's victory – again resembling Athena in *Eumenides*, who on her visit to the Troad had taken possession of Sigeium to be for all time the property of the Athenian people, as of course it was in Aeschylus' own day. Poseidon too, in *Glaucus of Potniae*, will have made a pledge for the future: that one far-distant day he would save Greeks, fighting on land, from the barbarians of the West, at the same time as he was saving Greeks, fighting at sea, from the barbarians of the East. In addition, finding himself now at Potniae, he may well also have made some reference to the battle of Plataea, or perhaps to the subsequent march on Thebes, during which the Athenian army must have passed through Potniae itself.

What then of *Phineus*? Phineus was saved from the Harpies, as we have seen, by the sons of Boreas and Oreithyia. Boreas and Oreithyia had played an important role in the campaign against the Persians. Early in the invasion, before the battles of Thermopylae and Artemisium, a large part of the Persian fleet was destroyed at Cape Sepias, in south-east Thessaly, by a north-easterly gale (Herodotus 7.188-90); the Athenians believed that this was the work of Boreas and Oreithyia, for whose aid they had prayed, and they afterwards established a sanctuary of Boreas just outside the city. Phineus was a prophet, and it would be natural enough if, in gratitude to the sons of Boreas, he foretold what Boreas would one day do to succour the distant heirs of the young men's grandfather, Erechtheus, and of their colleague on board the *Argo*, Theseus.

So Aeschylus' production of 472 may have contained in its first play a prophecy of the Sepias disaster; in its second, a narrative of Salamis and a prophecy of Plataea; and in its third, an allusion (or maybe more than an allusion) to the aftermath of Plataea, and a prophecy of Himera. There was after all a connecting link between the three: nothing other than the Persian War itself, together with the simultaneous attack on Greek Sicily by the Carthaginians.

It is not obvious how to link *Prometheus the Fire-Bearer* to this theme, and Aeschylus may indeed not have attempted to do so. But Prometheus had very close ties to Athens, the only place that we know of where he had any substantial cult; and in the play, the satyrs were shown both the benefits of fire (fr. 204b) and also its potential dangers (fr. 187a Radt = 206 Sommerstein; fr. 207). Aeschylus could thus, if he wished, have included in his script some allusions to the burning of Athens by the Persians and associated events. Whether he actually did so is another matter.

If Aeschylus' production of 472 was anything like what has been sketched out here, we can see it as an attempt to emulate Phrynichus' earlier commemoration of the Persian War in tragedy – but to do so in a totally different manner. Phrynichus, it seems, had written a suite of plays dealing directly with the war itself. Aeschylus creates a trilogy of which only the middle play straightforwardly dramatizes recent events; the preceding and following plays seem on the face of it to have no connection with the war at all – but they turn out, in different and devious ways, to foreshadow and foretell crucial moments in the struggle of Greeks and barbarians. And at least three plays of the production had strong Athenian connections.[28] The saviours of Phineus were Athenian on their mother's side, and Phineus' prophecy was of an event which had given rise to a new Athenian cult. *The Persians* centres on an Athenian victory gained in Athenian waters; Athens, its localities and its heroes are mentioned by name a total of eighteen times. Prometheus – very possibly made the subject of an Athenian drama for the first time – was very much an Athenian god, and his gift of fire was commemorated in a notable Athenian festival, the Promethia. Thus past and present were linked to Athens' glory as surely as they were a few years later on the walls of the Stoa Poikile, where the battle of Marathon kept company with the Amazon and Trojan wars (Pausanias 1.15.1-3).

Notes

1. If, as is likely, the order of stanzas in the manuscript tradition has been disturbed, and lines 93-100 properly belong between 113 and 114. The ensuing discussion is based on the text as thus transposed.

2. *Hybris* may be defined as wilful and contemptuous disregard of the proper dignity (*timê*) of another. The victim may be human or (as here, cf. 744-51) divine, an inferior or a superior. In many contexts 'outrage' makes a good one-word translation of *hybris*, as does the archaic 'contumely'; 'arrogance' sometimes; 'pride' never. The best account of the concept of *hybris* is Fisher 1992.

3. These and other terms relating to lyric structure are explained in §7.5 below.

4. Literally millions: Greeks believed that Xerxes' army numbered between two and three million men (Herodotus 7.185 and 228).

5. Throughout the play Persians frequently use this word of themselves.

6. It is true that Athenian women also often dressed in the Dorian style, and that this style, being simpler and more austere than the Ionian, made a sharper contrast with the luxury of Persian dress; it remains also true that Aeschylus *could* have chosen to identify this woman clearly as an Athenian, and that he has in fact chosen not to.

7. An effect repeated in the Queen's final response to the Messenger's report (see below) and again at the turning-point of *Seven against Thebes* (653-5).

8. I have discussed this passage in the sequence in which it is presented by the manuscripts and by most editors, but it is in fact likely that the Messenger's two couplets at 272-3 and 278-9 should change places: in 274-7 the chorus already know that the catastrophic battle was fought at sea, something which is mentioned in 278-9 but not in 272-3. See Sier 2005: 410-14.

9. Nor because the landing was led by Aristeides; see §12.3.

10. Indeed Mardonius himself does not even figure among the fifty or so commanders named in the play. To mention him would risk diluting Xerxes' responsibility for the disaster.

11. Here and in the following stanza, 'took' translates *agagen/agagon* 'led, conveyed', and 'their slayer(s)' translates *apôlesen/-san* 'lost (them), destroyed (them)'.

12. The ghost's complaint that the earth is being 'beaten and scratched' (683) can imply nothing else. Orestes and Electra probably do likewise, unavailingly, in *Cho.* 489-96 (cf. Euripides, *Electra* 678).

13. *Stichomythia* is a form of dramatic dialogue consisting of speeches of one line each by (normally) two speakers in alternation.

14. In antiquity, as now, the name Bosporus (or Thracian Bosporus) normally denoted the strait between Byzantium (Istanbul) and Chalcedon, leading to the Black Sea. In this scene, however, and probably also (by implication) in *Supp.* 544-6, Aeschylus treats the name as an alternative designation for the Hellespont (Dardanelles); so too Sophocles, *Ajax* 884.

15. Throughout the last twenty lines of the Darius scene, Xerxes is consistently thought of as a loved and loving son rather than as a king (832, 834, 837-8, 847, 850-1).

16. Cnidos (892) is on a peninsula, not an island – but the Cnidians had tried to make it an island to avoid a Persian occupation in the time of Cyrus (Herodotus 1.174).

17. Ideas like these are prominent in the reading of *Pers.* presented by Rosenbloom 2006.

18. I use this word in the sense (or one of the senses) in which it is now familiar in English. There are situations in Aeschylus, including this one, to which this English word might aptly be applied, but I should make it clear that Aeschylus does *not* apply the Greek word *nemesis* to such situations: when he uses the word at all (which, in the surviving plays and fragments, is only twice: *Seven* 235, fr. 266.4) it means merely 'indignation'.

19. The arguments presented in this section are developed more fully in Sommerstein 2010b.

20. Potniae was a village just south of Thebes; Aeschylus apparently placed the death of Laius there (fr. 387a; see §5.5).

21. Featuring, among others, Aërope (who became the mother of Agamemnon and Menelaus) and her Cretan father Catreus.

22. One of three entirely separate characters of this name who appeared in three different Aeschylean plays. The other two were a fisherman of Anthedon (in Boeotia) who ate a herb that made him immortal (*Glaucus the Sea-god*) and a son of Minos of Crete who drowned in a vat of honey but was brought back to life by the seer Polyidus (*The Cretan Women*). Ovid (*Ibis* 555-8) ingeniously imprecates upon his enemy the fate of all three of these Glauci.

23. Any scribal confusion between these two titles would have been much more likely to lead to a corruption in the *other* direction, since *pontios* 'of the sea' – together with its homonym, the Roman family name Pontius, familiar to every Christian scribe because of Pontius Pilate – is more than twenty times as frequent in Greek texts as *Potnieus* 'of Potniae'.

24. I use the masculine pronoun for convenience; there is nothing in the text as transmitted that definitely determines the gender of the speaker.

25. Except in so far as they came to be identified with places visited by Odysseus in the course of his wanderings.

26. Aesch. fr. 36b.2 col. II 9.

27. So, at any rate, the Sicilian Greeks said. In reality, of course, Hamilcar will have been sacrificing to one of the gods of his own city – probably Melqart, whom Greeks usually identified with Heracles but sometimes with Poseidon.

28. Perhaps all four did. *Glaucus of Potniae* contained a narrative of a chariot-race in which there was a multiple pile-up (Aesch. fr. 38). The similar narrative in Sophocles' *Electra* (680-762) also includes a pile-up (724-30) and may well be partly modelled on the Aeschylean narrative. In Sophocles, when on the last lap Orestes also crashes, the only driver left in the race, and therefore the winner, is an Athenian (cf. 731-3). Did Aeschylus likewise make an Athenian the winner of the race in which Glaucus perished? It may be relevant that Aeschylus' *khorêgos*, Pericles, was descended on his mother's side from a family (the Alcmeonidae) with a long history of chariot-racing victories in the major Games (Pindar, *Pythian* 7, esp. 10-13); we shall see later (§12.3) that in *The Persians* Aeschylus had alluded to a triumph of another kind achieved by Pericles' father, Xanthippus.

5

The Theban Plays

A tetralogy produced in 467, comprising *Laius*, *Oedipus*, *Seven against Thebes* and the satyr-play *The Sphinx*. It won first prize, defeating Aristias (who was presenting plays composed by his father Pratinas) and Polyphrasmon. The third play survives, together with small fragments of the others.

5.1. *Seven against Thebes*

The title is unlikely to be original, since the city and people of Thebes are never mentioned under those names anywhere in the play, being referred to instead by names derived from Cadmus, the founder of the city. Probably when the play was originally produced, as part of a connected tetralogy, it did not have a separate title; in the later fifth century, however, it seems to have been restaged on its own (when it greatly impressed the rhetorician Gorgias), and it was known to Aristophanes in 405 by its present name.[1]

Oedipus is dead. His sons, Eteocles and Polyneices (see Genealogy, p. 317), have quarrelled over his property and the succession to his kingship, and Polyneices has been forced (647-8) into exile; going to Argos, he has persuaded the Argive king Adrastus to launch an expedition against Thebes. When the play opens, the city has for some time been under siege.

In the opening scene Eteocles addresses the armed male citizenry. He reminds them of their duty to their motherland, informs them that according to the advice of a prophet (presumably Teiresias) a major attack is imminent, and orders them to man the walls and gates at once. The citizens accordingly leave, and a moment later a scout, sent out earlier by Eteocles, enters and reports to him that seven of the enemy leaders have sworn to destroy Thebes or perish in the attempt; his latest news is that they are drawing lots to decide which of the city's seven gates each shall attack. He urges Eteocles to make defensive arrangements promptly, and leaves to gather further intelligence. Eteocles, left alone, prays to 'Zeus, Earth, the gods that dwell in the city, and the mighty vengeful Curse of my father' to save the *city* from destruction (69-71); it is known (788-90) that Oedipus before his death had cursed his sons, saying that they would divide their inheritance sword in hand, and Eteocles' prayer is thus in effect that the fulfilment of the curse, as armies battle to decide the brothers' competing claims, may not lead to the obliteration of Thebes. He then leaves, presumably to make his dispositions for the defence of the gates.

The chorus of Theban maidens (cf. 110) then rush on in terror and panic. They have brought offerings for the gods of the city, whose images stand on what is later called an 'acropolis' (240), doubtless the mound at the rear of the *orkhêstra* (see §2.1). Terrified by the noises made by the attacking army, especially their horses and chariots (84-6, 89, 100, 103, 123-4, 151-5, 158-61), they pray passionately to the gods and goddesses, individually and collectively, to deliver Thebes from its peril. Their noise, in turn, brings Eteocles back. He harangues them furiously (182-202), denouncing women in general in unmeasured terms and especially the danger their present manifestations pose to public morale, and ordering them, on pain of death, to return to their homes. They do not move, but instead, in song, explain the cause of their fears, while Eteocles in blunt spoken triplets argues that they are only making things worse. Eventually he persuades them to be silent and himself prays to the gods of the city (271-8), vowing rich offerings from the enemy spoils in the event of victory. He asks them to echo this prayer in a self-controlled and dignified manner and then leaves, saying that he is going to station 'six men with myself the seventh' at the seven gates. The chorus, left alone, ignore the spirit of his instructions; they do indeed pray to the gods (301-20), but during the greater part of their song they are reflecting, in no confident mood, on the dangers facing their city and themselves – fire, slavery, exile, death, bereavement, plunder, forced concubinage.

The Scout and Eteocles return in quick succession (Eteocles, as we shall see in §5.2, is accompanied by attendants carrying his weapons and armour), and there begins a scene, occupying nearly one-third of the play (369-676), known variously as the 'shield scene' and the 'seven *Redepaare* [pairs of speeches]'. Gate by gate, in clockwise sequence, the Scout describes the seven attacking warriors, their appearance, character and boasts, and especially the devices (and in some cases mottoes) on their shields. Seven times in reply Eteocles nominates a Theban champion to defend one of the gates, each time a man who by his birth or personality, or because of the device on his own shield, makes an appropriate opponent for this particular enemy. The text has left scholars in some doubt whether Eteocles is actually choosing the defenders in immediate response to the Scout's account of the attackers, or whether some or all of his choices have already been made (see §5.2). Each of his speeches is followed by a short choral stanza in which the maidens, while still expressing their fears, pray for the defence to be successful.

The first five *Redepaare* establish a simple and predictable pattern. Each of the attackers is noisy, boastful, menacing, often blasphemous; each of the defenders is a quiet, determined man of action; and on each occasion Eteocles finds specific grounds for confidence in success, and is able to turn the arrogant devices on the enemy's shields into prophecies of doom for their bearers (thus the shield of Tydeus, which shows the moon dominating the night sky, is said to presage that the night of death will fall on Tydeus' eyes). To none of these gates does he assign himself. Attacking the sixth (Homoloïd) gate is the prophet Amphiaraus, a man of the highest character, who had joined the expedition against his will and his better judgement, and is raising his voice not in boastful threats but in loud denunciations of Tydeus as a murderer and a cause of disaster to Argos, and of Polyneices (here mentioned for the first time in the play) as a traitor to his native land (570-89). Amphiaraus has no device on his shield ('for he does not wish to be thought a man of valour, but to *be* one', 592). Eteocles laments the fate that has placed so good a man in such evil company, predicts (as indeed Amphiaraus had predicted himself) that he will fall in the battle, and duly nominates an appropriate opponent, leaving himself to defend the seventh gate.

And then he learns that the enemy leader who is attacking that gate is his own brother, eager either to die or to take vengeance on the man who dishonoured and exiled him, and displaying on his shield the picture of himself being brought back home by the goddess of Justice (631-48). With this information the Scout has done his duty and departs; and once again, as after the Scout's earlier exit, Eteocles' inner thoughts burst forth:

> O race whom the gods drive mad, whom they hate with a great hate!
> O my family, family of Oedipus, fit only for tears!
> Ah me, now my father's curses are fulfilled! (653-5).

Then, however, he seems to calm down, deconstructing the message of Polyneices' shield in his usual way, insisting that Polyneices and Justice have never had anything to do with one another, until the moment comes when he has to name the man to fight against Polyneices:

> Trusting in this I shall go and face him
> myself: who else could do so with greater right?
> Ruler against ruler, brother against brother,
> enemy against enemy I shall face him. Give me at once
> my greaves, protection against spear and arrow (672-6).

The chorus desperately try to dissuade Eteocles from what they see as his insane resolve (in an exchange that in many ways echoes in reverse the earlier one in 203-63), but to no avail. Eteocles' perception is that the fate foreshadowed for him and for the whole royal family from the time of Laius (691), confirmed by the curse of Oedipus (695-7, 709) and obscurely predicted in his own dreams (710-11) has now come upon him and cannot be avoided but only met with dignity and courage. It is likely that during his exchange with the chorus Eteocles is putting on his armour piece by piece (see §5.2); and with the words 'When the gods send evil you cannot escape it' (719) he goes to the seventh gate, to kill or be killed by his brother – except that the audience know he will kill *and* be killed.

The chorus sing of the Erinys, the embodiment of the curse of Oedipus now about to be fulfilled. They trace the origin of the family's sorrows to Laius, who disobeyed a thrice-repeated oracular warning 'to die without issue and save his city' and begot Oedipus (742-52); Oedipus slew his father and married his mother, and having at one time been held in unparalleled honour for saving Thebes from the Sphinx, he blinded himself and cursed his sons in the frenzy of his distress at discovering what he had done (778-90). That curse, the chorus conclude, now seems on the point of coming true.

A messenger brings what should have been tidings of joy: the battle is won, the city is saved. But this news is quickly overshadowed by his other message, that Eteocles and Polyneices have killed each other. On the messenger's departure the chorus reflect sombrely on the fulfilment of the curse; and then (848-60) the two bodies are brought in.

From this point it is likely (see §5.6) that the text has been altered and expanded by a producer or producers in the later fifth or fourth century. As it was known to later antiquity, and as it is found in the medieval manuscripts, the play continues thus. Antigone and Ismene, the sisters of Eteocles and Polyneices, come on stage (861-74). An elaborate lyric lament is sung over the two brothers, treating them with complete impartiality and emphasizing the responsibility of malevolent divine powers (875-960): the manuscripts are inconsistent on the question whether this lament is sung by the two sisters or by sections of the chorus, but its content strongly suggests the latter, and 866-70 confirms that the chorus are to sing before the sisters do. There follows a further lament (961-1004) in brief, broken, responsive iambic phrases, which as we have it is clearly meant to be sung antiphonally by Antigone and Ismene, with the chorus contributing refrains. At the end of this lament the question of burial is raised, and it seems to be decided that the brothers will be buried among the royal tombs, even though this will be 'a grief to their father as he sleeps close by'.

Now, however, a herald enters announcing the decision of 'the people's councillors' that while Eteocles is to be buried with full honours, Polyneices must be cast out unburied and unlamented to feed the dogs (1005-25). Antigone retorts that she will perform Polyneices' burial herself, whoever may forbid it; the herald argues with her inconclusively and departs (1026-53). The chorus divide into two groups, and the bodies are carried off separately, Antigone and half the chorus going to bury Polyneices while Ismene (presumably) and the rest of the chorus escort the bier of Eteocles.

5.2. Steps to catastrophe

Eteocles, as we have seen, considers his terrible fate to be essentially the result of events long past; and others in the play – the chorus and the Messenger – agree, referring not only to the curse of Oedipus but also, three times (750, 802, 842), to the 'ill counsel' of Laius in disobeying Apollo and begetting an heir. Yet at the same time we can see in the play itself how the catastrophe gradually crystallizes out of a perfectly intelligible, humanly credible sequence of events: once again, as in *The Persians*, we have to deal with 'divine' and 'secular' causation operating in parallel (see §11.3). Within the play, the fate of Eteocles and Polyneices results from the natural flow of events and from decisions taken by Eteocles. Whether these decisions, and others which Eteocles may have taken earlier, are themselves to be regarded as 'ill-counselled', or even the product of a deranged or possessed mind (as the chorus think, and as many critics have thought too), may be left for later consideration (see §5.3).

At the start of the play there is no anticipation in Thebes that either Eteocles or Polyneices will fight in person at all. In the opening scene the citizens are in armour[2] but Eteocles is not, and all his exhortations are in the *second* person plural. They are, as it were, the marines on board the ship of state, to be posted on the 'decks' (*selmata*) of the wall-towers (32-3), while Eteocles himself is the helmsman (2-3). Similarly when the Scout brings his report of the preparations by the Seven to attack the gates, there is no indication that Polyneices is among them. Of course Eteocles knows that his brother is with the enemy army, and he has his father's curse well in mind (69ff.), but he has no reason to anticipate a personal combat: a battle between forces supporting, respectively, his and his brother's claims to the Theban throne would be quite enough to fulfil the words of the curse.

While Eteocles is away, presumably making rapid dispositions (cf. 57-8, 65) to meet the impending assault, the situation within the walls is suddenly thrown into peril by the panic of the young women (the chorus). Eteocles comes back to quell this, and it is some time before he can resume his task; and when he does, his intentions seem to have changed, as he announces he is going to post at the gates 'six men *with myself the seventh*' (282-4). There was no hint of this at any earlier stage; Eteocles, alone among Theban men of military age, is not even equipped for combat; and everything encourages us to suppose that he has made a spur-of-the-moment decision in an effort to raise the people's, and especially the women's, morale. In fact it seems to make little impression on them ('my heart cannot sleep for fear' they sing, the moment he leaves), and it represents a large step nearer disaster.

Eteocles wished to complete making his postings before the arrival of urgent news forced him into immediate action (285-6). After the choral song, he and the Scout are both seen hastening back (369-74): the urgent news has come – Tydeus will be attacking the Proetid Gate the instant that Amphiaraus declares the omens to be favourable (377-9). Because of the interruption caused by the women, Eteocles has had much less time than he had expected in which to make his dispositions. Has he completed all of them, or some of them, or none? Much of our understanding of the great central scene will depend on whether we consider this a valid question to ask of the text, and, if we do, on how we answer it. The most various views have been held. Many critics have been attracted by the idea that when he comes on stage at the beginning of this scene, Eteocles is accompanied by six Theban warriors who then go out, one by one, as he assigns them to their stations, thus more and more obviously isolating Eteocles as the destined opponent of Polyneices, who (we can easily guess – though no one on stage can) is going to be attacking the seventh and last gate. Unfortunately this hypothesis has no sufficient support in the text, which contains no indication of the entry, the presence or the exit of these six champions.[3]

Taplin 1977: 149-56 nevertheless wished to maintain that Eteocles is actually assigning the defenders to their various gates, one by one, during the course of the scene; but given that the defenders are not on stage, and given that there is no sign whatever that Eteocles sends messengers out to convey his orders, he fails to find a plausible way in which this idea could be got across to an audience (before the days of walkie-talkie radios and mobile phones). If Aeschylus had wanted his spectators to understand that no decisions about postings had been taken before the beginning of this scene, he had available to him easy ways to make this unambiguously clear; instead he chose to do something quite different.

We must start, rather – as Wilamowitz 1914: 76 saw – from a consideration of the tenses of the verbs used by Eteocles in announcing his decisions. These form a very clear and very curious pattern:

I	I *shall post* (*antitaxô*) against Tydeus the excellent son of Astacus	(407f)
II	Against him *has been posted* (*tetaktai*) a fiery spirit, warlike Polyphontes	(447f)
III	Megareus *has been sent* (*pepemptai*), a man whose hands do his boasting for him	(473f)
IV	Hyperbius *has been chosen* (*hêirethê*) as the man to face this man	(504f)
V	There *is* (*estin*) to face this Arcadian ... a man who does not boast ... Actor	(553-5)
VI	Against him we *shall post* (*antitaxomen*) ... warlike Lasthenes	(620f.)
VII	Trusting in this I *shall go* (*eimi*) and face him myself	(672f)

Since the gates form a circle, with Gate I next to Gate VII (so that Amphiaraus, at Gate VI, is within shouting distance of Tydeus at Gate I: 571-5), not only are the three past (aorist or perfect[4]) tenses adjacent to one another (II, III, IV), but so are the three future tenses (VI, VII, I); the present tense, which could be understood either way, lies between these two blocks. The odds are about nine to one against such a pattern having arisen by chance. Can we make dramatic sense out of the apparent inconsistency? Indeed we can.

At the beginning of the scene, since Eteocles does not speak, we are left unsure whether he has had time to complete his dispositions or whether – as 285-6 hinted might be possible – he has been interrupted. The uncertainty continues through the Scout's first speech and the first dozen lines of Eteocles' reply, and then the future verb in 408 reveals that the task had been left incomplete. The tenses used in Eteocles' other speeches fill out what proves to be a coherent pattern. Eteocles has selected and posted defenders for the second, third and fourth gates, and probably also for the fifth, but has not yet done so for the sixth, seventh and first, which adjoin each other on the east side of the city, and which are being attacked (as it happens, though Eteocles does not yet know this) by the three outstanding figures among the Seven, Amphiaraus, Polyneices and Tydeus.

Of course we only perceive this pattern as the scene progresses, and only at 672-3 is the last detail filled in. At each stage we do not know whether Eteocles has a choice or whether he is already committed. At the first gate he has a choice – and his opening line, 'I would not tremble before any man's accoutrements' (397), suggests that he may go himself against the formidable Tydeus. But he chooses Melanippus. Then at the next four gates, each time the crucial verb comes to the king's lips we find that the choice has already been made; and he comes to the sixth gate with only one chance left to miss Polyneices – himself, of course, still not knowing that Polyneices is one of the Seven at all. And that one chance proves in fact to be no chance; for at the sixth gate is Amphiaraus, who is known to be doomed to perish if he enters the battle (587-9, 615-18) and whom therefore Eteocles cannot possibly choose as his own opponent, since if the king is to fight at all he must not be seen to be choosing a position of no danger.

Thus throughout the scene there is a continual interplay between knowledge and ignorance – and of the four parties concerned (Eteocles, the Scout, the chorus and the audience) no two are ignorant of the same things. The audience know, from their background knowledge of the legend, that Eteocles and Polyneices will fight each other, and can guess (with increasing confidence as the scene goes on) that Polyneices will prove to be attacking the seventh gate; they do not know how much freedom of choice Eteocles will have about where to post himself. Eteocles knows that three or four of the gates already have defenders assigned: he does not know in advance who the attackers are, nor which gate each one will attack, nor (above all) that his brother is among them. The Scout does know who the attackers are; he does not seem to know (cf. 425, 470) that some of the defenders have already been posted, nor does he know (cf. 650) that Eteocles has undertaken to defend one gate himself. And the chorus know only that they and Thebes are in danger – until Eteocles makes his fateful decision and the chorus, having followed each of his first six speeches with fervent prayers to the gods in metres dominated by the highly emotional dochmiac,[5] follow his seventh with a fervent appeal to *him* in spoken iambic trimeters (677-82). Knowledge and ignorance, of course, can be no new theme in a trilogy whose central figure, Oedipus, killed his father in ignorance and married his mother in ignorance.

Up to 652 it is circumstances that conspire to put Eteocles in a position where he must either fight his brother or publicly renounce his promise to defend a gate and so incur the shame of failing to complete what he has put his hand to. He makes choices, as we have seen, but he makes them in ignorance of a vital fact. But when knowledge does come to him, he is still offered another choice and another chance, when the chorus-leader urges him to let some other Theban fight Polyneices (679-80), adding explicitly a little later that he will not be called a coward if he withdraws in such circumstances (698-9). This time it is he himself who knowingly embraces his doom; and in all probability the last stages of his journey to death are marked by the donning of his armour, piece by piece, between 675 and 711.

As this interpretation of the passage remains controversial, it is necessary to defend it here. The *prima facie* evidence for it is simple. In the last lines of his last long speech (675-6), having announced that he will go to fight his brother, Eteocles calls for his greaves. Now when a warrior arms, he puts on his greaves *first*: this is the rule in all the arming-scenes in the *Iliad* (e.g. 3.330), for the simple practical reason that once the warrior is clad in his body-armour he will not be able to bend down. It follows, first, that at the moment of speaking 675-6 Eteocles is wearing no armour, and secondly, that he leaves the scene fully armed,[6] as would anyway be suggested by 717 where he speaks of himself as a *hoplitês* or heavy-armed soldier. And from that, in turn, it follows that he must put his armour on during the exchanges that follow 676.

Very strong arguments would be necessary to establish that these indications in the text are misleading. In fact only one argument relating specifically to this scene has been brought forward by recent opponents of the above interpretation. This is that, in the words of Taplin (1977: 159), if Eteocles were arming himself during this passage 'the audience's attention [would be] torn between the action and the highly demanding words of the scene. ... Could such powerful words [as those spoken by Eteocles] be accompanied by action independent of them?' One might well agree that the answer to that last question should be 'no'. But there is no need to suppose that Eteocles is speaking and putting on armour simultaneously. He can perfectly well arm himself during the passages which are sung by the chorus or spoken by their leader. Between 677 and 711 there are five such passages: precisely enough for Eteocles to put on (*a*) his two greaves and (*b*) his corslet, then (*c*) buckle on his sword, (*d*) put on his helmet and (*e*) take his shield in his left hand and spear in his right. He will not, of course, be doing all the work himself: the attendants who till now have been carrying his gear will help him on with it. Meanwhile he is listening to, and answering, the words of the chorus, and his actions, alternating with his words, show in a different way but (if one may so put it) with even more ironclad finality that he is not to be persuaded. This is not the only pivotal passage in Aeschylus where the attention of the audience must be divided between the actions of one group of persons and the words of another: consider *Eumenides* 711-33 where Apollo and the Erinyes conduct a strenuous altercation while the councillors of the Areopagus, going one by one to the voting-urns, cast their ballots to determine Orestes' fate.

If we reject the idea of an arming-scene, moreover, we must find an alternative that is consistent with the text, and none can be found. If Aeschylus had meant to send Eteocles off at 719 still unarmed, he would not have written 717 in its present form and probably would not have allowed Eteocles to say at 715 'I am whetted, and your words will not blunt me'. The only alternative is to suppose that Eteocles is in armour from the start of the play or (better) from the time of his re-entry at 372; but then we have to delete lines 675-6, in which Eteocles calls for his greaves. Such a deletion brings no other benefit, and it would ruin the conclusion of Eteocles' speech. It would destroy the carefully crafted structure of 674-5 with its three pairings 'ruler against ruler, brother against brother, enemy against enemy', of which 'the first and third are natural enough ... the middle term is unnatural and appalling' (Hutchinson 1985: 152), and it would make the speech end with justificatory argument where the transmitted text makes it end, like Eteocles' first speech in the play (31-5), with orders for immediate action.[7]

Having decided, then, to fight his brother, Eteocles has himself accoutred for that fight, while engaging in an exchange with the chorus which represents the last chance for his doom to be averted. At least, that is how the chorus see it; Eteocles does not. All his replies to them either assert or presuppose that his doom is inevitable, and in that belief he goes to meet it. The chorus continue to argue as though they believed that the doom was not inevitable – that on the divine level what is happening is but a passing storm (705-8), and that on the human level Eteocles will not be put to shame if he refrains from the fratricidal combat (698-9, 716; contrast 683-5, 717). Which is right?

5.3. Character and curse

Oedipus cursed his sons. The approximate terms of that curse can readily be reconstructed from *Seven* 766-7 and 788-90: 'May you quarrel, and come to a bitter reconciliation, and divide your inheritance with iron.' The two sons killed each other, and in the play this is seen by Eteocles before it happens, and by the chorus before it is known to have happened, as the fulfilment of the curse; nor are we given the least reason to suppose them wrong. At the same time we have already seen that this does not in any way preclude our asking: to what extent, as Aeschylus presents their story, are Eteocles and Polyneices helpless victims of the curse once it has been uttered, and to what extent are their personalities, characters and decisions responsible for their fate? For the time being we shall consider only that part of the story which appears in the surviving play (on earlier events see §5.5) and concentrate mainly (though not entirely) on Eteocles, as being the brother whom we meet there in person.

In the first place, it can be said that the war between Thebes and Argos, and therefore the duel of the two brothers, would never have happened had it not been for the quarrel and the exile of Polyneices. The quarrel itself was part of Oedipus' curse, and in the surviving play there is no clue to its cause; but Aeschylus does take the trouble to give us three opinions about its rights and wrongs. Two of these are the opinions of Polyneices and Eteocles themselves, each of whom, not surprisingly, considers himself wholly in the right and his antagonist wholly in the wrong. Polyneices (who positively *desires* to kill his brother, if necessary at the cost of his own life: 633-6) proclaims his conviction of right by the device on his shield, which shows the goddess of Justice leading him home (644-8; cf. *Ag.* 1607), and expects the native gods of Thebes to be on his side (639-41) against his 'degrader and banisher' (637). Eteocles' retort is that Polyneices has never had anything to do with Justice – not in birth, in childhood, in adolescence or in manhood, and certainly not in this attack on his native land (664-71); but he makes no response to the charge implicit in Polyneices' reported words, that he had expelled his brother from Thebes unjustly. Before we hear either of these rival claims, however, we have already heard the opinion of Amphiaraus on the same question. Amphiaraus is a man of the highest character in respect of justice and all other virtues, by the testimony of those against whom he is fighting (568-9, 592-4, 598, 610); moreover he is likely to sympathize with innocent victims of fate or circumstance, being one himself. He does not see Polyneices as such a victim. He condemns him in the strongest terms for the same reason as Eteocles does – for attacking the land of his birth, and its gods, with a foreign army (580-6). But that does not mean that he believes Eteocles had been right to force Polyneices into exile. On the contrary, 'what *justice*,' he asks Polyneices, 'can quench the mother-source?' (584). If Amphiaraus had thought Polyneices to have been in the wrong in the original quarrel, he would have said so, just as he condemns Tydeus as a murderer with reference to crimes committed before *he* came to Argos (572-4). Rather, Eteocles had been wrong to banish Polyneices, and Polyneices wrong to seek restoration in the way he did. The motivation of both is not far to seek: each wanted sole control of Thebes and of Oedipus' property.[8] Many a pair of brothers have quarrelled for that reason, both in fiction and in reality, without needing a paternal curse to make them do so.

Polyneices, as we have seen, is determined to take personal revenge on Eteocles, either by death or exile. Up to 652 Eteocles betrays no corresponding personal animus against Polyneices, and almost seems to be doing all he can to *avoid* a personal conflict. Initially he has no intention of taking part in the battle at all. It is the panic of the women, caused by the frightening sights and sounds beyond the walls, that is decisive in that regard: it prompts him to announce, in the hope of bolstering morale, that he will defend a gate himself, and it also leaves him with enough time to begin posting Theban champions at the gates but not with enough time to complete the job. Eteocles' initial reaction to the panic (181-202) is highly misogynistic, and some have thought it ill-judged; but the survival of Thebes and its people (including the women themselves) is at stake, and Eteocles would not be doing his duty if he did not immediately repress this dangerous emotional outburst[9] (just as he represses his own emotions at 656-7). Once he has decided to fight in person, he is lapped for a long time in the fog of ignorance that we have already examined, until he learns that the seventh gate is being attacked by his brother. We know what agency took Polyneices to that gate, and it was not human: the Seven chose the gates they were to attack by lot (55-6), or, otherwise put, they left the choice to the gods.

Thus while in Aeschylus' presentation Eteocles and Polyneices are both to blame for the war itself (as indeed are others, especially Tydeus), once the war has begun Eteocles at any rate can hardly be said to have had any responsibility for the chain of circumstances that puts him where he stands at line 653. Polyneices may be another matter: he is eager, as we have seen, for a personal confrontation with his brother, and he was prepared to take an oath (46-8) to *destroy Thebes* or die in the attempt. (How this squares with his wish, expressed in 647-8, to *possess* his native city and house, is a question he might not have been able to answer, any more than Hippias would have found it easy to answer a parallel question about Athens in 490 BC.)

From 653 onwards Eteocles behaves like a complete fatalist. The terrible coincidence that he has reserved himself to defend the same gate which his brother has been chosen by lot to attack is seen by him – and surely rightly, in terms of the audience's world-view – as the work of a malevolent divine power. It is also seen by him as evidence that that power is determined (we might say) to get him, and that further evasive action on his part will merely incur disgrace (683-5) without bringing safety. But while this is the constant burden of his words in 653-5 and in 683-719, the words which lie between (656-76) tell a different tale. Having condemned Polyneices as one with whom Justice (*Dikê*) has never had anything to do, he proceeds to declare that he will fight Polyneices himself and to ask 'who else could do so with greater *right* (*en<u>dik</u>ôteros*)?' The repetition should set alarm bells ringing; so too should the following set of phrases whose incongruity we have already noted, 'ruler against ruler, brother against brother, enemy against enemy'. Polyneices' claim that Justice was bringing him back to Thebes was rejected (both by Amphiaraus and by Eteocles) on the ground that it was an attack on the land of his *fathers* (582, 585, 668), on the land that was itself his *mother* (584). Eteocles' claim that

Justice singles him out as the proper person to fight Polyneices is to be rejected on the similar grounds that Polyneices is his *brother*, as the chorus-leader at once points out (681, cf. 718). Yet to Eteocles it is precisely the fact of their kinship that *makes* it fitting that they should fight each other! In almost the first word of this speech he had spoken of his family as one driven mad by the gods (653). In the last five lines he proves this true.

Now in our culture, to say that a person is mad or insane is officially[10] to absolve him from responsibility for his actions, to make blame unjust and punishment inappropriate. Ancient Greeks in general did not think in that way, even though they, like us, could regard insanity as a species of the genus 'disease' (*nosos*). This seeming oddity may well be connected with the fact that ancient Greek culture seems to have been what has been called a 'results culture', one in which, generally speaking, the effect of an action matters more than its intent.[11] A public benefactor would be honoured just as much if it was well known that he had made his benefactions precisely for the purpose of improving his standing with the public; indeed he would sometimes publicly and, it would seem to us, unnecessarily avow this motive in court later on.[12] A general who through no fault of his own lost a campaign he was expected to win would be almost as ill advised to return to Athens afterwards as one who had been guilty of corruption or treason. And similarly, a wicked deed could not be excused simply because it resulted from a mental sickness; indeed one often finds that the very fact of committing wicked deeds is cited as *evidence* of mental sickness, by enemies of the perpetrator determined to punish him. Sometimes they will use words meaning 'mad' and 'wicked' as if they were interchangeable (see Dover 1974:128-9, 148-9).

So it is quite likely that many of those who saw *Seven* in 467 BC thought *both* that Eteocles in 653-719 was insane, or possessed, or under the influence of a delusion, *and* that he was resolved to commit a terrible crime for which it was right to hold him responsible. And just as his earlier crime of expelling Polyneices can be explained by his desire for power and wealth, so this new crime can probably be explained by the same sheer hatred of Polyneices on Eteocles' part that Polyneices evidently has for him.[13] The chorus speak of anger (678), of 'spear-mad delusion' and 'evil lust' (687-8), of a 'yearning to bite raw flesh' (692). If one thing is certain it is that, whatever his previous intentions or desires were, at this moment Eteocles *wants* to fight his brother.

What happens when they actually meet Aeschylus does not tell us: the Messenger and the chorus simply reiterate, in constantly varying words, that they have killed each other. We learn two details: first, that both received their fatal wounds on the left side (887) from a spear (962); second, that one of the two (there is no way to tell which) 'struck having been stricken' (961). This implies a dénouement similar in principle to that described in detail in Euripides' *Phoenician Maidens* (1404-24): one of the brothers (Eteocles in Euripides' version) inflicts a fatal wound on the other, but the latter with his last strength thrusts his weapon into his killer's body. The fratricide may well have been described in more or less this way in the cyclic epic, the *Thebais*.

The play ends with the two brothers lying dead side by side. Their mutual hatred has achieved its desire. Both human and superhuman agencies have been at work to bring this end about. On the human level, the brothers quarrel about power and possessions, and a fierce mutual hatred develops between them, which comes to fill first Polyneices' mind and then Eteocles' to the exclusion of virtually everything else. Eteocles, however, had kept this hatred under firm control for a long time, in the interests of his community (see §5.4); it burst out only when he found that events had conspired to set him face to face with his brother. *That* was no (living) human being's work. Like most individuals, in fiction or history, whose fate is truly tragic rather than merely pathetic, Eteocles, the tragic hero of *Seven*, is both victim and agent.

5.4. *Oikos*[14] and *polis*

From the beginning the fate of the house of Laius had been interwoven with that of the city of Thebes: from the time when Laius was warned 'to die without issue and save his city' (748-9). We cannot tell with assurance how the interrelationship of these two destinies was handled in the first two plays of the trilogy (but see §5.5); and if we are tempted to be over-confident in reconstruction, we will do well to consider whether we could possibly have guessed, without the full text, how it is handled in the third.

For something like three-fifths of the play, with the exception of one single passage, one might almost say of one single line (70), the entire attention of the *dramatis personae* is concentrated on the danger to Thebes. The city is being besieged by an enemy, and an assault is imminent. It is not mentioned that the king's brother is in the besieging army. On the contrary, everything is done to emphasize the enemy's alienness, even to the extent of implying that they speak a foreign language (170): it is striking that while the besiegers' horses and chariots strike particular terror into the hearts of the Theban maidens, nothing in the text indicates that Thebes itself has any horses at all. (Both these details, as has often been observed, would remind Athenians of the recent history of their own city, attacked and burnt by a barbarian enemy at a time when there was no Athenian cavalry.)

If the play had been preserved to us only as far as line 630, it could very properly be characterized, with Vellacott 1961: 16, as 'above all a play … about the successful defence of a strongly walled city', or, with Gorgias and Aristophanes, as 'a drama replete with the spirit of war'. The armed citizens thronging the *orkhêstra* in the opening scene; Eteocles' patriotic harangue; his orders to man the defences; the prompt arrival of the Scout; his grim report of the oath of the Seven to destroy Thebes or perish, and his urgent request for the defence of the gates to be organized; Eteocles' prayer for the safety and freedom of the city; the panic of the maidens; their evocation of the sights, and especially the sounds, that have inspired their terror; their fervent prayers to the gods of the city; Eteocles' ferocious condemnation of them as a positive danger to the city, and the arguments culminating in his own prayer; the chorus's fearful prognostications of what may follow defeat – all these build up to a powerful picture of a community facing an external, armed menace that puts its existence in immediate peril. In these 368 lines the root of *polis* occurs fifty-two times. No individual leader on either side is mentioned except Eteocles and, once, Adrastus (50).

In the 'shield scene' the focus shifts somewhat, from the community as a whole to the seven champions who will be taking the major responsibility for its defence; but both they and the enemy leaders who are attacking the various gates are at first seen more as threats to, or protectors of, the community than as rounded and distinct individuals. We are told nothing, for instance, about the rich family and personal history of Tydeus; both he and his colleagues, as they are presented here, are little more than names attached to largely identical character-sketches, emphasizing boasting and blasphemy and menace to Thebes. The first four defenders are essentially their opposites, blameless in character and devoted to the *polis*. Punctuating the speeches, the chorus endlessly echo the same ideas.

The procession of warriors begins to become less anonymous with the fifth of the Seven, Parthenopaeus (526-49). In character he is the same as the others, but at least he differs in appearance and age, and unlike them he has an identified homeland (Arcadia), and at least one identifiable, though unnamed, parent (the huntress Atalanta, cf. 532).[15] Neither Eteocles nor the chorus is sensitive to these nuances. The stereotype is violated far more strongly when we come to Amphiaraus. Not only are his splendid personality and character fully portrayed and his words quoted at length, but through those words Tydeus acquires far more individuality (571-5) and Polyneices springs into dramatic existence for the first time. But Amphiaraus' opponent is as sparely portrayed as his predecessors were, and the chorus's sixth stanza is almost interchangeable with the other five; even the passage in which Amphiaraus is reported as upbraiding Polyneices (576-86) concentrates on Polyneices as an enemy not of his brother but of Thebes. It is still the city whose future is at stake.

And yet, near the start of the play, we heard Eteocles making a prayer:

> O Zeus and Earth and you gods that dwell in the city,
> and you, mighty vengeful Curse of my father,
> do not, I pray, let my *city* be captured by foes
> and uprooted out of Hellas in utter destruction! (69-72).

If we know the terms of Oedipus' curse (and we probably heard them in the previous play; see §5.5), we know it had nothing directly to do with the city. And the word *polis* is followed in the Greek by the little particle *ge*, whose English equivalent is an extra stress on the word, and which implies a contrast with something else: if the gods, and the Curse, are to save the *city* from destruction, who or what else may they destroy if they choose? For the Eteocles of this part of the play the natural answer is: himself. He has just been eloquent on the citizen's duty to his motherland; he is aware that in the event of defeat he will be held personally to blame (5-9); his decision to take part himself in the fighting is made without direct prompting. As a good ruler he is as willing as his subjects must be to sacrifice his life, if necessary, to preserve the community. And his mention of the curse implies that he suspects the curse may require some such sacrifice on his part. There is no reason why he should suspect anything more sinister. The audience know better; and for them that particle *ge* is full of irony.

The beginning of the pay-off comes when the Scout reveals that Polyneices is attacking the seventh gate. He too boasts and threatens – but not against Thebes, which he claims he has come to possess, not to destroy; rather against his brother. Amphiaraus may see him as impiously assaulting the gods of his fatherland, but he sees himself as deserving their patronage (639-41). The conflict is no longer being presented as Thebes versus a foreign enemy: it is now a civil, a fraternal war. The Scout does not perceive the change; his last words – echoing the opening lines of the play – are 'You yourself must decide how to captain the city' (652). Eteocles has not so much perceived the change as changed along with it. In his ensuing speech the city is not mentioned, only the doom of himself and his house (653-7), his loathing of Polyneices (658-71), and his determination to fight him (672-6). The chorus try to bring him back to his role as 'captain' of Thebes, pointing out that there are plenty of other 'Cadmeans' available to fight 'the Argives' (679-80), but to no avail. Eteocles' ship is no longer the ship of state, but the ship of the house of Laius, running before the wind to the waters of Hades (690-1). The chorus have to argue with him on his own terms, and the city is not mentioned again in the scene. Eteocles is bent on fighting his brother, fulfilling oracle and curse, and slaking the hatred of the divinities; the chorus are bent on avoiding this insane horror. Eteocles wins.

The long choral ode that follows is sung at the very time when the fate of the city, and of the chorus themselves, is being decided around the walls; but it concerns itself almost exclusively with the fate of the house of Laius. Of the song's ten stanzas, only one (the sixth) is devoted to the theme on which the chorus had harped unceasingly from their first entry to line 630:

> Now, as at sea, waves of trouble roll upon us;
> one falls, but it raises up another, three-taloned,
> which crashes right around the city's high stern;
> and for protection between us and it

stretches the narrow thickness of this wall.
I fear that together with the princes
the city may be overwhelmed (758-65).

The fear is still there; but it is now expressed abstractly. Gone are the vivid pictures of a terrible future which filled an earlier song (287-368). The peril of the city is a mere consequence of the fall of the royal house. The song, whose midpoint is the stanza just cited, begins and ends with other fears far more starkly expressed:

I shudder to think of the destroyer of houses,
the goddess unlike other gods,
the prophet of evil all too true,
the Erinys of a father's curse,
fulfilling the furious imprecations
of the deranged mind of Oedipus ... (720-6).

... and now I tremble
lest the ... Erinys fulfil that curse (790-1).

Enter then a Messenger with news of victory ('this city has escaped the yoke of slavery') to which the chorus do not respond at all. On the contrary, their first question ('What is this further untoward news for the city?', 803) is provoked by the first enigmatic report of what has happened at the seventh gate. The Messenger tries to balance joy and sorrow (814ff.), but even he, by the end, is putting far more emphasis on the latter (811-13, 815-19).

In 822-31 (assuming – which is doubtful – that these lines are genuine) the chorus ask themselves whether they should rejoice in the deliverance of the city or lament the death of the two princes. They proceed, at any rate, to do the latter exclusively. The deliverance of the city is never mentioned again; nor, down to 1004 (on 1005-78 see §5.6), is any distinction made between the brother who died saving Thebes and the brother who died having sworn to destroy it. The only difference between Eteocles and Polyneices is that the latter had been in exile (979, 991); everything else that is said of them is said of both alike. These lyrics are entirely centred on the brothers. The city figures in them as the object of the brothers' ambitions, the bone of their contention (cf. 882); its men are the pawns of their quarrel (cf. 922-5), its women lament their loss. The whole perspective has changed.

Was the perspective of the first 630 lines, then, a false one? Were Eteocles and the chorus misperceiving a conflict between brothers as a struggle against a foreign enemy? By no means. The words of Amphiaraus are sufficient proof of that. The danger to Thebes was real enough. But Polyneices had created that danger; and Eteocles, as his prayer when alone showed, was well enough aware of what lay behind and beneath the patriotic façade. Had Laius died without issue, the city would have been safe. He begot a son: the city was saved, but only just – and mourned as if it had been conquered. The chorus had feared 'that together with the princes the city may be overwhelmed' (764-5). In its immediate context, and in the context of the first three-fifths of the play, that had meant: we fear that the quarrel of the princes may result both in their deaths and in the capture and destruction of the city. But if we remember these words during the subsequent scenes, they will bear a different meaning: we fear that the extinction of the royal house may itself be a crushing blow to the city. And this apprehension comes true.

We have been given, during the play, a variety of stage-pictures of Thebes: the armed male citizenry; the frantic maidens; Eteocles leading them in prayer; Eteocles attended by his armour-bearers (cf. §5.2), about to decide whom he will fight; Eteocles as a hoplite going to his death. The stage-picture with which we end is one of two dead warriors and of mourning women. Thebes is not only without a ruler: dramatically speaking, it is without its men. We see the mourning of the chorus; we hear of the mourning of the *polis*, its walls, its soil (900-2); the men of Thebes are not mentioned even as grieving. It seemed that the play was going to be about how Eteocles saved the *polis*: it has turned out to be about how Eteocles and Polyneices between them destroyed it. Eteocles' prayer was not granted after all. Ruin has set up her trophy at the gates (957-8). Laius preferred the perpetuation of his *oikos* to the safety of the *polis* – and as a result his descendants have lost both.

This interpretation, it will be observed, assumes that the play ends at 1004 – or at any rate that 1005-78 is not the original ending; for in those seventy-four lines the *polis* appears as very much a going concern, complete with a new government, and the house of Laius too turns out not to be extinct after all. On the authenticity of the ending see §5.6.

5.5. The tetralogy

The tetralogy of which *Seven against Thebes* is the third play began, we know, with *Laius*; and there is very little else that we do know directly about that play. We possess, in effect, three pieces of information. A small scrap of papyrus (*Oxyrhynchus Papyri* 2256 fr.1) appears to tell us that Laius was the opening speaker. In addition we know that somewhere in the play the exposure of the infant Oedipus was mentioned, with the detail that he was left in a cooking-pot (fr. 122), and there was mention at another point of a murderer who tasted and spat out his victim's blood (fr. 122a) – an act intended to ward off the vengeance of the victim's Erinyes, which like all such acts in Aeschylus will have been futile; it is hard not to see this as coming from an eyewitness report of the death of Laius, and yet the ancient authorities are in agreement that blood-tasting was associated with planned, premeditated murder, which the killing of Laius cannot have been. Probably then, as in Sophocles' treatment, the initial eyewitness report was misleading as to the nature of the attack. There are also a number of other fragments which are not explicitly ascribed to this play by ancient sources but whose content suggests they may come from it. The most important and most plausible of these is one of two or three lines (fr. 387a) describing the road-junction at which the murder took place – not near Daulis on the way to Delphi, where Sophocles put it, but at Potniae, just a mile or so out of Thebes in the direction of Plataea. No doubt this passage comes from the same eyewitness report. It has generally, on the Sophoclean model, been assigned to *Oedipus*, but in view of fr. 122a it is much more likely that Laius' death was reported in the play in which he had been the principal character. If this is correct, then we are left with virtually no direct information about the second play: only the statement that it was one of five Aeschylean plays which seemed to contain allusions to the secrets of the Eleusinian Mysteries (see Chapter 1; it may be relevant that there was a sanctuary of Demeter and Kore at Potniae).

Our best evidence for the content of the first two plays does not come from these scanty fragments but from *Seven against Thebes* itself, especially the choral ode 720-91, which gives us a clear basic story, though not all of this can have been *enacted* in the first two plays.

The first event mentioned (745-9) is the oracle given 'three times' to Laius at Delphi 'to die without issue and save his city'; the point of 'three times' is presumably that Laius, having received this unfavourable response, inquired twice again in the hope that Apollo might relent, but received the same response each time. His defiance of the oracle is explained in a phrase (750) which is textually uncertain, but which in view of two later passages (802, 842) must have referred to his 'ill counsel' or 'imprudence' (*aboulia*; in 802 *dysboulia*). In Euripides' *Phoenician Maidens* (21-2) the begetting of Oedipus is ascribed to drunkenness or lack of self-control; Sophocles says nothing about the matter at all. In Aeschylus' treatment it seems to have been a quite deliberate disobedience – indeed 842 seems actually to speak of Laius' 'disobedient *plans*'.

We next hear that Oedipus – evidently after killing his unknown father (cf. 752) – came to Thebes and rescued the city from 'the man-snatching demon', the Sphinx (776-7); after which he was made king and married the widow of Laius. Eventually he discovered the truth about himself, and 'in the madness of his heart performed two evils' (781-2); Hutchinson 1985:xxiv-xxv has shown that the evils in question are the putting out of his eyes (783-4) and the cursing of his sons (785-90). It follows that in Aeschylus' presentation the curse must have been very closely associated with the discovery and the self-blinding. The chorus of *Seven* do in fact tell us the motive for the curse (785-6) – but once again the crucial phrase is corrupt and obscure; however, it is tolerably clear that Oedipus is being described as *epikotos trophas*, a phrase most easily interpreted as 'angry about his maintenance', and this fits well with the statement of a scholiast on Sophocles' *Oedipus at Colonus* (1375) that Aeschylus' treatment of

Oedipus' curse was 'similar' to the story in the epic *Thebais* (fr. 3 West) according to which he cursed his sons because they slighted him in the distribution of cuts of meat from a sacrifice. If Oedipus was being maintained by his sons, that implies that in the second play he was an old man – a very different figure, then, from the vigorous ruler familiar to us from Sophocles' *Oedipus the King*; indeed he would resemble more, in some respects, the Oedipus of *Oedipus at Colonus* – who, as it happens, is shown cursing his sons, and emphasizes the maintenance (*trophê*) that he received from his daughters and not from them (*Oedipus at Colonus* 341, 352, 446, 1265, 1362-9). Thus it would be in his old age, retired (like Peleus or Laertes in the Homeric epics) from active rulership, cared for by his sons in a manner that aroused his bitter resentment, that the Aeschylean Oedipus learned the truth about Laius' death and about his own marriage; and on learning it, he blinded himself and cursed his sons, whom he already had cause to hate and who now, as living reminders of the horrors of his past, were loathsome to him beyond bearing. As we have seen (§5.3), the curse ran: 'May you quarrel, and come to a bitter reconciliation, and divide your inheritance with iron.' This reflects the earlier, and the milder, of two versions of Oedipus' curse found in the *Thebais* (that of fr. 2 West); the other version (fr. 3), explicitly dooming the sons to die at each other's hands, was used later by Sophocles (*Oedipus at Colonus* 1387-8) but was apparently avoided by Aeschylus.

One matter to which we have no surviving clue is the fate of Oedipus' mother-wife. In one tradition (familiar from Sophocles, and found as early as *Odyssey* 11.277-80) she hanged herself as soon as she became aware of the truth; in another, which appears first in the Lille papyrus of Stesichorus (*GL* 222A) and was used by Euripides in *The Phoenician Maidens*, she survived and later tried to reconcile her warring sons. *Seven* offers no trace of the latter version (for the reference to the mother in 926-31 does not prove she is alive), and it is therefore on the whole likely that Aeschylus made the mother's death follow closely on the discovery. If so, she may have appeared on stage in *Oedipus*, though this is by no means certain.

With Oedipus' curse the choral ode in *Seven* ends, leaving a significant gap; for the next point of the story that we can be sure of finds Polyneices (and Tydeus) in Argos, persuading Adrastus to lead an army against Thebes. His assertion that Eteocles forced him into exile is, as we have seen, almost certainly true, and so probably is his claim that this was an unjust act; but we do not know what caused it, and there is no direct evidence as to whether or not it was part of the action of *Oedipus*. Aeschylus neither mentions nor denies the accepted tradition that Polyneices and Tydeus both married daughters of Adrastus, but probably he takes it for granted; it seems to be implicit in Amphiaraus' denunciation of the pair (especially Tydeus) in *Seven* 571-86.

Other passages in *Seven* may offer us a few further scraps or hints. We learn, for example, that at some time Eteocles has had a dream, or rather dreams, about the division of his father's property (710-11). It is not unknown in tragedy for an oracle, or a prophetic dream, to be mentioned for the first time when it is fulfilled or on the point of fulfilment (cf. *Pers.* 739-41, 800ff.); but in such cases we are regularly told what it was that the oracle said or the dreamer saw, so that we can understand in what sense the prophecy is being fulfilled and, where relevant, how its addressee had previously misinterpreted it. Eteocles' words here are much too vague to fulfil such a function, and they therefore presuppose (even more than does Clytaemestra's reference to her dream in *Cho.* 928) an earlier and fuller account of the matter, which can only have come in the second play.

Such is the material we have for reconstructing the two lost plays of the trilogy. In addition we have one negative datum. Oedipus' defeat of the Sphinx cannot have been part of, or have occurred during, the action of any of the plays of the trilogy, since it was the subject of the satyr-play that followed. Since Oedipus regularly confronts the Sphinx as soon as he comes to Thebes, this makes it unlikely that he was a character at all in the first play; he can have appeared only in the second.

The principal event of the first play, we have concluded, was the death of Laius. That happened when he was on a journey; and as he was in Thebes at the start of the play, Aeschylus must have given him a destination to go to and a reason for going. The dominant tradition – alluded to, it seems, by the one word *theôros* 'on a sacred mission' in Sophocles, *Oedipus the King* 114, and made explicit by Euripides in *Phoenician Maidens* 35-7 – was that he was going to Delphi to inquire whether the son born to him, whom he had had exposed in infancy, was alive or dead. This is not easy to square with a killing at Potniae, which is nowhere near the road from Thebes to Delphi: in Aeschylus' treatment Laius was travelling southwards. Might he have been going to Corinth, having heard a rumour (or been told by an oracle) that his son was living there? Or had the Sphinx already come to Thebes, and was Laius travelling in search of someone who could save Thebes by answering her riddle? Had he even, maybe, heard that Polybus, king of Corinth, had a son with a remarkably acute intellect? It is likely, at any rate, that in one way or another Laius' journey was connected (whether he himself knew it or not) with the son whom he had thought dead, and whose exposure was mentioned somewhere in the play. (What motive, by the way, can Aeschylus have assigned for the exposure, given that he had made the begetting of the child an act of wilful defiance? Did Laius repent of that defiance, too late? Or did he receive a further oracle telling him that his son would kill him?)

We can thus dimly perceive two scenes in the first play: one near its beginning, in which Laius explained his impending departure from Thebes and the reason for it, and another near the end, in which one of his servants returned to tell – perhaps with misleading details – the story of his death. The play may have ended with the return of his body to Thebes amid lamentation.

The second play, as Hutchinson 1985: xxiv-xxix has shown, is likely to have contained three major events, in this order: Oedipus' discovery of the truth about himself and his marriage; his self-blinding; and his curse upon his sons. Oedipus, as argued above, is an old man retired from active rulership, but still believed to be the son of Polybus of Corinth and still honoured by the citizens as the saviour of Thebes from the Sphinx (cf. *Seven* 772-7). His sons are managing his property, and Thebes, on his behalf, but they, not having been born when the Sphinx was vanquished, have shown less respect for Oedipus than do the citizenry, and less than he deserves as their father. Eteocles at least can hardly wait for Oedipus to die, whereupon he intends to seize sole control of kingship and inheritance. He has had, though, more than once, a mysterious dream about the division of that inheritance, apparently involving 'a foreigner from Scythia' who cast lots between the brothers (cf. *Seven* 710-11, 727-33, 941-6): for educated spectators this would be reminiscent of, yet strangely different from, the course of events in Stesichorus (*GL* 222A), where the brothers draw lots at the suggestion of their mother and of Teiresias, Eteocles getting the kingship and the palace, Polyneices leaving Thebes with all the movable property such as gold and livestock – and it would mislead them about the subsequent course of events in the drama. Only at the end of the trilogy will they discover that the 'Scythian' of the dream was identical with the 'iron' of Oedipus' curse (*Seven* 727-30, 941-3); for iron was first worked by the Chalybes, whose land (differently located by different poets and ethnographers) is here assumed to lie in Scythia.

Somehow or other (we cannot tell how, but can be fairly sure the development was quite different from what we find in Sophocles' *Oedipus the King*[16]) it is revealed that Oedipus is both the killer and the son of Laius. His mother-wife (probably) commits suicide. Oedipus blinds himself, and in the full kindling of his long-smouldering anger against his sons he curses them. These events, rising to such a climax, are enough to fill a play of typical Aeschylean length; it is unlikely that the brothers' quarrel, which Oedipus had anyway predicted, was part of the action, though the death of Oedipus may have been.

Of the events intervening between Oedipus' death and the beginning of the action of *Seven*, some are mentioned or alluded to in *Seven* itself; some were probably familiar enough to be taken for granted;[17] and some may be deliberately left vague, such as the cause of the quarrel and of Polyneices' exile. For the understanding of *Seven* it suffices at the outset to know the bare essentials: that the brothers did quarrel, that Polyneices left Thebes and went to Argos, that he persuaded Adrastus to lead an expedition against Thebes.

It will be seen that our real knowledge of the first two plays is rather slight: even when we can be fairly confident what the key events were, we can have little idea how the dramatist handled them. We can, however, discern the main movements of the action so far as it concerns the *oikos/polis* theme (see §5.4). The tension embodied in this theme was first set up, before the action of the trilogy began, by the oracle given to Laius, which made the extinction of the family a necessary condition for the survival of the city. Laius fought hard against the oracle, and when he found himself unable to persuade Apollo to change it, he disobeyed it, thus putting Thebes in jeopardy. Too late, he changed his mind, and took the only course by which he thought he could save the city without bringing on himself the pollution of murder: he exposed the infant Oedipus, but paradoxically the city was saved from the Sphinx by the very child that Laius left to die. That child, though, having become the killer of Laius, was himself already polluted, and soon by his incest became doubly so; and the discovery of that incest provoked Oedipus' curse which resulted in the final destruction of the family and the narrowly escaped mortal peril of the city – except that in *Seven* these issues are presented in the opposite order.

The paradox of Oedipus and the Sphinx warrants some further reflection. Oedipus, we may take it, was the only man who could have defeated the Sphinx. What then would have happened if he had never been born, as would have been the case if Laius had obeyed the oracle? At first sight it might seem that Thebes would then have been destroyed. But in that case the oracle would have been falsified. We must therefore infer that if Oedipus had not been born, the Sphinx would never have come to Thebes in the first place; that she was *sent* there as part of Laius' punishment – and indeed a line quoted by Aristophanes (*Frogs* 1287 = Aeschylus fr. 236) from the satyr-play *The Sphinx*[18] does seem to speak of her being sent. And who sent her? The evidence of *Seven* suggests that in Aeschylus' treatment the answer was 'Apollo', for he is more than once named as Laius' divine enemy and punisher (691, 745, 800-2). If my second suggestion above (p. 87) about the reason for Laius' journey is correct, Apollo by sending the Sphinx is the cause not only of Oedipus' triumph (and therefore of his incest) but also of the death of Laius. Thus was Laius' 'transgression punished swiftly' (*Seven* 743) – but not finally, for its consequences 'remained to the third generation' (*ib.* 744-5) to put Thebes in mortal peril a second time.

*

A remarkable vase-painting in Würzburg (*LIMC* Oidipous 72), first published by Simon 1981, almost certainly illustrates the satyr-play *The Sphinx*. Five richly-dressed individuals, holding sceptres, sit on covered chairs facing the Sphinx, apparently listening to her with some alarm. They must be the chorus of a play, and one would take them for Theban elders (like the seated Persian elders in Phrynichus' play); but their faces are those of satyrs. How do satyrs come to be Theban elders? Simon has put forward an ingenious suggestion. Creon, the brother of Laius' widow, and acting ruler of Thebes after Laius' death, has held a meeting of the state council to discuss the crisis facing Thebes from the menacing presence of the Sphinx. The news of the killing by the Sphinx of Creon's son, Haemon, causes the shocked elders (who would be a group of mutes, like the citizens at the beginning of *Seven*) to cast down their robes and sceptres in token of mourning; Creon proclaims the offer of the throne of Thebes, and the hand of his sister, to whoever can defeat the Sphinx. As soon as he and the elders have left, the satyrs appear, excited by the prospect of wealth, power and (at least for one of them) a noble and presumably attractive wife; finding the discarded accoutrements of the councillors, they promptly dress up in them – and then the Sphinx suddenly appears (perhaps out of the ground, like Darius in *The Persians*). At the moment captured by the painting the Sphinx may possibly be propounding her famous riddle. In the play the satyrs, or their 'father' Silenus, may have made some attempts to answer it. Another vase-painting (see Trendall & Webster 1971: 32) shows a single satyr, again elderly, again holding a sceptre, and displaying a bird to the Sphinx. The riddle (already familiar in Aeschylus' time, for it is indirectly alluded to in *Ag.* 81) is reported in various forms, but in all of them it asks which is the animal that can have two or three or four feet; and birds might be held to come close to meeting the requirements, since they have two feet yet could be colloquially classified among *tetrapoda* by a fifth-century Greek (Aristophanes, *Clouds* 659-61). If this was a failed attempt by Silenus to answer the riddle, his life will then have been in danger, and this may have been the cue for the arrival of Oedipus, who will have solved the riddle, destroyed the Sphinx (who may have sunk back into the earth, this time for ever), liberated Thebes and saved Silenus and the satyrs from their peril;[19] in a surviving fragment of the play (fr. 235) someone (Silenus?) proposes that Oedipus should be awarded a crown – but the phraseology implies that he has also, just previously, proposed that someone else (he himself?) should be given some other reward (the kingdom and Iocaste?)

5.6. The ending of *Seven*

Up to line 1004 of *Seven*, virtually the whole weight of the ending of the play, and therefore of the trilogy, is placed on the extinction of the house of Laius, whose last heirs lie dead before us, to the complete exclusion (as we have seen) of thoughts of the recent preservation, or the future destiny,[20] of the city of Thebes, whose living male citizens do not appear on the scene. But then there follows, in the manuscripts, a passage in which the house of Laius proves to have descendants (though female ones) still living, and Thebes to have a functioning government (referred to in an odd phrase as 'the *probouloi* of the people'). The scene introduces the theme of whether or not Polyneices shall be buried, and then leaves it up in the air as the two bodies are carried out separately, with no indication what will be the result of Antigone's defiance. Such inconclusive endings are regular enough, as we might expect, in Aeschylean plays which stand first or second in their trilogies; and it is not surprising that in the early nineteenth century, when the contents and order of the Theban tetralogy were still unknown, conjectural reconstructions of it took it for granted that *Seven* could not have been the third play (it was generally supposed to have been the second), nor that once the ancient production-notice (preserved in the tenth-century Medicean manuscript, and since confirmed by a papyrus) had been published in 1848 it began to be suspected that the ending had been added, or fundamentally remodelled, under the influence of Sophocles' *Antigone* and maybe also of Euripides' *Phoenician Maidens*. At present, probably the majority of specialists would agree that the ending as we have it is not Aeschylus' work, though its genuineness still occasionally finds defenders. I will not here rehearse all the arguments on both sides, but will indicate what seem to me the main considerations.

The basic objection to the final scene is that Antigone and Ismene have no place in a play about the complete destruction of the descendants of Laius (691, 720, 813, 877, 881-2, 951-5); indeed 926-31 arguably excludes their existence, since a woman with two daughters living could hardly be spoken of as 'wretched ... beyond all women who are called mothers of children' given the number of mothers, both in myth (e.g. Niobe) and in real life, who are bereaved of *all* their offspring. The inference that the two daughters have been inserted into a play in which they did not originally appear is confirmed by the extraordinary way in which they are introduced. The following is an (only slightly jaundiced) paraphrase of the anapaestic lines chanted by the chorus as the sisters enter:

> Here come Antigone and Ismene. They are obviously going to sing a lament over their brothers; but we really ought to sing before they do. Hail, most unhappy sisters! We grieve for you with the utmost sincerity (861-74).

It is clear that the author of these lines envisaged Antigone and Ismene remaining silent while the chorus sang 875-960, and then themselves singing 961-1004 responsively. What is not clear – if the author was Aeschylus – is why he should have adopted such a perverse arrangement. There is no dramatic point in it: both considerations of emotion, and the usual conventions of the Greek lament in and out of tragedy, would lead us to expect that the sisters would *lead* the lament with the chorus playing an accompanying role – as indeed happens in 961-1004. If the author of the anapaests was not Aeschylus but a later adaptor, everything becomes clear. The adaptor wanted to have Antigone on stage for the final scene, to lament her brothers and insist on burying Polyneices. Since the lament in 961-1004 is written for two principal voices, not one, he had to have Ismene as well.[21] But he could not give the sisters 875-960 too, since then the chorus would have nothing to sing at all. He thus had two not very good options to choose from – either to break up the lamentation-scene by bringing the sisters on after 960, or to have them on from the beginning but keep them silent for a long time – and chose the latter. In doing so he also sundered the choral lament 875-960 from 854-60 which are clearly meant to lead up to it.

Once it is accepted that Antigone and Ismene are later additions to the play, 861-74 must automatically be condemned, and so too must 1005-78 – for though only the middle section of this scene (1026-53) directly involves Antigone, the beginning (1005-25) exists only to set the stage for her defiance, and the conclusion (1054-78) presupposes that defiance (the chorus divide into two groups accompanying the bodies off separately, contrary to the assumption underlying the whole of 800-1004 that the two brothers are one in death). The entire scene is a dramatic absurdity: a Herald arrives, solemnly proclaiming a decree of the city's government (whose members, incidentally, he seems to have brought along with him, cf. 1025 'these Cadmean authorities'),[22] and then tamely leaves without taking any steps at all to see that the decree is enforced (and without specifying the punishment for breach of it – no doubt because the later audience, familiar with Sophocles' and Euripides' treatments, would take it for granted that the penalty was death).

There is no reason to doubt the genuineness of the choral ode 875-960; indeed this is virtually guaranteed by the contortions into which, as we have seen, the interpolator was forced in order to fit in the entry of the sisters before this ode began. The antiphonal dirge in single short lines (961-1004) has from time to time been suspected, but its only objectionable feature comes in lines 996-7:

(A) Oh woe! (B) Oh grief!
(A) – to the house. (B) – and to the land.
996 (A) But most of all to me.
997 (B) And to me even more.

These two lines – which are the sole lyric expression of *individual* grief for the two brothers in the play – must have been written to be sung by the sisters. Hence defenders of the authenticity of the ending argue that the lines, embedded as they are in what most consider a genuine context, show that the sisters belong to the original play; while some deleters argue that they are, on the contrary, evidence that 961-1004 is part of the interpolation. Neither inference is compelling. The two lines may themselves have been inserted into a genuine passage precisely in order to make that passage plausible on the lips of the sisters: it would be obviously absurd to have them sing over the bodies of their brothers a sobbing antiphon that made no reference at all to their personal grief. Moreover, the lines are isolated metrically in their context (they are the only dochmiacs in the otherwise iambic final section of the lament, 989-1004), and 997 is suspect linguistically. The dirge was probably written originally for the leaders of two divisions of the chorus, with the whole chorus singing the refrains 975-7 and 986-8. It is likely that when the new ending was added, some lines were cut from the original ending. When in the original play the chorus departed, they must have taken the bodies of the two brothers away with them for burial; they must therefore have reached a decision as to where that burial shall take place, and at 1004 they are still deliberating that question.

The original play, then, ended as follows: choral reflections on the news of the brothers' death (822-47); arrival of the two bodies (848-60); choral lament (875-960); antiphonal dirge for two solo voices and chorus (961-1004 – except for 996-7 – plus a few further lines now lost); *exeunt omnes*. The structure and sequence of the laments are strongly reminiscent of those which conclude *The Persians*, and this may well have been a frequent pattern in early tragedy. It is not surprising, however, if it was thought unlikely to appeal to later audiences, especially if *Seven* was then being produced on its own, without the two preceding plays; and some later producer commissioned a poet of uneven talent[23] to write some anapaests to cover the entrance of Antigone and Ismene, a couple of lyric lines to insert in the dirge, a confrontation between Antigone and a Herald, and a split exit for the chorus, with the object of spicing up the conclusion of the play with reminiscences of one of the most famous tragedies ever written, Sophocles' *Antigone*.[24]

Notes

1. Gorgias fr. 24 Diels-Kranz; Aristophanes, *Frogs* 1021.
2. This is shown by Eteocles' orders to them in 30-4; these are urgent instructions to be executed immediately ('off, all of you, to the battlements and the gates ... hurry') and do not envisage the citizens first going home to fetch and put on their equipment.
3. The manuscripts do make Eteocles refer to Melanippus in 408, and to Megareus in 472, as 'this man' (*tonde*); but there is independent reason to believe that 408 requires emendation and that 472 is spurious.
4. The Greek perfect is not, strictly speaking, a past tense, but I am applying that term to it here in order to emphasize that the perfect and aorist tenses alike indicate that the persons named have been chosen already.
5. A metre, common in tragedy, rare elsewhere, and associated with moments of heightened emotion, whose basic form is ⏑ ⏑ – ⏑ – with many variants (e.g. ⏑ ⏑ ⏑ – ⏑ –, – ⏑ ⏑ – ⏑ –).
6. It will, I hope, be agreed that we cannot suppose him to make his exit wearing his greaves but *without* the rest of his armour.
7. This discussion of *Seven* 675-711 owes much to Bernard Knox's review of Taplin 1977 in *The Times Literary Supplement* (6 October 1978); see the reprint in Knox 1979 (at p. 83).
8. Cf. 711, 727-33, 788-90, 816-17, 906-7, 944-5, and especially the expressive idiom of 882-3, literally 'you have seen bitter monarchies', i.e. 'your desire for sole rule has borne bitter fruit'.
9. Though there is a good case for the view that he does so in a clumsy and not

very competent way (see Stehle 2005): he is at least as careless as the women are about using words of ill omen, and he brusquely interrupts their prayer at 182 just when they have with difficulty found the appropriate tone and language to use.

10. I say 'officially' because in practice, at least in cases of homicide, those close to the victim frequently demand that the perpetrator be made to suffer regardless of his mental state.

11. The difficulty some well-educated people today have in comprehending such a value system is well illustrated by the shock with which a colleague once greeted a remark of mine, apropos of a famous line of T.S. Eliot, that I would always rather have someone 'do the right deed for the wrong reason' than do the wrong thing for the right reason.

12. See e.g. [Lysias], *For Polystratus* 31; Lysias, *Defence against a Charge of Subverting the Democracy* 13.

13. It may be significant that certain lines in Eteocles' speech have a notable concentration of *p*-sounds, as if he were spitting out his hatred (see lines 661-2, 669-71).

14. An *oikos* (lit. 'house') is the continuing group consisting of all males descended, in the paternal line, from a (normally recent) common ancestor, together with their dependants. A woman transfers on marriage from the *oikos* of her father to that of her husband. Henceforward *oikos* will often be rendered by 'house'.

15. In the transmitted text it is further mentioned that he is paying a debt of nurture to Argos (548), which might be thought to entitle him to at least a modicum of sympathy; but it is possible that this line is an interpolation (see Hutchinson 1985: 129).

16. Except that, as in Sophocles, Oedipus himself was largely responsible for discovering his own guilt: Sophocles' *Antigone* (51), which was produced earlier than *Oedipus the King*, presupposes this by calling Oedipus' crimes 'self-detected' (*autophôra*).

17. Aeschylus seems to have counted on a fairly ample knowledge of the legend among at least some of his audience. For example, there is independent evidence (*Thebais* fr. 9 West; Sophocles, *Antigone* 1303) that in some accounts of the war two of the defending Theban champions were killed in addition to Eteocles, namely Melanippus and Megareus – just the two whose death is envisaged as a possibility in the 'shield scene' of *Seven* (419-20, 477).

18. So, at any rate, says a scholiast on the *Frogs* passage; it is possible, however, that he or his source is merely guessing and that the line actually comes from *Oedipus*.

19. This would seem to require three actors (Oedipus, the Sphinx and Silenus), but there is reason to believe that in the two-actor period Silenus in satyr-plays could be regarded as a semi-detached member of the chorus (cf. Chapter 9).

20. Two passages, 843-4 and 902-3, have been thought to refer to apprehensions that the city may yet be destroyed in fulfilment of the oracle of Laius, and to the Epigoni as the agents of that destruction; but 843 (*merimna d' amphi ptolin*) is more likely to mean 'there is grieving throughout the city' (cf. 849 *diplain merimnain* referring to the 'double grief' for the two dead brothers) than 'there is apprehension about the city's fate', and in 902-3 the text has probably been tampered with (the scholiast's paraphrase was clearly written to explain a different text).

21. Thus, when the Herald enters, there will be three speaking actors on stage – in a tragedy (contrast n. 19 above) a further indication that the Herald scene is not part of the script acted in 467.

22. Why does the author invent this anonymous and anachronistic body of *probouloi*, instead of following Sophocles and ascribing the decree to Creon as the new monarch? He wants to end (as the original text had done) with both the brothers' bodies being taken off for burial. Therefore, if the burial of Polyneices is prohibited, Antigone must not only defy the prohibition but do so openly. It would be unimaginable for Creon to tolerate such an insult to his personal honour and authority. In Euripides, he successfully (at least for the time being) prevents Antigone from acting (*Phoenician Maidens* 1627-72); in Sophocles, she does not announce her intentions in advance (except to her sister). Here, therefore, Creon is replaced by a group of magistrates, and the personal sting of Antigone's defiance is thus diffused and weakened; even this group, moreover, is kept silent, leaving Antigone to oppose and defeat (in words) not the rulers of the *polis* but their humble mouthpiece.

23. Unless indeed the producer and the poet were one and the same person, Aeschylus' son Euphorion; M.L. West 2000: 351-2 points to significant parallels between *Prometheus Bound*, which is very probably Euphorion's work, and the additions to *Seven*.

24. An additional motive for the new ending may have been to provide employment for a third actor. Normally, in revivals of Aeschylean plays which had originally used only two actors, it would be possible to satisfy a three-man troupe by giving each of them at least one speaking part. *Seven* is unique among surviving Greek plays in having originally had a total of only two speaking parts, and the third actor in the troupe might well not have been too pleased at having to sit out a complete play; the added ending gives him a role (and indeed the chance to play Antigone!).

6

The Danaid Plays

A tetralogy produced a few years after the Theban tetralogy, possibly in 463, comprising *The Egyptians*, *The Suppliant Maidens*, *The Danaids* and the satyr-play *Amymone* (for the order of the plays see §6.2). It won first prize, defeating Sophocles and Mesatus. *The Suppliant Maidens* survives, together with fragments of the other plays amounting in total to about thirteen lines.

6.1. *The Suppliant Maidens*

Danaus and Aegyptus are brothers, descended from Epaphus (see Genealogy, p. 317), the child whom the Argive Io conceived by the 'touch and breath' of Zeus (15-18, 40-7, 313-15, 571-89) after having been driven from Argos to Egypt in the form of a cow by the jealous anger of Hera. Danaus has fifty daughters,[1] Aegyptus fifty sons. The brothers have quarrelled and warred in Egypt (cf. 741-2), and Aegyptus seems to have been victorious.[2] Either a cause or a result of the war was a demand by Aegyptus for the daughters of Danaus (hereafter 'the Danaids') to be given to his sons in marriage. The Danaids find the thought of such a marriage abhorrent – though in *The Suppliant Maidens* itself they never make it completely clear why this is so – and their father has taken a ship and fled with them from Egypt, making for Argos, their ancestral home. When the play begins they have just landed; the scene is on the coast near Argos, with an elevation topped by altars and images of the city's gods.

The Danaids, who form the chorus of the play, enter, each carrying the wool-wreathed olive branch that is the emblem of the suppliant. They pray to the gods of Argos to greet them kindly, and to drown 'that arrogant teeming swarm of males, the sons of Aegyptus' (29-30) who are pursuing them across the sea. Then in a lengthy song (twenty-one or twenty-two stanzas, including refrains) they affirm their own Argive descent (recalling the tale of Io, as they will many times again; see further §6.5), hymn the power of Zeus (86-103), and pray again to him and the other Olympians to uphold their just cause and save them from this hateful marriage. If their prayers are ignored, they plan to shame Zeus (who as their ancestor ought to protect his descendants) by 'supplicating the ever-hospitable Zeus of the Dead [Hades] with nooses instead of olive-branches' (157-60): a remarkable attempt to blackmail the supreme god, and one that seems to ignore the fact that the sons of Aegyptus are also Zeus' descendants.

Danaus probably entered at the same time as the chorus, and has been keeping a lookout from the 'hilltop'. He now tells his daughters that he sees signs of the approach of an armed force (180-3), and instructs them to join him at the sanctuary (188-96), which they do; and presently to the *orkhê-stra*, thus vacated by them, there enters Pelasgus, king of Argos and of all Greece (250-9), with a martial retinue. He asks the alien-looking newcomers where they are from; they reply, to his amazement, that they are Argive (274-5), and proceed to prove it by telling the story of Io and tracing their descent from her. Asked why they have fled from Egypt, they explain that they are trying to avoid marriage – or 'slavery' as they call it (335) – to the sons of Aegyptus, and ask him to give them protection if their cousins demand their surrender; which, as he immediately realizes (342), involves the risk of a major war.

There ensues a tense, if not overtly violent, struggle. Pelasgus is clearly not only reluctant to involve Argos in war, but doubtful about the prudence and justice of supporting the Danaids (cf. 338, 344); on the other hand, if their cause *is* a just one, he dare not offend Zeus the patron of suppliants (Zeus Hikesios) by rejecting them.[3] His first line of defence is to plead (365-9) that he cannot on his own authority consent to the Danaids' request: they are supplicating the city, not himself, and the citizens must decide. The Danaids, assuming that the king of Argos is an absolute ruler of the usual 'barbarian' kind, treat this as an evasion of responsibility on his part (370-5). Pelasgus next argues (387-91) that the Danaids must prove they have the right under Egyptian law to refuse marriage with their cousins; their emotional but evasive reply (392-6) strongly suggests that they have no such right and know it – but even if Pelasgus were to draw that inference, he cannot take the risk, to himself and his people, of acting on it. He sees no way out of his dilemma, and the Danaids keep tightening the screw. Finally they unveil a threat (echoing their earlier attempt to blackmail Zeus) in the face of which he is utterly helpless:

> DANAIDS[4]
> Hear now the end of my many respectful words.
> PELASGUS
> I hear; speak on; it will not escape my ears.
> DANAIDS
> I have sashes and girdles which hold my robes together.
> PELASGUS
> No doubt that is very proper for women.
> DANAIDS
> Well, with these, I tell you, a splendid scheme can be contrived.
> PELASGUS
> Speak on; what are these words you are going to utter?
> DANAIDS
> If you do not make a firm promise to our group –
> PELASGUS
> What is this girdle-scheme going to achieve for you?

DANAIDS
It will adorn these statues with a new set of votive tablets.
PELASGUS
That is a riddle. Speak your meaning plainly.
DANAIDS
From these divine images – forthwith – to hang ourselves.
PELASGUS
The words I hear are words that lash my heart.
DANAIDS
You understand; I have opened your eyes to see clear. (455-67)

Pelasgus is left with no choice. To risk the anger of Zeus Hikesios is bad enough; to have a shrine of all the gods polluted by death, and unnatural death at that, is unthinkable. He accepts the inevitable. Danaus is told (480-9) to take his daughters' suppliant-branches and place them on altars in the city, as a first step to prepare public opinion for the risk of war; he departs to do this, escorted and guarded at his own request (492-9) by men of Pelasgus' retinue (who are told to say as little as possible about him, 502-3). The maidens are asked (506-16) to descend from the shrine to a 'level meadow', i.e. the *orkhêstra*; Pelasgus intends to leave them alone there while he and Danaus address the Argive assembly, and dramatically it would have been more logical if he had allowed them to stay in the sacred place – but then the three major choral songs soon to be sung (524-99, 625-709, 776-824) could not have been accompanied by dancing.

The Danaids repeat their prayer to Zeus to defend them and drown their enemies (524-30), and emphasize their claim on him by a much fuller retelling of the story of Io, in particular her long wanderings and how they were ended in Egypt by Zeus whose touch and breath gave being to Epaphus. They end by reasserting (592-9) the boundless power of Zeus, with the clear implication that if he fails to help them it will not be from lack of strength but from lack of willingness.

Whether or not Zeus will help the Danaids, the Argive people have certainly done so. Danaus, returning from the city, exultantly reports (600-24) that in response to a persuasive speech by Pelasgus, the Argives have voted unanimously to grant the family full protection and asylum as resident aliens (*metoikoi*); no one, whether citizen or foreigner, is to molest them, and if anyone tries to do so all Argives are to go to the family's aid on pain of exile and disfranchisement. Pelasgus in his speech, we hear, emphasized the danger of pollution and of the wrath of Zeus Hikesios; he said nothing (that we are told) about the danger of war. The maidens sing an enthusiastic song of blessing on the Argive people; but the blessings they invoke include that of peace (663-6, 701-3) which at present seems anything but likely, *unless* Zeus has granted the Danaids' repeated prayers and destroyed their enemies at sea.

He has not. Danaus, back at his lookout post, announces the arrival of 'the ship' with its dark-limbed, white-clad crew (713-20), and almost at once the first ship is followed by a whole fleet (721). His daughters are naturally terrified, but their father urges them to put their trust in the Argives' promises, and arguing that the army will take a long time to land (764-72) he goes off again to Argos to summon help: should help be slow in coming, they will always be able to flee to the sanctuary (730-1).

After a choral song of high apprehension, there bursts on to the scene (825ff.) a party of Egyptians led by a herald. At this point our text becomes incoherent, partly through corruption in the single manuscript on which the text of this play depends, partly because the Egyptians appear to be singing in broken Greek. At any rate the Danaids flee in panic to the shrine. They are ordered in rough language to come at once to the ship. They curse their enemies wildly and invoke the gods; the herald displays his *hybris* by replying 'I do not fear the gods of this place' (893). He and his men are just on the point of dragging the Danaids off by force when Pelasgus arrives with troops and orders him, in the name of the Argive *polis*, to desist. The Danaids, he says, may be taken with their own consent and not otherwise (940-1). The herald treats this as a declaration of war (950) and departs with his men.

It is clear that the Danaids cannot any longer stay in this vulnerable spot (which in any case is no place to spend the night), and Pelasgus invites them to come to the city, where they will have a wide choice of residences (954-65). He then departs, leaving behind some of his men (954^5) to escort the Danaids to Argos; they ask him to send their father to join them.

When Danaus comes, however, he gives no indication of having been sent by Pelasgus. Indeed he seems to have established already a powerful position at Argos in his own right. He too is now accompanied by armed men: the Argives have assigned him a personal bodyguard (985-8). He speaks at considerable length (991-1013) on the moral dangers facing young girls in a strange city: his anxiety on this score has seemed excessive to many critics, given what we have heard of his daughters' own feelings, but the explanation of it may lie elsewhere in the trilogy (see §6.2). Danaus' daughters, at any rate, reply reassuringly, and all is now ready for the party to leave for Argos.

The Danaids sing in honour of Argos and its gods – except Aphrodite whom they reject (1031-3). Now, however, another group of voices take over; and these sing in *praise* of Aphrodite (1034-42), express fear of 'evil sorrows and bloody wars' (1043-4), reflect on the implications of the fact that the enemy's voyage to Argos was both swift and safe, and wonder if marriage is really so terrible a fate (1047-51). Who are these singers? The text indicates that two groups of persons other than the Danaids are present – Danaus' Argive escort (cf. 985) and the Danaids' own maidservants (cf. 977-9) – and in principle the song 1034-51 might be assigned to either group; but to assign it to the Argives probably requires less special pleading.[6] The intervention gives rise to an altercation (1052-61) between the Argives (or the maidservants) and the Danaids, the former warning the latter to 'make your prayer moderate' and 'avoid going too far in regard to the gods'. The Danaids can hardly be said to heed the warning: they end the play virtually as they had begun it, praying to Zeus – the Zeus who, 'laying a healing hand on Io, freed her from her troubles' (1064-7) – to avert the hated marriage and 'give victory to the women'. With that, all depart for the city, and the lines are drawn for war.

6.2. The tetralogy

As good a summary as any of the fundamental outlines of the Danaid myth is to be found in the prophecy given to the Danaids' ancestress, Io, by Prometheus in *Prometheus Bound* 853-69. There is, moreover, special reason for believing that this passage was composed with the Aeschylean version of the myth specially in mind. Not only was *Prometheus Bound*, even if not actually the work of Aeschylus, in all probability produced under his name by a member of his family (see §8.5); the prophecy itself contains, in the image of the doves and hawks (857), a clear echo of *The Suppliant Maidens* (223-5), and there is nothing in it that is inconsistent with that play or with the fragments of the other Danaid plays. Prometheus has been prophesying to Io her future experiences. She will come, he says, to Egypt[7] and there be made pregnant, just as the Danaids recall she was, by the touch of Zeus' hand, and give birth to Epaphus:

> And fifty girls, the seed of his fifth generation,
> will come back to Argos, not of their free will,
> fleeing the kindred wedlock
> of their cousins, who, with hearts driven by passion,
> hawks not far behind the fugitive doves,
> will come hunting marriages they should not be hunting;
> but a god will begrudge them their cousins' bodies,
> and the Pelasgian land will be moistened with blood
> shed by female slayers, when they are audaciously laid low of a wakeful night;
> for each woman will rob her husband of life,
> dipping a two-edged sword in his blood. …
> But one of the girls will be charmed by desire so as not
> to slay her bedfellow; her purpose will be blunted,
> and of the two alternatives she will choose
> to be called a coward rather than an unclean murderer.
> She will be the mother of a royal race in Argos …

and (adds Prometheus) the ancestress of the man (Heracles) who will one day set him free.

This evidence makes it highly probable that Aeschylus followed in essentials the usual version of the Danaid legend. The Argives, we see, for all the loyalty and determination they show in the surviving play, were unable to prevent the marriage which the Danaids so detested; but the new brides, all but one of them, killed their husbands on the wedding night. The one who did not, we know from other sources, was called Hypermestra, and her husband Lynceus, and they became king and queen of Argos – from which it follows that both Pelasgus and Danaus must have been either dead, or possibly in exile, by the end of the trilogy. Pelasgus, it has often and probably rightly been suggested, died in battle against the Egyptians. Danaus is regularly assumed in other versions of the story to have been the planner of the multiple murder, and often he is said to have punished or attempted to punish Hypermestra for not having taken part in it.

Our direct evidence about *The Egyptians* and *The Danaids* is very limited. Of the former, indeed, we possess but a single word. From *The Danaids* we have three fragments, two of which give significant information. One (fr. 43), though obscure and probably corrupt, seems to refer to the ceremony of 'awakening' the bridal couples on the morning after the wedding, and it is therefore likely that the action of this play was set on the day after the murders. The ceremony is spoken of as something about to happen rather than as something that has happened, suggesting that the action opened early on the morning in question, before the murders had been discovered. The other fragment (fr. 44) comprises seven lines of a speech by Aphrodite:

> The holy Sky yearns to pierce the Earth,
> and desire seizes Earth to join in union;
> the rain falls from the Sky's fluid abundance
> and makes Earth conceive, and she brings forth for mortals
> grazing for their flocks, corn for their sustenance,
> and the fruit of trees. From this wedlock of the rains
> come to birth all things that are; and of this I am a cause.

This affirmation by the goddess herself of the universality of her power, which the Danaids had sought to reject (cf. *Supp.* 1031-3), is evidence that in this play, in one way or another, the action of the Danaids (and their father, if as is almost certain he was involved in plotting it) was condemned, and Hypermestra vindicated. It is of course obvious that *The Danaids* stood later in the trilogy than *The Suppliant Maidens*, and it was universally thought to have been the final play of the trilogy long before a papyrus fragment of a production-notice (*Oxyrhynchus Papyrus* 2256, fr. 3) confirmed that it was.

The titles, and therefore the order, of the first two plays have not survived on the papyrus, but until very recently it was generally agreed that *The Suppliant Maidens* was the first play and *The Egyptians* the second. *The Egyptians*, it was thought, was probably concerned with preparations for the marriages, perhaps in the aftermath of a battle in which Pelasgus had been killed, after which Danaus had taken over power in Argos and undertaken to end the war. It was not immediately clear how he and his daughters could have contrived their murder-plot, given that the title implied a chorus of Egyptians; but one could imagine, for example, that the Danaids formed a secondary chorus, hatched the plot with their father in an early scene, and departed before the main chorus entered.[8]

However, there is an anomaly in *The Suppliant Maidens* itself that points in a different direction. Danaus' last speech in the play (in particular its second half, 996-1013) betrays an almost desperate anxiety that his daughters shall at all costs preserve their virginity and value it 'more than life itself' (1013). This, to be sure, would be an anxiety that every Greek father would feel, to some degree, until he had got his daughters safely married; but no other father, in a surviving text, makes such a song and dance about the matter, and Danaus' tirade is all the more remarkable because his daughters have not given the slightest indication of any tendency to go astray. What is more, Danaus says in effect (1006-7) that if they do go astray, they and he will have endured much suffering and a long sea-voyage for nothing. We learn here, in other words, that when Danaus refused the proposal of Aegyptus for a mass marriage of their children, and fled with his daughters from Egypt, it was not, or not solely, because he objected to a marriage alliance with Aegyptus' family in particular; it was because he did not want his daughters to be married *at all* – because he wanted them to remain permanent virgins.

The Danaids' own utterances, long before the reassuring reply they give their father (1014-7), suggest that they fully share his attitude. They do, of course, frequently express their loathing of their cousins, but there is also ample evidence of a general detestation of men, sex, and marriage. They equate marriage with slavery (335-7) and pray that they may never be 'subject to the power of males' (392-3). The very phrase 'the beds of men' prompts them to a cry of horror (142, 152), they wish for death 'before an abominated man touches my flesh' (788-90, cf. 796-9, 804-7) and they frequently dwell on the miraculous conception of Epaphus.

These attitudes, particularly that of Danaus, are extremely abnormal. For the father or guardian of a young woman deliberately to keep her unmarried was considered one of the most grievous wrongs that could be committed against her. Even in myth, there are few who do this, and they normally have some very powerful motivation. Aegisthus and Clytaemestra keep the latter's daughter Electra unmarried for fear that she may bear a son who would ultimately take revenge for the murder of her father Agamemnon; Acrisius imprisons his daughter Danaë because an oracle has told him he will be killed by his grandson. Might Danaus have a similar motivation?

In some known versions of the myth, he certainly does. There are several accounts[9] in which Danaus' rejection of Aegyptus' proposal for a marriage alliance results from an oracle he had received, to the effect that he would be killed (in some versions) by his son-in-law[10] or (in other versions) by a son of Aegyptus. But there is nothing whatever in *The Suppliant Maidens* itself that could for a moment make us suspect even the existence of such an oracle; nor can we assume that Aeschylus was able to take knowledge of it for granted as a regular part of the myth, for we know that in one quite recent poetic version of the story (Pindar, *Pythian* 9.112-16, performed in 474) Danaus not only survived[11] but actually arranged new marriages for his daughters. Either, then, Aeschylus has deliberately left his audience mystified on this important issue, to be enlightened only much later in the trilogy (a common technique of modern drama and fiction, but hard to parallel in anything we know of classical tragedy) – or else they had been informed about the oracle in a *preceding* play. If so, that play can only have been *The Egyptians*.[12]

Such a hypothesis accounts for considerably more than the attitude of Danaus and his daughters, in the surviving play, to sexuality and marriage. It greatly eases reconstruction of *The Egyptians*. That play need no longer be supposed to have dealt with the making of the murder-plot, or with marriage negotiations at Argos: it was set in Egypt, with a chorus no doubt of Egyptian nobles or elders,[13] and dealt with the earlier stages of the dispute between Aegyptus and Danaus. There are, moreover, certain allusions in *The Suppliant Maidens* to earlier events which are decidedly cryptic if we suppose that no play preceded *Supp.* The Danaids say to their father that the sons of Aegyptus are 'insatiate of battle' and add 'I speak to one who knows' (741-2). This implies that Danaus has waged war against them in Egypt – and this is the only reference in *Supp.* to this war. Why was it not mentioned at the beginning of the play? Because – we can now see – the audience already knew, from the preceding play, that there had been such a war, and further reference to it at that stage was unnecessary. Again, two passages in *Supp.* imply that under Egyptian law the sons of Aegyptus have the right to claim possession of their cousins regardless of the latter's own wishes or of their father's – but this emerges in a strangely indirect way. First Pelasgus asks whether such a law exists (387-91) and receives an evasive answer; later the Egyptian Herald speaks of the Danaids as items of his (meaning his masters') lost property (916-20), and asks (932-3) 'who shall I say took away from me this group of cousin women?' as if, again, they belonged to him by right. Such a right was utterly alien to Greek society (in which no free woman whose father was alive and *compos mentis* could ever be taken in marriage without his consent) and requires far clearer explanation than it ever receives in this play; again, such explanation is likely to have featured in *The Egyptians*.

The outlines of the plot of *The Egyptians* can now be discerned. Danaus is king of Egypt. He has, however, no son to succeed him, and the Egyptian people, as represented by the chorus of Egyptian notables, are anxious about the future of their kingdom. His brother Aegyptus comes to him with what might seem an admirable proposal: let Danaus' daughters be married to Aegyptus' sons, thus keeping both rulership and property entirely within the one family (cf. *Supp.* 338). Danaus, however, has been told by an oracle (probably that of Zeus Ammon, to Greeks the best known of all foreign oracles) that he will be killed by the bedfellow of his daughter,[14] and he refuses. Aegyptus, slighted, seeks and secures the support of the people against Danaus, and now, if not earlier, he invokes an Egyptian law according to which a woman's closest kinsman has the right to demand – indeed to *take* – her in marriage regardless of her or her father's consent. On his claim being rejected, he declares war on Danaus – probably with the enthusiastic support of the chorus – and the play may have ended with him going out to battle, perhaps accompanied by his sons as a secondary chorus (this would be the only opportunity in the trilogy to bring them on stage).

If this view of the structure of the trilogy is correct, it has important consequences for the understanding of *The Suppliant Maidens*. Danaus at least is systematically deceiving the Argives: neither they nor any other Greek *polis* would have been willing to support him had they known that they were fighting for his right to keep his daughters in permanent spinsterhood. It is less clear whether his daughters are also parties to the deception – whether, in other words, they are aware of the oracle. If, as is likely (see above), the oracle came from Zeus, and if the Danaids knew of it, their repeated and confident prayers for the support of Zeus would be so marvellously foolish that it is more likely that we are to suppose they do not know. Their father, in whose hands they are like the pieces on his game-board (cf. *Supp.* 12), must then have brought them up from childhood to look on marriage not as a natural and inevitable stage in life but as a fate literally worse than death. There were other versions of the myth in which the Danaids seem to have had a highly abnormal and indeed, by ancient Greek standards, a highly unfeminine upbringing: the dithyrambic poet Melanippides, a younger contemporary of Aeschylus, describes them (*GL* 757) as fond of hunting and chariot-driving, and a fragment of an early epic called the *Danais* (fr. 1 West) speaks of them *arming themselves,* as if for battle, beside the Nile.

Denys Page (in Denniston & Page 1957: xviii) thought he knew what happened in *The Danaids*: 'somebody was put on trial, and Aphrodite spoke for the prosecution or defence – whether of Danaus, because forty-nine daughters had killed their husbands; or of the fiftieth, because she had not.' We certainly know that Aphrodite spoke; we do not know that it was at a trial that she spoke, and there are reasons for believing that it was not. What we know of her speech would be irrelevant to a trial of Danaus, whose crime was not to have rejected Aphrodite but to have planned a multiple murder.[15] It would fit better as a defence of Hypermestra, and it has been pointed out that a tradition of such a trial existed at Argos in the time of Pausanias (second century AD);[16] but such a tradition could have had other sources than Aeschylus, and there are serious difficulties with the supposition of a trial of Hypermestra. What was her crime? Putting it at its highest, and even supposing that she was aware of the oracle, what she did was to disobey an order by her father to murder her husband, the 'justification' for the order being that her husband belonged to a group of fifty, one of whom was destined to cause her father's death. If Danaus had asked the Argives to punish his daughter for an 'offence' like that, it would not have needed Aphrodite's intervention to secure her acquittal. Danaus might well, on the other hand, have punished Hypermestra on his own authority, and several later authors (Horace, Ovid, pseudo-Apollodorus) know a version of the story in which he imprisoned her.[17]

The reconstruction of *The Danaids* should start from a different point. If we are right to suppose that the story began, for Aeschylus, with an oracle telling Danaus that he would be killed by his son-in-law, then it must have ended with the fulfilment of the oracle; that is, with the death of Danaus through the action of his only surviving son-in-law, Lynceus.[18] We have several other relevant scraps of information and inference. We have already seen that the action of the play began early in the morning following the night of the murders. It is widely accepted, too, that Danaus must by this stage have become *tyrannos* of Argos; the grant of a bodyguard to him by the Argive assembly (*Supp.* 985-8) was the classic first step towards the position of *tyrannos*, as exemplified by the career of Peisistratus in Athens or of Theagenes in Megara (see Aristotle, *Rhetoric* 1357b30-6). Thus Lynceus, in bringing about the death of Danaus, will not only be fulfilling the original oracle and taking personal revenge for the murder of his brothers, but also liberating the Argive people from a despot. Any reconstruction of *The Danaids* must also include some means for Lynceus to escape the wrath of Danaus until he is able to take action against him, and must provide a context for the speech of Aphrodite; and in view of her strong affirmation of the universality of the sexual principle, it is highly likely that the play and the trilogy ended with the making of new and more acceptable marriages for the Danaids.

There may well be several reconstructions that meet these requirements, and the one which follows is offered only *exempli gratia*: it is not fact, but speculation based on the data and inferences mentioned in the previous paragraph and on other known accounts of the legend. To keep the reader in mind of this while avoiding the constant use of expressions like 'may have been' and 'perhaps', the reconstruction is printed in italics.

The play began with the entry of Lynceus in disguise – perhaps in the garb of a slave or peasant. He narrated recent events – the war between Argives and Egyptians, the death of Pelasgus, the assumption of power by Danaus, his agreement to the marriage of his daughters to Aegyptus' sons as a condition of peace, and the murder of all but one of the bridegrooms by their brides during the night just past. He himself had been spared, and smuggled out of the house of death, by his wife Hypermestra; he would now lie low in or near Argos and await an opportunity to take revenge on Danaus who had planned the murders. Lynceus departed, and another character entered, perhaps a servant of Danaus ignorant of his master's plot; this character described the previous day's wedding festivities and went off to organize the 'awakening' of the couples. Then the Danaids entered as chorus, carrying the daggers with which they had committed the murders.[19] *Presently Danaus arrived, with guards escorting Hypermestra. He announced his discovery of her 'treachery', consigned her to prison, and departed to hold a meeting of the Argive assembly where he would demand, under dire threats, information on the whereabouts of Lynceus. Later the events of the assembly were reported to the Danaids by a messenger. After Danaus' speech (he said) an unknown young man had said he knew where Lynceus could be found, and asked for authority to act and armed men to assist him. On being granted these with the consent of Danaus, he had revealed that he was Lynceus, denounced Danaus as a murderer, had him arrested and taken away for execution, and himself been acclaimed king of Argos. After an agitated choral song, Lynceus and Hypermestra entered, appropriately escorted, as king and queen.*[20] *Lynceus was about to order the arrest of the Danaids when Aphrodite appeared. She explained the essential innocence of the Danaids (who, as was shown earlier, did not know of the oracle given to their father) and the true guilt and motive of Danaus, who had sought to negate and frustrate her universal power. Her eloquence reconciled the Danaids to marriage, and persuaded Lynceus to pardon them and purify them from the pollution of bloodshed. The Danaids dropped their daggers and declared their acceptance of their destined role; Lynceus undertook to give them in marriage, perhaps to the young Argive warriors forming his own escort – in dramatic terms the very same men who at the end of the previous play had warned the Danaids not to hold Aphrodite in contempt. The play ended with a procession very similar to that which ended 'The Suppliant Maidens', but this time it was a wedding procession, led by Aphrodite and by Lynceus and Hypermestra, the founders of the new royal house of Argos.*

If anything like this reconstruction of the trilogy is correct, it will have had three major themes, all converging in the climactic event of the death of Danaus. The first, and probably the least important, would be that familiar theme of Greek myth, the folly of attempting to evade the fulfilment of an oracle. The second theme would be a political one, centring on the deception of the Argive people by Pelasgus (who leads them into war without their realizing it until too late) and by Danaus (to whom they give the means by which he seizes absolute power as *tyrannos*). The third and arguably the dominating theme would be that of the nature of marriage. This theme began with Aegyptus, for good family reasons, wanting a certain marriage for his sons, while Danaus, for understandable (but not excusable) personal reasons, wanted no marriage at all for his daughters. In the next generation the brainwashed Danaids reject marriage root and branch (and therefore – though they never understand this – reject one of the cornerstones of the organized *polis* society which they bless and praise so highly in *Supp.* 625-709), while for the sons of Aegyptus marriage is a matter of mere forcible seizure and possession, as exemplified by the behaviour of the Herald. Between these opposites, radical conflict is inevitable, and it is all too predictable that it issues in murder. A third way is first pointed to by the secondary chorus, probably as we saw consisting of Argive spearmen, in *Supp.* 1038-42 when they sing of Aphrodite's companions Desire, Persuasion, Harmony and Eros, implying that any true and good union of the sexes must be based upon these; it is confirmed by Aphrodite herself, who speaks among other things of the *mutual* desire of the primeval couple Sky and Earth (fr. 44.1-2), and it is embodied in the marriage of Lynceus and Hypermestra. That is what marriage should be: based on mutual desire and affection, the foundation of the order of the universe, the order of the *polis* and the order of the *oikos*. That is the affirmation with which the Danaid trilogy may well have ended, and it would not be unfitting if at its end those same Argive spearmen became the Danaids' new bridegrooms.

*

There was one Danaid apart from Hypermestra who had a name and a story of her own. This was Amymone, and she was the subject of the satyr-play which followed the trilogy. Several surviving accounts of her myth introduce a satyr; this is so unusual in mythographic narratives as to raise a strong presumption that these accounts are derived from Aeschylus' play. The story as they tell it is as follows.

Amymone went out into the countryside. According to some she was sent by her father to fetch spring water for some ritual purpose, could not find a spring, and fell asleep with fatigue; according to others she went out hunting (cf. p. 104), threw a spear at a stag and accidentally hit a satyr. At any rate the satyr attempted to rape her. She called for help to Poseidon, who appeared at once, put the satyr to flight – and thereupon himself deflowered Amymone; in due course she gave birth to a son, Nauplius, and at the site of these events Poseidon created the spring of Lerna.

My use of the ambiguous verb 'deflowered' is designed to cover an uncertainty among our sources as to whether Amymone was raped by Poseidon or whether she consented: some accounts (all in Latin, not Greek) speak explicitly of rape, others use expressions like 'lay with' which leave the question open; the one Greek account, by pseudo-Apollodorus (*Library* 2.1.4), says that '*Amymone* lay with *him*' [italics mine], which implies consent fairly strongly. And, as several scholars have seen, persuasion by Poseidon and consent by Amymone would create in the satyr-play a close, if distorted and burlesqued, echo of the main theme of the trilogy: an attempt to effect sexual union through forcible seizure is forcibly prevented, and superseded by a consensual, mutually desired and fruitful union under divine auspices, associated with water and with the fertility of the soil (cf. fr. 44).[21] It is hard to be sure whether Aeschylus brought Amymone to Lerna for hunting or in search of water, but the latter has the advantages that it would link the beginning of the play with its end and would explain why Amymone calls for help to Poseidon rather than some other deity.

6.3. Lyrical tragedy?

This (without the question-mark) was the title of the first chapter of Kitto 1961, which dealt with *The Suppliant Maidens* as the sole surviving example of this phase of the tragic genre. When the first edition of Kitto's book had appeared in 1939, it had been almost universally believed that *Supp.* was – possibly by a long way – the earliest surviving Greek tragedy. Since we now know this belief was incorrect, it may be instructive to consider the very substantial arguments which then seemed to favour it.

(1) First and foremost stood the extraordinary prominence in this play of the chorus and of lyric. Of the play's 1073 lines, only 480 or 45% consist of spoken dialogue, and the chorus are an active participant in every scene except that between Pelasgus and the herald (911-53). Since the history of the tragic chorus is largely a history of its diminishing dramatic role, it seemed natural to suppose that we had here an early phase.

(2) There was (and is) strong reason to suppose that in addition to the main chorus the play had *two* singing subsidiary choruses, one of Egyptians (825 or 836 to 865) and another either of Argive soldiers or of the Danaids' maidservants (1034-62), both of whom engage in lyric dialogue with the Danaids. No other known tragedy has three choruses, and none has lyric dialogue between two independent choruses (as opposed to dialogue between sections of one chorus).

(3) Related to these points is the fact that little effective use is made of the second actor. In 176-233 Danaus appears to be in charge of the party of refugees, but when Pelasgus appears, Danaus, while still on stage, says and does nothing for some 250 lines; he is not even allowed to give his name (his daughters do that for him, 321). As Kitto says (1961:23), 'the play is in all essentials single-actor drama up to the point where Danaus is able to do something useful by going into Argos'. Later in the play, too, Pelasgus is rather artificially cleared off the scene before Danaus arrives.[22] It is as if Aeschylus were reluctant at this time to write two-actor scenes. In *The Persians* and *Seven* most of the major scenes (Queen-Messenger; Queen-Darius; Eteocles-Scout) involve two actors, and while there is still a tendency for a new arrival to speak with the chorus first, the second actor is never kept waiting anything like as long as Danaus. Since in the *Oresteia* Aeschylus uses *three* actors and uses them well, it was hard to suppose that he would be so apparently clumsy with two actors a few years earlier.

(4) The elaborate and often exotic spectacle (on which see §6.4) suggested an early date, it being assumed that tragedy evolved away from such extravagance and towards what was thought of as the classical restraint of Sophocles.

(5) Even allowing for the fact that the play was one part of a trilogy, the plot seemed simple and slight. The Danaids sought asylum at Argos; it was granted; and an Egyptian ultimatum was rejected. Nothing decisive happened, in sharp contrast with *Agamemnon* and *Choephoroi* (or even *Prometheus Bound* with its apocalyptic ending).

And then in 1952 the publication of a tiny fragment of papyrus revealed that the play was produced in competition with Sophocles, and therefore no earlier than 470.[23] At first attempts were made to reconcile what was now known with what had always been believed: perhaps the production-notice in the papyrus referred to a restaging, possibly after Aeschylus' death; perhaps the play, or the tetralogy, was written early in Aeschylus' career but for some reason was not produced until much later. But these were always desperate shifts, and it is not now seriously disputed that the play was both written and produced in the decade 470-60.[24] How had scholars managed to get it so wrong? Let us review the arguments set out above, in reverse order.

(5) Aeschylean plots are frequently simple by the standards of later tragedy; even less, after all, happens in *The Persians*, where, prosaically speaking, the only difference between the situation at the beginning and at the end is that by the end the defeat at Salamis (and the coming defeat at Plataea) are known about in Susa; and what would we think of *Agamemnon* if it had ended at or about line 1073? Nor is it entirely true that nothing decisive happens in *The Suppliant Maidens*: the reception of the Danaids is almost as decisive an event for Argos as the reception of Helen was for Troy, leading as it does to a major war, the death of the king and the establishment in power of a *tyrannos* – and the spectators watching *Supp.* had a fairly good idea, in general terms, of these coming developments.

(4) It is not obvious that there is vastly more extravagant spectacle in this play than in, say, *Eumenides* (see §§7.3 and 7.6). One cannot help suspecting[25] that some critics may have been influenced by the fact that this is the only surviving Greek tragedy in which the majority of the persons on stage are dark-skinned and of African origin, and by a subconscious assumption that 'true', 'mature' Greek tragedy ought to be about white Europeans: placing *Supp.* early conveniently relegated the two plays with mainly or entirely 'barbarian' *dramatis personae* to the protohistory of the genre. But to be fair, the 'spectacle' argument served largely to confirm a belief already held on other grounds, and principally on the basis of arguments **(1)-(3)** above: the predominance of the chorus, the two subsidiary choruses and the slight use made of the second actor.

All these features of *Supp.* seem in fact to be reflections of the author's deliberate decision to do, in this play, something very unusual: to make the chorus in effect the leading character. There is a very good reason why this was not normally done. Tragedy was about the actions and sufferings of men and women who were out of the normal run, of exceptional people; and exceptional people normally come as individuals, not as groups of twelve or fifteen indistinguishable persons. Nor does myth in general provide suitable groups for this purpose: most tragic choruses are not given by the myth but invented *ad hoc* by the author. The Danaids were a very special case: a large group of persons whose actions, culminating in the killing of their husbands, were eminently suited for tragedy, but who could appear in tragedy only as a chorus, since the only individuals among them who had distinct personalities, Hypermestra and Amymone, were untypical of the group and could not act as its representatives.[26] On the other hand Danaus could not be suppressed altogether: even had Aeschylus not decided to build the trilogy as a whole around the fulfilment, by his death, of an oracle once given to him, the story needed him anyway as ruler of Argos at a crucial stage. In *Supp.*, therefore, he had to be there, but could not be allowed to eclipse his daughters. And hence they, not he, were made to take the lead in supplicating Pelasgus. From the refugees' own point of view that was sound tactics: young girls, vulnerable and defenceless (or so it would seem), would make more persuasive suppliants than a middle-aged man – not for nothing did Athenian defendants make a practice of bringing their sorrowing, fearful children into court with them.

The prominence of the chorus itself accounts for the prominence of lyric. The chorus-leader, throughout Greek tragedy, can of course engage in dialogue with the actors, but it is an almost invariable convention that the chorus-leader never makes *long* speeches, and in this play the leader's longest speech is of five lines (328-32). If the chorus are to be foregrounded as a leading character, they *must* sing a great deal, since only thus, within the conventions, can they present themselves on a large canvas. Likewise, if the central character is to be a collective one, it makes sense to introduce other collective characters who can be balanced against them: it may be significant that the other surviving Aeschylean play in which the chorus is prominent as a dramatic character in its own right, *Eumenides*, is also the play that comes nearest to having two subsidiary choruses like *Supp.* (Athena's temple-staff, who sing, and the members of the Areopagus Council, who are silent but whose votes decide Orestes' fate; see §§7.3 and 7.6.5).

A parallel may also be worth adducing for the long neglect of Danaus, from a play not of the 460s but of the 420s – the *Suppliant Women* of Euripides. Adrastus has come to Eleusis, with the mothers of the Seven against Thebes whose expedition he had led, to beg Theseus for Athenian assistance in securing the burial of the Seven. At first (113-262) he represents the petitioners as their main spokesman; later (cf. 354) Theseus takes him to an assembly of the Athenians. At 381 Theseus returns, giving instructions to a herald who is to be sent to Thebes; he is also accompanied again by Adrastus, but the text at this point gives no clue to it, and if Adrastus had not burst out at 513 (in response to a Theban herald) with 'You utter villain!' and been firmly silenced by Theseus ('it is for me to reply to this man') we would not even know he was present until 589. Apart from the exclamation just mentioned, he does not speak from 262 to 734. We need not go into the dramatic reasons for this; my purpose is merely to show that it could be done, even a generation after Aeschylus' death.

Nevertheless it could still be that in the context of the 460s *Supp.* had a slightly archaic feel about it. Sophocles was already competing, and would soon be suggesting or supporting the introduction of a third actor; and the silence of Danaus is rather different from the silence of Adrastus. It is one thing for Adrastus to be kept quiet by Theseus because Theseus wants to deal with the Theban herald himself, and quite another thing for Pelasgus to address himself exclusively to the daughters of Danaus when their father is present and even after they have called Pelasgus' attention to him (319-21), especially given that Greeks did not expect women to speak in public if it could possibly be avoided: Aeschylus' ploy does seem a rather clumsy device. No doubt Taplin 1977: 204 is right to claim that 'the dramatic technique is calculated', but that is not the same as saying it is fully satisfactory; and when Taplin adds that 'a good audience whose concentration has been captured will not even notice Danaus', one cannot help observing that at 319-21 they are actually *made* to notice him. In total effect *Supp.* is far more like one-actor tragedy than any other Aeschylean play, *Agamemnon* (cf. §2.2) not excepted. *Agamemnon* is nearly one-actor drama much of the time because, though there are often two actors present, they usually for some assignable reason fail to communicate with each other, as when Clytaemestra refuses to listen to what the Herald has to say or when Cassandra refuses to answer Clytaemestra. *The Suppliant Maidens* is nearly one-actor drama for the quite different reason that the characters are kept out of one another's way. Pelasgus ignores Danaus not for any motive of his own but because the author does not want the chorus to be overshadowed, and after 523 the two men are never on stage together.

But when all is said and done, *The Suppliant Maidens*, as a play of the 460s, differs in degree and not in kind from the rest of the Aeschylean corpus. It may well have differed too from the other plays of its own trilogy, as *Agamemnon* so notably does from *Eumenides*. The dramatic interest in *The Egyptians* is likely to have centred much more on Danaus and Aegyptus than on the chorus, and in the third play, on almost any view of its content, the Danaids' die was already cast and the characters whose action could affect the outcome were Danaus, Lynceus and Aphrodite. Aeschylus, as the *Oresteia* shows, was a master of variation in pace and style. In *Eumenides* he was to make the chorus *a* principal character. In *Supp.* he made the chorus *the* principal character; but the Danaids, unlike the Erinyes, during much of their play had an individual, Danaus, attached to them, and Aeschylus had a difficult problem in handling him, to which perhaps no wholly satisfactory solution existed. What this shows is not that the author of *Seven*, soon to be the author of the *Oresteia*, had temporarily forgotten how to construct a play, but that he was never afraid to experiment and take risks with his audience. And we happen to know that his gamble paid off: the production won first prize.

6.4. Movement and spectacle

> *The Suppliants* ... is a play of movements and multitudes. The scene is filled, and vacated, by very large throngs of persons, for the most part of dusky complexion and unfamiliar costume. There is a moment when we stop to ask, how many persons are in sight? On a mound or platform are Danaus and his fifty daughters, each (unless the poet misleads us) with an attendant girl; in the scene below are a herald and his Egyptian escort, presumably equal in number to the screaming women whom they would carry away; to them enters the king of Argos with a bodyguard presumably equal in number to the Egyptians whom they repulse. Can the total be less than 203? The multitudes, the outlandish costumes, the black faces, the threats of the one party and screams of the other, compose a scene without parallel in the remains of Greek Tragedy.

Thus Denys Page, in the introduction to his edition of *Agamemnon* (Denniston & Page 1957: xxx); in a footnote he admits that 'assuming a Chorus of 12, contrary to the surface evidence' the number of performers can be reduced to 51, and we may add that if the maidservants are regarded as a post-Aeschylean addition (see p. 118n.6) it will fall to 39. This may still be, in Page's words, 'a considerable crowd', but it is less than the 50 who took part in every performance of dithyramb in the same *orkhêstra*, and is of the same order as the number on stage at the end of *Eumenides* (see §7.6.5) and indeed at some moments of certain plays of Euripides.[27] It remains true that *The Suppliant Maidens* contains more distinct and distinctive groups of persons, and more and more varied large-scale group movements, than almost any other extant tragedy. In this section I will attempt to catalogue the significant movements that take place during the play.[28] Within the acting area there are two basic locations, the *orkhêstra* floor and the altar-mound; beyond it there are two basic directions, that to the city of Argos and that to (or rather from) the shore, the sea and Egypt.

1 — The Danaids enter from the seaward direction. The anapaestic passage 1-39 accompanies their march into, and perhaps round, the *orkhêstra*; by 40 they are in position to dance and sing. Danaus, entering with or after them, goes straight to the mound at the rear, which serves him as a look-out point.

209-31 — The Danaids, on their father's direction, approach the mound, make obeisance to a number of gods individually and then (222) to all the gods of the sanctuary collectively, and then go on to the mound (after 223) and sit down in the pose of suppliants.

233 — Pelasgus enters from the direction of Argos, accompanied by soldiers; there is at least one chariot (181, 183), in which (if there is only one) he will be riding. The number of

soldiers is uncertain; it need not be large, but there must be enough to provide separate escorts for Danaus and Pelasgus when they respectively leave for Argos. Taplin's guess (1977: 201) that there were about a dozen men may well be correct.

490 Danaus descends from the mound.

504 Danaus leaves for Argos, with some (probably half) of Pelasgus' men as escort.

516-23 On Pelasgus' instructions (508) the Danaids move down to the 'level meadow' of the *orkhêstra*. Pelasgus with his remaining retinue leaves for Argos. These two movements must of course be co-ordinated, since the Danaids will be occupying the space which Pelasgus' men are vacating.

600 Danaus returns (alone) from Argos.

624 Danaus goes up to the mound, whence at 713, looking seaward, he sees the Egyptian fleet arriving.

733 At some point Danaus must descend from the mound, and the commencement of the epirrhematic dialogue (see §7.5) between him and his daughters, in which they repeatedly seek comfort from him (734, 748), is an appropriate moment.

775 Danaus again leaves for Argos.

825 A party of Egyptians, led by a herald, enter from the seaward direction.[29] Since they have come to seize the Danaids and take them away, there are probably again about twelve of them, whether or not they constitute a chorus in the sense of having words to sing as a group. The herald, by the nature of his status, cannot have been armed, and the other Egyptians probably are not armed either: they have not come to fight anyone but to take possession of what they regard as their property (cf. 918, 932-3).

825-35 The Danaids break into panic; at 832 they rush to the altars for sanctuary.

885 The Herald and his men begin to advance towards the mound, as if intent on dragging off the Danaids off by force, though they never actually take violent action (at 925 the Herald is warned not to lay a finger on the Danaids, not condemned for having done so).

911 Pelasgus enters from the Argos direction with armed soldiers, probably as many as at 234 (they will again divide into two groups later); this time there is no sign of chariots (with the Egyptians occupying much of the *orkhêstra*, chariots would be in the way).

928 The Herald retreats from the mound (Pelasgus' warning at 925 suggests that at that moment he had not yet moved).

951 The Herald and his men leave, going towards the seashore.

954-65 Pelasgus detaches (probably) half his men to serve as an escort for the Danaids.

966-76 Pelasgus leaves for Argos with the remainder of his men, and as they go they are replaced in the *orkhêstra* by the Danaids who now finally leave the altar-mound; the combined movement is similar to that at 516-23.

980 Danaus arrives from Argos with an escort of spearmen. These are very likely the same performers who left with Pelasgus shortly before; they no doubt merge with the Danaids' own escort to form once again a group of twelve.

1073 Danaus, his daughters and the Argive escort all leave for Argos; the text does not allow us to determine how they were arranged. This is the *seventh* occasion in the play when armed Argive soldiers have marched into or out of the acting area; they have been involved in more such movements than any other individual or group in the play.

The following table shows how the two main zones of the acting area are occupied at various stages of the play; the passages omitted from the table are transitional ones, in several of which the *orkhêstra* is vacated by one group and almost immediately occupied by another.

	Orkhêstra floor	*Altar mound*
1-209	Danaids	Danaus
233-504	Pelasgus and soldiers	Danaus and Danaids
524-599	Danaids	[vacant]
625-733	Danaids	Danaus
734-775	Danaus and Danaids	[vacant]
776-824	Danaids	[vacant]
836-910	Herald and Egyptians	Danaids
911-965	Herald and Egyptians (till 951) Pelasgus and soldiers	Danaids
980-1073	Danaus, Danaids and soldiers	[vacant]

6.5. Io

The Danaids are descendants of Io. This fact is clearly basic to the presentation of them in *The Suppliant Maidens*. They speak and sing of her story over and over again. The myth existed in various forms; its simplest presentation in our play is in the interrogation of the Danaids by Pelasgus (291-324). Io was a priestess of Hera at Argos. Zeus fell in love with her *and slept with her* (295-6); this became known to Hera, who turned Io into a cow – whether out of a jealous desire to hurt her, or in order to frustrate Zeus, or both – *but Zeus coupled with her again in the form of a bull* (300-1). It is significant that the two events which I have italicized are mentioned only in the interrogation (when it is vital for the Danaids to demonstrate that the story of Io as known to them precisely corresponds with the story of Io as known to the Argives[30]) and that in all their many lyric references to Io the chorus never speak of them; it is as if they wanted to believe, contrary to facts they know, that Io always remained a virgin. It is probably significant too that these early consummations of Zeus' desire for Io do not sit altogether easily with the story of the miraculous conception of Epaphus, for since in Greek myth generally 'the beds of gods are never unfruitful' (*Odyssey* 11.249-50) one would have expected Io to have been pregnant long before reaching Egypt.[31] The second, tauriform copulation appears in this form in none of the many other surviving versions of the Io story, and was presumably invented by Aeschylus. Aeschylus, in other words, is going out of his way at this stage to associate Io firmly, right at the outset of her story, with the affirmation, not the rejection, of sexuality – an association which he then has the Danaids totally ignore.

Hera's next move was to set the hundred-eyed Argus to guard Io (303-5), and when Argus was slain by Hermes she sent a gadfly (306-8) which drove Io from land to land until she reached Egypt; there Zeus made her pregnant by the touch of his hand (Greek *epaphê*) and she gave birth to Epaphus, whose daughter was Libya, whose son was Belus, whose sons were Danaus and Aegyptus.

Such is the plain story. To the Danaids Io is the symbol and evidence of three things above all: their claim on the Argives, their claim on Zeus, and the superfluity of sex. They constantly recur to the conception of Epaphus: they are the descendants of one who was brought into being without sexual union, without *gamos* – and in their pedigree as given to Pelasgus (314-21), only one parent in each generation is mentioned.[32]

Their first reference to Io introduces all these themes:

> ... the land of Argos, whence was created our stock,
> which boasts descent from Zeus through his breath and his touching
> of the gadfly-driven cow (15-18).

The themes are restated more discursively in the choral song that follows (40-56). Formally this song is an appeal to the Argives to recognize the Danaids as their kinsfolk; but its first stanza does not mention the Argives and puts all the emphasis on Zeus, who is named twice, and on Epaphus. Epaphus' name is the last of five closely-spaced words beginning with the prefix *ep(i)-*,[33] which could be strung together to mean 'breath and touch created the aptly-named Epaphus'. The idea of Io as evidence of a claim on Zeus becomes explicit later in the long *parodos*, when the Danaids pray to Zeus to ensure that 'the offspring of a highly-honoured mother' avoid 'the beds of men' (139-43) and warn him that if he spurns their prayers he will be justly censured for 'having dishonoured the child of the cow, whom he himself created and begot' (167-74).

The claim on Argos that Io represents is formally stated in the dialogue with Pelasgus, beginning with the first thing the Danaids tell him about their identity ('we claim to be Argive by race, the offspring of the cow who bore a fine child', 274-5), and continuing through their account of Io's history to conclude:

> Now that you know my ancestral race
> please act to succour this company of Argives (323-4).

Pelasgus accepts the claim, and the chorus make no further mention of it. The claim on Zeus remains, and as soon as Pelasgus has departed the Danaids sing an entire ode of ten stanzas (524-99) which is almost entirely about Io, beginning with a firm reminder to Zeus, 'the Toucher of Io' (535), that they are his descendants (527, 533, 536-7), and continuing with an extended description of Io's wanderings, which began in the Argive pastures (540) and ended in Egypt, 'the bountiful pasture-meads of Zeus' (558), to which she came as 'a maddened creature driven by Hera' (564). One of the countries through which she passed *en route* – apparently Phoenicia and/or Palestine – is spoken of as 'the land of Aphrodite, rich in wheat'.[34] This is the first mention of Aphrodite in the play, and it is Aphrodite's enemies that make it; but Io had passed through it without stopping, to find rest in a land whose patron was Zeus; and Zeus 'with painless strength' (576) ended her suffering and tears and by his touch (592) and his breath (577) gave her a son whose divine parentage was recognized by the whole land (584-5). And then the chorus go back to their reason for telling this tale:

> On whom of the gods could I more appropriately call,
> whose deeds give me a greater right to claim his aid?
> My very father, the Lord who begot me with his own hand,
> the great, wise, ancient artificer of my race,
> the all-resourceful, Zeus god of fair winds (590-4).

Zeus' answer to this prayer, as we have seen, is to send fair winds (!) to speed the pursuing ships in safety to Argos (cf. 734-5, 744, 1045-6); and for a long time after the Danaids learn this they make no more appeals to Zeus in the name of Io, but only as god of suppliants (811-5 and probably 885-92). With the return of Pelasgus and the dismissal of the Herald, however, they recover confidence: they pray for support to all the gods of Argos (except Aphrodite, 1031-3), and in the very last song of the play they invoke the memory of Io again:

> May Zeus the King prevent
> a hateful marriage with evil men,

> Zeus who gave Io a good release from her sorrows
> by covering her with his healing hand,
> making violence kindly (1062-7).

That last phrase, 'making violence kindly', recalls the 'painless strength' of 576 which referred to the same action, and the two together give us a crucial clue to the attitude to sex which Danaos has implanted in his daughters. They see it as a form of bodily violence, an infliction of pain, a wounding.[35] Now perhaps we understand the cry of pain they uttered at 142 = 152, demanding that Zeus allow

> the offspring of a highly-honoured mother
> to avoid the beds of men – ah, ah! –
> unmated and unconquered.

No wonder they dwell so eagerly on the end of the Zeus-Io story, while suppressing its beginning. No wonder that each will be willing to take to her marriage-bed a dagger, to wound before she is wounded, and that all but one use it. Danaus has done his work well. Myth to the Greeks was among other things a powerful instrument of education and socialization, and its use and abuse was already a matter for discussion by thinkers such as Xenophanes, with whose work, as we shall see later (§11.5), Aeschylus was familiar. By its positive and negative images it helped to train the boy for his future role as citizen and warrior, the girl for hers as wife and mother. In *The Suppliant Maidens* we can see how the myth of Io has been used to train girls *away* from their socially 'proper' role. It may not be accidental that the play contains no trace of any *other* role for the Danaids. In many versions of the myth, as we have seen, including some of the oldest, they engaged in 'masculine' pursuits like chariot-racing, hunting and war. There is nothing of this in *The Suppliant Maidens*. Pelasgus does indeed think briefly that the strange women who have come to his city may be the 'man-shunning, meat-eating Amazons' (287-9); but he rejects the identification because they have no bows and arrows (288). Even Amymone, as we have seen, probably went to Lerna, in Aeschylus' version, not to hunt but for the quintessentially 'feminine' task of fetching water. Aeschylus' Danaids, as their father has moulded them, are not women who try to live a man's life. They are women who have no meaningful life to look forward to at all. Towards the end of *The Suppliant Maidens* Danaus warns them to 'value chastity more than life' (1013) – having just betrayed the unnaturalness of this demand by an emphatic assertion of the power of sexual desire (997-1005) – and they assure him they will. The phrase could be understood in three senses, and in reference to the Danaids it would be true in all of them. In the first place, rather than lose their virginity, the Danaids are prepared to *die*, as they have already said and proved. In the second place, rather than lose their virginity, they are prepared to *kill*, as they will prove later. And in the third place – though they are as little aware of this as their father is apparently aware of the internal contradictions of his own position – rather than lose their virginity, they are prepared to *endure the living death* of permanent spinsterhood and childless old age. Or do they suppose that Zeus in his good time will grant them the same blessing which they believe him to have granted Io?

Notes

1. There is no reason to doubt that these were represented in *Supp.* and *The Danaids* by the usual chorus of twelve. The Aeschylean chorus represented a group, not a group of a precise size: we are not, for example, meant to imagine that an outburst of panic by twelve women threatened the safety of Thebes, or that there were only a dozen mourners over the bodies of Eteocles and Polyneices.

2. And hence, presumably, to have become undisputed king of Egypt and given his name to the country. In *The Suppliant Maidens* the country is called 'Egypt' only by the herald representing Aegyptus' sons (873); the family of Danaus, and the Argives, refer to Egypt and Egyptians as the land and people of the Nile (e.g. 3-4, 281, 308).

3. It was not necessarily impious to reject a supplication (Naiden 2006). A supplication was essentially a plea for justice, and the person supplicated was perfectly entitled to reject a plea that was not in accordance with justice. It was only *once he had accepted it* that he became bound by a religious duty not to betray the suppliant.

4. As usual in spoken dialogue, the chorus-leader would speak in the name of the whole chorus.

5. Reading *philois* with the manuscript; *philais* (Schütz) would refer to the Danaids' maidservants, on whom see below.

6. The strongest argument for the maidservants is that the passage 977-9, in which the audience's attention is specially drawn to them, is utterly pointless if they are not about to take a distinctive role in the action. If on other grounds it is preferable to assign 1034ff. to the Argive escort, there is a strong case for deleting 977-9, which could have been added by a later producer who wanted to swell the ranks of the final procession; see Sommerstein 1995: 120-1. For a possible role for the Argives of the escort at the end of the trilogy, see §6.2. Another possibility (Hester 1987) is that the dissenting voice is that of Hypermestra, the future rebel (see §6.2); there is no other known case of an individual character stepping, as it were, out of the ranks of the chorus, but Hypermestra must certainly have been an individual character in *The Danaids*, and if she can step out of the chorus *between* plays, why should she not do so *within* a play?

7. By a different route from that described in *Supp.* 540-64; but that was inevitable once the decision had been taken to bring her to the remote region of Scythia, near the outer Ocean, where Prometheus is.

8. Another possibility was that the title as transmitted in most sources was incorrect, the true title having been *Aegyptus* as the play is named in the Byzantine *Etymologicum Gudianum* (ζ578 de Stefani); several authors, including Euripides, bring Aegyptus to Argos with or after his sons.

9. Scholia to *Prometheus Bound* 853; to Euripides, *Orestes* 872; to *Iliad* 1.42 and 4.171; and to Statius, *Thebaid* 2.222 and 6.269.

10. Aeschylus may have made the oracle say 'the bedfellow of your daughter' or

the like, without restriction to legitimate wedlock. The scholium on *Iliad* 4.171 mentions that Danaus had advised his daughters 'to resist by force *those who tried to rob them of their virginity*'.

11. Presumably thanks to a reconciliation with Lynceus; cf. [Apollodorus], *Library* 2.1.5.

12. In the first edition of this book – following Rösler 1993, who in turn was modifying a proposal by Sicherl 1986 – I argued for the same conclusion on the basis of a scholium on *Supp.* 37 which Sicherl, Rösler and I took to mean that the Danaids were determined to resist marriage 'for fear of their father being killed'. Garvie 2005: xviii-xix has shown that we were wrong. The scholiast is trying to explain why, according to the Danaids, 'Right forbids' their cousins to force them into marriage; and his explanation is that to do so is improper 'because their father has not <yet> been killed'. If Danaus were dead, his daughters, under Athenian law, would automatically be married to the nearest kinsmen who claimed them (in this case the sons of Aegyptus – Aegyptus himself, it may be presumed, would waive his own claim); as he is alive, he and he alone has the right to give them in marriage when, and to whom, he wishes. But the case for placing *The Egyptians* first does not by any means depend solely on the evidence of this scholium. (What the scholium *does* tell us is that later in the trilogy Danaus *will* meet a violent end.)

13. Not of the sons of Aegyptus, who would have been called *Aigypti(a)dai*, not *Aigyptioi*.

14. Since Danaus needs to keep this information secret, it can have been communicated to the audience only in a soliloquy, i.e. in the prologue of the play.

15. There is some reason (based on Euripides, *Orestes* 871-3, with scholia) to suspect that in Phrynichus' treatment of the Danaid story, Danaus was prosecuted before the Argive people by Aegyptus. This in itself makes it likely that if there was a trial in Aeschylus' play, the accused was *not* Danaus.

16. Pausanias 2.19.6; see Rösler 1993:16-20 (pp. 189-93 of the English version in Lloyd 2007).

17. Horace, *Odes* 3.11.45; Ovid, *Heroides* 14; [Apollodorus], *Library* 2.1.5.

18. We would have direct evidence of this if Casadio 1993 is right to suggest that Archilochus fr. dub. 305 West, whose source is the wildly inaccurate John Malalas, is really a citation not of Archilochus but of Aeschylus; Malalas' statement is that 'Lynceus made war against King Danaus, killed him, and took his kingship and his daughter'.

19. A reprise with variation of their entry in *Supp.* carrying suppliants' olive-branches; it is probably significant that in *Supp.* 21 these branches are termed *enkheiridia*, a word which means literally 'things held in the hand' but whose normal meaning in ordinary usage is 'daggers'.

20. Hypermestra must have been silent in this scene (since the two speaking actors will have been playing Lynceus and Aphrodite), and may have been silent on her earlier appearance too.

21. We cannot tell for certain how fr. 13 ('It is your destiny to be mated and mine to mate') fitted into this structure; but the language is less that of a wooer than of one who considers himself entitled by right to the possession of the woman addressed, and the speaker may well be Silenus, leader of the satyrs, trying unskilfully to persuade Amymone to accept a union which he is determined she shall not escape in any case (compare the treatment of Danaë in *The Net-Haulers*, see Chapter 9).

22. This sequence may well in fact have a dramatic point in creating the impression that Pelasgus is, as it were, on the way out as a ruler, and Danaus on

the way in; it became important to do this once Aeschylus had decided that the actual assumption of power by Danaus would occur between plays rather than within a play.

23. This is the date given for Sophocles' début by the chronicle of Eusebius; Plutarch (*Cimon* 8.8-9) says that Sophocles' first victory, in 468, came with his first production. The less romantic alternative is more likely to be correct.

24. Even Scullion 2002: 87-101, who argues that on structural and stylistic grounds there is a good case for placing *Supp.* in the middle 470s, finally accepts that, in the absence of any evidence that Sophocles' career began that early, '470 ... is in the end perhaps the safest guess' (p. 101).

25. Not without documentary evidence; see the passage by Page quoted at the beginning of §6.4.

26. Contrast (for instance) those other husband-killers, the Lemnian women (see Chapter 3), whose best-known individual, Hypsipyle, is the leader and inspirer of their enterprise.

27. Thus between lines 87 and 364 of Euripides' *Suppliant Women* there are present on stage fifteen mothers, fifteen maidservants (cf. 72, 1115), at least seven boys (cf. 106-8), Adrastus, and Theseus and Aethra each with attendants, a total unlikely to be less than 44.

28. I omit consideration of the Danaids' maidservants, since it is doubtful whether they figured at all in the original production (see above). Some remarks have been made previously (§2.2) about masks and costumes in *Supp.*

29. It is uncertain, owing to the state of the text in 825-35, exactly when the Egyptians enter; I follow M.L. West 1990b: 152-4.

30. A fact acknowledged by Pelasgus at 310.

31. As indeed Aeschylus' contemporary Bacchylides (19.39-42) supposed her to have been. Bachvarova 2001 has argued that in Aeschylus too we are meant to understand that Epaphus was conceived at Argos, and that Zeus's touch in Egypt served merely to ease his birth; but how is an audience supposed to know that when the Danaids say that their race is descended from Zeus 'through his breath and his touching' (17-18) and that 'Zeus the Toucher begot [Epaphus] with his hand' (313, cf. 592) they are lying?

32. It was normal enough to trace one's descent through the male line only; but when the line being traced included a female (such as Libya here) it was usual to mention the father of her child, especially if (as in this case) it was a god (Poseidon).

33. *epipnoias* 'breath', *ephapsin* 'touch', *epônumian* 'significant name', *epekraineto* 'fulfilled, effected', *Epaphon*: these five words occupy 20 out of a sequence of 30 syllables.

34. The reference is probably to the famous temple of Aphrodite (Astarte, Ashtoreth) at Ascalon, said by Herodotus (1.105) to be the oldest temple of Aphrodite in the world.

35. Aphrodite too, in *The Danaids*, will speak of sexual penetration as a wounding (fr. 44.1) – but a wounding which the female partner (here Earth) desires as passionately to undergo as the male does to effect.

7

The *Oresteia*

The tetralogy known as the *Oresteia*, comprising *Agamemnon*, *Choephoroi*, *Eumenides* and the satyr-play *Proteus*, was produced in 458, the *khorêgos* being one Xenocles of Aphidna. It won first prize. The first three plays survive in their entirety, except that most of the first half of the prologue of *Choephoroi* is missing. Of *Proteus* we have six fragments totalling 17 words.

7.1. *Agamemnon*

The scene is before the palace of the Atreidae, Agamemnon and Menelaus, at Argos (for their family relationships see Genealogies, p. 318). It is the tenth year since the two kings, with most of the city's warrior youth, sailed for Troy to avenge the abduction of Menelaus' wife Helen by the Trojan prince Paris. It has been prophesied that within this year Troy will be captured, and Agamemnon's wife Clytaemestra, 'a woman with the counsels of a man' (11), has posted a man to watch nightly from the palace roof for the lighting of the last of a chain of beacon-fires which it has been arranged will signify the fall of the city. This watchman opens the play and the trilogy. He describes the hardships of his watch and laments the sorry state of the household. Then he sees the fire in the distance, shouts and dances for joy, proclaims the news for Clytaemestra to hear inside the house, and disappears within.

Presently there arrive at the palace a group of elderly and respected Argive citizens, who form the chorus of the play. They have come to ask Clytaemestra the reason why sacrifices are being made and incense burnt at all the altars of the city. But first they reflect on the mission of Agamemnon and Menelaus, sponsored by Zeus (Zeus Xenios, the patron of hospitality, because Paris had abused the hospitality of Menelaus) yet sure to involve great suffering for Greeks as well as Trojans (40-71); and when Clytaemestra does not immediately come out to meet them, they sing at length (104-257) about the events that occurred at the time the expedition set out: an omen; its interpretation by the prophet Calchas; the long delay caused by adverse winds at the port of Aulis; Calchas' advice on how this could be ended; Agamemnon's reluctant but decisive acceptance of this advice, and his sacrifice of his daughter Iphigeneia. Midway in this narrative, with no obvious connection with it (though as we shall see [§7.5], the metrical-musical pattern assures the listener that at some deeper level there *is* a connection), they sing three stanzas which have become known as the 'Hymn to Zeus', and the last of which in particular has often been seen as embodying ideas fundamental to the trilogy:

Zeus – whoever he may be, if that
is the name that he likes to be called,
then by that name I address him:
weighing all things in the scale,
I can find nothing to compare
save Zeus, if one would truly cast off
the burden of fruitless anxiety.

Not even he who was formerly great,
puffed up with the confidence of invincibility –
he shall not even be spoken of as 'the late';
and he who was born later is gone,
having met his vanquisher:
one who enthusiastically calls on Zeus with songs of victory
will be wholly in his right mind –

Zeus who put men on the road to wisdom,
who laid down and made valid
the law 'by suffering, learning'.
There drips before the heart, instead of sleep,
the pain that reminds of suffering; and good sense
comes to one against one's will.
Violent, it seems, is the favour of the gods
who sit on the august bench of command (160-83).

That last phrase 'violent ... is the favour' is an inverted form of the same oxymoron that was applied twice in *The Suppliant Maidens* to the touch by which Zeus made Io pregnant (see §6.5).

Clytaemestra comes out of the palace, and tells the elders that Troy is in the Argives' hands. They do not at first believe her, but when she gives a vivid (and largely conjectural) account of how the beacons carried the news from Troy to Argos (281-316), followed by an equally vivid (and wholly conjectural) word-picture of life in the captured city (320-37), they are completely convinced, and proceed to praise the gods for having punished the crime of Paris – though before long their reflections on this lead to disturbing thoughts about Greek bereavements and about popular resentment against the Atreidae: 'I have an anxiety that waits to hear about something done under cover of night; for the gods do not fail to take aim at those who have killed many' (459-62). Agamemnon will be returning to a situation of great danger – though the audience know that this danger comes not, as the elders suppose, from his subjects but from his wife.

Agamemnon's herald now arrives (503). He greets the soil and the gods of his native land and announces the impending homecoming of the victorious king. He is about to go into the palace when Clytaemestra forestalls him by coming out and, without giving him a chance to speak to her, gives him a message for her husband (to come home at once, where he will find an adoring people and a faithful wife) and immediately withdraws (587-614). The elders then ask the herald about Menelaus (of whom he has so far said nothing) and learn that there has been a terrible disaster: a great storm has scattered the Greek fleet and wrecked a large part of it, and Agamemnon's ship is the only one known to have come through safely (636-80). With this the herald departs, and the chorus sing of Helen, who had once seemed to be a blessing on Troy but turned into a curse. This leads them to reflect (750-82) on the law of life that deeds of impiety or *hybris*, to which the wealthy and fortunate are particularly tempted, often 'breed' further deeds of the same kind – a law, we can see, that applies not only to Helen or Paris or the Trojans. Prosperity plus moral sense equals safety; prosperity minus moral sense equals deadly peril.

Upon these words, Agamemnon enters, riding in a carriage, magnificently arrayed. At his side, silent and motionless, sits a young woman, in the garb and accoutrements of a prophet of Apollo, who is easily identified as Cassandra, the daughter of Priam, awarded to Agamemnon at the distribution of human and other spoils. The chorus greet him, and warn him against disaffected citizens (783-809). He congratulates the gods of Argos (and himself, perhaps rather too much) on the victory, while making no reference of any kind to the thousands of Argive dead; he assures the elders that he will be on the alert for disloyalty and punish it severely. As he is about to step down from the carriage and enter the palace, he, like the herald, is forestalled by Clytaemestra (855). She delivers a fulsome speech of welcome, and orders her servants to spread a costly, delicate crimson fabric along Agamemnon's path into the palace (905-11), as if to advertise both the almost superhuman status of the conqueror of Troy and the wealth of a royal house that can afford such blatant waste. Agamemnon, who has found his wife's flattery excessive, is extremely reluctant to accept an honour likely to arouse the resentment both of men and of gods, but she contrives to persuade him that it is the right thing to do (arguing that 'he is not enviable who is not envied', 939) and he surrenders, insisting only on taking off his shoes first, and asking Clytaemestra, with remarkable insensitivity, to give a kind reception to 'this foreign woman' Cassandra (950-5). He then marches over the fabrics and into the palace, to the accompaniment of a speech by his wife which to the audience (but to no one on stage, except Cassandra) has highly sinister overtones; and as he enters his house for the last time, she raises her hands to heaven and prays (973-4):

> Zeus, Zeus, god of fulfilment, fulfil my prayers,
> and take good care to fulfil what you are going to fulfil!

Agamemnon's return has left the elders apprehensive: an inner voice is telling them that something terrible is going to happen, and their reason is unable to silence this voice. Their words (975-1034) are as obscure as their thoughts are confused, but they seem to feel, as before, that Agamemnon is in danger because he is a shedder of blood and because his prosperity has become too great. Meanwhile Cassandra is still sitting in the carriage. Clytaemestra comes out and invites her into the palace. Cassandra does not reply, indeed gives no indication of having heard her, and Clytaemestra retires defeated. Then, on the kindly request of the chorus-leader, Cassandra does step down from the carriage – only to cry out in horror (1072-3) at the sight of the pillar and altar of Apollo Agyieus standing before the house – 'Apollo my destroyer' she cries, with a play on the literal meaning of the name, 'for you have utterly destroyed me a second time' (1081-2). And presently she begins to experience, and describe, visions in which she sees both past and future atrocities committed in this palace. The past atrocities are those connected with Agamemnon's father and uncle, Atreus and Thyestes, and are recalled here for the first time in the play: Thyestes seduced the wife of Atreus, and Atreus in revenge invited Thyestes to a feast at which he was made to eat unknowingly the flesh of his own children. The future atrocities are those now impending, the murder by Clytaemestra of her husband and of Cassandra herself.

The elders understand what Cassandra says about Atreus and Thyestes, but completely misunderstand her prophecies of what is now to happen: the idea of Agamemnon being killed by a woman is so incredible that it simply fails to register with them. Cassandra, in fury with Apollo (who, being in love with her, had blessed her with the gift of prophecy – and then, when she rejected his advances, cursed her with the destiny of never being believed), tears off and tramples on her prophetic insignia (1264-72). She prophesies the coming of 'another to avenge us, a mother-slaying offshoot, an avenger of his father' (1280-1). She prays for an easy death; has a last moment of revulsion as she approaches the door of the palace, for her the gate of Hades; and goes inside.

Cutting across the reflections of the elders come two loud cries from within (1343, 1345). 'I think,' says the chorus-leader, 'that the deed has been done', and the elders proceed to take counsel together. Assuming that Agamemnon has been killed by a group of political malcontents, the majority favour immediate action to nip in the bud what seems to be a *coup d'état* aimed at establishing a 'tyranny' (1355, 1365). They are then, however, persuaded out of this by a group which argues that there is no proof yet that the king is dead at all, and it is agreed that the first thing to do is discover exactly what has happened. At this moment the scene of death is revealed to them and the audience. Agamemnon is lying dead in a silver bathtub, pierced by three wounds, enveloped from head to foot in what looks like a robe of fine material, except that it has no holes for head or arms. Cassandra lies beside the tub. Over them stands the triumphant murderer, Clytaemestra, bloody sword in hand. In defiant speeches (1372ff., 1412ff., 1431ff.) she glories in her deed and challenges the elders to a trial of strength, confident in the support of Aegisthus (the surviving son of Thyestes), her adultery with whom she brazenly avows. She pooh-poohs the elders' denunciations of her, and to their laments for Agamemnon, their 'most kindly guardian' (1452), she replies that he treacherously killed her daughter, and that she herself will see to his burial. The elders remain unconvinced (1560-4):

> Here comes one reproach to meet another,
> and it is a hard struggle to judge:
> the plunderer is plundered, the killer pays.
> But it remains while Zeus remains on his throne
> that he who does must suffer: that is his law.

Clytaemestra for her part declares her willingness to make a bargain with 'the daemon of the house of Pleisthenes':[1] she is prepared to sacrifice most of the family's wealth for the sake of ending the sequence of intestine murders among its members (1567-76).

Before the chorus can comment on this, Aegisthus enters, accompanied by an armed guard, in peacetime the hallmark of the *tyrannos*. Hailing the 'welcome light of the day that has brought justice' (1577) he gives a tendentious version of the family's recent history[2] and announces that he has taken over Agamemnon's property and the rulership of Argos. When the elders protest, insulting him for his alleged cowardice and calling him 'woman' (1625), he threatens them with the crudest forms of repression; but they defy him and express their hopes for the return of Agamemnon's son Orestes 'to become the triumphant killer of both these two' (1648). Orestes, we had earlier been told, had been sent away to Phocis by his mother, ostensibly for his own safety in case of political unrest (877-86), really no doubt in order to leave the Argive throne free for future children of Clytaemestra and Aegisthus.

Faced with this public call for his assassination, Aegisthus orders his guards to take action; the elders proclaim their readiness to die rather than submit to tyranny, and Aegisthus grimly replies that 'die' is just the right word (1653). But now Clytaemestra intervenes, begging her 'dearest of men' not to shed further blood, and urging the elders to disperse quietly to their homes. Both parties are reluctant to comply, but eventually Clytaemestra steers her lover into the palace, saying 'you and I, ruling this house, will order everything properly', and the elders are left with nothing to do but depart, which they do in silence, as presumably, at the same time but in the opposite direction, do Aegisthus' guards.

7.2. *Choephoroi*[3]

It is some seven years after the death of Agamemnon. Two young men, one of them bearing a marked resemblance to Agamemnon especially in the colour and texture of his hair, enter as if arriving from a journey; they are Orestes and his friend Pylades, the son of his foster-father Strophius (cf.

Ag. 881), and traditionally his assistant in effecting his revenge. Orestes advances to the tomb of Agamemnon and begins to pray there. The first half of his prologue speech has been lost from the only manuscript, but several certain or probable quotations or paraphrases of parts of it have survived in other ancient sources, particularly in Aristophanes' *Frogs* (1123-76) where Euripides is made to single out this prologue for critical analysis. Orestes first, we can see, prays to Hermes to be his ally, and then calls on his father in Hades; and he deposits at the tomb a lock of his hair as a belated mourning-tribute (6-7). Just as he completes the rituals he sees a group of women (the chorus) approaching, clad in black, carrying jugs of some liquid (no doubt on their heads as women habitually did); another woman, of higher status, accompanies them, whom Orestes recognizes as his sister Electra. He and Pylades move out of the way as the women enter the *orkhêstra* and approach the tomb.

The chorus proves to be composed of middle-aged to elderly (cf. 171) palace slaves of Asiatic origin; they have rents in their clothes and gashes in their cheeks. They sing of how a woman in the palace (not named, but easily identifiable) had a terrifying dream during the night, which has been interpreted as signifying that 'those below the earth are wroth with their slayers in angry censure' (40-1); she has therefore now sent them with drink-offerings to Agamemnon's tomb, though they are certain that there can be no 'atonement when blood has fallen to the ground' (48, cf. 61-74). They reflect also on how the once unchallengeable reverence of the people for their rulers has vanished, so that now consent to government is based on nothing but fear (54-60); they themselves, however, remain devotedly loyal to Agamemnon and his family, whom they still call 'our masters' (53, 82).

Electra advances to lead the group in the act of presenting the offerings. She asks the advice of the chorus on how to perform the rite, and how to frame the accompanying prayer, given that she is acting on behalf of a mother who is hateful both to her and to the spirit of Agamemnon. They encourage her to make the offering as if it were her own, and to pray for blessings on 'all who hate Aegisthus', including especially Orestes, and then, as regards 'those responsible for the murder', to pray for the coming of some god or man … and here Electra asks, significantly, 'do you mean a judge (*dikastês*) or an avenger (*dikêphoros*)?' (120). The chorus-leader brushes the distinction aside: 'Say simply: one who will kill them in requital.' But Electra asks again: 'And is this a righteous thing for me to ask of the gods?' to which the response is: 'To repay your enemy with evil? Of course!' It is worth noting that the avenger for whose coming the chorus hope is apparently *not* identical with Orestes, an impression that will be confirmed in a moment when Electra prays for the return of Orestes (138-9) and for the coming of an avenger (142-4) as if they were two entirely separate things.

After her prayer and the pouring of the drink-offerings (which is accompanied by a short choral song combining lamentation and the wish for an avenger), Electra suddenly sees the lock of hair that Orestes had left at the tomb. She recognizes its resemblance to her own, and guesses it must be that of Orestes – sent from abroad, perhaps. The discovery unleashes a torrent of emotion within her (183ff.), and she cannot decide whether to believe the offering really comes from Orestes or not. Then she sees a 'second piece of evidence' (205), two sets of footprints, one of which closely resembles her own in shape. She is almost out of her mind with the tension: 'agony is here, and blasting of the wits' (211).

Orestes, listening to this, can wait no longer, and comes forward to tell his sister that 'you have come into view of that which you have long prayed for'. Electra, who has not seen Orestes since he was a small boy, does not know what he is talking about, and when he says 'I am he' (219) she at first does not believe it; but he proves his identity by producing a cloth embroidered by Electra herself, and with great rejoicing she accepts him as her beloved brother. Orestes prays to Zeus to give his aid to 'the orphan offspring of the eagle-father who died in the woven toils of the terrible serpent' (247-9), reminding him that his own credibility is at stake (for if he fails them he will 'no longer be able to send mortals signs they will believe', 258-9). The chorus-leader warns him and Electra to moderate their rapture for fear they may be noticed and denounced to the rulers, 'whom I long to see one day perish in the pitchy ooze of the fire' (267-8). The chorus still seem to assume that it will be someone other than Orestes who brings about that desirable consummation. But Orestes knows this cannot be so. Apollo at Delphi has explicitly ordered him to kill the murderers of his father, under threat of the most appalling physical, mental and social sufferings if he fails (269-96); he has no choice but to obey this oracle, and in any case has other sufficient motives of his own for the deed – his grief for his father, his exclusion from his rightful inheritance, and the disgrace to Argos of being ruled by 'two women' (298-305).

Orestes, Electra, Pylades (who remains silent) and the chorus now stand before the tomb and pray, one after another, to the ghost of Agamemnon for his aid, in what is at the same time a delayed funeral lament – for Agamemnon was buried in secret, without proper lamentations and without the presence of his children (430-50). This *kommos*,[4] as it is often called, is a vast lyric complex taking up almost one-sixth of the whole play. It is addressed first to Agamemnon, then (from 380) to Zeus and the underworld powers including the goddesses of vengeance, the Erinyes. Before the end, however, Orestes becomes the addressee (439ff., 451ff.) as the chorus, and to some extent Electra, strive to prepare him mentally for the hard task ahead; and he himself states explicitly (434-8) that he intends to kill Clytaemestra, though he adds that once he has done it his wish is for his own death. At the end of the *kommos* the chorus sum up its grim message:

> It is for the house to apply the dressing
> to cure these ills, and it cannot come from others
> outside, but only from its own members
> through cruel, bloody strife:
> such is the song of the gods beneath the earth (471-5).

The *kommos* is over, but Orestes and Electra continue to make prayers (now spoken) to their father. It seems likely that they expect his ghost to appear (as that of Darius did) to bless or advise them; in 489-96 their entreaties rise to a climax, and they may beat the earth to summon him up; but he does not come. Still they go on praying for his help, until the chorus-leader suggests that it is time for action (510-13).

First, however, Orestes asks why Clytaemestra sent the drink-offerings, and thus we hear for the first time the details of her dream. She dreamed she gave birth to a snake, dressed it in infant clothes and suckled it – and it sucked out a clot of blood, whereupon she woke up screaming. Orestes immediately interprets the dream as referring to himself ('I shall become a snake and kill her', 549-50), and proceeds at once to outline his plans. Electra is to go inside (for hereabouts the *skênê*, representing the palace, comes back into the action) and 'look after matters in the house' (579); the chorus are to maintain secrecy; Orestes and Pylades, disguised as travellers from Phocis, will seek admission to the house and kill Aegisthus, preferably where he sits on Agamemnon's throne (as usually represented in contemporary vase-painting, see §7.4). Nothing is said about Clytaemestra. Orestes and Pylades depart to prepare their disguise; Electra goes into the palace (she will take no further part in the play). The chorus reflect on the monstrous deeds of women – Althaea who killed her son Meleager, Scylla who killed her father Nisus, the proverbially wicked Lemnian women who killed their husbands – but can find nothing to compare with the deed of Clytaemestra, now about to be avenged by the sword of 'the child ... [who] at long last is being brought to the house by the deep-thinking Erinys' (649-51).

Orestes and Pylades return, looking like poor travellers carrying their own bundles (cf. 675). Orestes knocks on the palace door and asks to see someone in authority, preferably a man (664), as he has important news. It is, however, Clytaemestra who appears. The visitor explains that a certain Strophius of Phocis had asked him to convey to the parents of Orestes the news that Orestes was dead, and to seek their instructions on whether his ashes should be sent back to Argos. Clytaemestra bursts out in intense (though, as we shall discover, pretended) distress, but in face of the equally pretended embarrassment of the visitor assures him that his bad news will make no difference to the hospitality he receives, and instructs a servant to show the two men to the guest-rooms. The avengers are within the palace; the chorus pray to Earth, to Agamemnon's tomb, to 'guileful Persuasion' and to Hermes to lend their aid in the coming contest.

The expected confrontation with Aegisthus, however, does not as yet take place. Instead, out of the palace, weeping, comes Orestes' old nurse Cilissa. Aegisthus, we learn, is not at home, and Cilissa has been sent to fetch him. She is heartbroken at the death of the baby she reared, and reminisces about him in what some have thought excessive and undignified detail; she is almost as distressed by the happiness this event has brought to Clytaemestra and Aegisthus. The chorus-leader, discovering that Cilissa's instructions are to tell Aegisthus to come with his bodyguard, suggests that she 'amend' the message (773) and tell him to come alone 'so as not to frighten the informants' (771). Cilissa is somewhat baffled by the woman's evident optimism, but goes off to do as she asks, leaving the outcome to the gods. The chorus are now able to pray at greater length to appropriate gods for Orestes' success, but in so doing they bring before us more vividly than ever before the horror of what is going to happen:

> And you [they sing, apostrophizing Orestes], when your turn comes to act,
> and she cries to you 'My child!',
> have no fear, but shout back 'My *father's* child!',
> and complete an act of destruction that carries no blame (826-30).

But before that crisis is reached, Aegisthus must be disposed of. In Homer and in art this was the high point of the story. Aeschylus deals with it almost casually. Aegisthus arrives; makes an official-sounding statement that, according to report, Orestes is unfortunately dead, but that it will be necessary to question those who brought the report and establish whether it is reliable; and goes inside with the famous last words 'He'll not deceive a mind that has its eyes open' (854). The chorus breathlessly wonder whether the house of Agamemnon is destined for ruin or for liberation. A cry is heard from within; the chorus move away, anxious not to appear involved; a servant bursts out, crying 'Aegisthus is no more', and knocks and shouts at the 'women's doors' for Clytaemestra; she appears, probably looking as if just roused from sleep, asks what is the matter, and is told 'The dead are killing the living'; she understands at once and calls for a 'man-slaying axe' (which she apparently never gets); and then Orestes strides out of the house and says, without prelude, 'It's *you* I'm after; *he's* been satisfactorily dealt with' (892).

Clytaemestra, with no weapon of the ordinary kind, uses the oldest weapon of all. Calling Orestes 'my child', she displays her breast to him and bids him 'respect' (or 'feel shame before') the source of his infant nourishment. At last the true nature of what he has to do stands inescapably before Orestes. He turns to Pylades and asks 'What shall I do? Shall I, for shame, forbear to kill my mother?' (899). And Pylades, who has not said a word all through the play, finds voice and says (900-2):

> What then becomes in future of the oracles of Loxias
> delivered at Pytho, and of firm-pledged oaths?
> Hold all men your enemies rather than the gods.

As many have said, it is as if Apollo had spoken. Orestes becomes resolute and implacable. In a stichomythia Clytaemestra tries to defeat him in argument as she once defeated Agamemnon, but he parries every thrust, and the scene ends with Orestes and Pylades entering the palace sword in hand, driving Clytaemestra before them to her death.

The chorus, while sparing some grief for the two victims (931), nevertheless rejoice unstintingly in the liberation of the house. Then Orestes appears, like Clytaemestra in the previous play, standing over a male and a female corpse; but while, like Clytaemestra, he is holding a bloodstained sword in one hand, he holds in the other the wreathed olive-branch of a suppliant (cf. 1035). For the time being this is left unexplained, as Orestes displays to the chorus, the Argive people and the gods the dead 'twin tyrants of the land' and also the bloodstained robe-net which had been used to murder Agamemnon, denouncing Clytaemestra and asserting that the robe is proof that he was justified in killing his mother (988-9).

Presently Orestes feels that he is losing his grip on mental normality (1021-5), and hastily makes a declaration which is the turning-point of the whole trilogy:

> I say I slew my mother not without right,
> the polluted killer of my father, hated by the gods.
> And as the prime inducement that made me do this audacious deed
> I name Loxias, the Pythian seer, whose oracle declared to me
> that if I did this I should be free from blame and condemnation,
> but if I failed – I shall not speak of the punishment;
> for no archer could shoot to the height of those sufferings (1027-33).

We never heard this before. When Apollo commanded Orestes to carry out the double murder, he threatened him, we knew, with terrible suffering if he disobeyed. What we did not know was that Apollo also promised that Orestes *would suffer no penalty if he obeyed.* Accordingly Orestes now announces his intention to go as a suppliant to Delphi and seek Apollo's protection.

The chorus encourage him to remember the glorious aspect of what he has done: he has liberated not only his house but the whole city (1046). But on their words 'easily cutting off the heads of two serpents' (1047), he suddenly seems to see other serpents (1048-50):

> Ah, ah! I see loathsome women, like Gorgons,
> with dark garments, and wound around
> with many, many serpents! I cannot stay!

Since Orestes has already indicated that he feels on the edge of madness, and since only he, not the chorus (nor the audience), can see these apparitions, we do not know as yet whether they have objective reality (as his mother's Erinyes) or whether, as the chorus tell him, they are only the fancies of his mind. All we know is that for him at any rate they are so powerful and so terrifying that, rather than making a dignified departure for Delphi, he breaks and runs off in panic. The chorus are left to reflect on the 'third tempest' that has come upon the royal house. There have been the feast of Thyestes, the murder of Agamemnon, and now:

> And now in turn from somewhere has come a third saviour –
> or should I say death?
> Where will it come to completion, where will the power of Ruin
> be put to sleep and cease?

7.3. *Eumenides*

The traditional title of this play means 'The Kindly Ones', a euphemistic name applied to groups of chthonic (underworld) goddesses in various cults. It was certainly applied later (as in Euripides' *Orestes*) to the goddesses of vengeance, the Erinyes, who pursued Orestes and were afterwards placated, but the name Eumenides is nowhere used in this play. The Erinyes are indeed in the end renamed, but their new name is *Semnai Theai*, 'the Awesome Goddesses' (1041).

The play begins at Delphi. The Pythia, the prophetess of Apollo, prays to all the gods of Delphi (1-31) and goes into the temple, inviting those who wish to consult the oracle to enter in due order. Almost at once she rushes out again, having seen a terrifying sight: a man sitting at the sacred 'navel-stone', holding a bloodstained sword and a suppliant-branch, and close by him, asleep, a group of monstrous female beings whom she can hardly describe. She departs, and presently the scene she has portrayed is revealed to the audience. The suppliant, Orestes, prays for Apollo's aid, and Apollo at once appears, saying 'I will never betray you' (64), and tells him to flee to Athens where he is to clasp the ancient olive-wood image of Athena Polias and where 'we will have judges of these matters and words that charm, and will find means to release you permanently from these troubles' (81-3). Hermes will guard Orestes on his travels. Orestes departs, and Apollo withdraws.

To the still-sleeping Erinyes (for such they are) there appears, as in a dream, the figure of Clytaemestra, who reproaches them for their inactivity and urges them to pursue and destroy her murderer (94-139). They stir in their sleep, making noises like those of hounds in the chase, and finally awake to discover to their horror that Orestes is gone – stolen away, they sing, by that young 'thief' of a god, Apollo (140-78). Then Apollo himself reappears, bow in hand, and orders them out of his sanctuary. They attempt to argue with him: they claim that by accepting Orestes into the temple he has himself polluted it, he retorts that they are operating a double standard by condemning Orestes for killing his mother while condoning Clytaemestra's killing of her husband. The Erinyes reaffirm their determination to harry Orestes, and depart on his trail; Apollo reaffirms his determination to protect his suppliant, whose 'wrath is fearsome, both among mortals and among gods, if I willingly betray him' (233-4).

Orestes re-enters. The scene is now the temple of Athena Polias on the Acropolis at Athens, and Orestes clasps her image as instructed. Close behind him arrive the Erinyes, tracking him, like hounds, by the scent of blood, and exulting in his certain destruction; Orestes, however, calmly prays to 'the sovereign of this land, Athena' to come to his aid, promising that in return 'she will gain, without fighting, myself, my land, and the Argive people as faithful, honest, and eternal allies' (289-91). While he waits to see if she will respond, the Erinyes sing what they call a 'binding song' (306), weaving, as it were, a spell around Orestes to put him in their power, but also affirming and describing that power which can reduce the proudest man to ruin.

At last Athena appears (397), and asks, with a courtesy that contrasts markedly with Apollo's attitude, who her strange visitors may be. The Erinyes identify themselves, say that they are pursuing Orestes because he has killed his mother, and ask Athena to judge the issue, feeling she deserves 'worthy reverence in return for worthy reverence' (435). Orestes, asked to 'state his country, family and experiences, and rebut their accusation' (437-8), first emphasizes that he has been purified of his blood-pollution and is no danger to those with whom he comes into contact; then he says who he is, admits that he killed his mother, but claims that he did so to avenge his father's murder and on the orders of Apollo. He too asks Athena to judge the case, adding that he will accept her verdict whatever it may be (469).

Athena refuses to make a decision on her own authority: the matter is too important, and the Erinyes, if slighted, can do too much damage to the Athenian people. Instead she will establish 'judges of homicide … for all time' (483-4); and she departs to organize this tribunal, requesting the contending parties to prepare their evidence and arguments (485-6).

The Erinyes sing of the appalling consequences that will ensue if Orestes is victorious in the coming trial: murder will run riot through the world, and men will call in vain on Justice and the Erinyes. There is a place for fear in human hearts, for what man and what community will reverence justice if they have no fear of anything (517-25)? They set out a stern and simple moral code, reminiscent of much that was said by the chorus of *Agamemnon*, and graphically warn that he who wantonly transgresses it will be utterly destroyed (provided, of course, that the Erinyes' power is not undermined as it would be by Orestes' acquittal).

The trial is now ready to begin, inaugurated by Athena (566-73) with the blast of a trumpet and a herald's proclamation. Apollo unexpectedly arrives to bear witness for Orestes. The Erinyes, as prosecutors, cross-examine the accused, forcing him into the position of having to deny, absurdly as it seems, that mother and son are blood relations (606). At this point he appeals to Apollo to tell the jury (consisting of ten or eleven Athenian citizens) whether he acted justly in killing his mother. Apollo affirms that he did: Orestes was obeying his oracle, and he has 'never said anything from the prophetic throne, whether concerning a man or a woman or a community, except on the instructions of Zeus, father of the Olympians' (616-18), so that to condemn Orestes is implicitly to rebel against Zeus. Zeus, as the divine Father and King, is bound to be particularly outraged by the death of an Agamemnon at the hands of a woman – and Apollo describes that death in all its degrading detail (631-5). The Erinyes, however, retort that this alleged concern of Zeus for fatherhood sits ill with his treatment of his own father, Cronus, whom he had notoriously imprisoned; this leads to an ill-tempered altercation in which Apollo in turn is eventually forced to deny any blood-tie between the 'so-called mother' and 'her' son. Unlike Orestes, however, he is able to bring persuasive arguments for this position: the mother is not truly a parent at all, but only the 'nourisher' of the implanted male seed; witness Athena who was born without a mother (traditionally from the head of Zeus). The Erinyes find no answer to this, and Apollo ends by reiterating Orestes' earlier promise to establish an eternal alliance between Athens and Argos.

Before the jury vote, Athena delivers a speech formally establishing her new court and identifying it with the Council of the Areopagus, which still judged cases of intentional homicide in Aeschylus' time (but had recently been deprived of considerably wider powers of great political importance: see §12.1), and giving 'advice to my citizens for the future' to respect the Council and its laws, and to observe certain vital political and moral principles – the very same principles enunciated by the Erinyes in their song before the trial began:

> I counsel my citizens to cherish and practise
> the mean between anarchy and despotism,
> and not to banish fear entirely from the city;
> for who among mortals is righteous, if he fears nothing? ...
> This Council, untouched by thought of gain,
> reverend, sharp in anger, a watchful sentinel
> over a sleeping land, I now establish (696-706).

The jury vote, one by one, to the accompaniment of an altercation between Apollo and the Erinyes, each trying to influence the voters at the last minute, with the Erinyes making dire threats against the land and people of Athens. Athena then announces that she is voting for Orestes and that an equal vote will result in his acquittal (it is disputed whether these are two separate statements or two ways of saying the same thing). The votes are counted amid anxious comments from those whom the result will affect, and finally Athena declares that the votes are equal and that Orestes has been acquitted.

Orestes joyfully gives thanks to Athena, Apollo and Zeus the Saviour, and swears that in his posthumous capacity as a 'hero' he will prevent, by evil omens and other means, any attempt by an Argive army to attack Attica, while conferring blessings on Argos if she remains loyal to her alliance with Athens. He then departs homewards, 'an Argive again, dwelling on his father's estate' (757-8). Apollo departs also, and there remain only Athena, her people, and the Erinyes.

The Erinyes sing a song of rage against the 'younger gods', threatening to poison the soil of Attica and destroy fertility and life there. Three times Athena tries to soothe them, arguing that they have not really been dishonoured, promising them cultic worship if they remain in Athens, begging them not to harm the Athenian land or promote civil strife among its people (858-66), working ingeniously on their pride:

> I will bear with your anger, for you are older,
> and you are thereby also far wiser than I;
> yet Zeus has also given me no mean intelligence.
> And if you go to the country of another nation
> you will long for this land like lovers, I declare;
> for the time that is coming will bring greater glory
> to these citizens, and you will possess
> a glorious abode near the house of Erechtheus
> and receive from processions of men and women
> more than you could ever get from any other people. ...
> Such is the choice that now I offer you,
> well doing and well done by and well honoured
> to be sharers in this land which the gods love most of all (848-57, 867-9).

The Erinyes remain defiant still; but at the fourth attempt Athena succeeds by appealing to their sense of justice: it would be *unjust* for them to harm the Athenians who are offering them the right of residence and splendid honours (888-91). To this the Erinyes reply not with another song of fury but with a hesitant question: 'Lady Athena, what abode do you say I am to have?' – and the struggle is over: 'I think you are going to charm me, and I withdraw from my wrath' (900). Athena bids them invoke all manner of blessings on the Athenian people in every field except that of war, which she will see to herself (903-15); and they proceed to do so in a song which is punctuated by passages chanted by Athena in which she hymns their vast power, warns the Athenians against offending them, thanks 'Zeus of Assemblies' (Zeus Agoraios) for granting her the gift of successful persuasion, and assures the Athenians that by honouring the Erinyes, and the principles of justice for which they stand, they will infallibly prosper.

Rejoice, rejoice [conclude the chorus] amid your well-deserved wealth,
rejoice, people of the city,
who dwell close to the virgin
daughter of Zeus, loved and loving,
wise in due season:
you are under the wings of Pallas,
and her Father reveres you ...

Rejoice, rejoice again, I repeat,
all you in the city,
both gods and mortals!
Dwelling in the city of Pallas
and revering me who sojourn here
you will have no cause to complain
of the experiences of your life (996-1002, 1014-20).

Athena now gives instructions for a great procession, representing the whole community of Athens, to escort the Erinyes to their new home between the Areopagus and the Acropolis; over the black or dark grey costumes of the Erinyes are draped crimson robes, like those worn by *metoikoi* (resident aliens) in the festival procession at the Panathenaea, and under their new name of *Semnai Theai* they march off, escorted by the councillors of the Areopagus and the female staff of Athena's temple, accompanied by the light of torches, the sound of song, and the joyful cries (*ololugmoi*) of those on stage and probably of the audience too.

*

The satyr-play *Proteus* dealt with the visit of Menelaus and Helen to Egypt, described in *Odyssey* 4. In Homer, Menelaus is detained for twenty days by contrary winds on the island of Pharos, and forced to live unheroically on fish; *Proteus* contained a reference to fish flavoured with *garum* (fr. 211) and to the sea-goddess Eido or Eidothea, who in Homer had advised Menelaus how to force her father Proteus, 'the Old Man of the Sea', to give him information and advice (fr. 212). The satyrs may be on the island as a result of shipwreck (as in Euripides' *Cyclops*); perhaps they give assistance to Menelaus and escape with him. There are features of this plot that reflect aspects of *Agamemnon*, in whose narratives of the past Menelaus and Helen were prominent: in particular, Menelaus is once again in the same position that he and Agamemnon were in at Aulis, and perhaps the satyrs are as eager to rape Helen (cf. 6.2 and *Cyclops* 179-80) as the Achaean leaders were to sacrifice Iphigeneia; but if Aeschylus followed Homer here, Menelaus was required merely to return to the Egyptian mainland and make *animal* sacrifices, after which he could sail home across calm seas to a peaceful future. Proteus may, as in Homer, have told Menelaus about Agamemnon's murder; did he perhaps also prophesy Orestes' revenge, and bring the tetralogy to a symmetrical conclusion by instructing Menelaus to give his daughter Hermione to Orestes in marriage?[5]

7.4. Aeschylus and his predecessors

The murder of Agamemnon by Clytaemestra and Aegisthus was one of the most famous of the 'Return-stories' (*Nostoi*) attached to the saga of the Trojan War. The earliest known version of the story is that presented in Homer's *Odyssey*, principally in books 3, 4 and 11, in narratives told (i) to Telemachus, son of Odysseus, by Nestor, (ii) to Telemachus by Menelaus (reporting what he was told by Proteus), and (iii) to Odysseus by the ghost of Agamemnon. These accounts tell in all essentials a consistent story, a story unique among all forms of the legend known to us in that Clytaemestra is kept free of direct guilt for the murder of her husband. Even her adultery is slightly extenuated, it being mentioned that she resisted Aegisthus for a long time and only yielded when Agamemnon was already on his way home from Troy (3.272-7). Agamemnon, driven off course by the storm that scattered the Greek fleet, landed in an outlying part of his kingdom, near the home of Aegisthus. Aegisthus, informed by a spy of Agamemnon's arrival, treacherously invited him to a feast, set twenty men in ambush in the hall, and killed Agamemnon and his whole party (4.512-37). Clytaemestra is associated with the murder only in one passage, by Agamemnon's ghost (11.409-53), and in curiously ambiguous terms. Agamemnon regards her as responsible, together with Aegisthus, for his death, but all he says of her personal actions is that she failed to close his mouth and eyes and that she slew Cassandra. Since he also speaks of her as a 'crafty plotter' (11.422) we are probably to understand that she took part in the *planning* of the murder; but there is a conspicuous silence as to her part, if any, in its execution. Seven years later Orestes came home to Mycenae 'from Athens' and killed Aegisthus. No direct mention is made of the death of Clytaemestra, but we are told that Orestes made a funeral feast over both of them (3.309-10) and that on the day of this feast Menelaus came home.

Since this was and is the oldest surviving version of the legend, it is tempting to privilege it as the 'original' form. It contains, however, internal evidence that this is not the case, above all in the evasive treatment of Clytaemestra's death and of her part in Agamemnon's. Why is Telemachus told of Clytaemestra's funeral but not of how she died? The account seems designed to leave him thinking that Clytaemestra committed suicide, in shame or in grief; but why is this left inexplicit? The only reasonable answer is: because, in terms of a legend so well established as to be unalterable, it would not have been true. Homer has an obvious reason not to want to present Orestes as a matricide: he has decided to make Orestes into a model which Telemachus is to be urged to emulate (cf. 1.298-302). Hence the killing of Clytaemestra must be glossed over; hence, too, no mention must be made to Telemachus of her part in the killing of Agamemnon – though in book 11, when Telemachus is not present, more latitude can be given, and Agamemnon, while maintaining formal consistency with the earlier accounts by not claiming that Clytaemestra killed him with her own hands, does imply that she had a weapon and does say four times, directly or by implication, that she was guilty of his murder (11.429-30, 432-4, 444, 453).

We can therefore be confident that in Homer's time the story was already strongly established that Aegisthus and Clytaemestra plotted together to kill Agamemnon, and that Orestes returned later from exile to kill both of them. And all versions of the story other than Homer's assume this basic outline. The details that vary can be considered under the following headings: **(1)** the motivation of Clytaemestra; **(2)** the motivation of Aegisthus; **(3)** how and where the murder was committed, and the respective roles of the two murderers; **(4)** Orestes' exile; **(5)** his consultation of the Delphic oracle; **(6)** the method and details of his revenge; **(7)** its aftermath.

Our evidence for the story as it was told between Homer and Aeschylus consists of a substantial number of artistic representations of various episodes from it, one intact literary text (the eleventh Pythian ode of Pindar, probably performed in 474 BC [6]) and fragments of, or references to, five or six others, the most important of which are the cyclic epic *Nostoi*, the *Catalogue of Women* ascribed to Hesiod, and the *Oresteia* of the lyric poet Stesichorus. Stesichorus is known to have been active about the middle of the sixth century, and the other two poems mentioned may have taken their present shape about the same time (though much of the material contained in them is probably older).

(1) In Aeschylus' treatment, Clytaemestra has three clear motives for the murder of Agamemnon: revenge for the sacrifice of Iphigeneia; resentment against her husband for his sexual infidelities during the war, and in particular for bringing home Cassandra; and her love for Aegisthus. A possible fourth motive – the resentment of a stronger intellect at being dominated by a weaker merely because she is a woman – is not avowed but is not hard to detect. This fourth motive is probably original with Aeschylus: it fits well with the thematic concerns of the *Oresteia* in general (see §7.8). The second and third motives are already present in Homer, at least by implication, despite his downplaying of Clytaemestra's whole role in the murder. The history of the first is more complex.

The sacrifice of Iphigeneia is nowhere mentioned by Homer, but it may well be, once again, that he deliberately avoided doing so; the link between the sacrifice and Agamemnon's murder goes back at least to Stesichorus, for the sacrifice was narrated in some detail in his *Oresteia* (cf. *GL* 215, 217), and even in the *Iliad* there may well be considerable irony when Agamemnon (1.106ff.) first attacks the seer Calchas for always saying evil things (in later tradition it was regularly Calchas who had made known to Agamemnon the demand of Artemis for the sacrifice) and immediately thereafter declares that he prefers the captive girl Chryseis to his wife (the only mention of Clytaemestra in the *Iliad*) and very much wants to have her in his home!

A striking fact about the more explicit pre-Aeschylean (and indeed post-Aeschylean) accounts of the sacrifice of Iphigeneia is that she is not normally thought of as having been actually killed. Either (as in the cyclic epic, the *Cypria*, and most later versions) she is removed from the altar by Artemis and a deer substituted, or else (as in the *Catalogue of Women*) it is not she that is killed but a phantom in her shape. The latter substitution would not be known to other mortals,[7] and there might have been considerable tragic possibilities in making Clytaemestra's hatred of her husband spring from a crime of which she *mistakenly* believed him guilty. Aeschylus could have exploited these, had he wished, for example by making Iphigeneia's survival known through Cassandra; he did not, and we should not foist the idea upon him by claiming that his audience 'must have' assumed it. In Aeschylus, Agamemnon truly is guilty of his daughter's murder. Moreover, the guilt is much more strongly *his* than perhaps ever before: so far as we know, no one before Aeschylus had envisaged Agamemnon as killing Iphigeneia with his own hand. In the *Cypria* and the *Catalogue* the sacrifice is performed by the Greeks collectively; about the other pre-Aeschylean accounts we have no definite information on this point. Aeschylus emphasizes overwhelmingly the father's personal role in the act, and presents it as the consequence of a decision taken by him alone (*Ag.* 205-17).

(2) The motive of Aegisthus, in Aeschylus, is simple: revenge for the murder of his brothers, and the feeding of their flesh to his father, by Atreus. Since Aegisthus is already in Homer son of Thyestes, this motive, or something like it, probably goes back to the beginning of the tradition, though Homer never refers to any quarrel between Thyestes and Atreus (indeed *Iliad* 2.106-7 is virtually incompatible with one) and lays more emphasis on the sheer wickedness of a man who desired Clytaemestra, desired power, and let nothing stand in the way of either aim. Aeschylus may have simplified the story in some respects. From him we learn simply that Thyestes committed adultery with Atreus' wife, that he and Atreus quarrelled over the kingship, and that Atreus banished him and later treacherously invited him back and served him the 'Thyestean feast'. From other sources we learn how these elements fit together: through Atreus' wife, Thyestes obtained the golden ram which was the symbol of the kingship; the all-seeing Sun, knowing of these crimes which were hidden from mortals, created a portent (reversing the direction of its path across the sky) which made the truth known to Atreus. By omitting the golden ram and the portent, Aeschylus has turned a tale of myth and magic into one of power, revenge and cruelty. There is indeed a singular lack of truly supernatural elements in the *Oresteia* – until the Erinyes appear.

Another detail omitted by Aeschylus (indeed implicitly denied) is the unnatural birth of Aegisthus. In the usual tradition Thyestes had two sons, and Atreus (as one might expect) killed both of them, and subsequently drove Thyestes into exile a second time. Told by an oracle that he could gain vengeance against Atreus only if he begot a son by his own daughter, Thyestes acted accordingly, and the offspring of this incest was Aegisthus. Thus Aegisthus, the worst man of his generation, is given a suitably tainted pedigree. In Aeschylus, however, he is already born before his father's final exile, and is expelled as a baby together with his father. It is not explained why Atreus should thus spare a potential avenger, and one is tempted to look for some strong reason why Aeschylus should have reshaped the story in just this way. The main reason is probably to make the story of Aegisthus as close as possible a parallel to that of Orestes: both are exiled in infancy, both return as adults to avenge their fathers. The incest would be a distracting irrelevance.

(3) In Homer, Agamemnon is king of Mycenae and Menelaus of Sparta; but there also seems to be some awareness of a tradition according to which the two ruled jointly at Sparta or nearby Amyclae. Two details in the *Odyssey*, indeed, only make sense on this assumption. When Telemachus asks Nestor about Agamemnon's death, the first thing he wants to know is 'where was Menelaus?' (3.249); and Agamemnon on his voyage home is said to have been driven out to sea by a squall when on the point of rounding Cape Malea (4.514-16), which he would have had to double to reach a Laconian port, but which is nowhere near any route from Troy to the Argolid. Certainly a tomb of Agamemnon was shown at Amyclae (Pausanias 3.19.6). The majority of the lyric poets – Stesichorus, Simonides, Pindar – place Agamemnon's palace at Sparta, so that Pindar can speak of 'Laconian Orestes'; only the early and obscure Xanthus (*GL* 700) may have located him at Argos. Aeschylus retains the idea of a joint kingship, but transfers it (ignoring Mycenae) to Argos – assisted in this by Homer's frequent use of *Argeioi* 'Argives' to denote the Greek army at Troy and his description of Agamemnon (*Iliad* 2.108) as ruling over 'many islands and all Argos', but motivated in all probability by other considerations which will be discussed later (§12.1).

Traditionally, as we have seen, Agamemnon was murdered by Aegisthus and Clytaemestra acting together. Stesichorus' version of Clytaemestra's dream, however, in which she sees 'a snake with the top of its head all bloodied' (*GL* 219), implies that Agamemnon was killed with an axe and therefore by Clytaemestra (for Aegisthus would have used a sword); and in the very earliest artistic representation that we have of the event, a seventh-century terracotta plaque from Gortyn in Crete, Clytaemestra is the killer (here using a sword) while Aegisthus merely holds the victim down. Other artistic treatments have Aegisthus playing the main role; in some both partners have weapons. What we find nowhere before Aeschylus is what he has given us: Clytaemestra as sole killer, with Aegisthus not even there.

As to how the murder was carried out, there are two basic versions before Aeschylus. One is the Homeric, in which Agamemnon is killed, with his companions, at a feast, 'as one might kill an ox at the manger' (*Odyssey* 4.535). Homer *may* have invented this, since it so very neatly foreshadows the death of Penelope's suitors in the main action of the *Odyssey*; on the other hand, it is also an appropriate revenge for the 'Thyestean feast' and it is perhaps more likely to be a traditional element. The other is essentially the version we find in Aeschylus, the stratagem of the bath and the enveloping robe. This is certainly not Aeschylus' invention. For one thing, if it were, the audience would not be able to understand the obscure and riddling references to it made before the event by Cassandra. For another, the robe actually appears on an Attic vase of the early 460s, now in Boston[8] – where, however, it is Aegisthus who is attacking the victim with a sword, while Clytaemestra runs up behind with an axe. No bath is shown, but Agamemnon's hair, and especially his beard, look very much as if they were freshly washed and not yet groomed. Moreover, as March 1987: 96 observes, Agamemnon has already been stabbed once by Aegisthus, who is clearly about to strike a second time, and Clytaemestra's axe-blow will thus be the third; this seems to reflect a precise literary account (perhaps that of Simonides), which Aeschylus will have adapted with his three blows (two to fell the victim, a third when he had fallen) all struck by Clytaemestra (*Ag.* 1384-7). This cannot however have been the original version of the bath-and-robe story. As several scenes in the *Odyssey* show, it is a woman's, not a man's, task to attend a hero in the bath; there must therefore once have been a form of the bath-and-robe story in which Clytaemestra put the robe on her husband and Aegisthus killed him – deception, as so often in Greek thinking, being viewed as feminine and force as masculine. The Boston vase represents a combination of this version with another (probably due to Stesichorus) in which Clytaemestra and Aegisthus attacked Agamemnon together, *not* at the bath, with axe and sword respectively. Simonides may have been responsible for the combination. We can thus perhaps trace the evolution of the two main variants of the murder approximately as follows.

Variant A (Feast)

(A1) Aeg. kills Ag. with sword. Clyt. kills Cassandra (with axe?). *Homer* (*c.* 700-675 BC?)

(A2) Aeg. wounds Ag. with sword. Clyt. despatches him with axe blow (and kills Cass. too?). *Stesichorus* (*c.* 550).

Variant B (Bath)

(B1) Clyt. bathes Ag., and after bath puts enveloping robe on him. Aeg. kills him. *Xanthus* (*c.* 600?)?

(B2) Clyt. puts robe on Ag., leaves him helpless and goes to fetch axe; then as in A2. *Simonides* (*c.* 500-475).

(B3) Clyt. puts robe on Ag. and kills him herself with sword (see §7.6.4); Aeg. not present. *Aeschylus* (458).

(4) In all versions except Homer's, Orestes' place of exile is in Phocis, at the house of Strophius; and he returns to take his revenge in the company of Strophius' son Pylades. In Homer, however, he comes home 'from Athens' (*Odyssey* 3.307), and Pylades is not mentioned. Which is the older version? Almost certainly that involving Strophius. He and Pylades have little existence except as figures in the Orestes story. Pylades appeared already in the *Nostoi*; and in the *Catalogue of Women* mention was made (Hesiod fr. 194 Merkelbach-West = 137b Most) of a sister of Agamemnon and Menelaus, named Anaxibia, who looks very much as though she had been invented for the purpose of becoming the wife of Strophius and so making Pylades a cousin of Orestes.[9] Once again, then, it is likely that Homer has altered tradition, and once again his motive was probably to reinforce the parallel between Orestes and Telemachus: Telemachus, if his father does not return, will have to act alone against the suitors, and therefore Orestes is presented as having acted alone against Aegisthus. That, then, is why his place of exile is moved away from Phocis. It may then be futile to ask why Athens was chosen instead. Possibly some of the later Athenian legends linking Orestes with Athens (see below) were already in existence in Homer's time, but even if they were there is no evidence that they were known outside Attica until Athenian tragedy gave them panhellenic publicity. Homer may well have chosen Athens almost or quite at random; it may be relevant that he had had occasion to mention 'holy Sunium, the cape of Athens' less than thirty lines earlier (3.278) and that no other suitable mainland city was anything like so fresh in his memory.

According to Stesichorus and Pindar, Orestes at the time of his father's murder had been rescued, and smuggled out of the palace, by his nurse (called Laodameia by Stesichorus, Arsinoe by Pindar;[10] Aeschylus keeps the nurse, gives her a very different function, and gives her the lowly name of Cilissa, 'woman from Cilicia'). There also seems to have been a tradition that ascribed a role in the rescue to Agamemnon's herald Talthybius, and several artistic representations show him returning home with Orestes and assisting in his revenge; possibly then in Stesichorus the nurse handed the boy over to Talthybius to take to safety. Aeschylus alters this well-established story and has Clytaemestra herself send Orestes away at some unspecified time before Agamemnon's return: the innovation is all the more noteworthy because in the most recent of the earlier literary accounts, that of Pindar, the nurse is said to have rescued Orestes *from Clytaemestra* (*Pythian* 11.17-18). She who in Pindar is bent on killing her son, in Aeschylus sends him away from possible danger. The innovation highlights the contradictory and impossible position into which Clytaemestra has put herself: she is wife to Aegisthus and also mother to Orestes and Electra, and she cannot help but betray one or the other loyalty. In the end, according to Cilissa, she welcomes the news of Orestes' death as much as Aegisthus would (*Cho.* 737-43), though both publicly profess to regard it as a great misfortune (*Cho.* 691-9, 840-3).

(5) Our earliest definite evidence for Apollo's patronage of Orestes is in Stesichorus (*GL* 217), according to whom Apollo in person gave Orestes a bow to ward off the Erinyes of his mother. It is likely, however, that the tradition is older. Phocis is very close to Delphi; Pindar makes Pylades the owner of the site of the stadium where the races were held at the Pythian Games; according to Pausanias (2.29.4) the father of Strophius was Crisus, the eponym of Crisa, a site less than two miles from Delphi. From Stesichorus onwards, at any rate, Apollo's endorsement of Orestes' revenge becomes a fixed feature of the myth (though Pindar contrives to skate round it). Aeschylus gives it what seems to be a new twist by at first emphasizing (*Cho.* 269ff.) not Apollo's protective promises but his threats of terrible suffering if Orestes does *not* carry out the vengeance. The result is that in Aeschylus, Orestes, while not exactly a reluctant avenger, is also not an eager one: he takes the vengeance because 'the deed has to be done' (*Cho.* 298). We do not know how Orestes' personal attitude to the vengeance and particularly to the matricide was presented by Stesichorus and other earlier poets.

(6) Orestes returns home and kills Aegisthus and Clytaemestra: so much is universally agreed, except that Homer, as we have seen, for his own reasons glosses over the matricide. Some of the events leading up to the killings were also well established in the tradition before Aeschylus. The meeting and mutual recognition of Orestes and Electra at their father's tomb, with a lock of Orestes' hair as the recognition-token, goes back at least to Stesichorus; the role of Electra in the story may have been important from quite an early stage, for Orestes needs to have an ally inside the palace to further his plans. A number of terracotta reliefs of the early fifth century show Electra, Orestes, Pylades and a fourth figure meeting at the tomb, to which Electra has come with a drink-offering for her father's spirit: Aeschylus may or may not be innovating when he has Clytaemestra send the offerings in an attempt to appease her victim. Clytaemestra's ominous dream also figured in Stesichorus' poem: she saw a serpent come towards her with the top of its head all bloody, and then it turned into Agamemnon: Aeschylus keeps the serpent but has Clytaemestra dream of giving birth to it and suckling it, and blood comes not from the serpent's head but from Clytaemestra's breast. Both poets clearly presuppose the regular identification of the serpent with the spirit of vengeance (in archaic art Erinyes are usually shown in this shape), but Stesichorus emphasizes the dead husband, Aeschylus the living and matricidal son.

The evidence of art points strongly to a fixed canonical order for the killings: Aegisthus first, then Clytaemestra. This order is logical (the man, presumed to be the stronger adversary, must be taken by surprise and disposed of first), and it seems so firmly entrenched that even when, in Aeschylus, Orestes finds Aegisthus not at home, and Clytaemestra comes out to greet the visitor, neither Orestes nor the audience thinks of doing anything but gain entry to the house and wait for Aegisthus to arrive.

In *Choephoroi*, Orestes' plan is that he and Pylades will disguise themselves as Phocian travellers and seek admission as guests to Aegisthus' palace; and then, he goes on, 'if I pass the bar of the outer door and find him on my father's throne ... then before he can say "where is the stranger from?" I will make a corpse of him' (*Cho.* 571-6). This scenario has a very long pedigree in art, going back at least to the first quarter of the sixth century. In many versions Clytaemestra tries to defend Aegisthus, often with an axe, and is in turn restrained by one or more allies of Orestes (the nurse, Talthybius, Electra or Pylades). In the 460s Aegisthus is more than once shown playing a lyre, the better to indicate his feeling of utter security at the moment of attack. Aeschylus first leads his audience to expect that something like this scenario will be repeated, and then gives them something very different. Orestes makes no mention beforehand of the idea of giving a false report of his own death; this is not because it is something he thinks of on the spur of the moment when confronted with Clytaemestra (already at 659 he tells the doorkeeper that he has news for the family) but because Aeschylus wants to keep it from the audience – which suggests that it is an innovation, overlaid on an earlier conception in which Orestes and Pylades sought admission to the palace simply as travellers from abroad.

Since in all versions Orestes has at most one male companion of warrior age, it must have been taken for granted by Aeschylus' predecessors that Aegisthus had no armed men within call. Aeschylus in *Agamemnon* had given Aegisthus a company of 'spear-bearers' like a typical *tyrannos* (and like Danaus in *The Suppliant Maidens*); in *Choephoroi* he goes out of his way to make it clear to the audience that these guards are not on hand but somewhere away from the palace (766-9), and they are *kept* away at the crisis thanks to the willingness of Clytaemestra's slaves – the nurse and the chorus – to disobey and pervert the orders of their unworthy masters.

With Aegisthus dead, it remains to dispose of Clytaemestra. In art, as we have seen, for at least a century before Aeschylus, she is often by this stage armed with an axe, and sometimes she is shown plainly threatening to kill her son. In Aeschylus too she calls for an axe, and with the same intention (for she speaks of it as a 'man-quelling' axe, *Cho.* 889) – but she does not get it; and so, perhaps for the first time in the history of the legend, she meets Orestes unarmed and is killed in cold blood.

Looking at the story thus far, the greatest innovation Aeschylus appears to have made is in the emphasis he places on the masculinity of Clytaemestra – or what appears as such to others, especially the Argive elders – and her domination over all the men with whom she comes into contact (cf. §7.8). Linked to this is the removal of Aegisthus from all active participation in the murder of Agamemnon, and, corresponding to this in turn, the downgrading of the importance of his own death: he could hardly have a less significant role in *Choephoroi* without being absent from the play altogether, and in *Eumenides* not a word is said of him. We have also noted that Aeschylus seems to have been the first to have Agamemnon perform the sacrifice of Iphigeneia with his own hand; that he omits, elides or de-emphasizes details tending to suggest that Clytaemestra had, or ever had had, murderous intentions towards her son, and even makes her, in a sense, save his life by sending him away from Argos; that he avoids, as long as possible, referring to Apollo's promise to protect Orestes; that he has Clytaemestra meet her killers unarmed and helpless. Almost all these changes can be ascribed to a single motive: to make Clytaemestra the central figure of the trilogy. She alone appears in all three plays: in the first she commands the action throughout, and dominates every other person except Cassandra; in the second, her death, not that of Aegisthus, is the climax; in the third her ghost exercises authority even over divinities. She is given a plethora of motives for killing Agamemnon; her own death, on the other hand, is made as problematic, as disturbing, as possible, and is allowed to be justified by two considerations only: firstly that it is the punishment of a woman who killed a husband, a father, the head of an *oikos*; secondly that it was commanded by Apollo and therefore indirectly by Zeus – and even then half an Athenian jury find the justification insufficient. Clytaemestra is the tragic hero of the *Oresteia*.

(7) But Clytaemestra departs from the trilogy well before its end. With the completion of Orestes' revenge the basic story, on which virtually all sources agree, comes to an end, and is replaced by a variety of traditions, many of which seem to be designed to claim a link between some particular locality and this famous saga. They divide into two main classes, one centring on Orestes' madness, the other on his persecution by the Erinyes of his mother. Aeschylus' treatment belongs to the latter group, but little is directly known about his precursors outside Athens; the pursuit is occasionally represented in archaic art, and Stesichorus, as we have seen, had Apollo give Orestes a bow to ward the Erinyes off.[11]

We know, independently of Aeschylus, of two important Athenian legends involving Orestes. One told how he came to Athens as a polluted fugitive, forbidden as such to speak to anyone or to share food or drink with another; it was the day of the Choes (part of the Dionysiac festival of the Anthesteria), and to avoid embarrassing Orestes it was ordained that *all* those celebrating the festival should drink from separate vessels and in silence – a practice which thenceforth became a permanent feature of the Choes feast.[12] This story may be echoed at certain points in the *Oresteia* (for example in *Eum.* 448ff or in the description of Thyestes' feast in *Ag.* 1594ff.), but the main basis of the action of *Eumenides* is the separate Athenian story of Orestes' trial for murder on the Areopagus.

Of the many witnesses to this story Aeschylus himself is the earliest, and artistic representations begin only after him. Later accounts, however, contain many details that do not derive from Aeschylus and cannot reasonably be motivated as deliberate alterations of the Aeschylean version, so that it can confidently be assumed that the story was already in existence. If so, the later evidence suggests that it took approximately the following form. Orestes came to Athens, fleeing from the vengeance (not of the Erinyes but) of one or more kinsmen of Clytaemestra or Aegisthus or both. Possibly after supplicating Athena, he was granted a trial, before a jury consisting of the great Olympian gods, on the Areopagus, which had taken its name from an earlier trial there by a similar tribunal, when Poseidon had prosecuted his fellow-god Ares for the murder of Poseidon's son Halirrothius. Orestes was acquitted, and presumably returned home vindicated to reign in peace (the 'happy ending' is common to all the varied accounts of Orestes' fortunes so far as they are known).

What Aeschylus has done is, in the first place, to combine the story of Orestes' persecution by the Erinyes and protection by Apollo with that of his trial at Athens. Apollo's protection now includes, as a fundamental element, the advice to supplicate Athena Polias at Athens and the promise of a trial, at which Apollo himself appears as Orestes' witness and advocate; and the Erinyes, from being Orestes' physical *pursuers*, become his forensic *prosecutors* (Greek used the same verb, *diôkein*, both for 'pursue' and for 'prosecute'; similarly the defendant in a trial was called 'the fugitive', who was said to be 'captured' if convicted and to have 'escaped' if acquitted). In the trial itself the divine jury is replaced by a human one, the prototype of the Areopagus council of Aeschylus' own time and more broadly of all the courts of justice of fifth-century Athens; but there is still divine participation, for the trial is presided over not by an Athenian king but by Athena. Orestes' trial is no longer one of a series of mythical murder trials, but the first ever held (*Eum.* 682), so that it marks the transition from punishment by private vengeance to punishment by judicial sentence; and Orestes is acquitted on an equal vote, resolved in his favour through a ruling by Athena. What Aeschylus has created here is more than a mere modification of an existing myth: it is fundamentally a new myth with a new meaning, some aspects of which are explored in §§7.8, 7.9 and 12.1 below.

Even more is this true of what follows. The last quarter of *Eumenides*, after the final departure of Orestes, shows Athena successfully endeavouring to persuade the Erinyes to calm their furious anger against Athens and to dwell in its soil as the *Semnai Theai*, spirits potent both for evil and, if they and what they stand for are properly respected, for good. What else is known about the *Semnai Theai*, notably the cult they received and the importance of their sanctuary as a place of refuge for those in fear of enemies, suggests a profile quite unlike that commonly associated with Erinyes, and it is likely that when Aeschylus identified the *Semnai Theai* of Athens with the Erinyes who had pursued Orestes, he was making a startling innovation which, if his audience accepted it, would revolutionize their understanding of the significance of both groups of deities.

7.5. Metre and music

The importance of song and dance in Greek tragedy made it, in some respects, much more like what we should call opera than drama. Indeed, when the modern genre of opera was created in Italy about 1600, its creators believed that they were reviving Greek tragedy. The analogy should not be pressed too far. In modern opera, the music is normally completely dominant over the words, and the sound of the latter is held to be so much more important than their sense that opera, unlike drama, is normally performed in the language of the writer, not that of the audience; the writer or 'librettist' himself, however, is often treated as an insignificant figure, the opera being thought of as 'by' the musical composer alone; and the performers are trained as singers, not as actors. So far as we can tell, the balance in fifth-century Athens was different. Partly this will have been because of the nature of the music itself: sung always in unison, and accompanied by a single instrument (the *aulos* or double pipe) rather than an orchestra, it will have tended to bring out the words more clearly rather than obscuring them. At any rate the fifth-century dramatists were not afraid to couch exchanges and reflections of the highest dramatic importance in the form of song; and whereas on the modern stage the language of song is normally simpler syntactically than that of dialogue, on the Athenian stage, especially in the hands of Sophocles, it was often more complex and compressed. Writer and composer were of course one and the same person, but contemporary critics seem to have thought of the dramatists as primarily artists in words. Aristophanes in his Aeschylus-Euripides contest in *Frogs* deals with music (very entertainingly) in only one of the five rounds of the contest (1249-1364). Plato in various works has much to say about tragedy and much to say about music, but usually thinks of them in separate compartments;[13] in *Gorgias* (502b-d) he treats tragedy as a species of oratory. The etymological connection of the words *tragôidia, tragôidos*, with *ôidê* 'song' was recognized, and Euripides can use *aoidos* 'singer' to mean 'poet';[14] but professional tragic performers were normally called not *tragôidoi* but *hypokritai*. At the same time, however, it is not an insignificant fact about popular perceptions of the genre that *tragôidia* eventually came to mean just 'song', as *tragoudi* does in modern Greek.

With minor exceptions (in particular, a few papyrus fragments of Euripidean lyrics[15]) the music of Greek tragedy is lost. More strictly, its *melodies* are lost, together with the choreographic figuring of the dances. What have survived, though, are the *rhythms* of music and dance alike; for Greek poetry was based on the time-values of syllables.[16] In Aeschylus, too, the rhythms of lyrics are often clear, simple, and persistent, and it is possible, as Scott 1984 has shown, to give on their basis quite a firm outline of the musical structure of a play.

Before we examine *Agamemnon* from this point of view, a word is in order about the basic structuring of tragic song. In Aeschylus there are two principal types of lyric architecture. The first is *strophic structure*, normally used in songs sung exclusively by the chorus. Such a song will consist of paired stanzas; the number of such pairs in a song is unlimited (the opening song of *The Suppliants* has eight; the choral songs of *Agamemnon* have respectively six, three, four and two). The stanzas within each pair (the *strophe* and *antistrophe*) are identical in rhythm, syllable for syllable, subject to minor and, in general, strictly defined permissible variations. Sometimes strophe and antistrophe may end with (or have appended to them) verbally identical refrains; sometimes an unpaired stanza may stand between strophe and antistrophe (as a *mesode*) or may conclude a sequence of strophic pairs (as an *epode*). A song may be introduced by a passage, of any length, in anapaestic rhythm (based on the unit ⏑⏑–⏑⏑–, either half of which may be replaced by –– or less often –⏑⏑); these passages were chanted rather than sung, and are thought to have been accompanied by marching evolutions rather than by dance. During a strophic choral song the principals are nearly always either offstage or inactive.

The second main type of lyric architecture is *epirrhematic structure*. This is normally used in lyric, or rather semi-lyric, dialogues between the chorus and an actor. Usually the actor either speaks in iambics or chants in anapaests while the chorus, in alternation with him, sing a series of short stanzas forming strophic pairs. The actor's contributions normally likewise form pairs, those within each pair being of equal length. Typical is the exchange between Pelasgus and the Danaids in *Supp.* 348-417. The chorus sing six stanzas forming three strophic pairs; each stanza except the last is followed by a five-line iambic speech by Pelasgus in which he explicitly takes up a word or idea from the stanza just sung.

Aeschylus plays many variations on these basic patterns, up to the vast structure of the laments and prayers at Agamemnon's tomb in *Cho.* 306-478 which is written for two actors and chorus and consists of eleven strophic pairs (some of them in interlaced order, two of them with internal speaker-division) and four anapaestic chants; but the underlying structures always remain recognizable. We may now consider the music of *Agamemnon*.

The chorus of Argive elders begin with a long chant in (no doubt slow) marching anapaests. This is conventional: the length of the chant, 115 metrical units (*metra*), compares with 123 *metra* in the corresponding prelude in *The Persians* (1-64) and 77 in that of *The Suppliant Maidens* (1-39). The basic function of these preludes is for the chorus to introduce themselves and explain the situation; in this play of course much of the necessary exposition has already been provided by the Watchman, and the chorus can acquaint us with the remoter and deeper background to the current state of things. They end with an appeal to Clytaemestra to tell them the reason for the sudden flurry of sacrificial activity. There is no reply, and their thoughts turn back to the past, to the omen which, at the moment when the army set out for Troy, gave assurance that it would be victorious.

They describe this omen in a rhythm which is almost entirely dactylic (its *metron* is – ∪ ∪ or – –), the rhythm of Homer and of heroic achievement (the first and the penultimate line of each stanza are indeed heroic hexameters). The expedition is setting out on its way with confidence. But the strophe ends with a check: the last line (120) is not dactylic but iambic, a metre which has associations *inter alia* with laments, and its meaning too is negative (the hare caught by the eagles is 'cheated out of its last race'); and there follows a curiously equivocal dactylic refrain ('cry alas, alas, but let the good triumph!').

The antistrophe (122-39) has the same rhythm, but sinister thoughts arise earlier than in the strophe (131) as Calchas expresses his fear that Artemis may be wrathful against the army, and when the refrain comes again it feels thoroughly appropriate. There follows what will initially be perceived as the beginning of a second strophic pair, in which at first dactylic rhythm alternates with iambo-choriambic (based on the *metra* ∪ – ∪ – and – ∪ ∪ –); the latter rhythm appears nowhere else in the *Oresteia*, but it is found occasionally elsewhere in Aeschylus; its connotations are not clear. From 148 to the end the stanza is exclusively dactylic, with three successive hexameters towards the end (155-7); but there is nothing heroic about its content, which plainly foreshadows the sacrifice of Iphigeneia and the murder of Agamemnon, and by the time we hear the third refrain the mood is grim indeed.

Then the expected antistrophe fails to materialize: there is a complete change of mood and metre. What we thought was a second strophe proves to have been an unpaired epode. The chorus are now singing the praises of Zeus. They sing it in a rhythm dominated by one of the simplest of lyric units, the lekythion (– ∪ – ∪ – ∪ –), which occurs more than 250 times in the *Oresteia*, often bringing with it recollections of the thoughts of this 'Hymn to Zeus', especially perhaps in some of the lyrics of *Eumenides* (490-565, 916-1020) where it is the dominant rhythm.

But the 'Hymn to Zeus' is not a self-contained unit of song. As usually reckoned, it consists of one and a half strophic pairs (160-83). The second antistrophe (184-91) is the beginning of the narrative of the events at Aulis, and retrospectively it ties the 'Hymn' closely to those events: Zeus is the sole source of relief from anxiety, Zeus is triumphant and all-powerful, Zeus has established the law 'learning through suffering' – and Zeus caused the sacrifice of Iphigeneia. The lyric structure establishes Zeus' responsibility for the atrocity of Aulis even though in the actual narrative he is never referred to.

Once that link has been established, the dominant rhythm changes, at 192, to one which will appear again and again throughout the play, often in connection with events and actions which are in one way or another parallel to those of Aulis, or with reflections on those events – in sum, on *actions that cry out for retribution.* This 'Aulis-rhythm', as I shall call it, is well illustrated by the first two lines of the new movement (192-3), which are both of the same form:

⏑ – ⏑– – ⏑ – ⏑ – –

This precise structure (formally 'iambic *metron* plus ithyphallic') is repeated a total of 30 times in *Agamemnon.* More generally, the rhythm of the Aulis narrative is iambic with frequent syncopation, the basic iambic *metron* ⏑ – ⏑ – being time and again reduced to ⏑ – –, – ⏑ –, or even – –. If these reduced *metra* of three or two syllables were given the same time-value as a full *metron* of four, the effect would be to slow down the song and dance in a mood of hesitation and uncertainty. At the end of each stanza the rhythm temporarily changes to the quicker choriambic. This change does not always have the same effect, though it tends to come at moments when crucial steps are being taken towards the horror of the sacrifice. At 199 it accompanies the hopeful news that Calchas had announced a 'remedy' for the storm – but before the strophe ends the remedy has reduced the Atreidae to tears. In the antistrophe, at 212, the choriambics mark the moment when Agamemnon moves towards a resolution of his dilemma by posing the question – unanswerable, because wrongly formulated (see §11.2) – 'how can I become (*genômai*) a deserter?' At 225 the change of rhythm occurs in the middle of the phrase 'he brought himself to become (*genesthai*) the sacrificer of his daughter'; at 235 it comes when Iphigeneia is being hoisted aloft like a beast and gagged. In the last strophic pair of the ode the choriambs appear only fleetingly at the very end, and the Aulis-rhythm is left beating in our ears as the avenger of Iphigeneia appears on stage for the first time.

After Clytaemestra has convinced the Elders that Troy has indeed fallen, we expect that they will sing a song of triumph, and the anapaestic prelude (355-66) seems to confirm our expectation. But when the actual lyrics begin, the chorus resume the Aulis-rhythm. Once again they are singing not so much of the Argive victory, as of acts that cried out for retribution: in this case the acts of Paris. Once again there is a change of rhythm at the end of each stanza, but this time the change is more clearly marked, and the final section is metrically identical in every stanza throughout the three strophic pairs of this ode, so that it serves musically (though not verbally) as a refrain. It comprises, each time, two pherecrateans (– x – ⏑ ⏑ – –) followed by a glyconic (– x – ⏑ ⏑ – ⏑ –) and another pherecratean. An identical refrain or coda is found, also six times, in a choral ode of *The Suppliant Maidens* whose metrical structure is otherwise very different (625-709); that ode is devoted throughout to praise of and blessings on the Argives, and it is likely that the refrains carried music that matched this mood. Here the words of the codas are completely in harmony with the rest of the song, and the music may have been designed to suit it too. It seems that codas of this kind could be musically shaded to suit their surroundings.

Setting the codas to one side, in the main body of the successive stanzas the Aulis-rhythm continues without a break from the beginning of the ode to line 448. By then the thought has passed from the deeds of Paris and Helen to another act that cries out for retribution: the act of Menelaus and Agamemnon in taking so many Greek fathers, husbands and sons to their death 'for the sake of another man's wife'. On these words the rhythm shifts, as it did in the previous ode, from syncopated iambic to choriambic, as it begins to seem as though the Atreidae are under threat from an enraged Argive public and (in the antistrophe) from Zeus and the Erinyes. The main body of the ode, having begun with the 'stroke of Zeus' directed at Paris and the Trojans (367), ends with the 'thunderbolt from Zeus' (470) cast at 'those who have killed many' (461) such as the Atreidae.

The structure and thought of the ode are complete, but the chorus continue to sing what proves to be a rather formless epode (475-88). Its rhythm is similar to that of the preceding stanzas, especially the last two, but in 485-7, where the Elders are speaking slightingly of the credulity and excitability of women, there is a very high frequency of 'resolution' (replacement of a long syllable by two short ones), so that five iambic *metra* contain 25 syllables instead of the normal 20, as if women's excited chatter were being derisively mimicked.

The next choral ode (681-782) begins in the same rhythm as the Hymn to Zeus. This is doubly appropriate: as at the start of the Hymn, the Elders are thinking about names, and the name they are thinking about is that of Helen, Zeus's daughter. At the start of the ode, however, only they themselves know this; it is not till 687 that their words begin to make it clear that they have Helen in mind, and at that precise point the rhythm changes to one dominated by the colon ∪ ∪ – ∪ – ∪ –, the anacreontic. The anacreontic, unlike some other lyric verse-patterns, is actually common in the work of the poet from whom it takes its name, in Anacreon's songs of wine and love and luxury. It suits Helen and the 'delicate curtains' of 690-1 well; it suits rather less well the actual subject-matter of most of the strophe, which is armed pursuit, strife and destruction. The antistrophe (699-716) is articulated in the same way. It begins in lekythia with a comment on the appropriateness of an (ambiguous) word (and on the wrath of Zeus Xenios); continues in anacreontics with the wedding-song of Helen and Paris (705-8); and ends, still largely in anacreontics, with the very different song, of lament and loathing, which the Trojans sang when they understood the consequences of that marriage. The verse and the music, like Helen, retain the outward form that speaks of beauty and of love, even when the inward reality is catastrophe.

The same contrast is illustrated by the fable of the lion-cub (717-36). This is told in very unpretentious metrical patterns – glyconic/pherecratean, dactylic, iambic, each repeated two or three times before shifting to another. There is no contrast between the patterns themselves; the contrast lies in the way in which the very same patterns (and of course the very same melody) are used first, in the strophe, to describe the pretty kitten-like creature loved by young and old, and then, in the antistrophe, to describe the havoc wrought by the adult lion.

The third strophe continues the pattern of incongruities. It begins with lines strongly reminiscent of the Aulis-rhythm, and in this rhythm it describes a voluptuous, bewitching vision (737-43):

> At first, I would say, there came to Ilion's city
> a thought of windless calm,
> a gentle ornament of wealth,
> a soft dart of the eyes,
> a flower of desire that stings the heart.

At this point the metre changes to anacreontic and the related ionic (based on the unit ⏑ ⏑ – –), which one would have thought utterly appropriate for the theme that seems to have been embarked upon. Immediately and perversely the poet leaves this theme: these symposiac metres are used to speak of the 'evil outcome of the marriage' brought about by an Erinys who is at least partly identified with Helen. Perhaps that is the point. Helen and the Erinys could not be separated. Paris and the Trojans thought they could have one without the other, as the owner of the lion-cub thought he could have the kitten and not the killer. Both were wrong. So Helen is spoken of in a rhythm appropriate to the Erinys, and the Erinys in a rhythm appropriate to Helen.

By leaving the subject of Helen midway in a strophic pair the poet contrives, as at the end of the Hymn to Zeus, a close connection between what has gone before and the ensuing general reflections on *hybris* and justice: what has been said about Helen should be taken as illustrating these reflections. There is still incongruity. The antistrophe considers whether wealth or wickedness is the basic cause of persistent disaster in a family. The claims of wealth are considered in the Aulis-rhythm; those of wickedness in ionics and anacreontics. Logically it should have been the other way about. But wealth and wickedness, like Helen and the Erinys, are hard to separate (cf. 773ff.); something on which we may have particular cause to reflect when a moment later we see Agamemnon. In the final strophic pair the Aulis-rhythm predominates: we are still to be thinking in terms of actions that cry for retribution when, also a moment later, we see Cassandra – even if everyone on stage is going to ignore her existence for the space of 167 lines. Cassandra, we may note, has been brought across the sea, like Helen, to a 'marriage' which is no true marriage and which will bring disaster to him who brought her.

When Agamemnon has entered the palace for the last time, the chorus sing an ode dominated by lekythia; of 56 verses in the song, 30 are of this form. The song is one of bewilderment, and, like the previous ode (which also began with lekythia) and the Hymn to Zeus, it opens on a question to which the chorus find no answer. The only change of rhythm that lasts for any length of time comes at the beginning of the second strophe and antistrophe (1001-7 = 1018-24, though the strophe is corrupt) at a point when the chorus are affirming almost the only thing of which they can feel certain, the irrevocability of death.

All the lyrics thus far have been choral songs based on a strophic structure (incidentally of decreasing length: 154, 122, 102, 60 lines, not counting anapaestic preludes which would make the trend even stronger). The first part of the Cassandra scene is epirrhematic, but in an abnormal way. At first the normal pattern is completely reversed. Cassandra *sings*, and the chorus-leader *speaks* iambic couplets in reply (1072-1113): thus the extreme agitation and prophetic insight of Cassandra are contrasted with the matter-of-fact incomprehension of the Elders:

> CASSANDRA
> Apollo, Apollo,
> Apollo Agyiates, my destroyer!
> Ah, where have you brought me? To what house?
> CHORUS-LEADER
> To the house of the Atreidai; if you don't know that,
> I'll tell you, and you'll find it's no lie (1085-9).

Or again:

> CASSANDRA
> This testimony convinces me:
> these are babies bewailing their slaughter
> and the roasted flesh that their father devoured.
>
> CHORUS-LEADER
> Actually we had heard of your reputation as a seer,
> but we don't require any prophets (1095-9)

– for all the world as if he were replying to a job application.

Cassandra's utterances grow longer and longer as the scene proceeds: in successive strophic pairs they are of 14, 26, 34, 49 and 53 syllables. As her visions become more detailed, some of her agitation is communicated to the chorus, who from the fifth strophic pair (1121) begin to sing themselves, and from the sixth (1140) abandon spoken iambics altogether. Their song is in essentially the same rhythms (iambic and dochmiac) as hers. At the same time Cassandra herself seems to become slightly calmer as she contemplates her own fate rather than that of Agamemnon, and in the last two strophic pairs she ends each utterance with two spoken iambic trimeters (first in 1138-9). Thus in the end the traditional balance has been partly, but only partly, restored: the utterances of the chorus are further from ordinary speech than those of the actor, but only slightly further.

When Cassandra departs, the chorus chant what might be the anapaestic prelude to a further ode, but the ode never comes: on the last words of their chant, 'who of mortals can boast that he was born to a fortune free from harm, *when he hears this*?' (1341-2) we hear the cry of the stricken Agamemnon. In two other late plays of Aeschylus the act-dividing function of a choral song is performed, in the last quarter of a play, by an anapaestic chant alone (*Supp.* 966ff., *Cho.* 855ff.): this is in accordance with the tendency already noted for choral songs to become shorter as a play proceeds.

After the appearance of Clytaemestra, standing triumphant over the two bodies, there is a complex epirrhematic scene between her and the chorus, in which, unusually for scenes of this type, no two successive phases are alike. It is structured as follows:

(1) *1407-1447.* Choral strophe and antistrophe (dochmiac and iambic, indicating, as often and as in the Cassandra scene, emotional agitation) answered by Clytaemestra in speeches of substantial and roughly equal length (14 and 17 lines). The length of the speeches, as well as their arrogant assurance, suggests that Clytaemestra has the upper hand in this debate, and indeed in their next utterance the chorus abandon direct denunciation of her and wish for their own death.

(2) *1448-1480.* Choral strophe and antistrophe, beginning with dochmiacs but shifting into the Aulis-rhythm when they speak (1450-4, 1470-4) of the death of Agamemnon and the evil domination of Clytaemestra. The strophe, but not the antistrophe, is followed by a long coda, partly in anapaests (sung, not chanted) and partly in iambics and dochmiacs; this coda, like the two other codas later in the scene, begins with a vocative introduced by the cry *iô*, and its introduction may suggest that the chorus are finding difficulty in containing their grief within proper formal bounds. Clytaemestra replies (1462ff., 1475ff.) in anapaestic chants of identical length (11 *metra* each): she is thus more on a level with the chorus than previously.

(3) *1481-1529.* Choral strophe and antistrophe, beginning in aeolo-choriambic rhythms but shifting midway to patterns related to the Aulis-rhythm to affirm the role of Zeus in all that has happened (1485-8) and the certainty of further bloodshed in future (1509-12). Both strophe and antistrophe are followed by identical codas, rhythmically similar to the coda of (2) but longer (77 syllables as against 63). Clytaemestra again replies in anapaestic chants, but the second (in which she reminds the chorus of what her husband did to Iphigeneia) is substantially longer than the first (owing to textual uncertainties we cannot say precisely how much longer).

(4) *1530-1576.* Choral strophe and antistrophe entirely in the Aulis-rhythm: most of the strophe expresses bewilderment and fear, but the antistrophe affirms the certainty that 'it remains true, while Zeus remains on his throne, that the doer must suffer' (1563-4). The strophe alone is followed by a grieving coda, much the longest of the series (106 syllables). Clytaemestra's replies are again anapaestic, the second again substantially longer than the first.

The chorus's rhythms tell two parallel stories. One is of initial shock replaced by increasingly open grieving, represented by the lengthening codas. The other is the gradual, and eventually complete, replacement of the emotional dochmiac and allied metres by the Aulis-rhythm which throughout the play has expressed the demand for and the certainty of retribution. Once this process is complete, once the chorus have found the bedrock of certainty and know that in one respect at least Zeus can after all be absolutely trusted, they need no longer grieve; their last antistrophe is followed by no coda, and their subsequent defiance of Aegisthus is far more impressive than their earlier ineffective attempts to save Agamemnon. Clytaemestra, as the epirrhematic principle theoretically demands, has the last word; but from the time when she abandoned speech for anapaestic chant she has ceased to be absolute master of the discussion, and she ends in self-contradiction. The chorus have proclaimed that Zeus' law guarantees the doer must suffer, and that the house is 'glued' to catastrophe; Clytaemestra says they are quite right (1567) and forthwith attempts to make a businesslike deal with the *daimôn*.

Such are some of the ways in which we can perceive Aeschylus using the rhythm of music and dance to stress key ideas and moments in *Agamemnon*. No doubt he used other techniques that we can no longer perceive. We can see, too, that some of the long-running patterns we have discerned were continued into the rest of the trilogy, though they are also joined by others: the Asiatic women slaves of the second play, the Erinyes of the third, each have typical song patterns of their own, but both can also use some of the same rhythms as the Argive elders, especially that built around the lekythion. The striking thing about Aeschylus, in comparison with Sophocles and (usually) Euripides, is the perceptibility of these patterns. It will not have taken a connoisseur to appreciate how Aeschylus exploited them; only a listener with an ear for rhythm and for a tune, or a watcher with an eye that could recognize a repeated dance-movement. No wonder the chorus of Aristophanes' *Frogs* were shocked by Euripides' assertion that he could prove Aeschylus to be a 'bad songwriter' (*Frogs* 1249-50), having always assumed that he was 'the man who, of all poets down to the present day, had composed by far the most and the finest songs' (1252-6).

7.6. Visual dimensions

7.6.1. The house. As was shown in §2.1, the *Oresteia* is the earliest surviving tragic production which we can be confident was performed in a theatre with a visible building at the back of the acting area; and Aeschylus makes use of this new resource to the fullest extent. The trilogy, for most of its length, is about the vicissitudes of the 'house' of Atreus – that is, both the palace and the family that inhabited it: most of the words for 'house' in poetic Greek – *oikos, domos, dôma,* etc. – were capable of bearing either meaning (cf. 5.4).

If the dwelling is part of his scene-setting, the dramatist can, if he wishes, make the *oikos* itself 'almost an actor in his drama' (Kitto 1956: 31). In the *Oresteia* Aeschylus does this from the very first moment. For the first words of the trilogy are spoken, from the roof of the house, by a character who is at that moment invisible, at least to many of the spectators;[17] and briefly, until we realize who the speaker is, it will seem as though the house itself was praying to the gods to release it from its troubles (*Ag.* 1). The typical Aeschylean device of ring-composition (see p. 47) indicates that this is no flight of fancy; for at the end of the Watchman's speech, refusing to spell out the causes of the anxiety he evidently feels, he says 'The house, were it to find voice, could tell it most clearly' (37-8). And at various other crucial moments through the trilogy the house does find voice, or is spoken of as doing so: directly after the prologue, when Clytaemestra within the house utters the cry of joy which the watchman bade her raise at 28 (not included in script, but cf. 587); at the moment of Helen's fateful departure, described in the second choral song (408-26), when its anonymous 'spokesmen' lament its woes and those of Menelaus; in the prophecies of Cassandra, who hears infants bewailing their slaughter (1096) and the song of those unwanted house-guests, the Erinyes (1186-92); at the moment when Agamemnon is struck down (1343-5); in the nocturnal shriek of Clytaemestra, recalled twice in *Choephoroi* (32-7, 535), when in her dream she was bitten by her serpent-child; in the ungracious grumbling of the doorkeeper behind the still-closed door (*Cho.* 657); and in the last cries of Aegisthus (*Cho.* 869).

In each of the first two plays, one of the issues can be expressed as 'who speaks for the house of Atreus?' In *Agamemnon*, is it Agamemnon – or Clytaemestra, dragging Aegisthus after her – or is it only such characters as the watchman and Cassandra who can be said to have the good of the house truly at heart? In *Choephoroi*, is it Clytaemestra and Aegisthus, or is it the 'united company' (458) of their opponents, Orestes, Electra, the chorus of palace slaves, not to mention the nurse Cilissa? In each case the issue is pointed up visually by the dramatist's handling of movements between the house and the exterior.

In *Agamemnon* (see Taplin 1977: 299-300, 306-8, 324) almost all such movements are controlled by Clytaemestra, the 'watchdog of the house' as she aptly calls herself (607). Time and time again (255-8, 587, 855, 1035) she appears at the door, always at her own moment, never because she has been summoned; on two of these occasions, and also at 1372 where she appears on the *ekkyklêma* (see below), her appearance forestalls an entry into the palace by another person or persons. She re-enters the house likewise at her own moment, often leaving others on stage without explanation or leave-taking. No other person (except Cassandra) goes into the house, except at a time and in a manner of Clytaemestra's choosing. No other person comes out of the house at all. And all those, *including* Clytaemestra, who do enter the house through that door, are going in to their violent deaths, whether immediate (Agamemnon and Cassandra) or delayed (Clytaemestra and Aegisthus), so that Cassandra is literally accurate to speak of the door of the house as the gate of Hades (1291). Cassandra is the only person who defeats Clytaemestra, ignoring her orders and going into the house at *her own* moment and in freedom. At the end of the play the exit of Clytaemestra and Aegisthus, together, into the palace marks the public declaration of their union and recalls the movements of various other couples, enacted or described: the departure of Helen, with Paris, through this same door (407-8); the meeting, not side by side but face to face, in front of the door, of Agamemnon and Clytaemestra, and their passages through it, one after the other, a few seconds apart, stage-managed by Clytaemestra; the arrival of Agamemnon and Cassandra in a carriage, like bride and groom, after which Agamemnon treats her well-being as his wife's responsibility (950-5) and they enter the palace separately at an interval of 358 lines.

In *Choephoroi* the action is at first centred on Agamemnon's tomb, but the house is not forgotten. First Electra (233-4), then both Electra and Orestes (264-8), are warned to guard their tongues for fear their presence may be betrayed to the rulers. Earlier on, too, very unusually, the chorus (accompanied by Electra) have actually, it seems, entered from the *skênê*[18] – the first persons in the trilogy to do so, other than Clytaemestra; and though they have come out by her instructions, they are hostile to her and sabotage her orders. The palace is made the focus of the action again by the frequent references to it and especially to its door (*Cho.* 561, 565, 569, 571) in Orestes' speech outlining his plans, not long before he and Pylades knock at that same door, and it remains so from then to the death of Clytaemestra. But how different things are now from the way they were in *Agamemnon*! In scenes totalling only 279 lines, no less than five characters come out of the palace (Clytaemestra twice, the Nurse, another Servant, Orestes and Pylades); Aegisthus is the only character who is never seen emerging from the door. Clytaemestra exercises little control over their movements, though she thinks she does: she admits two Phocian travellers to the house – but in fact she has admitted her murderers; she sends the Nurse on an errand – but the Nurse delivers a different message; she summons Aegisthus – and she is summoning him to his death. She does not even exercise much control over her own movements: both times she appears she has to be summoned, and the second time she is apparently asleep behind a barred door (877-82). By then the door has virtually ceased to be any kind of barrier to the movement, or even the vision, of others: four characters come out of it within a maximum of 24 lines

(875-99), Orestes' appearance at the central door forestalls Clytaemestra's intention of entering it[19] (892), Aegisthus' corpse can be seen through the door from outside by the characters though probably not by the audience (892-3, 904), and the words and movements of the Servant in 875ff. will create the impression that the action being viewed is occurring not in front of the house but in its internal court (on these matters see further §7.6.6). Inside and outside merge as the authority of Clytaemestra dissolves; by 930 a new authority has been established as Clytaemestra, who before had always entered the house at her own sovereign volition, is forced through the door by Orestes and Pylades to her death.

In *Eumenides*, while the fortunes of 'houses' in various senses of the word (from the royal house of Argos to the temple of Apollo at Delphi, from Athenian families to the edifice of universal justice) are of as great consequence as ever, the visible house on stage, the *skênê*, is functional only in the opening, Delphic scenes, and the barrier between interior and exterior plays a role only in the two halves of the Pythia's prologue. Thereafter at Delphi we are *inside* the temple, just as when Orestes comes to Athens he is apparently inside the temple of Athena.

7.6.2. Tableaux and scene changes. It was argued in §2.1 that for the *Oresteia* Aeschylus had available the device now usually called the *ekkyklêma* – though perhaps 'device' is too grandiose a term for so simple and untechnological an object. The *ekkyklêma* should be thought of not as a mechanical contrivance but as a convention. It is significant that in later tragedy its use is often preceded by an instruction to 'open the doors'. What is seen on the *ekkyklêma* is, in principle, what one might see looking into the house through an open door. If the tableau was simply set up inside the *skênê*, the audience would not be able to see it; therefore it is displaced forwards to a position where they can.

The three *ekkyklêma* tableaux of the *Oresteia* all show victims of the Erinyes, but in other respects the first two of them resemble each other much more closely than either resembles the third. In both a killer, holding a bloodstained sword (see §7.6.4), stands over the bodies of his or her two victims, a man and a woman, describes the iniquities of the victims, and affirms the justice of the killing. In both scenes, too, the entangling robe that trapped Agamemnon is displayed – though in *Ag.* it is tight around the body, while in *Cho.* it is spread out to its fullest extent (983). There are important differences, however, not only, obviously, in the moral standing of the two killers and the impression their apologias make, but also in the visual presentations. Three features of the tableau in *Ag.* are particularly grotesque: the fact that the killer is a woman, who by all the rules of society ought not to be wielding a sword at all; the fact that not only her hands and sword are bloody, but also her clothes (1389-92; when she appears as a corpse in *Choephoroi*, and as a ghost in *Eumenides*, there will again be blood on her clothes, for different reasons); and the silver bathtub in which Agamemnon is incongruously sprawled. A correspondingly incongruous feature of the tableau in *Cho.* is the suppliant-branch which Orestes is holding in his left hand, and which is left unexplained for over sixty lines (cf. 1035).

In the third tableau, which is revealed directly after *Eum.* 63, Orestes is shown exactly as he had appeared at the end of the previous play (cf. 40-5), but he is now transformed from killer to victim. However, he is not lying down; he is sitting or kneeling at the sacred navel-stone. His pursuers have failed to slay him, and indeed they seem themselves at this moment dead to the world. And, crucially, whereas the previous two tableaux had remained unchanged for long periods, this one is transformed almost as soon as we see it by the appearance of Apollo, with the result that the 'victim' departs on his feet and the 'killers' remain immobile.

The *ekkyklêma* in tragedy is usually a temporary device: at some point the display has to be removed and the fiction of an interior scene abandoned. Often the fiction was never very rigorously maintained in the first place. In *Agamemnon* the corpses are still visible when Aegisthus enters; his first speech ends with an expression of delight at 'having seen this man in the toils of Justice' (1611) – which implies that the body is still wrapped in its entangling robe; and Agamemnon is still 'this man here' as late as 1643. At 1672-3, however, when Clytaemestra and Aegisthus go into the palace, it will not do to have a corpse-laden trolley in the way. The trolley can conveniently be withdrawn when attention is centred on the threatening confrontation between the chorus and Aegisthus' guards (1649-53). Possibly Clytaemestra had previously stepped down from it; possibly she disappeared inside with it, and then came out unsummoned yet again at 1654 to impose her will on the male world. Almost throughout the section of the play when the *ekkyklêma* was in use, it would be artificial to ask what persons or objects are inside the house and what outside. Physically, everyone and everything is outside. At first it is clear that Clytaemestra and the corpses are notionally within, and she makes this explicit at 1379; but thereafter the only continuing reminder that this is supposed to be an interior scene is the presence of the bathtub, and no one would suppose (for example) that Aegisthus and all his guards are imagined as being inside the palace in 1577ff.

If *Choephoroi* had survived without *Agamemnon*, we might well have wondered whether it was justifiable to assume the use of the *ekkyklêma* at all in 973ff. Orestes speaks first as the liberator of the city (*Cho.* 973) before he mentions the house, and the murderous robe is displayed to the heavens[20] which can only be done in the open air (though it could be done, we should remember, in the internal *courtyard* of a house). The parallel with *Agamemnon* makes it overwhelmingly probable that the tableau in *Cho.* was presented in the same way, even though nothing at all in the words of the text signals an interior scene. Orestes must step off the trolley fairly early, for he must be near the robe when it is displayed and its display will require plenty of space. The robe is still visible at 1015, but thereafter there is no deictic reference either to it or to the bodies; from 1021 attention is centred on Orestes himself (where at 973 he had said 'Behold the twin tyrants of the land', now at 1034 he says 'Behold me'), and probably the trolley with the bodies was withdrawn, and the robe taken away, during the short choral chant 1018-20.

In *Eumenides*, for the only time in surviving tragedy, an *ekkyklêma* tableau breaks up before our eyes, leaving the platform empty. It begins with Orestes at the navel-stone and Erinyes[21] asleep on chairs (cf. 46-7); presently Apollo also appears. But at 93 Orestes leaves and Apollo withdraws; from 140 the Erinyes awake and constitute themselves as a chorus in the *orkhêstra*, and the *ekkyklêma* platform is deserted. Its use, however, has had the effect that the whole acting area is now imagined to represent the interior of the temple; for Apollo cannot order the Erinyes 'out of this house ... get away from the inner prophetic shrine' (179-80) unless they are still in that house and close to that shrine. Probably the platform, with the navel-stone on it, is still visible, and Apollo reappears in the same place as before.

Immediately afterwards another interior scene is created, not, however, by means of the *ekkyklêma* but by the older, purely verbal technique employed briefly at *Persians* 140ff. Orestes enters; he approaches and then clasps an image which his words identify as the ancient olive-wood image of Athena Polias (242). Since that image was, as everyone knew, inside her temple on the Acropolis, the acting area will automatically be taken to represent the interior of that temple; the image will be best placed in the centre of the *orkhêstra*, at or near the *thymelê* (see 2.1), since only thus can the chorus completely surround Orestes while weaving their binding-spell about him (299-396). This localization of the action remains valid when Athena herself arrives, the image being mentioned as late as 446 and the temple at 474; but though at 488 Athena says that after choosing judges for the case she will 'come back', when she does return it is clear from the start, when trumpeter and herald are ordered to assemble the people, that the trial is being held in an outdoor, public place, eventually identified (685) as the Areopagus.[22] Various material impedimenta have to be provided for use during the trial (see below), and at the same time as they are being brought on the image of Athena can be unobtrusively taken away.

7.6.3. Clothing. A fair amount can be deduced about the dress of several characters, individual and collective, in the *Oresteia*, both from what is said in the text and from representations in art (especially those which date from the decades immediately following the first production of the trilogy). In some cases, as will be seen, costume proves to be of high thematic importance.

Clytaemestra. It is not clear whether there is anything distinctive about Clytaemestra's costume in *Agamemnon*. Probably she dresses in the normal manner associated with noble women in tragedy, with white the predominant colour; for when she describes with relish how she was bespattered by the jet of her husband's blood (1389-92) the dark stains ought to be clearly visible. We should not be tempted, because the chorus compare her to a raven (1473) or a spider (1492), to suppose that she wore black; no doubt, as she eventually avows, she has all the time been mourning for Iphigeneia, no doubt she is the personification of an Erinys, but when Agamemnon returns she must 'seem to be rejoicing' (1238) and could not greet him in mourning garb. In *Choephoroi*, on her first appearance (668ff.), she may wear a similar (but clean) costume; on her second (885ff.), when she has apparently been wakened from sleep, she may give the impression of having dressed hurriedly, perhaps wearing only her inner garment (*chiton*) without the overgarment (*himation*) and/or with dishevelled hair.[23] As a ghost in *Eumenides* she will wear this same *chiton*, in which she was killed, but now marked with rents and bloodstains (*Eum.* 103).

Agamemnon makes his first (and only) entry as the conqueror of Troy. Both the preceding choral song (cf. especially *Ag.* 691, 741, 752, 773-82) and much that is said in the 'crimson cloth' scene will make us think of wealth and luxury and their attendant dangers; and Agamemnon arrives riding in a carriage like the queen of Persia (see §2.2). He ought therefore to be dressed with special magnificence, probably in a brightly coloured, embroidered robe, a little like the Greek stereotype of an oriental ruler.[24] The fabric of the cloths on which he is invited to walk may be rather similar; these cloths are repeatedly spoken of as 'raiment' (921, 960, 963). Agamemnon later appears again, dressed in another luxurious and brightly coloured robe (*Ag.* 1383, *Cho.* 1013), but one which envelops him completely and has received a fresh 'dye' of blood (*Cho.* 1012-13), having been pierced in three places; this robe, often also spoken of as a net (*Ag.* 1115-16, 1382; *Cho.* 492, 998-1000; *Eum.* 460), will be displayed to the world years later by Orestes, and recalled by him and Apollo later still before and during his trial.

Cassandra. We know from *Ag.* 1264-70 (when she tears it off and tramples on it) that Cassandra was wearing a distinctive 'oracular dress' (as she calls it) and that it included a garland around her neck. The text offers no clue to the nature of the dress itself, but it may well have been an *agrênon*, a loose-knit woollen robe, looking like a net, which is said to have been worn by seers (among others) and which would have obvious thematic links with the robe in which Agamemnon dies (see above) and with other metaphorical nets that feature in the imagery of the trilogy. Cassandra, unlike Agamemnon, succeeds in breaking out of her net, and (as the chorus note in some bewilderment) freely *chooses* to go to her death.

Orestes and Pylades. A series of artistic representations of Orestes' meeting with Electra (see Prag 1985: 51-7 and pll. 34b, 35b-d, 36b), dating from the decades following the production of the *Oresteia*, show Orestes garbed as a traveller, with a hat (normally a broad-brimmed *petasos*) either on his head or slung round his neck. This then is how he will have appeared in *Choephoroi*, except that he and Pylades also carried their own baggage-bundles (cf. 675). In the opening scenes the hat was probably slung over his shoulders (cf. 230 where he invites Electra to put the lock of his hair, which she is holding, at the place from which it was cut), but when he approaches the palace he may have it on his head in order to conceal this hair which so much resembles Electra's (174-6) and presumably Agamemnon's. After the death of Aegisthus concealment is unnecessary, and one might expect the hat to have been discarded; but in post-*Oresteia* vase paintings showing Orestes hounded by the Erinyes the hat is nearly always present (though normally not on the head), and probably therefore Orestes retained it throughout. His partner Pylades will have been dressed very similarly; on two vase-paintings showing the pair of them they are almost indistinguishable except that one (presumably Orestes, as being of higher status) has a patterned border to his cloak and the other does not.

Electra and the chorus of 'Choephoroi'. The chorus is dressed in black (*Cho.* 11). Mourning choruses are not unknown in tragedy (Euripides' *Suppliant Women* and *Trojan Women* are surviving examples), but this case is an abnormal one because the death for which the chorus are mourning is that of a master, not a relative, and occurred several years previously. Their clothes have also been torn in grief (26-31); later we shall be seeing other garments with rents in them (see above). Electra also wears black clothes (17-18), but it is unlikely that they are torn. Hence the principal singers in the *kommos* will be Orestes wearing white and Electra wearing black; the same colour contrast has appeared earlier in the trilogy in connection with another pair of siblings, Agamemnon and Menelaus, who were identified by Calchas with the two eagles that attacked the hare, 'one black, one white at the rear' (*Ag.* 113-24).

The Erinyes are described by Orestes, when only he can see them, as 'dark-robed and woven around with many serpents' (*Cho.* 1049-50), and by the Pythia as resembling Gorgons or Harpies (though without wings) and wearing a costume not fit to be worn either in the gods' sanctuaries or in men's homes (*Eum.* 46-56). Artistic representations influenced by the *Oresteia* (see Prag 1985: 48-51 and pll. 30, 31, 32a) tend to show them dressed in light, flimsy, short-skirted *chitons* which leave their arms bare, with vertical line-shading indicating a dark colour; they often have snakes coiled around their heads and arms. This would suit the textual references well; the costume is certainly one that no respectable contemporary Greek female, human or divine, would dream of being seen in. Their masks were probably not exceptionally ugly as has often been supposed (see p. 31n.20), but they appear to have been dark in complexion (cf. *Eum.* 52), a colour always associated with *males* in Greek art; both this and their revealing costume (never normally worn by females on the tragic stage) would suggest that the Erinyes, despite their championship of the mother's rights, are themselves, like Athena (another mature virgin), something less than fully female (see §7.8). At the end of *Eumenides* (1028) the Erinyes, now *Semnai Theai*, are reclothed in crimson robes (no doubt these were simply draped over their dark garments); this serves the double purpose of avoiding having them take part in a joyful procession in an ill-omened garb and of identifying them as *metoikoi* (cf. 1011, 1018) who, we are told, wore robes of this colour in the procession at the Panathenaea.[25]

Apollo appears with Orestes on vase-paintings later than 458 as a very young-looking god, his bordered white garment draped over one shoulder, and wearing a laurel crown.

Athena, we know, wore the 'aegis' (*Eum*. 404). This is represented in art as a garment (now short, now long, and often scaly) fringed with tassels or with snakes, either worn over the shoulders (as is most likely in drama) or hung over the left arm. Since it has a *kolpos* (hanging fold at waist level) it may be rather longer and looser than usually portrayed. Athena's martial aspect would be sufficiently indicated, as in more than one relevant vase-painting, by a helmet and spear.

7.6.4. Weapons and implements. At one moment while Orestes, after having killed Clytaemestra, is justifying his action and displaying to the world and the gods the entangling robe used in the murder of Agamemnon, he says (*Cho*. 1010-1):

> Did she do it or did she not? This robe
> bears witness for me of how Aegisthus' sword dyed it.

Why *Aegisthus'* sword? Aegisthus, we know, was not even present when Agamemnon was killed; Orestes claims to have executed him not for murder but for adultery (990), and all his efforts are being bent to assert the guilt not of Aegisthus but of his mother. Aeschylus, then, envisaged Clytaemestra as killing Agamemnon not with an axe (as in many literary texts and artistic representations, especially those involving the bath and robe – see §7.4) but with a sword (cf. *Ag*. 1262, 1528), and specifically Aegisthus' sword. It follows too that when Clytaemestra is seen directly after the murder she must be holding that sword; and further, that when Aegisthus arrives from elsewhere shortly afterwards and makes his boastful, exultant speech over his dead enemy, he himself does not have a weapon. Thus when at the end of *Agamemnon* Clytaemestra leads him into the palace, in reversal of the normal order of society (and, as Greeks believed, of nature) she is armed and he is not. No wonder the chorus address him as 'woman'.

It may be worth while to examine what weapons and weapon-like objects other characters are seen holding or wearing during the *Oresteia*. With one important exception these objects are all long and thin. The first such objects we see are the walking-sticks of the Argive elders (*Ag*. 76, 81);

these are a mark of old age, yet they are not so very unlike the staff or sceptre which is the mark of royalty, and it is striking that when the sticks are first mentioned they are actually called *skêptra* (75, cf. 43) while not long afterwards the royal sceptres of Agamemnon and Menelaus (who are certainly *not* old men) are called *baktra*, a poetic variant of *baktêria* 'walking-sticks' (202, cf. *Cho.* 362). The elders, of course, carry these sticks throughout *Agamemnon*, and no doubt use them to emphasize important utterances both in speech and in song, for example when threatening Clytaemestra after Agamemnon's murder (1407ff., especially 1429-30 'you are yet destined ... to pay for stroke with stroke') and at an even more dramatic moment which will be mentioned presently.

There is no sign that Clytaemestra has anything in her hands during any of her appearances on stage before the murder. The first principal who does will be the Herald, who carries the distinctive staff which is his badge of office. He is presently followed by Agamemnon and Cassandra. Agamemnon probably both carries a sceptre as king, and wears a sword as the warrior who conquered Troy; these emblems of civil and military power would fit particularly well with the conclusion of his speech on arrival, when he speaks both of taking counsel in public assemblies (844-7) and of removing any ills in the body politic by 'burning or cutting' (848-50). And yet he, in the crimson-cloth scene, is conquered by his wife, who wields no weapons except those of the intellect. Cassandra is also carrying a *skêptron* (1265) of a very different kind, probably a staff adorned with laurel leaves, an emblem of her status as a prophet of Apollo; in 1264ff. she breaks it and throws it away, an extraordinary act of sacrilege which has attracted curiously little notice from scholars.

After the murder, as we have seen, Clytaemestra appears with a bloodstained sword in her hand, which she will brandish defiantly on lines such as these (*Ag.* 1403-6):

> I say, and it is all the same whether you wish
> to praise or blame me: this is Agamemnon,
> my husband, a corpse, the work of this right hand,
> an artisan of justice.

Aegisthus, on the other hand, is conspicuously unarmed, but he is accompanied by a guard of 'spear-bearers' (*doryphoroi*, cf. *Cho.* 769). The guard also wear swords, and at 1651 they are ordered to get them 'ready, hilt-foremost', i.e. to have hand on hilt in a position where the sword can be instantly drawn for action. The chorus-leader replies 'I am hilt-foremost too, and do not refuse to die', and it seems as though the elders are ready to fight against swords and spears with walking-sticks, until Clytaemestra intervenes.

The text of *Choephoroi* does not make it clear whether Orestes and Pylades wear swords in the early part of the play. It is striking, however, that vase-paintings showing their meeting with Electra and datable *later* than 458, unlike the few that are earlier, regularly show the two men dressed not as warriors but as travellers, sometimes carrying staffs but normally not weapons; one may therefore reasonably suppose that this is how Aeschylus portrayed them.[26] Another important hand-held object hereabouts is the lock of Orestes' hair, which he dedicates at his father's tomb in the prologue and which Electra holds from 164 until at least 230, afterwards presumably returning it to its place.

If this is correct, no weapon of any sort will be seen in *Choephoroi* until Orestes emerges from the palace at 892, accompanied or followed by Pylades. He and Pylades are explicitly posing as travellers when they approach the house at 653. Aegisthus, who lets others (Clytaemestra and his guards) do his fighting for him, is almost certainly unarmed as he was in *Agamemnon*, particularly since the Nurse's false message told him to come with a light heart (772) and not to frighten his visitors (771). At the same time, sharp bronze is insistently present in the *words* of Orestes and especially of the chorus (576, 584, 639, 647-8, 729, 859-60, 883-4). Aegisthus is killed; Clytaemestra is roused, calls for an axe but never gets it – and out come Orestes and Pylades with their drawn swords.

After the murder, and likewise at the beginning of *Eumenides*, Orestes still has his sword, now bloodied, but he also holds a suppliant-branch in his other hand (1035). Of the other personages who appear in the Delphic scenes of *Eumenides*, the Erinyes and the ghost of Clytaemestra seem to be empty-handed, but the Pythia perhaps holds a laurel-twig in her right hand. Apollo appears twice, in different roles and probably with different accoutrements. At his first appearance (64) he is a purifier and protector, and to judge by vase-paintings he will have held a long laurel-bough in his left hand. When he reappears, however, at 179, he is an archer, and he may well have his bow drawn back ready to shoot. On the divine level, as on the human level in the previous play, the normal relationship of the genders has seemingly been re-established: in contrast with what we saw in *Agamemnon*, males (Orestes, Apollo) are armed, females (the Pythia, the Erinyes, the ghost of Clytaemestra) are not.

But at Athens things are less clear. Orestes claims no longer to have polluted hands, and there is no sign that he now has a sword: in his final pledge of an eternal alliance between Argos and Athens (762-74) he does not promise to fight physically himself, but to bless or curse the Argives from his tomb according as they respect or violate the pact; and a little earlier, when he thinks of committing suicide in the event of defeat (746), he envisages a death not by the sword but by the noose. Athena, on the other hand, in all probability *does* appear in armour and carrying a spear: she has come from taking possession of captured enemy territory (398-402), Orestes had appealed to her as a warrior goddess (292-6), and her own specific blessing on the Athenians is a military one (913-15, cf. 864-5). The oxymoron 'a woman's spear' appeared twice earlier in the trilogy (*Ag.*

483, *Cho.* 630), in difficult contexts but clearly implying that females and spears did not go naturally together. But if the female is Athena, they do.

In the trial scene the herald's staff makes a fresh appearance (566), as does a new hand-held object, the trumpet (567), normally a military appurtenance but here proclaiming a session of a lawcourt. And then we meet another weapon, which within a civilized community ought to be mightier than a sword: the pebble with which a juryman casts his vote (the only object in this entire series which is not long and thin). Once the metaphorical voting-pebbles of the gods decided the fate of Troy (*Ag.* 813-17) and the Argive elders debated and voted ineffectively on how to react to the possible murder of Agamemnon (*Ag.* 1348-71); now the silent dropping of actual pebbles into urns saves Orestes and inaugurates a new way to respond to violence within the community, the sword being reserved for responding to violence from outside.[27]

One more kind of long thin hand-held object has still to be introduced: the torches (*Eum.* 1005, 1022, 1029, 1041-2) which illuminate the final procession. In spite of all the talk there has been throughout the trilogy of light and fire in all sorts of contexts, only now is fire actually seen on stage. The long night of violence has ended at last. In this final procession only one person carries a weapon, and that person is Athena.

7.6.5. Silent performers. Traditionally the lists of *dramatis personae* prefixed to Greek plays, whether tragic or comic, include only those personages who speak. It may be worth while to examine what non-speaking performers are shown by the text to have been on stage at various times during the performance of the *Oresteia*.

Attendants. It is generally assumed (cf. §2.2) that any person of high status would normally be attended by one or more slaves, of whom the text would not take notice except when they were ordered to do something special. Such attendants, as in real life, would normally be of the same gender as the principal. Leaving aside the special case of Aegisthus' guards, the passages in the trilogy at which notice is taken of such attendants are *Ag.* 908ff., when Clytaemestra's slaves spread out the crimson cloth in front of Agamemnon; *Cho.* 712-15, when Clytaemestra orders a slave (of unspecified gender) to take the 'Phocian visitors' to suitable guest-chambers; and *Cho.* 983ff., where Orestes orders the entangling robe to be displayed. Agamemnon also was probably attended at his victorious homecoming, perhaps by a few soldiers; the carriage in which he arrived would have been drawn by horses or mules, and the attendants could be disposed of by having them take the animals away. In the earlier scenes, when Clytaemestra is posing as the dutiful wife of an absent lord, she would no doubt take care, as Penelope does in the *Odyssey*, to have a maid or two with her when speaking to men from outside the family such as the Elders and the Herald. After the murder, on the other hand, she would be on her own, just as she committed it on her own. In *Choephoroi*

Orestes makes a point of saying that he and his companion have carried their own luggage (675) instead of being accompanied by slaves as travellers in real life (and comedy) normally were; Aegisthus also, as we have seen, arrives alone. In *Eumenides* Orestes is of course alone as a fugitive. The Pythia must be alone too; her only possible attendants would be the priests of the temple, and when she leaves the scene she entrusts the protection of the sanctuary not to them but to Apollo himself.

Aegisthus' bodyguard. These 'spear-bearers', whose presence stamps Aegisthus as a *tyrannos*, may well be equal in number to the chorus they confront. It is possible that their captain has a one-line speaking part (*Ag.* 1651).[28] In *Choephoroi* Orestes' allies contrive to keep them out of the way, and Aegisthus is alone.

Trial scene. The Areopagite jurors (who number either ten or eleven; see §7.3) have one of the most important non-speaking roles in all drama, for their votes decide a major issue of the trilogy. Two (or possibly four) of them have the further function of counting the votes (*Eum.* 742-3). There are also present in this scene a herald (566) and a trumpeter (567-9).

Final procession. At *Eumenides* 1005 is signalled the arrival on stage of a group whom Athena describes first as 'these escorts' and later (1024-5) as 'the handmaids who guard my image'. At the same time various properties are brought on, presumably by these same persons: torches (1004), one or more animals for sacrifice (1006) and crimson robes (1028). Since, according to the scholia (with which modern scholars generally agree), these female 'escorts' sing the concluding lyrics (1032ff.), they are not strictly non-speaking performers, but they may conveniently be considered under the same heading. The description of them in 1024-5 shows that they are the staff of the temple of Athena Polias, which consisted of women and girls from aristocratic Athenian families; other evidence indicates that this staff comprised three adults (including the priestess) and, at any given time, at least four children and perhaps several more. Two of this group will have carried the torches, and another, or others, will have led the sacrificial animal(s). Since the procession must also have included everyone else who was on stage at the time (the chorus, the Areopagites, Athena, the herald and trumpeter) it will have comprised a minimum of 32 persons and probably more.

Citizen crowds? At three moments in the trilogy the text assumes the presence of a large number of anonymous citizens. In *Cho.* 973ff. Orestes speaks as though to a public meeting of the Argive people, laying emphasis on the civic aspects of his actions (973, 975) in a manner which would be inappropriate if his sole audience were the chorus of female slaves, and calling 'all the Argives' to bear witness for him when the time comes to do so (1040-1). In *Eum.* 566ff, Athena orders the trumpeter and herald to call 'the host' to order so that her court can begin its work. And at the end of *Eum.* the processional escort (or perhaps one of their number, presumably the priestess) calls on 'all the people of the land' first to keep silence (1035,

1039) and then to utter a cry of joy (1043, 1047). It is not likely that in any of these scenes an actual stage-crowd was brought on. It is noteworthy that in the trial-scene those who are asked to keep silent are 'the whole city *for all time*' (572), an expression which corresponds to Athena's explanation that her speech inaugurating the Areopagos court is addressed to 'my citizens for the future' (707-8); this seems a strong indication that it is *the theatre audience* that is being called to order and is expected to listen carefully. It is reasonable to make the same assumption in the other two passages. In *Cho.* 973ff. Orestes, at least at first, is on or near the *ekkyklêma*, right at the back of the acting area, and must have been speaking straight at the audience in any case; and at the end of *Eumenides* it is highly appropriate for the Athenian people in the theatre to celebrate with cries of joy the inauguration of a cult which, as they have been explicitly told, offers blessing to them and their descendants for ever. Stage-crowds of citizens are not unknown in Greek tragedy (witness the opening of *Seven against Thebes* or of Sophocles' *Oedipus the King*); but in the *Oresteia*, especially towards the end when the relevance of the action to the contemporary world is a vital feature (see further §12.1), a stage-crowd representing a citizen body distinct from the audience would not be appropriate. It is somewhat otherwise in *Agamemnon* where the citizen-body of Argos is represented by the chorus, whose role as helpless spectators of the ruin of their city is not one in which the dramatist would wish to cast his own audience.

7.6.6. The murder scene in 'Choephoroi' (869-934). This scene, especially in its first half, represents quite a challenge for theatrical reconstruction, and it may be worth while to examine the questions that arise, some possible solutions and the arguments bearing on them. Our basic assumptions are that the arrangement of the acting area was as described (for the end of Aeschylus' career) in §2.1, with an *orkhêstra* and a *skênê* with an uncertain number of doors in its façade, and that the dramatist could make use of a maximum of three speaking actors. What the text offers us is this: it should be remembered that the marginal speaker-indications were inserted by ancient editors and are not properly part of the transmitted text.

A cry of distress is heard within (869). The chorus decide to 'stand away from the action that is reaching completion' (872). Someone cries out that Aegisthus is dead and calls urgently 'Open up right away, and undo the women's doors with bars' (878-9); receiving no reply, he complains that everyone is asleep and asks 'Where is Clytaemestra? What is she doing?' (882). Either the same person, speaking 'aside', or the chorus-leader, remarks that Clytaemestra is now very close to a well-deserved death (883-4). Clytaemestra appears, asks what is the matter, is told 'the dead are killing the living' (886), and calls for an axe (889). Then Orestes appears, saying 'It's *you* I'm after; *this* man's been satisfactorily dealt with'

(892) – referring to Aegisthus, whom he again calls 'this man (here)' in 904 and 907. Clytaemestra tries to stop him by urging him to 'respect this breast' which he once sucked (896-8). Orestes asks Pylades whether he should spare his mother. Pylades tells him he must at all costs obey the word of Apollo. Orestes accepts his advice and says to Clytaemestra 'Follow me; I want to slay you next to this man' (904). She resists and argues, but to no avail; on Orestes' last words, 'You killed whom you should not, now suffer what you should not' (930), the scene ends, and the chorus-leader comments that she grieves for the two victims but that it would have been a greater evil if 'the eye of the house' had been extinguished.

The following questions arise:

Where do the chorus move in 872-4, and why are they made to move? Whatever their movement is, it is presumably reversed in 931-4 after which they are again in their normal position in the *orkhêstra*, ready to perform the next ode. 872 ought to imply that they group themselves well away from the *skênê*. The effect of this is to concentrate all attention on the fast-moving events closer to the *skênê*. It also creates a moment of heightened tension, since the chorus are evidently uncertain whether Aegisthus or Orestes has been killed. And it avoids any uncomfortable questions arising about exactly where the chorus are supposed to be, when they had previously been outside the house (cf. 848-50) and yet the action is now (from 875) proceeding in its internal courtyard (see below).

Who is the speaker of 875-82? Clearly someone who regards himself as a servant of Aegisthus, whom he calls 'master' in 875.

What are his movements and actions? Since he refers to 'women's doors', and since Clytaemestra eventually answers his calls and appears on stage, it is reasonable to assume that the door at which she appears is to be understood as being the door of the women's quarters of the palace. It follows also that the servant must himself be visible on stage by the time he calls for the doors to be opened; therefore he must have come out of the interior space in which Aegisthus has just been killed.[29] Since no sane dramatist would have a character first come out through a door and then call frantically for that same door to be opened, there must have been at least two doors in the *skênê* façade. The servant will come out through one of the doors and begin shouting and knocking at the other. Greek houses normally had only one door communicating with the outside world, so on seeing two doors in use the audience will have understood that they were to imagine the action as being set in the internal courtyard of the house.

If there are two doors, which of them is the main, central door to the skênê? From 892 to the end of the scene only one door is in question: the door out of which Orestes and Pylades come, leaving Aegisthus dead behind them, and through which Orestes seeks to drive his mother to kill her beside her paramour (904, 906). Both for symmetry in this scene itself, and for effective mirroring of the scene in which Agamemnon walked into the palace to his death, this ought to be the central door. Therefore the Servant, also coming from the place where Aegisthus died, comes out of this door and knocks at a subsidiary door at which Clytaemestra appears. Thus this entry by Clytaemestra differs from all her previous entries in the first and second plays; she enters by an inferior door and probably in a state of toilette less than perfect for a royal person (see §7.6.3).

Who speaks 883-4? There are objections both to the Servant and to the chorus-leader as the speaker, but either assignment can be defended in dramatic terms. If the Servant speaks, the words are inconsistent with his grief at the death of Aegisthus and the urgency with which he summons Clytaemestra to take notice of her danger – but on the other hand they may reflect his delayed awareness that he no longer needs to conceal his real feelings towards the usurpers, and help to explain his failure to fetch the axe a moment later. If it is the chorus-leader who speaks, it is surprising that she should do so here and only here in the scene, particularly when the chorus were so anxious just now to dissociate themselves from the action – but on the other hand the clear evidence that Aegisthus is dead has removed her greatest anxiety, the risk to the life of Orestes (cf. 861-2, 934). The unemphatic pronoun *autês* 'her' in 883 tells somewhat in favour of assigning the couplet to the Servant, who has just referred emphatically to Clytaemestra by name.

How is the Servant removed from the scene? 889 seems to be designed in part as a means of achieving his removal.[30] It is addressed to 'someone', i.e. anyone who hears and is willing to help; the Servant is the only person present at that moment, and under his mistress's eye he must obey. He most likely goes off into the men's quarters from which he came. Before he can return with the axe, Orestes appears, and the Servant ceases to be relevant. One might speculate whether to suppose that he never intended to obey the order or that he was rendered harmless by Orestes and Pylades, but there are too many other things happening for a spectator in the theatre to indulge in such thoughts.

Can the audience see Aegisthus? This would only be possible if his body were brought out on the *ekkyklêma*, and that in turn would entail Clytaemestra being killed 'beside him' in full view of the audience. As is well known, violent deaths do not occur on stage in Greek tragedy (the one apparent exception in surviving plays, the suicide of Ajax in Sophocles, was probably so arranged that the death occurred just out of view).[31] Hence the audience will be expected to assume that the body, though invisible to them, is visible to the characters on stage through the open door.

What visible action, if any, accompanies Clytaemestra's words 'respect this breast'? The actor playing Clytaemestra, like all actors on the Athenian stage, was male; but comedy provides ample evidence that feminine anatomical features could where appropriate be indicated (by padding and painting) on the bodysuits which actors wore under their costumes. This may well have been unprecedented in tragedy, but it would not necessarily have been thought undignified, any more than is the gesture by Hecuba to Hector in *Iliad* 22.80 on which this passage is modelled or similar gestures by the mothers of other heroes such as Callirrhoe in Stesichorus' *Geryoneis* (*GL* S13) and Iocaste in Euripides' *Phoenician Maidens* (1568). Hecuba is said to have 'drawn open the fold of her dress, and held up her breast with her other hand'; probably Clytaemestra will have been made to do exactly the same. Whether invented by Aeschylus or inherited from the lyric tradition, the gesture became famous; Clytaemestra does it (offstage) in Euripides' *Electra* (1206-7) and it is recalled in his *Orestes* (527, 841). It is ingeniously transformed in another Euripidean play, *Andromache* (McClure 1999: 194-5). The distraught Hermione, dreading the anger of her husband after the failure of her plot to murder Andromache and her child, appears at 825 with her hair disarranged, her clothes torn *and her breast exposed*, and refuses her nurse's advice to make herself look decent (832-5) and/or to go inside; and while she is still outside, and still in the same state, who should appear but ... Orestes (881), whose knees she immediately rushes to clasp, and with whom she presently runs off? Hermione is, of course, the daughter of Helen (who famously used the same ploy to save her life[32]) and the niece of Clytaemestra.

When does Pylades enter? A director who was free to use as many actors as he wished would almost certainly bring Pylades on at 892 together with Orestes, by whose side he has been throughout the play. This, however, would most likely require a fourth actor,[33] since the Servant is certainly present until 886 and probably until 889, and there is no other scene in extant tragedy where a fourth speaking actor is required (except in the case of child parts, for which an exception was evidently made because child parts could not be doubled with adult ones). In Hellenistic times the three-actor rule was erected into an aesthetic canon, but in origin it was probably no more than a device to secure a measure of equality among the festival competitors, like the comparable rule which fixed the size of the chorus. Competition rules are made to be observed (MacDowell 1994: 326); and fifty years later we find Sophocles in *Oedipus at Colonus* resorting to some quite artificial expedients, such as (apparently) splitting the part of Theseus between two or even three actors and (certainly) making Ismene an important speaking character in some scenes while keeping her silent in others, in order to avoid a breach of this rule. Hence we are not entitled here to assume four actors if the scene can be performed with three; and it can be so performed, provided Pylades' entry is delayed until shortly before Orestes addresses him at 899. As Garvie 1986: l has noted, the delay can itself be seen as serving a dramatic function, namely that of isolating Orestes. The killing of Clytaemestra must on the human level be his act alone, for Pylades' part is irrelevant to the conflicts that will follow; and in the present scene Pylades' role is no longer that of a subordinate partner but that of Apollo's spokesman.

How is the exit of Orestes and Clytaemestra managed? Orestes' 'follow me' at 904 implies that he is nearer to the central door than Clytaemestra is. Therefore, unless their relative positions somehow change, he cannot alone drive her through the door (as he does Aegisthus at the end of Sophocles' *Electra*); possibly he drags her in, but more likely Pylades places himself on her other side and the two together force her through the door.

7.7. Imagery

Perhaps no work of Greek literature – perhaps few works in any literature – have a richer or more complex texture of imagery than the *Oresteia*. There are literally dozens of motifs that crop up time and again through the trilogy, sometimes in the form of a casual use of a word, sometimes as a striking simile or metaphor, sometimes in concrete, visible form on stage; and most of them soon acquire more and more sinister connotations, which they retain through almost the whole of the action, only to shed them all towards the end of *Eumenides* when the very same words come to convey a message of joy.

Let us take two typical motifs and follow them through the trilogy: the theme of dew (or more generally of things that drip) and the theme of young creatures. And let us note, right at the start, that these two motifs, like almost any other pair that might have been chosen, are interrelated. The Greek word for dew, *drosos*, can denote the generative seed of men or animals, and therefore, like *sperma* 'seed', it can also mean 'offspring', so that lion-cubs can be called 'the *drosoi* of lions' (*Ag.* 141). Another dripping liquid with which young creatures have much to do is the mother's milk, which figures repeatedly in the trilogy in various connections, and which provides a link, in turn, to the important theme of nourishment (*trophê*). And if dew-like liquids thus attend life's beginning, life can likewise end violently amid drops of blood, so that the *drosos* motif can be linked not only with the birth and growth of young creatures but also with their death. And both our chosen themes, as we shall partly see, are further linked to other themes in a web of almost inexhaustible complexity.

The theme of dew is introduced, quite casually, in *Ag.* 12 by the Watchman describing the discomforts of his watch:

> And when, abroad at night, I keep my dew-soaked couch,
> my couch not watched over by dreams ...

Not only 'dew-soaked' but also 'abroad at night' and 'dreams' are going to become thematic notions, as are Fear and Sleep, mentioned later in the same sentence; indeed the whole of the Watchman's speech is like an overture to the *Oresteia*, introducing in thirty-nine lines some twenty-five or thirty notions that are going to recur again and again throughout the trilogy[34] – though for the moment few of them appear more than once.

Drops of liquid appear next at 69, in the form of libations poured out to the gods – libations which are said to be incapable of placating their 'inflexible anger' – and in company, once again, with several other thematic ideas (persuasion, sacrifice, fire, wrath); and there follows the curious and arresting use of *drosoi* in reference to lion-cubs (141), already mentioned. But at this stage it is far from clear how Aeschylus is going to exploit this theme.

Its first emphatic presentation is in the 'Hymn to Zeus' (179), in close connection with the principle 'learning by suffering':

> There *drips* before the heart, instead of sleep,
> the pain that brings suffering to mind

– this uncomfortable dripping being portrayed as antagonistic to sleep as it was in the words of the Watchman. From now on most of the dripping liquids we hear of will indeed, in one way or another, put us in mind of suffering – though not for a long time will there be any sign that anyone is learning from this suffering. Before very long, human blood is flowing, the blood of Iphigeneia. There is only one direct reference to this (209-11), when Agamemnon pictures himself

> defiling a father's hands
> with streams of a slain maiden's blood
> next the altar;

but just before the actual slaughter the theme reappears in two expressions which by their very inappropriateness point up the horrible unnaturalness of what is taking place. First (239) we seem to see Iphigeneia's saffron-coloured robe 'poured to the ground', falling from her like a dash of yellow liquid; and then we hear (246) how she had often in her father's house sung the paean 'with the third libation' – when red wine was poured out in honour of Zeus the Saviour, as red blood is about to be poured in order that the agent of Zeus Xenios may shed more blood at Troy.

In the following scene we return to early morning dew, in an obvious reprise of the Watchman's opening statement of the theme (334-7):

> Now they are dwelling in captured Trojan houses,
> released from the frosts and dews
> of the open air, and like happy men
> they will sleep all night long with none to keep watch

– though the very next lines will remind the audience that this 'release' was at best temporary. Later (560-2) the Herald will have more to say about the hardships of the campaign:

> The rain from the sky, the dew on the grass from the ground,
> drizzled and soaked us, a persistent plague,
> filling the wool of our clothes with animal life

– a euphemism for lice, which are never mentioned by their proper name (*phtheires*) in tragedy.

Presently, however, this comparatively harmless nuisance gives place to more sinister variations on the theme. In the lion-cub parable of 717-36 two dripping liquids are highlighted which in this trilogy are going to stand in an unnaturally close relationship: one is blood (732), but the other is mother's milk (718-19: the lion-cub 'loved the nipple' but was reared 'without milk'). These of course contrast not only as symbols of birth and of death, but also in colour: the exploitation, verbal and visual, of colour in the *Oresteia* deserves a study to itself. Lions and blood are linked again soon after, when Agamemnon speaks of his army as a lion that has 'licked its fill of royal blood' (828) – and here the verb 'licked', like 'fawning' in the parable (725-6), in turn links the lion to that less noble, but in the *Oresteia* equally thematic, animal, the dog.

We next find the drip theme in a new and surprising form (887-8):

> For me the copious fountains of weeping
> have run dry, and there is not a drop in them.

These words of Clytaemestra's are of course deceptive in intent; and yet one can well imagine that her tears did indeed flow plentifully, not for her absent husband but for the daughter of whom she must for the present make no mention. One may indeed now feel that it was precisely the flow of Iphigeneia's blood that set going all the other flows that we have heard of – the dew of Troy, the blood of its princes, the dew of the palace roof, the mother's tears – as it will also soon cause the flow of more blood. It is almost immediately after this that the crimson vestments are spread out in front of Agamemnon, looking like blood flowing down the palace steps. Clytaemestra may persuade her husband to see it only as a gushing flow of purple dye, to which a price label can be attached (959-60); but *we* know it represents something beyond price.

And now the chorus use the idea of blood flowing to the ground to state one of the basic truths on which the trilogy is founded, and to give us – though they seem not to see it themselves – a reason why Agamemnon's death is certain (1018-21):

> But when the black blood has once fallen
> to the ground in front of a man,
> who can call it up again by incantations?

Clytaemestra may hypocritically invite Cassandra to share the lustral water of ritual hand-washing (1037), but we know what liquid she really has it in mind to pour out, and she has referred to it herself before the end of the same short scene when she pictures Cassandra as a mettlesome young horse, chafing at the bit and 'wasting her strength in bloody foam' (1067). And throughout the Cassandra scene the liquids that drip are all of a deadly nature, either blood or poison (1090-2; 1121-3):

> A house loathed by the gods …
> where men are slaughtered and the ground is bespattered.

> Saffron-coloured drops run to my heart,
> the same that for men who fall by the spear
> accompany the rays of their sinking sun of life

– alluding to a belief that in moments of terror (such as the chorus are now experiencing, and such as a mortally wounded man might be supposed to experience) the blood drains to the heart leaving the rest of the body pallid ('saffron-coloured').

> Like one who compounds a drug,
> she will also put into the potion something to pay me out with (1260-1).

> Instead of my father's altar, a chopping-block awaits me,
> which will be hot with my red blood when I am struck (1277-8).

> I pray to receive a well-aimed stroke,
> that I may close these eyes without a struggle,
> my blood flowing out in easy death (1292-4).

And as Cassandra approaches the palace door and recoils:

> The house breathes blood-dripping murder! (1309).

At last she goes into that house. And then Agamemnon is struck down, and for the first but not the last time we hear of a blood-dripping *sword* (1351); and very shortly after, we see the murderess holding that sword and obscenely rejoicing in the drops of blood as if they were – drops of fertilizing dew; this is where all the dew-imagery of earlier scenes was leading (1389-92):

> He jetted out rapid spurts of blood
> and struck me with a black shower of gory dew
> which gave me no less joy than is given to the crops
> by the Zeus-given moisture when the buds come to birth.

The linkage of death and birth is there again, but there is also something more: in Clytaemestra's pleasure, and in the way she describes it, there is a strong erotic element. A moment later we are invited to think of the almost equally obscene idea of a *libation* of blood (1395-6).

Now that actual bloodshed (as distinct from the memory of bloodshed) has at last entered the trilogy, it generates a new kind of liquid flow, of which we shall hear more (1427-8):

> The blood-dripping deed has made your mind mad:
> the drops of blood on your eyes are clear to see.

In the following epirrhematic dialogue between Clytaemestra and the chorus, references to this theme tend to strike the note that now blood has begun to flow, it will be impossible to put an end to it (1478-81; 1509-12; 1533-4):

> Because of him [the *daimôn* of the house] there grows a passionate
> desire to lick blood,
> and before the old wound heals, there is a fresh flow of pus.
>
> With yet more streams of kindred blood
> the black Spirit of Violence forces his way through
> to reach the point where he will furnish
> satisfaction for the clotted blood of devoured children.
>
> I listen with dread for the noise of a bloody rain
> that will make the house collapse: what has ended is but a drizzle.

That, in *Agamemnon*, is almost all: Aegisthus, who appears shortly after, is not one to be deeply affected by the shedding of blood (but for Clytaemestra's intervention he would have had the elders of Argos butchered without turning a hair), while the chorus are roused by his arrogance from their mood of despair into one of fierce resentment and nearly of violent resistance. But nothing can cancel the truth of what has been said.

The first half of *Choephoroi* is dominated, so far as this theme is concerned, by the flow of another kind of liquid to the ground: the pure drink-offerings to the dead, honey, milk, wine and water. But the flow of blood can never be far from our thoughts, particularly as these drink-offerings are intended, it seems, by Clytaemestra as some sort of atonement for her act of blood (cf. *Cho.* 48, 66-74); and before long the theme is applied in gorier and grislier ways than we have yet heard, when the chorus hope they will one day see Aegisthus and Clytaemestra 'die in the pitchy ooze of the fire' (268), i.e. be coated with pitch and burnt alive, with the pitch on their skins bubbling and spitting as it boils.

We are presently reminded that 'it is the law that drops of blood spilt on the ground call for further blood' (400-2), and the chorus, summing up the message of the whole first half of the play, insist that the old wound in the house of Atreus, which is still oozing pus, can be healed only by 'its own members, through cruel, bloody strife' (466-75). This kind of thing we have heard before; but now comes something new. For it is not just any blood that Orestes is going to have to shed, not even just any kindred blood; it is his mother's blood, and now the imagery begins to focus on this point, by means of the linkage (first established in the lion-cub parable) between blood and milk. Clytaemestra dreamed she gave birth to a serpent, which sucked out a clot of blood with her milk (533, 543-6): the breast that Orestes sucked is the breast that he will make to bleed.

The theme next appears in a most unexpected form: the next dripping liquid of which we hear tell is none other than that with which the infant Orestes bedewed his nappies (756-7). Into this rather distasteful fluid he converted his mother's milk, and gave his nurse a hard time at the wash-tub. But then, as the Nurse now remarks, he didn't know what he was doing (753), his bodily organs ran without central control (757). The Orestes of today will, with full knowledge and full intent, be converting his mother's milk into something far more evil and making a stain that no washerwoman can cleanse.

At last mother and son confront each other. She displays to him the breast from which he once drew milk. Can he now draw blood from it? After the long stichomythia we are given the answer: he is the serpent (928); he will suck her blood. Things have come full circle. We are back where we were after Agamemnon's death. Orestes appears with another reddened sword, and points to where his father's blood can still be seen on the robe in which he was entangled (1012-13), where it ruined that other, harmless product of liquid drops, the brightly-hued dyes of the robe. And then, suddenly, the blood on his hands generates fresh blood in horrifying fashion (1048ff.):

> ORESTES
> Ah, ah! These ghastly women, like Gorgons,
> with dark robes, and coiled around
> with teeming serpents ... the wrathful hounds of my mother!
> CHORUS
> The blood is still fresh on your hands;
> that is why confusion has fallen upon your mind.
> ORESTES
> O Lord Apollo, there are more and more of them!
> And from their eyes they drip a loathsome stream

(or, if we follow the manuscript, 'loathsome blood'). Henceforth the 'endless flow of blood' (as Lebeck 1971 called it) will be embodied in the persons of the Erinyes; and though at present only Orestes can see them (and it), soon we all will.

At the beginning of *Eumenides* we first hear about, and then see, Orestes at Delphi, dripping blood (according to the Pythia) from his hands and sword (41-2), and surrounded by the Erinyes who 'drip loathsome drops from their eyes' (54). Then Orestes comes to be described as a wounded fawn (246), whom the hounds, the Erinyes, track by the trail of blood he leaves behind him – blood which has already (they claim) polluted the sanctuary of Delphi itself (164-8), blood which the Erinyes will drink down (183-4, 264-6, 302, 333), as the serpent who was Orestes once drank blood from his mother's breast. Their fitting home, according to Apollo, would be 'the den of a blood-lapping lion' (193) – which of course harks back to the lion-cub parable, to the lion that licked the royal blood of Troy (*Ag.* 827-8), and to much else.

When the action resumes at Athens, the Erinyes are still tracking Orestes by his trail of blood and eager to suck him dry, but Orestes himself claims that he no longer has blood on his hands (probably, too, he is no longer wearing a sword: see §7.6.4). He has been purified – by sprinkling with blood and water (449-52); for almost the first time in the trilogy, drops of liquid appear to be working good instead of evil. The blood of purification, incidentally, is specifically said to be that of 'a young suckling beast'; thus yet again the two contrasting liquids, white milk and black blood, are brought into close connection.

The arrival of Athena gives a new twist to the theme of deadly dripping liquids, as she foresees that

> if they [the Erinyes] do not achieve a victorious outcome,
> then their injured pride will hereafter drip venom
> which will fall on the ground as a terrible, unbearable pestilence
> (477-9).

For the time being this idea is not developed, and indeed no more is heard of the theme until the middle of the trial-scene, when Apollo restates a familiar maxim, forgetting how easily it can be used against him:

> When a man has once died, and the dust has sucked up
> his blood, there is no rising again (647-8).

The Erinyes naturally pounce on this, and point out that one who has 'poured out on the ground his mother's blood, which is the same as his own' (653) has excluded himself by his pollution from sharing in the pure and holy lustral water at sacrifices. Apollo's reply takes us back to the very beginning of life: the young living thing is created, not from the mother's milk or even from the mother's blood, but from the father's seed (658-61).

On that particular line of argument, one can go no further. But Athena in her speech to the jury and to her 'citizens of the future' takes no notice of it. It is a bright and clear, not a dark or opaque, liquid that has the most prominence in her speech:

> If you pollute clear water with an influx
> of mud, you will never get a drink (695-6).

As we shall see elsewhere (§12.1), the precise interpretation of this remark is disputed, but there certainly must be some relation between this 'clear water' and the council which Athena is establishing to judge and punish the shedding of blood. In the past, the flow of blood has always led to the flow of fresh blood. In Orestes' purification, the stain of blood was washed away by blood and water together. Now it is to be purged by the clear, sparkling water of judicial determination.

But though the 'endless flow of blood' may thus have been staunched, there is still that other threat from the Erinyes hanging over Athens; Apollo may make light of it (729-30), but neither Athena nor her people can afford to. After the departure of Apollo and Orestes, the chorus spell out the threat in full:

> Venom, venom, shall I discharge from my heart, causing sorrow to
> avenge my sorrow,
> to drip upon the land, unendurable; and from it will arise
> a canker bringing leaflessness and childlessness ... (782-5 = 812-15).

But this is the end of the theme in its sinister form; for at 900 the Erinyes 'move away from their anger', and in tune with this, the *drosos* theme shifts – as every other theme does in this part of *Eumenides* – from a theme of darkness to a theme of light. Almost the first of the stream of blessings which fill the conclusion of the trilogy are those which will come 'from the waters (lit. dew) of the sea' (904). We should indeed remember that the Erinyes are still capable, if they are offended, of bringing men 'a life whose eyes are dimmed by tears' (954-5). But men have the power to make sure, by their own actions, that this does not happen, and likewise to make sure that the dust does not 'drink up the black blood of the citizens' in civil strife (980). The purple dye from the sea (*Ag.* 958ff.) which once coloured the fabrics on which Agamemnon walked, and which was then mimicked by the blood that stained both his and Clytaemestra's garments, is seen again now at the end (1028) on the new robes given to the Erinyes, now *Semnai Theai*, to mark their participation as honoured 'resident aliens' (*metoikoi*) in that final procession modelled in part[35] on the procession of the Panathenaea, literally the festival of 'all those who belong to Athens' – or maybe 'to Athena'.

Such is the development and resolution of the theme of flowing and dripping liquids in the *Oresteia*. With the theme of young creatures I shall deal more briefly. During the greater part of the trilogy, almost all the young creatures (human or not) who are mentioned either are the victims of violence, or are destined themselves on reaching maturity to be the perpetrators of violence, or (often enough) both. The first of them are the young birds who are stolen from their nests (*Ag.* 49ff.) – helpless victims who would, however, have become predators and killers had they grown to maturity, like the eagles that kill the unborn young of the hare (119) who, like the young of all wild things, are dear to Artemis (140-3). Then, after long foreshadowing, comes the first young human victim, the daughter of Agamemnon, who is compared, as she comes to sacrifice, to a yearling goat (232) and a heifer (245); and, on the other side, the young Trojans caught in the 'net' of ruin and slavery (359-61). Like the *drosos* theme, the 'young creatures' theme then goes underground for some time, to reappear in fully-developed form in the fable of the lion-cub – the lovable, much-cherished infant (explicitly compared to a human baby, 723) that became a bloody killer. The oxymoron of the infant that kills is repeated when Agamemnon calls his army 'the nestling of the [wooden] Horse' (825) and, a moment later, a slavering lion – and soon afterwards we hear for the first time of another infant who will kill, as Clytaemestra explains why Orestes is gone from home (877ff.) and, shortly thereafter, speaks of the hope for a family's future that is all embodied in 'a father's only child' (898). Then another break; and then the overwhelming horror of the murder and dismemberment of the children of Thyestes (1095ff. and often again), with its echo in the death of Itys (1144) whose flesh, as the listeners will remember, was also served up to, and eaten by, his father.[36] Cassandra herself is another young victim; and before she leaves the scene she reminds us, too, of her own brothers, all killed in their youth (1305). Thereafter we are reminded constantly, now of Iphigeneia, now of the children of Thyestes; these, the murdered offspring, are the young creatures most in our minds at the end of *Agamemnon*.

In *Choephoroi*, on the other hand, the theme is mainly embodied in the living offspring, Orestes and Electra, who unlike most of their predecessors actually appear on stage, and are several times compared to young creatures, especially young birds; as we have seen, too, Orestes' infancy is recalled in two important passages (510-53, 749-63). We may note also, in the central choral song, partial parallels to Orestes and Electra in the young man (Meleager) who was killed by his mother (605ff.) and the young woman (Scylla) who helped to kill her father (614ff.). At the climax, when Orestes is about to commit the matricide, we and he are reminded over and over again that he is the child whom Clytaemestra bore and nurtured (897ff., 908, 910, 912, 920, 922, 928) – and whom she wronged (913, 915). *Choephoroi* concludes with a brief reference back to the children of Thyestes (1068-9); but they will not be mentioned again – nor has there really been anything to prepare us for the turn this theme will take in the next play.

Eumenides begins with the first scene of *happy* infancy in the whole trilogy (unless one counts the lion-cub): the birth and youth of Apollo (7-19). But that is before the Erinyes (who, according to Apollo, take a favourable and very un-Greek attitude to the castration of young boys: 187-8) have come into the play. Once these 'ancient maidens' (69) are with us, the theme concentrates on Orestes again – but now Orestes is no longer the biting serpent, but the fleeing fawn (111, 246), nearly caught in the same hunting-net that once was spread over Troy (112). At the same time other 'young' beings begin to play an important and direct part in the action: the 'young' gods, especially Apollo and Athena.

When Orestes the fawn, pursued by his mother's avenging hounds, has come to Athens, he gains a hearing by telling Athena that the blood of a sucking-pig (283, 450) has purified him. After that, however, little is heard of the theme for a long time, except in Apollo's argument on genetic parenthood. But like the *drosos* theme, the theme of young growth reappears powerfully in the Erinyes' threatened curses from 778 onwards, and in Athena's replies to them:

> A canker bringing leaflessness and childlessness ... (785 = 815).

> You will for all time receive sacrifices before childbirth (835-6).

> Do not plant in my country
> whetstones of bloody violence which warp the spirits
> of young men and make them mad with a rage that does not come from wine (858-60).

And then, like all the other themes, this one is stood on its head, and transmuted into an overwhelming promise of fertility and free growth of plant, animal and human life alike, safe from all violence and suffering (except in glorious and successful wars with foreign enemies); I quote two typical passages only, both sung by the Erinyes:

> And may no blast blow that would do harm to trees ...
> so that the scorching heat, which robs plants of their buds,
> shall not pass the boundary of this country;
> and let no terrible blight come upon them that would make the crops to fail.
> And may Pan nourish their flocks and make them prosper
> and bring forth twofold offspring
> at the appointed time (938-45).

> And I forbid the misadventures that make men perish before their time;
> and to lovely maidens,
> you gods who have the authority,
> grant lives in which they will win husbands (956-60; cf. 907-12, 922-6).

Nor is that quite the end. The procession at the end includes Athena's temple-servants, who sing the final song (see §7.6.5); and most of these were – young girls of noble birth: girls not destined to be lured to a cruel death like Iphigeneia, or to be locked away like dangerous animals and denied the right to marry as Electra was, but destined to perform honourable and life-affirming religious functions in the name of the *polis* and then to become the wives of citizens and, in due season, the healthy mothers of healthy and happy new citizens – who in turn will be spared the fate of the children of Thyestes, or that of those who died in the dubious war for Troy, or the terrible dilemma of Orestes; and the young animals and young plants to which young humans have so often been compared will flourish equally, to the blessing of the *polis*.

It has taken us this long to examine, incompletely, only two themes. There are scores of others, mostly at least as complex and ramified as these, and they are all interlinked. Thus the theme of young growth which we have examined, in particular that of young animals, is linked, especially but not exclusively through Orestes the fawn, with the idea of hunting. This in turn is associated with the ever-recurring images of hounds and of the net – both of which, at different moments, are presented visually on stage (the Erinyes as hounds pursuing Orestes; the robe, compared to a net, in which Agamemnon was entrapped). From hounds we can move to eagles (called the 'winged hounds of the Father' in *Ag.* 136), from eagles to omens, from omens to prophecy to Apollo to healing, and so on almost *ad infinitum*. Or to return to the net, the 'net' that Clytaemestra spread for Agamemnon was actually a rich, many-coloured robe, embodying the themes of wealth, colour and clothing; these same themes were also embodied in the crimson raiment on which Agamemnon trod, thus linking them to the theme of trampling or kicking down what is sacred – a metaphor which is more than once applied to a metaphorical altar (*Ag.* 381-4, *Eum.* 538-42), which suggests sacrifice, which is often equated with murder – and so on, once again, almost *ad infinitum*, or better, perhaps, in never-ending circles, since at almost any point in the chain one can find a connection back to various points touched on earlier. One can almost say that every important feature of human life (as human life was lived in Aeschylus' time) finds a place among the imagery of the *Oresteia*; and that is as it should be, because the well-being of all that is precious in human life depends to no small extent on the proper resolution of the issues that the trilogy raises.

7.8. Male and female

A theme which runs right through the *Oresteia*, both in word and in action, until it meets its resolution at the end, is that of the roles and relations of the two sexes. In contemporary Athens these were governed by well-defined conventions which placed men and women in almost entirely separate spheres, with all formal authority and all participation in civic life (except in religious functions) reserved for men. The *Oresteia*, almost throughout its length, is dominated by two females who persistently go against these conventions, one because she rejects them, the other because, being a goddess, she is exempt from them: Clytaemestra and Athena. The Erinyes too, those 'ancient maidens' with unfeminine complexions and clothing (see §7.6.3), rebel against the male-dominated Olympian hierarchy in the cause of a woman who rebelled against the male-dominated hierarchy of the *polis*. At the same time a long series of other women – Iphigeneia, Cassandra, Electra, the chorus of slave-women in *Choephoroi* – are forcibly prevented from playing their 'proper' social role. As to the men, they at first take their supremacy for granted: when the Elders are told, twice over, that Agamemnon will be killed by his wife, they cannot even understand what is being said, let alone believe it. But it happens; and by the end of *Agamemnon* Clytaemestra is in full control of everything and everyone, including her own little male parasite, Aegisthus. And when eventually the Areopagus court has to pronounce on the guilt or innocence of Orestes, and Athena has to give the decisive vote, the decision turns to a great extent on the question whether Clytaemestra's action was so counter to nature, so damaging to society, that it could justify the killing of a mother by her son. And the court rules, though by the narrowest possible margin, that it was.

The keynote, as we might expect, is struck right at the outset, when the Watchman explains that he is looking out for the beacon-fire bringing news from Troy on the orders of 'a woman's hopeful heart that thinks like a man's'. The last five words render the Greek adjective *androboulon*, which virtually sums up Clytaemestra's personality in a single word – particularly since the same word would also be capable of bearing the senses 'who wants a man' and 'who plots against a man (or husband)'.

Clytaemestra is not named here. And when another woman is mentioned, by the chorus, she too is not named, and she too is defined by her relation to men: 'a woman of many men' she is called (62) – Helen, who was Clytaemestra's sister. No one would ever think of *her* as a masculine woman, but she in her way has been as great a destructive force (63-7, 681ff., 1455-61) as Clytaemestra will be: women as such, it seems, are being presented as having something intrinsically evil about them.

But it soon proves that as well as being a doer of evil, woman in *Agamemnon* can also be a victim of evil – and the female victims include not only the innocent Iphigeneia, manhandled to the altar amid a sea of stony male faces (228-43), but also Clytaemestra herself, the 'guileful housekeeper, the unforgetting child-avenging Wrath' (155). The killing of Iphigeneia was a wrong to the mother as well as to the daughter, as in due course the mother will remind us – although the Elders seem no more aware of the fact than Agamemnon was.

When Clytaemestra at last makes her appearance, one thing about her very quickly becomes evident: she believes (quite rightly) that because she is a woman, men consider her to be of strictly limited intelligence and rationality, a prejudice which she resents intensely and will take every possible opportunity to disprove – subject to the overriding requirement that the strongest proof of her capabilities, namely her plot against Agamemnon, must remain secret until he is dead. Over and over again her resentment finds expression:

> You belittle my intelligence, for all the world as if I were a young girl (277).
>
> Such is the tale that I, a woman, have to tell you (348).
>
> And people said to me chidingly, 'Have beacons
> persuaded you to suppose Troy has already been sacked?
> How like a woman to let one's heart be lifted off the ground!' (590-2).
>
> You make trial of me as though I were a stupid woman (1401).
>
> Such is the advice of a woman, if anyone sees fit to learn from it (1661).

As the last quotation shows, the same chip is still on her shoulder even after her comprehensive triumph over every male character in the play; and not entirely without reason, for the Elders too, for all their amazement and horror, do not at any stage abandon their stereotype view of woman's nature. Her first triumph, anyway, in the beacon-scene, is only a very temporary one. The chorus-leader may tell her 'Lady, you speak intelligently, like a sensible *man*' (351), but by the time the Herald arrives the chorus are saying:

> It is what you would expect from a woman's rule
> to authorize thanksgiving before the facts are clear. ...
> A report voiced by a woman
> quickly dies and perishes (483-8).

In the choral song that separates these two utterances, we have met two other women, the causer and the victim of one and the same evil. The first is Helen, whose departure with Paris from the house of the Atreidai brought sorrow to the house, war to Argos and ruin to Troy (403-26). The other is anonymous:

> And all those who set forth from the land of Greece
> leave present in each of their houses
> a mourning woman of enduring heart (429-31).

This nameless woman represents thousands whose husbands or sons may any day return from Troy 'to each of their houses' as an urnful of ashes (433-44) because of a war fought 'for another man's wife' (448). We may recall, though, that there is another mourning woman in the palace itself, lamenting someone who died before the war began, at Aulis – and also, like the others (450ff.), thinking of revenge.

Clytaemestra next appears at 587, to address the Herald, and in spite of the superb imperiousness of her manner, brushing aside his message as not worth hearing and withdrawing before he can say a word, she nevertheless gives a fresh turn to the man-woman theme, in an ostensibly more conventional direction, by introducing the idea of the victorious warrior about to return to his loving and faithful wife. Clytaemestra is of course neither loving nor faithful, but from now to the climax she must play the part of a proper, subordinated, womanly woman. She will say all the correct things (855-76, 888-94) about how terribly anxious life without her husband has been – though she naturally will not dream of *criticizing* him for his long absence on necessary masculine business. She will explain (877-86) that Orestes has been sent away for his own safety – not on her initiative (a mere woman could not be expected to have the political insight to perceive the danger) but on the suggestion of Strophius. And she will give Agamemnon the most effusive welcome imaginable on his return, right up to the moment at which she offers to perform the duty which in heroic times, as Greeks imagined them, could be performed equally well by a maidservant or a princess and thus expressed most fully the subjected status of all women – the duty of attending her lord in the bath.[37]

Well before we reach that stage, however, we have had occasion (681ff.) to reflect much more fully on that other female destroyer, Helen. And yet she is in considerable measure presented as an 'object of strife' (687) rather than an agent: the wind, or Strife, or Wrath, conveys her to Troy (690-700), she is described in a long string of phrases – all in the neuter gender – not as a person but as a thought, an adornment, a look, a flower (739-43), and when the Trojans realize what her coming has brought them it is Paris whom they curse (714). The question of Helen's personal guilt is never really raised in this play. It is fairly clear that the Elders *believe* her guilty (cf. 1455ff.), but at no time do they, or anyone else, say anything to show that her elopement with Paris was her voluntary act. This does not mean that we are being encouraged to conclude that she was abducted by force; it does mean that the Elders are prepared to believe the worst of her without evidence, just as they are *not* prepared to believe the worst of Clytaemestra even when they have what should have been ample evidence – because the alleged crime of Helen is one that was thought to be typical of women, while the actual crime of Clytaemestra is not.

Agamemnon arrives, in what looks for a moment like a wedding procession – except that he has a wife already. No doubt, as was suggested above, her greeting is meant to strike him as just what one might expect from a devoted but rather simple spouse, and to judge by his reply that is exactly how it does strike him. Whereupon she takes him on in a contest of words and ideas, and beats him utterly while leaving him (943) with the impression that he is the winner; he expresses the truth, however, without realizing it, in his words 'I have been overcome into obeying you in this' (956), and walks into the palace on Clytaemestra's terms, anything but 'a man of final authority' (972) – though the Greek phrase used here, *andros teleiou*, could also mean 'a man fit to be sacrificed'. The housekeeper, the watchdog, has become the master of the house; and we know it, though only one other person on stage does.

That person is Cassandra; and she, as the first to understand what is going on, is also the first to give expression to the unnaturalness of it:

> Ah, ah! Look, look! Keep the bull away from the cow! (1125-6).

On this exclamation it is perhaps worth citing the note of Denniston and Page 1957 – both for what they see and for what they fail to see:

> 'Keep the bull away from the cow' at once suggests the meaning 'protect the cow from the bull'. Aeschylus means 'protect the bull from the cow', a reversal of the order of nature which would have been very effective if only he had reversed the phraseology accordingly.

It would be truer to say that the utterance gains most of its effectiveness precisely from the fact that the phraseology is *not* reversed. To any ordinary hearer (such as the Elders), Cassandra's words will indeed suggest that the bull is about to attack the cow. But the theatre audience are privileged: *they* know that, as is so often the case with the words of prophets and oracles, Cassandra means the exact opposite.

Before Cassandra returns to the matter of the coming murder, she speaks, in reply to the chorus-leader's questions, about one of her own two experiences of what it means to be a woman (1202-13). Her wooer was a god, but he behaved as a man might – only more so. He offered her a precious gift if she in return would give herself to him. She agreed. He gave her the gift. She then went back on her part of the bargain. The reaction of many a man under such circumstances would be – at least if he were malicious or vindictive – to do his best to ruin the girl's reputation;[38] and in his own way that is just what Apollo did. This was the first of the two occasions on which he has 'destroyed' her (1082); and 'destroyed' is hardly too strong a word, if a princess came to be spoken of as 'a vagrant, a mendicant, a wretched beggar-woman dying of hunger' (1273-4). Apollo, we may fairly say, believes as strongly as Agamemnon that subject to certain conventions, females exist for the pleasure and the service of males (no doubt bulls think much the same about cows). This parallelism between the thinking of male humans and of male gods will later receive far greater emphasis. We have so far had only one indication of the view that female divinities take: when Zeus sent his male eagles, who symbolized the male Atreidae, to kill a pregnant female hare, it was the female Artemis who retaliated. The only other female deities of whom we have heard anything significant thus far are the Erinyes, and little has yet been made of their gender any more than in the case of other feminine personifications like Justice and Strife. At present they are simply shadowy, semi-abstract spirits of wrath and vengeance, who seem to be serving Zeus and Apollo with marked fidelity; we have no more reason than Zeus and Apollo have to suppose that this state of affairs is likely to change.

Soon Cassandra is again foretelling the murder of Agamemnon, and this time making it much plainer that 'the female [is the] murderer of the male' (1231). And as ever, this is so much beyond the imagination of the Elders that it simply fails to register with them:

> By what man is this grievous deed being perpetrated? ...
> I do not understand how he will contrive to carry it out (1251-3).

Cassandra's reply to this is 'And yet I know the Greek language all too well' (1254), alluding, I suspect, to the fact that she has used the grammatical genders of Greek with perfect accuracy to specify the murderer as female[39] and has failed to get her message through: fifth-century Greek caricatures of the broken Greek of 'barbarians' more than once present them as unable to cope with this feature of the Greek language.[40] This is not the first time (see above on 739-43), nor will it be the last, that Aeschylus in this trilogy puts grammatical gender to thematic use.

And then the murder happens – and the Elders are still convinced, even after the event, that it is a man's, or rather several men's, doing (1355-7, 1363), until they see the truth, the tableau of the blood-spattered woman standing, warrior's sword in hand, over a male and a female corpse. And this woman speaks almost exactly as a man might have done; note especially her challenge, an absurd challenge if any other woman had flung it down:

> If you threaten me like that, take note that I am prepared
> that if you defeat me by force in fair fight
> you shall rule, but if god decides it the other way
> you will be taught a lesson and learn, rather late, good sense (1422-5).

At the same time, however, she has a motive for her action that only a woman could have, a motive that never occurred to the minds of the Elders or of Agamemnon. To them, Iphigeneia was merely '*his* own child' (1417); to her, she was '*my* beloved pangs' (1417-18), the being *she* had brought into the world amid pain and blood. Until now in the trilogy, motherhood has been no more than a word, and not often even that; from now on it will be a reality – a reality that not even Apollo (*Eum.* 657ff.) will be able to talk out of existence.

If the male characters have forgotten that women have maternal feelings, they can hardly be expected to remember that women also have sexual feelings – particularly since it was in the highest degree improper for them to give expression to those feelings in public. Clytaemestra now does just this (1431-47), avowing her adultery with defiant pride and giving full vent to her jealous resentment of Cassandra and all her other wartime supplanters, not without some rather coarse language (Aegisthus, she says, 'lights the fire on my hearth', an expression found in comedy to denote sexual activity; Cassandra is 'the *mast-rubber* of the ships' benches', a term which could well be, or be a modification of, a sailors' slang word for a prostitute).

Having now digested what has happened, the chorus place Clytaemestra side by side with her sister Helen (1453ff.) as a pair of destroyers, the instruments of the *daimôn* which 'by means of women holds a power that wounds my heart' (1470-1). But if there are to be dominant women, there must also be subservient men; and one of these presently appears. If Clytaemestra is the woman who is like a man, Aegisthus is the man who is like a woman (cf. 1625). He wears no sword (see §7.6.4), he did not go to war (1626), he had not the courage to kill Agamemnon with his own hand (1635), and (if, as I believe, Thomson 1938 was right to assign line 1651 to the captain of the guard) he is a failure even as a tyrant, being incapable of issuing direct orders for a massacre. Once Clytaemestra decides to intervene (1654) she has him very firmly under control. She may still profess to doubt whether anyone will take a woman's words seriously (1661), but her two short speeches, decisive in manner and decisive in effect, contrast most eloquently with the futile trading of insults between Aegisthus and the Elders, and when, before finally leading him into the palace, she says 'I and you will rule this house and order things well' we can have little doubt who will be doing the ordering. When she and her tame man depart, the two dozen other males on stage are left with nothing to do or say, and go off in silence. This is the only undisputed play of Aeschylus in which an actor, an individual character, has the last word. As the Watchman said right at the beginning (10-11), the woman is in power.

In the action of the second play, Clytaemestra for a long time seems to shrink back to something closer to the normal proportions of a woman. The first thing we hear of her is that she is sleeping in the 'women's chambers' (*Cho.* 36) – in segregated quarters, then, like any proper Athenian woman whose husband could afford them – and that a dream has frightened her out of her wits: the Clytaemestra of the previous play was frightened only in pretence, and approaches even the insatiable *daimôn* of the house not in fearful but in businesslike tones (*Ag.* 1567-76). There are other women on stage too, many more than before, and they too seem quite normal women: Electra mourning for her father and hoping for the return of her brother and the coming of a powerful avenger – it does not occur to her, as it does to her Sophoclean namesake and as it surely would to a Clytaemestra, that if all else fails it is her duty to take the role of avenger herself; and the chorus of slave-women, devoted to the memory of their master and to the duty of 'keeping the house in good order' (84). The only abnormality is in the relationship between Clytaemestra and her children; on the lips of Electra 'my mother' (90) all too plainly implies 'that evil woman', and later (241) she says of her 'her I hate with every justification'. The feeling is mutual, for Clytaemestra is a 'mother who has thoughts anything but motherly for her children' (190-1); she, as we know, is responsible for sending Orestes into exile, and she, it is plainly implied, is responsible for Electra's being kept unmarried. This abnormal, dishonourable treatment of Electra is not explicitly mentioned until 487, but it was well known in the tradition,[41] and the audience would be aware of it from the start. Electra is a woman who wants to *be* a woman, to fulfil a woman's proper role, and who is not being allowed to.

Such is the situation, and in the *kommos* (418-50) various aspects of it are re-emphasized. The detailed account of Clytaemestra's dream, in which she bore and suckled a snake, brings us back to the idea of motherhood: what offspring could so monstrous a woman bring forth, if not another monster? She may be trying now to live the life of a normal woman, but she cannot get away from her past.

It is now that we are reminded of a whole series of other acts of violence by women, introduced by a complex 'priamel':[42]

> Many are the fearsome, terrible evils
> that are bred by earth ...
> [and by sea, air and sky] ...
> but who can tell of the audacious pride of men
> or the passions [*erôtes*] of women ...?
> The reckless power of female passion [*erôs*]
> wins perverted victories over marital unions (585-600).

The first two illustrations of this principle, however, show women committing murder in traditionally feminine ways for traditionally feminine reasons. Althaea caused the death of her son Meleager (602-12) by quasi-magical means (burning a brand whose destruction was fated to end his life) in revenge for the death of her brothers. Scylla caused the death of her father Nisus (612-22), also by magical means (cutting off the lock of hair that gave him immortality), because she succumbed to the alluring glitter of gold. Neither killed with her own hands: Meleager died by what seemed to be natural causes, Nisus was killed by Minos and his men. Clytaemestra, on the other hand, herself killed her own husband and took command of her household (such is probably the implication of the difficult lines 629-30 in which the chorus seem to be saying that they honour 'a ... household ... in which a woman behaves like a woman' [Garvie 1986: 217]). There is no crime to which hers can be compared except that of the women of Lemnos (631-8), who killed their menfolk all by themselves without any assistance at all, whose motive (in the usual account) was exclusively that of sexual jealousy, and who proceeded to rule the island themselves and eventually to choose their own sexual partners (the Argonauts). That, to the Greek mind, is a topsy-turvy world comparable to the society of the Amazons (of whom we shall hear later), and that is the nearest parallel to what Clytaemestra has done.

It is after this ode that we first, in this play, see Clytaemestra; and she behaves as an utterly normal woman. She is able to offer hospitality, but hastily adds that if there is any serious business to be discussed 'that is a matter for men' (673). She hears of Orestes' death, and laments as a mother should – and as yet we are in no position to judge how sincere she is. She has the strangers taken to 'the men's guest-chambers' (712), another allusion (cf. 36, 878-9) to segregated accommodation within the palace, of which there was no mention in the previous play. And she concludes by saying that she will communicate the news to 'the ruler of the house' (716-17). Is she a changed woman, or trying to be? Or is she the same masculine female she always was? The answer comes in the first words of the Nurse:

> The woman in power has ordered me to summon Aegisthus ... (734-5).

Directly afterwards, too, we learn that Clytaemestra's grief was a pretence (737-40). For real (quasi-)maternal grief we need only listen to the Nurse herself, though she, we may assume, has never borne a child of her own. It is remarkable, incidentally, that of a total of thirty females who appear in the trilogy[43] (including two choruses, but excluding those who figure only in the final procession), Clytaemestra is the only one who has ever been a mother, with the possible (but unmentioned) exception of the Pythia. Nevertheless the Nurse has at least come close to fulfilling the proper role of a woman, and she is the first woman in the trilogy to have done so.

When Aegisthus is killed, Clytaemestra is apparently asleep behind the barred 'women's doors' (878). When danger threatens, she becomes her old self, calling for a 'man-slaying axe' (889); but if she is a killer, she is still also a woman and mother, and as woman and mother she makes the ultimate appeal to him who once sucked his food from her (896-8). The ensuing dialogue raises openly for the first time the issue, in the end to be crucial, of the relative importance of mother and father to the *oikos*. The answer the dialogue seems to imply is that the mother may nurture (*trephein*) the child (908, cf. 898), but the father by his labour supports (*trephein*) the mother and everyone else (921): ultimately it is by his efforts that the *oikos* can survive. This conclusion will in the end be endorsed by Athena. As Orestes himself recognizes, though, it does not make Clytaemestra's fate any less wrong (930).

In Orestes' speech over the two bodies much is made of the allegation that Clytaemestra and Aegisthus plotted and acted *together* (973-9, cf. 1011); and we may reflect that they are the only couple we see in the trilogy who *act* as a couple. Agamemnon and Clytaemestra never co-operate in any way at any stage; Agamemnon and Cassandra never exchange a word; Menelaus and Helen are separated before we first hear of them;[44] Paris and Helen are never mentioned as a pair. The idea of the couple is left to be represented solely by the two murderers. Only at the end of the trilogy are we offered a more positive presentation of the union of man and woman

(*Eum.* 835, 959-60), which can be symbolized by the divine pairing of Zeus and Hera (*Eum.* 214-18). Meanwhile, if *this* is what the notion of the couple means, it is hardly surprising that Orestes wants nothing to do with it (*Cho.* 1005-6).

Orestes has destroyed a foul female monster (994-6). But several of them have arisen in its place, as Orestes sees the terrifying Erinyes (whom both he and presently the Pythia speak of as 'women'). With their appearance (to him alone, for the moment) the male-female opposition is extended, for the first time since the Aulis ode, from the human to the divine plane.

Eumenides begins with male and female gods in delusive harmony – Phoebe presenting Delphi to her infant grandson Apollo (7-8), Athena and the Nymphs honoured alongside Dionysus, Poseidon and Zeus (21-9) – but presently the Pythia in turn sees the Erinyes. They too are females who do not play the female's proper role:

> grey virgins, ancient maidens, with whom no god
> nor man nor beast ever holds any intercourse (69-70)

– whether social or sexual. It is natural then that they regard the sanctity of marriage as being of no account (214-18); for Apollo, on the other hand, marriage comes within the province of three great gods (Zeus, Hera and Aphrodite) and also of that very Destiny (cf. 217) to which the Erinyes themselves owe their privileges and powers (cf. 173, 335, 392). Apollo stands behind Orestes, for the male; the Erinyes represent Clytaemestra and the female. No compromise seems possible.

But then the scene moves to the temple of Athena. Athena, like her city of Athens, had never been mentioned throughout the first two plays, not even in connection with the victory over Troy which she had done so much to secure (cf. *Eum.* 457); the first, seemingly casual reference to her is at *Eum.* 10. Athena, as Goldhill 1984: 259 finely put it, 'stands between and against the opposition ... of the sexes'; she is the virgin who is a warrior, the daughter who has no mother (whereas the Erinyes apparently have no father or at least never mention one). When Orestes calls to Athena to come to his aid, his last three lines (296-8) contain six nouns, adjectives and participles referring to her, every one of which is masculine in form – and the context, too, is a military one. Moreover, Athena is not only a commander, but also a ruler; here, and throughout the play, she and no one else is the head of the Athenian state. She is in fact a female who is far more thoroughly masculine than Clytaemestra ever was. The difference is that *her* masculinity – helmet, spear and all – was to every Athenian something natural and normal. There is, then, at least one female in the universe who plays a distinctly male role without causing the least offence to the most dedicated male supremacist. And perhaps only the society that, like Athena, incorporates both male and female elements in harmonious combination can hope for enduring success.

So when the conflict between Apollo (representing Orestes) and the Erinyes is resumed in the trial-scene, the presence and the presidency of Athena give it a new aspect; the alternative extremisms of the two contending parties no longer offer the only possible choices. The gender issue is brought to the forefront when Apollo is challenged (622-4) to explain why Zeus allegedly took the view that it was right for Orestes 'to hold of no account the honour due to his mother'. Apollo replies:

> It is not the same thing for a noble *man* to die,
> a man honoured with the sceptre given by Zeus,
> and that at the hands of a *woman*, not by the rushing
> long-range arrows of, say, an Amazon,
> but in the manner you shall hear of ... (625-9).

The Amazons, here referred to for the first time, will be mentioned again at greater length by Athena (685-90). Even more than the women of Lemnos (*Cho.* 631-8), they represent the nightmare of male imaginations: the women who live, to all intents and purposes, in a maleless society. There cannot be a self-sustaining[45] society consisting only of men (though men in all ages, and ancient Greek men more than most, have done their best to create sub-societies from which women were excluded). But there *could*, in principle, be a society consisting only of women, provided there were some males in existence somewhere who could be called in occasionally for reproductive purposes (either by permission or by compulsion) and for the rest of the time excluded and ignored. And such was the society of the Amazons as Greeks imagined it. The Amazons did all the things which Greeks thought most unfeminine, such as riding horses and shooting arrows. They took the field in war, and fought men and sometimes defeated them. When they bore children, they reared only the girls; the boys they either exposed or sold (whereas Greeks in real life did the opposite, more often than they cared to talk about). And in a famous Athenian myth to which Athena will presently allude, they made war against Athens. For their society was the very antithesis of the civilized *polis*, having no civic institutions, growing no crops, rearing no livestock and living by hunting and pillage; their father and patron is the god of violence, Ares (cf. *Eum.* 689). But, says Apollo now, Clytaemestra was a greater monstrosity even than they, and her killing of a leader of male society the most heinous murder imaginable. As to her claim, any woman's claim, to consideration on the ground of her role as mother, Apollo disposes of this with his celebrated biological argument (657-66) in which the nurturing womb becomes no more than a safe-deposit box (660-1).

Athena, as just noted, also has something to say about the Amazons; but although she recalls how they attempted to destroy her own city, she does not damn them out of existence or memory as Apollo might well have done. Instead she actually locates her new court of law in the place where they encamped and which takes its name from the sacrifices that they offered – an explanation of the name of the Areopagus which was almost certainly invented by Aeschylus. And just as the seemingly asocial Amazons are thus in a sense to be incorporated into Athena's good society, so will the seemingly asocial Erinyes be: neither can be wholly excluded from the city (cf. 698).

At one point, however, it does become necessary for Athena to choose between one sex and the other. She must vote for or against Orestes, for the rights of the male or of the female. And she chooses the male for essentially the same reason that was raised in the last dialogue between Orestes and his mother: because the male provides the livelihood (*Cho.* 921), or, as Athena here prefers to emphasize, the defence (*Eum.* 740) of the *oikos*. And the way she puts it implies (738) that this is also the judgement of Zeus. But it is no open-and-shut issue; the choice is as finely balanced as is the verdict in the trial; Athena only says 'I shall not respect the death of a woman *more*, when she had killed a man' – she does not say she will respect it less. In the last analysis the preservation of the *oikos* (and the *polis*) is what matters most – but the claims of the female cannot be simply discounted.

Nor are they. In her speeches of persuasion to the Erinyes, Athena promises that they will receive the sacrifices of women (834-6) before expanding this into a more general promise of honours from men and women alike (856); and the Erinyes themselves include among their blessings the prayer that men may not die before their time and, immediately after, that maidens may not remain unmarried (956-60). It is now taken for granted that it is in marriage that women will seek their fulfilment in life – there will be no more Helens or Clytaemestras; the prayer is that they shall not be denied that fulfilment by death (like Iphigeneia), enslavement (like Cassandra or the chorus of *Choephoroi*), or the malice of their guardians (like Electra). And if that is the role of the woman in the *oikos*, she also has an important role in the *polis*, not in the political but in the religious sphere: there were very many cults whose ritual was wholly or mainly in the hands of women, and among them the most important of all, the cult of Athena Polias. And so, in the final procession, while the political life of the city is represented by the male councillors of the Areopagus, its religious life is represented by the priestess of Athena, her women assistants, and her girl temple-servants. The all-male camp of Agamemnon at Aulis which put its girl-child to death is no more a proper society than the all-female camp of the Amazons before Athens, the Amazons who sell their boy-children as slaves. The *polis* must include both, and render to both their proper honour. The Erinyes were wrong, but so was Apollo.

To render to women their proper honour, of course, need not by any means imply equality: 'to each his (or her) due' is one thing, 'to each the same' is another. And during most of the trilogy it is women, not men, who have been presented as the encroachers and the infringers. And yet at the same time we have perhaps been invited to consider the loneliness and frustration that can be a woman's lot, especially when the man is away from home, and we have certainly been invited to reflect on the immense significance of motherhood, which simply cannot be discounted as easily as Apollo would have us suppose. The *oikos*, no less than the *polis*, needs both its male and its female components. The *oikos* of Menelaus was as maimed when Helen left it as that of Agamemnon (and many others in Argos) were when the war took their menfolk away; it is no accident that we are made to think of both these absences in the same choral song (*Ag.* 403ff.). And on the divine level, the universe and human society need the instinctive reactions of the Erinyes just as much as they need the civilized logic of Apollo – and in any case the Erinyes themselves can be just as logical as Apollo, and Apollo just as emotional as the Erinyes. Athena unites the best in both; and if Athena, the child of Zeus who had no mother, is 'wholly of the Father' (*Eum.* 738), Zeus does so too.

> Zeus is the Firmament, Zeus is Earth and Heaven,
> Zeus is the All and all that is beyond.

So said a character in Aeschylus' lost *Daughters of the Sun* (fr. 70). Dare we add that Zeus is Male and Female – the Father *and Mother* of gods and mortals, just as he was both father and mother to Athena? I am not certain that Aeschylus would have rejected that inference. For only so can Zeus be truly *teleios*, 'the Fulfiller' (*Eum.* 28) but also the Fulfilled, the *perfect* supreme divinity.

There is one gender-related fact about the conclusion of the trilogy that should not be overlooked. This is that for its last 270 lines, after the departure of Orestes, *no male utters a word*, even though there is a male group present (the councillors of the Areopagus) who at one point (949) are directly addressed. At the very end, when chorus-sized groups both of male and of female Athenians take part in the final procession, it is the females who sing; they command the male citizenry (probably both those on stage and those in the audience) when they should be silent and when they should give voice (1035, 1039, 1043, 1047); and the very last utterance of the *Oresteia*, cried out by the male Athenians at the behest of this female chorus, is a typically feminine shout of joy. This is not what a dramatist would have done whose primary aim, so far as gender was concerned, was to validate the unconditional supremacy of the male.

7.9. Justice and the gods[46]

The question 'what is the *Oresteia* about?' is perhaps not a very sensible one, but if one were compelled to answer it one would certainly wish to say that one of the most important things it is about is justice, or rather *dikê* in its three senses of 'right and wrong', 'punishment' and 'judicial proceedings'. And in questions of *dikê* the poet at every stage involves the gods.

The theme is introduced not, like so many others, in the prologue, but in the anapaestic prelude chanted by the Elders when they first enter (*Ag.* 40-71), in which we hear of two acts of *dikê*/punishment, one of which serves to illustrate the other: the punishment of the Trojans for the crime of Paris, and the punishment of the unidentified miscreants who robbed the eagles' nest (50-9). And in what is said about these certain principles are laid down which will also govern all the other acts of *dikê* /punishment of which we hear in *Agamemnon*.

In the first place, the very first appearance of a derivative of *dikê* (41) characterizes Menelaus as 'the great plaintiff (*antidikos*) against Priam', as if the Trojan expedition were a lawsuit; and thereafter, as Lloyd-Jones 1979 *ad loc.* notes, 'the issue between the Atreidae and the house of Priam is repeatedly described in legal language' (cf. 534-7, 812-17) – nor is it the only issue to be so described (cf. 1412-21). But this legal language is all metaphorical. When the gods voted to condemn Troy, they did so without having heard any spoken pleas (813-14), and their penalty – the utter destruction of a whole city – was both more drastic and more indiscriminate than anything a real lawcourt would dream of imposing. And in 40-9, the proceedings taken by Menelaus and Agamemnon as co-plaintiffs consist of a vast military expedition, and they are described as raising a loud and enthusiastic war-cry (49). They are fighting in a just cause – that is never disputed – but it is war and victory, not justice as such, that they truly have at heart. This will be equally true of Clytaemestra and Aegisthus, except that the justice of *their* cause is far more dubious; it will be much less clearly true of Orestes. The point being made is reinforced by the image of the robbed birds: they are of course victims of wrongdoing, but they are also birds of prey who, far from being lovers of justice and peace, themselves make a living by robbery and murder.

Secondly, these violent acts of justice are accomplished under divine auspices, and through the medium of the Erinyes. The god who hears the cry of the bereaved birds 'sends an Erinys against the wrongdoers' (59; cf. 462-8, 749, 991, 1119, 1186-93, 1433, 1580-1); in the human dispute, the role of the Erinys is played by the Atreidae whom Zeus Xenios 'sends' (61) against Paris. And in the same way, too, everything else that is done in the name of justice in *Agamemnon* is done, as the Elders later sing, 'through Zeus, the cause of all, the worker of all' (1485-6; cf. 355-69, 525-6, 581-2, 748, 973-4). The violent 'justice' of Agamemnon is not merely the justice of imperfect man; it is also the justice of Zeus, and if we think (as the Elders in the end seem to think) that some aspects of this justice are far from satisfactory, then Zeus cannot escape a share of the responsibility.

Thirdly, the justice here described is inexorable:

> Neither by burning sacrifices nor by offering libations ...
> will he [Paris] charm away the unbending wrath (69-71).

This will be as true of Clytaemestra, sending drink-offerings to the tomb of the husband she has murdered, as it is of Paris, or of Priam when he kills and sacrifices vast numbers of cattle (1168-9) in the hope of saving his city. If a man has 'kicked the great altar of Dike out of sight' (383-4) then 'none of the gods hears his prayers' (396). Very simply and very inexorably, though we hear it in so many words only towards the end of the play, 'he who *does* must *suffer*' (1564).

But fourthly, the justice of Zeus and the Erinyes strikes at the innocent almost as much as the guilty: Zeus Xenios in punishing Paris brings down great suffering 'on Danaans and Trojans alike' (63-7), and this point is greatly developed in what follows, as emphasis is repeatedly placed on the sufferings that the war brought to the Greeks (432-55, 517, 568-71) – beginning with the war's very first casualty, Iphigeneia. By causing her death, Agamemnon made it certain, even before he went to Troy, that he would himself become a victim of the same *dikê* that he was exacting from the Trojans, at the hands of his wife. And while it is Agamemnon himself who chooses to press on with his war at the cost of such a crime (on this see §11.2), we must wonder again about the role of Zeus. He wants the Trojans to be punished; and Agamemnon, though without knowing it, is his agent in this task. But he sends an omen which angers Artemis and causes her to intervene, in such a way that Agamemnon cannot do what Zeus wants done to Troy without ultimately bringing ruin upon himself. It seems, to say the least, a self-defeating kind of justice. If Dike can only act through wrathful violence, then every act of *dikê*/punishment will at the same time be a crime that requires punishment in its turn, and what the Elders say of Agamemnon will be true for all humanity:

> If he is to pay for the blood of former generations,
> to die for the dead and thereby to trigger
> more deaths in retribution,
> what mortal can boast that he was born
> to a destiny free from harm? (1338-42).

The august, and at first sight so attractively just, law of Zeus will ensure that there can be no security for any human being.

Is there any hope of anything different? Only, perhaps, in what was said in the 'Hymn to Zeus':

> Zeus who put men on the road to wisdom,
> who laid down and made valid
> the law 'by suffering, learning' ...
> Violent, it seems, is the favour of the gods (176-82).

There are two kinds of learning by suffering: there is learning, too late, by one's own suffering (cf. 250-1, 1425, 1619-23); and there is learning by taking warning from the suffering of others. If the 'suffering' in question is fatal, only the second kind of learning can be said to form 'the road to wisdom' in any useful sense; and nobody will give any evidence of having learned from suffering in that sense until we come to Electra and Orestes. In *Agamemnon*, on the contrary, everyone marches confidently, or at least hopefully, along the same path as those who have gone before, shutting their eyes to the implications of what their predecessors have suffered, and inevitably meeting the same fate themselves. Nobody has the least doubt that when one is wronged, one should take wrathful and violent revenge, and having done that, hope for the best (cf. 217, 854, 1568-76, 1638-42).

And the play shows how this works out. At first, attention is naturally concentrated on the punishment of the Trojans. Clytaemestra indeed warns that the Greeks may offend in their turn, as they will in fact do (338ff., cf. 527), but that may seem to be a separate issue: it is not *inevitable* that a victorious army will commit acts of sacrilege – though it is striking that that very average Greek, the Herald, treats the victory and the sacrilege as a single event, the act both of Agamemnon (530) and of Zeus (526, 582). But meanwhile, in the second choral ode (369-474), we find that there is after all an inevitability that will naturally lead to the destruction of the destroyers. We have seen (§7.5) how this song weaves a devious path from Paris to Helen to Menelaus to the war and its dead – its Greek dead, and their families mourning them back home in Argos:

> 'For the sake of another man's wife.'
> That is what men quietly mutter;
> and grief together with resentment steals over them
> against the chief plaintiffs, the Atreidae. ...
> The talk of citizens, coupled with anger, is a grievous thing;
> it is equivalent to a public curse.
> My anxiety waits to hear
> about something done under cover of night.
> For the gods do not fail to take aim
> at those who have killed many, and in time
> the black Erinyes reduce to helplessness
> him who is fortunate without justice ... (448-64).

Now if there was one thing that was inevitable about the Trojan expedition, it was that a great many Greeks would be killed in it (cf. 63-7). Now it appears that the Argives, or many of them, are angry at these deaths in a war which they consider to have been fought for no good reason (cf. 799-804), and that the Atreidae, the agents of the *dikê* of Zeus and the Erinyes (50-63), are destined to become victims of *dikê* – that is, of wrathful revenge – at the hands of the Argive people acting, in turn, as agents of the Erinyes (463) and of Zeus (469-70). That Zeus uses fallible instruments for the fulfilment of his purposes need not worry us: as Dover 1973: 65 briefly observed, the God of the Hebrew prophets is constantly presented as punishing the Israelites in precisely this way, through the agency of outside powers like Assyria and Babylon which are themselves sinful and are destined to be punished in their turn. A thief has no valid ground for complaint if another thief is set to catch him. But that cannot excuse the sufferings imposed by Zeus' plan for the punishment of Paris on the innocent Greek dead and their even more innocent kith and kin. It is perhaps here that we begin to suspect rather definitely that the flaw may lie in the current concept of *dikê* itself.

Shortly before the entry of Agamemnon, the chorus articulate some important principles underlying not only the events they have already recalled but also others which have not yet been mentioned or which still lie in the future. These principles are expressed at some length (750-82), but essentially boil down to two points: (1) that the goddess Dike rejects the wicked and honours the righteous (774-82); (2) that '*hybris* is wont to breed *hybris*' (763-6). Unfortunately these principles are not entirely compatible. What happens if a righteous person is the victim of an act of *hybris*? Dike demands that the crime be avenged; but it can only be avenged by the victim (or, if he is dead, his next of kin), and only through a fresh act of *hybris*, for which therefore the victim, the 'sufferer' turned 'doer', must inevitably pay in his turn – and so on, potentially *ad infinitum*. So far this has only been a theoretical possibility, since in *Agamemnon* none of the avengers has been a righteous person. But in the case of Orestes it will become actual.

Being now fully acquainted with the nature of divine justice, we are ready to see it at work upon Agamemnon. And a little later, we are also ready to be told, initially by Cassandra, about earlier instances of the same kind of *dikê*. Thyestes seduced the wife of Atreus (1193). Atreus in revenge deceived Thyestes into eating his own children's flesh. Thyestes' son in return seduced the wife of Atreus' son ... and so on, potentially *ad infinitum*. Agamemnon thus becomes the joining-point of two separate chains of vindictive justice (the other began with Paris), chains which, whatever Clytaemestra may hope (1567-76), are bound, by the law of the gods, to stretch on into the indefinite future (1279-84, 1318-19, 1338-42, 1533-6, 1563-6). Even the hopes which the Elders place in Orestes (1646-8, 1667-9) are sure, by the principles which they themselves have enunciated, to prove equally futile. Or are they?

It is Electra who offers the first sign that a change may be coming; and that in two ways. In the first place, as we have seen (§7.2), the organization of her prayer (*Cho.* 130-44) implies that while she longs for her father's death to be avenged, she does not envisage Orestes as the avenger: what she would like to happen – though as the world stands, it cannot and does not happen – is for the task of vengeance to be carried out by an independent third party; and the attitude of the chorus is the same (115-19, 160-3). That was not what Cassandra prophesied, and it is not what the Elders hoped for. In the second place, she is by no means sure that she desires even an independent avenger to act by violence, and here she differs from the chorus. When they urge her to pray for the coming of a liberator, 'some god or mortal', she asks in reply: 'Do you mean a judge, or an avenger?' (120). As Kitto 1956: 41 remarked, 'the chorus is not interested in Electra's distinction, but *we* may be'; and we may be interested too when she prays, unprompted, that she may be 'far more virtuous than my mother, and more pious in action' (140-1). That is not the sort of hope that anyone expressed in the previous play.

These hopes, though, seem doomed to disappointment. The avenger, as Cassandra knew and Apollo has decreed, can only be Orestes, and he will not be able to punish by judicial process (or even ask another to do so) but only by direct action, by deception and violence. And that is all the more tragic when we discover that Orestes, unlike all his predecessors, is devoid of guilty motives. He states, and we have no reason to disbelieve him, what his actual motives are:

> the command of the god, and my great grief for my father,
> and also I am hard pressed by being deprived of my property,
> to stop the people of the most glorious city in the world ...
> having thus to obey a pair of women (300-4).

Some critics have felt uncomfortable that Orestes should mention his property in this connection. They should not have done. Orestes is the rightful heir to Agamemnon's property, he has been cheated of what is his, and he is determined to get it back. What must indeed make us uncomfortable is not the motives for Orestes' act, but the nature of the act itself. As a minister of Dike, for the best of reasons, under a divine command, he is going to put to death two heinous criminals – one of whom is his mother. As always, therefore, though in a rather different way from before, the punishment of *hybris* is going to involve fresh *hybris*, since Orestes must resolve to set at nothing the honour to which his mother is entitled simply because she is his mother (cf. *Eum.* 624). What he does is both inevitable and intolerable, its nature perfectly summed up in the last words that Clytaemestra hears on earth, 'You killed whom you ought not, now suffer what you ought not' (*Cho.* 930). Equally intolerable are Orestes' future prospects. Had he refused to carry out the vengeance, he would have been harried and tormented by the Erinyes of his father (278-96). Having carried it out, he will be harried and tormented by the Erinyes of his mother (924). If Apollo and Zeus foresaw this (and we are given no indication that they did not), they seem quite unconcerned about it, as unconcerned as they were about the fate of all those other innocents who were destroyed as incidental victims of their grand schemes for enforcing *dikê*. Orestes may look forward, in the manner that Electra foreshadowed, to a trial and a judgement (987-8) on the issue of whether he killed his mother 'with justice' (cf. 1027); but for him, as for her, so far as we can yet tell, that option will not exist.

And then comes a revelation that changes everything (cf. §7.2):

> And as the prime inducement that made me do this audacious deed
> I name Loxias, the Pythian seer, whose oracle declared to me
> that if I did this I should be free from blame and condemnation
> (1029-32).

In other words, this time he who has done shall not suffer. The law that was going to remain 'while Zeus remains on his throne' is to be set aside, with no indication as yet of what new law, if any, is to take its place. The alliance between Zeus and the Erinyes is broken. And since we are left in no doubt, at the end of *Choephoroi*, that the Erinyes are persecuting Orestes just the same, it would appear that they are in effect defying, for the moment successfully, the will of the supreme god.

At the outset of *Eumenides* (19) it is, as it were, officially confirmed that Apollo has the backing of Zeus for all his oracular responses and therefore also for his support of Orestes; and presently, from his words and those of the Erinyes, we can perceive what kind of conflict now exists among the gods. On the one side are the old gods and the old law that were supposed to be eternal; on the other side, the 'young' Olympian gods (150, 162) and a new law that does indeed, as Electra and Orestes had hoped, put the idea of judgement (cf. 81, 224, 260) in the place of the idea of wrathful vengeance. The old gods are represented in the play by the Erinyes, though behind them looms the power of their sisters (961-2) the Moirai, the personifications of Destiny (173, 334-5, 392, 723-8, 1046). The younger gods are represented by Apollo, behind whom stands Zeus whose spokesman he claims to be. The old law is precisely that which was formerly championed by Zeus: he who has done must suffer – and at the hands of the Erinyes. Orestes is their quarry to be chased and caught and devoured (147-8, 230-1, 244-53), or their sacrifice, destined to feed them (299-305, 325-33). It is at first less clear what the new law is. At some moments (e.g. 619-21) Apollo seems to be saying: he who has done must suffer – unless Zeus orders otherwise. These two positions cannot be rationally reconciled. But Apollo says one other thing that will in the end make a reconciliation possible: he is prepared to submit the dispute to the judgement of Athena (224). Eventually, thanks to Athena's courteous reception of them, the Erinyes agree to do likewise (433-5). But even this can be no permanent solution. Indeed, it cannot even solve the immediate problem of Orestes; for Athena, who like Apollo and (as we shall later see) like Zeus feels a sense of responsibility for the well-being of mortals quite unlike anything the gods had shown before, cannot risk exposing her people to the consequences of either of the two choices open to her – rejecting her suppliant or rejecting the Erinyes – *without their consent*. And so it is that the case of Orestes becomes the occasion for the introduction, under divine auspices, of a kind of *dikê* unprecedented in the history of the world, *dikê* in the sense of judicial proceedings, a prototype and model for the future. The legal metaphors of *Agamemnon* will be turned into reality. The new law will be: he who has done must suffer – provided that a court of upright judges is convinced that he justly deserves to suffer.

A detailed comparison may be fruitful between this new justice and the old justice as it was described at the start of *Agamemnon* and repeatedly exemplified in the course of that play. In the old justice, drastic penalties were inflicted, without a hearing, by the agency of the enraged victims of wrong themselves or their next of kin. The new justice, on the other hand, satisfies the aspirations once expressed by Electra. It is administered by an authority independent of wrongdoer and victim alike. This authority will still be able to inflict drastic penalties, but it will first listen carefully to the pleas of both sides, itself saying nothing at all, giving its verdict merely by casting a pebble; and though it will still be 'sharp in anger' (*Eum.* 705), that anger will be narrowly directed against the wrongdoer alone – no longer will the innocent be indiscriminately involved in the punishment of the guilty. Here the ethic of the Areopagus stands in marked contrast to that still upheld by the Erinyes, who fully intend to ruin the innocent Athenian people (711, 719-20, 733, 780-7) if Athena does not decide the problem of Orestes in the way they think right. Since, too, the agent of punishment will not now be acting from guilty motives (like Clytaemestra or Aegisthus) or even for personal though honest reasons (like Orestes) but purely as an impartial servant of Dike, he will no longer himself be a criminal to be punished, so that *dikê* will not take the form of an unending cycle of vengeance but will be final and permanent, confirming instead of undermining the stability of society.

Nor is the justice of the Areopagus as utterly inexorable as was that of the gods of *Agamemnon*. To be sure, it must remain immune to bribery (*Eum.* 704, cf. *Ag.* 69-71) – even if the briber is a god (like Apollo in *Eum.* 667-73). But the representatives of the new justice *are* open to reasoned persuasion. Athena sharply rejects the suggestion that Orestes should be automatically considered guilty because he would not swear that he did not kill his mother (*Eum.* 429-32); he is to be allowed to advance and argue for a plea of justification. Hence, too, since argument and evidence will impress different minds in different ways, one must expect a jury to be divided in its opinions;[47] and the jury that tries Orestes is indeed divided, in sharp contrast to the gods who 'tried' the people of Troy and cast all their 'votes' in the same urn (*Ag.* 815-18).

One thing of cardinal importance remains unchanged. Justice still works under divine auspices as it always did, and under the ultimate control of Zeus, Athena being his deputy. But his primary agents are no longer the Erinyes but human judges, whom he holds firm in the path of justice by means of the judicial oath (cf. *Eum.* 483, 680, 710). Apollo, indeed, makes rather light of this oath, claiming that the authority of Zeus overrides it (621); but then he, like the Erinyes, is less interested in justice as such than in victory.

The same, of course, would be true of most real prosecutors and defendants in most real trials. That is to be expected in an adversary system. An Athenian went to court in order to get something out of his opponent (or to prevent the opponent from getting something out of *him*), and (in the absence of professional lawyers and their ethical codes) he would use any method, legitimate or illegitimate, in pursuit of this aim, that he thought he could get away with. Certainly that is how Apollo behaves; and so do the Erinyes, once they become seriously afraid of losing. And yet justice is done all the same – because so long as the *judges* are honest and intelligent, they will be able to see through and ignore the dishonesties of the contending parties; and the intelligence of *these* judges is guaranteed by the fact that they are Athenians (and the pick of the Athenians too, cf. *Eum.* 487), their honesty by the oath they have taken. They can offer justice as near perfect as human beings can provide.

But it is still *human* justice, no more. Athena has sat with the court in its inaugural session, and has cast a decisive vote, but that will not happen again. The old justice of Zeus and the Erinyes may have been extremely rough, but it was at any rate sure: sooner or later, every wrongdoer got retribution upon his head, unless (as perhaps in the case of Atreus) it was reserved for his descendants. No human lawcourt can ever hope to achieve such perfection. The Erinyes had claimed that they in particular were the natural avengers in those cases where human justice was helpless:

> Against whoever, like this man, does grave wrong
> and conceals his bloody hands,
> we present ourselves as upright witnesses for the dead
> and appear in full power as avengers of blood (316-20).

If they are deprived of this function, they warn, murder will run riot, and anarchy or despotism or both will ensue (490-529): 'Fear has its place, where it is a good thing' (517). With this Athena agrees absolutely:

> I counsel my citizens to cherish and practise
> the mean between anarchy and despotism,
> and not to banish fear entirely from the city;
> for who among mortals is righteous, if he fears nothing? (696-9)

In its immediate context this refers to the awe-inspiring institution of the Areopagus, but Athena may well also be looking further ahead in the hope of incorporating in the city those far more effective inspirers of fear, the Erinyes themselves.

And this she succeeds in doing – so that by a sublime paradox, those deities who most vehemently protested against the new form of Justice are made to be themselves its ultimate guardians. They will be as fearsome and implacable as ever; but their methods have changed in important ways from those with which *Agamemnon* made us familiar. They are now ready to bless the righteous individual or community (916-1020 *passim*) as well as cursing the unrighteous. They will no longer indiscriminately punish the innocent along with the guilty.[48] Nor will their justice be mediated through human avengers who will thus incur guilt in their turn; rather they will themselves act directly against those whose crimes have evaded human detection. Thus where formerly their activities caused *hybris* to breed fresh *hybris*, in future they will see that it perishes without offspring (cf. *Cho.* 806), so that as time goes by virtue and prosperity will continually increase (*Eum.* 853-4, 910, 990-5, 1007-9, 1017-20).

Such are the fruits of Athena's persuasion. But it is not only the Erinyes who are transformed in the course of the trilogy: Zeus undergoes a transformation too.[49] It is he, we are told, who presides over the moral chaos of the first play; it is he, we are told, who stands behind Apollo when Apollo intervenes to protect Orestes; it is he, we are told, in whose name and with whose aid Athena achieves the final reconciliation (*Eum.* 850, 973, 1045). Zeus is presented first, with great emphasis, as the guarantor of the law that 'he who has done must suffer', and then as sanctioning, at the risk of civil war among the gods, a violation of that law. In the first play the Erinyes are agents and emissaries of Zeus and the Olympians, working in perfect harmony with them; in the third the Erinyes and the 'younger gods' are at daggers drawn – and it is certainly not the Erinyes who have changed. Is there any alternative to supposing that there has been a change in Zeus?

Zeus, it will be recalled, 'put men on the road to wisdom, [and] laid down and made valid the law "by suffering, learning" '. It is not stated that that law applied only to mortals; and there is no reason why it should be so restricted, once we rid ourselves of the presupposition that gods must of necessity be eternal and immutable. In Greek philosophical thought this proposition was often, most notably by Aeschylus' contemporary Parmenides, taken as axiomatic; but it was quite otherwise with the gods of Greek cult, myth, poetry, art and popular belief. These gods, to be sure, were immortal; their existence had no end; but it *did* have a beginning. The gods were conceived and born, they passed through infancy and childhood, they came to maturity, and most of them (though not Athena or the Erinyes) produced children. They could also be thought of as developing mentally as well as physically. Repeatedly in *Prometheus Bound* (see Chapter 8) the tyrannical behaviour of Zeus is explained, and sometimes excused, by the fact that he is *young* and new to power. He is young in *Agamemnon* too – a vigorous and victorious wrestler (*Ag.* 168-75); Apollo is a wrestler also (*Ag.* 1206), a young lover whose anger flames as hot as his passion. Both may have much to learn; and by Zeus's own law, they must learn it by hard experience. Zeus will find that the inexorable working of his other law, 'he who has done must suffer', threatens to lead, through the matricide of Orestes, not only to the destruction of a morally innocent person (that would be nothing new), but also to the destruction of a royal house under Zeus's own patronage (cf. *Ag.* 43-4, 677-8, *Cho.* 246-63), and to the ruin of a *polis* (Argos) which, unlike Troy before it, has not as a community done anything wrong (see §7.10). Zeus will not allow this to happen. This doer shall not suffer, no matter how much the Erinyes insist that he shall. Orestes is saved; but in the process another innocent *polis*, Athens, comes to be threatened with ruin – and Zeus 'learns' some more. Apollo, that vehement hater of the Erinyes and all they stand for, fades out; Athena, the conciliator, takes his place as the representative of Zeus; and a mature humanity, 'wise in due season' (*Eum.* 1000), joins the matured gods in operating a system of justice that satisfies the legitimate aspirations of all.

This depiction of an evolving divinity and an evolving divine justice is itself almost unique in serious Greek literature, the Prometheus plays (see Chapter 8) offering the only real parallel. But a series of passages spread out through *Eumenides* imply an idea more startling still: that the gods are in some measure *responsible* to mortals and have obligations towards them, and that they stand to suffer if they break these obligations. Apollo says he will protect Orestes because the wrath of a betrayed suppliant 'is to be feared by mortals *and by gods*' (233-4). Athena is reluctant either to condemn or to acquit Orestes on her own responsibility, because in either case *she will incur wrath* (480-1) – the wrath of Orestes if she spurns him, or the wrath of the Athenian people whom the Erinyes will harm if she spurns *them*. Orestes describes Zeus as having *felt shame* (760) over Agamemnon's death, as if Zeus by allowing Agamemnon to be killed had failed in an obligation of honour towards him. Athena urges the Erinyes, 'being *goddesses*, not to put a blight upon *mortals*' land' (824-5), implying that it is improper for divinities to injure mortals unjustly. Later she tells her people that the Erinyes have great power 'among *the immortals*, among those under the earth, and among men' (950-3) – implying that they punish gods as readily as mortals. And lastly, and most astonishingly of all, the Erinyes tell the Athenians that Zeus 'reveres you' or 'stands in awe of you' (1002), using a verb (*hazetai*) whose proper application is to the reverence of mortals for gods or for the sacred.

Ideas of this kind can be paralleled only in Old Comedy, where in Aristophanes' *Peace* and *Wealth* we find men attempting, with success, to call the gods, and in particular Zeus, to account for their misgovernment of the universe. In *Eumenides* the gods are never *actually* called to account; but they are conscious that they *might* be if they act unjustly towards mortals – and therefore they do not so act. The power of Fear, which the Erinyes personify, is as effective in holding gods to their duty as in holding mortals to theirs. The Erinyes, once the agents of the gods for causing indiscriminate havoc among mortals, become *inter alia* the guarantee that the gods themselves will pay due reverence to the rights and dignity of mortal humanity.

7.10. A tale of three cities

The *Oresteia* is political in two senses. The connections between the trilogy and specific political issues of concern to Athenians in 458 BC will be explored in a later chapter (§12.1). In a more general sense the trilogy is political because it is concerned throughout with the behaviour and the fortunes of human beings in *polis* communities, three of which come under particular scrutiny: Troy which dominates the opening of the trilogy, Argos which dominates the middle and largest section, and Athens which dominates the conclusion. The three stand in contrast to one another morally and politically. Morally, Troy can be seen as the unjust city that earns destruction; Athens as the just city that will earn glorious prosperity (provided only that it remains a just city); and Argos as the city whose people desire justice (as their representatives, the chorus of *Agamemnon*, clearly testify) but which finds itself continually dragged down by the hybristic acts of successive rulers. Politically, Troy is a (stereo)typical 'oriental' monarchy; Athens is a Hellenic commonwealth with no ruler but Athena; and Argos is again in an intermediate state, at first possessing both a king and a decision-making assembly (cf. *Ag.* 844-6) but ultimately falling under the sway of a tyrant, Aegisthus, from whose rule of terror (*Cho.* 54-60) Orestes is its liberator (*Cho.* 302-4, 973, 1046-7). The trilogy begins with the shining out of fire to signal the fall of Troy; it ends with the shining out of fire to herald the rise of Athens.

To say that Troy dominates the opening of the trilogy is perhaps something of an exaggeration, but not a very great one. The first three choral odes all commence, and continue for some time, on the theme of the crime of Paris and its consequences (*Ag.* 40-71, 355-408, 681-782); the third, indeed, stays with that theme to its end, even if much of what is said in it also has ironic application to the situation in Argos. The war, and the capture and sack of Troy, are also the main subject of the prologue, of Clytaemestra's first scene (258-354), and of half the Herald scene (503-86), not to mention the beginning of Agamemnon's entry-scene (783-828); and even then there is still to come one of the most powerful scenes of the play, in which the Trojan Cassandra will be in command of the stage.

Cassandra is one of the innocent sufferers – like the cattle and sheep that her father sacrificed (1168-9); but we are left in no doubt that the *polis* as a whole deserved its fate. It is not just a case of the crime of one man staining the whole city by association (395); the city itself was party to the crime (532), for it welcomed Paris and Helen and celebrated their 'wedding' with enthusiasm (700-8), and like the man who reared the lion-cub (717-36) it should have known better. The result was utter destruction, emphasized repeatedly in the play: the adult males are dead, the rest of the population enslaved (326-9); city and countryside are both laid waste, temples and altars destroyed, the very seed perished from the soil (525-8); even as Agamemnon speaks on his return to Argos the ruins are still smouldering and smoking (818-20). Wrongdoing and destruction are two of the three main elements in the picture we are given of Troy; the third is wealth. Troy was rich in cattle (127-8); Paris spurned the altar of Dike through 'surfeit of wealth' (382, cf. 376); the Greek army has brought home abundant spoils (577-9); Helen brought to Troy 'a delicate adornment of wealth' (741); Dike shuns the combination of 'gold-bespangled dwellings with unclean hands' (776-8); the embers of the burning city 'send forth rich puffs of wealth' (820). The fullest treatment of this theme comes in the purple-cloth scene, when Agamemnon refuses to be adulated 'in the fashion of a barbarian' (919) but in the end yields and does what a Priam would have done in similar circumstances (935) – namely, conspicuously waste a precious possession, knowing himself so rich that its loss will not be noticed. All in all, Troy provides us with an initial paradigm of how not to run a city: wealth plus wickedness equals catastrophe.

In Troy (so far as we hear in Aeschylus' presentation) there was no political authority except the king: the people of Troy do indeed ratify the actions of Paris, but they do so not in a decision-making assembly (as in the *Iliad*, e.g. 7.345-79) but at a wedding feast. So it was, perhaps, in Argos in the days of Atreus and Thyestes; in what we are told about them, the Argive people have no part to play at all. But in the dramatic present it is otherwise. The citizen-body of Argos is represented on stage by the Elders, and there are also other Argive citizens off stage – including those who fight and die in the war against Troy. For the Trojan War, as presented in this play, was an undertaking not of 'the Hellenes' (as the Persian War of 480-79 had been) nor of 'the Achaeans' (as usually in Homer) but rather, to use fifth-century terminology, of 'the Argives and their allies'. The two principals, Agamemnon and Menelaus, are both Argives, as is the Herald, the only representative of the common troops that we meet; and the army as a whole is called 'Argive' (45, 198, 267, 573, 577, 652, 824) almost as often as it is called 'Achaean' (108, 185, 189, 269, 320, 538, 624, 649, 660). Like fifth-century Athens, Argos is thought of as making war at the head of a confederacy of *poleis*, and one of Agamemnon's reasons for going ahead with the sacrifice of Iphigeneia is that he fears he will lose his allies otherwise (213; see §11.2). He also has to consider, throughout, the feelings of his own people. We hear from the Elders, who say it to Agamemnon's face, that they disagreed strongly with his original decision to launch the expedition (799ff.); we hear also that the heavy casualties have brought popular resentment against the royal house to a point where a plot against their lives must be regarded as a possibility (445-60), and Clytaemestra can plausibly explain that Orestes was sent abroad for his own safety because of the dangers of 'noisy popular anarchy' (877-85). Agamemnon himself believes that the malcontents are a small minority, motivated by jealousy (830-40), who can easily be isolated by the calling of an assembly (845) and then dealt with by 'surgical' methods (849). Who is right about this, neither we nor Agamemnon ever learn; but the Elders do have the advantage of having lived in Argos during the past ten years, and if feeling against the rulers was already strong during the war it will not become weaker now it is known that, of the thousand ships that set out (45), only one has returned.

Then comes the shattering climax of Agamemnon's murder. It literally shatters the chorus, who proceed to argue with one another as twelve distinct individuals (1348-71), and it also shatters the structure of the Argive state. The Elders are all convinced that if there has been an assassination, it has been a political act, and the first suggestion that is made is to call out the citizens in force to defeat the plotters (1348-9) whose 'opening moves are the signals for tyranny' (1354-5). And although the revelation that Clytaemestra is the murderer seems to prove them wrong, they are not in fact all that wrong. At first, now that they have found that Agamemnon was not after all killed in a *coup d'état*, they envisage his killer being dealt with by the ordinary mechanisms of a well-organized *polis* (cf. 1410-11), an attitude which is rightly characterized by Clytaemestra in judicial language (1412-21). But the mechanisms of the *polis* have been subverted. First Clytaemestra declares her complete confidence in the protection of Aegisthus (1432-7); it is striking that from that moment the Elders cease to speak of her being punished by the *polis* and hope only for her punishment by the gods. And then, for this play, the *polis* theme is climaxed by the entry of Aegisthus with the bodyguard of spearmen who constitute the visible evidence that the Elders were right after all: Argos *is* going to be subjected to a *tyrannos* (1633). They try to speak to him in the same manner in which they had earlier spoken to Clytaemestra:

> I say that you will pay the penalty and that your head,
> be sure of it, will not escape the curses and stones the people will fling
> (1615-16).

Aegisthus' reply shows that talk of that kind is very obsolete indeed. He proposes to rule by naked terror, 'bonds and pangs of hunger' (1621, cf. 1641-2), his régime financed by the confiscated possessions of Agamemnon (1638); and though the Elders with futile heroism resist him at the willing sacrifice of their lives (for it 'would not be the Argive way to fawn on an evil man', 1665), there is nothing really to be done but curse the despot and hope for the return of Orestes (1646-8, 1667). The *polis* has failed to save itself, and can now only be saved by violence coming from outside – and violence of a particularly horrendous kind.

During most of *Choephoroi* we are encouraged to think more of the ills of the house than of those of the city. The scene is first at the tomb of Agamemnon, where his son and daughter both bring offerings, and then before the palace where the son will confront the mother; and the chorus are not now male citizens of the *polis* but female servants of the household.

Orestes' companion, too, is a non-Argive. Nevertheless we are soon reminded that the city as well as the house is suffering:

> The irresistible, indefeasible, invincible reverence
> that formerly transfixed the ears and hearts of the people
> has departed, and men are afraid ... (*Cho.* 54-8).

The Argives obeyed Agamemnon because they revered him; they now obey Aegisthus simply because they are terrified not to. They are, in fact, no longer in the position of citizens but in that of slaves, just as in a rather different sense Orestes and Electra are (132-7). This is one of the things Orestes finds intolerable, to think of

> the people of the most glorious city in the world ...
> having thus to obey a pair of women (302-4).

But that, for more than 600 lines, is all. From the *kommos* to the murder the action is viewed entirely from the standpoint of the *oikos*, and the same is true even of the mythical *exempla* in the choral ode 585-651 (we are told that Scylla caused the death of her father but not that she caused the capture of her city). In all this time only one phrase points to what is to follow: in 864 the chorus look forward to the prospect of Orestes winning 'lawful rulership over the city'. Aegisthus is killed; his tyranny is not mentioned. Orestes and Clytaemestra argue over rights and wrongs; nothing is said of Agamemnon's position as ruler of Argos. The chorus celebrate the cleansing of the house; they say nothing of the cleansing of the state. Then Orestes appears standing over his two victims, and his first words are 'Behold the twin tyrants of the land!' (973). These words imply a citizen audience, a role into which the theatre audience may have been conscripted (see §7.6.5). Throughout the ensuing scene we are encouraged to view Orestes *both* as matricide *and* as tyrannicide: from the point of view of the *oikos* he is a polluted outcast, from that of the *polis* an admired hero. Orestes himself, indeed, tends to forget what he has done for the *polis*, but the chorus cannot: 'You have liberated the whole city of Argos' (1046). But the liberator of Argos cannot even remain in Argos to receive his congratulations.

With that, the trilogy ceases to be concerned with the Argive *polis* as such (except in its fifth-century role as an ally of Athens: see §12.1). We have seen Argos first in a state of political instability, then bloodily enslaved, and at last bloodily liberated; there must surely be a better way of running a *polis* than this. And so, although Argos, and the confirmation of his own rights there, still matters a great deal to Orestes, the centre of 'political' interest from the start of the third play is rather Athens, referred to in *Eum.* 10 (as 'the shipfaring shores of Pallas') for the first time in the trilogy.

At first Athens is simply a location – the place where Orestes is to supplicate Athena and submit to her judgement; and allusions to an Athenian alliance with Argos (*Eum.* 289-91) and to Athenian possessions in the Troad (398-402) do not really change this. For at this stage there is dramatically hardly any difference between Athens and Athena; *she* is promised Argos as an ally, *she* is envisaged waging war in Africa or Europe, *she* has taken possession of conquered Trojan land. Athens as a human community enters the scene only at 470-83, when Athena declines to judge the issue between Orestes and the Erinyes herself because of the possible effects on her citizens, and instead announces that she will enlist the best of them to judge it with her in a court whose institution will endure for all time. Thus the first and essential function of the *polis* is seen as the enforcement of justice upon and between its members; and whereas Argos was represented on stage by the feeble if valiant Elders, armed only with sticks which were no defence against the swords of the tyrant's men, Athens is represented, silently, by the councillors of the Areopagus, whose *physical* weapon (cf. §7.6.4) is a feebler one still – a mere pebble – but who are armed *spiritually* with the same irresistible, invincible awe of which the chorus of *Choephoroi* had sung.

It is at the same stage that the Erinyes, those utterly asocial and anti-social creatures (as both we and Apollo had imagined), also begin to take an interest in the nature of the good society:

> Who would still revere Dike
> if he nurtured no fear in his heart –
> man or city, it makes no difference?
> Reject the life of anarchy
> and reject life under despotism (522-8).

In the Argive situation in *Agamemnon*, there had been elements both of anarchy and of despotism – anarchy in the dimly-envisaged popular murmurings and conspiracies against the rulers, despotism in the successful *coup* of Aegisthus. The law and justice were equally powerless against both. And they will always be powerless unless they are reinforced by fear and reverence – as Athena too insists when she declares that the Areopagos must have '(the) reverence and inborn fear of the citizens'[50] and so 'restrain wrongdoing by day and night alike' (690-2). This the Areopagos can do, and will do, provided that it is vigilant and incorruptible (704-6) and provided 'the citizens themselves do not make innovations in the laws' (693) – whatever precisely that may mean (see §12.1).

In the end the good society has two prerequisites. One is the right machinery; the other is the right spirit. Athena has supplied the Athenians with the right machinery – so long as they stick to it. Only a healthy Fear (698-9) can supply them with the right spirit; and this fear the Erinyes are harnessed to inspire. Thus the Athenians with their matured understanding (1000) will be fully aware of the benefits of justice and the harm done by injustice, will maintain their unity, avoid civil strife (858-66, 976-87), and be blessed with all the blessings that Athena and the Erinyes call down upon them in the last scenes of the trilogy. The Trojans had nothing like the right spirit, and they had no constitutional machinery at all. The Argives, some of them – the Elders, for example, and later Orestes – did have the right spirit, and they also had constitutional machinery of a sort; but when that machinery proved unable to prevent Atreus from committing a vile child-murder, unable to prevent Agamemnon from embarking, without adequate reason, on a war which may have been victorious but was also calamitous, and from sacrificing his daughter in order to go ahead with that war – then the *polis* broke down, for the aggrieved had no other redress but to plot murder in return; and the result, as we saw, was first anarchy and then despotism. Atreus and Agamemnon were able to get away with their abuses of power because they were *too* powerful and too wealthy to be restrained by the laws of the *polis*: hence the emphasis placed in *Eumenides* on the principle that even the richest and the proudest cannot hope to avoid the penalty of their wrongdoings (368ff., 553ff., 934ff.). And thus the trilogy that began with the wealth, the wrongdoing and the destruction of Troy ends with the wealth (*Eum.* 946, 996), the virtue and the prosperity of Athens.

Notes

1. Pleisthenes is a shadowy name in the family to which Agamemnon belongs, found at several different points in its genealogy (Gantz 1993: 552-6). Most often he is a son of Atreus who dies young and whose children, Agamemnon and Menelaus, are then adopted by their grandfather; it is hard, though, to understand why Thyestes should curse *his* descendants (1602) rather than his father's (Atreus, after all, might yet have other children), and it is simpler to suppose that Aeschylus is treating 'Atreus' and 'Pleisthenes' as alternative names for the same person, like 'Paris' and 'Alexandros'.

2. He speaks of Atreus' expulsion of Thyestes from Argos as if it resulted merely from a political struggle between the brothers (1583-6), making no reference to Thyestes' adultery with Atreus' wife, of which we know from Cassandra (1193).

3. This title, usually and not very informatively translated as 'The Libation Bearers', means 'Women bringing drink-offerings to a tomb', referring to the chorus.

4. *Kommos* properly means 'lament', but the word is often used by students of Greek tragedy (following Aristotle, *Poetics* 1452b24-5) in the more specific sense of a lament, wholly or mainly sung, in which, as here, both the chorus and one or more actors take part. Sometimes the term is extended to include passages of similar structure which are not laments.

5. For some further speculations see Griffith 2002: 237-54.

6. The *Eleventh Pythian* is in honour of a successful runner, Thrasydaeus of Thebes. This name appeared in the Pythian victor-list for a boys' race in 474 and for a men's race in 454; it is not known whether the later victor was the same person as the earlier, or another of the same name. Either way, the ode almost

certainly belongs to 474: it makes no mention of any previous victory by Thrasydaeus (only by members of his family), and, in a manner typical of odes for boy victors, it has a great deal to say about the honorand's father even though he had apparently never gained any athletic triumphs himself. See Finglass 2007: 1-19.

7. Euripides in *Iphigeneia in Tauris* (783-5, cf. 564-7) manages to get away with claiming that Artemis substituted a deer for Iphigeneia without anyone present noticing (Agamemnon still thought he was killing his daughter, and everyone in Argos assumes her to be dead). How even a goddess could have contrived this is far from clear.

8. Reproduced in Prag 1985 pl. 3, March 1987 pl. 32, Shapiro 1994: 128 fig. 89, and in many other places.

9. As he is in Euripides, *Iphigeneia in Tauris* 918; in Pausanias 2.29.4, and in the scholia to Euripides, *Orestes* 765, 1233, his mother is Anaxibia (other sources give her other names).

10. The fifth-century mythographer Pherecydes (fr. 134 Fowler) has Aegisthus kill the nurse's own son by mistake for Orestes; it is not clear whether we are to take this as an accident, or whether in this version the nurse (here named as Laodameia) actually substituted her own child for her master's.

11. We also hear of a local variant on this story, from Arcadia, in which Orestes takes sanctuary at the altar of Artemis at Parrhasium and the goddess protects him from the Erinyes (Pherecydes fr. 135 Fowler).

12. Euripides, *Iphigeneia in Tauris* 947-60; Phanodemus fr. 11 Jacoby; Plutarch, *Moralia* 613b, 643a; and scholia on Aristophanes, *Acharnians* 961 and *Knights* 95.

13. As in the discussions of poetry, including tragedy (377c-398b), and of music (398c-400c) in the *Republic*.

14. Euripides, *The Madness of Heracles* 1315, 1346.

15. See M.L. West 1992; Pöhlmann and West 2001.

16. In the descriptions of metrical patterns below, – denotes a long syllable, ∪ a short syllable (normally about half the time-value of a long), and x an 'anceps' (a position which can be occupied by a long or short syllable indifferently).

17. He is keeping watch in a reclining, not a standing position. This is implied by *koimômenos* 'taking my night's rest' (*Ag.* 2) and *eunên* 'couch' (13), and confirmed by his anxiety about falling asleep (14-17): one cannot fall asleep standing on a roof, with nothing to lean against. The actor would inevitably be seen by spectators in the higher tiers, but he would be invisible to those closer to the performing space. Probably the Watchman jumps to his feet on seeing the beacon-light (21/2); in the prologue of *Eumenides*, contrariwise, the Pythia, having entered the temple and seen the Erinyes, reappears crawling on all fours (*Eum.* 36-8).

18. This is shown by what Orestes says in 13-15: he knows that the women are connected with the palace even before he sees Electra among them. See Scullion 1994: 72-7. In the next play the chorus will once again enter from the *skênê* (below, n. 21).

19. Thus echoing in reverse an important visual motif of the previous play, as will his appearance after the murder (see §7.6.2).

20. The 'Father' who is asked by Orestes to look down on it is Zeus, not the Sun; see M.L. West 1990b: 262-3, deleting line 986 with W.S. Barrett.

21. Not the whole chorus (for whom there would not be space); most likely three (note the chorus-leader's words in 140, 'Wake that one, as I am waking you'). Later, and perhaps already, three was the canonical number of the Erinyes; the audience will have been taken by surprise when more of them appeared from the *skênê* (probably between 143 and 147) so as to make up a complete chorus.

22. Scullion 1994: 77-86 argues that the imaginary location remains on the Acropolis throughout, and that Orestes continues to clasp the image of Athena until the moment she declares him acquitted (752-3); he never mentions 566-9 or engages with the implications of that passage for the setting of the trial.

23. Each of these features appears in some artistic representations of the death of Aegisthus from the 470s and 460s; in one, by the Berlin Painter (Prag 1985: pl. 17), both appear together.

24. Dickey 1996: 94 has observed that Agamemnon and Xerxes are the only mortals in surviving fifth-century Greek tragedy to be addressed as *basileu* 'king', a form of address which in prose literature implies extreme deference and is scarcely ever used by a Greek speaking to a fellow-Greek.

25. Photius, *Lexicon* s.v. σκάφαι, citing Menander fr. 147.

26. Orestes is carrying a pack (560, 675), so presumably is Pylades, and we can if we wish suppose that his sword is hidden inside it.

27. On the contrast between the 'voting' in *Agamemnon* and the voting in *Eumenides*, see also Bowie 2009: 229-30.

28. See Sommerstein 2010c: 104-7.

29. The possibility cannot be in principle excluded that he appears at a window or on the roof and calls *down* into the house (like the Watchman at *Ag.* 25ff.); but even so, his specific mention of the 'women's doors' indicates that the door through which Clytaemestra presently appears is not the same one as that behind which Aegisthus has been killed and from which Orestes and Pylades will emerge.

30. See, however, below, on the question of Pylades' entrance.

31. On the conventions governing the presentation of violence in Greek drama, see Sommerstein 2004.

32. As we were reminded earlier in *Andromache* (627-31).

33. It is just possible that if the Servant exited at 886 (with 889 being addressed not to him specifically but to anyone who happened to be in earshot), the actor would have had time to change mask and costume and reappear (through the same door) as Pylades at 892; but this would be, by a considerable margin, the fastest change known in tragedy (though paralleled in Menander's *Dyskolos*, where Gorgias and Sostratus exit at 873 and one of the two actors must re-enter – again through the same door – as the slave Getas at 879).

34. The following thematic words and notions, all of which recur at intervals throughout the trilogy, make their first appearance in the Watchman's speech: dance (23, 31), *dikê* (3), dogs (3), dream (13), dripping liquids (12), *euphêmia* (auspicious speech) (28), fear (14), fire (9), healing (17), hope (11), house (18, 35-7), *khairein* (rejoicing) (22), *kharis* (favour/delight) (24), light and darkness (21-3), male and female (11), messengers (21, 30), nocturnal activity (12), *ololygê* (cry of triumph) (28), *philia* (friendship or kinship) (34), *polis* (29), *prepein* (conspicuousness) (6, 30), release from trouble (1), silence (36), sleep (14-15), song (17), *symphora* (sad or happy event) (18, 24), torches (8), watch-keeping (2).

35. 'In part', because it is also partly modelled on the great annual procession in honour of the *Semnai Theai* themselves (Demosthenes, *Against Meidias* 115; Philo, *That Every Virtuous Man is Free* 140; scholia to Sophocles, *Oedipus at Colonus* 489).

36. Itys was the son of Tereus and Procne. When Procne learned that Tereus had raped her sister Philomela, she took revenge (with Philomela's assistance) by killing Itys and serving his flesh to Tereus to eat. When Tereus discovered this, he tried to kill both women, but the gods prevented this by transforming both them and Tereus into birds; Procne became a nightingale, and laments Itys in song to this day.

37. Cf. *Odyssey* 3.464-9 and 4.47-50, where Telemachus is bathed and dressed, at Pylos by the *daughter* of Nestor, at Sparta by the *maidservants* of Menelaus.

38. As the poet Archilochus was said to have slandered Neobule after her father had broken a promise to give her to him in marriage.

39. She has referred to the murderer in the feminine gender six times between 1107 and 1127, and about seven times more between 1228 and 1237.

40. The most spectacular case is that of the Scythian archer in Aristophanes' *Thesmophoriazusae*, who in lines 1109-1225 makes fifteen gender blunders at an average rate of one every fifteen words. In Timotheus' lyric nome *The Persians* a Phrygian is made to call Artemis 'my great god' in the masculine gender (*GL* 791.160).

41. It goes back at least as far as Xanthus, a precursor of Stesichorus, according to whom Agamemnon's daughter, originally named Laodice, was called Electra by the Argives because she was kept unmarried (*alektros*, lit. 'unbedded') by Aegisthus and Clytaemestra (*GL* 700).

42. A 'priamel' is the modern critical term for the literary device that consists in listing a series of examples of some quality as a build-up to the introduction of what is claimed to be the supreme instance of that quality; e.g. 'Some say a host of cavalry is the fairest thing on the black earth, some say a host of infantry, some say a fleet of ships, but I say it is whatever one loves' (Sappho fr. 16.1-4).

43. Clytaemestra, Cassandra, Electra, the Nurse, the Pythia, Athena, and the choruses of *Choephoroi* (twelve) and *Eumenides* (twelve).

44. And the Herald reports the disappearance of Menelaus (*Ag.* 624-5, 674-9) without mentioning that Helen was with him – after which the Elders meditate on the coming of Helen to Troy (681-749) without making any reference to her departure thence or to Menelaus. The couple are reunited, dramatically speaking, only beyond the end of the trilogy, in the satyr-play *Proteus*.

45. This qualification is added to exclude monastic communities, which are wholly dependent for their continued existence on reproduction and child-rearing outside the community, a process in which the community members take no part (except sometimes in the later stages as teachers). The Amazons, on the other hand, bore and reared their own (female) children.

46. This section is an expanded version of Sommerstein 1989a: 19-25. I am grateful to Cambridge University Press for permitting me to include this material in the present work.

47. Assuming that, like all Athenian juries, it voted without first holding a discussion.

48. *Eum.* 934-5 ('Crimes coming from his forebears hale a man before their [the Erinyes'] tribunal') is often cited as showing that the Erinyes will still, as formerly, punish descendants for the crimes of their ancestors; but the person being punished here is not innocent (in 936 he is called 'loud-mouthed', i.e. boastfully confident of his invulnerability, cf. *Eum.* 368, 561), and if his crimes come 'from his forebears' it is because he has inherited their character defects, as did the lion-cub of *Ag.* 717-36, or Aegisthus (an adulterer, son of an adulterer), or Agamemnon (a child-killer, son of a child-killer).

49. On the matters discussed in this and the next paragraph see further §11.6.

50. I have bracketed the first 'the' to suggest the ambiguity, inherent in the phraseology of the Greek, as to whether the citizens are to revere and fear the Areopagites, or vice versa (see §12.1).

8

The Prometheus Plays

The date of production of *Prometheus Bound* (*Desmôtês*) is not known, and in modern times its Aeschylean authorship has come under suspicion (see §8.5). It was produced together with *Prometheus Unbound* (*Lyomenos*), of which there survive fragments in Greek totalling about 36 lines, as well as a passage of 28 lines in a Latin translation by Cicero. We have no firm information about the other plays in the production; the question of a possible 'Prometheus trilogy' is discussed in §8.4.

8.1. *Prometheus Bound*

The scene is a deserted region in the furthest part of Scythia (1-2). Four persons enter. One is Hephaestus, the god of fire and metalwork; another is Prometheus, the god who, according to a myth narrated by Hesiod (*Theogony* 516-616), stole fire from the gods and gave it to mortals. Prometheus is being held prisoner by the third and fourth characters, who are presently named (12) as Kratos and Bia, Power and Force, obedient agents of Zeus (12-13) who has instructed Hephaestus to clamp Prometheus to the rocks in punishment for his theft, 'so that he may learn to accept the *tyrannis* of Zeus and abandon his man-loving ways' (10-11). Hephaestus is very reluctant to carry out these orders, but is bullied and even threatened (67-8) by Kratos into doing so, and leaves as soon as he can. Kratos lingers a moment or two more to taunt Prometheus (whose name means 'Forethought'), asking him whether he can forethink of a device to escape from his bonds.

Prometheus, who has not yet uttered a word, is now left alone, and cries out to the elements to 'behold what I, a god, suffer at the gods' hands' (93). He hears the sound of someone or something approaching, and is briefly alarmed; but it proves to be a band of nymphs, daughters of Oceanus, who will form the chorus of the play. They sympathize warmly with Prometheus' plight, faced with the 'inflexible' resolve of Zeus (164); Prometheus, however, predicts that Zeus will one day have need of him, because Prometheus knows 'the new scheme by which he will be robbed of his sceptre and his honours' (170-1) and will refuse to reveal it until he is released and compensated (173-6), after which he and Zeus will join in sincere friendship (190-2).

In reply to an inquiry by the chorus, Prometheus explains how he came to fall foul of Zeus. In the struggle between Zeus on the one side, and

Cronus and the Titans on the other, for the rulership of the universe, Prometheus, on the prophetic advice of his mother Themis (here identified with the Earth-goddess Gaia), warned his brethren, the Titans, that they must seek to prevail by craft and not by force. They refused to heed him, and Prometheus and his mother then went over to the side of Zeus who defeated the Titans by the aid of their counsels. When Zeus was established in power, he resolved to destroy the human race (231-3); Prometheus prevented him from doing so, and it is for this that he is being punished. In particular, he planted 'blind hope' in mortals' hearts (248-50), so that they would no longer know beforehand when they were to die, and he gave them fire 'with which they will learn many skills' (254). He says that he was in error (266), never having supposed that his punishment would be so heavy; but he invites the chorus to descend from their 'winged vehicle' (see §8.3) and learn from him about the future, and they duly alight.

A visitor makes a flying entry, riding on a 'four-legged bird'. He is Oceanus, father of the chorus (who however take no notice of him, nor he of them[1]) and father-in-law of Prometheus. He advises Prometheus to moderate his hostility towards Zeus, and promises to do what he himself can to secure his release. Prometheus, reminding him of the fate of other enemies of Zeus such as Atlas and Typhos, tells him not to endanger himself to no purpose, and makes it clear that his offer is unwelcome, and Oceanus departs. The chorus sing of how all humanity is grieving with and for Prometheus, and Prometheus tells them of how he enabled mortals to acquire the arts of civilization, from arithmetic and writing to medicine and divination. This leads on to some cryptic remarks about a possible future overthrow of Zeus, on which Prometheus refuses to elaborate because in keeping this secret lies his hope of eventual freedom.

There now enters an extraordinary spectacle, a young woman with a cow's horns, singing and dancing wildly as if being harassed by an invisible insect. Prometheus recognizes her as Io (cf. §6.5), loved by Zeus and on that account tormented by Hera. When she learns who he is, she asks him to foretell her future destiny, but at the request of the chorus she first tells them the story of what she has already suffered. Zeus had repeatedly propositioned her in dreams; she eventually told her father; he sought the guidance of oracles and was told to expel Io from his home or else his entire family would be destroyed; he reluctantly obeyed; Io immediately found that she had grown horns, was tormented by a gadfly and watched over by the hundred-eyed monster Argus; Argus was killed, but the gadfly remained and has driven her from land to land. Prometheus carries the narrative on into the future, telling Io she will wander through many remote and fantastic regions on the edges of the world until she finally reaches Egypt (her route is quite different from that described in *Supp.* 540-64). In the middle of this prophecy a casual remark (756) again raises the issue of the possible overthrow of Zeus, and Prometheus lifts the curtain a little further on this prospect: Zeus will be overthrown by his own folly (762) when he mates with a female who is destined to 'bear a son greater than his father' (768). Prometheus of course refuses to identify the female in question until he is released from his captivity, but the audience will realize at 768 that the reference is to Thetis, for whom Zeus and Poseidon were suitors until this prophecy was revealed, whereupon she was married off to the mortal Peleus and fulfilled the prophecy by becoming the mother of Achilles.[2]

Having brought Io, in prospect, to Egypt, Prometheus proves the genuineness of his prophetic power by telling her some details of her past wanderings which she herself had omitted to mention, and then moves further into the future, telling her how Zeus will restore her to full humanity and, by the touch of his hand, make her pregnant with Epaphus; how the descendants of Epaphus, the Danaids, will return to Argos, and what will befall them there (see Chapter 6); how one of them will be the ancestress of a royal house from which will spring 'a bold man, renowned for archery, who will release me from these sufferings' (871-3) – a person whom the audience will easily identify as Heracles (cf. Hesiod, *Theogony* 526-34). At this point Io is again stung by the invisible gadfly and dances off. The chorus pray to be spared the misfortune of being loved by a god (887-907).[3]

Prometheus, now in almost triumphant mood, views in his mind's eye the coming downfall and humiliation of Zeus, for whom, he proclaims, he 'cares less than nothing' (938). As if in response to this Hermes, the messenger of Zeus, arrives to demand in Zeus' name that Prometheus reveal, without obscurity or mystification, the identity of the female whose child will overthrow him. Prometheus contemptuously refuses; nothing will make him reveal his secret, unless he is released from his bonds. Hermes warns him that if he is obdurate, he will first be swallowed up by the earth (1016-19) and when at long last he is restored to the light Zeus will send an eagle every day to tear his flesh and feast on his liver (1021-5). The chorus suggest that Prometheus would be well advised to submit, but he remains adamant. Hermes then warns the chorus to leave Prometheus for their own safety, but they insist on standing by him; to do otherwise, they say, would be cowardice and betrayal (1066-70). Hermes gives them a final warning and leaves, and immediately thereafter there erupts a great elemental tempest, through which Prometheus cries out the last words of the play: 'O my honoured mother, O thou Sky round which the world's luminary circles, do you see how unjustly I suffer?'

8.2. Structure, logic and action

For Aristotle (*Poetics* 1450b23-1451a35), the content of a tragedy had to consist of a single complete 'action' (*praxis*) whose component events were linked together by 'probable or inevitable' connections. *Prometheus Bound* might well seem to fall down badly on both criteria. If we ask what single complete action it portrays, we might indeed answer 'the punishment of Prometheus by Zeus' – and it would be no objection to this that Zeus does not actually appear in the play, because he never normally does appear on stage in Greek drama of any kind (though, as we shall see later, *Prometheus Unbound* may have been an exception). But many of the events of *Prometheus Bound* are not part of Prometheus' punishment and have little or no causal connection with each other: this is particularly true of the Io episode, the longest in the play, which has no causal linkage at all with anything that precedes it and only a very tenuous linkage with the Hermes episode that follows. It probably has an important function in preparing for the action of the following play (see §8.4), but that could have been performed much more briefly. The play, moreover, has an obvious central character (Prometheus himself) who does nothing. Not only is he literally immobilized; even his words generally have no effect, except to bring further suffering on himself. He tells Io her future and that of her descendants, but it makes no difference to Io's movements, which are controlled by the pestilent gadfly in any case. His dialogue with Oceanus has the negative result that Oceanus will do nothing to help him. The chorus at the end show admirable courage and loyalty, but this comes entirely from themselves; Prometheus has not asked for it.

And yet in another sense something very important *has* happened during the play. At its beginning we see Prometheus as a helpless sufferer, victim of the cruel tyranny of Zeus, looked on with sympathy by all mortals and many divinities but irretrievably doomed to appalling suffering that is made even worse by the fact that he foresees it all (101ff.). At its end Prometheus, though in appearance even more completely crushed, in fact holds the whip hand, and it is Zeus who is doomed to catastrophe. As once before (204-13) craft has defeated force.

The engine of this transformation is our growing awareness of Prometheus' secret and the power it gives him. If we examine the action analytically as though it were a real event, we will deduce that this secret – the prophecy regarding Thetis – must have been known to Prometheus from the start. But it is not known to the audience; or rather, they have no way of knowing that it is going to be in any way relevant to the play. At first Prometheus is pure victim, so much so that for the first 87 lines he does not speak, even when directly addressed (by Hephaestus, more in sorrow than in anger, in 18-35, and tauntingly by Kratos in 82-7). When he does speak (88-127), his words express in turn grief, indignation which he knows to be futile, resignation, and fear; he finds no support except from the inanimate elements (88-91);[4] he can see no hope and refers to no possibility of release. He thinks himself hated by all the gods (120-2); even Hephaestus, for all his sympathy, not only acquiesced in but put into effect Zeus' terrible sentence. He knows that mortals have reason to love him, but mortals are powerless in Zeus' universe.

When Prometheus hears the beating of wings (124), the audience may well suppose, and may well suppose Prometheus to know (cf. 101-3), that Zeus's terrible eagle is already at hand; in Hesiod (*Theogony* 523) the eagle is mentioned immediately after the binding. But instead he hears the voices of a group of young females, and their first words are 'Fear nothing; this is a friendly band' (128). Moreover, they have come here despite the opposition of their father (130-1); it is far from matching the audacity of Prometheus' defiance of *the* Father, but it does show that Prometheus has those who will take practical steps, and break convention (cf. 134), to express their solidarity with him, and who are ready to criticize Zeus (149-51, 162-7). Prometheus at first remains fixed in grief and self-pity (136-43, 152-9), but from 168 he begins to envisage for the first time a positive future and begins to hint that he has a secret connected with a danger threatening Zeus. The chorus hardly notice, let alone believe, the significance of what he is saying (178-85); but the seed has been planted in the spectators' minds.

Prometheus' next speech is important in various ways for the movement of the play. By narrating his past services to Zeus he adds monstrous ingratitude to the list of Zeus' wrongs against him. Once before, when the Titans spurned his advice, he joined their enemies and took part in their destruction; it may therefore be no empty boast if he claims to be able to do the same to Zeus who has treated him so much worse. We learn, too, whence he gets his knowledge of the future: from his mother Themis (209, cf. 18) who is, we are told, identical with Gaia, one of the oldest of all divinities – and *the* oldest of *prophetic* divinities (cf. *Eum.* 1-2). This Prometheus is therefore in a very different position from the Prometheus of Hesiod, whose parents were the Titan Iapetus and the Oceanid Clymene, and who simply endured his bondage until released by Heracles. And we begin to hear what his gifts have meant to mortals, who, starting on the brink of complete destruction, have acquired fire and hope, and will in due time advance further (254). Prometheus, we know, has hope too, and 271-3 suggests we are going to hear more about it:

> And now do not lament my present sufferings,
> but come down to the ground and listen to my fortunes
> to come, that in the end you may learn it all.

Fulfilment of this promise, however, is forestalled by the arrival of Oceanus. Oceanus introduces a possibility not considered thus far: perhaps it may be possible, if Prometheus is suitably co-operative and penitent, to secure a pardon from Zeus. Having seen Zeus at work, as represented by Kratos and Bia, and recalling how he treats his benefactors and how he was prepared to treat mortal humanity, we may well feel Oceanus is being wildly over-optimistic: Prometheus confirms this for us by the examples of Atlas and Typhos, while making no reply at all to Oceanus' advice to him to moderate his own language and behaviour.

Oceanus, in short, hopelessly underrates both the tyrannical arrogance of Zeus and the latent power of Prometheus; his well-meaning intervention is irrelevant.

Prometheus' next speech (436-506) shows us how, by his aid, the power of mortals over their environment is growing. At 254 their acquisition of the arts of civilization still lay in the future; now it is described as already an accomplished fact – though it has been observed that the arts of war, and of civic and political life, are missing from the list. Nevertheless mortals do seem to have been put in a position where they can survive by their own efforts and even enjoy some luxuries (466, 502). At the same time Prometheus feels, and makes us feel, more conscious of his own power: where previously he had thought in terms of using his secret to re-establish friendship between himself and Zeus (188-92), he now sees it purely as a weapon to secure his own release (522-5); where formerly he had spoken of that release being effected by Zeus (175), he now speaks of it as an 'escape' (513, 525); and he emphasizes the paramount importance of not divulging the secret prematurely. He is no longer merely a mere captive and victim of Zeus; he has become a powerful enemy.

This is the point at which the Io episode is inserted. It reveals to us, no longer in general terms but by the arresting presentation of a single concrete case, the full extent of the *hybris* with which Zeus (and Hera too) treat human beings, so that we are fully prepared for the moment when Prometheus, on whom Zeus had once pronounced sentence, will pronounce sentence on Zeus. It increases the solidarity between Prometheus, the chorus, and humanity (we have seen that by its end the chorus seem to have forgotten that they are divine). And it uncovers more of the future, including the further development of human potentialities and something of the nature of the threat facing Zeus, as well as a renewed suggestion of the possibility that Zeus himself may be capable of change for the better.

Hitherto, all the participants in the action have been gods. 'Mortals' have been an anonymous collectivity. Only once (in the choral song 397-435) has the text been more specific, and it is striking that the nations mentioned there as grieving for Prometheus – those of Asia, Colchis, Scythia and Arabia – conspicuously omit the Greeks. Io is an individual mortal, and a Greek too. She lived among all the benefits of the civilization described in 436-506; her father lived in a substantial house with separate accommodation for the women (646, 665, cf. 450-1), he kept sheep and cattle (653, cf. 462-5), he was able to consult oracles (658-70, cf. 484-99). And yet none of this availed Io or her father anything against the lust of Zeus and the jealousy of Hera. If Io had received from a young man the sort of messages she received from Zeus, and told her father of them, Inachus would not have engaged in anxious consultation of oracles: he would have taken direct and drastic action, and the man would have been lucky to escape with his life. Zeus simply assumes that every attractive human female is automatically available to him. Hera is no better: she is determined to frustrate Zeus, and does so without regard to what the innocent human involved may suffer in the process. It is entirely appropriate that Io's sufferings are attributed, by Prometheus and by Io herself, indiscriminately to Zeus (578, 672, 736, 758-9) and to Hera (592, 600, 704) – whereas in *The Suppliant Maidens*, where Io's descendants the Danaids are concerned to enlist Zeus as an ally, they are attributed to Hera alone.

It is appropriate also that after we have heard what Zeus and Hera are prepared to do for the sake of sexual desire and sexual jealousy, we should learn that sexual desire will work the downfall of Zeus (764, cf. 864). Zeus is not all-powerful; he is inferior not only to Destiny and the Erinyes (516-18) but also to Eros. Had it not been so, Prometheus' revelation at 764 would have relieved Zeus of all anxiety: he had only to remain faithful to his legitimate spouse Hera, and he would be safe for ever. The story of Io has shown that that is not in Zeus' nature, and it is fitting that the tormentors of Io should fall by the same means. This theme also accounts for the inclusion in Prometheus' last speech, at what might seem disproportionate length, of the story of the Danaids. The Danaids' cousins, like birds of prey (857), will follow them to Argos 'hunting marriages they should not be hunting' (858), and all but one will perish on their bridal night. Zeus had pursued Io in the opposite direction, from Argos to Egypt, for a similar purpose; he will pursue others in the future, including (unless he is warned) Thetis – and it is here that Prometheus interposes the wish 'May such a consummation come to all my enemies!'

But of course (as the audience know long before they see *Prometheus Unbound*) this downfall of Zeus is not in fact destined to occur: Zeus is still master of the universe. Prometheus' release will be the price of his survival. There are other important things which *are* destined to occur, and of which Prometheus tells in the course of his prophecies to Io (707-35, 790-815, 829-76). I will deal with these under two heads: the development of humanity, and the development of Zeus.

Io's wanderings will at first take her among a long series of (in Greek terms) uncivilized peoples, some of them the very antithesis of (Greek) civilization: the Scythians who live in covered wagons (709-10), the Chalybes who hate strangers and live near the 'aptly named' River Hybristes (714-17), the 'man-hating' Amazons who will one day dwell near a promontory called 'the stepmother of ships' (723-7), the Gorgons and Graeae who figure in the legend of Perseus (793-800, cf, p. 38), the one-eyed Arimaspians (804-5). Over and over again she is warned 'do not go near them' (712, 715, 800-1, 807). Eventually however she will reach Egypt; and Egypt is presented as being, like Greece, a land of *poleis* (846) where it is possible for Greeks to found a 'colony' (*apoikia*, 814-15), and where Io's son will establish a kingdom over the whole country (851-2). His descendants will likewise reign over the *polis* of Argos (869); and from their line will spring the supreme example of the power mortal humanity can attain, Heracles, whose stupendous achievements were too well known to require mention except for the most relevant, the release of Prometheus. Previously Prometheus had spoken, first of being released by Zeus, then of bringing about his own release; now it is a mere mortal (if a very exceptional mortal) who will be able to release him. Zeus is beginning to seem quite weak! And Heracles is not the only exceptional mortal whose birth destiny has in store: we have after all been reminded, by the allusion to the prophecy about Thetis, that in the following generation there will be an Achilles.

These last speeches of Prometheus to Io also, however, indicate that there may be, now or in the future, another side to Zeus. The first evidence of this actually comes in a narrative of *past* events (829-41). When Io came to the oracular sanctuary of Zeus at Dodona, the 'speaking oak-trees' hailed her as 'the glorious bride-to-be of Zeus' (834-5) – which, uncongenial as it may be to Hera, at least suggests a greater degree of respect on Zeus' part than did the dream-message in which Io was informed that Zeus wished to 'arouse Aphrodite' with her and invited her 'not to spurn union with Zeus' but to meet him in the meadows of Lerna 'so that the eye of Zeus may find relief from its longing' (650-4). And when Zeus does at last meet Io in Egypt, the first thing he will do is restore her to her right mind and presumably to fully human form (848), the second will be to give her a child *without* any violation of her body (849-51). This is a Zeus we have not heard of in the play before: a Zeus who is thoughtful, compassionate, self-controlled. For the moment this Zeus is still in the future. By a crudely realistic chronology it is, of course, the fairly near future, but the fact remains that in *this* play we will not be seeing anything of this kind actually happening. We may also recall, when we hear a little later about Heracles, that he, the liberator of Prometheus, will be a son of Zeus.

Prometheus, who at the start seemed to be an isolated and doomed rebel, is now perceived as having both the predominant feeling and the fundamental forces of the universe behind him in his struggle with Zeus, as with tremendous authority (though still clamped to his rock) he thunders out his condemnation, introducing new elements like the curse of Zeus's father Cronus (910-12) which makes his son's downfall seem inevitable, the vision of Zeus's supplanter wielding weapons mightier than the thunderbolt of Zeus or the trident of Poseidon, and the final exultant picture of Zeus' future destiny of 'slavery' (927). When Hermes arrives, Prometheus, who suffered in silence the taunts of Zeus' other minion Kratos, does the taunting himself:

> Ah, I see coming Zeus' footboy,
> the new tyrant's menial. …
> Your words are pompous and full of pride
> considering they come from the gods' lackey. …
> I can assure you I wouldn't exchange
> my sufferings for your servitude (941-2, 953-4, 966-7).

Hermes may make demands with menaces, but Prometheus knows that if he has the strength to say 'no', and to endure the pain that will ensue, he cannot be defeated. He says 'no', with the maximum of defiance and contempt, and the chorus, now representing all the victims of Zeus' tyranny, volunteer to share his fate. The play may end with Prometheus thrust into the underworld, and crying out to earth and sky on the injustice of it; we know, too, that the torment of the eagle is still to come; but for Zeus the outcome has been failure. He failed to destroy the human race; he has failed to deprive them of fire and the other skills Prometheus gave them; and he has failed to secure the one piece of information that is essential to his own safety. At the beginning of the play the silence of Prometheus was a mark of his powerlessness. At the end, though he has had more to say than everyone else put together,[5] his silence on the one point that matters is a mark of his predominant power. And it is that movement in the balance of power that constitutes the real action of *Prometheus Bound*.

8.3. Problems of staging

To judge purely from its text, *Prometheus Bound* ought to be the most scenically spectacular of all Greek tragedies. Certainly of all Greek tragedies it is the one whose staging is at first sight hardest to envisage within what is otherwise known or reasonably supposed about the configuration and resources of the Athenian theatre. In what follows I shall assume, in the light of the evidence about the play's date considered below (§8.5), that it was written for a theatre with a *skênê*, similar to the theatre in which the *Oresteia*, or Sophocles' *Ajax* and *Antigone*, were produced, and with an *ekkyklêma* and *mêkhanê* available.

The place of Prometheus' binding. Prometheus is bound to a rock or cliff (15, 20, 31, 117, etc.). This implies that he has his back to a vertical surface. The only vertical surface which we know to have existed in the acting area is the front wall of the *skênê*. This must therefore have been the place which Prometheus occupied throughout the play. If he was immediately in front of the central door (cf. below) he would be the central feature of the scenic picture almost from beginning to end. He cannot have been bound to the door itself, but may have been clamped (see below) to a large board placed against the closed door.

The manner of Prometheus' binding. Prometheus' bonds are described as being put around his arms, chest and legs (52, 55, 71, 74, 81) and then nailed to the rock (56, 76) so as to 'squeeze' or 'choke' him (58). This describes a punishment similar to the Athenian form of execution called *apotympanismos*, in which the criminal was stripped and clamped by neck, arms and legs to a board which was then stood up vertically, leaving the man 'hanging' with his feet off the ground until he either died of exposure, heat, dehydration, etc., or (perhaps at sunset, if he lived that long) was strangled by the tightening of the neck-clamp. In Prometheus' case emphasis is similarly put on exposure, heat and dehydration (22-4, 147, 269), though since he is immortal it will be of indefinite duration and will include the cold of night, and deprivation of sleep, as well (25, 32). Perhaps for the same reason, since there can be no question of putting him to death, Prometheus is clamped at the chest instead of the neck.

Such a binding is easy to stage, provided certain precautions are taken. It is possibly significant that there is no reference to Prometheus being in a 'hanging' position; indeed 32 implies that he is 'standing upright' on his feet, and in that position he could remain without distress for the duration of the play (he would, moreover, have been in the shade of the *skênê* front, which faced north). However, an additional element is introduced at 64-5, when Hephaestus is ordered to drive a wedge 'right through his chest'. Dramatically the object of this is to inflict on Prometheus a pain beyond human imagining, since what is done to Prometheus would instantly kill any mortal: it is the part of Hephaestus' task whose performance pains *him* the most (66). Theatrically it could be handled in various ways, e.g. by pretending to hammer the wedge in while actually *fastening* it to the chest-clamp.

The movements of the chorus. The text gives us to understand that the chorus arrive flying (124-5, 129) 'in a winged vehicle' (135). They must, however, be in a position where they can see Prometheus (141, 144, 244-6), though it is not absolutely essential that he should be able to see them (he knows who they are without being told, 138-40, but this *might* be due to his prophetic powers[6]). Later he asks them to 'come to the ground' (272) and they respond by leaving their 'swift-moving seat, and the holy heavens traversed by birds' for the 'rocky earth' (278-81). The general pattern is not unlike that in *Seven* and *The Suppliant Maidens* where the chorus at first occupy an elevated position and then are instructed to descend, presumably from the *pagos/okhthos* to the floor of the *orkhêstra* (see §2.1). Here, however, the references to a 'winged vehicle' and a 'swift-moving seat' imply inescapably that until 277 the chorus are, or are to be imagined as, seated in a vehicle or vehicles.

In the first edition of this book I took the view (a modification of a proposal by Fraenkel 1954) that the chorus entered at ground level, some of them riding in wagons and others on foot (perhaps pushing the wagons). This now seems to me inconsistent with their clear statement in 280 that they are in 'the holy heavens traversed by birds'. They must be well above ground level. We cannot suppose that they were brought on by means of the *mêkhanê*: that could not carry a whole chorus, and after they had finished using it there would not be time for the crane to be swung back and prepared for the entry of Oceanus (see below). We are therefore driven to the solution adopted by Griffith 1977: 143-4 and 1982: 109-10: the wagon or wagons must have been rolled out on to the *skênê* roof. If that is where the chorus are, then when they are told to 'come to the ground' they will have disappeared within or behind the *skênê* building. Probably they remain out of sight until after Oceanus' departure (396), and then come out of the *skênê* to take up a normal choral position in the *orkhêstra*; this is the easiest way to account for the complete absence of any interaction between them and their father while he is present. This staging involves two features unique in what we know of classical Athenian tragedy. Nowhere else does a chorus enter at roof level, and nowhere else does a chorus which has temporarily left the scene return without there being any indication of movement in its words. But any other hypothesis would involve even greater difficulties.

The entry of Oceanus. Oceanus, according to his own words, is transported to and from the scene by a 'four-legged bird' (286, 395) which is seen by Prometheus and presumably by the audience (286). It is spoken of as if it were a horse (cf. 287 'guiding [it] without a bit'), and it is reasonable to assume that Oceanus is mounted on it like (e.g.) Bellerophon on the flying horse Pegasus, and therefore that he is brought on and off by the *mêkhanê*. His steed may be a griffin (a lion with eagle's wings). Oceanus perhaps dismounts on arrival; at 394 the crane-operator may have made the beast bob up and down as if impatient to be off, after which Oceanus remounted and departed.

The final cataclysm. The elemental convulsions described in 1080-8 are no problem theatrically since they will have been left to the imagination, aided by music and one or two sound-effects such as thunder (cf. Sophocles, *Oedipus at Colonus* 1456ff.; Aristophanes, *Clouds* 392). The phenomena mentioned are all such as could have been reasonably represented in that way, with a strong emphasis on thunder, lightning[7] and wind. The serious staging issues are **(1)** what happens to Prometheus and **(2)** what happens to the chorus.

(1) If Prometheus is attached to a board directly in front of, and indeed resting on, the central doors of the *skênê*, and these doors are suddenly opened (inwards, which was the normal direction of opening for house doors), the board with Prometheus on it will fall back into the dark interior. Certainly in satyr-play and comedy, and possibly also in some tragedies, the *skênê* door could be treated as an entrance to the underworld (cf. too *Ag.* 1291). Danger to the actor would be avoided by having men ready to stop the board hitting the floor and drag it back clear of the doors, allowing them to be closed again. Alternatively Prometheus might have been standing throughout the play on the *ekkyklêma* trolley, and at the end this might have been withdrawn into the interior; but this is less likely, since it might be confusing given that the *ekkyklêma* seems to have had in tragedy the well-established function of revealing *interior* scenes, and it is part of Prometheus' punishment that he is to be bound not in some cave but in the open air, exposed to sun, rain, wind and cold.

(2) Hermes' first warning to the chorus (1058-62) merely advises them to leave the place to avoid the stunning sound of Zeus' thunder, and does not imply that they are any closer to Prometheus than their normal place in the *orkhêstra*. After their defiant assertion of loyalty to Prometheus, however, Hermes tells them they have no one but themselves to blame if they are 'caught by disaster' (1073), 'cast into suffering' (1075) or 'enmeshed in the impenetrable net of ruin' (1078-9), language which is hardly apt to describe a mere risk of temporary mental disorientation. It is likely therefore that during 1063-70 the chorus group themselves closely about Prometheus (cf. 1067 'I am ready to suffer whatever must be suffered together with him'). What happens thereafter? We do not want the chorus to be taken down to the underworld with Prometheus, since we would be left wondering what became of them when Prometheus came up to earth again. There seems little alternative but to have them scatter in terror, their loyalty and courage no match for the awesome power of Zeus (just as the civic courage of the Elders, at the end of *Agamemnon*, is no match for Aegisthus' armed guards, and they depart leaving him and Clytaemestra in control). Prometheus' last words (1091-3) may imply that as in 88ff. when he likewise appealed to the elements to behold his plight, he is now again alone with them, all other sentient beings having disappeared.

8.4. The Prometheus trilogy?

We know of three plays about Prometheus, besides *Prometheus Bound*, that were ascribed in antiquity to Aeschylus – or rather we know of three titles of such plays: *Prometheus Unbound* (*Lyomenos*); *Prometheus the Fire-bearer* (*Pyrphoros*); and *Prometheus the Fire-kindler* (*Pyrkaeus*).

The last-mentioned play, *Fire-kindler*, can be dismissed from consideration so far as concerns the production of which *Prometheus Bound* formed part, because we know that it belonged to a quite different production: it was, in fact, the satyr-play produced together with *Persians* and other plays in 472. Two ancient quotations (fr. 187a Radt = 206 Sommerstein, and fr. 207) show that Prometheus in this play brought fire to the satyrs, who were fascinated by this new toy and unaware that it could be dangerous; one of them was so delighted with the flame that he wanted to kiss and hug it, and Prometheus had to warn him 'You'll mourn for your beard, like the goat in the story'. Several vase-paintings show satyrs, often accompanied by Prometheus, carrying fire in fennel-stalks (in one of which, according to tradition, Prometheus had first brought it to earth). We have a papyrus fragment of a choral song (fr. 204b) which almost certainly comes from this play: the chorus sing and dance in praise of fire and of Prometheus and look forward, in typical satyric fashion (see Chapter 9), to further celebrations in the agreeable company of nymphs.

We are fairly well informed about *Prometheus Unbound*. In addition to actual quotations or translations from its text, *Prometheus Bound* itself and its ancient annotations are of considerable help. It is from two such notes, for example, on lines 511 and 522 of the surviving play, that we know for certain that *Unbound* was its direct sequel. Another, on line 167, speaks of Zeus amorously chasing Thetis round the Caucasus until stopped in his tracks by a warning from Prometheus; since, so far as we know, it was only in the Aeschylean Prometheus plays that Prometheus was associated with the Zeus-Thetis-Peleus myth, and since other evidence shows that ancient scholars believed (rightly or wrongly) that *Prometheus Unbound* was set in the Caucasus, there is very strong reason to believe that the commentator was referring to *Unbound*. There is also the evidence of the list of characters prefixed to *Bound* in the manuscripts: this list includes two characters who do not appear in *Bound*, Ge (= Gaia, Earth) and Heracles, and since Heracles certainly appeared in *Unbound* it is a fair guess that Ge, the mother of Prometheus (*Bound* 210), appeared there too. Forward references in the text of *Bound* itself are of limited help, since they may be misleading; but we can at least be fairly sure that somehow or other Prometheus' startling prediction (190-2) will be fulfilled and he and Zeus will be reconciled in friendship, and that a crucial feature of the reconciliation will be the communication by Prometheus to Zeus of the secret about Thetis (this last point is confirmed by references in later writers[8]).

We may reconstruct the action tentatively as follows. The scene is the same as in *Prometheus Bound*. Having been swallowed up by the earth at the end of *Bound*, Prometheus has now returned to the light (cf. *Bound* 1020-1), but he is still chained to his rock. The play opened, like *The Persians* and *The Suppliant Maidens*, with the entry of the chorus, composed of Prometheus' brethren the Titans, who must therefore have been released by Zeus from their underground prison. The release of the Titans is not a mythical innovation,[9] but its introduction here, right at the start of *Unbound*, indicates that there has indeed, as foreshadowed in Prometheus' prophecy to Io (see §8.2), been some sort of change in Zeus – and may set us wondering how far this change has gone, and whether there has been any corresponding change in Prometheus. When the Titans have described their journey across the earth, in a geographical catalogue resembling those of the Io scene of *Bound* (frr. 190-2), it is Prometheus' turn to tell them of his sufferings, especially the torments inflicted by the eagle (fr. 193, preserved in Cicero's translation), and we discover that so far as Prometheus is concerned Zeus has not softened at all. Prometheus' own morale does not now seem high (though it should be remembered that Cicero may not have translated the whole speech); doubtless the poet wanted this play, like *Bound*, to be marked by an upward movement, a gradual brightening, and for this purpose it was necessary to start at a fairly low point.

Then Heracles arrives. He is on an expedition to seek the golden apples of the Hesperides in the far west, and is therefore badly out of his way; possibly he asks Prometheus for help, but at any rate the dreaded eagle is soon seen approaching – and Heracles, with a prayer to Apollo (fr. 200), raises his bow and shoots it. We cannot be sure of Heracles' motive, but most probably he was presented as simply acting on impulse, as he often does in other stories, here out of the same sympathy for Prometheus that has been felt by every other character in both plays except Kratos and Hermes. Very possibly he did not even reflect that he was killing the sacred bird of his father and frustrating his father's will. At any rate he does not release Prometheus from his bonds: one late source[10] says he was afraid of his father's anger, but it may simply be that the bonds, crafted by Hephaestus himself, were beyond human power to unloose. For what he *has* been able to do, Prometheus is immensely thankful, and speaks of him as 'beloved son of a hated father' (fr. 201). He proceeds to give Heracles directions on how to reach his destination (frr. 195-7, 199); after which Heracles departs, leaving Prometheus still chained.

We have little clue to the part played by Prometheus' mother Gaia-Themis, but one possibility is that she arrived after the departure of Heracles and played a part in some ways similar to that of Oceanus in the first play, advising Prometheus to relent and reveal his secret now that the crisis for Zeus is imminent.

Enter now Thetis, fleeing from Zeus – a second Io, though a divine one; and here, as in *The Weighing of Souls* (see Chapter 3), it seems highly likely that Zeus appeared on stage in person.[11] It is true that (as noted above, §8.2) Zeus is never normally a character in tragedy, because of the general rule, valid from Homer onwards, that while other gods may, and often do, come down to the earth on which we mortals tread,[12] Zeus does not. But this general rule has a general exception. Zeus can and indeed must come down to earth whenever he has sexual business to transact with a human female (such as Io). Thetis of course is divine, not human, but her home is in the sea rather than the heavens or Olympus, and Zeus therefore must come down to earth in quest of her. Probably he finds her, as Peleus later did, on the seashore, and she flees from him until she comes to where Prometheus is. On the arrival of Zeus, shortly afterwards, Prometheus must make the decision on which the outcome of the drama, and the fate of the universe, depend. He reveals his secret, and thereby saves both Thetis and Zeus. Thetis, he says, is the female who is destined to bear a son mightier than his father, and Zeus must therefore at all costs leave her alone. Prometheus has now saved Zeus twice, once in the war with the Titans and once now; and in gratitude Zeus releases him from his bonds, or orders him to be released, and may also have given him compensation in the form of cultic honours at Athens. However, Zeus's own dignity also has to be preserved, and Prometheus will continue to expiate his original offence by the token punishment of 'binding' his finger with a ring of stone and iron, and his head with a garland (fr. 202 and Hyginus, *Poetica Astronomica* 2.15) – though this is an ambiguous sort of punishment, since the garland might also be a symbol of victory, and it is also decreed that *mortals* will henceforth wear garlands on all *festive* occasions in *honour* of Prometheus. Thetis, of course, will be married to the mortal Peleus.[13] As for the human race, Prometheus has made it impossible for Zeus to destroy them, and it may be that now (if the myth told by Protagoras, in Plato's dialogue of that name,[14] is to a significant extent based on *Prometheus Unbound*) Zeus himself gives to humans one piece of knowledge which, on the evidence available to us, they do not seem to have had from Prometheus, namely the knowledge of how to live in society, or as Protagoras is made to put it 'restraint and justice'. It would be appropriate to end with the gift of these virtues to man, since we have just seen them being established for the first time among the gods, who have learnt at last, as never before, how to live together in peace. It may not be a coincidence that the man of this particular generation who was traditionally regarded as being pre-eminent in these very virtues was none other than Peleus.[15] On the other hand there was reference earlier in *Prometheus Unbound* to at least one and probably two peoples who already practised the social virtues, the 'righteous and hospitable' Gabii (fr. 196) and the 'law-abiding' Scythians (fr. 198).

Everything mentioned above, down to and including the institution of garland-wearing, was part of *Prometheus Unbound*, and it is almost certain that the other aspects of the final settlement, if included in the Prometheus play-sequence at all, also figured in that play and not in a third play to follow: the reconciliation at the end of *Unbound* could no more have been followed by a further sequel than could the reconciliation at the end of *Eumenides*. This leaves us with the problem of accounting for the evidence concerning another Prometheus-play called *Prometheus Pyrphoros* (*Prometheus the Fire-bearer*).

This evidence is as follows: **(1)** *Pyrphoros* is listed, between *Desmôtês* and *Lyomenos*, in the catalogue of Aeschylean plays found in the tenth-century Medicean manuscript (which omits the satyr-play *Pyrkaeus*). **(2)** The Roman author Aulus Gellius (second century AD) quotes from *Pyrphoros* a line ('keeping silent where silence is proper, and saying what is appropriate') which is almost identical with *Choephoroi* 582. This is the only textual fragment ascribed to this play. **(3)** An ancient commentator on *Bound* 94 states that 'in *Pyrphoros* <Aeschylus> says that <Prometheus> was bound for thirty thousand years'.

With three *Prometheus* titles available (other than *Pyrkaeus*), and knowing the fondness of Aeschylus and his contemporaries for composing connected trilogies, the temptation is strong to posit a Prometheus trilogy made up of the three plays. But where can *Pyrphoros* be placed? It cannot, as we have seen, follow *Unbound*, since by the end of *Unbound* everything of any dramatic value that one could possibly envisage Prometheus as doing or suffering has already happened. The title *Pyrphoros* might well suggest that it would be better to place this play first in a trilogy and suppose that its subject was Prometheus' theft of fire (M.L. West 1979; Griffith 1982: 282-3). So much, however, is said in the surviving play about this and its antecedents as to suggest that there is very unlikely to have been another play before it. In a speech like *Bound* 199-241, for example, it is fairly clear that Prometheus is giving information to the chorus not so much because *they* need it as because the audience do – and this would be pointless if the audience knew it all already. In fact, given the *Prometheus Bound* that we have, and given what we know of *Unbound*, there is no room for a third play either preceding or following them – at any rate, not a play about Prometheus. This need not alarm us: we have already seen (Chapter 3) that there are other cases in the Aeschylean corpus where we can identify two connected plays but there seems to be no third, and where the hypothesis of a 'dilogy' is not unreasonable. Unless such a dilogy was produced at the Lenaea,[16] it must have been accompanied by a third play (as well as the usual satyr-play), but we have no clue to this play's identity.

If *Prometheus Pyrphoros* was not the third member of a trilogy with *Bound* and *Unbound*, what was it? The most likely answer, as Brown 1990 has shown, is that *Pyrphoros* is simply a variant form of *Pyrkaeus*, the title of the satyr-play of 472. It would, indeed, be a more accurate title than *Pyrkaeus* for that play: we know that Prometheus did 'bear' or 'bring' (*pherein*) fire to the satyrs, and neither in what we know of the satyr-drama, nor anywhere else, is he ever described as having 'kindled' it – he is never the creator of fire, only its stealer and purveyor. There are other cases of such minor variation in the distinguishing epithets attached to plays of the same name by the same author;[17] in this case the corruption of *Pyrphoros* to *Pyrkaeus* will doubtless have been due to recollection of another play with a similar epithet, Sophocles' *Nauplios Pyrkaeus*, in which Nauplius really did kindle a fire (the fire that lured the Greek fleet, homeward bound from Troy, on to the rocks of Euboea).[18] The hypothesis that *Pyrphoros* and *Pyrkaeus* are identical accounts best, too, for the ancient evidence about *Pyrphoros*: item (3) above is on the face of it inconsistent with *Bound* and *Unbound*, in which Prometheus' binding and release are separated by the thirteen generations from Io to Heracles (774) which could not possibly be taken to span thirty thousand years, whereas in a separate, and probably earlier, satyr-play – in which Prometheus' binding might have been associated, as it is in Hesiod, with the very origins of the human race as we know it – nothing need have prevented it being assumed that his sufferings were of prodigiously long duration.

8.5. The question of authenticity

The authenticity of the Prometheus plays was never questioned in antiquity, so far as we know, and in Roman and Byzantine times *Prometheus Bound* became the most popular of all Aeschylean plays. Doubts about the Aeschylean authorship of *Prometheus Bound* in its present form were first expressed only in 1856, and not till 1911 was it first suggested that the play might have been composed in its entirety by another dramatist. To some extent the objections have been based on content, it being thought that a poet of Aeschylus' generation could not have written a play that treated Zeus in such a hostile manner; but though the portrayal of Zeus as a tyrant in *Prometheus Bound* is done with unusual consistency and emphasis, it is not obvious that the dramatist is being more disrespectful to him than the highly-regarded Hesiod was when he claimed that Zeus had deliberately pretended to be deceived by Prometheus, in the matter of the division of sacrificial meat, so as to have an excuse for inflicting harm on mortals although the latter are not described as themselves having done him any wrong (*Theogony* 550-2). Within the Aeschylean corpus, *Agamemnon* is hardly a shining tribute to the wisdom and benevolence of Zeus (see §7.9); of course we see a different side of Zeus in *Eumenides*, but then we have evidence that the same is true of *Prometheus Unbound*, in which Zeus first releases the Titans (for no reason, so far as we know) and then not only releases Prometheus (which one might be inclined to discount, as a surrender to blackmail) but probably rewards or compensates him. The more serious difficulties with the ascription of *Prometheus Bound* to Aeschylus are features of language, metre, style and technique which collectively tend, in the eyes of many scholars (see above all Griffith 1977), to separate the play from the undisputed works of Aeschylus (though significantly not from *Prometheus Unbound*, so far as our evidence for the latter goes), to associate it with the literary and intellectual trends of a period some time after Aeschylus' death, and to suggest in some respects a lower level of dramaturgical competence than is elsewhere characteristic of Aeschylus.

It is not within the scope of this book to consider in detail the technical issues involved, but there are one or two things that can relevantly be said.

In the first place, independently of the question of the authenticity of these plays, there has been a good deal of study of features of Aeschylus' language and style that seem to evolve over time, and these rather consistently tend to make *Prometheus Bound* the latest of all by what seems a considerable margin. Yet the *Oresteia* is known to have been produced only two or three years before his death, and we would thus have to assume that Aeschylus' style had changed with remarkable rapidity in his last years – unless *Prometheus Bound* is by someone else.

Secondly, *Prometheus Bound*, while full of eloquent set speeches, is sometimes not very felicitous in fitting them into scenes and effecting transitions between them. The Io episode is particularly full of fussy and futile discussion of what shall be said to whom and when. Prometheus twice refuses to answer Io's questions about himself for no good reason except that the audience already know the answers (615, 621); having for a time refused to tell Io her future destiny because it might distress her (624-8), he asks her to satisfy the mere curiosity of the chorus – who are, he reminds her, her aunts – by telling them the equally distressing tale of her past sufferings (631-9); he arbitrarily gives her the choice of hearing the end of his prophecy about herself or learning the identity of his own future liberator (775-81) and then agrees to reveal the former to her and the latter to the chorus (782ff.) as if both would not be listening the whole time – and then, when he does tell Io how her wanderings will end, he says explicitly that he is speaking to the chorus as well (844-5). There is nothing like this in the other surviving plays of Aeschylus.

Thirdly, the undisputed plays of Aeschylus all have a high and fairly constant proportion of sung lyric; the percentage of sung verses ranges from a minimum of 32.5% (in *Eumenides*) to a maximum of 50.0% (in *The Suppliant Maidens*). In *Prometheus Bound* the corresponding percentage is a mere 16.6%; that is, this play has only about half as much sung lyric even as *Eumenides*. This small body of lyric includes two actor solos with no choral participation (114-19, 565-608); elsewhere in Aeschylus actors sing only in alternation with the chorus. Of actual choral lyric *Prometheus Bound* has only 136 lines (12.4% of the text); the lowest figure in the other six plays is 28.3% in *Choephoroi*. In these respects *Prometheus Bound* behaves like a play of the second half of the fifth century, and is within or even slightly below the range of variation shown by Sophocles (all lyrics, 18.5%-27.2%; choral lyrics, 12.5%-18.2%) and in the earlier tragedies of Euripides (13.6%-23.6% and 10.0%-18.7% respectively); its profile, in fact, most nearly resembles that of Euripides' *Medea*, which was produced as late as 431. Of chanted anapaests, on the other hand, *Prometheus Bound* is very fond, having proportionately more than any Aeschylean play (12.6%; *The Persians* comes second with 11.0%). They include a solid block of 54 lines which conclude the play, and in which Prometheus, Hermes and the chorus all take part; such endings in anapaestic dialogue are not uncommon in Sophocles and Euripides, but the only one of comparable length is that of Euripides' *Electra*, produced *c.* 420 (68 lines). This fondness for chanted anapaests appears to have been equally characteristic of *Prometheus Unbound*; we have three (possibly four) separate quotations from the words of the chorus on or immediately after its entry (frr. 190-2 and perhaps 203) and all are anapaestic.

Fourthly, what lyrics there are in *Prometheus Bound* exhibit some metrical patterns common in other fifth-century poetry but not used elsewhere, so far as we know, by Aeschylus; in particular, two choral odes (526ff., 887ff.) are in 'dactylo-epitrite' rhythm, which is frequent in the work of all the major lyric composers of the period (Pindar, Bacchylides, Sophocles, Euripides) *except* Aeschylus.[19] On the other hand, the syncopated iambics and lekythia, whose ubiquity in the *Oresteia* we noted earlier (§7.5) and which are also very common in Aeschylus' earlier plays, are almost entirely absent from *Prometheus Bound*, and the few iambic stanzas (160ff., 901ff.) have a high frequency of resolution which is also uncharacteristic of Aeschylus. On these and other grounds it has been said (Griffith 1977: 67) that 'were the choral lyrics of *Prom.* all that we possessed of an anonymous tragedy, we would on metrical grounds reject absolutely the idea that Aeschylus could be their author'.

And yet there are other arguments that do tend to associate the Prometheus plays with Aeschylus. There is the very fact of their being a *sequence* of plays forming a close unity, a phenomenon characteristic of Aeschylus and his contemporaries but comparatively rare in the later fifth century. There is the fact that the sequence shows a movement, typical of several known Aeschylean trilogies, from more violent to more restrained methods of effecting divine and human purposes (see pp. 40-1), and that this movement is bound up, as in the *Oresteia* (and, so far as we know, nowhere else in Greek literature; see §§7.9 and 11.6), with an apparent evolution in the nature of Zeus. There is a further link with the *Oresteia* in the direct presentation on stage of a conflict between gods (contrast, say, Euripides' *Hippolytus* where there is plainly a conflict between Aphrodite and Artemis but they never meet on stage), a conflict, moreover, of vital importance to the future of the human race. And there is the absence of any evidence that ancient scholars, who are known to have regarded a considerable number of tragedies and comedies (including one tragedy attributed to Aeschylus[20]) as doubtfully or wrongly ascribed, ever had any doubts about the authorship of the Prometheus plays.

Before attempting to reconcile these apparently contradictory considerations, something should be said of what can be deduced about the date of the Prometheus plays. No direct ancient evidence about the date of production survives, as it does for all the other extant Aeschylean plays, and we have to depend on the less certain evidence of echoes in these plays of, and echoes of these plays in, other contemporary texts. These give us a fairly firm lower bound. It is generally accepted that Aristophanes, *Knights* 836 ('You who have arisen as the greatest of benefactors to all mankind') is modelled on *Prometheus Bound* 613; *The Knights* was produced early in 424. An earlier comedy, Cratinus' *Wealth-gods*, of which a substantial papyrus fragment has survived (Cratinus fr. 171), contained a chorus of Titans[21] who had at one time been imprisoned (lines 20, 21) but who have now come in search of their brother (lines 25-6); it is hard not to associate this with the Titan chorus of *Prometheus Unbound*, and the vocabulary of the passage contains much that is reminiscent of *Prometheus Bound*. Political references in the papyrus fragment suggest that it belongs to the early years of the Peloponnesian War and most probably to 429 or 428; hence the Prometheus plays can be no later than 430. An upper bound is less easy to define. The plays are almost certainly later than the Danaid trilogy, since the image of the hawks and doves in *Bound* 857 seems to reflect the use of the same image in *Supp.* 223ff. where it is much better integrated with its context; so we can probably set 460 as an upper terminus. The same upper limit is indicated by the fact that *Prometheus Bound*, unlike *Supp.* but like the *Oresteia* and almost all known later tragedies,[22] requires three actors. Various other parallels (with Pindar's fourth Olympian ode, probably performed in 452; with Sophocles; with Herodotus; with the sophist Protagoras and the mythographer Pherecydes) have been put forward as suggesting a date around 440 (M.L. West 1979) or in the late 430s[23] (Bees 1993). What the evidence regarding date does strongly suggest is that the Prometheus plays are very unlikely to have been *produced* by Aeschylus in his lifetime: whether or not they were wholly or partly written by him, they were almost certainly presented to the public by someone else.

Now we are told[24] that Aeschylus' son Euphorion was victorious on four occasions with previously unperformed plays of his father's – or with what he *said* were previously unperformed plays of his father's. It is further known that Euphorion also wrote and produced tragedies on his own account. This suggests, as West and others have seen, an explanation of the curious contradictions in the evidence about these plays – plays universally ascribed to Aeschylus in antiquity, typical of Aeschylus (especially *late* Aeschylus) in their structure, plot and ideas, yet bearing in their detailed craftsmanship the mark of a somewhat later period and a somewhat inferior talent. The least implausible explanation of the origin of the Prometheus plays is that they are the work of Euphorion, but that he entered them for the festival as the work of his father. Possibly he had composed them on the basis of a sketch or synopsis left by Aeschylus; possibly, as West prefers to suppose, he hoped that his own work would have a better chance of success if he presented it as his father's. At any rate the plays were entered in the festival records, from which the scholars of Alexandria derived their information, as the work of Aeschylus; and if anyone was sceptical at the time about Euphorion's claim, their doubts left no permanent record. If this is right, we have a tragedy which can truly be called both Aeschylean and non-Aeschylean: Aeschylean in concept, but not in execution.

Notes

1. Probably because the chorus are offstage in this scene (see §8.3).

2. The story had been told by Pindar in *Isthmian* 8.27-52 (performed in 478), but was probably much older.

3. This may seem incongruous, given that the chorus were originally introduced as themselves divine beings; no allusion, however, has been made to their divinity since line 636.

4. Even his mother, Gaia-Themis, is addressed here only as 'Earth, mother of all', as if an elemental power on a par with the sky, winds, rivers, etc.; contrast 1091.

5. From the point when Prometheus first speaks (88) to the end of the play there are 1006 lines, of which Prometheus speaks 546.

6. Or he might even be supposed to have inferred it from the fact that they are daughters of one father (130), divine (since they have means of aerial transport), and live in a cave (133).

7. There would be no need to simulate lightning; in real life we often miss seeing the lightning flash, but when we hear the thunder we take it for granted that there has been lightning too.

8. The earliest of these is the philosopher Philodemus (*On Piety* p. 41 Gomperz), a contemporary of Cicero.

9. It is mentioned by Pindar (*Pythian* 4.291) as if well known, and probably appeared in the text of Hesiod's *Works and Days* known to him and Aeschylus between what are now lines 173 and 174, where two overlapping papyrus fragments present five lines, absent from the medieval manuscripts, stating *inter alia* that Cronus was set free by Zeus and now reigns over the heroes in the Isles of the Blest.

10. 'Probus' on Virgil, *Eclogue* 6.42.

11. This is the clear implication of the scholia to *Bound* 167 (see above); the scholiast explicitly speaks of Zeus being engaged in an erotic pursuit across a terrestrial landscape. M.L. West 1979: 144 (cf. 2000: 346n.45) has Hermes appearing as Zeus's emissary, as in *Bound*, this time to demand the surrender of Thetis; but why should Zeus have abandoned a race which, as the more powerful god, he was certain eventually to win?

12. I use this expression to allow for the fact that Zeus is sometimes, especially in the *Iliad*, located not in heaven but at the top of a mountain (e.g. Olympus, Ida) – which, though part of the earth, was almost as remote from mortals as the sky was.

13. It will also be necessary, as part of the final settlement, for a way to be found to fulfil the condition laid down by Hermes in *Bound* 1026-9 as necessary for Prometheus' release: 'some god [must appear] to be [Prometheus'] successor in suffering and [be] willing to go down to rayless Hades'. This has long, and rightly, been associated with the story in [Apollodorus], *Library* 2.5.4, 2.5.11, that the centaur Cheiron, having been painfully and incurably wounded by Heracles' arrow, longed to die but was unable to do so until 'Prometheus gave to Zeus one who would become immortal in exchange for him'. The two passages of [Apollodorus] have been much and unnecessarily emended to bring them into conformity with *Bound* 1026-9; in fact, as Robertson 1951 showed, they are consistent with the *Bound* passage as they stand, once it is recognized that the 'one who would become immortal' is none other than Heracles. Cheiron is Prometheus' 'successor in suffering' because, like Prometheus, he is enduring torments that threaten to be unending because he cannot die; Prometheus, with the ingenuity that is typical of him, finds a solution that enables Cheiron to end his ordeal, Heracles eventually to become a god, and himself to secure final release.

14. Plato, *Protagoras* 320c-322d, especially 322a-d.

15. Pindar, *Isthmian* 8.28, 44; Aristophanes, *Clouds* 1061-7; Plato, *Republic* 391c.

16. A possibility that cannot be excluded, since tragic contests at the Lenaea were first held in the late 430s, and we shall see in §8.5 that *Prometheus Bound* and *Unbound* may well have been produced about that time.

17. Thus each of Euripides' two plays about Hippolytus has two alternative distinguishing epithets: *Kaluptomenos* and *Katakaluptomenos* for one, *Stephanêphoros* and *Stephaniâs* for the other.

18. I will discuss this play, and edit its fragments, in Sommerstein & Talboy (forthcoming).

19. Dactylo-epitrite metre is based on various sequences of the units – ∪ ∪ – ∪ ∪ – and – ∪ –, usually with a 'link-syllable' separating successive units.

20. The 'spurious' (*nothoi*) version of *The Women of Aetna*.

21. They had once, they say (line 12), been called Wealth-gods (*Ploutoi*), whence the title of the play.

22. The only known exception is Euripides' *Alcestis*, which could, if desired, have been performed by two actors.

23. In which case a plausible date would be 431, when Euphorion is known to have defeated Sophocles and Euripides (Euripides' production included the surviving *Medea*). The objection of M.L. West 1990b: 71 – that 'no one abbreviating Aristophanes' Hypothesis [to *Medea*] would have been likely to eliminate a reference to such a well-known play as *Prometheus*' – is not a strong one; of the Hypotheses transmitted with the text of surviving tragedies, only one (that of *Seven against Thebes*) gives the titles of the plays produced by rival competitors.

24. *Suda* ε3800.

9

Aeschylean Satyr-drama

Productions in the tragic competition at the City Dionysia nearly always ended with a satyr-play: a farcical treatment of some story from heroic saga, into which were intruded a chorus of the half-bestial beings (slaves of Dionysus) called satyrs and their 'father' Silenus, beings in almost every respect the very opposite of heroic and devoted in the main to the service of Dionysus, the consumption of wine and the pursuit of nymphs. The satyrs are often presented as slow of understanding, and are hardly ever successful unaided in any of their undertakings: when, as often, they begin a play as prisoners or slaves, they normally owe their eventual release to human intervention. They are thus inferior to humans both ethically and in terms of power: they can be called 'beasts' (*Net-Haulers* 775) even by their friends (Euripides, *Cyclops* 624). In general, indeed, the whole of the value-system presupposed by tragedy is inverted in satyr-play: only intelligence and ingenuity are at a premium in both. As poetry, on the other hand, satyr-play resembles tragedy quite closely: diction, syntax and metre are broadly similar in the two genres and clearly distinct from those of comedy, though satyr-play does admit (especially in the speeches and songs of the satyrs themselves) some types of lexical items which tragedy normally excludes.

We now possess a fair amount of satyr-play text from each of the three major tragic dramatists. One complete satyr-play by Euripides, *The Cyclops*, survived, uniquely, via the medieval manuscript tradition. From Sophocles we now have extensive papyrus fragments of *The Trackers* (*Ikhneutai*) and a fair amount of text from two other plays. And from Aeschylus, substantial parts of two satyr-plays became known during the twentieth century. Two papyri, probably parts of the same book though now a thousand miles apart (in Florence and Oxford) and published separately in 1933/4 and 1941, give us all or part of some 90 lines of *The Net-Haulers* (*Diktyoulkoi*); another, in several fragments, contains about the same amount of *The Sacred Delegation, or At the Isthmian Games* (*Theôroi* or *Isthmiastai*). All these Aeschylean texts were found at Oxyrhynchus in Egypt, all are written in the same hand, and they seem to form part of a multi-volume set which may once have contained Aeschylus' complete works (other fragments of this collection include those of *Prometheus the Fire-bearer* mentioned in the last chapter, and those of *The Myrmidons* discussed in the next).

The subject of *The Net-Haulers* was the arrival at the island of Seriphos of the floating chest containing Danaë and her infant son Perseus, who had been set adrift by Danaë's father, Acrisius, king of Argos; the chest was discovered by Dictys, brother of the king of Seriphos, and he took mother and child under his protection. The play seems to have been about as long as an average Aeschylean tragedy, for one of the papyrus fragments, from a scene which is certainly not the last of the play (see below), includes a line which is marked in the margin as number 800 (whereas Euripides' *Cyclops* has only 709 lines in all). It may be that in Aeschylus' time, when tragedies were mostly shorter than those of Sophocles or Euripides, satyr-plays were longer.

What appears to be the first fragment (46a) contains a dialogue between two persons, one of whom (but it is not clear which) is likely to be Dictys; the other may or may not be Silenus. They are apparently fishing together from the shore with a net, and one of them draws the other's attention to a large object which they at first think is a giant fish. They cast their net over it and try to haul it in, but it is too heavy for them, and one of them calls for the entire local population to come to their assistance. Here the fragment ends. Another papyrus fragment (46c) *may* come from a later scene in which several persons are hauling on the chest with a rope, but their efforts are still not succeeding and further assistance is being called for; it is by no means certain, however, that this fragment belongs to *The Net-Haulers* at all (the vital word 'rope' is partly restored, two letters being missing).

In our last and most important fragment (47a; lines 765-832) the chest has evidently been brought to land. Dictys is nowhere to be found, and Silenus and the satyrs have got possession of Danaë and the baby. A plausible suggestion is that the appeal for help in fr. 46a was answered by the satyrs, accompanied by Silenus (if he was not present already, cf. above); that with their help Dictys hauled in the chest; that when it was opened and found to contain Danaë the satyrs developed a strong amatory interest in her (see below); and that Dictys, alarmed but unable by himself to save her from so large a group, went off to get help, leaving Silenus and the satyrs temporarily in control of Danaë.

When our main fragment opens, Silenus has apparently decided to make Danaë his wife. He makes extravagantly solemn promises to be her faithful protector and champion (765-9) and claims that the baby is babbling happily at him as if he were its nurse (770-2). Danaë, appalled and terrified, appeals to the gods, asking if they are going to abandon her to be outraged by these 'beasts' (773-6); she thinks briefly of suicide, but instead appeals desperately to Zeus (the father of her child), complaining that *he* was mainly responsible for her plight but *she* has paid the whole of the penalty for it (782-5).

Silenus and the satyrs take no notice of Danaë, and instead they sing to the child, their song interspersed with clucking noises (the note *poppysmos* denoting these appears in the papyrus after lines 792 and 802). They claim

(786-95) that the child is smiling or laughing at them, in particular at their spotty bald heads and their great erect phalli ('what a willy-loving little chick!' they comment, in the nearest approach to downright obscene language to be found in surviving satyric texts). Silenus encourages the child to come to his arms (802-7): he will learn to hunt, share his mother's and (step)father's bed, and grow up to live like the satyrs (808-20). The chorus then, in chanted anapaests, declare that it is time to go and celebrate the marriage, saying with considerable wishful thinking that 'I see this bride already very much wants to satiate herself with our love' (824-6), having been on her own at sea for such a long time (827-9) and now beholding 'the flower of our youth' (830). Here the papyrus ends, but the *play* cannot have ended there: Perseus was not after all brought up by the satyrs, and though in the myth Danaë was indeed sought in marriage against her will, it was by king Polydectes, Dictys' brother. Hence the impending exit of the chorus must have been prevented, presumably by the return of Dictys, with assistance, to rescue Danaë and Perseus.

Beyond this we can say little more of the plot of the play. We may note, however, that the scene from which fr. 46a comes must have been an early one, since the chorus of satyrs are not yet present (otherwise the fishermen would have turned to them for help at once rather than summoning the local farmers, herdsmen and so on). Yet when fr. 47a begins we are already at line 765. This suggests that between these two scenes there were others to which we have no clue; in particular a substantial scene, together with one or even two choral songs, may have intervened between the hauling-in of the chest and its opening, during which the satyrs may have eagerly anticipated what they might do with the treasure they no doubt imagined it to contain, and Dictys perhaps tried to restrain them from opening the chest.

This reconstruction, and most others that have been suggested, require three actors (since Dictys, Danaë and Silenus would at one point all be on stage together). This would normally be taken as indicating that this was a late play, but it is possible that in satyr-plays Silenus was considered as a semi-detached member of the chorus. His position is certainly a unique one in Greek drama: only in satyr-plays was the dramatist obliged invariably to include one particular character.

It may be worth while considering the nature of possible thematic links between the satyr-play and the tragedies that preceded it. There is clearly a parallelism between the satyrs and Polydectes who also sought to marry Danaë against her will. The future envisaged by Silenus for Perseus as a hunter of fawns, martens and porcupines (808-9) – not, be it noted, of nobler game such as boars, lions or adult deer – contrasts sharply with the heroic role he played in the tragedies, imposed on him by Polydectes. Yet the connections are not only a matter of grotesque distortion or inversion. Danaë's speech raises a serious issue about the role of Zeus, and may make us wonder how much ethical difference there is between the behaviour of

Zeus to Danaë and that of Polydectes or Silenus, or indeed Acrisius. It is likely (see Chapter 3) that the preceding play may have included the killing of Polydectes by Perseus: Zeus could not thus suffer for what he did, but possibly the eventual triumph of Perseus and the rescue of his mother were represented as Zeus' amends to them. In that case Danaë's appeal to Zeus in *The Net-Haulers* will have been received by spectators in the light of their knowledge that it was ultimately answered. The fact remains that at the time when she makes that appeal, Danaë can with good reason feel that Zeus (783-4), her father (780-1) and the satyrs (775-6) have treated her with about the same degree of beastliness.

The fragments of *The Sacred Delegation* are much harder to interpret. The scene is at the temple of Poseidon at the Isthmus of Corinth. When the first fragment begins, someone (whom I will call 'the Inventor') is giving the satyrs painted likenesses of themselves. They admire these greatly, remarking on their perfection ('all they need is a voice', fr. 78a.7;[1] 'my mother would think it was me if she saw it', *ib.* 13-17), and fix them on the façade of the temple, remarking that they will 'stop travellers in their tracks' (*ib.* 20-1). It has been suggested that the satyrs, who are intending to compete in the Isthmian Games (see below), are hoping thus to scare away possible opponents.

At this point someone (very likely Dionysus) enters and says to the satyrs 'I *thought* I'd find you here' (fr. 78a.23). The satyrs, it seems, have been trying to evade this person, but have left very plain evidence of their movements (*ib.* 24ff.). The state of their phalli, furthermore, shows that they are in training as athletes (*ib.* 29-31; perhaps specifically as wrestlers, cf. the mention of their arms in 35) when they ought to have been concentrating on dancing and not 'damaging my property' (i.e. their own bodies) (*ib.* 32-5). Evidently he has been training them to dance at a choral festival (cf. fr. 78a.71-2 + 78c.37-8)[2] – it is not clear where – and they have revolted, absconded to the Isthmus, and decided to take part in the athletic games instead, with the help of the Inventor.

Dionysus ends by cursing the satyrs (fr. 78c.2), after which their spokesman, no doubt Silenus, complains that they are being wretchedly lodged and treated like slaves (*ib.* 5, 7); although the text is too full of gaps to be certain, it is not unlikely that, with typical effrontery, Silenus is asking Dionysus to sympathize with the satyrs in the hardships they are suffering as a result of running away from Dionysus! After a gap in the papyrus, we find Dionysus in turn complaining (fr. 78a.65ff.) that the satyrs are slandering him, saying that he is 'no good with iron' and a 'cowardly, womanish being', and speaking slightingly of his dances which 'no one, old or young, misses if he can help it' (fr. 78c.37-8); he warns them that they will weep for this and for their insistence on competing in the games (*ib.* 39-41). The satyrs reply that whatever he may threaten, they will never leave the temple (*ib.* 43ff.); their short song may or may not be accompanied by Dionysus' exit.

At this point, in the view of many scholars (e.g. Lloyd-Jones 1957: 544-6), the Inventor returns, bringing the satyrs some 'new toys, fresh from the adze and the anvil' (fr. 78c.49-52). The chorus-leader at first does not want them, but is told that they are suited to 'the speciality you have taken up' (*ib.* 56); in other words they are a form of athletic equipment, and since they were made with adze *and* anvil, and therefore contain both wood and metal, they could well be javelins (javelin-throwing was one of the components of the pentathlon event). The chorus-leader then apparently asks what they are for (*ib.* 57) and is told that they are 'very well fitted for joining in the Isthmian Games' (*ib.* 58); the text gives out a few lines later.

Another possibility, favoured among others by Taplin 1977: 421-2, is that it is not the Inventor who reappears with the 'new toys' but Dionysus himself – in which case they are likely to be instruments of bondage, possibly iron shackles and a wooden collar. Their association with the satyrs' new occupation will then be ironical – if the satyrs persist in their determination to be athletes, this is what they will get; and in the ensuing few lines the satyrs will be protesting that they cannot possibly compete chained in the Games while Dionysus, still ironically, assures them that his new gift is just what they need for the purpose. This solution is probably the preferable one; there is no clear indication of an exit for Dionysus (who is still being addressed at fr. 78c.48, the last line before the alleged return of the Inventor) or of an entrance for another character, and fr.78c.41-2 (cf. 45) is plainly a threat of punishment by Dionysus, which we would expect to be followed up.

Of the play as a whole we can say little, on this evidence, except that it seems to involve a contest for the loyalty of the satyrs between Dionysus, who wants them to dance, and the Inventor, who encourages them to become athletes, perhaps with some ulterior motive. Much might become clearer if the Inventor could be confidently identified, but in fact it is not even clear whether he is a mortal (Sisyphus, Daedalus, Theseus and even Heracles have been suggested) or a god (such as Hephaestus or Poseidon[3]). The contrast may be between the traditional rustic simplicity of the satyrs' usual world (cf. fr. 78c.7) and the urban sophistication represented by the great temple of Poseidon, by the Inventor's new technologies, and by the elaborate and expensive training of athletes (cf. fr. 78a.35 – and the complaints of the rustic Strepsiades in Aristophanes' *Clouds* about his son's mania for chariot-racing). Since the satyrs cannot permanently abandon their own nature, it is safe to assume that in the end they rejected the urban world and stayed with Dionysus. The play appears to be a late one, since the fixing of the portraits to the temple presupposes the existence of a *skênê*. The associated tragic plays cannot be identified; but *The Priestesses* (which also requires a *skênê*, and which cannot be assigned to any connected trilogy) may have been one of them.

On the satyr-plays *The Sphinx*, *Amymone*, *Proteus*, *Prometheus the Fire-bearer*, *The Chamber-makers* (?) and *Circe*, see §§5.5, 6.2, 7.3, 8.4, 10.1 and 10.2 respectively.

Notes

1. References are as in Radt 1985. In Sommerstein 2008, following Henry and Nünlist 2000: 14-16, Radt's fragments 78a and 78c are combined into one fragment (numbered 78c) and the lines renumbered into one sequence.

2. In the Henry-Nünlist reconstruction these lines are consecutive.

3. So far as I can discover, no one has yet identified the Inventor with Poseidon; but the satyrs do regard Poseidon as their new protector (frr. 78a.22, 78c.46-47), and no one would be better qualified than he to give them guidance about what it is religiously proper to do in his sanctuary (fr. 78a.2).

10

Slices from Homeric Feasts

The title of this chapter is based on a saying attributed to Aeschylus himself. In the *Deipnosophistai* (*Intellectuals at Dinner*) of the second-century AD writer Athenaeus (8.347d), one of the characters, Ulpian, speaks of 'the admirable and glorious Aeschylus' as having said that 'his tragedies were slices of fish taken from the great banquets of Homer'. Isolated apophthegms of this kind are always suspect, but there is some corroboration from two much earlier sources. On the one hand Aristophanes in *The Frogs* (1040) makes Aeschylus claim to have 'moulded' the virtues of his heroic characters, such as Patroclus and Teucer, on the models provided by Homer; on the other, the only surviving fragment of the comedy *The Cooks*, by the fourth-century dramatist Anaxilas (fr. 19), seems to speak of certain 'little fish' as being 'much better for baking than those of Aeschylus'.

If Aeschylus did make this notably modest comment on his own art (which is quite in keeping with other evidence about his attitude to it: see pp. 8, 10), he probably meant by 'Homer' not just the *Iliad* and the *Odyssey*, but the whole of what later came to be called the Epic Cycle and perhaps, even more broadly, the entire corpus of archaic narrative epic.[1] The Epic Cycle proper, as eventually defined, included one poem on primordial times (the *Titanomachy*), three on the house of Oedipus and the Theban wars (the *Oedipodeia*, *Thebais* and *Epigoni*), and eight (including the *Iliad* and *Odyssey*) on the Trojan War and its aftermath; and all this material was sometimes attributed to Homer. So, we know, were some other early epics, such as *The Sack of Oechalia* (on the last exploits of Heracles). Already in the fifth century there was considerable scepticism about the attribution to Homer of epics other than the *Iliad* and *Odyssey*, but there is no reason to believe that Aeschylus shared this. In this chapter, however, I wish, as a sample of Aeschylus' lost tragedies, to examine the two tetralogies in which he attempted to do nothing less than transpose the *Iliad* and *Odyssey* themselves, or at least their crucial portions, into dramatic form.

The two trilogies differ notably in their structure. The action of the *Iliad* is highly concentrated in time and space, and Aeschylus was able to include in his Iliadic trilogy all the major turning points of the latter two-thirds of the poem, from the Embassy of book 9 to the ransoming of Hector's body at the end, with only minor gaps in the action between the three plays. In his Odyssean trilogy, on the other hand, he had to jettison many of the most memorable portions of the *Odyssey* and concentrate on particular episodes, covering others perhaps in prophecies or in retrospective narratives.

10.1. The Iliadic tetralogy

The tetralogy based on the *Iliad* comprised *The Myrmidons*, *The Nereids*, *The Phrygians* (also called *The Ransoming of Hector*) and an unknown satyr-play (see below). The first and third plays were set in the hut of Achilles (cf. fr. 131.3-4): there being at the time no *skênê*, an interior setting could easily be imagined by the audience if the words so directed them. The second play, with its chorus of sea-goddesses, may have been set on the seashore nearby (cf. *Iliad* 1.348-61); but there is some artistic evidence (see below) suggesting that each of the three plays began with the same tableau of a seated, silent Achilles. Probably we should suppose that the performing area was imagined as vaguely representing Achilles' section of the camp, with Achilles taken to be sitting inside his hut but, in the absence of any visible building, able to converse with Myrmidons or Nereids who in real life would have been likely to congregate outside it.

Aristophanes in *The Frogs* (911ff.) makes Euripides complain of Aeschylus' habit of making a character, 'some Achilles or Niobe', sit silent on stage, with veiled head, for a long period at the beginning of the play while the chorus sang 'four strings of lyrics non-stop on the trot'. The ancient commentators on *The Frogs* are not certain whether to associate the reference to Achilles with *The Myrmidons* or *The Phrygians*. The latter is supported by the evidence of the ancient life of Aeschylus, but there is in fact no reason to choose: Aeschylus might very well have used a seated, silent Achilles twice (just as in the *Oresteia* he repeated the tableau of the killer, sword in hand, standing over a male and a female victim), though in the first play his silence would be due to wrath, in the third (like Niobe's) to grief.

The Myrmidons began, we know, with the chorus of Myrmidons (Achilles' own men) asking him, in chanted anapaests and then in song, why he was ignoring the plight of the Greek army and remaining in his hut instead of coming to their assistance. He will have made no reply, even when they implicitly accuse him, as they seem to have done, of cowardice (fr. 132a4.i.2) and of betraying the army (fr. 132a8.5). In Homer, Achilles was visited by an embassy sent by Agamemnon and the army, consisting of Ajax, Odysseus and his own old tutor Phoenix, all three of whom make speeches. Aeschylus could not have reproduced such an embassy in a two-actor play, but we are fortunate to have direct papyrus evidence (fr. 132b) that Phoenix was a character and that it was he who coaxed Achilles out of his silence. The fragment comprises the end of a speech by Phoenix and the beginning of one by Achilles. Phoenix seems to be saying that he has no further 'charm' to soothe Achilles' anger, having said everything he can think of, and that it is now up to Achilles to decide how to act. Achilles replies that for a long time, while many evil things have been said about him, he has remained silent and said nothing in return. Homer's Achilles complains of many things, but not of being slandered; for this play, however, we have some evidence that harsh words have been used of Achilles even by his own followers, and they may well have told him that (as in the case of Ajax in Sophocles' play) his enemies and rivals in the army are using even harsher ones. In what may be the end of this same speech (fr. 132c.1) Achilles mentions the possibility that the army may stone him (presumably as a traitor) and appears to make the hyperbolical assertion that even if he is stoned to ribbons he will not abandon his stand. Then he says something like this (the papyrus has lost three to six letters from the beginning of each line):

> Shall I, for fear of the Achaeans, set myself in motion, with a spear
> in the hand which is now idle through anger because of that evil
>   shepherd [Agamemnon]?
> If all on my own, as our allies claim,
> I caused so much harm by my absence from battle,
> then I am *everything* to the Greek army,
> I say that straight out and unashamedly (fr. 132c.7-12).

On a previous occasion he had saved the whole army when it was on the point of being shamed and routed by one man[2] (*ib.* 15) – and yet someone dares to accuse him of treason (*ib.* 20)?

At the end of this performance someone seems to say that Achilles is in the wrong ('this is in no way appropriate', *ib.* 34) and speaks of 'reconciliation' and 'propitiation' (*ib.* 35-6) – at which point the papyrus breaks off.

The situation and personalities are distinctly different from those assumed by the *Iliad*. Homer's Achilles was conscious of his superiority and bitterly resentful at being slighted in the matter of Briseis. Aeschylus' Achilles boasts loudly of his superiority and is contemptuous not only of Agamemnon but also of the other leaders (cf. fr. 132c.13-14). As for the cause of his anger, while we shall see that it is likely that Briseis played some role in the action of the trilogy, the surviving fragments of *The Myrmidons* make no reference to her, and, as we shall see, in Aeschylus' treatment Achilles' *grande passion* is for Patroclus. The emphasis which he puts, in his first words, on the evil tongues of his enemies, suggests that we are to understand rather that he has been angered principally by repeated depreciations, on Agamemnon's part, of his value to the army. At any rate, as in Homer, the action seems to have reached an impasse, and Aeschylus indeed caps Homer by leaving his Achilles unmoved not only by appeals and promises but even by threats of death.

After the failure of the chorus and of Phoenix, it can only, as in Homer, have been Patroclus who persuaded Achilles to (partly) relent. Nothing survives of the scene in which he did so, but we know from Plato's

Symposium (180a) and from several quotations from later parts of the play (frr. 135-7) that Aeschylus presented Achilles as being in love with Patroclus, and Patroclus could well have appealed to him in the name of that love. All we do possess from this part of the play is two snatches from a description of the firing of one of the Greek ships (frr. 133, 134).

Achilles will have sent Patroclus out to fight, and a little later a messenger will have come to narrate what ensued. The Aristophanic Aeschylus (*Frogs* 1041) speaks of Patroclus as one of the greatest of his martial heroes, and such a speech would offer the only opportunity for his heroism to be brought into the play; this may well have been the speech containing the 'Scamanders and ditches and bronze griffin-eagles on shields' ridiculed by the Aristophanic Euripides (*Frogs* 928-9). It is possible that the messenger did not know of Patroclus' death and reported only that he had pursued the enemy to the very walls of Troy, leaving Achilles in the same state of ignorance in which Homer shows him in *Iliad* 17.401-11.

It is likely that in Aeschylus, as in Homer, the shattering truth was brought to Achilles by Antilochus, the son of Nestor (whom Achilles addresses in fr. 138); the news was accompanied, or soon followed, by the mangled body of Patroclus himself – which, while it devastates Achilles emotionally, does not revolt him physically, so great is his love for the dead man (fr. 137). One quotation (fr. 135, cf. 136) shows Achilles reproaching Patroclus for having betrayed him, in strongly erotic language:

> You did not respect the sacred bond of the thighs –
> O, so ungrateful for those countless kisses!

This monstrous complaint, by the man who sent Patroclus to his death, is fully worthy of the blindly egotistical Achilles that we met in the scene with Phoenix. Another fragment displays his touching yet wholly self-centred grief:

> Bewail me who live, Antilochus,
> more than him who is dead; for my world has disappeared (fr. 138).

But it seems that with reflection he begins to realize his responsibility for what has happened:

> This is like the tale they tell in Africa
> of an eagle that was struck by an arrow
> and said, when he saw how it was flighted with feathers,
> 'Thus we are vanquished not by another,
> but by our own plumage!' (fr. 139).

It is still Achilles' disaster more than it is Patroclus', but he sees it is a self-inflicted one. And he burns for instant revenge on Hector: 'Arms, arms I need!' (fr. 140). But he has no arms; Patroclus was wearing them, and they are lost. Achilles, who at the beginning of the play was torpidly inactive in the face of enormous pressure to act, is now desperate to act and unable to do so. Here, or shortly after, the play must have ended.

The Myrmidons may be said to be based on *Iliad* 8.1 to 18.342, as seen from Achilles' standpoint (he was almost certainly on stage from beginning to end). This section of the epic covers two days and an intervening night; it is likely, though not certain, that Aeschylus combined the two days into one. He probably had no embassy from Agamemnon. Phoenix was himself a Myrmidon; indeed Homer does not explain how he came to be available for an embassy from the main army to Achilles when one would have expected him to be in Achilles' section of the camp already. In Aeschylus he probably came forward as an older, more respected, more eloquent representative of Achilles' own loyal followers than the young warriors of the chorus. Antilochus will thus have been the only non-Myrmidon to appear in the play;[3] the other *dramatis personae* seem to have been Achilles, Phoenix, Patroclus, a messenger and the chorus. Aeschylus will also have omitted, or rather postponed, the arrival of Thetis and the Nereids to console Achilles, which in Homer *precedes* the recovery of Patroclus' body (18.35-148); Thetis and the Nereids belong to the next play.

Of this play, *The Nereids*, we have little definite knowledge;[4] the surviving fragments amount to only some 23 words. In Homer the Nereids came with Thetis to comfort Achilles immediately after he learns of the death of Patroclus, and Thetis returned alone the next morning (19.3-39) bringing new armour for Achilles. Since we know (see above) that at the end of *The Myrmidons* Achilles was already anxious to fight and calling for armour, it is likely that for his second play Aeschylus conflated Thetis' two visits into one, and that this was presented as taking place on the morning after the action of the previous play. The arming of Achilles must have been a pivotal scene in *The Nereids* (cf. §5.2 on the arming of Eteocles): an armed warrior Achilles, going out to battle, would contrast sharply with the brooding or mourning Achilles of *The Myrmidons*.

Apart from the arrival of the chorus ('crossing the expanse of the sea where dolphins swim', fr. 150) and the arming scene, only one other event of the play is positively attested by surviving evidence. The only preserved spoken line of the play (fr. 153) reads 'Let fine, delicate cloth be cast around his flesh': this must refer to funeral attire for Patroclus (cf. *Iliad* 18.352-3). In Homer the body of Patroclus is washed and clothed on the evening of the day he is killed; if Aeschylus postponed this episode he did so for a reason, and one possible reason, coherent with what we have seen of the presentation of Achilles in *The Myrmidons*, would be to portray Achilles as so self-centred, so determined to revenge upon Hector the injury done to himself, that he does not even think of preparing his beloved friend for burial. If this is the object of the postponement, it would be most effective if Patroclus' body was dressed in its grave-clothes only after Hector had been killed.

The play may then have proceeded roughly as follows, corresponding approximately to *Iliad* 19-23. Achilles is mourning over the body of Patroclus, perhaps in the very same position in which we left him at the end of the previous play; the body is naked and bloody as when we last saw it. The chorus of Nereids enter, attempt to console him and perhaps join with him in lamenting Patroclus; they are presently followed by Thetis, who brings Achilles' new armour, made by Hephaestus. He puts it on, and as he does so he seems to become a new man (cf. *Iliad* 19.12-18). This whole sequence was probably long and slow, with much song, rather like the first half of *Choephoroi*; it may well have included some equivalent to the poignant dialogue of *Iliad* 18.70-126, with Thetis endeavouring in vain to keep Achilles out of the fighting because she knows that if he kills Hector his own death will soon follow. Achilles will have left for the battle, like Patroclus the previous day; presently another messenger will have reported his triumph and the death of Hector. Achilles apparently refused to gloat over his fallen enemy (fr. 151), using the same argument that the Homeric Odysseus uses at the climax of the *Odyssey* (22.411-12). Is his fury already beginning to abate? At any rate he can hardly, after saying this, have maltreated Hector's corpse as he does in the *Iliad*, though the body may well have been brought on stage, as Patroclus' had been at the end of the previous play, and left lying there while Achilles devoted his attention to preparing for Patroclus' funeral. The play may have ended with renewed lamentation for Patroclus by Achilles and the Nereids (cf. *Iliad* 23.4-23). It seems like a tragic full-close – except that the body of Hector will remind us that there is still unfinished business.

The ancient commentators on Aristophanes' *Frogs* say that the reference there to the silence of Achilles relates to the third play of the Achilles trilogy, *The Phrygians*; but Aeschylus' ancient biographer more precisely says that in this play Achilles for a long time remains veiled and does not speak 'except for a short dialogue with Hermes at the beginning'. In Homer (*Iliad* 24.103-40) it is Thetis who conveys to Achilles the instructions of Zeus that he must give up the body of Hector for ransom: Aeschylus replaces the mother with a more impersonal divine messenger, who approaches Achilles with rather cold exposition:

> Whether you choose to benefit the dead
> or to injure them, it makes no difference;
> <for the lot of dead men is to be without sensation>
> and incapable of pleasure or pain.
> But *our* [i.e. the gods'] retribution is more powerful,
> and Justice exacts the penalty due to the wrath of the dead (fr. 266).

We do not know what answer Achilles gave to Hermes, but clearly the god must have failed to move him from his set grief, and once again, as in *The*

Myrmidons, he sat silent and veiled as the chorus entered. They were Phrygians (i.e. Trojans), escorting Priam and the ransom he brought for Hector, and their exotic dances were well remembered over half a century later – witness a character in an unidentified comedy of Aristophanes (fr. 696):

> ... I saw those Phrygians,
> when they came with Priam to ransom his dead son,
> making lots of dance-movements like *this* and like *this* and *this* way ...

Their *parodos* was followed by the arrival of Priam who appealed to Achilles to allow him to ransom his son's body. We do not know what he said or how he said it, except for one or possibly two touches. Priam spoke, as in Homer, of his own old age, saying 'I have almost kept the watch of my life' (fr. 265). And someone said of Hector:

> That man was softer than mulberries (fr. 264).

It is now widely accepted, following Dover 1964, that this is a cruel jest at Hector's expense, based on *Iliad* 22.373-4; and certainly in the fourth century a boxer, say, who had been beaten black and blue, could be said to 'look like a basket of mulberries' (Alexis fr. 275). But to whom and in what context *in this play* could Achilles say such a thing about Hector? And why 'was', which ought to show that the reference is not to the dead but to the living Hector? Vastly preferable is the older interpretation which sees Priam as the speaker and the subject as the gentleness of Hector's character. In Homer it is above all Helen who recalls this (*Iliad* 24.767-75): Aeschylus cannot bring Helen into his play, and it is appropriate that the same thought should be put into the mouth of Priam, the only other Trojan (according to Helen) who showed the same kindness towards her as Hector did. I suggest that Aeschylus may have ingeniously altered the basis of Priam's appeal. In Homer he appeals to Achilles in the name of Achilles' father – and is more successful than he could have expected, in part because Achilles knows, as Priam does not, that his father is destined never to see him again. His implicit argument then was 'I am like your father; you would have pity on your father; so have pity on me'. In Aeschylus, I suspect that the appeal was in the name of Achilles' beloved Patroclus, the gentleness of whose personality is emphasized in the *Iliad*; its rationale will have been: 'Patroclus was gentle, and you loved him dearly; Hector was gentle, and I loved him dearly; so let me do my last service to Hector as you did yours to Patroclus'. And Achilles is persuaded: persuaded, perhaps for the first time in the trilogy, to take seriously the feelings of someone other than himself or (to some extent) Patroclus. Hector is ransomed against his own weight in gold. This startlingly literal realization of Achilles' hyperbolical words of *Iliad* 22.351-2 is positively attested by two ancient commentators on that passage and confirmed by a word meaning 'of equal weight' cited from our play (fr. 270) by the lexicographer Hesychius. Aeschylus is not necessarily presenting Achilles as greedy for material gain: rather, as in Homer, Achilles accepts the ransom that Priam happens to bring.

We know one other detail about this play. At some point someone was addressed, or referred to, as 'child of Andraemon of Lyrnessus, from whence Hector brought his beloved wife' (fr. 267). This finds no precise explanation in the *Iliad*, where the only Andraemon mentioned is on the Greek side, the father of Thoas, leader of the Aetolians (2.638 etc.), and where Andromache's home town is not Lyrnessus but Thebe (6.395-8). Briseis, however, did come from Lyrnessus (though her father was named Briseus, not Andraemon), and Lyrnessus and Thebe were sacked by Achilles in the course of a single expedition (2.688-93). It is likely, therefore, that Briseis is the person referred to here. Aeschylus presumably altered Andromache's place of origin to increase the sense of quasi-brotherhood between Achilles and Hector. Both Achilles and Hector took women from the same town; that town was sacked, and the natal families of both the women were destroyed; Andromache is already a widow, and soon Briseis will be one too (except that Briseis was never even a wife). It must have been Achilles who mentioned Briseis, perhaps in a retrospective account of the events leading to the death of Patroclus and Hector. It is not likely that Briseis herself had a speaking part, since she could not have spoken while Achilles and Priam were both on stage; the text of fr. 267 as preserved (which is slightly defective) does not tell us whether or not she was present as a silent character.

Like all tragedies, the play must have ended with the departure of the chorus; they will have been accompanied by Priam, and the body of Hector will either have been carried off (as that of Ajax is in Sophocles' play) or perhaps taken on a wagon (as in Homer). In the *Iliad* Priam leaves quietly before dawn, but Aeschylus, being unable to include in his play the laments of the Trojans in the city (*Iliad* 24.696-776), very probably made his Trojan chorus sing laments for Hector before they departed, in which Priam will have joined; and if my suggestion above about the awakening of new sensibilities in Achilles is correct, it would be appropriate for Achilles to take part in the mourning also. Doubtless too, as in Homer (24.582-90), Achilles took part personally in preparing the body of Hector for its funeral rites, as he had done for Patroclus.

Perhaps no Aeschylean trilogy can have been so completely dominated as this one by a single character. In all probability Achilles was on stage throughout the trilogy except for that portion of *The Nereids* when he is on the battlefield; and even then he will have been kept before the audience's minds by a messenger-speech almost entirely taken up with his exploits. In accordance with Aristotle's insight into the basic differences between epic and tragedy, all the peripheral 'episodes' of the *Iliad* are stripped away, and nothing is allowed to distract from the emotional travails, and the actions and inactions, of Achilles, who matures from a total egotism, tempered perhaps only by his passionate love of Patroclus, to a broad human sympathy that includes even his enemies.

It has been attractively suggested that a papyrus fragment (fr. 451l Radt = 78a Sommerstein), which to judge by the reference to 'these beasts' (15) appears to be satyric, may come from the final play of the Iliadic tetralogy, since Priam is apparently a character (12) and there is reference to *Teukris* (25), i.e. the Trojan land or city or a Trojan woman. The word *thalamon* 'chamber', often 'bridal chamber' (22), suggests that a marriage may be involved (cf. also *platis* 'wife', 26), and also suggests an association with the Aeschylean play-title *Thalamopoioi*, 'Chamber-builders'. More than a century ago Wecklein 1893:413-4 suggested that *Thalamopoioi* might have been inspired by *Iliad* 6.243-50 in which Priam's palace is described:

> This was fashioned with smooth-stone cloister walks, and within it
> were embodied fifty sleeping chambers [*thalamoi*] of smoothed stone
> built so as to connect with each other; and within these slept,
> each beside his own wedded wife, the sons of Priam.
> In the same inner court on the opposite side, to face them,
> lay the twelve close smooth-stone sleeping chambers of his daughters
> built so as to connect with each other, and within these slept,
> each by his own modest wife, the lords of the daughters of Priam
> (tr. Lattimore).

Wecklein thought that Aeschylus had adapted this idea to another story involving fifty married couples, that of the Danaids; he believed that *Thalamopoioi* was an alternative title for *The Egyptians* (taken as the middle play of the Danaid trilogy; see §6.2). But the papyrus suggests that the adaptation may have been more direct. I consider it highly likely that *Thalamopoioi* was written around the marriage of one or more of Priam's children, with the satyrs (as so often) in the role of reluctant labourers building the marriage chamber(s) and (as so often) threatening physical interference with a beautiful bride (most likely Andromache, cf. fr. 267, though Helen has also been suggested).

10.2. The Odyssean tetralogy

The action of the *Iliad* is concentrated in one place and in a short space of time; its major tragic events, from Achilles' rejection of the pleas of the 'embassy' to the death of Hector, occur within a span of forty-eight hours. The action of the *Odyssey*, if in this we include (as Aeschylus did) the events narrated by Odysseus in his tale to the Phaeacians, covers a period of ten years and a wide range of real and surreal locations, from Ithaca to the gates of Hades. A single day in the *Iliad* (the day on which Patroclus is killed, corresponding approximately to the day comprised in the action of *The Myrmidons*) takes Homer 5,405 lines to describe; the two longest single days in the *Odyssey* (the two days that Odysseus spends in disguise in his own house, ending with the slaying of the suitors and his reunion with Penelope) occupy only 1,693 and 1,582 lines respectively. Whereas therefore the action of Aeschylus' three Iliadic tragedies is essentially continuous (there is, to be sure, an interval of some days between *The Nereids* and *The Phrygians*, but nothing of significance happens in it except the funeral of Patroclus), in his Odyssean trilogy he has perforce to be selective and in particular to choose for dramatic treatment only one episode from all of Odysseus' earlier adventures.

The episode he chose was the *Nekyia*, the visit to the underworld (or rather to its portals) in book 11 of the *Odyssey*. This episode was in fact especially suitable for adaptation as a two-actor tragedy, since Odysseus throughout it converses with only one spirit at a time, and it could be linked forward easily to later stages of the story through the information Odysseus receives about the state of affairs in Ithaca, retrospectively from his mother (*Odyssey* 11.152-224) and prospectively from Teiresias (*ib.* 90-151). His play was later given the name *Psykhagôgoi* (*The Ghost-raisers*). Its setting was a lake or marsh (*limnê*) at which there was believed to be an entrance to the underworld (frr. 273, 273a), probably either Lake Avernus in Italy or the marshes by the river Acheron at Ephyra in Thesprotia (Epirus) where there was an oracle of the dead (*nekyomanteion*). The chorus consisted of local inhabitants (worshippers of Hermes, god of communication between living and dead) who advised Odysseus on the offerings and prayers necessary to bring up the spirits of the dead from below. The only other substantial fragment of this play that survives is one evidently spoken by Teiresias in which he prophesies Odysseus' death: the bizarre and undignified nature of his end (his head will be pierced by the sting of a sting-ray concealed in the excrement of a sea-bird) has not surprisingly led some scholars to insist that *The Ghost-raisers* must have been a satyr-play, but the chorus's self-description in fr. 273 surely rules this out, and this account of Odysseus' death may well have had precedents in late epic. We have no other solid information about the play, but it is hard to see how it can have had much movement or tension:[5] its main theatrical impact must have been achieved through the incantations of the chorus and the appearance of one spirit after another from below (however this was contrived). This was apparently enough to establish it firmly in Athenian theatrical memory: the chorus of Aristophanes' *Birds*, produced in 414, evoke (1553-64) a mock *Nekyia* with Socrates as the *psykhagôgos*, the cowardly Peisander in the role of Odysseus wanting to meet a spirit (his own) and Socrates' yellow-complexioned friend Chaerephon coming up from below like Teiresias – or rather like a bat!

Perhaps the most serious difficulty for an early fifth-century tragic dramatist tackling the *Odyssey* was how to handle the climax of the epic, the killing of Penelope's suitors. He would have no way to dramatize this event directly. The suitors could figure in a tragedy only as a chorus; and not only was a chorus of villains a rarity in tragedy, but more importantly it was impossible for a chorus to be killed. It followed that a play based on this part of the *Odyssey* could not be set in the hall of the palace, which the suitors dominated. The obvious alternative setting was the upper chamber where Penelope lived, and this appears to have been Aeschylus' choice, though he may not have defined the location very precisely in order to avoid raising questions about the propriety of a strange man being admitted to that part of the house. The chorus, almost certainly, consisted of Penelope's maidservants; Penelope (after whom the play was later named) will have been present throughout, with Odysseus arriving and departing. Only one line of the play (fr. 187) survives, but it is enough to show that the interview between Penelope and Odysseus, described in *Odyssey* 19, was a major scene of the play. In this line Odysseus describes himself as 'a Cretan of noble lineage' (cf. *Odyssey* 19.172ff.). Later scenes may have included a narrative (by the nurse Eurycleia?) of Odysseus' triumph over the suitors, followed by the reunion of Odysseus and Penelope (both modelled on *Odyssey* 23); but here we are in the dark.

The conclusion of the *Odyssey* has been much criticized, both in ancient and in modern times, and many scholars have regarded part or all of the last 624 lines of the poem (from 23.297) as a post-Homeric addition. The main events which occur in this portion of the *Odyssey* are the secret departure of Odysseus, Telemachus, and the faithful swineherd and oxherd from the city, leaving Penelope in the palace; the journey of the suitors' souls to Hades and their reception there; the meeting of Odysseus and his aged father Laertes; an assembly of the Ithacans, dominated by the kinsfolk of the suitors, where a majority decide to take violent revenge on Odysseus; a brief battle at Laertes' farm; and a final reconciliation imposed by Athene on the instructions of Zeus. It seems that Aeschylus too may have found this ending unsatisfactory, for he discarded it entirely in favour of another, either of his own invention or modelled on the cyclic epic, the *Telegony*.[6] The title of his third play, *Ostologoi* (*The Bone-gatherers*), recalls *Odyssey* 24.415-17:

> The people came ... from their several places,
> to gather, with groaning and outcry, before the house of Odysseus.
> They carried the corpses out of the house, and each one buried
> his own ... (tr. Lattimore).

In Aeschylus' play, however, when the suitors' relatives entered Odysseus' palace, they found there not only the young men's corpses but also Odysseus. He has not escaped to the countryside; he has stayed put. From the two surviving fragments (fr. 179, 180) it appears that the bodies were on stage, and that Odysseus spoke of the insulting treatment the suitors had meted out to him when he had been in the palace in the guise of a beggar – humiliations even greater than those described in the *Odyssey*: using his head as a target for wine-flicking (*kottabismos*) or throwing a chamber-pot at him which smashed and emptied its contents all over his face. This enabled Aeschylus not only to bring the suitors, who must have been much talked about earlier, physically into the play (if only as corpses), but to some extent to characterize them individually: Eurymachus was mentioned (fr. 179.1) and said to have been 'no less' insolent than, presumably, Antinous (the only suitor who, in Homer, is more important and more vicious than Eurymachus); the thrower of the chamber-pot may have been Antinous himself, the only suitor who in the *Odyssey* actually hits Odysseus with an impromptu missile (a footstool, 17.462-4). Thus whereas the Homeric Odysseus, after killing the suitors, beats a retreat and then prepares to fight, the Aeschylean Odysseus stands his ground, argues and attempts to persuade. And he must have been successful, either by his own eloquence or perhaps with the help of Athena's; at any rate, by one means or another, the suitors' relatives (who formed the chorus of the play) were convinced that revenge would not be justified, and the Odyssean trilogy, like the Iliadic, ended with the reconciliation of enemies through the power of words and with laments for those who had perished.

The satyr-play of the Odyssean tetralogy was *Circe*, based evidently on *Odyssey* 10. It is an attractive suggestion (Seaford 1984: 106) that the satyrs were herding Circe's pigs, as they herd sheep in Euripides' *Cyclops* and cattle, apparently, in Sophocles' *Inachus*; Odysseus, as in *Cyclops*, will have liberated them as well as his companions.

It will be seen that we know much less about the Odyssean plays than we do about the Iliadic ones. This may be because they were less read in later antiquity, and hence less likely to be quoted or to yield surviving papyrus fragments. It would be fascinating to know exactly how Aeschylus remodelled the end of the *Odyssey*, or how he interpreted the interview of book 19, where modern critics are deeply divided over the extent to which, and the level of consciousness at which, Penelope may be understood to suspect that the alleged Cretan beggar is actually her husband. This, however, is beyond our knowledge.

Notes

1. For an excellent guide to what is known about, and what survives from, the poems (other than the *Iliad* and *Odyssey*) that made up this corpus, see M.L. West 2003.

2. Probably Cycnus, at the time when the army first landed; the story was dramatized by Sophocles in *The Shepherds,* the fragments of which I will be editing in Sommerstein & Talboy (forthcoming).

3. Indeed, so far as our actual knowledge goes, he is the only non-Myrmidon Greek to have a role anywhere in the trilogy. Achilles' jealous Greek enemies or rivals are an external presence only, whom we hear about but never meet – like

the Atreidae and Odysseus in lines 134-1039 of Sophocles' *Ajax*, a play which may owe a great deal to this Aeschylean model. Aeschylus' trilogy was much more exclusively centred on Achilles and his emotions than Homer's epic: it was an *Achilleis* rather than an *Iliad*.

4. So little that it has been possible for M.L. West 2000: 341-3 to argue that it came third, not second, in the trilogy and that its subject was the death of Achilles. Against this, note that (i) a series of vase paintings (*LIMC* Achilles 510-25) shows Thetis and the Nereids bringing new armour to an Achilles who is often shown sitting muffled just as in *The Myrmidons* and *The Phrygians*; (ii) fr. 296 Radt = 150a Sommerstein ('For all Troy sees light because of Hector's good fortune') would most naturally be said after Hector's day of triumph on which Patroclus was killed, but before his death – i.e. in a play that followed *The Myrmidons* and preceded *The Phrygians*; and (iii) fr. 151 (see text above) shows that at some point in the play Achilles returned from battle safe and victorious.

5. Unless the information he received from Teiresias (and perhaps also from his mother Anticleia) led Odysseus to make, and to announce, a major decision affecting the future development of the plot, e.g. to return home in disguise rather than openly and/or to test his wife and slaves (cf. *Odyssey* 11.441-3, 455-6).

6. The opening sentence of Proclus' summary of the *Telegony* speaks of the suitors being buried by their families; this shows that the *Telegony* began, not where our *Odyssey* ends, but somewhat earlier, perhaps after 23.296. This may, indeed, have been one reason why two great Hellenistic scholars, Aristophanes of Byzantium and Aristarchus, regarded 23.296 as the end of the *Odyssey*.

11

Aeschylus, the Gods and the World

11.1. Puppets of the gods?

Greek tragedy differs from most Western fiction (dramatic and other) of the last few centuries in that its characters often explicitly ascribe events, especially disastrous events, to the direct purposive actions of personal divine beings whom they do not regard as being universally benevolent. Such events are also frequently spoken of as having been foretold by prophets or oracles, or as the result of a curse uttered by some outraged victim of a past wrong, or as divine punishment for such a wrong falling on the head not of the original wrongdoer but of his or her descendants. Many modern minds find such a manner of speaking and of thinking irredeemably alien, and one often hears or reads, whether from media drama critics or from undergraduates, that in Greek tragedy the characters have no freedom of choice but are 'puppets' in the hands of 'fate' or of the gods, or that the action of a play consists essentially in the working out of a predetermined divine plan, usually with the unspoken corollary that such a drama cannot be of any possible interest to modern humans who believe that their destiny is in their own hands. Since the undergraduates do not usually go on to explain why in that case they think Greek tragedy worth studying, nor the drama critics why their editors think it worth while to cover performances of it, we would appear to be in the presence of a triumph of cliché over clear thinking.

In what, let us ask, does the supposed alienness of the Greek tragic world-view consist?

It is not an alien assumption that human events are sometimes determined by forces too powerful for humans to resist successfully. That happens every time there is a natural disaster. It is true that the normal twenty-first-century reaction to such a disaster is to look for someone to blame (and preferably to sue), but in many cases it has to be recognized that no human being can with any pretence of rationality be held responsible. Some of the most influential modern philosophies of history and society, moreover, have maintained that the major developments of human history are determined by the working out of inevitable social and economic laws which generate irresistible winds of change. And at an individual level, we are familiar with psychological theories which explain the anti-social behaviour of adolescents or adults by reference to childhood traumas of various kinds, with sociological theories which explain it by reference to social or economic deprivation, and with biological theories which explain it by reference to genetic inheritance. I here hold no brief for or against any of these theories. I merely note that they exist and are well known. It simply is not true that modern humans believe, without qualification, that their destiny is in their own hands.

It is not an alien assumption, either, that the sins of one generation can be visited upon another. It is, indeed, a truth (if an inconvenient one) that is now being shouted at us daily from the rooftops. The folly or the ignorance of adults may infect their child, from the moment of its birth, with a fatal virus. The greed and the carelessness of humanity today may leave an uninhabitable planet as an inheritance to our descendants, say, a hundred years hence. It is true that these statements are, or ought to be, based on scientific investigations whose methods and principles were unknown to Greeks of Aeschylus' day; but it needs no scientific training, nor any insight into alien thought patterns, to understand (for example) Kipling's epitaph on the dead of the First World War:

> If any question why we died,
> Tell them, because our fathers lied.

Related to this, sometimes identical with it, is the principle, equally familiar to us, that the sins of superiors may be visited on their subordinates. The 'fathers' of Kipling's epitaph are not only the previous generation, but also the old men (politicians) who failed to prevent the war in which the young men (soldiers) met their deaths, just as Xerxes 'heaped Hades with Persians'. Again we have no difficulty comprehending this: we may object, and rightly, when a state inflicts collective punishments, but we know that life itself often does so whether we like it or not.

There remain three presuppositions of Greek tragedy, in this area, that may with some justice be considered alien to us: **(1)** that the future can be predicted with certainty by persons with appropriate training or inspiration; **(2)** that it can be determined by prayers or curses; **(3)** that the superhuman forces of the universe are embodied in, or are controlled by, personal beings with psychological motives resembling those of humans. But none of these necessarily takes us into an incomprehensible thought-world.

(1) Prediction of the future is something we all do all the time, though with varying degrees of confidence and success. In some fields we too believe it can be done with certainty. No one, for example, on 11 August 1998, would have been prepared to place a bet, even at the most extravagant odds, that there would not, exactly one year later, be an eclipse of the sun, which would be total in certain parts of Cornwall. Again, it is certain that if a kilogram of pure uranium-238 is sealed up underground today and the seal is broken 4,500 million years hence, there will be 500 grams of uranium remaining, the rest having decayed into other elements. Most of us, however, do not think that future events affecting *human beings* can be predicted with that kind of certainty. Ancient Greeks did so believe (as do that not insignificant minority today who provide astrologers and their like with a comfortable living); but they also believed that the predictions actually offered to inquirers were hard to interpret and were often fulfilled in a sense other than their literal one. It was the responsibility of the person to whom the prediction was made to determine its possible meanings, and then so to plan his future that the prediction was fulfilled in the most favourable or least damaging way. This applies even to the most notorious of all Greek tragic prophecies, the one given to Oedipus at Delphi that he would kill his father and marry his mother: for there are other ways of killing one's father than by striking him down (cf. Sophocles, *Oedipus the King* 969-70), and one may metaphorically 'sleep with one's mother' by being buried in the soil of one's native land (cf. Herodotus 6.107). It was not the witches' fault if Macbeth chose to take the fulfilment of their prophecy into his own hands by killing Duncan, and it was not Apollo's fault if Oedipus forgot why he had come to Delphi in the first place, viz. to dispel doubts voiced at Corinth about his parentage (*Oedipus the King* 779-89).

(2) Curses have gone out of fashion. Many people pray to a divinity for the well-being of themselves, of those they love, and of humanity in general: few indeed pray for harm to come upon their enemies, let alone seek to make such prayers more effective by inscribing them on lead tablets as Greeks did throughout antiquity. Curses play an important role in many Greek myths, but they are not as important in Greek tragedy as they are sometimes said to be. Indeed they are not even always effective. In the surviving plays ascribed to Aeschylus there are three curses of significance. The most famous is the so-called 'curse on the house of Atreus', or, to be more precise, the curse uttered by Thyestes when he discovered that his brother Atreus had given him the flesh of his own children to eat (*Agamemnon* 1599-1602). This curse is an impressive event as Thyestes' surviving son Aegisthus describes it, but it can hardly be said to cause the death of Agamemnon (since Aegisthus had a duty of revenge anyway, curse or no curse, and other less honourable motives besides), and in any case it was not fully effective. Thyestes' words were 'So perish all the race of Pleisthenes' [= Atreus, see p. 209n.1]; and the race of Pleisthenes did *not* perish, for Menelaus and Orestes survived. It was, in fact, Thyestes' own line that became extinct. The curse of Oedipus on his sons is a powerful force in *Seven*, but we saw in Chapter 5 that it is far from being the only cause of their death at each other's hands. The other curse is one said to have been uttered against Zeus by his father Cronus (*Prom.* 910-12), and we know that this curse failed even though it was the curse of a god: Zeus was not in the end overthrown.

(3) We can recognize readily enough, when we think about it, that human beings often are effectively powerless in the face of superhuman forces. We can recognize that the world can be cruel, and that minor wrongdoings or innocent mistakes or even acts intended as benevolent can have catastrophic consequences, sometimes lasting for decades or centuries. But we do not today think of the forces that bring these events about as being wielded by divinities who act from the same kinds and mixtures of motives as we do ourselves, and who as well as being vastly our superiors in power and immortality are at least our equals in selfishness and spite. All major modern religions are unanimous in proclaiming that divine power is a power of and for good – and then seeking, with varying degrees of ingenuity and of success, to account on that assumption for the extreme if intermittent cruelty that the world, created and governed by this divine power, can display.

Ancient Greeks also wanted to believe that the gods were good. From Homer to Menander,[1] when the miscreant meets his deserved fate or the innocent is triumphantly vindicated, we sometimes hear the observer exclaim 'So there are indeed gods in heaven!' But alongside and in tension with this view of the world there was always another. That there were gods could not be seriously doubted: too many things, on a large and a small scale, happened in the world for which there was no other adequate explanation. That there was evil in the world, and that it was not always remedied, was even more certain. If one assumed that the gods were reliably good, it would have to follow that the evils of this world were compensated for in another, after death: such was the doctrine of certain mystery-religions, but it did not square with the widespread perception of the afterlife as, for almost all, a dreary and joyless shadow-existence in the realm of Hades beneath the earth. The only alternative was to suppose that the gods were not reliably good, that they were as capricious as wind and weather (which, after all, among many other things, they controlled). The morally offensive nature of the Greek gods is thus a corollary of the morally offensive nature of the universe in which their worshippers lived. If we find it hard to come to terms with, it is not because there has been a fundamental change in our perception of the universe, but because there has been a change in our concept of divinity, a change which began in Aeschylus' own time with a few philosophers (notably Xenophanes) who saw the tension described earlier in this paragraph as a contradiction. For some people today the very word 'god' may be so loaded with the connotations of the new concept that in discussions of Greek tragedy, even without a capital letter, it is hopelessly misleading. In view of this there is something to be said for eschewing the word altogether and using instead a word like 'Power' (a capital letter is in order here, as a reminder that the power meant is superhuman). I will continue to use 'god(dess)', but readers, especially religiously-minded ones, must take care to remember that these are gods who demand not faith in an ideal but recognition of a reality.

The working of the Aeschylean gods is remarkably consistent. At least in the extant plays (other than *Prometheus*), they impose no arbitrary dooms. Rather, they hold humans rigidly to the consequences of their own[2] or their rulers' or their community's actions and decisions. Sometimes, as in *The Persians*, the process is simple. Sometimes it is quite complex. Laius defies a clear oracular warning to remain childless; this leads to his death at his son's hands, followed by the latter's incestuous marriage; this in turn puts the ageing Oedipus into the power of sons who have a grudge against him, and whose slighting treatment of him provokes his curse; the sons' quarrel puts the whole city of Thebes in danger of destruction. The gods' role in all this is essentially to close loopholes: there was a god's hand in it when Laius and Oedipus, not knowing each other, came to the same place at the same time, and again when Eteocles found that Polyneices was attacking the gate which he had reserved for himself to defend. Similarly in the Danaid trilogy it was apparently Zeus who saw to it that the sons of Aegyptus arrived safely at Argos in pursuit of the Danaids, and it was surely Aphrodite who influenced Hypermestra to spare Lynceus, events without which Danaus would have escaped his deserved doom; but before he meets that doom, suffering in plenty has already come not only to the hybristic sons of Aegyptus but also to the innocent Argives.

In the next section I will examine what may at first seem a striking counterexample to my assertion that the Aeschylean gods impose no arbitrary dooms, the matter of the sacrifice of Iphigeneia.

11.2. Agamemnon's dilemma

Clytaemestra kills Agamemnon in revenge for his sacrifice of Iphigeneia at Aulis: she makes this very clear several times after the event (*Agamemnon* 1412-21, 1524-9, 1555-9). This is certainly not her only motive (see §7.4), but that it is a genuine motive is beyond doubt, not least because the connection is clearly indicated from the start, for those who know the story (as of course the audience do), in the words of Calchas (150-5). And yet it may at first appear that the extent of Agamemnon's guilt for the death of Iphigeneia is open to some question, indeed that he had little or no choice in the matter.

Agamemnon and Menelaus have been sent by Zeus (60-2, cf. 362ff., 525-6, 581-2, 748) to avenge upon the Trojans the outrage against Zeus' law of hospitality committed by Paris. As they set out on their expedition, Zeus sends a favourable omen. This omen, according to Calchas, angers Artemis (131-52). One might be tempted to take much of Calchas' language metaphorically: perhaps when he says that Artemis is angry with 'the winged hounds of her Father' and hates the eagles' feast, he means that she is angry with the Atreidae, whom the eagles represent (122-5), because of what they intend to do to Troy, symbolized by the hare. This, however, is ruled out by 140-3, where Artemis' anger is associated with her benevolence towards the young of wild creatures: no wild creatures will be killed in the sack of Troy, only domestic livestock (128-30) and, above all, humans (326-9). Artemis is angry about the omen itself. The omen was sent by Zeus. One would therefore expect her to retaliate against Zeus. Instead Calchas fears, correctly, that she may retaliate against Agamemnon and the army, who are in no way responsible for the event that has angered her. This part of the story is an innovation by Aeschylus, for we know that at least one earlier version existed (that of the *Cypria*) in which Artemis' anger was the result of an offence by Agamemnon, who shot a stag and boasted that he was a better archer than Artemis. Aeschylus apparently does not want Agamemnon to be responsible for the crisis in this way.

Through no fault of Agamemnon, then (it seems), he finds himself in a position in which he is required to sacrifice his daughter or the expedition will not be able to sail. The leaders of his army are eager for the war (214-16, 230); nor can the army stay much longer at Aulis, or it will starve (188-98). If the expedition is disbanded, Agamemnon will be failing in a mission in which he is the agent of Zeus, and failing also in his obligations towards his allies who will regard him as a deserter (212-13). He has therefore no alternative but to do the horrendous act of sacrificing his own daughter, and thereby to make certain his own humiliating death. And this is the work of Zeus, who by sending the expedition and also sending the omen has for no reason given caused Agamemnon, who (as we have been reminded) holds his throne and sceptre from Zeus (43), to forfeit his life.

We can, of course, try to supply Zeus with a reason. One popular line of escape at this point is to say that the death of Iphigeneia is part of a divine plan to fulfil the curse of Thyestes and avenge the latter's children: Iphigeneia must die in order that Clytaemestra may have a motive to kill Agamemnon and so fulfil the curse. There are two problems with this theory. One is that nothing whatever is said about Thyestes or his children (including Aegisthus) for nearly another thousand lines. The other and more serious is that no one, at any point in the trilogy, ever makes any connection of any kind between the two events. Cassandra says much about the children of Thyestes, but nothing about Iphigeneia; Aegisthus likewise. Clytaemestra says much about Iphigeneia, and once refers to the feast of Thyestes (1500-2), but never in the same context. If we wish to construct a scheme under which Zeus contrives the death of Iphigeneia in order later, through Clytaemestra, to punish Agamemnon for the murders committed by Atreus, we will have to do so without any help or encouragement from the poet. In any case, there was no need for Zeus to go about things this way, given that Agamemnon was already hated by Aegisthus as the son of Atreus, and would soon be hated by the Argives as responsible for the death of many of their sons and husbands (429-60). The city would already hold an ample number of potential regicides. Why have an innocent maiden killed merely in order to add one more to that number?

Such is the case for holding that Agamemnon is the essentially innocent victim of an arbitrary doom inflicted either foolishly or maliciously by

Zeus. It requires, however, closer examination, for it rests on the assumptions that Agamemnon is under a duty (1) to Zeus and (2) to his allies to undertake the expedition, and that if he abandoned it he would be committing an offence so serious that the sacrifice of Iphigeneia might reasonably seem the lesser evil; and these assumptions are highly dubious.

If it would be an offence against Zeus to abandon the expedition, this would be the strongest possible argument that Agamemnon could use to convince himself and others of the rightness of the sacrifice, and it therefore becomes very remarkable that in his soliloquy quoted by the chorus (206-17) he makes no mention of it. The chorus, moreover, later on, tell Agamemnon to his face that at the time when the expedition set out they thought he was utterly foolish to embark on so great a war for the sake of Helen (799-804), and before then they have spoken in disparaging terms, and in the context of the sacrifice of Iphigeneia, of 'the war to take revenge over a woman' (225-6) – and 'a woman of many men' at that (62). They could not have spoken so if they thought Agamemnon was under an obligation to Zeus to fight the war: it can never be foolish to fulfil an obligation to Zeus. Therefore that cannot be what they mean when they say that Zeus 'sent' the expedition. What they do mean was clearly seen by Dover 1973: 65. Zeus is *using* Agamemnon as his *instrument* for the punishment of Paris. Agamemnon musters and launches the expedition not because he has received some command from Zeus to do so, but because he wants to; early on the chorus describe him and Menelaus as 'uttering from their hearts a great cry for war' (49, cf. 228-30). The reasons for his enthusiasm are not given explicitly, no doubt because they can easily be assumed to be the same as the reasons for which any ruler embarks enthusiastically on a war he expects to win: glory and material gain – both of which he achieves.

What of the duty to the 'allies' that seems to be implied in 212-13? Nothing outside this five-word sentence suggests that Agamemnon is under any obligation to the non-Argive leaders and communities who have joined the expedition. The Argives think of it as an Argive expedition undertaken on the initiative of the joint kings of Argos; they have invited others to share in the risks and rewards, and can if they choose withdraw the invitation. Agamemnon may well indeed consider himself under an obligation to Menelaus, as his brother and co-ruler; but Menelaus is as distressed by the proposed sacrifice as Agamemnon himself initially is (202-4), and no one is entitled to demand that revenge be taken on behalf of Helen's husband if Helen's husband himself does not want to take it. Agamemnon's phrase *xummakhias hamartôn* (213) has often been translated 'fail my allies', 'default on my alliance' or the like. It is, however, quite hard to derive that meaning grammatically, and, as Lloyd-Jones 1979 and Winnington-Ingram 1983: 83 have seen, there is a regular usage of the verb *hamartanein* which offers a sense that fits much better the assumptions of the context. If Agamemnon disbands the expedition, he will *lose* his allies (cf. e.g. 535 for this usage). He is the leader of a grand Greek coalition. He has put his hand to a great enterprise. If he now abandons it, climbing down in the sight of them all, he will suffer (or so he fears) a shattering blow to his prestige: his leadership, his *hêgemonia*, will be gone. They will scorn him as a deserter (212), never mind that it is logically impossible to desert an expedition initiated by oneself. To be their leader he must follow them: not duty but political expediency, combined with his own continuing determination to have his war, impels him to carry out the sacrifice. He could have chosen otherwise. At least one scholar (Page in Denniston & Page 1957: xxvi-xxvii) has argued that if Agamemnon had refused to sacrifice Iphigeneia the other commanders would have done so in any case, forgetting that Iphigeneia was not yet at Aulis and that only her father could compel her to be brought there. He could have told the troops: 'We can only sail against Troy if I sacrifice, that is murder, my own daughter. None of you would be willing to do that to his child, and I am not willing either. Menelaus, whose wrongs I asked you to avenge, would rather forgo his vengeance, and give up hope of recovering his wife, than compel me to commit so foul an act. I am deeply grateful for your willingness to give us aid, and I will reward you accordingly from my great wealth, but now I must ask you to go home.' He might or might not have lost his allies; he would have saved not only his own life but many thousands of others.

And, of course, the purpose of Zeus would have failed. But Zeus's purposes do not fail. When he decided to make Agamemnon the instrument of his plans for the punishment of Paris, he knew well enough what manner of man Agamemnon was: the man we will see later in the play, a man devoted to power and prestige, who in his speech at homecoming (810-54) does not mention the casualties and has nothing to say to or about their grieving relatives, while devoting some twenty lines to alleged political malcontents and the measures he will take ('by cutting or burning', 849) to render them harmless; a man who would rather accept honours fit only for a god than forgo any of the glory due to a conqueror; a man who, having resolved on a war, will allow nothing, nothing at all, to stand between him and the waging of it. In that sense it was inevitable that Agamemnon would sacrifice his daughter. But that does not mean he had no choice. It only means that Zeus chose the right man for his job.

From the same perspective we need not be alarmed to discover that, as Page puts it (Denniston & Page 1957: xvi n.1), 'it is the will of Zeus that Troy shall be taken ... but also that anybody responsible for many deaths (as the taker of Troy must be) shall be severely punished' (cf. 461-74). To be an agent of the will of Zeus is not a guarantee of moral rectitude or divine favour. Clytaemestra, after all, was also an agent of the will of Zeus. The sack of Troy is the greatest of a series of acts spread out through the *Oresteia* which are both just punishments and terrible crimes. Such, in the *Oresteia*, is the nature of vengeance. Such therefore also are the gods who preside over and direct it.

11.3. Maradona and Farmer Jones

We saw in the previous section that the Trojan war occurs by the will of Zeus and also by the will of Agamemnon. Zeus wants it in order to punish Paris; Agamemnon wants it, apparently, in order to gain power, prestige and booty. It is meaningless to say 'It is the will of Zeus, therefore it had to happen; Agamemnon's wishes and motives are irrelevant'; for if that were so, Aeschylus has misled us seriously by showing Agamemnon coming to a decision without giving any indication that that decision was somehow controlled by Zeus. It would be equally misguided to say 'It was Agamemnon's war; the reference to Zeus is merely a poetic device to indicate that it was just and natural retribution for the crime of Paris', because there is far too much in the *Oresteia*, as well as in other plays, that cannot be understood in that allegoristic framework – beginning with the intervention of Artemis. Moreover, the pattern is one that occurs repeatedly both in the *Oresteia* and elsewhere.

The death of Agamemnon is the work of Clytaemestra and Aegisthus, acting for a variety of reasons: in Clytaemestra's case, revenge for Iphigeneia and resentment of Agamemnon's sexual infidelities including the bringing home of Cassandra; in Aegisthus' case, revenge for his father and brothers, and the desire to acquire Agamemnon's power and wealth (*Ag.* 1638-9); in the case of both, their guilty mutual love. But it is also the work of Zeus (*Ag.* 461-2, 1485-8), of the Erinyes (1186ff.), and of the *daimôn* of the house, using Clytaemestra and Aegisthus as their instruments for punishing the crimes of Agamemnon (including the deaths for which he was responsible at Troy) and also those of Atreus.

The death of Cassandra is the work of Clytaemestra, acting out of a jealous hatred which she makes very evident in *Ag.* 1440-7. But it is also the work of Apollo, avenging Cassandra's deception of him (1080-2, 1202ff., 1275-6).

Orestes is commanded by Apollo, who was speaking for Zeus (*Eum.* 19, 616-21), to kill Clytaemestra and Aegisthus; Apollo backed his command by threatening Orestes with the wrath of the Erinyes in case of disobedience. But Orestes, having spoken of these things, at once adds that even if he were to ignore the word of Apollo, 'the deed must still be done' (*Cho.* 298) for various purely 'secular' motives: Orestes' grief for his father, his right to reclaim his inheritance, the shame of seeing Argos subservient to 'two women'.

Orestes is eventually acquitted 'thanks to Pallas, Loxias and Zeus the Third, the Saviour, who fulfils all things' (*Eum.* 754-61); but also thanks to the Athenian jurors who voted with Athena and to whose descendants, rather than to her, he promises the eternal fidelity of Argos (762-74).

The expedition of Xerxes is destroyed by 'Zeus the King' (*Pers.* 532ff.) and the gods in general, but also by the superior intelligence, tactics, discipline and morale of the Greeks, and by the unfriendly Greek terrain which decimated the army on its retreat. The Greeks were fighting for their freedom; so, we may feel, was 'the land itself [which] acts as their ally' (792); Zeus and the gods were concerned to punish the Persians for breaking the boundary between land and sea and between Asia and Europe. Xerxes is crucially deceived, before the battle of Salamis, by 'an avenging spirit or an evil *daimôn*' (354) and also by 'a Greek man from the Athenian forces' (355): and after recounting what the man said, the messenger remarks that Xerxes 'did not perceive the deception of the Greek or the resentment of the gods' (361-2).

Eteocles and Polyneices kill each other because of their deep hatred of each other, evidenced by Polyneices' words reported in *Seven* 636-8 and Eteocles' in 658-75. But their deaths are also the work of Apollo (800-2), in final requital for Laius' disobedience to his oracle, and of the Arai or Erinyes (955, cf. 946), the embodiments of their father's curse, not to speak of other powers such as Ares (945) and Ate (957).

The Danaids are granted asylum in Argos thanks to skilful, and somewhat duplicitous, political manoeuvring by King Pelasgus (*Supp.* 480-503, 600-24). Pelasgus' motive was fear of pollution and divine wrath if Argos were to reject the Danaids' supplication and they were then to carry out their threat to hang themselves in the sanctuary. But the decision was also, according to Danaus, the work of Zeus (624).

Thus almost every important event in Aeschylean tragedy is the fruit of parallel human and divine action, usually from different motives. This is by no means peculiar to Aeschylus. It is, indeed, even older than Homer: Homer does not assert, but assumes his audience know, that Achilles was killed by Paris and also by Apollo (*Iliad* 19.417, 22.359-60). He himself, at the beginning of the *Iliad*, says that the quarrel of Achilles and Agamemnon was caused by 'the son of Zeus and Leto' (1.8-9), but when he proceeds to the actual narrative we find that the quarrel was caused, not directly by the plague sent by Apollo, but by Agamemnon's angry reaction to Calchas' prescription for ending it. The official name for this early Greek thought-pattern is 'the principle of double determination', which may be thus expressed:

The involvement of divine hands does not relieve human ones of their responsibility.[3]

One is tempted to christen this the *Maradona Principle*, after a great Argentinian soccer player who in a World Cup match in 1986 scored a famous goal which he ascribed to the hand of God while some others felt that his own hand had (illegally) rather more to do with it. The principle is by no means restricted in its application to the ancient Greek world: as Kitto 1961: 68-9 pointed out, someone who after a Harvest Thanksgiving service said to a worshipper, 'But you can't have it both ways; who *is*, in your idea, responsible for the harvest, God Almighty, or Farmer Jones?'

would have shown, not that the worshipper's beliefs were incoherent, but that he himself did not understand what religion was all about.

In the *Oresteia* – unusually, for tragedy – the Maradona Principle is consciously and explicitly articulated and even argued over. After the murder of Agamemnon, the chorus reflect (1448-61) on the two women, Helen and Clytaemestra, who have determined his fate: Clytaemestra replies (1462-7) that they should not turn their anger against Helen, and approves (1475-81) when a moment later (1468-74) they lay the responsibility for what has happened on the *daimôn* of the house of Tantalus and ultimately (1485-8) upon Zeus. But having said firmly that everything has come about 'because of Zeus, the cause of all, the worker of all' (1485-6), the chorus, apostrophizing their dead king, immediately go on to use language implying that they blame Clytaemestra:

> Here you lie in this spider's web,
> having breathed out your life in an unholy death –
> ah me, a deathbed unworthy of a free man! –
> laid low by treacherous death at the hands
> <of your wife> with a two-edged weapon (1492-6).

And Clytaemestra protests at this:

> You assert that this deed is mine:
> but do not suppose I am Agamemnon's wife.
> Rather the old, bitter avenging spirit
> of Atreus who made that grim feast
> has taken the likeness of this dead man's wife
> and paid him out, sacrificing an adult to add to the young ones (1497-1503).

Clytaemestra, who had earlier proudly asserted her responsibility for Agamemnon's death, now seems to be denying it; but the chorus will not let her:

> That you are not responsible
> for this murder, who will testify?
> How, how? But an ancestral avenging spirit might have *partnered* you (1505-8).

Thus the Elders, having specifically asserted the responsibility of the *daimôn* and of Zeus, just as specifically refuse to let this negate the responsibility of the human agent. Clytaemestra does not argue the point further, and indeed will later say 'By me he fell and died, and I will bury him' (1552-3), while also hoping to end the sequence of violent deaths in the family by persuading the *daimôn* to leave the house (1568-76). The issue of the shared responsibility of a superhuman power is raised briefly again by Clytaemestra in her final dialogue with her son: 'Destiny [*Moira*], my child, is jointly responsible [*paraitia*] for these things' (*Cho.* 910) – to which Orestes merely replies that in that case Destiny is bringing about *her* death as well.

The role of Apollo in bringing about the death of Clytaemestra is of course peculiarly clear and undeniable; but it is just the sort of question that is apt to be disputed during a judicial proceeding. The precise placing of responsibility for a death, indeed, is a leading theme in the *Tetralogies* ascribed to Antiphon, sets of speeches for fictitious homicide cases composed probably in the third quarter of the fifth century. In the present case we might reasonably expect – and the analogy of the argument in *Agamemnon* points the same way – that Orestes will strive to minimize his own role and maximize that of Apollo, while his persecutors, the Erinyes, will maintain that Orestes was primarily if not solely responsible. What we actually find is the reverse. The first words the Erinyes say to Apollo are 'You are not *jointly* responsible [*metaitios*] for these things; you did it all and are *solely* responsible [*panaitios*]' (*Eum.* 199-200). Apollo at this stage neither accepts nor rejects this assessment of his responsibility, but we may well ask, if the Erinyes think Apollo is 'solely responsible', by what right they continue to harry Orestes. In a sense the answer is provided by Orestes himself, speaking later to Athena. He does not deny that he killed his mother, nor does he deny a share of responsibility for the act: 'Loxias,' he says, 'shares a joint responsibility [*koinêi* ... *metaitios*[4]] for these things' (465). In the trial itself this receives quasi-legal confirmation when the Erinyes ask Orestes by whose persuasion and by whose counsels (*bouleumata*) he committed the murder (593) and Orestes replies 'by the oracles of this god'; for in Athenian law the planner or counsellor (*ho bouleusas*) of a homicide was guilty in the same degree, and liable to the same penalty, as he who carried out the killing with his own hands. Orestes' defence is not that he was not responsible for the killing but that it was justified (468, 609-15); he and Apollo are both present at the trial, and both accept responsibility for Clytaemestra's death while arguing that it was justified by her murder of Agamemnon, that it was not the killing of a blood relation, etc.

The idea of shared divine and human responsibility is also made explicit, though less discursively, in connection with two other crucial events of the trilogy, the sack of Troy and the acquittal of Orestes. As regards the sack of Troy, Agamemnon's first words on his return have become notorious:

> First it is proper for me to address Argos
> and the gods who dwell there, who are jointly responsible [*metaitious*]
> with me
> for my return and for the justice I have meted out
> to the city of Priam ... (*Ag.* 810-13).

It was shown by Fraenkel 1950: 371-4 that there is nothing abnormal in a victor giving credit to the gods for his success and at the same time claiming credit for himself; and it fits in perfectly with the pattern we have already observed. At the same time one may suspect (and Fraenkel's parallels do nothing to dispel the suspicion) that Agamemnon is here being made to claim an excessive share of credit for himself. He speaks of 'the justice *I* meted out', completely eliding the gods (not to mention the rest of the army); and he claims a share of credit for his own safe return, when in the view of the Herald, who was on board the same ship, its survival was not due to Agamemnon nor even to the helmsman but to 'some god, no man' or to sheer good luck (661-70). But the significance of this passage certainly is not exhausted by its function of characterizing Agamemnon.

Lastly, the trial of Orestes. It is likely, as we have seen (§7.4), that if before Aeschylus a tradition already existed that Orestes was tried on the Areopagos, his judges had been the twelve gods. Aeschylus replaces these by a human jury, with Athena as president. Athena, however, does more than preside over the trial. Unlike the presiding magistrates in real Athenian courts, and (so far as we can tell) unlike the *basileus* in murder trials on the Areopagus, she herself votes among the jury (*Eum.* 735ff.). We need not now enter into the dispute over whether Athena's vote is or is not included among the votes which are counted and found to be equal, i.e. whether her vote breaks the tie or whether it makes the tie. It is sufficient for our purposes that she has a vote and declares how she will use it. Orestes is thus judged and acquitted not, strictly speaking, by a human jury, but by a jury consisting of ten or eleven humans and one divinity, sitting together and voting successively. The goddess is 'jointly responsible' for the outcome. And the idea is repeated, both verbally and visually, at the very end of the trilogy, when the Erinyes, now to become the *Semnai Theai*, wish joy to 'all those in the city, both gods and mortals' (1015-16) and are escorted to their new homes by a procession comprising male and female representatives of the Athenian people *and Athena* (1003-5, 1022).

All this does not mean, of course, that there are not some events which are caused purely by divine action without any human participation. Such events in fact occur in every surviving play of Aeschylus. It was a god who unseasonably froze the river Strymon and a god (the Sun) who melted the ice next morning, drowning a large part of the Persian army (*Pers.* 495-507). It was a god who caused the lots cast by the Seven against Thebes (*Seven* 55-6) to fall in such a way that Polyneices went to the seventh gate. It was a god, apparently Zeus, who gave the sons of Aegyptus safe and rapid passage to Argos (*Supp.* 1045-9). It was the gods who wrecked the Greek fleet on its voyage home from Troy (*Ag.* 648ff.), and it was a god who saved Agamemnon's ship amid the destruction. It was Apollo who threatened Orestes with the terrible wrath of his father's Erinyes if he failed to avenge Agamemnon's death, and while the verdict of the court that tried Orestes was a joint human and divine verdict, the decision to establish the court in the first place was Athena's alone. For Aeschylus, as for us, there are many events which are caused by no human action or decision; Aeschylus, and doubtless his public too, ascribed these events to divine action. But whenever a human being acts, he or she is responsible for that action and must bear the consequences of it, whether or not the action is also described as having been caused by a god. In the surviving plays of Aeschylus there are no exceptions to this principle.

What applies to action applies also in large measure to suffering. There are many innocent victims in Aeschylus' plays, but few if any who cannot with good reason blame a mortal as well as a god for their suffering. The countless Persian and allied dead of Xerxes' expedition were 'slain by Xerxes', as the chorus of *The Persians* say in so many words (923). The presumable death of Pelasgus in the Argive-Egyptian war is morally the responsibility of Danaus and his daughters, who deceived and blackmailed him into supporting their cause (and we saw in §6.2 that Danaus probably took advantage of Pelasgus' death to establish himself as *tyrannos*). There are all too many human culprits responsible for the deaths of the Trojan war: Paris, Helen, the Trojans who welcomed them and celebrated their adulterous 'wedding' (*Ag.* 705-8), Agamemnon who insisted on waging a great war for the sake of Helen and who afterwards destroyed the Trojans' sacred shrines (*Ag.* 527), his enthusiastic colleagues (*Ag.* 230) ... . Even Cassandra, who is killed by Apollo for reasons of sexual spite that would be meat and drink to the tabloid press of today, is also killed by Clytaemestra (for reasons of the same order, as it happens) and, not least, by the arrogant folly of Agamemnon in bringing her home to his wife's house. The only human being in the surviving Aeschylean corpus whose sufferings are due wholly and solely to the malice of a god is Io, in a play which is probably not by Aeschylus (Io also figures prominently in retrospective choral odes in *The Suppliants*, but the emphasis there is not on her sufferings but on the favour shown to her by Zeus, which the Danaids as her descendants claim should be shown to them also). It is true of Aeschylus, as in general it is true of the *Odyssey*, that, as Zeus is made to say at the outset of that poem,

> mortals put the blame on us
> gods, for they say evils come from us, but it is they, rather,
> who by their own recklessness win sorrow beyond what is given
> (*Odyssey* 1.32-4 tr. Lattimore).

11.4. Niobe and divine malevolence

The above discussion of human and divine responsibility in Aeschylus has been based on the surviving plays. This is inevitable. The lost tragedies, even those of which quite substantial fragments survive, are too incomplete to be used as evidence: we know *some* of the things that were done and said in these plays, but to draw firm conclusions from this evidence without knowing what *else* was done and said elsewhere in a play is a very unsafe procedure. For example, in a play which cannot be identified with certainty, Thetis bitterly reproaches Apollo. He, she says, was present at her wedding to Peleus, and sang a beautiful song extolling her blessedness and the glorious child (or children) she would bear, who would enjoy long life and freedom from sickness.

> And I supposed [she continues] that Phoebus' divine lips
> could not lie, instinct as they were with prophetic skill;
> But he, the same who sang that song, the same who attended that feast,
> the same who spoke those words, is the same who has slain
> my son (Aesch. fr. 350).

Plato (*Republic* 383a-c) found it intolerable that a poet should suggest that a god might be capable of lying. Aeschylus and his contemporaries would not have agreed. It was accepted that a god might deceive or mislead a mortal to tempt him into dangerous paths, as Zeus misleads Agamemnon in *Iliad* 2.1-36 (another passage that aroused Plato's ire) and Hector in *Iliad* 11.181-210. Apollo, however, being a god of prophecy, traditionally speaks only the truth (cf. *Cho.* 559, *Eum.* 615), and here he is accused not only of lying, but of lying to another divinity. But we do not know the context or the sequel. It is entirely possible, indeed probable, that before the end of this play, perhaps very shortly after this speech, Thetis herself made Apollo's words come true after all. Proclus' summary of the cyclic epic *Aethiopis* speaks thus of Achilles' funeral:

> Then they bury Antilochus [who had been killed by Memnon] and lay out the body of Achilles. Thetis comes with the Muses and her sisters [the Nereids] and laments her son; and after that Thetis snatches her son from the pyre and conveys him to the White Island

– a story which, with some variations, is frequently mentioned or alluded to by other archaic and classical poets,[5] who make it clear that Achilles was thenceforth immortal.

Another Aeschylean passage which offended Plato (*Republic* 380a) consists of a line and a half from *Niobe* which is implicitly presented as typical of the tragic approach to divinity:

> The deity plants a cause[6] in mortals
> when he wishes to ruin a house utterly (fr. 154a.15-16).

Taken at face value, this might seem to contradict everything we have been saying about divine action in Aeschylus. A god wishes to destroy a family, perhaps for no other reason than resentment of its prosperity (a popular belief rejected by the chorus of *Agamemnon*, 750-62). He therefore 'plants a cause' by inducing a member of the family to commit some grave wrongdoing which can then be punished – perhaps by afflicting the person with some form of mental blindness, perhaps by acting as an *agent provocateur* and tempting the person to do some wrong which (s)he would not have done otherwise. Such a god, surely, is not a parallel but an overriding cause, and it is doubtful whether the human wrongdoer is in any way to be blamed; the god indeed would be acting like the God of Martin Luther who 'by his own will ... makes us necessarily damnable'.[7]

Now we know what Niobe's offence was: she boasted that she had borne more children than the goddess Leto (*Iliad* 24.602-9). Her punishment for this was to have all her children slain by Leto's offspring, Apollo and Artemis. Since the boast was obviously a rash act, anyone who wants to exonerate Niobe must suppose that when she uttered it she was somehow not in control of her own mind and actions (as, for example, in Euripides' *Bacchae* Agaue is not in control of her mind when she kills her son Pentheus, and is not blamed or punished by her other kinsfolk for that action[8]). As it happens, we now possess a papyrus fragment of some twenty lines, including the two quoted by Plato, and it points in a quite different direction. The speaker appears to have continued:

> But, since one is mortal, one must cherish
> the [prosperity that comes from the gods] and not be rash in speech.
> [But those who] enjoy great good fortune never suppose
> that they will [come to grief] and lose the [prosperity] they possess.
> For [this woman,] elated by [her(?)] surpassing beauty ...

It now becomes evident that what we have here is a perfectly normal instance of the working of the Maradona Principle. The ruin of Niobe, which in the play she sits mourning, mute and motionless, is the work of a god who 'wishes to ruin [her] house utterly', but it is also the work of Niobe herself. She ought to have known better than to boast. But she was 'elated' or 'carried away' (*exartheisa*) by pride in (probably) her great beauty and her numerous children, and spoke rash words that were bound to provoke divine anger.

What then was the 'cause' which the deity planted in Niobe? The logic of the passage provides an answer. The deity plants a cause when he wants to ruin a family, *but* one must remember that prosperity is precarious and refrain from rash boasting. The only way to make a meaningful connection between these two statements is to suppose that in this case the 'cause' and the 'prosperity' are one and the same. A god gave Niobe a large family of beautiful children and thus *tempted* her into rash boasting, to her ruin. And while we may sympathize with a victim of temptation, we should also remember that temptation visits all of us constantly and that most of us, most of the time, do not succumb to it. The speaker of the passage, though evidently a person close to Niobe (most probably it is Niobe's nurse: see Sommerstein 2008: 163), clearly considers Niobe to have acted wrongly, however disproportionate the gods' retaliation has been.

It is more than possible, too, that the divine animus against Niobe and her family was neither arbitrary nor unmotivated. It is known that Niobe's father Tantalus was a character in the play (frr. 158, 159), and Tantalus was one of the most notorious of mythical offenders against the gods – his offences, too, are often thought of as arising from the same cause as Niobe's, the overconfidence induced by great prosperity. Thus Niobe, in the words of Garvie 1986: xxviii, has inherited 'not only guilt but a propensity to incur fresh guilt'. At some point in *Niobe* Tantalus reflects (probably) on his own errors and their consequences as well as his daughter's:

> My soul, which once was up above in heaven,
> has fallen to earth, and says this to me:
> 'Learn not to honour too much the things of mortal life' (fr. 159).

Thus Plato has once again misled us. The *Niobe* passage he quotes is not evidence that Aeschylean gods could make humans the puppets of their will, cause them to commit crimes and afterwards punish them for these same crimes. It is evidence only that Aeschylus saw those who enjoy great good fortune as being at great risk of succumbing to the temptation to think of themselves as no longer bound by the limitations and uncertainties of mortal existence, a principle most notably exemplified, in his surviving plays, by Xerxes, Paris (*Ag.* 369-402), and Agamemnon.

11.5. The ultimate realities behind the universe[9]

No simple formula can account for the ways in which Aeschylus portrays his gods; the same indeed applies to most other archaic and classical Greek poets. Sometimes, in the spirit of many parts of the *Iliad*, they are little but powerful, immortal human beings. Such is the Apollo who wooed Cassandra ('he was a wrestler,' she recalls [*Ag.* 1206], 'breathing delight on me') and who later takes revenge on her; the Hera who persecuted Io (*Supp.* 164-5, 291-311, 562-4, 586-7) and the Zeus who had seduced her but could not conceal the fact from Hera (*Supp.* 295-6); the Artemis who takes offence at the killing by Zeus' eagles of her protégés, young wild creatures, and, presumably because she is unable to strike back at Zeus, takes out her resentment on *his* protégés, the kings of Argos. But sometimes they are much more than that. The Zeus of the 'Hymn' in *Agamemnon* ('whoever he is', *Ag.* 160) is spoken of as the only means whereby one can 'cast off the vain burden of anxiety' (*Ag.* 165-7). The chorus of *The Suppliant Maidens* sing of Zeus in terms reminiscent of Xenophanes, a philosopher-poet of the previous generation:

He casts mortals down
from lofty hopes into utter destruction,
yet arms no force to do so –
everything gods do is done without toil:
he sits, and somehow he puts his thought into action
automatically, right from his holy seat (*Supp.* 96-103)

– or, as they put it later, 'he can effect a deed as rapidly as a word' (598-9). Apollo in *Eumenides* speaks similarly of Zeus: with the sole exception of raising the dead,

he can turn and arrange anything else,
this way and that, without effort, by his mere desire (*Eum.* 650-1).

This is no traditional personal god; he seems almost Aristotelian, and in another passage, to which I have referred before (§7.8), from the lost play *The Daughters of the Sun*, he seems to have absorbed all the other gods and their provinces into himself:

Zeus is the Firmament, Zeus is Earth and Heaven,
Zeus is the All and all that is beyond (fr. 70)

– a passage quoted with warm approval by the Christian writers Clement of Alexandria and Eusebius.[10]

It seems certain that Aeschylus was acquainted with the thinking and the writings of Xenophanes, who had written in hexameter verse of

one god, greatest among gods and men,
in no way similar to mortals either in body or in thought ...
[who] always remains in the same place, moving not at all,
nor is it fitting for him to go to different places at different times,
but without toil he shakes all things by the thought of his mind.
(Xenophanes fr. 23+26+25 Diels-Kranz, trans. Kirk *et al.* 1983)

and who also said (fr. 27) that all things (i.e. all living things) come from earth and end in earth, an idea echoed in *Choephoroi* 127-8. Xenophanes was born about 570 BC, spent much of his life in Sicily, and was still alive in 479/8; Aeschylus could well have become acquainted with his work on his own first visit to Sicily.

There is no way to make the Aeschylean passages quoted above consistent with the anthropomorphism found elsewhere in the corpus (of which Xenophanes would have vehemently disapproved), and we should not try. They represent one strand in Aeschylus' ways of thinking about divinity and the universe. They are not the whole of his thought on these things, but they are an important part of it.

To Aeschylus in this mood, the gods were not so much a group of superhuman persons as a device for talking about the power that causes the universe to be the way it is. Most often, when an individual name was given to this godhead, it was that of Zeus, the traditional supreme god – though it is a mistake to speak of Aeschylean 'monotheism', since the practice of speaking of divine power as a vague singular entity, which might be called *daimôn* or *theos* or *Zeus*, was at least as old as Homer and carried no dogmatic implications. Sometimes, in appropriate contexts, aspects of this ultimate reality might be called by other names. The Aphrodite who intervenes in *The Danaids*, and whose speech includes fr. 44 (see §6.2), is obviously not, or not primarily, the personal goddess who seduced Ares or Anchises or Adonis, who won the prize of beauty in the Judgement of Paris, whom Hera deceived during a battle before Troy, and so on: she is the universal power of sexuality, who is, as she says herself, the cause[11] of all plant life (and surely of animal and human life too – cf. *Supp.* 998-1005 – though these do not figure explicitly in the part of her speech that survives), the power associated with Zeus and Hera, the divine patrons of marriage, in *Supp.* 1034-5 and *Eum.* 213-16.

A universal reality of a darker kind is represented by the Erinyes, who during most of the *Oresteia* can almost be seen as the embodiments of Zeus' law that 'he who has done shall suffer' as they are, in mythical language, his agents for enforcing it. At the same time they are also the embodiments of wrathful vengeance, since in *Agamemnon* and *Choephoroi* that is the method by which this law is in fact enforced, and it is unquestionably (at least to an ancient Greek) a universal reality. In these two plays the Erinyes' power always acts through a series of wrathful human avengers – Atreus, the Greeks attacking Troy, Clytaemestra, Aegisthus, Orestes. After Clytaemestra's death there are no human avengers left to act, and the Erinyes must act, if at all, in their own persons – and it is at this stage that instead of merely being spoken about they begin to be seen, first by Orestes, then by the Pythia, and finally by everyone. In the final settlement the wrathful human avenger is abolished, or rather transformed into the prosecutor in a judicial proceeding, and the universal principle of requital represented by the Erinyes comes into play when, for whatever reason, the institutions of the *polis* fail to secure justice. One way or another, the universe will then get its own back, and the Erinyes are the personification of that principle. At the same time they are also personal divinities and therefore have personalities and psychologies of their own, being angered, for instance, when the younger gods fail to show respect for their age.

The Aeschylean play, of those we know, most dominated by these relatively impersonal divinities is *The Persians*. This is partly because the play, being set in the recent past, is not required to accommodate the well-established activities of this or that god in this or that myth. There would, however, have been no difficulty, had Aeschylus so wished, in portraying in the account of Salamis, or in the prophecy of Plataea, the intervention of personal deities angered by the Persian destruction of their sanctuaries; this Aeschylus has not done. Another and more important reason behind the treatment of the gods in this play is probably the dramatist's desire to have his audience think of the Persian catastrophe in a universalistic rather than a nationalistic mode: the catastrophe is to be seen as having been caused by gods, but not specifically by *Greek* gods.

Thus the overthrow of the Persians is ascribed variously to 'the gods' (283, 294, 347, 362, 373, 741, 749, 1005), to 'a god' (*theos* or *daimôn*: 93, 158, 345, 354, 454, 472, 495, 514, 515, 724-5, 742, 911, 921, 942), and to a supreme god whom the Persians are assumed to worship and who can reasonably be treated as equivalent to Zeus (532-6, 740, 827). Other individual gods – apart from those like the Earth and the Sun, which can be assumed to be the same for all nations, or semi-abstract powers like Moira and Ate – are mentioned only occasionally. Athena appears once as patron of Athens (347), and a sacred hearth of Apollo figures in an account of an omen (206); the minor god Pan provides local colour in the description of the island of Psyttaleia (449), much as the hero Ajax does for Salamis (307, 368, 596); Hermes and 'the king of those below' are asked to send up the ghost of Darius (629); and the power of the Sea, which Xerxes offended by 'yoking' the Hellespont, is given the name of Poseidon (750). None of these deities, except Poseidon, is directly associated with the Persian defeat. The total number of references in the play to the major Olympians, other than Zeus, is four: even the familiar use of 'Ares' as a metonym for 'war' is avoided in this play.[12] In *The Persians* divinity is essentially a unified and harmonious force imposing an intelligible cosmic order. Yet the audience who saw *The Persians* had just seen *Phineus* with its account of the monstrous (and probably god-sent[13]) Harpies who snatched the food from Phineus' table and were put to flight by the sons of the (divine) North Wind; and they were presently to see *Prometheus the Fire-bearer* in which the god Prometheus has just stolen fire from the god Hephaestus. And one may safely assume that Aeschylus did not expect them to leave the theatre suffering from mental indigestion after so varied a feast.

Aeschylus, and presumably his audience, unhampered by credal or philosophical dogmas, were able with ease to think of divinity in different terms in different contexts, and assumptions which a strict logician would have to regard as contradictory could happily coexist in the same play or even in the same choral song, where, for example, the 'Hymn to Zeus' is embedded within the account of Artemis demanding the sacrifice of Iphigeneia and thereby threatening to thwart Zeus's plan for the punishment of Paris, and itself contains mention of Zeus's own violent overthrow of a father who in turn had overthrown his. Yet in the end, so far as we can tell, the impression given is of a coherent and rational world-order. Injustice, impiety, *hybris* 'will out' and will sooner or later be punished, though often not before they have involved the innocent as well as the guilty in suffering; but 'if a house keeps on the straight path of justice, the fate of its children is ever fair' (*Ag.* 761-2, cf. *Eum.* 911-12, 992-5).

This concept of divine justice (*dikê*) is beautifully expressed in a scene, preserved for us on a papyrus fragment (fr. 281a), of a play that is certainly by Aeschylus (one line of the fragment is quoted elsewhere as his) but which has never been convincingly identified. A goddess is speaking; she says that Zeus, when he came to the Olympian throne, began to honour her greatly, and now sends her 'to anyone towards whom he is friendly', including the people of the land in which the play is set. Her interlocutor (probably the chorus-leader) asks her who she is, and she identifies herself as Dike[14] (line 15). She says that she prolongs the life of the righteous (line 17); what she does to the wicked (line 19) can no longer be read, but since the chorus ask her (line 20) whether she does it by 'charms' or by force, it is likely that she said she induced the wicked to change their ways. At any rate, she writes down their transgressions on 'the tablet of Zeus', which is opened and read on 'the day [that brings] them their ordained fate', presumably the day of their death (lines 21-3). She then seems to promise the chorus that their community will prosper if they receive her with good will (line 25); and to prove her power, she tells a tale (lines 30-41) of how she brought up a savage son of Zeus and Hera (who must be Ares, the god of war); as a child he practised shameless, indiscriminate, sadistic violence (lines 33-7), but evidently (though the remains of the papyrus now become very scanty, and soon give out entirely) she must have tamed him and persuaded him to attack only those who did not respect justice, leaving others in peace.[15]

A friendly reviewer of an earlier work of mine (Garvie 1991: 219) asked whether Aeschylus really believed that 'he who keeps his mental and moral balance, and respects justice, will find that his prosperity is secure' (Sommerstein 1989a: 178, paraphrasing *Ag.* 750-82 and *Eum.* 535-7). Perhaps not. Perhaps it would have been better to say that *only* he who respects justice will find that his prosperity is secure – for this is where the emphasis is placed, by Aeschylus as by Solon (cf. e.g. Solon frr. 4 and 13 West). And even then we must remember (as Niobe did not) that *all* human well-being is by its very nature temporary (though on the other hand the *oikos*, unlike the individual, can in principle prosper indefinitely). But we do not seem to be left at the end of an Aeschylean trilogy, as we often are at the end of a Euripidean and sometimes of a Sophoclean play, with a catastrophe beyond morally tolerable explanation. There are many failings in the characters created by Aeschylus, including some of the divine characters; there are many appalling horrors in the events he has enacted and narrated; but ultimately there is no tragic flaw in his universe.

11.6. Evolutionary theology

One feature of the world of the gods as created by Aeschylus is, so far as we know, unique to him and his immediate 'school'. This is the idea, which we have seen in the *Oresteia* and the Prometheus plays, that over the course of world 'history' the gods have matured in wisdom. Both the

Oresteia and the plays of the Prometheus-sequence involve a contrast between older and younger gods, and the younger gods behave, in the early stages, with all the rashness, arrogance and indeed *hybris* thought to be characteristic of young males.[16] Later in the action the gods come to behave with rather less energy and much greater wisdom. In both sets of plays the early activities of the young gods threaten to cause large-scale disaster – in the *Oresteia* to Argos and its royal house, in the Prometheus plays at one stage to the whole human race, at another to Zeus himself and hence to the future stability of the entire universe. In both, in the end, these same young gods establish a stable cosmic (and, in the *Oresteia* and perhaps in *Prometheus Unbound* also, a social) order, as well as a religious order in which the older gods (such as the Erinyes-Semnai, Prometheus, and perhaps also Cronus and Gaia) receive worship and honour alongside themselves; this cosmic-social-religious order is identical to that which prevails in Athens in Aeschylus' own day.

This pattern in late Aeschylean and sub-Aeschylean drama has already been examined in §§7.9 and 8.4 above. In this section I wish to take up two other matters related to it: the connection between progress in the divine and the human worlds, and the question whence Aeschylus may have derived this notion of a progressive divinity.

In the *Oresteia* the watchword of progress is 'by suffering, learning' (*Ag.* 176), and we saw in §7.9 that this is to be applied to mortals and gods alike (see further Sommerstein 1993). Human society too evolves, in the trilogy, from youthful folly to matured wisdom. In *Agamemnon* we meet the spoilt irresponsibility of Paris (who is compared to 'a boy chasing a bird on the wing', 394) and of the Trojans who made his crime their own, and the varying forms of *hybris* displayed by Thyestes, Atreus, Agamemnon, Clytaemestra and Aegisthus. Cassandra, to be sure, is endowed with wisdom by her prophetic insight, and the Elders by their age and experience, but both are powerless to influence events: Cassandra bears Apollo's curse of never being believed, and the Elders are as helpless to prevent Agamemnon's murder or bring its perpetrators to book as they had been, ten years before, to dissuade him from embarking on an expedition which they believed to be crazy. There are limits, too, even to their understanding: they interpret past events with assurance, but have no success at all in foreseeing the future until it is too late. Only at the very end of *Agamemnon* do they make an accurate prediction (1646-8, 1667-9).

In *Choephoroi* signs of improvement are evident on the human level well before they become so on the divine. We meet two new characters, a brother and sister, both young adults, both devoid of anything resembling *hybris*, both resolved to be party to an appalling deed not from any guilty motive but because the situation, and a god's command, leave them with no alternative. Even then, too, Orestes requires a long preparatory build-up, through the *kommos* and its aftermath, to be ready to do the deed, and hesitates in the final confrontation, while Electra, as we have seen, would rather have her father avenged by a third party (*Cho.* 119ff., 143; likewise the chorus in 160ff.) and/or have his murderers judged rather than killed summarily (120, cf. 122). There is no sign that any of the gods are moving in the same direction until we hear of Apollo's promise of protection less than fifty lines from the end of the play (1029-33), and that passage comes in the middle of a scene in which Orestes first feels himself going mad and then is driven away in flight by the Erinyes. Since Apollo is Zeus's son, and the Erinyes in *Agamemnon* were Zeus's agents, it is for the present entirely unclear where the supreme god stands.

In *Eumenides* the position of Zeus is soon clarified, but it also soon becomes clear that his representative Apollo, though admirably solid in defence of Orestes, will never be able to restore stability in the divine world, since he can neither reconcile nor destroy the Erinyes. Athena, on the other hand, has both the power to destroy (for she has access to Zeus's thunderbolt, *Eum.* 826-8 – though now, in contrast with *Ag.* 469-70, it is not in active use but locked up as a last resort) and the wisdom to reconcile, which she likewise ascribes to Zeus (850, 974) and uses successfully twice over. The human characters of *Eumenides* are the Pythia, Orestes and the Athenians (as represented by the Areopagite judges). The Pythia, like that other Apolline prophetess Cassandra, has vision but no power – though unlike Cassandra she has Apollo as a friend instead of an enemy. Orestes in his first scene says very little (*Eum.* 85-7), but in his second, though beset by the bestial Erinyes, he delivers an admirably constructed speech (276-98) which bears out his claim, made in its first line, to have been taught by adversity, and which begins to present him as potentially a holder of great power through his promise to make an eternal alliance between Argos and Athens. In the end, restored to Argos by the court's verdict, he speaks both as its present king and as a future cult-hero capable of controlling the actions of Argives through all future generations (762-74).

But the supreme example of human wisdom and power in the *Oresteia* is constituted by the judges of the Areopagus – in effect, the Athenian people. They judge what is in effect a dispute between gods; they see through the distortions and sophistries, the promises and threats, of the contending parties, and give, each for himself, a silent decision that contrasts notably with the voluble debate and collective indecision of the Argive elders in *Ag.* 1348-71 (cf. Bowie 2009: 229n.81); Athena follows them to the voting-urns, and the vote of each of them counts for the same as hers. When their votes are counted and the outcome declared, their verdict binds both Apollo and the Erinyes: the Erinyes may fulminate against Athens, but it never occurs to us to suppose that they might ignore the verdict and resume their pursuit of Orestes. These men are well worthy to receive from Athena the responsibility for safeguarding her city for the future, to be hailed by the Erinyes as 'wise in due season' (*Eum.* 1000), and to be 'revered' (1002) by Zeus himself. At the end of the trilogy the gods, who always had power, have learned wisdom; mortals, who at the outset had either had power (or the illusion of power) without wisdom or else (limited) wisdom without power, have been able to combine the two in an Athens unmatched in the world for virtue, for honour and for victory (*Eum.* 700-3, 776-7, 851-4, 869, 910-15, 917-20, 990-5, 1000, 1012, 1031).

In the Prometheus plays it is harder to see this pattern of parallel advance in the divine and human worlds, because the surviving fragments of the second play make relatively little reference to human civilization. We can, however, observe the contrast between the only two human characters who appear in the two plays – Io in the first play, who is a pure victim, not even fully human in form, her mind deranged (*Prom.* 581, 673) and her movements enslaved to the will of a mere insect, and Heracles in the second, the embodiment of heroic power, prepared to kill the eagle sent by his own divine father. Within *Prometheus Bound* the human race as a whole is first seen as threatened with total destruction (231-6), then as raised from helplessness (442-57) by Prometheus' gifts of knowledge and skill; and we have seen that *Prometheus Unbound* may have had something to say about man's acquisition of the moral and social virtues – 'restraint and justice' in the words ascribed to Protagoras – at the same time as the gods too, and Zeus in particular, seem to be acquiring these same virtues.

The suggestion that the *Oresteia* and the Prometheus plays posit a 'progressive' notion of divinity has often been scouted because it would represent something unique in Greek thought, and it is worth while to consider what precursors and precedents Aeschylus may have had for this idea.

Perhaps the clearest specific piece of evidence for a 'progressive' divinity in these plays is the unilateral release by Zeus of the Titans, of which we learn at the beginning of *Prometheus Unbound*. We have seen (§8.4) that this is mentioned by Pindar in his fourth Pythian ode, performed in 462, as a well-known mythical 'fact', and that both he and the *Prometheus* poet probably derived the idea from their text of Hesiod's *Works and Days*. The release of Prometheus himself, too, would have rested, for a fifth-century reader, on the authority of Hesiod (*Theogony* 521-34), so that Aeschylus would have found in *each* of the two major Hesiodic poems a story of Zeus first imprisoning an enemy and then allowing him to be freed.[17]

The more general pattern of development, from more violent to gentler methods of rule, is implicit in more than one myth of primeval times, some included in the Hesiodic poems, some not: for example in the legend of the Flood (itself connected with Prometheus who is said to have been the father of Deucalion, the Greek Noah, and to have advised him on the building of his ark[18]) and, most importantly, the framework story of the *Theogony* on the successive generations of the gods, each ruler violently overthrown by his successor, until Zeus conquers his last opponents and assigns to the gods their respective spheres of rule 'when the blessed gods had completed their labours' (881). More significantly still, it is also implicit in Homer, especially in the *Iliad*. Repeatedly in that poem, in scenes among the gods, there are references to episodes of horrific violence perpetrated by Zeus. We find Zeus seizing Hephaestus by the foot and hurling him down from heaven (1.590-4); threatening to whip disobedient gods, or cast them down to Tartarus, or pull up earth and sea and gods and all and hang them from a spur of Olympus (8.7-27); threatening to strike Hera and Athene with a thunderbolt (8.403-5); and picking up other gods and throwing them around his palace (14.257) or from heaven to earth (15.23-4) while hanging Hera in chains from the sky with two anvils tied to her feet (15.18-22). Other gods fear he may do the same again, making no distinction between guilty and innocent (15.135-7, cf. 1.580-1). But it is not quite fair to say with Kirk 1990: 296 that 'flinging disobedient deities out of Ol[y]mpos is a favourite punishment by Zeus'. In the course of the *Iliad* he never once actually uses violence against another god (though he does allow them to fight each other, always without any decisive effect). Zeus' violence against gods either belongs to the *past*, or else it belongs to the world of *unfulfilled possibilities*, of things threatened or feared. The impression given is that once upon a time Zeus ruled by the actual use of brutal force, but now the mere fear of it is sufficient for him to maintain his supremacy – which is exactly parallel to the development we have observed in the *Oresteia*. It is true that Zeus' *language* is still often brutal, and the other gods are anxious not to cross him; but even this changes during the course of the *Iliad* itself. After book 15 there are no further references to violence by Zeus against gods, whether past or hypothetical. Thereafter, indeed, far from showing brutality to gods, Zeus is most often found pitying mere mortals (16.433ff., 17.201ff., 19.340ff., 22.168ff., etc.). In the Battle of the Gods in books 20 and 21 Zeus sits and watches, and at the end of it he does not even follow up the complaint of his beloved daughter Artemis against his not very beloved wife Hera (21.505-13). And in our last three meetings with Zeus in the *Iliad*, he first gives a tactful decision which satisfies Apollo without angering Hera (24.65-76), then orders Achilles to surrender Hector's body, indicating that he is angry but making no specific threats (24.104-19), and lastly gives Iris a message for Priam ending with seven lines of much-needed reassurance (24.152-8): a transformed Zeus to match the transformed Achilles of this last episode, who is aware of the anger within him that has had such terrible consequences before now and takes special precautions to prevent it from bursting out again (e.g. 24.581-6). In the Prometheus plays the 'old' and the 'new' Zeus are separated by about thirteen generations. In the *Oresteia* they are separated by seven years (if we follow the chronology of the *Odyssey*). In the *Iliad* the brutal Zeus of books 1-15 and the almost kindly Zeus of the rest of the poem are separated by no more than one or two *hours*!

I am not trying to father a 'progressive' theology on Homer. Within the *Iliad* there is no essential change in the pattern of Zeus' actions (as distinct from his words); it is just that the poet chooses to present him under a different aspect, probably mainly in order to guide the emotions of his listeners in the latter part of the poem where tragic pathos is so much more important than violent heroic action. Nevertheless, from the point of view of a reader a couple of centuries later, familiar with Hesiod and probably with other cosmogonies both mystic and philosophical, the presentation of Zeus in the *Iliad* could well be interpretable in terms of a development from violence and chaos towards order and harmony and/or of a maturing process comparable to that which is observable in Achilles. Aeschylus' evolutionary theology may well have been Homeric in inspiration. But like its Homeric precursor, it could only be effective on a broad canvas. It may be for that reason, rather than for any reason to do with his religious beliefs, that Sophocles, who in his own way owed just as much to Homer but who seems not to have favoured the trilogy form, made no use of evolutionary theology. A generation later, no highly-educated Athenian could any longer have taken such an idea seriously: by then, either the universe was moral (in which case the gods were perfectly good and always had been) or it was amoral (in which case the gods were either amoral also, as usually in Euripides, or else did not exist). The gods of the *Oresteia* and the Prometheus plays could not have been created later than the 430s, and probably could not have been created earlier than the 470s or so. No wonder we do not find anything truly comparable before them or after them.

Notes

1. *Odyssey* 24.351; Menander, *Dyskolos* 639.
2. In the first edition of this book I added 'or their ancestors'. I now think this was wrong. Föllinger 2003 (esp. 319-20) argues persuasively that the Aeschylean gods never punish the innocent arbitrarily for the sins of their ancestors; rather, the actions of past generations shape the circumstances under which their descendants take decisions, decisions for which they nevertheless have a responsibility of their own. This does not exclude the possibility that the crime or error of one person may lead by a fairly short chain of causation to the suffering of innocent members of his/her family (as in the case of Niobe, to be considered in §11.4); it does exclude the possibility of the gods storing up a grudge and taking it out on an innocent descendant long afterwards.
3. Alternatively (Buxton 2007: 182): 'The omnipresence of divine influence on human action in tragedy does not negate the importance of human choice.'
4. *metaitios* is an emendation (the manuscripts have *epaitios*, which appears again two lines later); but in any case *koinêi* is enough to show that joint, not sole, responsibility is being ascribed to Apollo.
5. Pindar, *Nemean* 4.49-50 has Achilles living on the White Island ('a bright island in the Euxine sea'; so too Euripides, *Andromache* 1260-2); elsewhere (*Olympian* 2.79-80) he places him in the Isles of the Blest. Ibycus (*GL* 291) and Simonides (*GL* 558) had spoken of his being taken to the Elysian fields.
6. Or 'guilt' or 'responsibility' (*aitia*).
7. Martin Luther, *De servo arbitrio*, tr. Watson & Drewery 1969: 138.
8. Together with her sisters, she had been driven mad by Dionysus as punish-

ment for denying his divinity – and their father Cadmus *does* blame them for that, and rightly (*Bacchae* 1297, 1302).

9. In the first edition of this book I wrongly attributed this phrase to Robinson (1963), who in fact never used it.

10. Clement of Alexandria, *Stromateis* 5.14.114.4; whence Eusebius, *Preparation for the Gospel* 13.13.41.

11. Or rather the *joint* cause (*par-aitios*): cf. §11.3.

12. For comparison, the number of explicit references to major Olympians other than Zeus is 33 in the authentic part of *Seven*, 23 in *The Suppliant Maidens* (despite the dominance of Zeus in the thoughts of the chorus), 10 in *Agamemnon* 1-1071, and 15 in *Choephoroi*.

13. We do not know what the reason was, in Aeschylus' account, for the Harpies' persecution of Phineus, but when later sources do give a reason they say the Harpies were sent by Zeus or the Sun-god to punish Phineus for some offence (Asclepiades fr. 31 Jacoby; Apollonius Rhodius, *Argonautica* 2.178-93).

14. Hence the play – of which we have at least one more small fragment (fr. 281b) and very possibly a third, more substantial one (fr. 451n) – is often referred to as 'the Dike Play'.

15. This *may* have prompted the eulogy of peace which we find in fr. 451n.

16. It is noteworthy that the young gods who are presented as behaving in this way are always in fact male – Zeus, Kratos and Hermes in *Prometheus Bound*, Zeus and Apollo in the *Oresteia* – while the young goddess Athena in *Eumenides* has a far more equable temperament and shows proper respect for her elders; it is no accident that Athena is never mentioned in the first two plays of the *Oresteia*, even in connection with the capture of Troy and the subsequent storm, both of which were traditionally in large measure her work.

17. This interpretation of Hesiod may well in fact have been wrong. In the passage cited Heracles is said to have freed Prometheus from his 'distress' (*Thg.* 528) but is *not* explicitly said to have freed him from his bonds, and later in the *Theogony* (616) we are told that Prometheus is still 'restrained by great bonds'. But anyone who overlooked the later passage would be likely to understand the earlier one to mean that Prometheus was set at liberty, particularly since another poem ascribed to Hesiod, the *Catalogue of Women* (Hesiod fr. 2 Merkelbach-West = 3 Most), made him the father of a son (Deucalion, see above) whose mother was Pandora, the woman whom Zeus created at the same time as he originally imprisoned Prometheus.

18. The first consecutive account is in [Apollodorus], *Library* 1.7.2; but the comedy *Promatheus or Pyrrha*, by Aeschylus' Sicilian contemporary Epicharmus (frr. 113-20), presupposes the story.

12

Aeschylean Drama and the Political Moment

It has emerged sufficiently in the course of this book that Aeschylean tragedy is deeply concerned with issues regarding the collective life of human communities, issues that are in the broad Greek sense 'political' because they concern human beings in their capacity of citizens (*politai*). With political matters in the narrower modern sense tragedy was in theory not supposed to concern itself. From the time when Phrynichus' *Capture of Miletus* was banned and its author fined in 493, no tragedy again took its theme directly from a matter of current political controversy; and Sophocles and Euripides, while they almost certainly do from time to time make allusions to living issues of contemporary politics, do so in a subtle, indirect, generalized manner, so that modern interpreters are often in doubt whether any allusion is intended at all. In Aeschylus' time this convention was less firmly established, particularly since, as we shall see, politicians themselves were capable of using tragedy as an instrument of their competitive struggles. The last play of the *Oresteia*, though still set like the preceding plays in the heroic age, contrives to make explicit reference to highly specific current issues of domestic and foreign politics; and *The Persians* actually enters the arena in support of identifiable individuals in political life. It has been argued (indeed, I argued in the first edition of this book) that *The Suppliant Maidens* does so too; but its date, and the chronology of the 460s, are too uncertain for such an argument to be safely based on them. But even the 472 and 458 productions, taken together, imply a dramatist who as a person is definitely associated with a particular faction or tendency in Athenian politics, though at the same time well capable of subordinating factional interest to the broader unity and well-being of the *polis*. And while *The Suppliant Maidens* cannot be shown to address specific topical issues or personalities, it has an intense interest in the workings and pitfalls of democratic government that merits close attention. I will therefore examine all three dramas – in reverse chronological order, since the *Oresteia* is much the richest in relevant material.

12.1. *Eumenides* and 459/8[1]

Few times in Athenian history can have been so full of hopes and dangers, both at home and abroad, as the three or four years that followed the political and diplomatic revolution of 462/1. Until then, ever since the ostracism of Themistocles a decade or so before (see §12.3), Athenian politics had been dominated by Cimon, whose foreign policy had been firmly based on friendship with Sparta and continuation of the war against Persia. In 462 he had persuaded the Assembly to send a large force of hoplites, which he himself commanded, to help Sparta suppress a Helot revolt in Messenia. But before long the Spartans, 'fearful,' says Thucydides (1.102.3), 'of the audacity and the revolutionary temper of the Athenians ... lest they might be persuaded to support the rebellion', sent the Athenian force away. This was perceived by the Athenians as a mark of disgrace, since they were the only allied contingent to be thus dismissed, and in this way the Spartans succeeded at a stroke in ruining the political career of the best friend they ever had at Athens. The Athenian Assembly promptly withdrew from the alliance with Sparta which had remained in being, despite various strains, ever since the Persian invasion of Greece nearly twenty years before, and made new alliances with Sparta's enemy, Argos, and also with Thessaly. At the first opportunity, too, Cimon himself was banished for ten years by ostracism. At some time during the same year (perhaps earlier, when Cimon and his troops were still abroad) Cimon's leading political rival, Ephialtes, proposed and carried a decree which effected a major constitutional change.

The Council of the Areopagus was composed of all those who had held one of the nine archonships, magistracies which since 487/6 had been filled by lot but whose holders were still drawn exclusively from the two highest property classes. It exercised various powers, of which the most important politically seem to have been the examination of the official conduct of outgoing magistrates (called *euthynai*) and the trial of serious crimes against the state brought before it by the procedure called *eisangelia*. What happened in the late 460s is most easily intelligible if Cimon, relying on the support of the class from which the Areopagus council was drawn, had been using these procedures to drive opponents out of public life, as Themistocles in the 480s had used ostracism and as Cleon in the 420s was to use the popular courts.[2]

Already before 462 Ephialtes had begun to mount a campaign against the members of the council, prosecuting several of them for bribery (cf. *Eum.* 704). Now he successfully proposed to deprive it of most of its powers – which, he asserted, it had acquired recently and illegitimately – and to leave it only with what were allegedly its original functions. Of these the only one of consequence was the trial of charges of homicide[3] and malicious wounding. Henceforth Athens was a democracy in the most absolute sense, unlimited legislative power being vested in the Assembly of all citizen men, unappealable judicial power in the popular courts (*dikastêria*) whose jurors were chosen by lot from among all citizen men over thirty who wished to serve.

Shortly after this, Ephialtes died one night, suddenly and unexpectedly, in circumstances which convinced most people that he had been murdered. According to the Aristotelian *Constitution of Athens* (25.4) the murderer was a foreigner, Aristodicus of Tanagra; he may indeed have been convicted of the crime (or else fled the country to avoid trial), but many seem to have thought that he was really acting on behalf of others, for Antiphon, who was alive at the time, says (*On the Murder of Herodes* 68) that the *murderers* of Ephialtes were never discovered. Popular suspicion (whether or not justified) will certainly have fallen on those who had opposed Ephialtes' reforms. In 459/8 virtually all democrats must have believed implicitly that their leader had been murdered at the instigation of diehard enemies of his and their cause – and that these men were still walking free in the city.

But they made no attempt to take the law into their own hands. Instead, under the leadership now of Pericles, they concentrated on continuing the process of democratizing the political institutions of Athens from top to bottom. The sovereign control of the people in assembly over policy *decisions* was already established; it remained, however, to secure, so far as possible, popular control over the preliminary *formulation* of policy, for which the Council of Five Hundred (consisting of representatives of the 139 demes, chosen by lot) was largely responsible, and also over its subsequent *execution* by the Council and the various boards of magistrates. The method adopted was to institute the payment of salaries out of public funds to councillors and magistrates, and of a daily attendance fee to the jurors of the *dikastêria*. Salaries would to some extent encourage relatively poor men to put themselves forward for the lotteries whereby councillors and magistrates were chosen; the payment of jurors would ensure that magistrates accused of corruption or maladministration would be tried by a tribunal in which supporters of the new order predominated. The process of democratization affected the Areopagus council itself by 457, when the property qualification for the nine archons was substantially lowered, perhaps increasing as much as tenfold the numbers eligible for these positions and hence for membership of the Areopagus council.

During the same few years Athens began to pursue a foreign policy of remarkable audacity. Having already, by her alliance with Argos, ranged herself among the enemies of Sparta, she proceeded to make a further alliance with Megara, which had just seceded from the league headed by Sparta and was actually at war with Corinth, the second most powerful member of that league. About the same time she gave offence both to Sparta and to Corinth by capturing Naupactus at the neck of the Corinthian Gulf and settling there the survivors of the Messenian rebels.

Athens was thus committed by 459 to a war against Corinth which was almost bound to become, if indeed it had not become already, a war against Sparta and her whole alliance; and in this war it was Athens that first took the offensive both by land and by sea. At the same time Athens was also at war with Aegina, and at one moment, when her main army was engaged in the siege of Aegina town, she had to send a scratch force of under- and over-age soldiers to defend Megara against a Corinthian invasion – which they successfully did. And even that was not enough for the Athenians. The state of war still continued between them and Persia, and in this same year an expedition of 200 Athenian and allied ships was sent to Cyprus; but an appeal for aid came from Egypt, where a revolt had broken out against Persian rule, and the expedition was diverted there, so that soon Athenian troops were fighting a land war in Africa, laying siege to the 'White Castle' in Memphis, the ancient capital of the Pharaohs. This was the greatest armed force that had sailed from Greece to fight on non-Greek soil since the days of Agamemnon. In this first year of what is now usually called the First Peloponnesian War, the Athenian dead probably numbered between 1500 and 2000:[4] these twelve months of fighting cost the lives of about one in every twenty adult male Athenian citizens.

But if there were perils abroad, there were also perils at home. Whether or not it was true that Ephialtes' death had been the work of irreconcilable opponents of the new political order, events were soon to prove that such a group existed and were prepared to go to any lengths to re-establish their ascendancy. Either in 458 or in 457 these Athenian oligarchs were encouraging the Spartan-led army, then in Boeotia, to invade Attica in the hope that the democracy might be overthrown before the 'Long Walls' being built between Athens and Peiraeus could be completed. The plan miscarried, because the democrats got wind of it and marched out to confront the Peloponnesians at Tanagra; the latter, though victorious in the ensuing battle, suffered heavy casualties and afterwards merely went home, leaving the Athenian democrats free to make themselves masters of most of central Greece. But no one could say that the Athenian 'Right' had not done their best to bring about the defeat and humiliation of their own city. On the 'Left', too, there will surely have been those who talked of taking violent and indiscriminate revenge on those who had murdered Ephialtes, or who might have done so, or whose friends might have done so. Never between 508/7 and 411 was Athens in more danger of plunging into a bloody civil conflict. In the spring of 458 she was at a crossroads of her history, from which she might go on to greatness or to ruin.

Many of the anxieties of the day are reflected, in a general way, all through the *Oresteia* (cf. §7.10), notably in the presentation of the domestic and external politics of Argos in the first play, as in the doubts of the Argive elders over whether the Trojan war was justified or worth while (*Ag.* 799-804), the fears expressed by them and by Agamemnon of popular unrest or a *coup d'état* (445-60, 807-9, 844-50, 1354-5, 1365), and the contempt for the ordinary citizen expressed by the new 'tyrants', Clytaemestra and especially Aegisthus (883-5, 1617-42, 1662-72). In *Eumenides*, however, once Athens becomes the scene of action, Aeschylus goes much further by repeatedly making clear allusions to highly topical matters: the alliance with Argos; war in general and the Egyptian expedition in particular; the danger of civil strife; and the role of the Areopagus council.

The Argive alliance. Three times in *Eumenides*, with increasing emphasis (289-91, 669-73, 762-74), Athena and her people are promised, by Orestes and Apollo, that in return for favourable treatment of Orestes they will gain Argos as an ally for ever; in the third passage Orestes takes oath that he, in his posthumous capacity as a hero, will ensure that the Argives faithfully abide by this alliance. Thus the political and military alignment of Athens and Argos – which was hardly three years old – is presented as having been continuous since the heroic age, and the Athenians are offered the strongest of assurances that they can rely implicitly on Argive fidelity. It is taken for granted that the alliance is a great and unmixed blessing for Athens; a proposition with which not all Athenians would necessarily, in spring 458, have agreed. It is, incidentally, so far as we can tell, solely for the sake of these contemporary allusions that Agamemnon's capital is located in the *Oresteia* at Argos rather than at Mycenae as in Homer.[5]

War. In Orestes' first prayer to Athena (*Eum.* 292-6) he pictures her as a military commander, fighting perhaps on the plain of Phlegra (where she had fought in the Battle of the Gods and Giants) *or in Africa.* Athena had traditionally been born at Lake Tritonis in Libya, but there was no tradition of her being involved in a *battle* there; and an audience who had just been reminded, by mention of the Argive alliance, of the great war in which their city was engaged, and who then heard tell of Athena 'aiding her friends' in Africa, could not help thinking of the vast Athenian force even then fighting on the banks of the Nile, in which so many of *their* friends were serving. Later on in the play Orestes and Athena, in wishing good fortune upon Athens, both give prominence to the blessing of victory in war (777, 915, 1009), and the war-god Ares is named, most unusually, as one of Athens' principal divine patrons (918). But what is most strikingly indicative of the attitude of many Athenians – and presumably of Aeschylus – at this time is Athena's extraordinary blessing on her people in 864: 'may you have external war, *and plenty of it*'. The multiple conflicts in which Athens was currently engaged, far from being a grievous burden, are presented as a divine *boon* enabling Athenians to win glory for themselves and their city (865, 914). The decisions taken by a majority of Athenian citizens between 460 and 457 strongly suggest that this view was no individual aberration.

Civil strife is vehemently deprecated both by Athena (858-66) and by the Erinyes (976-87), who also both warn (526-8, 696-7) against the opposite evils of anarchy and despotism to which civil strife so often leads. Particular emphasis is laid on the danger of 'passion for revenge' leading to 'tit-for-tat murders' and ultimately to 'the city's ruin' (980-3) – highly relevant, of course, to the main plot of the trilogy, but also to the possibility of attempts at revenge upon the alleged killers of Ephialtes. It would be a great error to suppose that three years after this event, passions must necessarily have cooled. It may be significant that when, not long afterwards, the Athenians found themselves in control of Boeotia, their first significant action there was to demolish the walls of Tanagra (Thucydides 1.108.3), the home town of Ephialtes' suspected assassin Aristodicus, thus venting their anger on an external scapegoat without risking civil peace at home.

The Areopagus council. An important feature of the trial of Orestes is a speech by Athena, directed mainly to 'my citizens for the future' (707-8), in which she formally establishes the Areopagus council, speaks highly of the benefits it can confer on the Athenian people, and warns them against damaging changes:

> Upon this hill, reverence
> and inborn fear of the citizens shall restrain
> wrongdoing by day and night alike,
> so long as the citizens themselves do not make innovations in the laws:
> if you pollute clear water with an evil influx
> of mud, you will never get a drink.
> I counsel my citizens to cherish and practise
> the mean between anarchy and despotism,
> and not to banish fear entirely from the city (690-8).

What laws, and what innovations, are referred to in 693? Many different interpretations have been offered. Is the point being made simply the general one, a commonplace of classical Greek thought, that the laws of a *polis* should not be lightly altered, especially perhaps (given the subject of the trial in progress) the laws of homicide? Or does the context of the speech, which is a speech about the Areopagus council, indicate that the laws which are not to be changed are laws about that council? And if so, what is the *status quo* which is being commended? The *status quo* of 462, which Ephialtes had altered so radically, handing over many of the Areopagus' functions to councils and courts many of whose members would indeed be viewed by aristocrats as little better than 'mud'? Or the *status quo* of 458, which according to the reformers was no innovation at all but a restoration of the 'ancestral' state of things by the removal from the Areopagus of what were said to be 'added' powers (Aristotle, *Constitution of Athens* 25.2)? And if the latter, is the new *status quo* being defended against reactionaries, or against ultra-radicals, or both? Or has Aeschylus designed this passage precisely in order to leave it unclear which of these various positions Athena is upholding?

All these views have had their advocates during the last two centuries. It is important to distinguish in this connection between the political attitudes and preferences of Aeschylus the Athenian citizen, and the directions in which Aeschylus the dramatist may have sought to influence the views of his public. Another part of the passage quoted above may be significant for both: 'reverence and inborn fear of the citizens shall restrain wrongdoing by day and night alike' (690-2). In the Greek this sentence is so expressed that it is impossible to determine grammatically (1) whether it refers to reverence for, and fear of, the Areopagus council on the part of the citizenry or to reverence for, and fear of, the citizenry on the part of the Areopagus council, and accordingly (2) whether it is the citizenry or the Areopagus council that is to be restrained from wrongdoing. An adjustment to the language at any one of at least three points could have obviated this ambiguity; it is therefore most unlikely that the ambiguity is accidental, and this increases the likelihood that the uncertainties in the interpretation of 693-5 are likewise not due merely to our ignorance but are part of the poet's design.

It would seem, therefore, that in the spring of 458 Aeschylus did not want to be seen to be partisan on this highly controversial issue of domestic politics. There is indeed a sharp contrast between the references to external and to internal politics in *Eumenides*. Externally, Aeschylus has no hesitation in avowing strong support for the war policy and the Argive alliance. Athens is embattled on many fronts. Her young men's lives and perhaps (pending completion of the Long Walls) her very survival are in danger. In such circumstances support for the war effort can reasonably be seen as the duty of every loyal citizen; at any rate, whether in ancient or in modern times, the 'war party' invariably do see things in that way and do not hesitate to say so with emphasis. On matters of internal politics no explicit stand is anywhere taken. In contrast with *The Suppliant Maidens* a few years before (see §12.2), there is no reference, direct or indirect, to democracy, and the very words *dêmos* 'the people' and *plêthos* 'the masses' are never used, the Athenian people being referred to instead as 'the citizens' (*astoi* or *politai*) or 'the host' (*laos* or *stratos*). In the internal affairs of Athens Aeschylus in this play publicly espouses one principle only: the vital importance of avoiding anything that might lead to civil conflict. Everyone could agree that crime must be repressed, the country defended, and anarchy and despotism avoided (though they might well differ on what they *meant* by anarchy or despotism). Everyone could agree that the Areopagus council (which still had the literally vital function of judging murders, including political murders) must be respected, vigilant, upright and incorruptible. These things are said by Athena, and some of them by the Erinyes also, with the utmost clarity. All else is ambiguous, and (as was already seen by Wilamowitz 1893: ii 341) each spectator will understand it in the light of his own preconceptions.

But the ambiguity noted above in 690-2, together with other evidence, enables us to define with confidence Aeschylus' personal political views at this time. Crucial here are his three emphatic references to the Argive alliance and his treatment of an abundance of war as a blessing. We can put him down without hesitation as a strong supporter of the line taken by Ephialtes and Pericles in foreign policy and an opponent of the pro-Spartan orientation favoured by Cimon. From this alone it does not necessarily follow that he was also a strong supporter, or a supporter at all, of the new radical democracy at home. Thucydides, after all, was both a cynic about democracy (in whose view the Athenian constitution of 411/0, which disfranchised well over half the citizen body, was the best he had known[6]) and perhaps the greatest admirer we know of Pericles as statesman and strategist. Consider though the ambiguity of 690-2. Athena's speech as a whole is one of praise of the Areopagus council – praise which some have considered excessive if applied to a 'mere' murder court. Yet it includes a passage capable of two equally valid readings, one of which warns the Areopagus against wrongdoing, says that it will only be effectively restrained from this if it respects and fears the citizen body at large, and adds (693) that such respect and fear can only be guaranteed if the Areopagus confines itself to its traditional functions and does not arrogate further powers to itself. Since this reading goes against the grain of, and to a considerable extent subverts, the praise of the Areopagus in the rest of the speech, it is unlikely that Aeschylus would have made it available unless it represented his own views. Two further details point the same way. The Areopagus, if it is to be faithful to the will of its divine founder, must be *incorruptible* (704); all democrats will have recalled that Ephialtes, before his final assault on the council's powers, had prosecuted several of its members for bribery. And the Areopagus is to restrain the citizens, or the citizens are to restrain the Areopagus, from crime *by day or night* (692); it was during the night that Ephialtes had been killed (Diodorus Siculus 11.77.6), and it is hardly extravagant to suppose that members of the Areopagus council, many of whom were his personal as well as political enemies,[7] were widely suspected of having been involved in the plotting of his murder.

Aeschylus thus appears in 459/8 as a committed supporter of the new democracy and the main lines of its external and internal policies, who is nevertheless anxious to conciliate rather than suppress its defeated opponents – just as Athena strives to conciliate the Erinyes as they smart under their humiliating defeat by the 'new/young'[8] rulers of the universe and to offer them an honoured place in the Athenian *polis*, knowing how much damage they are capable of doing to Athens if she is foolish enough to treat them with contempt as Apollo did. His praise of the Areopagus council, while as we have seen not unequivocal, involves a definite opposition to any further significant reduction in its powers or prestige: it will be, so Athena says unconditionally, a 'council of judges for ever' (684), and its members constitute the representation of the male citizens of Athens in the final procession. The warnings against 'anarchy' as well as 'despotism', and against tit-for-tat murders, reinforce the implication that danger to the stability of the *polis* can come from Left as well as Right. It would appear that this position was one that had other influential advocates at the time, doubtless including Pericles: at any rate the Areopagus council did retain its homicide jurisdiction, we know of no witch-hunt against anti-democrats at this time nor of any political assassinations until the eve of the oligarchic coup of 411, and Cimon himself, when he returned (perhaps early, by special decree) from his ten-year exile, was elected a general and given a major command.

12.2. *The Suppliant Maidens*

As we saw in Chapter 6, the date of the Danaid trilogy is not firmly established. It must be earlier than the *Oresteia*, but cannot be earlier than the début of Sophocles; that is, it must belong to one of the years 470-459. The date of 463 sometimes quoted rests on the assumption that the opening letters of the papyrus fragment of the ancient production-notice, *epiar*, are the beginning of *epi Ar[khedêmidou]* 'in the term of office of Archedemides', who was archon in 464/3 and the only one in the relevant period whose name begins with the required letters; but another possible continuation is *epi ar[khontos ...]* 'in the archonship of ...' which would give us no clue to the precise year, and this latter restoration finds some support in the fact that a papyrus production-notice of one of the Theban plays, in the same hand and from the same book, quotes its date in the form *epi arkhont. [Theag]enidou*. The date of the trilogy must therefore be regarded as uncertain (within the limits quoted above).

In the surviving play of the trilogy, *The Suppliant Maidens*, there are no direct political allusions. Attempts to link the favourable portrayal of Argos to issues of Athenian foreign policy in the 460s are unconvincing: if Aeschylus had had contemporary Athenian-Argive relations at the front of his mind, he would never have given King Pelasgus the speech (254-9) in which he claims to be ruler of all Greece, including Epirus and Macedonia and by implication including Athens itself. There are, however, at least two features of the play that seem designed to give Athenians food for thought about their own political system.

In the first place, Argos is presented as a democracy. Although it has a king, he is so plainly dressed that the Danaids cannot tell whether he is ruler, priest or private citizen (247-8, cf. 932-3), and he refuses to commit the *polis* to their support without the approval of the *dêmos* (365-9, 398-401). When the *dêmos* meets in assembly, the event is described in terms that would exactly fit a meeting of the Assembly of fifth-century Athens, with generous use of technical and semi-technical terms such as *edoxe* and *dedoktai* 'it is resolved' (601, 605), *psêphisma* 'decree' (601, cf. 943), *metoikein* 'have the status of a resident alien' (609), *atimos* 'deprived of citizen rights' (614); the Assembly expresses its approval of the king's proposal not by acclamation (as in Homer or in contemporary Sparta) but, as at Athens, by show of hands (604, 607-8, 621). The very word *dêmokratia* 'democracy' itself appears, thinly disguised, for the first time in a surviving Greek text (Ehrenberg 1950: 522): the Danaids ask what has been the majority decision of 'the controlling hand of the *dêmos*' (<u>*dêmou*</u>

kratousa kheir, 604), and later pray that 'the people, who control the city' (*to damion to ptolin kratunei*) may act with justice and wisdom towards both citizens and foreigners (698-703). Despite having previously assured Pelasgus that 'you are the *polis*, you are the people' (370), they clearly now recognize where sovereignty in Argos rests: whatever Pelasgus' theoretical prerogatives may be, in practice decision lies with the people. One may well suspect that all this is relevant to debates in the late 460s over the extent, if any, to which the sovereign competence of the Assembly should be restricted, for example by the Areopagus council in its role as 'guardian of the laws'.

And yet, although the Assembly is clearly recognized as sovereign, in the play it is expertly manipulated by Pelasgus into taking a decision whose full implications are concealed from the people until too late and whose merits Pelasgus knows to be dubious. Pelasgus is in an acute dilemma. A group of foreigners, claiming an ancestral connection with Argos, has taken sanctuary at, and deposited the wreathed olive-branches of supplication on, a public Argive altar. They seek the assistance of Argos against enemies from their own country. The justice of their cause is uncertain (see pp. 97. 103). If their plea is accepted, it will involve Argos in war with Egypt. If it is unjustly rejected, an offence will have been committed against Zeus Hikesios. Pelasgus is at first unable to reach a decision (438-54), but when the Danaids threaten to hang themselves in the sanctuary, thus polluting it and incurring the wrath of all the gods of Argos, he decides that war, terrible and dangerous though it is, is the lesser evil. He cannot, however, embark on war without the approval of the people, and proceeds to take careful steps to ensure that he wins that approval.

To begin with, Danaus is instructed to place suppliant-branches on the other altars of Argos, so that all the citizens may be aware of the supplication (480-4), Pelasgus be protected against hostile comment (484-5), and public opinion be won over to support of the Danaids and hostility to their oppressors (486-9). Pelasgus' original intention was apparently that Danaus should go to Argos alone, and when he asks for an escort (492-9) Pelasgus sends a detachment of soldiers with him with the significant orders to keep their mouths shut (502): he does not want the nature of the crisis to become public knowledge except through himself and Danaus – and even Danaus must be carefully briefed on what he is to say (519).

When the Assembly met, we are told, Pelasgus made a speech putting enormous emphasis on the danger of pollution, and of the wrath of Zeus Hikesios, if the plea of the suppliants was disregarded (615-20). It was apparently not necessary for Danaus to speak: as soon as they had heard Pelasgus, without waiting for the formal putting of the question by the herald (622), the people voted unanimously (607) in favour of the resolution which Pelasgus had presumably proposed, in approximately the following terms:

> That Danaus and his daughters be granted the status of free resident aliens in Argos, with immunity from seizure and spoliation by any person whether a resident of Argos or not; and that if an attempt is made to use force against them, any Argive citizen who does not come to their aid shall be exiled and lose his citizen rights (609-14, slightly paraphrased).

Danaus, at the end of his enthusiastic report of the Assembly's proceedings, speaks of the people being readily persuaded by Pelasgus' 'oratorical twists'; this phrase (Greek *dêmêgoroi strophai*) is clearly intended by Danaus to be complimentary, but in ordinary Attic usage both words, especially the second, carried distinct connotations of dishonesty. And Pelasgus *has* been dishonest. He knew that he had a choice between two dangerous courses: the course he chose was the less dangerous, but dangerous it certainly was (474-7). Yet with a speech which, so far as we are informed about it, made no reference to any possibility of war, he has secured assent to a resolution which commits every Argive to 'come to the aid' of the refugees if an attempt is made to seize them by force. If such an attempt is backed by an army – as Pelasgus himself expects it to be – and if the Argives obey the new decree – which they are bound to, on pain of disfranchisement and exile – Argos will be at war. Thus the Argive people have voted for war with Egypt, without being aware they have done so. The wool has been well and truly pulled over their eyes.

Accordingly, when he confronts the Egyptian herald, Pelasgus speaks and acts as one who has a popular mandate for war. The herald claims a right to seize the Danaids. Pelasgus orders him off. The herald asks to whom he is speaking (932-3) and says that refusal of his demands will mean war (934-7). Pelasgus refuses to give his name (938) because he is speaking for his entire people who are solidly determined not to hand over the women without their consent (942-9). The herald: 'It looks like war, then; may the males win.' Pelasgus: 'The Argives are more masculine than you beer-drinkers.' Exit the herald. In effect he has declared war, his declaration has been accepted by Pelasgus, and Argos is involved in a major conflict for which it never knowingly voted. And we are fairly certain what the outcome of this conflict was (see §6.2): as a result of a battle which can at best have been drawn, the Argives lost both their king and (in substance, if not in name) their democracy, and found themselves the subjects of a *tyrannos* in the person of Danaus, who then decided to let his daughters marry their cousins after all and forthwith proceeded to bring upon Argos the very pollution that Argos had fought to avoid, by having the cousins murdered. Such are the consequences of Pelasgus' abuse of the democratic process.

Whether all this was perceived by its audience as reflecting some current or recent events in which they had been involved we cannot tell. It will certainly have been perceived as reflecting a situation in which they *might* at any time be involved. In the ideology of Athenian democracy it was axiomatic that the people must be on their guard against deception, either by their own politicians or by foreigners seeking their support (Ober 1989:156-77). On the other hand, Pelasgus in deceiving the people was not intending to harm them; quite the contrary, he was trying to ensure that, of the two alternative decisions open to them, they chose the one which he rightly thought to be better for them (or at least less bad), and in doing so he had no hidden selfish aim contrary to the interests of the community. Had he made clear the likelihood of war, would the people still have voted as they did – not unanimously, perhaps, but at least by a majority? Certainly they would not have done so with such alacrity, and so forestalled the expression of opposing views; and had such views been aired, they might well have carried the day. So are there, after all, circumstances in which it is not wrong to deceive the people? Pelasgus' methods, and their outcome, would leave the Athenians with a great deal to think about.

12.3. *The Persians* and 473/2

We have seen that *The Persians* is a play of Persian tragedy, not of Athenian triumph. Some fifty Persian leaders who took part in the war (and all of whom, except Xerxes, are stated or understood to have been killed) are mentioned by name; of the Greeks, not one. Yet such a play could not help but remind Athenians vividly of the peril they had faced, of the victory they had won, and of how they had won it; and there are moments when this aspect of the play comes particularly to the surface – one thinks in particular of the paean and battle-cry of the advancing Greeks at Salamis (388-405) and the chorus's roll-call of lands no longer ruled by Persia (869-902) which bears a curious resemblance to the membership of the Thracian (869ff.), Hellespontine (876ff.), Island (880ff.) and Ionian (897ff.) divisions of the new Athenian-led Delian League.

And although no individual Greek is mentioned by name, one individual Greek certainly is mentioned without being named: the guileful man who induced Xerxes to order his fleet to patrol the exits from Salamis bay all night by telling him the Greeks were about to flee (353ff.) and thereby, as the Messenger tells the tale, effectively won the battle before it had begun. This man, as everyone knew, was Themistocles, whether acting in person or by an agent (Herodotus 8.75). There are other moments too at which Themistocles' name will have come to mind. One comes only a few lines before the passage just mentioned: when the Messenger is asked whether Athens is still unsacked he replies 'While she has men, she has an impregnable wall' – which, according to Herodotus, is essentially what Themistocles said to the Corinthian who taunted him as a man without a country ('We have a city and a country greater than yours while we have two hundred ships and their crews', Herodotus 8.61). And the constant emphasis throughout the play on the fact that the Persians have been defeated *at sea* and *by ships* may make many reflect that most of those

Greek ships were the ships that Themistocles had persuaded the Athenians to build, against some opposition, in the years before 480, with a windfall of silver from the mines of Laureium (cf. 238) which others had wanted to use for other purposes. Salamis, the victory that more than any other was Themistocles' own, is given central treatment in the play. Marathon, the victory of Miltiades the father of Cimon, always thought of in later generations as Athens' greatest achievement, is mentioned just once directly (475) and twice obliquely (236, 244), each time in a single line. Plataea, which at the supposed time of the action still lies in the future, is treated more extensively (803-22) but is presented as a 'Dorian', i.e. a Spartan, victory, with no mention of Athenian participation.

The Athenian army at Plataea was commanded by Aristeides, who had been ostracized in 483/2 and, together with others, recalled in the crisis; for some years he seems to have co-operated with Themistocles, but he may have broken with him in the late 470s (perhaps indeed this rupture helped to secure Themistocles' ostracism). To ignore the Athenians at Plataea was thus to ignore Aristeides. It has often been suggested, however, that one episode of the battle at Salamis is given undue emphasis in *The Persians* in order to give credit to Aristeides: the destruction of the Persian troops on the islet of Psyttaleia by a force led by Aristeides acting, so Herodotus implies, on his own initiative. This incident is narrated by the Messenger in lines 441-64. But so far as the Greek side is concerned, he tells the story quite differently from Herodotus. According to Herodotus (8.95), Aristeides 'took with him many of the Athenian hoplites who were stationed along the shore of Salamis and landed them on Psyttaleia'. Aeschylus on the other hand implies (somewhat implausibly) that the Greeks who landed on Salamis were the same who had fought the sea-battle:

> When the god
> gave the Greeks the glory in the battle of ships,
> the same day they clothed their bodies
> in fine bronze armour, leaped from their ships, and surrounded
> the whole island, so that our men were at a loss
> where to turn (454-9).

Nor, it seems, are all of them hoplites, since they at first attack the Persians with stones and arrows (459-61). As throughout the actual fighting, no leader is mentioned: it is 'the Greeks' who fight, collectively. In the nine lines describing their attack on Psyttaleia there are nine verbs and participles referring to the attackers: all are plural, and none has an expressed subject. Psyttaleia as presented here, though it required the Greeks to put on armour and fight on land, is not a separate engagement but a part, though an important part, of the general slaughter that followed the rout of the fleet, in which every Persian or ally who could be caught was killed whether in the water (424-8) or on land.

One other individual Greek would have been of particular interest to those responsible for the production of *The Persians*: Xanthippus, whose son Pericles was Aeschylus' *khorêgos*. He had been the Athenian admiral in 479, succeeding Themistocles, had taken part in the battle of Mycale, and had been responsible for the siege and capture of Sestos, whence he had brought home the cables of Xerxes' bridge of boats over the Hellespont to be dedicated in Athenian temples:[9] that bridge and its cables duly find prominent mention in the play (65-73, 112-13, 130-1, 722-5, 745-50) and are made, as we have seen, into the very symbol of Xerxes' arrogant impiety.

But Themistocles is the main 'unspoken hero' of *The Persians*. We know that at some time in the late 470s Themistocles lost popularity and was ostracized; but the chronology of this period is notoriously uncertain. We cannot therefore tell whether Aeschylus was seeking in some measure to defend Themistocles' record at a time when he was already under attack, or whether he was paying to a popular hero a tribute for which he could expect popular endorsement; but it is perhaps significant that he should have felt it necessary in 473/2 to return to a theme which had been handled by Phrynichus, with memorable success, perhaps only four years earlier, and we may note too that Themistocles' rival Cimon had since then gained great prestige by the capture of Eion and Scyros and the restoration to Athens of the bones of Theseus. On the whole it is most likely that part of the aim of *The Persians* was to keep memories of Themistocles' achievements fresh when they were threatening to fade and to help protect him against the possibility of prosecution or ostracism; if so it failed, or at best perhaps postponed his fate for a year or two.

12.4. Aeschylus, prophet of democracy

The domination of Athenian politics by Cimon, from the middle 470s until 462,[10] was strongly reflected in the Athenian arts world. The exploitation of the arts to promote the public image of a ruler was no new thing: it had been practised to great effect by the Peisistratids in Athens in the sixth century, and in Cimon's time the tyrants of Sicily – Gelon and Hieron of Syracuse, Theron of Acragas – were carrying on the tradition. Cimon himself was perhaps the first political leader in a constitutional state to exploit the arts in this way on a large scale. In public building, the Theseion commemorated his victory at Scyros and his recovery of Theseus' bones; the paintings of the Stoa Poikile (originally the Peisianakteion, named after Cimon's brother-in-law, as the Metiocheion was named after his brother) linked the triumphs of the heroic age with Miltiades' victory of Marathon. In poetry, inscriptional and literary sources attest epigrams on public display, glorifying the victories of Miltiades and Cimon without naming them, and poems in honour of Cimon and members of his family were composed by Melanthius and apparently also by the philosopher

Archelaus (Plutarch, *Cimon* 4.1, 4.7). There is some evidence that Cimon sought to harness more distinguished poets than these to his publicity machine. Bacchylides' Theseus ode (18) is under considerable suspicion of describing Cimon under the guise of Theseus (Barron 1980). And whether or not it is true that Cimon was personally involved in Sophocles' first City Dionysia victory in 468 (see p. 7), it is far from impossible that Cimon and his faction tried to recruit Sophocles and use him to undermine the immensely popular Aeschylus, who, as we have seen, had already aligned himself with Themistocles and Pericles. A figure with Sophocles' features, indeed, could be seen in one of the paintings in the Stoa Poikile, playing a lyre,[11] a compliment by the artist Polygnotus similar to that which he paid to Cimon's sister Elpinice.

Unlike Cimon (and unlike Pericles), Themistocles was not an artistically-minded man. Like some of his successors on the 'left' of Athenian politics, he even cultivated a plebeian image, claiming (according to the near-contemporary Ion of Chios[12]) that he had never so much as learned to play the lyre; and the monuments of his building projects were not temples and stoai but fortifications and dockyards. But he does seem to have had a lively awareness, earlier and more strongly than Cimon did, of the unique potential of the dramatic arts for influencing public opinion. It was probably, as we have seen (p. 4), on his initiative that comedy was given an official place on the festival programme, with its licence to debunk the powerful and pretentious;[13] and in 476 he himself acted as *khorêgos* to Phrynichus for a production about the Persian War, at a time when Cimon was already conducting a new campaign against the remnants of Persian power in Europe. Pericles did likewise for Aeschylus (Phrynichus being probably dead) four years later.

Aeschylus had won his first victory in 484, in the middle of Themistocles' first period of ascendancy, and from then on, especially after Phrynichus' death, he may have won almost every time he competed: in this sense the story is perfectly credible (whether true or not) that by 469/8 questions were beginning to be asked about the impartiality of the judging panels. Both *The Persians* in 472 and the *Oresteia* in 458, as we have seen, have political implications that favour the policies supported by the Themistocles-Ephialtes-Pericles group, and no play of Aeschylus that we know of has implications telling in the contrary direction. At some moments he may have become one of the group's most important assets.

This is not to say that he was in any sense a mercenary. Doubtless, like almost every other Greek poet, he was capable of bending his art to the praise of a patron; doubtless indeed he contrived to do so for Hieron in *The Women of Aetna* (and perhaps also in *Glaucus of Potniae*, see §4.2). But there was a significant difference between the public-relations activities of Cimon and those of his opponents. Almost everything Cimon did in this field bears a personal and dynastic stamp: buildings are named after his relatives, poets praise his beauty and generosity, his followers hand out gifts to needy citizens on the street. Themistocles, Ephialtes and Pericles seem to have portrayed themselves as acting not only in the interests of, but also in the name of, the people. In later years Pericles dispensed enormous handouts (some of them in the form of employment) to needy and not so needy citizens, but these came not from his purse but from that of the state (and in the end mainly from the tribute paid by the 'allies'). Their slogan, at least by the late 460s and quite likely earlier, was *dêmokratia*, popular power. When Pericles in his turn launched a building programme that eclipsed Cimon's, there was never any question of *his* naming the buildings after members of his family!

Aeschylus' politics too, as they appear in his plays, are concerned more with principle than with personality, and this tendency increases with time. In *The Persians*, when Themistocles is under a cloud and possibly in danger, Aeschylus among other things reminds his audience of what they owe to him; but even in *The Persians* issues of principle are well to the fore, above all the contrast between Greek freedom and the irresponsible despotism of Persia. The Persian queen, who thankfully reflects that even if Xerxes is defeated he cannot be held to account and, if alive, will remain ruler of Persia (213-14), is surprised to hear that the Athenians 'are not called the slaves or the subjects of any man' and yet have a highly effective army (241-5). Freedom is the keyword of the Greek battle-cry at Salamis (403). After the chorus have heard of the Persian disaster, the climax of their grief-stricken reflections is the thought that

> men's tongues are no longer
> under guard; the people
> are let loose to speak freely,
> now the yoke of force has been removed (591-4):

the Greeks have won a victory not only for themselves but for the cause of freedom almost throughout the known world – and especially for those Greek communities (cf. 869-902) that once paid tribute (*dasmos*) to Persia 'by the constraints of lordship' (586-7) and now pay contributions (*phoros*, not yet a dirty word to the subjects of an empire not yet created) to the Delian League.

In *The Suppliant Maidens* we hear the chorus invoking blessings on a democratic state, with the watchword *dêmokratia* itself appearing twice, thinly disguised. Pelasgus has deceived the people (as Athenian politicians from Miltiades onwards were often accused of doing), but the people themselves have unquestionably done the right thing given the flawed and partial information that was laid before them, and at the end of the play we see their representatives, the Argive spearmen, physically protecting the Danaids because Argos has committed itself to their protection, even though they have and express severe doubts whether the Danaids' cause deserves to, or will, triumph. It may be that later in the trilogy the Argive people were undeceived and themselves overthrew the tyranny of Danaus.

In the *Oresteia* there is no detectable allusion to any individual Athenian, and it is significant that in *Eumenides*, for the only time in surviving tragedy, Athens in the heroic age is represented as having no king: its only ruler is Athena, and Orestes is tried by her and ten or eleven anonymous and silent citizens. The ideological language of democracy, as we have seen, is played down in *Eumenides* in favour of the importance of national unity – though of course this in practice means national unity in support of the existing régime; and warnings to the régime's opponents are balanced by warnings to its possibly over-enthusiastic supporters. A new Athens is being created, based not on the rule of one person or of one class but on the co-operation and mutual love (*Eum.* 984-5) of all and on striving for the common good (975, 1012-13) – but also on the fear (517ff, 698f.) which will serve to restrain the over-mighty (368ff., 553ff., 932ff.) from anti-social action or worse, so that no Atreus or Paris or Agamemnon will be able to bring the whole *polis* to ruin or near-ruin.

This new Athens is a community at war, and in *Eumenides* we are constantly reminded of this. But we hear little of its enemies. Sparta is mentioned once, obliquely and in a context by no means uncomplimentary: Athena tells her people that fear and respect of the Areopagus and what it stands for will give them a 'bulwark of safety ... such as no other race of men have, neither in Scythia nor in the land of Pelops' (700-3). The Scythians (or some of them, cf. Aesch. fr. 198) and the Spartans were famous for *eunomia* – for having good laws and observing them: this passage accepts that reputation as well-deserved and tells the Athenians they will be able to surpass it. Menelaus, who in other surviving tragedy is always a Spartan king and usually presented as contemptible, is in the *Oresteia* the 'beloved ruler' of Argos (*Ag.* 617-19). Athens is thought of not as a contender with other Greek states but as a leader and champion of Greece: in the Trojan war she was awarded a special prize of territory (*Eum.* 398-402) and in the future (Aeschylus' own present) she will be under the patronage of Ares as 'the fortress of the gods, the defender of Greek altars, the delight of Greek divinities' (918-20). This language implies that the prime enemy is Persia which had destroyed the temples and altars of these gods in Athens and in many other places; the Delian League had been founded partly to exact retribution for these crimes, and some years later, on Pericles' proposal, Athens would send heralds to all the states of Greece, friendly and unfriendly, to invite them to a congress which would discuss *inter alia* 'the sanctuaries which the barbarians have burnt' (Plutarch, *Pericles* 17.1). Athens, in fact, is the true successor of heroic Argos (and therefore appropriately allied with contemporary Argos), fighting for the Greek people and their gods against their common enemies (but with a better cause than Agamemnon had). The Delian League, after all, was thought of by Athenians as the legitimate successor of the league of 'the Greeks' which had fought the Persians in 480/79 and from which Sparta and her allies had chosen to withdraw, and the

League's treasurers were still called *Helleno*tamiae. That Athens and the League were also fighting against other Greeks is nowhere admitted. Even the three references to the Argive alliance make no allusion to the enemy against whom this alliance is directed (the only possible enemy mentioned is Argos itself, 765-71). This too can be regarded as part of the trilogy's general policy of internal conciliation. Virtually everyone was in favour of continuing the war against Persia; but those who were hostile to the new democracy were also hostile to the war against Sparta. Therefore that war is elided.

We need not suppose that Aeschylus himself had any serious doubts about the wisdom of Athens' current wars against fellow-Greeks; if he had, he would never have made Athena say 'May you have external war *and plenty of it*' (*Eum.* 864), nor indeed would he have laid so much emphasis on the Argive alliance, which, as he must have known perfectly well, was meaningless unless it was directed against Argos' neighbours Sparta and Corinth. But he knew that some Athenians did have doubts, and that to raise the issue might open internal wounds; nor need we deny that he may have cherished the hope that one day Athens would be the leader of a league of all the Greeks in which Sparta too would have a place.

The one political element that all Aeschylus' surviving plays share is the contrast between the powerful, self-interested individual in control of a state, and the community which ought to be in control of itself. In *The Persians*, Xerxes, the ruler 'like a god' with no responsibility to his people, destroys an empire (as Aeschylus portrays things) and causes the death of untold thousands of his subjects, while the Greeks, 'slaves and subjects of no man' and in the Messenger's narrative led by no commanders, fight with a discipline and system which amaze the Persians (399, 400, 417, 457-9) and secure not only their own freedom but that of many others. In the Theban trilogy the irresponsibility of Laius, the domestic tension between Oedipus and his sons, and the private quarrel between the latter, almost lead to the destruction of Thebes with its terrible consequences, graphically anticipated (*Seven* 287-368), for the Thebans and particularly the Theban women: the city is saved by the six men, modest in word but resolute in action, who defeat the boastful leaders of the invading army, while the house of Laius is annihilated. In the Danaid plays, Danaus certainly once, probably twice, involves an entire state in war, and later in mass blood-pollution, to cheat an oracle and secure (as he supposes) his personal safety, enlisting as his allies his deluded daughters and even the public-spirited king of Argos: but eventually the democracy which the Danaids praise proves its worth, with the help of Lynceus, by saving Argos from tyranny and the Danaids themselves from the unnatural lot (as all Greeks regarded it) of perpetual virginity. In the *Oresteia* powerful individual after powerful individual either ignores the interests of the community or else treats the state as his or her private property: for Troy the result is total destruction, for its captors the loss of 99.9% of their number dead or missing,[14] for Argos a degrading tyranny ended by a crime so appalling that the admired liberator is forced to flee and leave the city leaderless.[15] If Troy had been able and willing to force Paris to surrender Helen, or Argos to compel Atreus and Thyestes to resolve their disputes in a civilized manner; if the Argive elders had been able to prevent Agamemnon from launching a foolish war; if Clytaemestra's complaint against Agamemnon, or Orestes' against her, could have been brought before a judicial tribunal of their fellow-citizens – what misery might have been averted! Of course the same could be said of many other Greek tragedies; the difference is that in *Eumenides*, at Athens, the institutions that were lacking are created and put into operation, such that (once they have the backing of the Erinyes) no one, however powerful – not even a god, it is claimed (*Eum.* 951-2) – can defy them with impunity. And although the prototype of these institutions is the Council of the Areopagus, its judges are called not *bouleutai* but *dikastai* (*Eum.* 483, 684, 743) and thus equated with the judges of the new democratic *dikastêria*, ordinary citizens sitting in juries several hundred strong and receiving pay by the day. Consistently in Aeschylus the well-being of communities is threatened by the irresponsible acts of powerful individuals and sustained by the collective action of ordinary people.

Neither in Sophocles nor in Euripides is this the normal pattern. We may consider three plays of theirs which in some ways come nearest to the Aeschylean model. In Sophocles' *Ajax* the self-centred behaviour of Ajax does indeed threaten disaster to the community consisting of his family and his troops; but they are quite incapable of helping themselves and are saved in the end by the intervention of Odysseus.[16] In his *Oedipus the King* the plague at Thebes is in the first half of the play an essential part of the background against which the action unrolls; but the plague is caused by actions that were neither vicious nor irresponsible nor even intentional, and after line 685 it is never mentioned again. In Euripides' *Bacchae* the bigotry of Pentheus and the jealousy of Semele's sisters threaten disaster to Thebes; this might have been averted had Pentheus taken some notice of a herdsman's report from Mount Cithaeron (660-774), but Pentheus ignores it and goes to his death, leaving the Thebans without government and almost without any dramatic existence – for of those on stage in the final scene, some (the chorus) are foreigners and the others (Cadmus and Agaue) are on the point of going into exile. In most other Sophoclean and Euripidean plays the community, if present at all, are more spectators than victims, let alone actors. It is Aeschylus who constantly asks, with Shakespeare's Lucrece,

> Why should the private pleasure of some one
> Become the public plague of many mo[r]e? …
> For one's offence why should so many fall,
> To plague a private sin in general?[17]

And, unlike many tragic dramatists (but like Livy in the story on which Shakespeare based his poem), he provides an answer and a remedy. The answer to Lucrece's question is: because there are no institutional constraints whereby the 'many' can prevent the 'one' from acting as he pleases regardless of the consequences to others. The remedy is to create such constraints. This cannot be done in a state ruled by one man, since he will take care that the constraints do not apply to himself. In various parts of Greece it could be and was done in states ruled by a minority of the citizenry, but (as usual in Athens during most of the fifth century) this option is ignored, the antithesis to democracy being not oligarchy but tyranny. It certainly cannot be done in a state of anarchy. Democracy remains, then, as the only form of government that can in principle reliably control and contain the consequences of the disputes, conflicts and crimes of individuals. And Aeschylus, who lived through the birth, growth and coming of age of Athenian democracy, is found over and over again embodying that proposition in memorable dramatic forms. We have abundantly seen that that is not, by a long way, all there is to his plays, but it is enough to entitle him to be called the prophet, the forth-teller, of democracy.

Notes

1. This section is an expanded version of Sommerstein 1989a: 26-32. I am grateful to Cambridge University Press for permitting me to include this material in the present work.

2. Since almost all references to actual political trials in this period imply that the judges were not the Areopagus Council but the people, Ostwald 1993 has attractively proposed that what happened in political cases was that the Areopagus gave a verdict but that a convicted defendant could then appeal to the people. He argues, however, that there is unlikely to have been any provision for an appeal against an *acquittal*, and suggests that what triggered the crisis of the late 460s may have been *the acquittal of Cimon by the Areopagus* on a charge of corruption (cf. Plutarch, *Cimon* 14-15).

3. Strictly speaking only a minority of homicide charges were heard by the Areopagus Council; if the charge was of unintentional rather than intentional killing, or of 'planning' a murder which was not carried out, or if the victim was not an Athenian citizen, or if the killer admitted the act but claimed that for one reason or another it was not criminal, the case was judged by a body called the 'Referees' (*ephetai*), who had to be at least 50 years old (whereas the effective qualifying age for membership of the Areopagus Council was 31). It is widely believed, however, that the *ephetai* were none other than the senior members of the Areopagus Council itself. Note that Orestes is tried by the Areopagus Council although he pleads justifiable homicide.

4. One of the ten 'tribes', whose death-roll has survived, lost 177 men (*IG* i^3 1147).

5. Mycenae had been destroyed by the Argives a few years previously. Sophocles and Euripides, in their plays about the family of Agamemnon, call his city Argos or Mycenae indifferently; Aeschylus avoids the latter name entirely.

6. Thucydides 8.97.2.

7. If I am a classical Greek (and am not a direct or indirect disciple of Socrates – but in 458 Socrates was still a child), my personal enemies are those who have done harm to me or mine, and to whom therefore I have a right in justice, and may consider myself to have a duty in honour, to do harm in return.

8. Greek *neos* means both 'young' and 'new'.

9. Herodotus 8.131.3, 9.114.2, 9.120.4-121.

10. For a sketch of internal Athenian politics between 488/7 and 462/1 see pp. 4-8.

11. *Life of Sophocles* 5.

12. Ion fr. 13 Jacoby.

13. It was only some forty years later that comedy was hijacked by the Right and used as a political weapon against Themistocles' spiritual heirs such as Pericles and Cleon (see A.T. Edwards 1993).

14. Of course Menelaus (*Ag.* 674ff.), Odysseus (*Ag.* 841-4) and some others survived, but this is not known at Argos when Agamemnon returns. A thousand ships sailed (*Ag.* 45); one came home.

15. This point is not made explicitly in the text; but the chorus look forward to Orestes becoming ruler of the city (*Cho.* 865), hail him as its liberator (1046) and seek anxiously to dissuade him from considering himself an exile (1044-5, cf. 1042).

16. And, as Alex Garvie reminds me, the spectators' thoughts in the final scene will be focused not so much on the endangered community (even though its members – Tecmessa, Eurysaces, Teucer and the chorus – are still present) as on the honour of Ajax himself.

17. Shakespeare, *The Rape of Lucrece* 1478-84. Lucrece (Lucretia) is moved to reflect thus when she contemplates a painting of the siege and sack of Troy. Her rape by Sextus Tarquinius, and subsequent suicide, is in Shakespeare's poem, as it was in Livy 1.58-60, the cause that leads to the overthrow of the Roman monarchy.

13

Of An Age, or For All Time?

We live in an age of anxiety. Even when we have done our best to understand the significance of the gods' role in Aeschylus' dramatic world (see Chapter 11), we are uneasy with the idea of an essentially rational and just universe, all the more so when it is presented to us by a poet who is designated as tragic. Tragedy is supposed to be about insoluble problems. Less than half a century after his death Aeschylus was apparently too naïve for many of the intellectuals of the Sophistic Enlightenment. How can he have anything to say to us, another 24 centuries later? In this final chapter I shall explore this question with particular reference to three issues which matter as much to us as they did to Aeschylus' contemporaries. The first of the three is a major concern of Aeschylus throughout his surviving work; the other two will be discussed with special reference to the *Oresteia.*

13.1. War and peace

Under what circumstances is it morally permissible for a state to make war? Are there circumstances in which it is morally impermissible for a state *not* to make war? These are questions which will go on being asked as long as there are states (or even, alas, factions within states) whose interests conflict sharply enough to make one of a confronting pair feel that the conflict cannot be acceptably resolved except by force. It was a question that Aeschylus must have found himself constantly asking in his role as an Athenian citizen and soldier. His first production at the City Dionysia was probably in 499, a few months before the Athenian Assembly voted to send twenty ships to assist the Ionian rebels against Persia, a decision but for which the great Persian wars, Marathon, the sack of Athens – and also the Athenian Empire – would in all likelihood never have come to pass. His last was in 458, when Athens was at war simultaneously, and by her own choice, with the two most powerful enemies she could possibly have had. Of his four genuine productions that survive in whole or in part, war features prominently in every one, and in every case the justice of the war is called into question. Typically the wars result either from the excessive ambition of individual leaders, or from underhand and often dubious motives on their part; often both sides are to blame, though we usually find warm sympathy for the common troops and civilians who are caught up in the struggle. Except in *Eumenides* (to which we shall come presently) there is little sign that there can be such a thing as a just war, except when a people are forced to defend themselves against wanton attack.

This of course is what the Greeks do in *The Persians*, and as we have seen (§12.3) they are presented as doing it not under the direction of leaders, for none are mentioned even generically, but by a sort of collective will. There is never any doubt of the justice of their resistance, for they are fighting to defend all they hold dearest (402-5). Xerxes' aggression is attributed on one level to a divinity that took away his wits (724-5), but on another to the personal ambition of a foolish young man blinded by power and wealth and surrounded by foolish advisers:

> This is what bold Xerxes has been taught by associating
> with base men. They said that you [Darius] had acquired
> great wealth for your children with the spear, while he through
> cowardice
> was a stay-at-home warrior doing nothing to increase his patrimony.
> Hearing such reproaches often repeated by these base men
> he planned this march and expedition against Greece (753-8).

Winston Churchill, who had probably never read *The Persians*, said almost exactly the same in a famous essay about Kaiser Wilhelm II (Churchill 1937: 33-6); and the fallacious cry 'we must not disgrace the valour of our ancestors' is one that continues to be heard often enough in various parts of the world. We have seen also (see §§4.1 and 12.3) that Aeschylus may have been aiming, among other things, to encourage Athenians – the victims of Persia's aggression, and the successors to her power in the Aegean – to ask themselves questions about their own state's actions and policy, and translations and adaptations have continued to be used for that purpose.[1]

In *Seven against Thebes* one and the same conflict is viewed successively from two different angles. It first appears as the defence of Thebes against foreign aggressors (cf. §5.4). The aggressors' horses and chariots are spoken of in language elsewhere used of barbarian warriors such as Rhesus or Tereus, and it is implied that they do not speak Greek (170); their champions – at least the first five – are moral and for the most part physical monsters, sharply contrasted with the Thebans who oppose them. The Theban women are terrified, and vividly foresee their fate in the event of the city falling. Eteocles, as he competently organizes the defence and subdues a threatened panic, knows (unlike Xerxes) that in the event of defeat he will be held personally responsible (5-8). Then suddenly a reported remark of Amphiaraus begins to show things in a different light. While fiercely condemning Tydeus and Polyneices, he asks the latter 'What justice can quench the mother-source?' (584). Polyneices, that is, had a justified grievance against his brother (cf. §5.3): that is, it is a wrongful act by Eteocles that put the future of Thebes in jeopardy – but

Polyneices, who has attacked his own city, is in the wrong too. The Thebans themselves are caught between the two of them, and fear that their city may be destroyed along with its kings (764-5). A private family quarrel has involved an entire people. One disputant blazons Justice on his shield (642-8), but is quite ready (as the Peisistratids were in 490 and 480) to become the ally of those who aim to destroy his own city; the other is in the tragic position of leading his people in what they rightly see as a war of patriotic self-defence while he sees, equally rightly, that it is a personal quarrel arising from the curse of Oedipus – as he avows at the only moment of the play when he is alone on stage (69-77). Something not too unlike this has happened in many (mostly third-world) countries at various times in the last few decades, though often the personal quarrels have been disguised under party or ideological labels. Meanwhile good men like Amphiaraus are forced against their better judgement to take part, even a leading part, in a conflict they know to be impious and foredoomed. There has been many an Amphiaraus in these modern conflicts, and the faction leader who fights (like Polyneices) against his own fellow-citizens, alongside a foreign army aiming at conquest for their own ends, is an all too familiar figure. For Amphiaraus, and surely for Aeschylus, such conduct can *never* be condoned: *no* justice can quench the mother-source. So most Athenians would have thought too. Were they right? Do we, in fact, always take the same view?

The Danaid trilogy, if our reconstruction of its main lines is correct, contains two wars. Both result from the determination of Danaus never to give his daughters in marriage. The first is the conflict in Egypt between the brothers Danaus and Aegyptus. The second is in several ways even more disturbing. It involves the people of Argos, who had no connection at all with the original quarrel except that both disputants have an Argive ancestor four or five generations back. It is fought by them in the righteous and pious cause of protecting suppliants, which they have endorsed by a democratic vote as their duty; and yet that vote was procured through disingenuous political manoeuvring by a ruler who had severe doubts about the justice of the suppliants' cause and who concealed from his people even the possibility that war would be the result of the vote. Would the outcome have been different if Pelasgus had trusted his people and presented the situation fully and honestly to them? We have, and the original audience had, no way of *answering* that question; but no one who notices Pelasgus' duplicity can help *asking* it. In at least one modern situation that is in some ways parallel (the 1964 US Congress resolution on the Gulf of Tonkin, which was the legal basis for the ten-year American campaign in Vietnam) the answer to the corresponding question is in little doubt. Pelasgus, though, is in any case helpless before the Danaids' blackmail. A weak party, with a cause of dubious merit, puts a far stronger power (Argos, remember, rules the whole of Greece) in a position where it has effectively no choice but to undertake a dangerous war in the weak party's defence. Again this is a scenario which has been enacted often enough in the last hundred years. Aeschylus' verdict on all these matters is not too hard to see. The Argives have behaved with honour. Pelasgus may not have been quite the ideal ruler, but what he induced the Argives to do was what they would have had to do in any case, and his death expunges any guilt he may have incurred. The Danaids are dupes (with an irony they apparently fail to perceive, they pray that the Argives be granted the blessing of peaceful resolution of their international disputes, *Supp.* 701-3, at the very moment when they are making this impossible). It is their cynically manipulative father, ready to plunge both Egypt and Greece into war to save his own skin, who bears full responsibility for the evil results. That kind of thing still happens too, even if the rulers in question are more likely to be afraid of their electorate, or of a *coup d'état*, than of the fulfilment of an oracle.

We have already examined from various angles the presentation of war in the *Oresteia*. The Trojan War, though justified (and willed by Zeus) as the punishment of Paris' outraging of the laws of hospitality, is nevertheless wrong. The loss of Helen is simply not worth such a vast and costly response: the Argive elders saw that from the start, and when the cost is brought home to the Atreidae by the demand for the sacrifice of Iphigeneia, they see it too, and weep (*Ag.* 202-4). Agamemnon, however, has come too far to go back now without a disastrous loss of prestige (212-13; see §11.2): and he goes straight forward, to victory and also to ruin for his army, his city, his family and himself. He miraculously escapes death at sea only to be killed by his wife; and if he had miraculously escaped death at her hands, it might have been only to meet death at the hands of citizens enraged by the enormous loss of life for which he has been responsible (432-74). He could have avoided his fate only by not launching the war in the first place. Menelaus' grief at the loss of Helen is pitiable (410-28), but he is not the first man to have lost his wife: what right have he and his brother to seek a cure for their grief by bringing comparable or greater grief to countless others (429ff.)? The man, or the community, that is thinking of going to war must ask themselves more questions than the Atreidae did. They asked (1) 'do Paris and the Trojans deserve to suffer severely for what they have done to us?' and answered: yes. They asked (2) 'what can we hope to gain from this war?' and answered: revenge, Helen, booty and prestige. They asked (3) 'do we have a good chance of winning?' and were told by Calchas that it was a certainty (126-30). All these questions they were right to ask, and can be assumed to have answered correctly. But there was a fourth question which they did not ask until it was too late: 'what is it going to cost us, and will it be worth it?' That is a question that is still often not asked by those contemplating war, even when (which is by no means always) they have remembered to consider the first three. But then Agamemnon, when he set out from Argos, did not expect that *he* would have to pay the cost; nor did the other 'chieftains eager for war' (230) who were present at, and in agreement with, the sacrifice of Iphigeneia. A sovereign, democratic assembly, whose members would share at least equally with their leaders in the risks of a war but could not hope for an equal share of the glory, might have seen things more clearly.

The idea that emerges most strongly from all this is that those who are eager for war are very likely to be deceiving their public, or themselves, or both, and that often one will be mistaken to begin a war even when it seems that one is avenging, rectifying or preventing a grave wrong. Where does this leave *Eumenides*? In that play, after all, Athens is repeatedly wished success in war and even an abundance of wars, Ares is treated as one of her patron gods, and Athena is imagined fighting alongside her 'friends' in an African campaign. That campaign, to be sure, was against the Persians, and justifiable as revenge for their sacrilege in Greece (*Eum.* 919-21); but the risk being taken was enormous and might well be thought out of proportion to the prize. And although the inter-Hellenic conflicts of the moment are downplayed, Athenians could hardly be expected to forget about their existence when within months or weeks they might be required to march to battle against the most formidable army in Greece. Has Aeschylus, in writing *Eumenides*, forgotten about the implications of *Agamemnon*? Or is he surer than we might be that a democracy can be trusted not to go to war without good reason?

The explanation of the apparent paradox may lie in a basic feature of the ideology of Athenian democracy, already noted in §12.2. The sovereign people, it was recognized, sometimes made wrong decisions; but the blame for these decisions lay not with the people themselves, but with the speakers and advisers who had 'deceived' them into error, most probably for some corrupt motive.[2] The *dêmos* itself obviously could not possibly have malicious intentions towards itself, but it could be stupid, short-sighted or gullible, and it was common for democratic politicians to accuse it of being so and urge it to change its ways. This ideological construction is reflected in the work of Aeschylus. We have noted (§12.4) that in his plays other than *Eumenides*, the responsibility for wars rests with individuals – a Xerxes, an Eteocles and a Polyneices, a Danaus, an Agamemnon; only in *The Suppliant Maidens* of these five plays is a citizen assembly involved, and there the Argives are deceived by Pelasgus. In *Eumenides* the Athenians have no king or politician to lead them astray; the people are assumed to be wise (1000) and make their decisions intelligently (674, 1012-13); in the trial scene they pay as little attention to Apollo's attempt to bribe them as to the menaces of the Erinyes. If they bring the same critical perception to decisions on war and peace, then Athena's blessing will come true: they will wage no wars but victorious ones (913-15, 1009).

But will they, in reality, reach this high standard? Only four years earlier, after all, they had taken the decision to send help to Sparta against the Helot/Messenian revolt (see §12.1) – an expedition which ended in humiliation and which, had it succeeded, would only have strengthened a power that was soon to be Athens' enemy. And we know now, what Aeschylus and most of his audience did not know and did not believe, that the decision to send an expedition to Egypt was wrong too.[3] Their critical perception had failed: they misjudged the costs, or the odds, or both. It was not to be the last time that that happened at Athens.

Over the two decades up to the time of writing, the leading democracies of the world have repeatedly found themselves considering the choice of going or not going to war, and no international system has yet been devised that can guarantee that this choice will not sooner or later present itself again. If and when it does, those who have to take the decisions (which means all of us, for democratic governments have to take account of public opinion) could do worse than remember to ask themselves the four questions formulated above, to remember that some of those who seek intervention may have hands not much cleaner than those of Danaus or Polyneices, and to remember that, as Agamemnon failed to see even at Aulis, not every war in a righteous cause is a war that it is right to undertake. And having remembered all that, they must also remember (as many in the 1930s tragically forgot) that now and again there arises a potential Xerxes or worse, and that then, while the cost of fighting may be high, the cost of not fighting may be far, far higher.

13.2. Gender and *hybris*

In the field of interstate relations our world has really changed very little from that which Aeschylus knew. In the field of gender relations it has changed enormously. In the modern Western world males and females officially have equal rights, and virtually every occupation and activity is open to both alike; in many areas these rights and opportunities are guaranteed by law, and it is taken for granted that there should be a severe onus of proof on anyone who proposes that any differentiation be made between the treatment of men and women, to the disadvantage of the latter, for any reason or purpose whatever. In Aeschylean Athens, as at most times and places in human history, such a gender-blind society would have been thought an absurd impossibility. The socially significant activities of life were in principle either men's activities or women's, and whatever it was that required to be done, hardly ever was the gender of the person who was to do it a matter of indifference. Except in religious matters, the *polis* was essentially an association of citizen men, and the status of being a female citizen (*astê*) brought with it none of the self-enforceable public rights possessed by every male citizen (*astos*). The destiny of every female citizen was marriage and motherhood (which is why the denial of marriage to the Danaids and to Electra is such a shocking thing), and she could neither reject that destiny, nor normally refuse the husband chosen for her by her father or next of kin: indeed she might be validly and bindingly betrothed (as young women often are in Menander's comedies) without even being informed of the fact. A married woman was under the control of, and legally represented by, her husband; an unmarried woman (who would not normally be more than about fifteen years old) by her father, brother or designated guardian; a widow with children (one without children, if still of childbearing age, would always be remarried as soon as possible) by her sons, her son-in-law, or if the children were still young, by their guardian.

Aeschylus, particularly in the *Oresteia*, has been interpreted by some recent critics as affirming and validating the male-dominated order, and by others as questioning it. It is perhaps more accurate to regard him as taking it fundamentally for granted (as everyone else did) while emphasizing, in common with other tragic poets, that within it women had a legitimate status of their own which must not be infringed. In the public sphere this status was expressed through the many important religious functions that women performed, and women dominate the religious procession at the end of *Eumenides* and sing the processional hymn. In the private sphere women's legitimate status was outraged if they were denied marriage; or if they were treated like pieces of property, as the Danaids are by the sons of Aegyptus; or if they were robbed of their children, as Clytaemestra is of Iphigeneia; or if a husband brought a mistress into his wife's home, as Agamemnon does.

This may not at first sight seem very relevant to our culture, in which a woman cannot be denied marriage (except by her own choice, or by her own failure to find a mate) and in which, if she were subjected to any of the other indignities mentioned, she could obtain redress from the courts (as in Athens she could not, except with the aid of some male kinsman as her representative). There is, however, more than one kind of relevance.

Aeschylus' outstanding female creation, Clytaemestra, is a remarkable portrayal of a woman in power, all the more remarkable because it is almost entirely a creation of the imagination, since Aeschylus can never have met a woman who held such power or anything like it. What he will sometimes have met, however, is *men* who had come to hold power after being in a dependent position – poor men who had become rich and acquired an influential public position, or even freed slaves who had prospered and become slave-owners themselves: it was proverbial, as Clytaemestra herself is made to remark, that such people exercised power harshly (*Ag.* 1044-5, cf. *Prom.* 35). Clytaemestra is such a person. She has not only been dependent on a man who is mentally her inferior, but has been treated by him with contempt in persistent violation of the basic rules outlined above. In *Agamemnon*, as we have seen, her resentment against those who think themselves superior because they are male is obvious, fuelled by her own consciousness of intellectual superiority; after Agamemnon's death she clearly enjoys defying their hostility, and she ends by speaking of them as if they were dogs (*Ag.* 1672). She glories in the reversal of fortune whereby she can commit adultery with impunity while Agamemnon and his paramour can be killed; she stabs his dead body (*Ag.* 1385-7) and afterwards mutilates it (*Cho.* 439-43). She takes care to choose a partner in love and in rule who is devoid of leadership qualities and will be under her thumb. Such is the outcome that can be expected if a person, or a group, that has been treated with arrogant contempt (*hybris*) for a long period, comes to attain power. Such, after all, for many decades, was the nightmare of a large proportion of white South Africans, and but for two great men – a white man who conquered fear, and a black man who conquered revenge[4] – it might have become reality. Such has *been* the reality of many a social revolution. *Hybris*, as the Argive elders say, breeds *hybris*: the outraged will become outragers. And while in our world such situations arise most often in connection with race, class and religion, we are capable of responding in strong and varied ways to the portrayal of such a situation in connection with gender, as witness the controversies aroused in the early 1990s by the film *Thelma and Louise*.

Agamemnon never realizes that he is treating his wife with *hybris*. In his agonized reflections on the demand for the sacrifice of Iphigeneia, it never occurs to him to think of what her mother might feel, and on his return he speaks at some length (*Ag.* 830-44) of the (largely imaginary) jealousy, resentment and hostility of his colleagues at Troy, and on that which may exist at Argos, without ever thinking that he may have incurred the hostility of his wife. His long absence, about which Clytaemestra speaks with feeling that need not be entirely feigned, is for him suitable material for a rather feeble joke (*Ag.* 915-16). He is awarded Chryseis as a prize of war (*Ag.* 1439): of course he takes her. Later he is awarded Cassandra: of course he brings her home, and commits the crowning idiocy of asking his wife to take care of her (*Ag.* 950-5). Not many would be as foolish as that; but many then, and many now, treat others, without realizing it, in ways that make the latter feel deeply insulted – and too often those who do so are male and those to whom it is done are female. To avoid the recoil of *hybris* of which the elders sing, one must refrain from committing it; and a prerequisite for that is to be aware what kinds of action will be perceived as *hybris*. Athena achieves her triumph of reconciliation at the end of the *Oresteia* in part because, the first time she meets the Erinyes, she becomes aware just in time that she is speaking in an insulting manner, stops, and apologizes (*Eum.* 410-14; contrast Apollo, *Eum.* 180-97 etc.). The Erinyes, in their turn, never once insult Athena personally. As *hybris* breeds *hybris*, so respect will breed respect.

13.3. Justice, deterrence and retribution

The *Oresteia* is in one of its aspects a study in the contrast between what Gabriel Herman (1993) has termed 'tribal' and 'civic' codes of behaviour. The tribal code, which is reflected in Homer and in many of the plots of tragedy, and is practised in much of the rural Mediterranean world (and not only there) to this day, requires one, in Herman's words, 'upon being provoked, dishonoured, or injured, ... [to] react impulsively, violently, and at all costs, to inflict upon the offender an injury much graver than the one suffered'. The civic code is the one to which, in general, speakers in the Athenian courts claim to conform. According to it, an injured party 'should exercise self-restraint, should avoid violence, should compromise, and should attach as little importance as possible to the traditional code of honour. More important still, one should separate the reaction from the provocation ... by an appeal to the courts.'

In classical Athens the two codes uneasily coexisted. Over a century after the *Oresteia*, Lycophron, a client of Hypereides defending himself on a charge of adultery, claims that allegations about his behaviour on the woman's wedding day are absurd, because the bride's brother and a friend of his, both famous wrestlers, were present, and had he behaved as alleged he would have been strangled on the spot: 'who could have endured hearing such things said about his sister as they allege I said, without killing the man who said them?'[5] According to the civic code the answer to that rhetorical question would be 'any law-abiding Athenian', and a man who killed in such circumstances would have had no defence to a charge of murder. Yet what Lycophron says must be at least credible to the jury: the average Athenian must at least have been familiar with the notion that one who made a merely verbal assault on a woman's honour might expect to be repaid with instant death. On the other hand, some two generations earlier, as Herman elegantly shows from Lysias' speech *On the Killing of Eratosthenes*, a husband who killed an adulterer actually taken in the act does everything possible to portray himself as a man who cares little for traditional concepts of honour and much for the observance of law: 'it is not I who kill you,' he claims to have said to Eratosthenes, 'it is the law of the *polis*'.[6] Orestes had said something similar to his mother: 'not I will kill you, you will have killed yourself' (*Cho.* 923). On the whole the civic code was effective, largely because access to the courts was easy, their judgements were in general accepted by the community at large, and although enforcement of judgements was largely a matter of self-help, legal remedies and sanctions were available if such enforcement was resisted. But the old instincts of honour and revenge were often not far below the surface, especially perhaps in the years after the revolution of 462/1 and the murder of Ephialtes.

A notable feature of the tribal code, as presented in the *Oresteia*, is that avengers are presented as deriving intense pleasure and satisfaction from the act of revenge. Agamemnon and Menelaus 'utter a great shout of war from their hearts' (*Ag.* 49) as they lead the expedition against Troy. Clytaemestra, similarly, is spoken of by Cassandra as having raised 'a great shout of triumph, as when an enemy is routed in battle' (*Ag.* 1236-7) as the moment of revenge draws near. When she actually kills her husband, she takes what can fairly be called a quasi-erotic delight in the act (*Ag.* 1388-92) and also in the slaying of Cassandra (1446-7); the Elders do not merely suppose she must be mad but actually see madness in her eyes (1426-8). For Aegisthus the mere sight of his dead enemy offers a satisfaction that nothing in life can surpass, so that he would now die happy (1610-11) – an expression which equates his joy with that of the Herald on returning to the native soil he had never expected to see again (539-41, cf. 503-7). The Erinyes, those embodiments of wrathful vengeance, laugh over their victims' sufferings (*Eum.* 560) and are exhilarated by the prospect of a meal of blood (*Eum.* 253, cf. 191-2). Near the end of the trilogy this theme is encapsulated in two powerful phrases, both in prayers against civil strife: Athena speaks vividly of 'whetstones of bloody violence which warp the spirits of young men and make them mad with a rage that does not come from wine' (*Eum.* 859-60), the ex-Erinyes more bluntly of 'lust to avenge' (*orga poinas*) which makes men 'eagerly embrace their city's ruin through tit-for-tat murder' (980-3).

Anger is a powerful emotion; it is not for nothing that we still speak of anger being 'slaked' as if it were thirst, and the slaking of anger, like the satisfaction of other basic physical and emotional needs, can be intensely pleasurable. Uncontrolled, however, it nearly always carries the risk of grave damage to society. The first two plays of the *Oresteia* show what can happen – and terrible as are the events they portray, they are almost an idealization compared with what was to happen, say, in Corcyra thirty years later, or in Rwanda in 1994. Reflection on the legend, and on the tensions and dangers within Athenian society after the murder of Ephialtes, has led Aeschylus to ask a question that has gone on being asked ever since: *what is the purpose of punishment?* I know of no earlier explicit treatment of this issue.

In *Agamemnon* punishment, or vengeance, is inflicted in anger and its only purpose is to satisfy anger. The fact that punishment is often long delayed, even sometimes falling on a subsequent generation, is not evidence against this diagnosis: what happens is that the anger is stored up and brooded on, to become even more devastating than it would have been if acted on immediately. The avenger takes no thought for the future (at least not until *after* vengeance has been taken): vengeance is its own purpose.

In *Choephoroi* there has been a change, on the human level though not necessarily on the divine. Orestes is not acting in anger, whether fresh or bottled: if he were, the long mental preparation session of the *kommos* would have been unnecessary. His motives are almost all thoroughly rational (*Cho.* 297-305), and several of them are to do with setting wrongful situations right: the wrong of his own exclusion from his inheritance, the wrong of Electra's exclusion from marriage,[7] the wrong of the subjection of Argos to an unworthy pair of tyrants. Thus he cannot but look to the future, and he does, as do the chorus. He and his sister pray to their father's spirit for the restoration of their rights (479ff.) and look forward to bringing him offerings from their substance; the chorus envisage success in terms of freedom and of Orestes being master of Argos and of his ancestral wealth (863-5). But though these are his aims, his methods have to be the same as, or worse than, those of his predecessors, the methods of 'raw, bloody strife' (474), and as Electra and the chorus strive to arouse his anger by recalling the indignities inflicted on Agamemnon, Orestes, in contradiction to what he says elsewhere, expresses the wish to die after carrying out his vengeance (438). And at the end of *Choephoroi* it almost seems as though he might as well have done. Neither he nor Argos is any better off. Orestes is forced to flee, and despite the chorus's rejoicing in the liberation of Argos (1046-7) it has merely exchanged despotism for 'anarchy' (absence of government). Only Apollo's promise of protection now offers hope.

In the early part of *Eumenides* there is argumentative deadlock between Apollo, who says the Erinyes and their methods are obscene, and the Erinyes, who say they are doing their traditional duty, assigned by Moira. The arrival of Athena does not at first resolve the deadlock; the Erinyes, while accepting her as judge, do not modify their position that the killing of a mother (and other comparable crimes) demand an automatic reaction without regard to possible mitigating circumstances (*Eum.* 425-32).

But after Athena has gone to select her judges, it is the Erinyes themselves who introduce an idea entirely new to the trilogy:

> Now is the overthrow of ordained
> laws, if victory goes
> to the dangerous plea
> of this matricide.
> *This event will straightway unite*
> *all men in freedom from inhibitions* (*Eum.* 490-5).

Orestes' acquittal, that is, must at all costs be prevented, not because it is an insult to the Erinyes, nor because their anger demands that he suffer, nor even because he deserves to suffer for what he has done, but *because it will encourage criminal behaviour in others.* This note continues to be struck in what follows. More parents can expect to be struck down by their children (496-8); the Erinyes, by not pursuing murderers, will unleash every kind of death (499-502) for which a cure will be sought in vain (503-16). There is a place for Fear in men's minds, and without it neither an individual nor a community can be expected to practise justice (517-25).

That is the answer the Erinyes give now to the question 'what is the purpose of punishment?' *The purpose of punishment is the prevention of crime.* And Athena agrees:

> Upon this hill, reverence
> and inborn *fear of the citizens shall restrain*
> *wrongdoing* by day and night alike ... .

> I counsel my citizens to cherish and practise
> the mean between anarchy and despotism,
> and not to banish fear entirely from the city;
> for *what man observes justice if he fears nothing?* (690-2, 696-9).

It follows, in the first place, that the infliction of punishment must not be left to the victims or their representatives, who will be moved by anger and 'lust to avenge'. Athena has put decisions regarding the punishment of homicide into the hands of an impartial body of representatives of the community, who hate crime but do not have personal reason to hate the alleged criminal, and who will base their decisions on a rational assessment of the case (*Eum.* 674-5). In the fullness of time her people will make similar provision for the trial of other offences. And it follows, in the second place, that the question these judges must ask themselves is not 'what does this criminal deserve to suffer?' but 'what punishment, if any, will it be for the good of the community to inflict upon him?'

The philosophy of punishment here presented is one of deterrence; the word 'fear' is prominent. There will be less crime if those who might be tempted to it (as Paris was by Temptation, daughter of Ruin: *Ag.* 385ff.) are shown convincingly that it will not pay. The third pillar of subsequent penology, reformation, is not considered. This is because no punishments existed which could serve such a purpose – except indeed in the disciplining of children and of slaves; it was left to Plato, especially in *The Laws*, to devise a system that made punishment into a form of education. Aeschylus, I think, would have agreed with the views which Plato in an earlier dialogue attributes to Protagoras:

> For no one punishes a wrongdoer with no other thought in mind than that he did wrong, unless he is retaliating unthinkingly like an animal. Someone who aims to punish in a rational way doesn't chastise on account of the past misdeed – for that wouldn't undo what is already done – but for the sake of the future, so that neither the wrongdoer himself, nor anyone else who sees him punished, will do wrong again (*Protagoras* 324a-b, tr. C.C.W. Taylor).

'Retaliating unthinkingly like an animal' is precisely what Atreus, Agamemnon, Clytaemestra and Aegisthus are presented as doing; there is no more rationality in their desires (as opposed to their schemes for giving effect to those desires) than in the actions of the lion of *Ag.* 727-36. Such unthinking retaliation nearly ruined Argos, and in 458 BC, if not restrained, it would be capable of ruining Athens, with an almost unlimited potential to create misery for the innocent.

Popular discussions of punishment today tend to be polarized between the retributivist and reformationist positions, often thought of as 'hard' and 'soft' respectively.[8] In part this is because both retribution and reformation can easily be discussed in terms of individuals. It makes a good news story to interview the dead child's mother who expresses satisfaction that the murderer will never be free again, or indignation that the hit-and-run driver was given only three years. It makes a good feature programme to interview the ex-criminals who are now leading an honest life thanks to careful and kindly supervision and training, and those who have helped them to achieve this. It is impossible to interview those who have been tempted to commit crime but deterred by the fear of detection and punishment: they may not even be aware of the fact, and if they are, they are not likely to admit it. The result is that even some professional criminologists are capable of talking and writing as if retribution and reformation were the only possible purposes of punishment. Retribution, as Aeschylus saw, appeals to some very basic instincts. Reformation appeals to others, in particular to the instincts underlying parental care and training. Deterrence does not appeal to instincts at all; it appeals to reason, and in the age of the sound-bite it takes an exceptional intellect to make an appeal to reason in the sixty seconds the media will usually allow.

The rejection of unthinking retaliation, of knee-jerk retributivism, does not entail being soft on crime. The council of the Areopagus certainly was not; those convicted of murder by it were sentenced to death, and death, in some cases by *apotympanismos* (see §8.3), was either the obligatory or an optional penalty for a wide range of other offences tried by ordinary juries. Plato retained it in *The Laws* for those serious criminals whom he thought beyond reformation (including – with terrible irony, for a devoted disciple of Socrates – those who engaged in certain heretical religious practices[9]). In *Eumenides* the Erinyes, who in future will pursue those who evade human justice, may be as savage under the new dispensation as they ever were under the old (*Eum.* 932-7, 954-5). There is no general answer to the question whether punishment should be severe or mild. The ultimate, if perhaps unattainable, object of penal laws is to create a society free of crime; the ultimate object of punishment is to do away with itself:

> Out of these fearsome countenances
> I see great benefit for my citizens:
> if you always kindly confer great honour
> on these kindly powers, you will in every way
> lead the city and the land
> on the straight path of justice and splendour (*Eum.* 990-5).

To punish severely, in appropriate cases, is right and necessary – and, in the long run, kind, as Athena implies in the passage just quoted. To derive pleasure from inflicting punishment, no matter how deserved, or from seeing it inflicted, is wrong and may be disastrous. It is wrong too, in a more subtle way, to base punishment on an emotional reaction to the particular crime or criminal, instead of on the general interests of the community. It is not easy to hold that balance. It is not easy to respond to the conviction of a murderer not with 'Serve him right' or 'I hope he fries' (cf. *Cho.* 267-8) but with 'Now we're that little bit safer'. And when people take the law into their own hands in a way that arouses sympathy – say a woman kills a persistently brutal husband, or a group of neighbours tie up and beat a youth suspected (perhaps for good reason, though without legally acceptable evidence) of a series of burglaries – it is not easy to remember that in the not so long run more innocent people will suffer if the offenders are not sent to prison than if they are, as others follow their example with more dubious justification. The civic code is unnatural. But so is civilization. And if we want the one – so Aeschylus suggests – we must accept the other.

13.4. The good society

In two plays of Aeschylus, *The Suppliant Maidens* and *Eumenides*, the chorus are made to sing a long prayer calling down blessings on a *polis* (Argos and Athens respectively) which has accepted them as residents (*metoikoi*). The two prayers are for much of their length closely parallel (though each contains features of its own appropriate to the singers or the context), and between them they may be thought to constitute a recipe for a successful society. We could do worse, in concluding this chapter and this book, than to see how the recipe looks after twenty-four or twenty-five centuries. The greater part of both songs is taken up with wishes for prosperity and freedom from suffering; but each concludes with a prayer, in different terms, that the *polis* be well governed. I have translated the two prayers on the next page. I offer no commentary except where a phrase needs explanation; I will leave readers to reflect for themselves on what follows and on how it may apply (not always literally) to our own day.

Suppliant Maidens 698-709

May the people, who rule the city,
properly protect the dignities of the citizens
and rule with foresight and with good counsel for the common weal.
With foreigners may they accept
painless judgement under fair agreements[10]
before arming the god of war.
And may they ever honour the gods who dwell in the land
with the native ancestral honours,
bearing of laurel boughs and sacrificing of oxen;
and may there be honouring of parents too,
which is written third in the ordinances
of Justice supreme in honour.

Eumenides 976-87

I pray that Faction,[11] insatiate of evil,
may never rage in this city;

and may the dust not drink up the dark blood of the citizens
and then, out of lust for revenge,
eagerly embrace the city's ruin
through retaliatory murder;
rather may they give happiness in return for happiness,
resolved to be united in their friendship
and unanimous in their enmity;
for this is a cure for many ills among men.

Notes

1. A notable and highly controversial recent example was the 1993 adaptation by Peter Sellars, set against the background of the Gulf War of 1991, on which see E.M. Hall 2004 (esp. 176-85).

2. An attitude with which Thucydides had little patience, remarking that when the Athenians learned of the catastrophic failure of the Sicilian expedition 'they were angry at those politicians who had been enthusiastic for the expedition, *as though they themselves had not voted for it*' (Thucydides 8.1.1).

3. The expedition ended, four or five years later, in utter disaster (Thucydides 1.109-10).

4. Since only one of their names is universally known today, I here name them both: F.W. de Klerk and Nelson Mandela, who were jointly awarded the Nobel Peace Prize for 1993.

5. Hypereides, *For Lycophron* 7.

6. Lysias, *On the Killing of Eratosthenes* 26.

7. Orestes nowhere explicitly mentions this, but it is clear from 252-6 that he regards Electra as a victim equally with himself.

8. I am not claiming that such discussions *always* elide considerations of deterrence, but they certainly do so very often.

9. Plato, *Laws* 910c-d.

10. The reference is to *symbola*, interstate agreements under which disputes were referred to arbitration under rules specified in the agreement.

11. Greek *stasis*, factional strife, usually violent.

Genealogies

1. The House of Laius

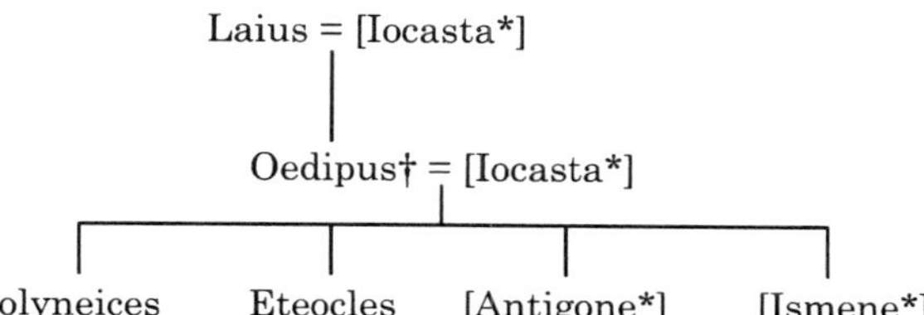

*The mother-wife of Oedipus is not, so far as we know, named in the Theban tetralogy. Antigone and Ismene appear in the ending of *Seven* as transmitted but probably did not appear in the original play (see §5.6).

†Exposed as a baby and taken to Corinth, where he was brought up by Polybus and Merope, believing himself to be their son.

2. The Danaids and their ancestors

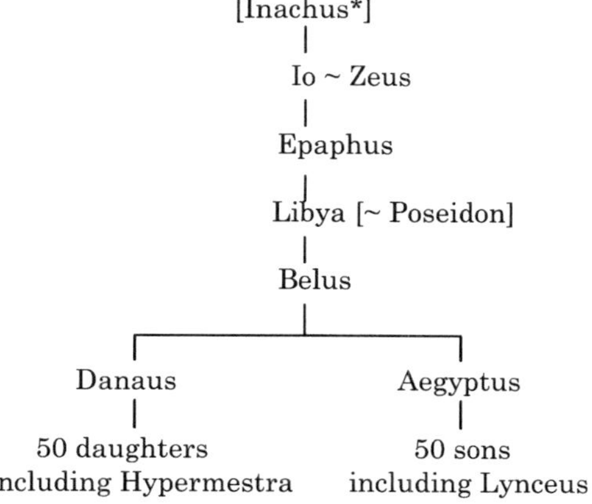

*The father of Io, and the father of Belus, are known from other sources but are not (so far as our evidence goes) identified in the Danaid trilogy.

3. The family of Agamemnon and Menelaus

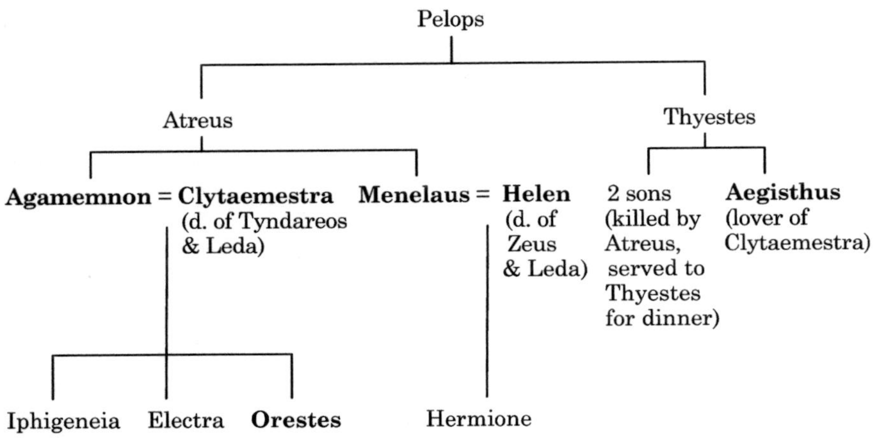

Bibliographical Guide

Where a modern work originally written in another language has been translated into English, it is referred to in this Guide by the date of publication of the translation, and appears in the List of References under that date but with the date of original publication in brackets, thus 'Lesky 1983 [1972]'.

General

Texts, translations and commentaries

The standard critical edition of the seven surviving plays of Aeschylus is M.L. West 1990a, whose accurate, informative and economical critical apparatus, and the invaluable linguistic information supplied in his introduction, make it essential for specialists despite its high price; those who simply want a good text of the seven plays between one pair of covers may well remain content with Page 1972.

For the ancient commentary material (*scholia*) preserved in the medieval manuscripts, see the editions of Dähnhardt 1894 and Massa Positano 1963 (for *The Persians*), Herington 1972 (for *Prometheus Bound*), and O.L. Smith 1976, 1982 (for the other plays).

The standard edition of the fragments of lost plays is Radt 1985, which also includes all the ancient evidence relating to Aeschylus' life and work and ancient critical comment thereon. Radt's numbering of the fragments is based on that of Nauck 1889; many works published between about 1960 and 1985 use instead the very different numeration of Mette 1959, and they do not always warn the reader of this. There is a richly annotated Spanish translation of all the Aeschylean fragments, with extensive introductions to each play, by Lucas de Dios 2008.

The new Loeb edition (Sommerstein 2008) includes a freshly constituted text, with facing translation, of the seven plays and of fragments containing at least the equivalent of one line of continuous text.

All seven surviving plays have been edited with commentaries in English during the last sixty years (the asterisked editions also include a translation):

The Persians: Broadhead 1960; E.M. Hall 1996*; Garvie 2009 (see also Belloni 1988).
Seven against Thebes: Hutchinson 1985 (see also Lupaç & Petre 1981).
The Suppliant Maidens: Friis Johansen & Whittle 1980; Sandin 2003 (lines 1-523 only).
Oresteia: Thomson 1966.
Agamemnon: Fraenkel 1950*; Denniston & Page 1957 (see also Bollack & Judet de la Combe 1982, Judet de la Combe 2001).
Choephoroi: Garvie 1986 (see also, on the lyrics only, Sier 1988).
Eumenides: Podlecki 1989*; Sommerstein 1989a.
Prometheus Bound: Griffith 1982; Podlecki 2005a*.

Complete translations of the seven plays include, besides the Loeb edition mentioned above, Ewans 1995 + 1996 (with 'notes' which in fact constitute a detailed study of the staging of the plays), Collard 2002 + 2008 (a very accurate rendering of West's text, with excellent annotations and bibliography); and Shapiro & Burian 2003 + Burian & Shapiro 2009.

Separate translations of the *Oresteia* are numerous. Among the most noteworthy are Lloyd-Jones 1979 (annotated) and Meineck & Foley 1998; Fagles & Stanford 1977 (annotated) is a good example of poet-scholar collaboration; [Headlam &] Thomson 1938 (facing Greek text, with commentary) is notable for its attempt to reproduce in the lyrics the rhythms of the Greek. In recent decades there have been some performance-orientated 'translations' of great merit (e.g. Raphael & McLeish 1979, Tony Harrison 1981), but they nearly always omit, telescope or transpose important sections of text.

Among separate translations of other plays suitable for the serious student may be noted, in addition to those asterisked above:

The Persians: Podlecki 1970 or 1991 (both annotated).
Seven against Thebes: Dawson 1970 (annotated).
The Suppliant Maidens: Friis Johansen [& Smith] 1970 (facing Greek text); Burian 1991.
Prometheus Bound: Thomson 1932 (facing Greek text, with commentary).

Bibliographies and other study aids

Wartelle 1978 aims to list all scholarly work on Aeschylus from the first printed edition until 1974. *L'Année Philologique* records publications annually, with brief summaries of articles and references to reviews of books; all of its records, from its foundation in 1924, are now available online (www.annee-philologique.com/aph/). Italie 1964 catalogues the occurrences, constructions and senses of words used in the plays and fragments (supplementary word-list, without annotation, in Radt 1985: 515-19).

General works

Aeschylus, unlike Sophocles, suffers from a shortage of recent general studies; the best are Gagarin 1976, Rosenmeyer 1982 (concentrating on poetic and dramatic technique, and organized by topic rather than by play), Winnington-Ingram 1983 (essentially a revised collection of articles), Herington 1986, Court 1994 and Lossau 1998. Taplin 1977, though nominally devoted to 'the dramatic use of exits and entrances', is an unmatched study of many aspects of Aeschylean dramatic and theatrical technique. Gruber 2009 discusses the roles and functions of the Aeschylean chorus. There are some good introductions to Aeschylus in books dealing more generally with Greek tragedy, e.g. Winnington-Ingram 1985, Lesky 1983: 37-114, Kitto 1961: 1-114, Görgemanns 1979, Zimmermann 1991: 26-55, Latacz 1993: 86-160, Saïd 2005. McCall 1972, Hommel 1974, Segal 1983: 13-137, and Lloyd 2007 are anthologies of articles. Conacher 1980 + 1987 + 1996 presents critical readings of all seven plays.

On aspects of Aeschylus' language and style see Stanford 1942, Earp 1948, Fowler 1967, Sideras 1971, Sansone 1975, Petrounias 1976, and Matino 1998.

On the transmission of the text see Dawe 1964, M.L. West 1990a: iii-xxiv and 1990b: 319-54; on the transmission of ancient texts generally, Reynolds & Wilson 1991.

The literary and artistic evidence for the myths used by Aeschylus (as by other early poets) is set out by Gantz 1993; the artistic evidence is presented and discussed, with full illustration, in *LIMC*. Föllinger 2003 is a study of Aeschylus' treatment of myth.

Chapter 1. The Life and Times of Aeschylus

The principal ancient sources for the history of Greece, especially Athens, in Aeschylus' lifetime are Herodotus for the period down to 479 (especially 5.55-103 and 6.85 onwards); Thucydides 1.89-108 (from 479 to the mid 450s); Aristotle, *The Athenian Constitution* 17-26 (probably in fact the work of a pupil, and based on patchy sources uncritically handled, but containing much good information not otherwise available); Diodorus Siculus 11; Plutarch's lives of Themistocles, Aristeides, Cimon and Pericles (based mainly on fourth-century sources, but including material from two gossipy contemporaries, Ion and Stesimbrotus, and from Craterus' collection of state decrees); surviving contemporary inscriptions (for a selection of inscriptions of historical significance see Meiggs & Lewis 1988: 19-83, 309-10; for those relating to dramatic competitions see Snell & Kannicht 1986: 3-52, 341-4 and Mette 1977) – and the plays of Aeschylus himself, especially but not exclusively *The Persians*. Crawford & Whitehead 1983: 147-321 offer a particularly rich and well-commented anthology of source material in translation.

Modern historical introductions tend to end or to begin about the time of the Persian invasions (conventionally taken to divide the 'archaic' from the 'classical' period); Ehrenberg 1973 is an exception. On the late archaic period see Forrest 1986, O. Murray 1993: 246-301, J.M. Hall 2007, Burn 1984, and Cawkwell 2005: 1-125; on the post-Persian War period, Meiggs 1972: 1-108, J.K. Davies 1978: 13-128, Powell 1988: 1-135, Osborne 2000, Hornblower 2002, Rhodes 2005, and (for a reconstruction differing sharply in many respects from the recent consensus) Badian 1993. The pivotal figure of Themistocles has attracted more attention than any other individual; see Podlecki 1975a, Lenardon 1978, Frost 1980. On the introduction of comedy to the City Dionysia, here regarded as part of Themistocles' populist policy, see A.T. Edwards 1993.

The ancient biographical tradition about Aeschylus (as about other poets) is to be approached with critical scepticism, though not necessarily as much as is shown by Fairweather 1974, Lefkowitz 1981 (who *inter alia* translates the biography transmitted in certain medieval manuscripts) or, in connection with Aeschylus' alleged epitaph, by Page 1981: 129ff. who assigns it firmly to the Hellenistic period (Sommerstein 1996 argues against this). On Aeschylus' Sicilian visits see Herington 1967, 1970; Lloyd-Jones 1971: 95-103; Griffith 1978; Basta Donzelli 2003.

On the early history of Athenian tragedy, and on Phrynichus and his contemporaries, see Lloyd-Jones 1966, Garvie 1969 (=2005): 88-140, Lesky 1983: 1-36, Herington 1985. On the City Dionysia* see Pickard-Cambridge *et al.* 1988: 57-101, Goldhill 1987, Osborne 1993; Csapo & Slater 1994: 103-21 present a selection of source texts.

For what is known regarding the later members of Aeschylus' family, including the known titles and surviving fragments of their plays, see Snell & Kannicht 1986 under the names of Euphorion I, Euaeon, Philocles I and II, Melanthius I, Morsimus, and Astydamas I and II.

*The name 'Great Dionysia', often used by modern writers, is anachronistic; it is not attested in our sources before about 330 (Aristotle, *Constitution of Athens* 56.4).

The reception of Aeschylus in the two generations after his death is discussed by Zimmermann 2005.

Chapter 2. Aeschylus' Theatre

On the Theatre of Dionysus, and the physical conditions of production in Aeschylus' time, see Pickard-Cambridge 1946, Dinsmoor 1951, Arnott 1962, Hammond 1972, 1988, Melchinger 1974, Taplin 1977: 434-59, 1978: 9-21, Newiger 1979, Simon 1982a, Gould 1985, Rehm 1988 and 1992, Green 1991, Green & Handley 1995, Wiles 2000: 89-127. For the evidence on which is based the theory of a quadrilateral *orkhêstra* see Pöhlmann *et al.* 1995 and Goette 2007 (*contra*, Scullion 1994: 3-66 and Wiles 1997: 23-62). On doors in the *skênê* see Dover 1966. On the *mêkhanê* and *ekkyklêma* see Hourmouziades 1965 (who concentrates on Euripides), Newiger 1990, and Mastronarde 1990.

On tragic actors see Ghiron-Bistagne 1976, Slater 1990, Heiden 1993, Easterling & Hall 2002; on the tragic chorus, Webster 1970, Pickard-Cambridge *et al.* 1988: 232-62, Winkler 1990 (who argues that they were of 'ephebic' age, i.e. 18-20); on costumes and masks, Pickard-Cambridge *et al.* 1988: 177-209, 362-3, Wiles 2000: 147-59. Marshall 2003 is an interesting study of the distribution of parts in the *Oresteia* and its possible implications.

On many matters discussed in this chapter, Taplin 1977 remains fundamental.

Csapo & Slater 1994 collect a wide range of ancient texts (in translation) relating to ancient theatres and the performances that took place in them.

On the artistic evidence relevant to fifth-century dramatic performances see Webster 1967 (catalogue), Trendall & Webster 1971, Green 1991.

The composition of the theatre audience is discussed, from very different points of view, by Goldhill 1997 and Sommerstein 1997. Henderson 1991 argues that women formed a not insignificant part of it. Pope 1986, Csapo & Slater 1994: 157-60, and Marshall & van Willigenburg 2004 attempt to reconstruct the judging procedure.

Chapter 3. The Tetralogy

The fundamental discussions of the Aeschylean tetralogy are Gantz 1979 and 1980. Radt 1985: 111-19 lists all the proposals that had been made, up to that date, for the reconstruction of trilogies and tetralogies. On particular groups of plays not discussed in later chapters, the following studies are of interest: (#4, *Lycurgeia*) M.L. West 1990b: 26-50, Jouan 1992; (#7, *Aethiopis* group) M.L. West 2000: 343-50; (#8, Ajax group) March 1993: 4-7; (#9, Dionysus at Thebes) Dodds 1960a: xxix-xxxiii, March 1989, Jouan 1992; (#11, Argonautic group) Deforge 1987; (#13, Perseus group) Goins 1997; (#14, Telephus group) Preiser 2000: 51-9.

The pattern in some trilogies of a 'movement from more barbaric to more civilized behaviour' has been emphasized especially by Herington (1965, 1970, 1986); see also Moreau 1985, and (on the role of persuasion in the process) Buxton 1982, esp. 105-14.

Chapter 4. *The Persians*

Book-length studies of *The Persians* in English are Michelini 1982, T.E.H. Harrison 2000 and Rosenbloom 2006; see also Paduano 1978 and the conference volume Ghiron-Bistagne *et al.* 1993. Other important studies include Adams 1952, Kitto 1966: 74-106, Alexanderson 1967, Winnington-Ingram 1973, Thalmann 1980, Saïd 1981, 1988 and 2002, Lenz 1986, Goldhill 1988, Pelling 1997b, Garvie 1999,

McClure 2006, Garvie 2007: 174-9, and Papadimitropoulos 2008; and *The Persians* is a fundamental text for the investigation of E.M. Hall 1989 into the figure of the 'barbarian' in Athenian tragedy and in Athenian fifth-century thought. Lazenby 1988 is an examination, by a noted historian of ancient warfare, of the play's account of the battle of Salamis; the battle is analysed in great detail, with the evidence of Aeschylus both exploited and assessed, in Wallinga 2005.

The discussion of the tetralogy in §4.2 is based on Sommerstein 2010b.

On ring-composition (p. 47) see Friis Johansen 1954: 32-48, Garvie 1969 (= 2005): 74-8, Griffith 1977: 207-9.

Chapter 5. The Theban Plays

There have been book-length studies of *Seven against Thebes* by Cameron 1971, Thalmann 1978, Zeitlin 2009, Berman 2007 and Torrance 2007 (see also the conference volume Aloni *et al.* 2002); other important general studies are Winnington-Ingram 1977, Jackson 1988 and Stehle 2005. The character of Eteocles has attracted much attention, being discussed from various angles by Lesky 1961a, von Fritz 1962: 193-226 (translated in Lloyd 2007: 141-73), Golden 1964, Podlecki 1964 and 1993, O.L. Smith 1969, Caldwell 1973, Brown 1977 and Lawrence 2007; see also more generally, on characterization in Aeschylus, Easterling 1973, and, with special reference to Eteocles' final decision, Long 1986, Nussbaum 1986: 38-41 and DeVito 1999. The 'shield scene' has been analysed by Fraenkel 1957, Bacon 1964, Wilkens 1974, Vidal-Naquet 1981a, Judet de la Combe 1987 and Johnson 1992. On the chorus, see Byrne 1997 and Roisman 2004 (esp. 95-7). Wiles 1993 explores visual aspects of the play and their relationship to the script. Ieranò 2002 and Zimmermann 2004 discuss Homeric resonances in the play.

The ending of *Seven* is regarded as spurious by all recent editors and commentators (except Lupaş & Petre 1981 who are non-committal); see also Dawe 1967, 1978, and Barrett 2007b. Lloyd-Jones 1959, Flintoff 1980 and Orwin 1980 defend its authenticity; Brown 1976 takes a middle course.

The earlier plays of the trilogy and their bearing on *Seven* are examined, usually with particular reference to the curse of Oedipus, by Burnett 1973, Thalmann 1982, March 1987: 139-48, and Sommerstein 1989b: 440-5; the play is a major focus of attention in the discussions of inherited guilt, curses, etc., by Föllinger 2003 and Sewell-Rutter 2007. On *The Sphinx* see Simon 1981.

On ancient Greek society as a 'results culture' (p. 79) see Adkins 1960 (overstated), Dover 1974, Cairns 1993.

Chapter 6. The Danaid Plays

Garvie 1969 (updated in 2005) is fundamental, though it does not supersede such earlier studies as Winnington-Ingram 1961, von Fritz 1962: 160-92 and Lloyd-Jones 1964. Subsequent valuable 'readings' of *Supp.* have included Burian 1974, Ireland 1974, Gantz 1978, Mackinnon 1978, Zeitlin 1992, des Bouvrie 1990: 147-66, Sicherl 1986, Rohweder 1998, Gödde 2000, Murnaghan 2005, Mitchell 2006 and Papadopoulou 2010. Grethlein 2003: 45-107, Bernek 2004, and Naiden 2004: 83-8 and 2006, have made important contributions on the theme of supplication and/or the play's connections with contemporary Athens. Sicherl's article stimulated much subsequent work on the reconstruction of the trilogy, including that of Rösler 1993 and Sommerstein 1995; Podlecki 1975b, like Garvie, had been thoroughly sceptical about the possibilities of any such reconstruction (cf. also

Hose 2006). Scullion 2002: 87-101 has valuably reminded us not to be dogmatic about the date of the play. On *Amymone* see Sutton 1974; on the Io myth see R.D. Murray 1958, Wehrli 1967, Yalouris 1990 and Calame 2000: 117-43.

Chapter 7. The *Oresteia*

7.1-3. Two excellent introductions to the *Oresteia*, with contrasting approaches, are Conacher 1987 and Goldhill 2004; four 'readings' of the trilogy, likewise contrasting, are provided by Kitto 1956 (esp. 1-86), Vickers 1973: 347-437, Goldhill 1984 (see also Goldhill 1986: 1-56 which is considerably more reader-friendly; Wiles 1987 subjects both Goldhill's books to a measured critique), and Rehm 1992: 77-108. Käppel 1998a is a major analysis of the structure and movement of the trilogy; see also Käppel 1998b on the changing role of the chorus.

Valuable studies of particular sections of the trilogy are numerous, and only a few can be mentioned here: Gantz 1983 and Thiel 1993 (on the chorus in *Ag.*); Bergson 1967, P.M. Smith 1980 and Weglage 1991 (on the 'Hymn to Zeus'); Schenker 1999 and Fletcher 1999 (on apparent changes of mind in *Ag.*); J.R. Wilson 1995 (on failure of communication in *Ag.*); Knox 1952 and Nappa 1994 (on the lion-cub parable in *Ag.* 717-36); Easterling 1973, Dover 1987b, Konishi 1989, Judet de la Combe 1990 and Crane 1993 (on the 'crimson fabric' scene); Morgan 1994 (on Cassandra, Orestes and Apollo); O'Daly 1985 (on the scene following Agamemnon's murder); Garvie 1970 (on the beginning of *Cho.*); McCall 1990 (on the chorus of *Cho.*); Hame 2004 (on the funeral rites of Agamemnon); Pontani 2007 (on Orestes' ruse in *Cho.*); Brown 1982, 1983, 1984, and Johnston 1999: 250-87 (on the presentation of the Erinyes; Brown 1984 is answered by Lloyd-Jones 1990b and Henrichs 1994); Porter 2005, Frontisi-Ducroux 2006, 2007, Easterling 2008, Revermann 2008, Bowie 2009, and especially Mitchell-Boyask 2009 (on *Eumenides*); Dyer 1969 and Sidwell 1996 (on the question of Orestes' pollution and purification); Gagarin 1975, Hester 1981, Seaford 1995 and Braun 1998 (on the vote of Athena). On the conclusion of the trilogy in its relation to the Panathenaea, and on other more or less probable echoes of myths and cults not directly connected with the Agamemnon-Orestes story and their possible significance, see Bowie 1993 (but note the cautions of Stinton 1986 on this type of interpretative strategy); the conclusion is also discussed by Taplin 1996: 198-9, Gredley 1996: 211-12, and Bacon 1999. Van Erp Taalman Kip 1996 and Garvie 1996 debate the unity of the trilogy and the points at which it may be subject to strain. Moreau 1998 discusses the portrayal and significance of lower-class characters in the trilogy (and also in *Seven*). On *Proteus* see Sutton 1984 and Griffith 2002 (esp. 237-54). For studies dealing with the narrative of the sacrifice of Iphigeneia see bibliography to Chapter 11.

7.4. On previous versions of the myth, and Aeschylus' transformation of them, there are five good recent studies: M. Davies 1968, Prag 1985 (the fullest, covering both art and poetry), March 1987: 79-98; Moreau 1990; and Shapiro 1994: 125-48. Knoepfler 1993 covers artistic representations of the story from the beginnings to Roman times.

7.5. The fundamental study of metre and music in the *Oresteia*, and in Aeschylus generally, is Scott 1984; see also Chiasson 1988 on the lekythion (cf. p. 148 above). For an account of Greek metre see M.L. West 1982 (or its abridged and simplified version, M.L. West 1987); Dale 1968 discusses the lyric metres of drama (both tragedy and comedy) at a more specialized level; Dale 1971-83 presents metrical analyses of all choral passages in surviving tragedy. Parry 1978 examines the functions of lyric in tragedy generally.

7.6. The best discussion of many of the topics of this section is to be found in Taplin 1977 and/or 1978. On Clytaemestra's weapon see M. Davies 1987 (axe), Sommerstein 1989c and Prag 1991 (sword), and Marshall 2001 (axe in later revivals?) On 'silent characters' I discuss only those who never speak at all; Aeschylus' ways of exploiting the silence in one part of a play of characters who speak earlier or later are the subject of a classic article by Taplin 1972 (and see §10.1 on Achilles and §11.4 on Niobe).

7.7. On Aeschylean imagery and thematics in general see O.L. Smith 1965, Fowler 1967, Sansone 1975, Petrounias 1976, Mossman 1996 and Conacher 1996: 115-49; on that of the *Oresteia*, Goheen 1955, Peradotto 1964, Zeitlin 1965, Lebeck 1971, Vidal-Naquet 1981b, Thalmann 1985, Roth 1993, and J. Heath 1999a, 1999b, 2005.

7.8. Gagarin 1976: 87-105 has an excellent discussion of gender issues in the *Oresteia*. Many valuable ideas on the subject await the patient reader of Goldhill 1984 (for the less patient, Goldhill 1986: 51-6 and 2004: 33-41 may be preferable). Winnington-Ingram 1948, meanwhile, remains a classic, though some have suspected the author (as some may suspect the present author) of wishful thinking; Burian 2006 too argues that the ending of the trilogy is not to be seen as presenting a purely masculinist ideology. Griffith 1998, contrariwise, argues that tragedy frequently seems to validate in the end the supremacy of the father in the *oikos* and the fatherly king in the *polis*. See also Zeitlin 1978, Podlecki 1983, Moreau 1994, E.M. Hall 1997, 2006: 60-183, and Foley 2001; also Moles 1979, Pulleyn 1997, and Sommerstein 2002: 154-7 on Clytaemestra's use of sexually suggestive language in the scene following Agamemnon's death, McCoskey 1998 on women and slaves in the trilogy, Mitchell-Boyask 2006 on Cassandra and Apollo, and McClure 1999: 70-111 on gender and language. Zeitlin 1999: 190-4 offers a new mythical perspective on Athena's role at the end of the *Oresteia*. On the Amazons see Boardman 1982, Tyrrell 1984, Hardwick 1990, Blok 1995.

7.9. Discussions of the theme of *dikê*, and of the role of the gods, are to be found in all general studies of Aeschylus and of the *Oresteia*, as well as in many books on early Greek religion and ethics, among which may be specially noted Lloyd-Jones 1971: 84-103 and Fisher 1992: 270-97. Specialized studies include Lloyd-Jones 1956, Fontenrose 1971, Euben 1982, Winnington-Ingram 1983: 132-74, and many works focusing on Agamemnon's decision to sacrifice his daughter (for which see on §11.2). The approach taken in the present section owes most to Kitto (1956: 1-86, 1961: 62-93, 1966: 38-74). P.J. Wilson 2006 analyses Aeschylus' thematic exploitation in the *Oresteia* of the use of the accusative case of *dikê* as a preposition (or more often a postposition) in the sense 'like, in the manner of'.

7.10. The 'political' aspects of the *Oresteia*, in the broad sense with which this section is concerned, are brilliantly discussed by Macleod 1982; see also Dodds 1960b, Easterling 1989, Meier 1990: 82-139, Meier 1993, Schaps 1993, Cartledge 1997, Griffith 1998, Chiasson 1999/2000, Goldhill 2000a, 2000b, Rhodes 2003, Carter 2004, 2007: 29-34, 58-63, M.L. West 2006, M. Heath 2006. Saïd 1993a considers the significance of Argos as a *polis* in tragedy; Podlecki 1986 and 1993 explore the relations between ruler and community in early tragedy. Thomson 1973 and Rose 1992 examine the 'politics' of the *Oresteia* and of Aeschylean tragedy generally from Marxist standpoints. Griffith 1995 explores the contribution of the *Oresteia*, and of Athenian tragedy generally, to the promotion of cohesion and solidarity between mass and élite in Athens.

Chapter 8. The Prometheus Plays

Good general treatments of *Prometheus Bound*, from various points of view, are Conacher 1980, Winnington-Ingram 1983: 175-97, Saïd 1985, and Stoessl 1988; see also Garzya 1965, Bollack 2006, Fowler 1957, Mossman 1996 (imagery), and Scott 1987 (chorus). White 2001 offers as good a case as can probably be made for the view that Prometheus is to be seen as short-sightedly frustrating the benevolent long-term plans of Zeus. On issues of staging see (besides Taplin 1977: 240-75) M.L. West 1979, Davidson 1994, Dyson 1994. Recent scholarship has tended to focus on the issues of authenticity, of date and of the trilogy, and to link these together; of the major studies, Griffith 1977, 1978 and 1984, Taplin 1977: 460-9, M.L. West 1979 and 1990b: 51-72, Bees 1993, Marzullo 1993, Lefèvre 2003, and (on theological grounds) Bees 2009: 260-309 regard the play as spurious, while Herington 1970, Dodds 1973: 26-44, Pattoni 1987, Lloyd-Jones 2003, and Podlecki 2005a: 195-200 defend Aeschylean authorship. On the trilogy (or dilogy, as the case may be) see M.L. West 1979 and Brown 1990; Fitton Brown 1959 is still worth consulting. Dougherty 2005 is a study of Prometheus the god, in which these plays are naturally a major focus of attention. S.R. West 1994 explores the connections (through the cyclic epic, the *Titanomachy*?) between the version of the Prometheus myth presented in these plays, so different from Hesiod's, and Near Eastern myths, especially those of the Flood.

Chapter 9. Aeschylean Satyr-drama

On satyr-drama in general see Sutton 1980 (esp. pp. 14-35 on Aeschylus), Seaford 1984: 1-48, Easterling 1997b: 37-44, E.M. Hall 1998 and 2006: 142-69, Griffith 2002, Seidensticker 2003 and 2005, and above all Krumeich *et al.* 1999 who have detailed discussions of every satyr-play of which fragments survive; on the satyr-plays of Aeschylus, Ussher 1977, Gallo 1981b, Simon 1982b, and Podlecki 2005b.

Chapter 10. Slices from Homeric Feasts

The most important discussions of the Iliadic plays are Schadewaldt 1936, Taplin 1972: 62-76 (some second thoughts in Taplin 1977: 423), Garzya 1995, Moreau 1996, M.L. West 2000: 338-43, and Michelakis 2002: 22-57; on the homoerotic aspect see Dover 1978: 197-8, and for the 'cruel jest' interpretation of fr. 264 see Dover 1964. Less work had been done on the Odyssean plays until the publication of fr. 273a in 1980; see now Katsouris 1985, Grossardt 2003, and Bardel 2005: 85-92 (earlier, Kudlien 1970).

Chapter 11. Aeschylus, the Gods and the World

Many relevant works have already been cited under other headings (especially §7.9), to which may be added Reinhardt 1949, Golden 1961, Herington 1965 and 1970, Grube 1970, Dodds 1973: 26-44, Gantz 1981, Otis 1981 and Moreau 1985. Garvie 1986: xxvii-xxxiv is a particularly sensitive discussion of many relevant issues, with abundant reference to earlier work. Two sharply contrasting views of Aeschylean theology are taken by Geisser 2002 and Bees 2009. S.R. West 1994: 148-9, discussing the Prometheus plays, finds significant Near Eastern antecedents for what I call (though she does not) their evolutionary theology. The basic notion of a development through the *Oresteia* in the gods' approach to justice is accepted by Bowie 2009: 229-30.

On ancient Greek religion see (successively, from introduction to comprehensive treatise) Parker 1986, Mikalson 2004, Easterling & Muir 1985, and Burkert 1985; but if you only read one book, it should be Parker 2005!

There are many discussions of Aeschylus' presentation of the sacrifice of Iphigeneia and of 'Agamemnon's dilemma'; it features in all comprehensive studies of the *Oresteia* and of *Agamemnon*, and various positions are argued in articles devoted to the topic by Lloyd-Jones 1962, Hammond 1965, Lesky 1966, Peradotto 1969, Dover 1973, Lawrence 1976 (cf. Sommerstein 1980a), M.W. Edwards 1977, and Nussbaum 1986: 25-50.

The principle of 'double determination' has perhaps been most clearly enunciated and argued for by Albin Lesky (1931, 1961b, 1966, 1983: 110-14); see also Kitto 1956, Saïd 1978: 152-78, Vernant 1981.

On the *Niobe* fragment quoted by Plato, and its context, see Lloyd-Jones 1971: 87, Gantz 1981: 24-5, Garzya 1987, 1990, Moreau 1995.

On Xenophanes see Guthrie 1962: 360-402, Barnes 1979: 82-99, Kirk *et al.* 1983: 163-80, Lesher 1992; on possible connections between Aeschylus and other contemporary or earlier philosophers, see Gladigow 1962 and Rösler 1970.

Chapter 12. Aeschylean Drama and the Political Moment

The matters discussed in this chapter have been most comprehensively considered by Podlecki 1966; see also de Ste. Croix 1972: 183-5 and Meier 1993: 62-165.

On the *Oresteia* see Dover 1957, Dodds 1960b, Macleod 1982 (sceptical of all allusions), Jones 1987, Meier 1990: 82-139, Sommerstein 1992 and 2010d, Bearzot 1992, Marr 1993, Rosenbloom 1995, Braun 1998, Pelling 2000: 167-77, and Carter 2007: 58-63. Bowie 1993, brilliantly if sometimes audaciously, discerns a further series of allusions to contemporary events in the trilogy through the medium of myth and ritual. On the Areopagus council and Ephialtes' reforms see Sealey 1964, Rhodes 1981: 283-91, 309-22, Carawan 1987, Cawkwell 1988, Wallace 1989, Saïd 1993b, Ostwald 1993, De Bruyn 1995 (who however deliberately ignores *Eumenides* as evidence) and Rihll 1995.

Ehrenberg 1950 pointed out the importance of *The Suppliant Maidens* for the early history of the concept of democracy. Various political interpretations of the Danaid trilogy are put forward in (*inter alia*) Forrest 1960, Sommerstein 1997: 74-9 (over-confident), Rohweder 1998, and Boedeker & Raaflaub 2005: 115-18; the treatment of Argos in these plays, in the *Oresteia*, and also in Euripides' *Suppliants*, is considered by Pattoni 2006.

On *The Persians*, see Pelling 1997b: 9-13 (sceptical of any relationship to internal Athenian politics) and Podlecki 1998: 11-15.

On Cimon's publicity machine see e.g. Webster 1969: 8-10, Barron 1972, 1980, and Castriota 1992.

Chapter 13. Of An Age, or For All Time?

I know of no systematic discussion of Aeschylus' presentation of issues of war and peace, though Winnington-Ingram 1983: 78-100 is important on the Trojan war. On the ideology of democracy and the role of leaders within it see Ober 1989, esp. 156-77 on the danger of the orator who 'deceives' or 'misleads' the people (cf. Dover 1974: 23-8).

On gender issues see on §7.8, adding Foley 1981: 127-68, 1993: 129-41, Loraux 1987, Zeitlin 1989, 1992, des Bouvrie 1990: 147-66, Sommerstein 1995. On *hybris* see Fisher 1992: 247-97.

The contrast between 'tribal' and 'civic' codes is applied to classical Athens by Herman 1993; see also Flaumenhaft 1989, Herman 1998, 2000, 2006, McHardy 2006 (and, for a very different view, Burnett 1998, esp. ch. 3 on *Choephoroi*). On theories of punishment in archaic and classical Greece, before Socrates and Plato, see Saunders 1991: 9-136.

References

Adams S.M. 1952. Salamis symphony: the *Persae* of Aeschylus. In White 1952: 46-54; reprinted in Segal 1983: 34-41.
Adkins A.W.H. 1960. *Merit and responsibility: a study in Greek values* (Oxford).
Alexanderson B. 1967. Darius in the *Persians*. *Eranos* 65: 1-11.
Allan W. 2001. *Euripides: The Children of Heracles* (Warminster).
Aloni A. *et al.* ed. 2002. *Atti del seminario internazionale 'I Sette a Tebe': dal mito alla lettura* (Bologna).
Arnott P.D. 1962. *Greek scenic conventions in the fifth century B.C.* (Oxford).
Bachvarova M.R. 2001. Successful birth, unsuccessful marriage: using Near Eastern birth incantations to interpret Aeschylus' *Suppliants*. *NIN* 2: 49-90.
Bacon H.H. 1964. The shield of Eteocles. *Arion* 3: 27-38; reprinted in Segal 1983: 24-33.
Bacon H.H. 1999. The Furies' homecoming. *CP* 94: 48-59.
Badian E. 1993. *From Plataea to Potidaea: studies in the history and historiography of the Pentecontaetia* (Baltimore).
Bakker E.J. *et al.* 2002. *Brill's companion to Herodotus* (Leiden).
Bardel R. 2005. Spectral traces: ghosts in tragic fragments. In McHardy *et al.* 2005: 83-112.
Barnes J. 1979. *The Presocratic philosophers. Vol. 1: Thales to Zeno* (London).
Barrett W.S. 2007a. *Greek lyric, tragedy, and textual criticism: collected papers* (Oxford).
Barrett W.S. 2007b. *Seven against Thebes*: the final scene. In Barrett 2007: 322-50 [written *c.* 1981].
Barron J.P. 1972. New light on old walls: the murals of the Theseion. *JHS* 92: 20-45.
Barron J.P. 1980. Bakchylides, Theseus and a woolly cloak. *BICS* 27: 1-8.
Basta Donzelli G. 2003. Eschilo a Gela. In Panvini and Giudice 2003: 95-8.
Bearzot C. 1992. Ancora sulle *Eumenidi* di Eschilo e la riforma di Efialte (in margine ad una pagina di Chr. Meier). *Prometheus* 18: 27-35.
Bearzot C. and Landucci F. ed. 2006. *Argo: una democrazia diversa* (Milan).
Beazley J.D. 1963. *Attic red-figure vase-painters*[2] (3 vols) (Oxford).
Bees R. 1993. *Zur Datierung des Prometheus Desmotes* (Stuttgart).
Bees R. 2009. *Aischylos: Interpretationen zum Verständnis seiner Theologie* (Munich).
Belloni L. 1988. *Eschilo: I Persiani* (Milan).
Bergson L. 1967. The Hymn to Zeus in Aeschylus' *Agamemnon*. *Eranos* 65: 12-24.
Berman D.W. 2007. *Myth and culture in Aeschylus' Seven against Thebes* (Rome).
Bernek R. 2004. *Dramaturgie und Ideologie: Der politische Mythos in den Hikesiedramen des Aischylos, Sophokles und Euripides* (Munich).
Betts J.H. *et al.* 1986. *Studies in honour of T.B.L. Webster. Vol. 1* (Bristol).
Bieber M. 1961. *The history of the Greek and Roman theater*[2] (Princeton).
Biles Z.P. forthcoming. Aeschylus' afterlife: reperformance by decree in 5th c. Athens? To appear in *ICS* 31-2.

Blok J.H. 1995. *The early Amazons: modern and ancient perspectives on a persistent myth* (Leiden).
Boardman J. 1982. Herakles, Theseus and Amazons. In Kurtz & Sparkes 1982: 1-28.
Boardman J. *et al.* ed. 1986. *The Oxford history of the classical world* (Oxford).
Boardman J. *et al.* ed. 1991. *The Oxford history of Greece and the Hellenistic world* (Oxford).
Boedeker D. and Raaflaub K.A. 2005. Tragedy and city. In Bushnell 2005: 109-27.
Bollack J. 2006. *Prometheus Bound*: drama and enactment. In Cairns & Liapis 2006: 79-89.
Bollack J. and Judet de la Combe P. 1982. *L'Agamemnon d'Eschyle: le texte et ses interprétations. 1.i: Prologue, parodos anapestique, parodos lyrique 1* and *1.ii: parodos lyrique 2-3, présentation du premier épisode, premier stasimon* (Lille).
Bowie A.M. 1993. Religion and politics in Aeschylus' *Oresteia*. *CQ* 43: 10-31; reprinted with minor updates in Lloyd 2007: 323-58.
Bowie A.M. 2009. Athens and Delphi in Aeschylus' *Oresteia*. In Goldhill & Hall 2009: 208-31.
Braun M. 1998. *Die 'Eumeniden' des Aischylos und der Areopag* (Tübingen).
Broadhead H.D. 1960. *The Persae of Aeschylus* (Cambridge).
Brown A.L. 1976. The end of the *Seven against Thebes*. *CQ* 26: 206-19.
Brown A.L. 1977. Eteocles and the chorus in *Seven against Thebes*. *Phoenix* 31: 300-18.
Brown A.L. 1982. Some problems in the *Eumenides* of Aeschylus. *JHS* 102: 26-32.
Brown A.L. 1983. The Erinyes in the Oresteia. *JHS* 103: 13-34.
Brown A.L. 1984. Eumenides in Greek tragedy. *CQ* 34: 260-81.
Brown A.L. 1990. Prometheus Pyrphoros. *BICS* 37: 50-6.
Burian P. 1974. Pelasgus and politics in Aeschylus' Danaid trilogy. *Wiener Studien* 8: 5-14; reprinted in Lloyd 2007: 199-210.
Burian P. 1991. *Aeschylus: The Suppliants* (Princeton).
Burian P. 2006. Biologia, democrazia e donne nelle *Eumenidi* di Eschilo. *Lexis* 24: 127-40.
Burian P. and Shapiro A. 2009. *The Complete Aeschylus, Volume II: Persians and Other Plays* (Oxford).
Burkert W. 1985 [1977]. *Greek religion, archaic and classical* trans. J. Raffan (Oxford).
Burn A.R. 1984. *Persia and the Greeks*^{2} (London).
Burnett A.P. 1973. Curse and dream in Aeschylus' *Septem*. *GRBS* 14: 343-68.
Burnett A.P. 1998. *Revenge in Attic and later tragedy* (Berkeley).
Bushnell R. ed. 2005. *A companion to tragedy* (Oxford).
Buxton R.G.A. 1982. *Persuasion in Greek tragedy: a study of Peitho* (Cambridge).
Buxton R.G.A. 2007. Tragedy and Greek myth. In Woodard 2007: 166-89.
Cairns D.L. 1993. *Aidôs: the psychology and ethics of honour and shame in ancient Greek literature* (Oxford).
Cairns D.L. and Liapis V. 2006. *Dionysalexandros: essays on Aeschylus and his fellow tragedians in honour of Alexander F. Garvie* (Swansea).
Calame C. 2000. *Poétique des mythes dans la Grèce antique* (Paris).
Caldwell R.S. 1973. The misogyny of Eteocles. *Arethusa* 6: 197-231.
Cameron H.D. 1971. *Studies on the Seven against Thebes of Aeschylus* (The Hague).
Carawan E.M. 1987. *Eisangelia* and *euthyna*: the trials of Miltiades, Themistocles, and Cimon. *GRBS* 28: 167-208.

Carter D.M. 2004. Was Attic tragedy democratic? *Polis* 21: 1-25.
Carter D.M. 2007. *The politics of Greek tragedy* (Exeter).
Cartledge P.A. 1997. 'Deep plays': theatre as process in Greek civic life. In Easterling 1997a: 3-35.
Casadio V. 1993. Aesch. fragm. novum? *Museum Criticum* 25-28: 67-70.
Castriota D. 1992. *Myth, ethos and actuality: official art in fifth-century B.C. Athens* (Madison).
Cawkwell G.K. 1988. *Nomophulakia* and the Areopagus. *JHS* 108: 1-12.
Cawkwell G.K. 2005. *The Greek wars: the failure of Persia* (Oxford).
Chiasson C.C. 1988. Lecythia and the justice of Zeus in Aeschylus' *Oresteia. Phoenix* 42: 1-21.
Chiasson C.C. 1999/2000. The Athenians and time in Aeschylus' *Eumenides. CJ* 95: 139-61.
Churchill W.S. 1937. *Great contemporaries* (London).
Collard C. 2002. *Aeschylus: Oresteia* (Oxford).
Collard C. 2008. *Aeschylus: The Persians and other plays* (Oxford).
Conacher D.J. 1980. *Aeschylus' Prometheus Bound: a literary commentary* (Toronto).
Conacher D.J. 1987. *Aeschylus' Oresteia: a literary commentary* (Toronto).
Conacher D.J. 1996. *Aeschylus: the earlier plays and related studies* (Toronto).
Connor W.R. 1990. City Dionysia and Athenian democracy. In Fears 1990: 7-32.
Court B. 1994. *Die dramatische Technik des Aischylos* (Stuttgart/Leipzig).
Craik E.M. ed. 1990. *'Owls to Athens': essays on classical subjects for Sir Kenneth Dover* (Oxford).
Crane G. 1993. Politics of consumption and generosity in the carpet scene of the *Agamemnon. CP* 88: 117-36.
Crawford M.H. and Whitehead D. 1983. *Archaic and classical Greece: a selection of ancient sources in translation* (Cambridge).
Cropp M. and Fick G. 1985. *Resolutions and chronology in Euripides: the fragmentary tragedies* (*BICS* Suppl. 43) (London).
Csapo E.G. 2007. The men who built the theatres: *theatropolai, theatronai,* and *arkhitektones.* In P.J. Wilson 2007: 87-115.
Csapo E.G. and Miller M.C. ed. 2003. *Poetry, theory, praxis: the social life of myth, word and image in ancient Greece: essays in honour of William J. Slater* (Oxford).
Csapo E.G. and Slater W.J. 1994. *The context of ancient drama* (Ann Arbor MI).
Dähnhardt O. 1894. *Scholia in Aeschyli Persas* (Leipzig).
Dale A.M. 1968. *The lyric metres of Greek drama*[2] (Cambridge).
Dale A.M. 1971-83. *Metrical analyses of tragic choruses.* 3 vols (*BICS* Suppl. 21.1-3) (London).
Davidson J. 1994. *Prometheus Vinctus* on the Athenian stage. *G&R* 41: 33-40.
Davidson J. and Rosenbloom D. ed. 2010. *Greek Drama IV* (*BICS* Suppl.) (London).
Davies J.K. 1978. *Democracy and classical Greece* (London).
Davies M. 1968. Thoughts on the *Oresteia* before Aeschylus. *BCH* 93: 214-60.
Davies M. 1987. Aeschylus' Clytemnestra: sword or axe? *CQ* 37: 65-75.
Dawe R.D. 1964. *The collation and investigation of manuscripts of Aeschylus* (Cambridge).
Dawe R.D. 1967. The end of *Seven against Thebes. CQ* 17: 16-28.
Dawe R.D. 1978. The end of *Seven against Thebes* yet again. In Dawe *et al.* 1978: 87-103.

Dawe R.D. *et al.* ed. 1978. *Dionysiaca: nine studies in Greek poetry by former pupils, presented to Sir Denys Page on his seventieth birthday* (Cambridge).
Dawson C.M. 1970. *The Seven against Thebes by Aeschylus* (Englewood Cliffs, NJ).
Deacy S. and Pierce K.F. 1997. *Rape in antiquity* (London).
De Bruyn O. 1995. *La compétence de l'Aréopage en matière de procès publics* (Stuttgart).
Deforge B. 1987. Eschyle et la légende des Argonautes. *REG* 100: 30-44.
Deichgräber K. 1974. *Die Persertetralogie des Aischylos* (Mainz).
Denniston J.D. and Page D.L. 1957. *Aeschylus: Agamemnon* (Oxford).
de Ste. Croix G.E.M. 1972. *The origins of the Peloponnesian War* (London).
des Bouvrie S. 1990. *Women in Greek tragedy: an anthropological approach* (Oxford/Oslo).
DeVito A. 1999. Eteocles, Amphiaraus, and necessity in Aeschylus' 'Seven against Thebes'. *Hermes* 127: 165-71.
Dickey E. 1996. *Greek forms of address from Herodotus to Lucian* (Oxford).
Dinsmoor W.B. 1951. The Athenian theater of the fifth century. In Mylonas 1951: 309-30.
Dodds E.R. 1960a. *Euripides: Bacchae*[2] (Oxford).
Dodds E.R. 1960b. Morals and politics in the Oresteia. *PCPS* 6: 19-31; reprinted in Dodds 1973: 45-63, and (with minor adjustments) in Lloyd 2007: 245-64.
Dodds E.R. 1973. *The ancient concept of progress and other essays on Greek literature and belief* (Oxford).
Döhle B. 1967. Die Achilleis des Aischylos in ihrer Auswirkung auf die attische Vasenmalerei des 5. Jahrhunderts. *Klio* 49: 63-149.
Dougherty C. 2005. *Prometheus* (London).
Dover K.J. 1957. The political aspect of Aeschylus's *Eumenides*. *JHS* 77: 230-7.
Dover K.J. 1964. Aeschylus, fr. 248 M. *CR* 14: 12.
Dover K.J. 1966. The skene in Aristophanes. *PCPS* 12: 2-17.
Dover K.J. 1973. Some neglected aspects of Agamemnon's dilemma. *JHS* 93: 58-69.
Dover K.J. 1974. *Greek popular morality in the time of Plato and Aristotle* (Oxford).
Dover K.J. 1978. *Greek homosexuality* (London).
Dover K.J. 1987a. *Greek and the Greeks. Collected papers, vol. I: language, poetry, drama* (Oxford).
Dover K.J. 1987b [1977]. The red fabric in the *Agamemnon*. In Dover 1987a: 151-60.
Dyer R.R. 1969. The evidence for Apolline purification rituals at Delphi and Athens. *JHS* 89: 38-56.
Dyson M. 1994. Prometheus and the wedge: text and staging at Aeschylus *PV* 54-81. *JHS* 114: 154-6.
Earp F.R. 1948. *The style of Aeschylus* (Cambridge).
Easterling P.E. 1973. Presentation of character in Aeschylus. *G&R* 20: 3-19.
Easterling P.E. 1989. City settings in Greek poetry. *PCA* 86: 5-17.
Easterling P.E. ed. 1997a. *The Cambridge Companion to Greek Tragedy* (Cambridge).
Easterling P.E. 1997b. A show for Dionysus. In Easterling 1997a: 36-53.
Easterling P.E. 2008. Theatrical furies: thoughts on *Eumenides*. In Revermann & Wilson 2008: 219-36.
Easterling P.E. and Hall E.M. ed. 2002. *Greek and Roman actors: aspects of an ancient profession* (Cambridge).
Easterling P.E. and Knox B.M.W. ed. 1985. *The Cambridge history of classical literature. Vol. I: Greek literature* (Cambridge).

Easterling P.E. and Knox B.M.W. ed. 1989. *The Cambridge history of classical literature. Vol. I Part 2: Greek drama* (Cambridge).

Easterling P.E. and Muir J.V. ed. 1985. *Greek religion and society* (Cambridge).

Edwards A.T. 1993. Historicizing the popular grotesque: Bakhtin's *Rabelais* and Attic Old Comedy. In Scodel 1993: 89-117.

Edwards M.W. 1977. Agamemnon's decision: freedom and folly in Aeschylus. *CSCA* 10: 17-38.

Ehrenberg V. 1950. Origins of democracy. *Historia* 1: 515-48.

Ehrenberg V. 1973. *From Solon to Socrates: Greek history and civilization during the sixth and fifth centuries B.C.*[2] (London).

Euben J.P. 1982. Justice and the Oresteia. *American Political Science Review* 76: 22-33; revised version in Euben 1990: 67-95.

Euben J.P. ed. 1986. *Greek tragedy and political theory* (Berkeley).

Euben J.P. 1990. *The tragedy of political theory: the road not taken* (Princeton).

Ewans M. 1995. *Aeschylus: The Oresteia* (London).

Ewans M. 1996. *Aeschylus: Suppliants and other dramas* (London).

Fagles R. and Stanford W.B. 1977. *Aeschylus: The Oresteia* (Harmondsworth).

Fairweather J. 1974. Fiction in the biographies of ancient writers. *Ancient Society* 5: 231-75.

Fears J.R. ed. 1990. *Aspects of Athenian democracy* (Copenhagen).

Finglass P.J. 2007. *Pindar: The Eleventh Pythian* (Cambridge).

Finglass P.J. *et al.* ed. 2007. *Hesperos: studies in ancient Greek poetry presented to M.L. West on his seventieth birthday* (Oxford).

Fisher N.R.E. 1992. *Hybris: a study in the values of honour and shame in ancient Greece* (Warminster).

Fitton Brown A.D. 1959. Prometheia. *JHS* 79: 52-60.

Flaumenhaft M.J. 1989. Seeing justice done: Aeschylus' *Oresteia*. *Interpretation* 17: 69-109.

Fletcher J. 1999. Choral voice and narrative in the first stasimon of Aeschylus *Agamemnon*. *Phoenix* 53: 29-49.

Flintoff E. 1980. The ending of the *Seven against Thebes*. *Mnemosyne* 33: 244-71.

Flintoff E. 1992. The unity of the *Persians* trilogy. *QUCC* 40: 67-80.

Foley H.P. ed. 1981. *Reflections of women in antiquity* (New York).

Foley H.P. 1993. The politics of tragic lamentation. In Sommerstein *et al.* 1993: 101-43.

Foley H.P. 2001. *Female acts in Greek tragedy* (Princeton).

Föllinger S. 2003. *Genosdependenzen: Studien zur Arbeit am Mythos bei Aischylos* (Göttingen).

Fontenrose J. 1971. Gods and men in the *Oresteia*. *TAPA* 102: 71-109.

Forrest W.G. 1960. Themistokles and Argos. *CQ* 10: 221-41.

Forrest W.G. 1986. Greece: the history of the archaic period. In Boardman *et al.* 1986: 19-49; reprinted in Boardman *et al.* 1991: 13-46.

Fowler B.H. 1957. The imagery of the *Prometheus Bound*. *AJP* 78: 173-84.

Fowler B.H. 1967. Aeschylus' imagery. *C&M* 28: 1-74 [published 1971].

Fraenkel E. 1950. *Aeschylus: Agamemnon* (3 vols) (Oxford).

Fraenkel E. 1957. *Die sieben Redepaare im Thebanerdrama des Aischylos* (Munich).

Friis Johansen H. 1954. Some features of sentence structure in Aeschylus' *Suppliants*. *C&M* 15: 1-59.

Friis Johansen H. and Smith O.L. 1970. *Aeschylus: The Suppliants. Vol. I* [no more published] (Copenhagen).

Friis Johansen H. and Whittle E.W. 1980. *Aeschylus: The Suppliants* (3 vols) (Copenhagen).

Frontisi-Ducroux F. 2006. L'étoffe des spectres. *Métis* n.s. 4: 29-50.
Frontisi-Ducroux F. 2007. The invention of the Erinyes. In Kraus *et al.* 2007: 165-76.
Frost F.J. 1980. *Plutarch's Themistocles: a historical commentary* (Princeton).
Gagarin M. 1975. The vote of Athena. *AJP* 96: 121-7.
Gagarin M. 1976. *Aeschylean drama* (Berkeley).
Gallo I. ed. 1981a. *Studi salernitani in memoria di Raffaelle Cantarella* (Salerno).
Gallo I. 1981b. Ricerche sull' Eschilo satiresco. In Gallo 1981a: 97-155; reprinted with addenda in Gallo 1992: 43-94.
Gallo I. 1992. *Ricerche sul teatro Greco* (Naples).
Gantz T.R. 1978. Love and death in the *Suppliants* of Aeschylus. *Phoenix* 32: 279-87.
Gantz T.R. 1979. The Aischylean tetralogy: prolegomena. *CJ* 74: 289-304.
Gantz T.R. 1980. The Aischylean tetralogy: attested and conjectured groups. *AJP* 101: 133-64; reprinted with minor updates in Lloyd 2007: 40-70.
Gantz T.R. 1981. Divine guilt in Aischylos. *Classical Quarterly* 31: 18-32.
Gantz T.R. 1983. The chorus of Aischylos' *Agamemnon*. *HSCP* 87: 65-86.
Gantz T.R. 1993. *Early Greek myth: a guide to literary and artistic sources* (Baltimore).
Garvie A.F. 1969. *Aeschylus' Supplices: play and trilogy* (Cambridge).
Garvie A.F. 1970. The opening of the Choephori. *BICS* 17: 79-91.
Garvie A.F. 1986. *Aeschylus: Choephori* (Oxford).
Garvie A.F. 1991. Review of Sommerstein 1989a. *JHS* 111: 219-20.
Garvie A.F. 1996. The tragedy of the *Oresteia*: response to van Erp Taalman Kip. In Silk 1996: 139-48.
Garvie A.F. 1999. Text and dramatic interpretation in *Persae*. *Lexis* 17: 21-40 (including discussion).
Garvie A.F. 2005. *Aeschylus' Supplices: play and trilogy*[2] (Exeter).
Garvie A.F. 2007. Greek tragedy: text and context. In Finglass *et al.* 2007: 170-88.
Garvie A.F. 2009. *Aeschylus: Persae* (Oxford).
Garzya A. 1965. Le tragique du *Prométhée enchaîné* d'Eschyle. *Mnemosyne* 18: 113-25.
Garzya A. 1987. Sur la Niobé d'Eschyle. *REG* 100: 185-202.
Garzya A. 1990. *Eschilo e il tragico: il caso della Niobe* (Naples).
Garzya A. 1995. Sui frammenti dei *Mirmidoni* di Eschilo. In López Férez 1995: 41-56.
Geerard M. *et al.* ed. 1990. *Opes Atticae: miscellanea philologica et historica Raymondo Bogaert et Hermanno van Looy oblate* (Bruges/The Hague).
Geisser F. 2002. *Götter. Geister und Dämonen: Unheilsmächte bei Aischylos* (Munich).
Ghiron-Bistagne P. 1976. *Recherches sur les acteurs dans la Grèce antique* (Paris).
Ghiron-Bistagne P. and Moreau A.M. ed. 1994. *Femmes fatales* (= *CGITA* 8) (Montpellier).
Ghiron-Bistagne P. *et al.* ed. 1993. *Les Perses d'Eschyle* (= *CGITA* 7) (Montpellier).
Gill C. *et al.* ed. 1998. *Reciprocity in classical Greece* (Oxford).
Gladigow B. 1962. Aischylos und Heraklit: Ein Vergleich religiöser Denkformen. *Archiv für Geschichte der Philosophie* 44: 225-39.
Gödde S. 2000. *Das Drama der Hikesie: Ritual und Rhetorik in Aischylos' Hiketiden* (Münster).
Goette H.R. 2007. An archaeological appendix [to Csapo 2007]. In P.J. Wilson 2007: 116-21.

Goff B.E. ed. 1995. *History, tragedy, theory: dialogues on Athenian drama* (Austin, TX).
Goheen R.F. 1955. Aspects of dramatic symbolism: three studies in the *Oresteia*. *AJP* 76: 113-37.
Goins S.E. 1997. The date of Aeschylus' Perseus tetralogy. *RhM* 140: 193-210.
Golden L. 1961. Zeus, whoever he is .... *TAPA* 92: 156-67.
Golden L. 1964. The character of Eteocles and the meaning of the *Septem*. *CP* 59: 79-89.
Goldhill S.D. 1984. *Language, sexuality, narrative: the Oresteia* (Cambridge).
Goldhill S.D. 1986. *Reading Greek tragedy* (Cambridge).
Goldhill S.D. 1987. The Great Dionysia and civic ideology. *JHS* 107: 58-76; revised version in Winkler & Zeitlin 1990: 97-129.
Goldhill S.D. 1988. Battle narrative and politics in Aeschylus' *Persae*. *JHS* 108: 189-93.
Goldhill S.D. 1997. The audience of Athenian tragedy. In Easterling 1997a: 54-68.
Goldhill S.D. 2000a. Greek drama and political theory. In Rowe & Schofield 2000: 60-88.
Goldhill S.D. 2000b. Civic ideology and the problem of difference: the politics of Aeschylean tragedy, once again. *JHS* 120: 34-56.
Goldhill S.D. 2004. *Aeschylus: The Oresteia*² (Cambridge).
Goldhill S.D. and Hall E.M. 2009. *Sophocles and the Greek tragic tradition* (Cambridge).
Goldhill S.D. and Osborne R.G. ed. 1999. *Performance culture and Athenian democracy* (Cambridge).
Görgemanns H. 1979. Aischylos: Die Tragödien. In Seeck 1979: 13-50.
Gould J. 1985. Tragedy in performance. In Easterling & Knox 1985: 263-81; reprinted in Easterling & Knox 1989: 6-29.
Grassi E. 1956. Papyrologica. *Parola del Passato* 11: 204-9.
Gredley B. 1996. Comedy and tragedy – inevitable distinctions: response to Taplin. In Silk 1996: 203-16.
Green J.R. 1991. On seeing and depicting the theatre in classical Athens. *GRBS* 32: 15-50.
Green J.R. and Handley E.W. 1995. *Images of the Greek theatre* (London).
Gregory J. ed. 2005. *A companion to Greek tragedy* (Oxford).
Grethlein J. 2003. *Asyl und Athen: Die Konstruktion kollektiver Identität in der griechischen Tragödie* (Stuttgart).
Griffith M. 1977. *The authenticity of Prometheus Bound* (Cambridge).
Griffith M. 1978. Aeschylus, Sicily and Prometheus. In Dawe *et al.* 1978: 105-39.
Griffith M. 1982. *Aeschylus: Prometheus Bound* (Cambridge).
Griffith M. 1984. The vocabulary of *Prometheus Bound*. *CQ* 34: 282-91.
Griffith M. 1995. Brilliant dynasts: power and politics in the *Oresteia*. *CA* 14: 62-129.
Griffith M. 1998. The king and eye: the rule of the father in Greek tragedy. *PCPS* 44: 20-84; the *Persians* section is reprinted in Lloyd 2007: 93-140.
Griffith M. 2002. Slaves of Dionysos: satyrs, audience, and the ends of the *Oresteia*. *CA* 21: 195-258.
Griffith M. and Mastronarde D.J. ed. 1990. *Cabinet of the Muses: essays on classical and comparative literature in honor of T.G. Rosenmeyer* (Atlanta).
Grossardt P. 2003. The title of Aeschylus' *Ostologoi*. *HSCP* 101: 155-8.
Grube G.M.A. 1970. Zeus in Aeschylus. *AJP* 91: 43-51.
Gruber M.A. 2009. *Der Chor in den Tragödien des Aischylos: Affekt und Reaktion* (Tübingen).

Guthrie W.K.C. 1962. *A history of Greek philosophy. Vol. I: The earlier Presocratics and the Pythagoreans* (Cambridge).
Hall E.M. 1989. *Inventing the barbarian: Greek self-definition through tragedy* (Oxford).
Hall E.M. 1996. *Aeschylus: Persians* (Warminster).
Hall E.M. 1997. The sociology of Athenian tragedy. In Easterling 1997a: 93-126.
Hall E.M. 1998. Ithyphallic males behaving badly; or, satyr-drama as gendered tragic ending. In Wyke 1998: 13-37.
Hall E.M. 2004. Aeschylus, race, class, and war in the 1990s. In Hall *et al.* 2004: 169-97.
Hall E.M. 2006. *The theatrical cast of Athens: interactions between ancient Greek drama and society* (Oxford).
Hall E.M. *et al.* ed. 2004. *Dionysus since 69: Greek tragedy at the dawn of the third millennium* (Oxford).
Hall J.M. 2007. *A history of the archaic Greek world c.1200-479 BCE* (Malden, MA/Oxford).
Hame K.J. 2004. All in the family: funeral rites and the health of the *oikos* in Aeschylus' *Oresteia. AJP* 125: 513-34.
Hammond N.G.L. 1965. Personal freedom and its limitations in the Oresteia. *JHS* 85: 42-55.
Hammond N.G.L. 1972. The conditions of dramatic production to the death of Aeschylus. *GRBS* 13: 387-450.
Hammond N.G.L. 1988. More on conditions of production to the death of Aeschylus. *GRBS* 29: 5-33.
Hardwick L. 1990. Ancient Amazons: heroes, outsiders or women? *G&R* 37: 14-25.
Hansen M.H. 2006. *Polis: an introduction to the ancient Greek city-state* (Oxford).
Harris E.M. and Rubinstein L. ed. 2004. *The law and the courts in ancient Greece* (London).
Harris E.M. *et al.* ed. 2010. *Law and drama in ancient Greece* (London).
Harrison G.W.M. ed. 2005. *Satyr drama: tragedy at play* (Swansea).
Harrison, Thomas E.H. 2000. *The emptiness of Asia: Aeschylus' Persians and the history of the fifth century* (London).
Harrison, Tony 1981. *The Oresteia* (London). Also in Harrison 1986: 185-292.
Harrison, Tony 1986. *Theatre works 1973-1985* (Harmondsworth).
Headlam W.G. and Thomson G. 1938. *The Oresteia of Aeschylus* (2 vols) (Cambridge).
Heath J. 1999a. Disentangling the beast: humans and other animals in Aeschylus' *Oresteia. JHS* 119: 17-47.
Heath J. 1999b. The serpent and the sparrows: Homer and the parodos of Aeschylus' *Agamemnon. CQ* 49: 396-407.
Heath J. 2005. *The talking Greeks: speech, animals and the other in Homer, Aeschylus and Plato* (Cambridge).
Heath M. 2006. The 'social function' of tragedy: clarifications and questions. In Cairns & Liapis 2006: 253-81.
Heiden B.A. 1993. Emotion, acting, and the Athenian *ethos*. In Sommerstein *et al.* 1993: 145-166.
Henderson J.J. 1991. Women and the Athenian dramatic festivals. *TAPA* 121: 133-47.
Henrichs A. 1994. Anonymity and polarity: unknown gods and nameless altars at the Areopagos. *ICS* 19: 27-58.

Henry W.B. and Nünlist R. 2000. Aeschylus, Dictyulci (fr. 47a Radt) und Isthmiastae (fr. 78a-d). *ZPE* 129: 13-16.

Herington C.J. 1965. Aeschylus: the last phase. *Arion* 4: 387-403; reprinted with minor revisions in Segal 1983: 123-37.

Herington C.J. 1967. Aeschylus in Sicily. *JHS* 87: 74-85.

Herington C.J. 1970. *The author of the Prometheus Bound* (Austin TX).

Herington C.J. 1972. *The older scholia on the Prometheus Bound* (Leiden).

Herington C.J. 1985. *Poetry into drama: early tragedy and the Greek poetic tradition* (Berkeley).

Herington C.J. 1986. *Aeschylus* (New Haven).

Herman G. 1993. Tribal and civic codes of behaviour in Lysias I. *CQ* 43: 406-19.

Herman G. 1998. Reciprocity, altruism, and the Prisoner's Dilemma: the special case of classical Athens. In Gill *et al.* 1998: 199-225.

Herman G. 2000. Athenian beliefs about revenge: problems and methods. *PCPS* 46: 7-27.

Herman G. 2006. *Morality and behaviour in democratic Athens: a social history* (Cambridge).

Hester D.A. 1981. The casting vote. *AJP* 102: 265-74.

Hester D.A. 1987. A chorus of one Danaid. *Antichthon* 21: 9-18.

Hexter R. and Selden D. ed. 1992. *Innovations of antiquity* (London).

Hommel H. ed. 1974. *Wege zu Aischylos* (2 vols) (Darmstadt).

Hornblower S. 2002. *The Greek world 479-323 BC*^{3} (London).

Hose M. 2006. *Vaticinium post eventum* and the position of the *Supplices* in the Danaid trilogy. In Cairns & Liapis 2006: 91-8.

Hourmouziades N.C. 1965. *Production and imagination in Euripides: form and function of the scenic space* (Athens).

Hutchinson G.O. 1985. *Aeschylus: Septem contra Thebas* (Oxford).

Ieranò G. 2002. La città delle donne: il sesto canto dell' 'Iliade' e i 'Sette contro Tebe' di Eschilo. In Aloni *et al.* 2002: 73-92.

Ireland S. 1974. The problem of motivation in the Supplices of Aeschylus. *RhM* 117: 14-29.

Italie G. 1964. *Index Aeschyleus*^{2} (Leiden).

Jackson E. 1988. The argument of *Septem contra Thebas*. *Phoenix* 42: 287-303.

Janko R. 1992. *The Iliad: a commentary. Volume IV: books 13-16* (Cambridge).

Jocelyn H.D. ed. 1993. *Tria lustre: essays and notes presented to John Pinsent* (Liverpool).

Johnson J.A. 1992. Eteocles and the posting decisions. *RhM* 135: 193-7.

Johnston S.I. 1999. *Restless dead: encounters between the living and the dead in ancient Greece* (Berkeley).

Jones L.A. 1987. The role of Ephialtes in the rise of Athenian democracy. *CA* 6: 53-76.

Joshel S.R. and Murnaghan S. ed. 1998. *Women and slaves in Greco-Roman culture: differential equations* (London).

Jouan F. 1992. Dionysos chez Eschyle. *Kernos* 5: 71-86.

Judet de la Combe P. 1987. Étéocle interprète: action et langage dans la scène centrale des Sept contre Thèbes d'Eschyle. In *Le texte et ses représentations* (Paris) 57-79.

Judet de la Combe P. 1990. La force argumentative du dérisoire: *Agamemnon* 931-43. In Geerard *et al.* 1990: 209-37.

Judet de la Combe P. 2001. *L'Agamemnon d'Eschyle: commentaire des dialogues* (2 vols) (Lille).

Käppel L. 1998a. *Die Konstruktion der Handlung in der Orestie des Aischylos* (Munich).
Käppel L. 1998b. Die Rolle des Chores in der Orestie des Aischylos: Vom epischen Erzähler über das lyrische Ich zur dramatis persona. In Riemer & Zimmermann 1998: 61-88.
Katsouris A.G. 1985. Aeschylus' Odyssean tetralogy. *Dioniso* 53: 47-60 [published 1985].
Kirk G.S. 1990. *The Iliad: a commentary. Volume II: books 5-8* (Cambridge).
Kirk G.S., Raven J.E. and Schofield M. 1983. *The Presocratic philosophers: a critical history with a selection of texts* (Cambridge).
Kitto H.D.F. 1939. *Greek tragedy*[1] (London).
Kitto H.D.F. 1956. *Form and meaning in drama* (London).
Kitto H.D.F. 1961. *Greek tragedy*[3] (London).
Kitto H.D.F. 1966. *Poiesis: structure and thought* (Berkeley).
Knoepfler D. 1993. *Les imagiers de l'Orestie: mille ans d'art autour d'un mythe grec* (Zürich).
Knox B.M.W. 1952. The lion in the house (*Agamemnon* 717-36). *CP* 47: 12-25.
Knox B.M.W. 1979. *Word and action: essays on the ancient theatre* (Baltimore).
Konishi H. 1989. Agamemnon's reasons for yielding. *AJP* 110: 210-22.
Kossatz-Deissmann A. 1981. Achilleus. *LIMC* i 37-200.
Kraus C. *et al.* ed. 2007. *Visualizing the tragic: drama, myth, and ritual in Greek art and literature* (Oxford).
Krumeich R., Pechstein N. and Seidensticker B. 1999. *Das griechische Satyrspiel* (Darmstadt).
Kudlien F. 1970. Zu Arats *Ostologia* und Aischylos' *Ostologoi*. *RhM* 113: 297-304.
Kurtz D.C. and Sparkes B.A. ed. 1982. *The eye of Greece* (Cambridge).
Latacz J. 1993. *Einführung in die griechische Tragödie* (Göttingen).
Lawrence S.E. 1976. Artemis in the *Agamemnon*. *AJP* 97: 97-110.
Lawrence S.E. 2007. Eteocles' moral awareness in Aeschylus' *Seven*. *CW* 100: 335-53.
Lazenby J.F. 1988. Aeschylus and Salamis. *Hermes* 116: 168-85.
Lebeck A. 1971. *The Oresteia: a study in language and structure.* Washington: Center for Hellenic Studies.
Lefèvre E. 2003. *Studien zu den Quellen und zum Verständnis des Prometheus Desmotes* (Göttingen).
Lefkowitz M.R. 1981. *The lives of the Greek poets* (London).
Lenardon R.J. 1978. *The saga of Themistocles* (London).
Lenz L. 1986. Zu Dramaturgie und Tragik in den Persern. *Gymnasium* 93: 141-63.
Lesher J.H. 1992. *Xenophanes of Colophon: fragments* (Toronto).
Lesky A. 1931. Die Orestie des Aischylos. *Hermes* 66: 190-214.
Lesky A. 1961a. Eteokles in den Sieben gegen Theben. *Wiener Studien* 74: 5-17.
Lesky A. 1961b. *Göttliche und menschliche Motivation im homerischen Epos* (Heidelberg).
Lesky A. 1966. Decision and responsibility in Aeschylus. *JHS* 86: 78-86; reprinted with minor revisions in Segal 1983: 13-23.
Lesky A. 1983 [1972]. *Greek tragic poetry* trans. M. Dillon (New Haven).
Lévy E. ed. 1983. *La femme dans les sociétés antiques: actes des colloques de Strasbourg (mai 1980 et mars 1981)* (Strasbourg).
Liapis V. forthcoming. *[Euripides]: Rhesus* (Oxford).
Lloyd M. 2007. *Oxford readings in classical studies: Aeschylus* (Oxford).
Lloyd-Jones H. 1956. Zeus in Aeschylus. *JHS* 76: 55-67.
Lloyd-Jones H. 1959. The end of the *Seven against Thebes*. *CQ* 9: 80-115.

Lloyd-Jones H. 1962. The guilt of Agamemnon. *CQ* 12: 187-99; reprinted with minor revisions in Segal 1983: 57-72.

Lloyd-Jones H. 1964. The 'Supplices' of Aeschylus: the new date and old problems. *Antiquité Classique* 33: 356-74; reprinted with minor revisions in Segal 1983: 42-56.

Lloyd-Jones H. 1966. Problems of early Greek tragedy: Pratinas and Phrynichus. *Cuadernos de la Fundación Pastor* 13: 11-33. Abridged version republished in Lloyd-Jones 1990a: 225-37.

Lloyd-Jones H. 1971. *The justice of Zeus* (Berkeley).

Lloyd-Jones H. 1979. *Aeschylus: Oresteia* (also issued as 3 vols: *Agamemnon, Choephoroe, Eumenides*) (London).

Lloyd-Jones H. 1990a. *The academic papers of Sir Hugh Lloyd-Jones: Greek epic, lyric and tragedy* (Oxford).

Lloyd-Jones H. 1990b. Erinyes, Semnai Theai, Eumenides. In Craik 1990: 203-11.

Lloyd-Jones H. 2003. Zeus, Prometheus and Greek ethics. *HSCP* 101: 49-72.

Long A.A. 1986. Pro and contra fratricide: Aeschylus *Septem* 653-719. In Betts *et al.* 1986: 179-89.

López Férez J.A. ed. 1995. *De Homero a Libanio* (Madrid).

Loraux N. 1987 [1985]. *Tragic ways of killing a woman* trans. A. Forster (Cambridge MA).

Lossau M. 1998. *Aischylos* (Hildesheim).

Lucas de Dios J.M. 2008. *Esquilo: fragmentos, testimonios* (Madrid).

Lupaş L. and Petre Z. 1981. *Commentaire aux Sept contre Thèbes d'Eschyle* (Bucharest/Paris).

MacDowell D.M. 1994. The number of speaking actors in Old Comedy. *CQ* 44: 325-35.

Mackinnon J.K. 1978. The reason for the Danaids' flight. *CQ* 28: 74-82.

Macleod C.W. 1982. Politics in the Oresteia. *JHS* 102: 124-44; reprinted in Lloyd 2007: 265-301.

March J.R. 1987. *The creative poet* (*BICS* Suppl. 49) (London).

March J.R. 1989. Euripides' *Bakchai*: a reconsideration in the light of vase-paintings. *BICS* 36: 33-65.

March J.R. 1993. Sophocles' *Ajax*: the death and burial of a hero. *BICS* 38: 1-36.

Marr J.L. 1993. Ephialtes the moderate? *G&R* 40: 11-19.

Marshall C.W. 2001. The next time Agamemnon died. *CW* 95: 59-63.

Marshall C.W. 2003. Casting the *Oresteia*. *CJ* 98: 257-74.

Marshall C.W. and van Willigenburg S. 2004. Judging Athenian dramatic competitions. *JHS* 124: 90-107.

Marzullo B. 1993. *I sofismi di Prometeo* (Florence).

Massa Positano L. 1963. *Demetrii Triclinii in Aeschyli Persas scholia*[2] (Naples).

Mastronarde D.J. 1990. Actors on high: the skene roof, the crane, and the gods in Attic drama. *CA* 9: 247-94.

Matino G. 1998. *La sintassi di Eschilo* (Naples).

McCall M.H. ed. 1972. *Aeschylus: a collection of critical essays* (Englewood Cliffs NJ).

McCall M.H. 1990. The chorus of Aeschylus' *Choephori*. In Griffith & Mastronarde 1989: 17-30.

McClure L. 1999. *Spoken like a woman: speech and gender in Athenian drama* (Princeton).

McClure L. 2006. Maternal authority and heroic disgrace in Aeschylus's *Persae*. *TAPA* 136: 71-97.

McCoskey D. 1998. 'I, whom she detested so bitterly': slavery and the violent division of women in Aeschylus' *Oresteia*. In Joshel & Murnaghan 1998: 35-55.
McHardy F. 2006. *Revenge in Athenian culture* (London).
McHardy F. *et al.* ed. 2005. *Lost dramas of classical Athens: Greek tragic fragments* (Exeter).
Meier C. 1990 [1980]. *The Greek discovery of politics* trans. D. McLintock (Cambridge MA).
Meier C. 1993 [1988]. *The political art of Greek tragedy* trans. A. Webber. (Cambridge).
Meiggs R. 1972. *The Athenian empire* (Oxford).
Meiggs R. and Lewis D.M. 1988. *A selection of Greek historical inscriptions to the end of the fifth century B.C.*[2] (Oxford).
Meineck P.W. and Foley H.P. 1998. *Aeschylus: Oresteia* (Indianapolis).
Melchinger S. 1974. *Das Theater der Tragödie: Aischylos, Sophokles, Euripides auf der Bühne ihrer Zeit* (Munich).
Mette H.J. 1959. *Die Fragmente der Tragödien des Aischylos* (Berlin).
Mette H.J. 1977. *Urkunden dramatischer Aufführungen in Griechenland* (Berlin).
Michelakis P. 2002. *Achilles in Greek tragedy* (Cambridge).
Michelini A.N. 1982. *Tradition and dramatic form in the Persians of Aeschylus* (Leiden).
Mikalson J.D. 2004. *Ancient Greek religion* (Malden, MA/Oxford).
Mitchell L.G. 2006. Greeks, barbarians, and Aeschylus' *Suppliants. G&R* 53: 205-23.
Mitchell-Boyask R. 2006. The marriage of Cassandra and the *Oresteia*: text, image, performance. *TAPA* 136: 269-97.
Mitchell-Boyask R. 2008. Review of P.J. Wilson 2007. *BMCR* 2008.05.24.
Mitchell-Boyask R. 2009. *Aeschylus: Eumenides* (London).
Moles J.L. 1979. A neglected aspect of *Agamemnon* 1389-92. *LCM* 4: 179-89.
Molyneux J.H. ed. 1992. *Literary responses to civil discord* (Nottingham).
Moreau A.M. 1985. *Eschyle: la violence et le chaos* (Paris).
Moreau A.M. 1990. Les sources d'Eschyle dans l'*Agamemnon*: silences, choix, innovations. *REG* 103: 30-53.
Moreau A.M. 1993. La tétralogie des *Perses* a-t-elle une unité? In Ghiron-Bistagne *et al.* 1993: 119-44.
Moreau A.M. 1994. La Clytemnestre d'Eschyle. In Ghiron-Bistagne & Moreau 1994: 153-71.
Moreau A.M. 1995. La *Niobè* d'Eschyle: quelques jalons. *REG* 108: 288-307.
Moreau A.M. 1996. Eschyle et les tranches des repas d'Homère: la trilogie d'Achille. In Moreau *et al.* 1996: 3-29.
Moreau A.M. 1998. Portrait des humbles dans le théâtre d'Eschyle (le Messager thébain, le Veilleur, le Héraut et la Nourrice d'Argos). *Cahiers de la Villa 'Kérylos'* 8: 27-42.
Moreau A.M. *et al.* ed. 1996. *Panorama du théâtre antique d'Eschyle aux dramaturges d'Amérique latine* (Montpellier).
Morgan K.A. 1994. Apollo's favorites. *GRBS* 35: 121-43.
Mossman J.M. 1996. Chains of imagery in *Prometheus Bound. CQ* 46: 58-67.
Murnaghan S. 2005. Women in groups: Aeschylus's *Suppliants* and the female choruses of Greek tragedy. In Pedrick & Oberhelman 2005: 183-98.
Murray O. 1993. *Early Greece*[2] (London).
Murray R.D. 1958. *The motif of Io in Aeschylus' Suppliants* (Princeton).

Mylonas G.E. ed. 1951. *Studies presented to David Moore Robinson on his seventieth birthday* (St Louis).
Naiden F.S. 2004. Supplication and the law. In Harris & Rubinstein 2004: 71-91.
Naiden F.S. 2006. *Ancient supplication* (Oxford).
Nappa C. 1994. *Agamemnon* 717-736: the parable of the lion cub. *Mnemosyne* 47: 82-7.
Nauck A. 1889. *Tragicorum Graecorum fragmenta*[2] (Leipzig).
Newiger H.J. 1979. Drama und Theater. In Seeck 1979: 434-503.
Newiger H.J. 1990. Ekkyklema und Mechane in der Inszenierung des griechischen Dramas. *WJA* 16: 33-42.
Nussbaum M.C. 1986. *The fragility of goodness: luck and ethics in Greek tragedy and philosophy* (Cambridge).
Ober J. 1989. *Mass and elite in democratic Athens: rhetoric, ideology, and the power of the people* (Princeton).
O'Daly G.J.P. 1985. Clytemnestra and the elders: dramatic technique in Aeschylus, *Agamemnon* 1372-1576. *MH* 42: 1-19.
Orwin C. 1980. Feminine justice: the end of the *Seven against Thebes*. *CP* 75: 187-96.
Osborne R.G. 1993. Competitive festivals and the polis: a context for dramatic festivals at Athens. In Sommerstein *et al.* 1993: 21-38.
Osborne R.G. 2000. *Classical Greece 500-323 BC* (Oxford).
Osborne R.G. and Hornblower S. ed. 1994. *Ritual, finance, politics: Athenian democratic accounts presented to David M. Lewis* (Oxford).
Ostwald M. 1993. The Areopagus in the *Athenaion Politeia*. In Piérart 1993: 139-53.
Otis B. 1981. *Cosmos and tragedy: an essay on the meaning of Aeschylus* (Chapel Hill NC).
Paduano G. 1978. *Sui Persiani di Eschilo: problemi di focalizzazione drammatica* (Rome).
Page D.L. 1972. *Aeschyli septem quae supersunt tragoedia[e]* (Oxford).
Page D.L. 1981. *Further Greek epigrams: epigrams before A.D. 50 from the Greek Anthology and other sources, not included in 'Hellenistic Epigrams' or 'The Garland of Philip'* (Cambridge).
Panvini R. and Giudice F. ed. 2003. *'Ta Attika': Veder greco a Gela* (Rome).
Papadimitropoulos L. 2008. Xerxes' *hubris* and Darius in Aeschylus' *Persae*. *Mnemosyne* 61: 451-8.
Papadopoulou, T. 2010. *Aeschylus: Suppliants* (London).
Parker R.C.T. 1986. Greek religion. In Boardman *et al.* 1986: 254-74; reprinted in Boardman *et al.* 1991: 306-29.
Parker R.C.T. 2005. *Polytheism and society at Athens* (Oxford).
Parry H. 1978. *The lyric poems of Greek tragedy* (Toronto).
Pattoni M.P. 1987. *L'autenticità del Prometeo incatenato di Eschilo* (Pisa).
Pattoni M.P. 2006. Presenze politiche di Argo nella tragedia attica del V secolo. In Bearzot & Landucci 2006: 147-208.
Pedrick V. and Oberhelman S.M. 2005. *The soul of tragedy: essays on Athenian drama* (Chicago).
Pelling C.B.R. ed. 1997a. *Greek tragedy and the historian* (Oxford).
Pelling C.B.R. 1997b. Aeschylus' *Persae* and history. In Pelling 1997a: 1-20.
Pelling C.B.R. ed. 2000. *Literary texts and the Greek historian* (London).
Peradotto J.J. 1964. Some patterns of nature imagery in the Oresteia. *AJP* 85: 378-93.

Peradotto J.J. 1969. The omen of the eagles and the *êthos* of Agamemnon. *Phoenix* 23: 237-63; reprinted with minor adjustments in Lloyd 2007: 211-44.
Perysinakis I.N. 2000. I trilogia tôn Persôn. In Sifakis 2000: 233-66.
Petrounias E. 1976. *Funktion und Thematik der Bilder bei Aischylos* (Göttingen).
Pickard-Cambridge A.W. 1946. *The theatre of Dionysus in Athens* (Oxford).
Pickard-Cambridge A.W., Gould J. and Lewis D.M. 1988. *The dramatic festivals of Athens*[3] (Oxford).
Piérart M. ed. 1993. *Aristote et Athènes* (Fribourg/Paris).
Podlecki A.J. 1964. The character of Eteocles in Aeschylus' *Septem*. *TAPA* 95: 283-99.
Podlecki A.J. 1966. *The political background of Aeschylean tragedy* (Ann Arbor MI).
Podlecki A.J. 1970. *The Persians by Aeschylus* (Englewood Cliffs NJ).
Podlecki A.J. 1975a. *The life of Themistocles: a critical survey of the literary and archaeological evidence* (Montreal).
Podlecki A.J. 1975b. Reconstructing an Aeschylean trilogy. *BICS* 22: 1-19.
Podlecki A.J. 1983. Quelques aspects de l'affrontement entre les hommes et les femmes chez Eschyle. In Lévy 1983: 59-71.
Podlecki A.J. 1986. *Polis* and monarch in early Attic tragedy. In Euben 1986: 76-100.
Podlecki A.J. 1989. *Aeschylus: Eumenides* (Warminster).
Podlecki A.J. 1991. *Aeschylus, The Persians: a companion with translation* (Bristol). (Revised edition of Podlecki 1970.).
Podlecki A.J. 1993. *Kat' arkhês gar philaitios leôs*: the concept of leadership in Aeschylus. In Sommerstein *et al.* 1993: 55-79.
Podlecki A.J. 1998. *Perikles and his circle* (London).
Podlecki A.J. 2005a. *Aeschylus: Prometheus Bound* (Oxford).
Podlecki A.J. 2005b. Aiskhylos satyrikos. In G.W.M. Harrison 2005: 1-19.
Pöhlmann E. and West M.L. 2001. *Documents of ancient Greek music: the extant melodies and fragments edited and transcribed with commentary* (Oxford).
Pöhlmann E. *et al.* 1995. *Studien zur Bühnendichtung und zum Theaterbau der Antike* (Frankfurt).
Pontani F. 2007. Shocks, lies, and matricide: thoughts on Aeschylus *Choephori* 653-718. *HSCP* 103: 203-33.
Pope M. 1986. Athenian festival judges – seven, five, or however many. *CQ* 36: 322-6.
Porter D.H. 2005. Aeschylus' *Eumenides*: some contrapuntal lines. *AJP* 126: 301-31.
Powell A. 1988. *Athens and Sparta: constructing Greek political and social history from 478 B.C.* (London).
Prag A.J.N.W. 1985. *The Oresteia: iconographic and narrative traditions* (Warminster).
Prag A.J.N.W. 1991. Clytemnestra's weapon yet once more. *CQ* 41: 242-6.
Preiser C. 2000. *Euripides: Telephos* (Hildesheim).
Pulleyn S. 1997. Erotic undertones in the language of Clytemnestra. *CQ* 47: 565-7.
Radt S.L. 1985. *Tragicorum Graecorum fragmenta (TrGF). Vol. 3: Aeschylus* (Göttingen).
Raphael F. and McLeish K. 1981. *The serpent son: Aeschylus' Oresteia.* (Cambridge).
Rehm R. 1988. The staging of suppliant plays. *GRBS* 29: 263-307.
Rehm R. 1992. *Greek tragic theatre* (London).
Reinhardt K. 1949. *Aischylos als Regisseur und Theologe* (Berne).

Revermann M. 2006. *Comic business: theatricality, dramatic technique, and performance contexts of Aristophanic comedy* (Oxford).
Revermann M. 2008. Aeschylus' *Eumenides,* chronotopes, and the 'aetiological mode'. In Revermann & Wilson 2008.
Revermann M. and Wilson P.J. ed. 2008. *Performance, iconography, reception: studies in honour of Oliver Taplin* (Oxford).
Reynolds L.D. and Wilson N.G. 1991. *Scribes and scholars: a guide to the transmission of Greek and Latin literature*[3] (Oxford).
Rhodes P.J. 1981. *A commentary on the Aristotelian Athenaion Politeia* (Oxford).
Rhodes P.J. 2003. Nothing to do with democracy: Athenian drama and the *polis. JHS* 123: 104-19.
Rhodes P.J. 2005. *A history of the classical Greek world 478-323 BC* (Oxford).
Riemer P. and Zimmermann B. ed. 1998. *Der Chor im antiken und modernen Drama* (= *Drama* 7) (Stuttgart).
Rihll T.E. 1995. Democracy denied: why Ephialtes attacked the Areopagus. *JHS* 115: 86-97.
Robertson D.S. 1951. Prometheus and Chiron. *JHS* 71: 150-5.
Robinson J.A.T. 1963. *Honest to God* (London).
Rohweder C. 1998. *Macht und Gedeihen: Eine politische Interpretation der Hiketiden des Aischylos* (Frankfurt).
Roisman H.M. 2004. Women's free speech in Greek tragedy. In Sluiter & Rosen 2004: 91-114.
Rose P.W. 1992. *Sons of the gods, children of earth: ideology and literary form in ancient Greece* (Ithaca NY).
Rosen R.M. and Farrell J.J. ed. *Nomodeiktes: studies in honor of Martin Ostwald* (Ann Arbor, MI).
Rosenbloom D. 1995. Myth, history and hegemony in Aeschylus. In Goff 1995: 91-130.
Rosenbloom D. 2006. *Aeschylus: Persians* (London).
Rosenmeyer T.G. 1982. *The art of Aeschylus* (Berkeley).
Rösler W. 1970. *Reflexe vorsokratischen Denkens bei Aischylos* (Meisenheim am Glan).
Rösler W. 1993. Der Schluss der 'Hiketiden' und die Danaiden-Trilogie des Aischylos. *RhM* 136: 1-22; English version, with a postscript, in Lloyd 2007: 174-98.
Roth P. 1993. The theme of corrupted *xenia* in Aeschylus' *Oresteia. Mnemosyne* 46: 1-17.
Rowe C.J. and Schofield M. ed. 2000. *The Cambridge History of Greek and Roman Political Thought* (Cambridge).
Rupp E.G. *et al.* 1969. *Luther and Erasmus: free will and salvation* (Philadelphia/London).
Saïd S. 1978. *La faute tragique* (Paris).
Saïd S. 1981. Darius et Xerxès dans les *Perses* d'Eschyle. *Ktèma* 6: 17-38.
Saïd S. 1985. *Sophiste et tyran ou le problème du Prométhée enchaîné* (Paris).
Saïd S. 1988. Tragédie et renversement: l'exemple des *Perses. Métis* 3: 321-41; English version, with minor revisions, in Lloyd 2007: 71-92.
Saïd S. 1993a. Tragic Argos. In Sommerstein *et al.* 1993: 167-89.
Saïd S. 1993b. Le mythe de l'Aréopage avant la *Constitution d'Athènes.* In Piérart 1993: 155-84.
Saïd S. 2002. Herodotus and tragedy. In Bakker *et al.* 2002: 117-47.
Saïd S. 2005. Aeschylean tragedy. In Gregory 2005: 215-32.
Sandin P. 2003. *Aeschylus' Supplices: Introduction and Commentary on vv.1-523* (Diss. Göteborg; reissued with corrections, Lund 2005).

Sansone D. 1975. *Aeschylean metaphors for intellectual activity* (Wiesbaden).
Saunders T.J. 1991. *Plato's penal code: tradition, controversy, and reform in Greek penology* (Oxford).
Schadewaldt W. 1936. Aischylos' 'Achilleis'. *Hermes* 71: 25-69.
Schaps D.M. 1993. Aeschylus' politics and the theme of the *Oresteia*. In Rosen & Farrell 1993: 505-15.
Schenker D.J. 1999. Dissolving differences: character overlap and audience response. *Mnemosyne* 52: 641-57.
Scodel R.S. ed. 1993. *Theater and society in the classical world* (Ann Arbor MI).
Scott W.C. 1984. *Musical design in Aeschylean theatre* (Hanover NH).
Scott W.C. 1987. The development of the chorus in *Prometheus Bound*. *TAPA* 117: 85-96.
Scullion S. 1994. *Three studies in Athenian dramaturgy* (Stuttgart).
Scullion S. 2002. Tragic dates. *CQ* 52: 81-101.
Seaford R.A.S. 1984. *Euripides: Cyclops* (Oxford).
Seaford R.A.S. 1995. Historicizing tragic ambivalence: the vote of Athena. In Goff 1995: 202-21.
Seaford R.A.S. 2005. Mystic light in Aeschylus' *Bassarai*. *CQ* 55: 602-6.
Sealey R. 1964. Ephialtes. *CP* 59: 11-22.
Seeck G.A. ed. 1979. *Das griechische Drama* (Darmstadt).
Segal E. ed. 1983. *Oxford readings in Greek tragedy* (Oxford).
Seidensticker B. 2003. The chorus of Greek satyrplay. In Csapo & Miller 2003: 100-21.
Seidensticker B. 2005. Dithyramb, comedy, and satyr-play. In Gregory 2005: 38-54.
Sewell-Rutter N.J. 2007. *Guilt by descent: moral character and decision making in Greek tragedy* (Oxford).
Shapiro A. and Burian P. 2003. *Aeschylus: The Oresteia* (Oxford).
Shapiro H.A. 1994. *Myth into art: poet and painter in classical Greece* (London).
Sicherl M. 1986. Die Tragik der Danaiden. *MH* 43: 81-110.
Sideras A. 1971. *Aeschylus Homericus* (Göttingen).
Sidwell K.C. 1996. Purification and pollution in Aeschylus' *Eumenides*. *CQ* 46: 44-57.
Sier K. 1988. *Die lyrischen Partien der Choephoren des Aischylos* (Stuttgart).
Sier K. 2005. Vorschläge zum Aischylos-Text. *Hermes* 133: 409-23.
Sifakis G.M. ed. 2000. *Kterismata: philologika meletimata aphierômena ston Io. S. Kambitsi (1938-1990)* (Iraklion).
Silk M.S. ed. 1996. *Tragedy and the Tragic* (Oxford).
Simon E. 1981. *Das Satyrspiel Sphinx des Aischylos* (Heidelberg).
Simon E. 1982a [1972]. *The ancient theatre* trans. C.E. Vafopoulou-Richardson (London).
Simon E. 1982b. Satyr-plays on vases in the time of Aeschylus. In Kurtz & Sparkes 1982: 123-48.
Slater N.W. 1990. The idea of the actor. In Winkler & Zeitlin 1990: 385-95.
Slater N.W. and Zimmermann B. ed. 1993. *Intertextualität in der griechisch-römischen Komödie* (= *Drama* 2) (Stuttgart).
Sluiter I. and Rosen R.M. ed. 2004. *Free speech in classical antiquity* (Leiden).
Smith O.L. 1965. Some observations on the structure of imagery in Aeschylus. *C&M* 26: 10-72.
Smith O.L. 1969. The father's curse: some thoughts on the *Seven against Thebes*. *C&M* 30: 27-43.

Smith O.L. 1976. *Scholia graeca in Aeschylum quae extant omnia: Pars I scholia in Agamemnonem Choephoros Eumenides Supplices continens* (Leipzig).
Smith O.L. 1982. *Scholia graeca in Aeschylus quae extant omnia: Pars II Fasc. 2 scholia in Septum adversus Thebas continens* (Leipzig).
Smith P.M. 1980. *On the Hymn to Zeus in Aeschylus' Agamemnon* (Chico CA).
Snell B. and Kannicht R. 1986. *Tragicorum Graecorum fragmenta (TrGF). Vol. I: Didascaliae tragicae, catalogi tragicorum et tragoediarum, testimonia et fragmenta tragicorum minorum*[2]. (Göttingen).
Sommerstein A.H. 1980a. Artemis in *Agamemnon*: a postscript. *AJP* 101: 165-9.
Sommerstein A.H. 1980b. *Aristophanes: Acharnians* (Warminster).
Sommerstein A.H. 1989a. *Aeschylus: Eumenides* (Cambridge).
Sommerstein A.H. 1989b. Notes on Aeschylus' 'Seven against Thebes'. *Hermes* 117: 432-45.
Sommerstein A.H. 1989c. Again Klytaimestra's weapon. *CQ* 39: 296-301.
Sommerstein A.H. 1992. Sleeping safe in our beds: stasis, assassination and the *Oresteia*. In Molyneux 1992: 1-17; reprinted with updates in Sommerstein 2010a: 143-63.
Sommerstein A.H. 1993. *Pathos* and *mathos* before Zeus. In Jocelyn 1993: 109-14; reprinted with updates in Sommerstein 2010a: 178-88.
Sommerstein A.H. 1995. The beginning and the end of Aeschylus' Danaid trilogy. In Zimmermann 1995: 111-34; reprinted with updates in Sommerstein 2010a: 89-117.
Sommerstein A.H. 1996. Aeschylus' epitaph. *Museum Criticum* 30/31: 111-17; reprinted with updates in Sommerstein 2010a: 195-201.
Sommerstein A.H. 1997. The theatre audience, the demos, and the *Suppliants* of Aeschylus. In Pelling 1997: 63-79; reprinted with updates in Sommerstein 2010a: 118-42.
Sommerstein A.H. 2000. The prologue of Aeschylus' *Palamedes*. *RhM* 143: 118-27.
Sommerstein A.H. 2001. *Aristophanes: Wealth* (Warminster).
Sommerstein A.H. 2002. Comic elements in tragic language: the case of Aeschylus' *Oresteia*. In Willi 2002: 151-68.
Sommerstein A.H. 2004. Violence in Greek drama. *Ordia Prima* 3: 41-56; reprinted with updates in Sommerstein 2010a: 30-46.
Sommerstein A.H. 2008. *Aeschylus* (3 vols) (Cambridge MA).
Sommerstein A.H. 2010a. *The tangled ways of Zeus and other studies in and around Greek tragedy* (Oxford).
Sommerstein A.H. 2010b. The Persian War tetralogy of Aeschylus. In Davidson & Rosenbloom 2010.
Sommerstein A.H. 2010c. Textual and other notes on Aeschylus. *Prometheus* 36: 1-22 and 97-122.
Sommerstein A.H. 2010d. Orestes' trial and Athenian homicide procedure. In Harris *et al.* 2010: 25-38.
Sommerstein A.H. *et al.* ed. 1993. *Tragedy, comedy and the polis: papers from the Greek drama conference, Nottingham, 18-20 July 1990* (Bari).
Sommerstein A.H. and Talboy T.H. (forthcoming). *Sophocles: selected fragmentary plays. Volume II* (Oxford).
Sourvinou-Inwood C. 1994. Something to do with Athens: tragedy and ritual. In Osborne & Hornblower 1994: 269-90.
Stanford W.B. 1942. *Aeschylus in his style: a study in language and personality* (Dublin).

Stehle E. 2005. Prayer and curse in Aeschylus' *Seven against Thebes*. *CP* 100: 101-22.
Stoessl F. 1988. *Der Prometheus des Aischylos als geistesgeschichtliches und theater-geschichtliches Phänomen* (Stuttgart).
Sutton D.F. 1974. Aeschylus' *Amymone*. *GRBS* 15: 193-202.
Sutton D.F. 1980. *The Greek satyr play* (Meisenheim am Glan).
Sutton D.F. 1984. Aeschylus' *Proteus*. *Philologus* 128: 127-30.
Taplin O.P. 1972. Aeschylean silences and silences in Aeschylus. *HSCP* 72: 57-97.
Taplin O.P. 1977. *The stagecraft of Aeschylus: the dramatic use of exits and entrances in Greek tragedy* (Oxford).
Taplin O.P. 1978. *Greek tragedy in action* (London).
Taplin O.P. 1993. *Comic angels and other approaches to Greek drama through vase-paintings* (Oxford).
Taplin O.P. 1996. Comedy and the tragic. In Silk 1996: 188-202.
Thalmann W.G. 1978. *Dramatic art in Aeschylus' Seven against Thebes* (New Haven).
Thalmann W.G. 1980. Xerxes' rags: some problems in Aeschylus' *Persians*. *AJP* 101: 260-82.
Thalmann W.G. 1982. The Lille Stesichorus and the *Seven against Thebes*. *Hermes* 110: 385-91.
Thalmann W.G. 1985. Speech and silence in the Oresteia. *Phoenix* 39: 98-118 and 221-37.
Thiel R. 1993. *Chor und dramatische Handlung im 'Agamemnon' des Aischylos* (Stuttgart).
Thomson G. 1932. *Aeschylus: Prometheus Bound* (Cambridge).
Thomson G. 1966. *The Oresteia of Aeschylus*[2] (2 vols) (Amsterdam/Prague).
Thomson G. 1973. *Aeschylus and Athens*[4] (London).
Torrance I.C. 2007. *Aeschylus: Seven against Thebes* (London).
Trendall A.D. and Webster T.B.L. 1971. *Illustrations of Greek drama* (London).
Tyrrell W.B. 1984. *Amazons: a study in Athenian mythmaking* (Baltimore).
Ussher R.G. 1977. The other Aeschylus. *Phoenix* 31: 287-99.
van Erp Taalman Kip A.M. 1996. The unity of the *Oresteia*. In Silk 1996: 119-38.
Vellacott P.H. 1961. *Aeschylus: Prometheus Bound, The Suppliants, Seven against Thebes, The Persians* (Harmondsworth).
Vernant J.P. 1981 [1972]. Intimations of the will in Greek tragedy. In Vernant & Vidal-Naquet 1981: 28-62.
Vernant J.P. and Vidal-Naquet P. 1981 [1972]. *Tragedy and myth in ancient Greece* trans. J. Lloyd (Brighton).
Vickers B. 1973. *Towards Greek tragedy* (London).
Vidal-Naquet P. 1981a. The shields of the heroes. In Vernant & Vidal-Naquet 1981: 120-49.
Vidal-Naquet P. 1981b. Hunting and sacrifice in Aeschylus' *Oresteia*. In Vernant & Vidal-Naquet 1981: 150-74.
von Fritz K. 1962. *Antike und moderne Tragödie* (Berlin).
Wallace R.W. 1989. *The Areopagus council to 307* BC (Baltimore).
Wallinga H.T. 2005. *Xerxes' Greek adventure: the naval perspective* (Leiden).
Wartelle A. 1978. *Bibliographie historique et critique d'Eschyle 1518-1974* (Paris).
Watson P.S. and Drewery B. 1969. *Luther: De servo arbitrio*. In Rupp *et al.* 1969: 99-334.
Webster T.B.L. 1967. *Monuments illustrating tragedy and satyr play*[2] (*BICS* Suppl. 20) (London).

Webster T.B.L. 1969. *An introduction to Sophocles*² (London).
Webster T.B.L. 1970. *The Greek chorus* (London).
Wecklein N. 1893. Studien zu den Hiketiden des Aischylos. *SBAW* (1893) ii 393-450.
Weglage M. 1991. Leid und Erkenntnis: Zum Zeus-Hymnus im aischyleischen Agamemnon. *Hermes* 119: 265-81.
Wehrli F. 1967. Io, Dichtung und Kultlegende. In *Gestalt und Geschichte: Festschrift Karl Schefold zu seinem sechzigsten Geburtstag* (Berne) 196-9; reprinted in Hommel 1974: ii 136-45.
West M.L. 1979. The Prometheus trilogy. *JHS* 99: 130-48; reprinted, with a postscript, in Lloyd 2007: 359-96.
West M.L. 1982. *Greek metre* (Oxford).
West M.L. 1985. Ion of Chios. *BICS* 32: 1-6.
West M.L. 1987. *An introduction to Greek metre* (Oxford).
West M.L. 1989. The early chronology of Greek tragedy. *CQ* 39: 251-4.
West M.L. 1990a. *Aeschyli tragoediae cum incerti poetae Prometheo* (Stuttgart). [The seven plays have also been published each as a separate volume.]
West M.L. 1990b. *Studies in Aeschylus* (Stuttgart).
West M.L. 1992. *Ancient Greek music* (Oxford).
West M.L. 2000. *Iliad* and *Aethiopis* on the stage: Aeschylus and son. *CQ* 50: 338-52.
West M.L. 2003. *Greek epic fragments from the seventh to the fifth centuries BC* (Cambridge MA).
West M.L. 2006. King and Demos in Aeschylus. In Cairns & Liapis 2006: 31-40.
West S.R. 1994. Prometheus orientalised. *MH* 51: 129-49.
White M. ed. 1952. *Studies in honour of Gilbert Norwood* (Toronto).
White S. 2001. Io's world: intimations of theodicy in *Prometheus Bound*. *JHS* 121: 107-40.
Wilamowitz-Moellendorff U. von, 1886. Die Bühne des Aischylos. *Hermes* 21: 597-622; reprinted in Wilamowitz 1935: 148-72.
Wilamowitz-Moellendorff U. von, 1893. *Aristoteles und Athen* (2 vols) (Berlin).
Wilamowitz-Moellendorff U. von, 1914. *Aischylos: Interpretationen* (Berlin).
Wilamowitz-Moellendorff U. von, 1935. *Kleine Schriften, Band I: Klassische griechische Poesie* (Berlin).
Wiles D. 1987. Reading Greek performance. *G&R* 34: 136-51.
Wiles D. 1993. The seven gates of Aeschylus. In Slater & Zimmermann 1993: 180-94.
Wiles D. 1997. *Tragedy in Athens: performance space and theatrical meaning* (Cambridge).
Wiles D. 2000. *Greek theatre performance: an introduction* (Cambridge).
Wilkens K. 1974. *Die Interdependenz zwischen Tragödienstruktur und Theologie bei Aischylos* (Munich).
Willi A. ed. 2002. *The language of Greek comedy* (Oxford).
Wilson J.R. 1995. Unsocial actors in 'Agamemnon'. *Hermes* 123: 398-403.
Wilson P.J. 2000. *The Athenian institution of the khoregia: the chorus, the city and the stage* (Cambridge).
Wilson P.J. 2006. *Dikên* in the *Oresteia* of Aeschylus. In Davidson *et al.* 2006: 187-201.
Wilson P.J. ed. 2007. *The Greek theatre and festivals: documentary studies* (Oxford).
Winkler J.J. 1990. The ephebes' song: *tragôidia* and *polis*. In Winkler & Zeitlin 1990: 20-62.
Winkler J.J. and Zeitlin F.I. ed. 1990. *Nothing to do with Dionysos?: Athenian drama in its social context* (Princeton).

Winnington-Ingram R.P. 1948. Clytemnestra and the vote of Athena. *JHS* 68: 130-47; revised version in Winnington-Ingram 1983: 101-31.
Winnington-Ingram R.P. 1961. The Danaid trilogy of Aeschylus. *JHS* 81: 141-52; revised version in Winnington-Ingram 1983: 55-72.
Winnington-Ingram R.P. 1973. Zeus in the *Persae*. *JHS* 93: 210-19; revised version in Winnington-Ingram 1983: 1-15.
Winnington-Ingram R.P. 1977. *Septem contra Thebas*. *YCS* 25: 1-45; revised version in Winnington-Ingram 1983: 16-54.
Winnington-Ingram R.P. 1983. *Studies in Aeschylus* (Cambridge).
Winnington-Ingram R.P. 1985. Aeschylus. In Easterling & Knox 1985: 281-95 (bibliography, pp. 761-4); reprinted in Easterling & Knox 1989: 29-43 (bibliography, pp. 177-80).
Wyke M. ed. 1998. *Parchments of gender: deciphering the body in antiquity* (Oxford).
Yalouris N. 1990. Io. In *LIMC* v 1.661-76 and v 2.442-52.
Zeitlin F.I. 1965. The motif of the corrupted sacrifice in Aeschylus' Oresteia. *TAPA* 96: 463-508.
Zeitlin F.I. 1978. The dynamics of misogyny: myth and mythmaking in the Oresteia. *Arethusa* 11: 149-84; revised in Zeitlin 1996: 87-119.
Zeitlin F.I. 1989. Patterns of gender in Aeschylean drama: Seven against Thebes and the Danaid trilogy. In Griffith & Mastronarde 1989: 103-15.
Zeitlin F.I. 1992. The politics of Eros in Aeschylus' Danaid trilogy. In Hexter and Selden 1992: 203-52; revised in Zeitlin 1996: 123-71.
Zeitlin F.I. 1996. *Playing the other: gender and society in classical Greek literature* (Chicago).
Zeitlin F.I. 1999. Aristophanes: the performance of utopia in the *Ecclesiazousae*. In Goldhill & Osborne 1999: 167-97.
Zeitlin F.I. 2009. *Under the sign of the shield: semiotics and Aeschylus' Seven against Thebes*[2] (Lanham MD).
Zimmermann B. 1991 [1986]. *Greek tragedy: an introduction* trans. T. Marier. (Baltimore).
Zimmermann B. 1995. *Griechisch-römische Komödie und Tragödie* (= *Drama* 3) (Stuttgart).
Zimmermann B. 2004. Aischylos und Homer. *Lexis* 22: 191-9.
Zimmermann B. 2005. La fortuna di Eschilo nel V sec. a.C. *Dioniso* n.s. 4: 6-13.

Index of Passages Cited

General Index

Except for the *Iliad* and *Odyssey*, and Greek words with lower-case initial, all main entries in *italics* are the titles of plays (or suites of plays) by, or ascribed to, Aeschylus. All these plays are listed alphabetically on pp. 11-12; this list is not referenced in the index. Bold font indicates major discussions. The abbreviation A denotes Aeschylus.